# WORKING AMERICANS

## 1880–2012

## Volume XIII:
## Educators & Education

# WORKING AMERICANS

## 1880–2012

## Volume XIII:
## Educators & Education

## By Scott Derks

A Universal Reference Book

Grey House
Publishing

| PUBLISHER: | Leslie Mackenzie |
| EDITORIAL DIRECTOR: | Laura Mars |
| ASSOCIATE EDITOR: | Diana Delgado |
| PRODUCTION MANAGER: | Kristen Thatcher |
| MARKETING DIRECTOR: | Jessica Moody |

| AUTHOR: | Scott Derks |
| CONTRIBUTORS: | Jael Bridgemahon, Jim DuPlessis, Katherine Gwaltney, Ellen Hanckel, Anne Mandeville-Long, Brenda Monteith |

| COPYEDITOR: | Elaine Alibrandi |
| COMPOSITION: | PreMediaGlobal, Inc. |

Grey House Publishing, Inc.
4919 Route 22
Amenia, NY 12501
518.789.8700 FAX 845.373.6390
www.greyhouse.com
e-mail: books@greyhouse.com

While every effort has been made to ensure the reliability of the information presented in this publication, Grey House Publishing neither guarantees the accuracy of the data contained herein nor assumes any responsibility for errors, omissions or discrepancies. Grey House accepts no payment for listing; inclusion in the publication of any organization, agency, institution, publication, service or individual does not imply endorsement of the editors or publisher.

Errors brought to the attention of the publisher and verified to the satisfaction of the publisher will be corrected in future editions.

Publisher's Cataloging-In-Publication Data

Derks, Scott.
  Working Americans 1880-2012 / by Scott Derks.

  v. : ill. ; cm.

Title varies.
"A universal reference book."
Includes bibliographical references and indexes.
Contents: v. 1. The working class—v.2. The middle class—v.3. The upper class—v.4. Their children.—v.5. At war.—v.6. Women at work—v.7. Social movements—v.8. Immigrants—v.9. Revolutionary war to civil war—v.10. Sports & Recreation.—v.11. Inventors & Entrepreneurs.—v.12. Our History Through Music.—v.13. Educators & Education.
  ISBN: 1-891482-81-5 (v.1)
  ISBN: 1-891482-72-6 (v.2)
  ISBN: 1-930956-38-X (v.3)
  ISBN: 1-930956-35-5 (v.4)
  ISBN: 1-59327-024-1 (v.5)
  ISBN: 1-59237-063-Z (v.6)
  ISBN: 1-59237-101-9 (v.7)
  ISBN: 978-1-59237-197-6 (v.8)
  ISBN: 978-1-59237-101-3 (v.9)
  ISBN: 1-59237-441-7 (v. 10)
  ISBN: 1-59237-565-3 (v. 11)
  ISBN: 978-1-59237-762-6 (v. 12)
  ISBN: 978-1-59237-877-7 (v. 13)

1. Working class—United States—History. 2. Labor—United States—History. 3. Occupation—United States—History. 4. Social classes—United States—History. 5. Immigrants—Employment—United States—History. 6. Economic conditions—United States—History. 7. Sports—United States—History. 8. Inventions—United States—History. 9. Inventions—United States—History. 10. Music—United States—History. 10. Education—United States—History. 1. Title.

HD 8066 .D47 2000
305.5/0973/0904

To my first teacher, Martha Lovell Hope Derks, and to those who exemplify educational excellence in my world: Rich Jones, Charlie Sigel, Don Armentrout, Brenda Monteith, and Alice Linder.

Exploring the diverse world of educators and education has been enlightening. We are all marked by our own experiences in the classrooms, a shape-shifting locale that transforms a group event into a personal, unique memory. Credit must be ladled on two newcomers, Jim DuPlessis and Katherine Gwaltney, for their excellent support, research and writing. Thanks and appreciation also go to contributors Anne Mandeville-Long, Bobby Long, Brenda Monteith, and Ellen Hanckel. Informational assistance was provided by Dr. Jan Rosemergy, deputy director and director of communications at the Vanderbilt Kennedy Center, Nashville, Tennessee; Amy Pottier, manager of technology support at the Vanderbilt Kennedy Center; Dr. Carl Haywood, professor emeritus, Peabody College of Education and Human Development, Vanderbilt University, Nashville; Mary Ellen Wilson, Order Services, Vanderbilt University Library; Scott Shanklin-Peterson, director of the Arts Management Program and associate professor in the School of the Arts at the College of Charleston, South Carolina; Terry K. Peterson, director of the Afterschool and Community Learning Network at the College of Charleston; Ken May, executive director of the South Carolina Arts Commission, Columbia; Millie Hough, communications director of the South Carolina Arts Commission; Christine Fisher, director of the Arts in Basic Curriculum project at Winthrop University, Rock Hill, South Carolina. Finally, my heartfelt appreciation to Laura Mars and Brandy, who make the grueling process of writing more fun.

# TABLE OF CONTENTS

## 1880 – 1899 INTRODUCTION

## 1900 – 1909 INTRODUCTION

# 1930 – 1939 INTRODUCTION

# 1940 – 1949 INTRODUCTION

# 1950 – 1959 INTRODUCTION

## 2000 – 2012 INTRODUCTION

# PREFACE

Welcome to the thirteenth volume of the Working Americans series that explores the social and economic lives of educators, including the practical and philosophical debates that molded American education from 1880 to 2012. The intensity of the debate was a clarion demonstration of the importance of education. There is little doubt that America's attempts at free, universal education, encompassing the high school years, contributed to its economic progress, innovation and ability to absorb millions of earnest immigrants seeking a better life for themselves and their children. The ability and willingness of thousands of teachers to guide and educate children in the midst of tumultuous social changes are compelling stories. They range from a young woman who taught Native Americans in the West, to architects who dreamed about the perfect learning environment, to educators who taught adults the fine art of woodworking. This volume explores the shifts in educational philosophy as educators wrestled with the role of phonics, English-only classes, integration, Title IX and the push for sex education programs in school. Along the way we meet a man who built "teacherages" so that rural teachers would have a place to live, librarians who were preparing for their "dream job," a teacher who rediscovered herself in the classroom, a man obsessed with the importance of the IQ test, and the formation of educational television. In all, there are 36 stories about the men and women who have impacted education philosophy or the opportunity to learn during the last 132 years.

As in the previous volumes, each profile is modeled on real people and events. As in the previous books in this series, most of the names have been changed and some details added based on statistics, the popularity of an idea or writing of the time. The real names of several educators were used for reasons of visibility, accuracy or sentimentality. They are: Corabelle Fellows, 1888; Margaret Haley, 1907; Dwight Heald Perkins, 1909; Abraham Flexner, 1910; Septima Clark, 1961; Mary Calderone, 1969; Joan Ganz Cooney, 1970; James Krenov, 1985; Scott Shanklin-Peterson, 1995; and Anne Mandeville-Long, 2012.

Every effort has been made to profile accurately the individuals' expertise, as well as home and work experiences. Letters, biographies, interviews, high school annuals, and magazine articles were consulted and used to ensure that the profiles reflected the mood of each decade and the feelings of the subjects. In some cases, the people profiled represent national trends, but mostly they represent themselves. Ultimately, it is the working Americans and their activities—along with their investments, spending decisions, passions and jobs—that shape the society and economy of the United States.

The first three volumes of *Working Americans: 1880-1999* explore the economic lives and loves of working-class, middle-class, and upper-class Americans through the eyes and wallets of more than 100 families. Employing pictures, stories, statistics and advertisements of each period, these intimate profiles study their jobs, wages, family life, expenditures and hobbies throughout the decades. Although separated by levels of wealth, each volume also captures the struggles and joys of a shifting

American economy and the transformation they brought to communities and families in the workplace, regardless of economic status. The fourth volume, *Their Children*, builds upon the social and economic issues explored previously by examining the lives of children across the entire spectrum of economic status. Issues addressed include parents, child labor, education, peer pressure, food, fads and fun. *Volume V: Americans at War* explores the life-changing elements of war and discusses how enlisted personnel, officers and civilians handle the stress, exhilaration, boredom and brutality of America's various wars, conflicts and incursions. *Volume VI: Women at Work* celebrates the contributions of women, chronicling both their progress and roadblocks, and highlighting the critical role of women in the front lines of change.

*Working Americans VII: Social Movements* explores the various ways American men and women feel called upon to challenge accepted conventions, whether the issue is cigarette smoking in 1901 or challenging the construction of a massive hydroelectric dam in 1956. *Working Americans VIII: Immigrants* examines the lives of first- and second-generation immigrants, with a focus on their journey to America, their search for identity, and their emotions experienced in the new land. *Working Americans IX: The Revolutionary War to the Civil War* steps back in time to chronicle the lives of 36 families from the 1770s to the 1860s, detailing their troubles and triumphs, whether they were farmers, postal clerks, whiskey merchants, lawyers or cabinetmakers. *Working Americans X: Sports and Recreation* tackles the diverse and ever-changing world of competitive sports in America from the viewpoint of the professional, the amateur, and the spectator. Along the way, we meet Olympic swimmers, basketball players who rarely play, boxers with extraordinary stamina, weightlifters of unbelievable determination, and weekend athletes thrilled by the opportunity to be in the open air.

*Working Americans XI* focuses on the inventors and entrepreneurs whose willingness to take risks transformed America. This romp through time unveils the efforts needed to invent zippers, vacuum cleaners and FM radio. Entrepreneurs establish insurance companies, launch restaurant chains, and seed companies with varying degrees of success.

The twelfth volume in this series, *Our History Through Music*, brings to life the harmonies of an amateur barbershop quartet and the Prince of Funk, George Clinton. This volume lifts up the diversity of American music embraced by opera singer Geraldine Farrar and guitar magician Wayne Henderson, as well as the role that advanced technology played in accurately broadcasting a rock band to the subtlety of recording in the age of multi-track tapes.

Each of these 13 volumes—embracing the lives of families throughout American history—strives to tell a story. A simple story of struggling, hoping and enduring. And if I've learned anything in the last 14 years of writing these books, it is that the American spirit lives on, maintains its free will, and endeavors to meet the challenges of the day. This spirit is alive and well, and still lives in America.

Scott Derks

# INTRODUCTION

*Working Americans 1880-2012 Volume XIII: Educators & Education* is the 13th volume in the *Working Americans* series. Like its predecessors, this work profiles the lives of Americans – how they lived, how they worked, how they thought – decade by decade. The earliest volumes focus on economic status or social issues. More recent volumes focus on a specific group of Americans – athletes in *Volume X* and musicians in *Volume XII*. This volume highlights American educators – from traditional teachers to unlikely mentors, from coaches to authors, from parents to program innovators. *Educators* depicts the classroom that is America – from natural environments to thoughtful buildings, from educational television programs to programs for children of immigrants, from war trenches to piano benches.

Arranged in 12 chapters, this newest *Working Americans* includes three **Profiles** per chapter for a total of 36. Each profile offers personal insights using *Life at Home, Life at Work* and *Life in the Community* categories. These personal topics are followed by historic and economic data of the time. **Historical Snapshots** chronicle major milestones. A variety of **News Features** puts the subject's life and work in context of the day. These common elements, as well as specialized data, such as **Selected Prices,** in currency of the time, punctuate each chapter and act as statistical comparisons between decades. The 36 individuals profiled in this volume represent all regions of the country, and a wide variety of ages and ethnic backgrounds.

In *Volume XIII: Educators & Education,* you will read about educators who:

- Travel to the Dakotas in 1881 to teach Sioux children;
- Design school buildings that encourage learning and community involvement;
- Teach young immigrants the importance of being American;
- Convince schools to buy and use IQ tests;
- Discover why Johnny can't read;
- Convince schools that sex education reduces teen pregnancy:
- Teach with armed officers posted outside their windows during desegregation:
- Tutor children in South Africa and Teach for America.

All thirteen volumes, regardless of economic status, time period, or specific focus, offer a unique look at those Americans whose talents, desires, motivations, struggles, and values shaped – and continue to shape – this nation. Without exception, the 437 individuals profiled in the thirteen volumes of this *Working Americans* series are working toward their version of the American dream.

Like its companion volumes, *Working Americans 1880-2012 Volume XIII: Educators & Education* is a compilation of original research (personal diaries and family histories) plus printed material (government statistics, commercial advertisements, and news features). The text, in easy-to-read bulleted format, is supported with hundreds of graphics, such as photos, advertisements, pages from printed material, letters, and documents.

All thirteen *Working Americans* volumes are "point in time" books, designed to illustrate the reality of that particular time. Some Americans portrayed in this 13th volume went on to realize fame and fortune, while others did not. What they all did, however, is help America find her voice, and many of their stories and struggles march on.

**Praise for earlier volumes –**

*" . . . this unique volume portrays music and musicians in America over the past 130 years. . . . The intent . . . is to profile individuals involved in music at all levels . . . and the publisher . . . achieves that lofty goal."*

*" . . . by arranging the people chronologically rather than alphabetically, users can see how industry changed over time and how ideas and inventions built upon each other. . . . an outstanding overview of the unique inventions and entrepreneurial efforts . . . This work is highly recommended for school libraries from middle school through high school as well as college libraries from community college through graduate school . It should also be found is public libraries of every size.*
**American Reference Books Annual**

*"this volume engages and informs, contributing significantly and meaningfully to the historiography of the working class in America . . . a compelling and well-organized contribution for those interested in social history and the complexities of working Americans."*
**Library Journal**

*"these interesting, unique compilations of economic and social facts, figures, and graphs . . . support multiple research needs [and] will engage and enlighten patrons in high school, public, and academic library collections."*
**Booklist**

*"[the author] adds to the genre of social history known as 'history from the bottom up' . . . Recommended for all colleges and university library collections."*
**Choice**

*"the volume succeeds at presenting various cultural, regional, economic and age-related points of view . . . [it is] visually appealing [and] certainly a worthwhile purchase..."*
**Feminist Collections**

B O C O D

O B O C O D

O A ● B O C O D

15. ● ● B O C O D

● A O B O C O D

16. O A ● B O C O D

17. O A O B

18. O

# 1880–1899

While the opulence and glitter of the Gilded Age was attracting all the attention, American education was in the midst of fundamental change. Since the 1830s, the common school movement had been reshaping education in America. Reformers believed that education was the key to creating a good society, especially when it reinforced Anglo-Protestant American culture. Thus, the schoolhouse was seen as a way to stabilize the political system, reduce tension between social classes, and eliminate crime. By the 1890s, with immigration accelerating every year, the schools had become the essential "flame" beneath the American melting pot.

This was a time of vast, accumulated wealth and an abundance of emerging technology—all racing to keep up with the restless spirit of the American people. The wealth propelled the founding of the New York Metropolitan Opera in 1883, and the restless spirit discovered its voice in the emerging popularity of ragtime music. The rapid expansion of railroads opened up the nation to new industries, new markets, and the formation of monopolistic trusts that catapulted a handful of corporations into positions of unprecedented power and wealth. This expanding technology also triggered the movement of workers from farm to factory, the rapid expansion of wage labor, and the explosive growth of cities. Farmers, merchants and small-town artisans found themselves increasingly dependent on regional and national market forces. The shift in the concentrations of power was unprecedented in American history. At the same time, professionally trained workers were reshaping America's economy alongside business managers or entrepreneurs eager to capture their piece of the American pie. It was an economy on a roll with few rudders or regulations. In this environment, the popular song industry known as Tin Pan Alley both prospered and dramatically influenced the taste and direction of American music.

Across America, the economy—along with its work force—was running away from the land. Before the Civil War, the United States was overwhelmingly an agricultural nation. By the end of the century, non-agricultural occupations employed nearly two-thirds of the workers. As important, two of every three Americans came to rely on wages instead of self-employment as farmers or artisans.

At the same time, industrial growth began to center around cities, where wealth accumulated for a few who understood how to harness and use railroads, create new consumer markets, and manage a ready supply of cheap, trainable labor. Jobs offering steady wages and the promise of a better life for workers' children drew people from the farms into the cities, which grew at twice the rate of the nation as a whole. The new cities of America were home to great wealth and great poverty—both produced by the massive migrations and influx of immigrants willing to work at any price. It was a time symbolized by Andrew Carnegie's steel mills, John D. Rockefeller's organization of the Standard Oil monopoly, and the manufacture of Alexander Graham Bell's wonderful invention, the telephone. By 1894, the United States had become the world's leading industrial power, producing more than England, France, and Germany—its three largest competitors—combined. For much of this period, the nation's industrial energy focused on the need for railroads requiring large quantities of labor, iron, steel, stone, and lumber. In 1883, nine-tenths of the nation's entire production of steel went into rails. The most important invention of the period—in an era of tremendous change and innovation—may have been the Bessemer converter, which transformed pig iron into steel at a relatively low cost, increasing steel output 10 times from 1877 to 1892.

The greatest economic event during the last two decades of the nineteenth century was the great wave of immigration that swept America. It is believed to be the largest worldwide population movement in human history, bringing more than 10 million people to the United States to fill the expanding need for workers. In the 1880s alone, 5.25 million immigrants arrived, more than in the first six decades of the nineteenth century. This wave was dominated by Irish, German, and English workers, but Scandinavia, Italy, and China also sent scores of eager workers, usually men, to fill the expanding labor needs of the country. To attract this much-needed labor force, railroad and steamship companies advertised throughout Europe and China the glories of American life. To an economically depressed world, it was a welcome call.

The national wealth in 1890 was $65 billion; nearly $40 billion was invested in land and buildings, $9 billion in railroads, and $4 billion in manufacturing and mining. By 1890, 25 percent of the world's output of coal was mined in the United States. Annual production of crude petroleum went from 500,000 barrels in 1860 to 63.6 million barrels in 1900. This was more than the wealth of Great Britain, Russia, and Germany put together.

Despite all the signs of economic growth and prosperity, America's late nineteenth-century economy was profoundly unstable. Industrial expansion was undercut by a depression from 1882 to 1885, followed in 1893 by a five-year-long economic collapse that devastated rural and urban communities across America. As a result, job security for workers just climbing onto the industrial stage was often fleeting. Few wage-earners found full-time work for the entire year. The unevenness in the economy was caused both by the level of change underway and irresponsible speculation, but more generally to the stubborn adherence of the federal government to a highly inflexible gold standard as the basis of value for currency.

Between the very wealthy and the very poor emerged a new middle stratum, whose appearance was one of the distinctive features of late nineteenth-century America. The new middle class fueled the purchase of one million light bulbs a year by 1890, even though the first electric light was only 11 years old. It was the middle class also that flocked to buy Royal Baking Powder (which was easier to use and faster than yeast) and supported the emergence and spread of department stores that were sprouting up across the nation.

# 1881 PROFILE

With two years of college under her belt and two years of teaching in northern Michigan, Mary Greene was ready for the educational change sweeping the nation.

## Life at Home

- When Mary Greene entered her tiny, one-room school in Wisconsin in 1881 for the first time, she was well aware of the educational reforms sweeping the prairielands.
- Industrialist Horace Mann—building off the ideas of Thomas Jefferson—had seen to that.
- A modern education required a standard curriculum, universal attendance and graduated steps to completion; Mary was proud to be at the center of the transformation.
- In 1778, Thomas Jefferson, while still a member of the Virginia Assembly, proposed that all children be guaranteed three years of public schooling.
- It was a radical concept that he believed was essential to the perpetuation of democracy.
- "General education will enable every man to judge for himself what will secure or endanger his freedom," Jefferson said.
- "But was it necessary?" asked his fellow landowners, who already paid a fee to send their children to private "dame schools"; besides, no one was sure that field hands needed the capacity to read William Shakespeare.

*Teacher Mary Greene was ready for educational reform.*

*Horace Mann was at the center of education reform.*

- The debate raged for decades.
- Despite a professed belief that free, universal education was essential to the perpetuity of democracy, by 1840 America still offered few educational opportunities to the children of its agrarian workers and industrial workforce.
- With no state supervision, inconsistent local budgets and a tepid commitment to instructing the masses, America's schools languished.
- Most of the schools offered an education linked to the Protestant Bible; the most common schoolbook was the New England Primer—used to teach reading and the fundamentals of Protestant catechism.
- The few older boys who went beyond the grammar school years studied mathematics, Latin and philosophy.
- Mary Greene was fully aware of the role Horace Mann played in changing attitudes for her sake.
- His personal inspection of 1,000 Massachusetts schools over a six-year period had demonstrated that most lacked adequate light, heat and ventilation.
- With no standardized textbooks, pupils spent hours memorizing or reciting passages from books they brought from home, no matter how dated or irrelevant they might have been.
- Mann supported a new system called "common schools" that would serve all boys and girls and teach a common body of knowledge that would give each student an equal chance at life.
- "It is a free school system, it knows no distinction of rich and poor…education, then, beyond all other devices of human origin, is the equalizer of the conditions of men, the great balance wheel of the social machinery."
- Mann proposed that the state establish both a taxation system adequate to meet the needs of the school and create standards or expectations on a statewide basis.
- Additional innovations included the introduction of school desk chairs with backs, standardized textbooks, a bell to signal the time and the visibility of a blackboard.
- Convinced that an educated citizenry benefited the entire community, he was also a major proponent of teacher education and universal taxation.
- Fearing any statewide control, local school boards attacked the plans vociferously, but the debate fully exposed the concept that everyone in society should pay for universal education.
- In 1879, a uniform grading program was instituted in Wisconsin.
- In 1881, for the first time, students would be formally charted on their progress.
- Mary had grown up in Wisconsin schools that mirrored the educational process that Mann criticized.
- During Mary's schooling, the role of the teacher was largely to oversee and monitor pupil behavior; there was no clear curriculum and no graduated steps to higher grades.
- Raised on a farm as one of nine children, Mary's father loved school so much that his parents agreed to extend his education to the sixth grade, whereas most of his classmates and siblings left school after three years.
- Her mother had had no formal education beyond Bible reading at home, and desperately wanted one of her children to acquire enough education to become a preacher, a teacher, or an undertaker, since all three guaranteed paying jobs.
- Growing up, Mary was taught to commit to memory words for public recitation; the person who possessed the best word memory was the most satisfactory pupil.
- Education experts speculated that since the object of education was to strengthen the innate properties of the mind, recitations served as the rigorous, muscle-building exercise children needed.

- Mary also experienced the custom of "boarding 'round," in which her teachers moved from house to house every two weeks, spending time in the home of each child who attended her school.
- Mary was thrilled when the teacher came to stay at her house; only years later did she realize that the custom was necessary because of the low wages paid to female teachers, and that few adults would wish to change their location every two weeks.

## Life at Work

- Mary Greene's first challenge as a newly hired teacher was to figure out when the school year started.
- Every year the school board set the dates for the start of the school year based upon the amount of school taxes that had been collected; the funds covered teacher wages and contingency.
- Only after the numbers were in could the local school board establish the calendar for the winter and summer terms—each running about four months.
- Generally, school attendance in the country was an erratic, seasonal activity based on the farming needs of the family, the opening day of hunting season, or the unexpected illness of a prized animal.
- In Otsego, Wisconsin, the summer term traditionally began after the spring planting of the potato crop, and the winter term started after the harvest.
- Some boys only attended school in the summer session.
- In years past, men were hired as schoolteachers in the winter term when boys were considered more obstreperous and difficult to teach; women were hired for the summer term.
- From 1867 to 1880, the one-room school in Otsego was served by 25 different teachers.
- It made for very poor continuity, and the skills of the students lagged.
- At the same time, women were beginning to dominate teaching.
- Women were considered more temperamentally suited to the teaching profession and would work for less.
- For the first time in years, the school board had contracted with Mary to cover the entire year, and told her they wished to break the cycle of frequently changing teachers.
- But unlike her predecessors, Mary was experienced in teaching and in the ways of politics.
- Before the school year had begun, she visited the most influential families in the area to demonstrate why an education should take precedence over potato farming; as important, she talked about the future as a time of change when their children would need the ability to read and write effectively.
- The community listened and threw its support behind education; they even embraced the statewide curriculum that established graded steps toward graduation using statewide standards, including an expectation that a child's education should last eight years.
- Using the plans distributed by the Wisconsin State Superintendent's Office, pupils were to be graded or grouped based on their abilities into one of three levels: primary form, middle form, and upper form.
- Movement from one grade to the next was to be determined based on a system of examinations.
- The year Mary arrived, the school was transitioning from the New England Primer to the McGuffey Reader.
- McGuffey Readers, including a primer, a speller, and five readers, had been around since 1836; nearly 100 million copies had been sold in the prior 34 years.
- The Readers were designed to become progressively more challenging with each volume; word repetition in the text was featured as a learning tool, helping to develop reading skills.
- Sounding out, enunciation and accents were emphasized, gradually introducing new words and carefully repeating the old.

*Outdoor recess for Wisconsin school children.*

- McGuffey also listed questions after each story to aid the teacher and assist in the statewide plan to establish grades.
- While Mary's youngest students, eager to catch up with their older brothers and sisters, loved the energy and focus of the new curriculum, the older students fought the changes.
- A year earlier, they knew exactly what was required to obtain high grades; now, everything was unfamiliar.
- So on the last day of the first week, the older students staged a strike by refusing to re-enter the classroom after recess.
- Mary simply ignored them while she taught the first graders and left the protest alone.
- One by one her charges, looking very sheepish, reappeared in her classroom.
- They all expected to be paddled—a punishment Mary avoided.
- "I don't plan to tell your parents what you have done," she proclaimed at the end of the school day, and "I expect no more student strikes—leave that to the unions that are fighting for workers' rights."
- The next day, Mary devoted the first hour of the day to explaining why change was taking place.
- She told her 28 charges that "what was good enough for pa is good enough for me" was no longer true.
- "The world is getting more competitive; hundreds of thousands of people arrive in America searching for work. They want jobs—your jobs—to raise their families."
- With that out of the way, she got out a map of Europe to show everyone where the immigrants were coming from, and then helped everyone with their arithmetic by demonstrating how many zeros were in 100,000—as in 100,000 new immigrants.
- She then used a horseshoe to demonstrate how to measure in inches—then she asked one of the boys to throw the horseshoe and showed how to measure in feet.
- Then a student brought in a plot of his family's property, and the next class was devoted to acres, divisions and calculating triangles.
- But when one of her quietest students brought in figures showing the shoulder height of her cows compared to their weight and asked how math could be used to determine the weight of cows in the field, Mary knew it was going to be a good year.

## Life in the Community: Otsego, Wisconsin

- Otsego, Wisconsin, got its start as a transportation center and functioned as a station on the Chicago, Milwaukee & St. Paul Railroad.
- Situated in the prairie region north of Madison, it served as the center of agricultural and dairy; potatoes dominated the agricultural crops throughout the county.

*Mary Greene outside her one-room school.*

- By 1881, amenities included a graded school, and Lutheran and Catholic churches, while the Modern Woodmen of America and the Catholic Order of Foresters added to the sociability of the area.
- The first settler to the area, Wayne B. Dyer, arrived in 1844 and erected a log house in which to live and entertain weary travelers.
- Being on the direct route between Milwaukee and Stevens Point, Dyer prevailed upon quite a number of travelers to settle around his hostelry, and by December 1847, the Post Office of Otsego was established.
- As other hotels were built, the village attained a fair degree of prosperity.
- In January 1849, the growing community was organized into a town to which was given the name of Otsego.
- The two largest cities nearby were Milwaukee and Madison.
- Madison was created in 1836 when former federal judge James Duane Doty, planning to build a city on the site, purchased over a thousand acres of swamp and forest land on the isthmus between Lakes Mendota and Monona.
- The Wisconsin Territory had been created earlier that year and was tasked with choosing a permanent location for its capital.
- Doty lobbied aggressively for the legislature to select Madison as the new capital, offering buffalo robes to the freezing legislators and promising choice Madison lots at discount prices to undecided voters.
- Doty named the city Madison for James Madison, the fourth president of the U.S., who had died on June 28, 1836, and he named the streets for the other 38 signers of the U.S. Constitution.
- Even though Madison was still only a city on paper, the territorial legislature voted on November 28 in favor of Madison as the capital, largely because of its location halfway between the new and growing cities around Milwaukee in the east and the long-established strategic post of Prairie du Chien in the west.
- When Wisconsin became a state in 1848, Madison remained the capital, and the following year it became home to the University of Wisconsin-Madison.

# HISTORICAL SNAPSHOT
# 1881

- Thomas Edison and Alexander Graham Bell formed the Oriental Telephone Company
- The city of Phoenix, Arizona, was incorporated
- Kansas became the first state to prohibit all alcoholic beverages
- Black colleges Spelman College in Georgia and the Tuskegee Institute in Alabama opened

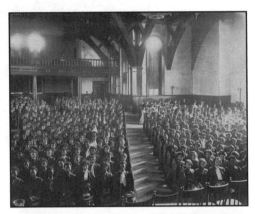

- The Four Dead in Five Seconds Gunfight erupted in El Paso, Texas
- The University of Connecticut was founded as the Storrs Agricultural School
- Clara Barton established the American Red Cross
- The USS *Jeannette* was crushed in an Arctic Ocean ice pack
- President James Garfield was shot by Charles Julius Guiteau and died 11 weeks later; Vice President Chester Arthur became the nation's twenty-first president
- Sheriff Pat Garrett shot and killed outlaw William Henry McCarty, Jr.—widely known as Billy the Kid—outside Fort Sumner, New Mexico

- Sioux Chief Sitting Bull led the last of his fugitive people in surrender to U.S. troops at Fort Buford in Montana
- The fifth hurricane of the Atlantic season hit Florida and the Carolinas, killing about 700
- Francis Howell High School in St. Charles, Missouri, and Stephen F. Austin High School in Austin, Texas, opened on the same day, September 12, putting them in a tie for the title of the oldest public high school west of the Mississippi River
- Atlanta, Georgia hosted the International Cotton Exposition
- In London, Richard D'Oyly Carte opened the Savoy Theatre, the world's first public building to be fully lit by electricity, using Joseph Swan's incandescent light bulbs
- The Gunfight at the O.K. Corral in Tombstone, Arizona, captured nationwide media attention
- The magazine *Judge* was first published
- New York City's oldest independent school for girls, the Convent of the Sacred Heart, was founded
- The United States National Lawn Tennis Association and The United States Tennis Association were established, and the first U.S. Tennis Championships were played
- The Vatican's archives were opened to scholars for the first time

## Selected Prices

Carriage, Wire or Wooden Wheels.............................................$12.35

China, 130-Piece Dinner Set....................................................$30.00

Fruit, Wine, and Jelly Press....................................................$3.00

Hotel Room, New York...........................................................$1.00

Music Box...........................................................................$2.50

Pocket Watch......................................................................$10.00

Suspenders.........................................................................$0.05

Violin.................................................................................$5.00

Whisk Broom Holder.............................................................$0.20

Woman's Storm Cape............................................................$8.25

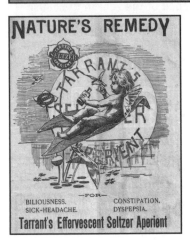

### "The Macnicol Case," *The Fitchburg Sentinel* (Massachusetts), January 1883:

The approaching trial of a Kentucky school teacher for various offenses of dress will decide the important question whether there is any particular style of dress which a schoolteacher must adopt, and whether certain peculiarities of dress are in themselves sufficiently immoral to justify the offenders removal from all connection with the great work of educating Kentucky's small boys.

It appears that Mr. Macnicol, of the Norville School District, has been charged by the ladies of his district with "official misconduct." The specifications are four in number. It is alleged that he does not wear a coat; that his trousers are so ragged as to expose portions of his body; that he wears only one suspender, and that he never puts on a pair of stockings. The charge and specifications are to be investigated by a School Commissioner, and the results of the investigation are awaited with intense anxiety.

There seems a strong possibility that the four specifications above cited will be sustained by sufficient evidence. It is said that witnesses without number may be made to testify to the condition of Mr. Macnicol's trousers and suspenders, and to his habitual rejection of coat and stockings. It does not follow, however, that the charge of official misconduct will be sustained. Whether a schoolteacher who is guilty of ragged trousers, of one suspender, and a dislike of coat and a dislike of wearing stockings is also necessarily guilty of "official misconduct" is a question of law rather than of fact.

There are many pleas which Mr. Macnicol can urge in defence of his conduct. He may insist that the so-called ragged condition of his trousers is due to an excessive love of neatness. What his indiscriminating accusers regarded as rents may be simply holes made by cutting out pieces of cloth that have become accidentally stained with ink. Or he may take the broad general ground that his trousers have been worn out in the cause of education and that the alleged rags are the glorious scars sustained while endeavoring to instill the multiplication table into the system of a boy peculiarly impervious to clubs and reason. There is no particular pattern of trousers prescribed by any school regulation which has yet been brought to his knowledge, and he can claim the same right to wear openwork trousers that his fair accusers claim for themselves in connection with open work stockings.

As to Mr. Macnicol's failure to wear a coat, it is merely an evidence of his zeal in the cause of education. How can a Kentucky schoolteacher hope to teach half-grown Kentucky boys with his coat on? If he "means business," and proposes to accomplish any real good, he must take off his coat. Does not the Kentucky preacher take off not merely his coat, but his collar, whenever he means to preach a really eloquent sermon? And did anyone ever hear of a Kentucky political orator or barroom debater who either spoke or argued with his coat on? Mr. Macnicol, if he is wise, will confess to teaching without a coat and glory in it. The ladies of the Norville School District are doubtless admirable women, but they know very little about teaching Kentucky boys if they fancy it can be done with a coat on. No coat ever yet made would last a Kentucky teacher for a single week if he did not take it off before grasping his cane and summoning a boy to come to him and acquire the first principles of arithmetic....

*Continued*

### "The Macnicol Case," ... *(Continued)*

It is to be hoped that Mr. Macnicol will be triumphantly acquitted. If he is found guilty of official misconduct, no schoolteacher will be safe who does not obtain written instructions from the ladies of the district as to which articles of clothing he must wear and who does not habitually dress in the presence of witnesses. And if women can dictate how the male schoolteacher shall clothe himself, men will have the right to say what clothes a female teacher must wear. From such a state of things, the acquittal of Mr. Macnicol alone can save us.

### Editorial, *The Cambridge City Tribune* (Indiana), May 29, 1879:

"The editor of the *Newcastle Mercury* is exasperated over the fact that the superintendent of the Cambridge City Schools receives $1,500 a year for his services, while "four lady teachers, each of whom performs her part well," receive "about the same amount in the aggregate." He will, no doubt, be shocked to learn that the superintendent of the Car Works at this place receives as much per year as three or four of the daily laborers in his employ, each of whom performs his part well. If Bro. Parker will direct his attention to the elevation of his own cheap school instead of meddling with what he acknowledges to be "none of his business," he will find full employment for his talents. We already pay our lady teachers more than they receive in most places, and give employment to two or three more of them than we should do if we did not have a superintendent who understands his business. It takes brains to secure attendance at school of 81 percent of all the persons in the district between six and 21 years of age; and for that kind of brains we are ready to pay at least fair market price.

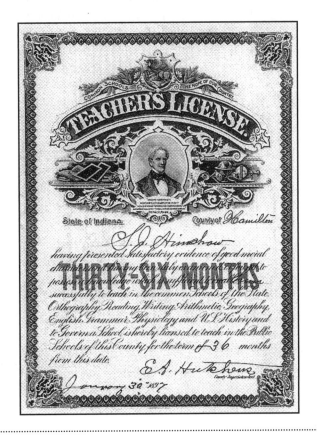

There is a snail-paced gait for the advance of new ideas.... People have more feeling for canals and roads than education."

—Thomas Jefferson, 1817

You crowd from 40 to 60 children into that ill-constructed shell of a building, there to sit in the most uncomfortable seats that could be contrived, expecting that with the occasional application of the birch they will then come out educated for manhood or womanhood.

—Horace Mann

### "Pay of School Teachers," *The Cambridge City Tribune* (Indiana), May 29, 1879:

On Friday our Public Schools completed their tenth year—eight of which have been under the supervision of the present superintendent. Eight pupils, having completed the full course of study prescribed in this school, received diplomas which will enable them to enter the freshman class in the State University without further examination—a similar privilege having been accorded them by Hanover and other Colleges. The number of graduates is greater than any former occasion; and the records of the school show a larger attendance than in any previous year—a larger one, we believe, than can be shown by any town of the same size in the state. Out of 726 persons entitled to the benefit of the Common School Fund, 588, or more than 81 percent have been enrolled—while few other towns show as high as 75, and some of them fall as low as 30 percent.... In the absence of a law making education compulsory, we doubt if our own town, or any other, will ever show a larger enrollment than during the past year....

In regard to teachers, also, our schools have made an advance upon all former years. During the past year, two teachers admirably qualified in every other way were compelled to resign on account of ill health; but their places were promptly supplied, and at the close of the term, there was not a single exception to the mental, moral and physical qualifications of the teachers employed, all of whom were emphatically first-class.

It is cheering to know that, notwithstanding these facts, our people have been subjected to no additional tax for educational purposes. From the year 1869 down to 1876, the school trustees found it necessary to levy a tax for "Special School Revenue," of $0.60 on each $100 worth of taxable property, in addition to the annual tuition tax of $0.25 levied by the Town Board. This made a total tax for school purposes of $0.75 on each $100. Last year, each board made a levy of only $0.20, and we believe they have done the same this year, so that our people can pay a total school tax of only $0.40, or a little more than half what they paid for the first half dozen years after the establishment of the schools. Yet we are told that the education of our children is costing too much, and that some of our teachers are receiving extravagant pay for their services. There is no doubt that we pay higher salaries in some schools we could name, and it is equally true that we could procure teachers of some sort for less money. Prof. Hall now has applications from 30 persons desiring to teach, many of whom would, no doubt, accept situations for $25 per month. But if experience in education matters has demonstrated any one thing beyond peradventure, it is this: that it don't pay to employ low-priced teachers and cheap superintendents.

## *The Authentic Life of Billy the Kid*, Pat Garrett, 1882:

(On the night of July 14, 1881, Sheriff Pat Garrett and his two deputies were hunting for the outlaw Billy the Kid. The residents of that section of New Mexico were sympathetic to the Kid and the lawmen could extract little information. Garrett decided to seek out an old friend, Peter Maxwell, who might tell him the Kid's whereabouts. As chance would have it, the Kid stumbled right into the Sheriff's hands. Garrett published his account of the incident a year after it happened.)

I then concluded to go and have a talk with Peter Maxwell, Esq., in whom I felt sure I could rely. We had ridden to within a short distance of Maxwell's grounds when we found a man in camp and stopped. To Poe's great surprise, he recognized in the camper an old friend and former partner, in Texas, named Jacobs. We unsaddled here, got some coffee, and, on foot, entered an orchard which runs from this point down to a row of old buildings, some of them occupied by Mexicans, not more than 60 yards from Maxwell's house. We approached these houses cautiously, and when within earshot, heard the sound of voices conversing in Spanish. We concealed ourselves quickly and listened; but the distance was too great to hear words, or even distinguish voices. Soon a man arose from the ground, in full view, but too far away to recognize. He wore a broad-brimmed hat, a dark vest and pants, and was in his shirtsleeves. With a few words, which fell like a murmur on our ears, he went to the fence, jumped it, and walked down towards Maxwell's house.

Little as we then suspected it, this man was the Kid. We learned, subsequently, that, when he left his companions that night, he went to the house of a Mexican friend, pulled off his hat and boots, threw himself on a bed, and commenced reading a newspaper. He soon, however, hailed his friend, who was sleeping in the room, told him to get up and make some coffee, adding: "Give me a butcher knife and I will go over to Pete's and get some beef; I'm hungry." The Mexican arose, handed him the knife, and the Kid, hatless and in his stocking-feet, started to Maxwell's, which was but a few steps distant.

When the Kid, by me unrecognized, left the orchard, I motioned to my companions, and we cautiously retreated a short distance, and, to avoid the persons whom we had heard at the houses, took another route, approaching Maxwell's house from the opposite direction. When we reached the porch in front of the building, I left Poe and McKinney at the end of the porch, about 20 feet from the door of Pete's room, and went in. It was near midnight and Pete was in bed. I walked to the head of the bed and sat down on it, beside him, near the pillow. I asked him as to the whereabouts of the Kid. He said that the Kid had certainly been about, but he did not know whether he had left or not. At that moment a man sprang quickly into the door, looking back, and called twice in Spanish, "Who comes there?" No one replied and he came on in. He was bareheaded. From his step I could perceive he was either barefooted or in his stocking-feet, and held a revolver in his right hand and a butcher knife in his left.

He came directly towards me. Before he reached the bed, I whispered: "Who is it, Pete?" but received no reply for a moment. It struck me that it might be Pete's brother-in-law, Manuel Abreu, who had seen Poe and McKinney, and wanted to know their business. The intruder

*Continued*

***The Authentic Life of Billy the Kid . . .*** *(Continued)*

came close to me, leaned both hands on the bed, his right hand almost touching my knee, and asked, in a low tone: "Who are they, Pete?" at the same instant Maxwell whispered to me, "That's him!" Simultaneously, the Kid must have seen, or felt, the presence of a third person at the head of the bed. He raised quickly his pistol, a self-cocker, within a foot of my breast. Retreating rapidly across the room he cried: "Quien es? Quien es?" ("Who's that? Who's that?") All this occurred in a moment. Quickly as possible I drew my revolver and fired, threw my body aside, and fired again. The second shot was useless; the Kid fell dead. He never spoke. A struggle or two, a little strangling sound as he gasped for breath, and the Kid was with his many victims.

# 1888 PROFILE

Although at first Corabelle Fellows did not know the language or customs of the Sioux, she trekked from Washington, DC, to the Dakotas to teach Sioux children nearly everything from arithmetic and reading to sewing and geography.

## Life at Home

- When Corabelle Fellows began her journey to the Dakotas in 1884, she'd never met an Indian, taught in a school or claimed any understanding of the Lakota, Sioux, people she intended to help.
- The headstrong, educated teen was determined to punish her Washington, DC, society parents for breaking up a potential love affair with an older man.
- Going to a place she had never seen to teach people she didn't know seemed to be a good idea—despite everyone's concerns for her safety.
- Only eight years earlier, the nation had been shocked to learn of Custer's last stand at the Battle of the Little Bighorn.
- That day in late June, the 7th Cavalry Regiment of the United States Army lost 278 soldiers in the most famous action of the Great Sioux War of 1876.
- It was an overwhelming victory for the Lakota, Northern Cheyenne, and Arapaho, who were led by several major

*Corabelle Fellows left a comfortable life in Washington DC to teach Sioux children in the Dakotas.*

war leaders, including Crazy Horse and Gall, inspired by the visions of Sitting Bull (Thathánka Íyotake).

- The "massacre," as it was immediately labeled, resurrected ancient fears of random and unprovoked Indian attacks, even though Little Big Horn was neither.
- When Europeans arrived in the New World, more than 200 distinctly different Indian cultures existed on the North American continent.
- The various tribal groups spoke mutually unintelligible languages and practiced widely different hunting, housing and living styles.
- They were distinctive in their differences, although habitually described as similar by popular culture in the Eastern press.
- Growing up in Glens Falls, New York, several Missouri communities, and Washington, DC, Corabelle loved her dolls, dressing the cat in the latest fashions and watching her photographer father employ his craft.
- As a child in Washington, she played on the steps of the U.S. Capitol building when Congress was in session and her father served as doorman, fell in love with the Corcoran Art Gallery and borrowed books from the Congressional library.
- Her mother had been educated in music, French, needlework and fine cookery; when no schools were available for Corabelle and her sister Marian, their mother taught them herself— six days a week—in the finer points of writing, reading, arithmetic, geography, physiology and sewing.
- "Always when we least expected it, mother would call us to her and demand the spelling of words, the boundaries of a state, the multiplication tables, or the poem she had set us to learn, or ask us to write a paragraph on the circulation of the blood," Corabelle recalled.
- The two girls sewed an hour each day and also routinely learned their catechism for Sunday.
- When her mother finally accepted Corabelle's decision to move West to teach Indians, she gave her a flatiron in hopes that "even in that outlandish place you will remember to keep your clothes pressed."
- Her mother staged an elaborate going-away party and arranged for Corabelle to attend the inaugural ball of President Garfield—to remind her of what she would be missing.
- Corabelle made the journey westward in late November 1884 to a school affiliated with the American Board of Commissioners for Foreign Missions, which had begun among the Dakota people in 1834.
- She cried frightened tears throughout most of the train ride from Washington to Springfield, Dakota Territory; "As we neared the end of the journey, I gradually achieved a calmer mind and a less swollen face," said Corabelle.
- The trip included bruising bumps, sleepless nights and swollen rivers that defied crossing; Corabelle was miserable.
- When she arrived at the Santee Reservation on the day before Thanksgiving, she stepped into "the most penetrating cold I had ever experienced."
- After years of work, the reservation's Normal School consisted of 18 buildings on 480 acres to accommodate the 206 students; the boarding school was at the heart of the mission— emphasizing religious training and industrial vocational school.
- School courses included farming, carpentry, printing and blacksmithing for boys, and sewing, cooking and housekeeping for girls.
- The school provided training in the reading and writing of the Dakota language, a path developed by white missionaries focused on Bible reading; at other times of the day, only English was permitted to be spoken.
- When the federal government insisted that only English be taught, the Missionary Society balked, saying the rules were "illegal, unscientific and irreligious."

## Life at Work

- Shortly after the five-foot-one, 100-pound Corabelle Fellows arrived at the Dakota reservation, she was given a new, Indian name.

- Even though "Corabelle" meant "beautiful girl," the Indian girls in Lakota looked into her eyes and rendered a separate verdict: Wichipitowan, or Blue Star.

- Everyone, it seemed, pronounced the rechristening appropriate; "You want a name of good meaning," she was told.

*Students knew little English and Corabelle knew no Sioux.*

- Her first class among the Sioux was composed of 15 Indian girls aged five to seven; Corabelle's assignment was to teach them how to sew.

- "They knew but little English. I knew no Sioux. But I could show them how…. I took each docile brown hand in mine and guided it to set fine hemming stitches in the squares of purple, orange, blue, and scarlet calico which they held. They sat on the circle upon little chairs and turned their large, bright black eyes on me unblinkingly. There was not a sound."

- Soon she was introduced to more students and taught classes in a variety of subjects: arithmetic, reading, etiquette.

- At night at her home, she received visitors, always in twos and threes; the Sioux, she learned, rarely went anywhere alone.

- "Blame and praise are thus equally divided, especially blame."

- The girls came for help with their lessons; the boys usually wanted to play dominoes.

- The girls also loved to finger her clothing—particularly silk or cotton dresses—drink coffee and listen to stories about what a city was like.

- The boys were fascinated by geography and quite readily grasped the relationship of one area to another; when she displayed several maps of the United States as they related to a world map, she was pronounced most knowledgeable and admired by the boys.

- Corabelle also assumed that the wisdom of replacing the culture of the Indian students with her own was a self-evident good.

- She gave children English first names and used their fathers' names as their last names, ignoring native understanding of naming practices.

- She also came to learn that her pupils were unchangeable gum chewers—in and out of the classroom.

- Gum was manufactured from the juice of the purple coneflower which they sliced and dripped into a pottery bowl.

- When the liquid was boiled down, the residue was a fine, rubberlike substance which could be chewed constantly.

- The boys chewed with much noise and swagger, she recalled years later; the girls were experts at snapping.

- After seven months of successful schooling, Corabelle was asked to take a new assignment among the "rougher Indians, who spoke a different dialect of Sioux."

- Six other teachers had failed to make it this far; unable to stand the cold, the food, the Sioux language or the odors.

- At the next reservation school site in Oahe on the Missouri River near Fort Sully, she learned the rhythm and customs of the Indians: why each tepee was set up exactly the same way, the process making of pottery, how to properly scrape an animal skin, and the art of lassoing an animal.

- One day she was invited to go hunting for beans with the women of the village; the children showed her how to find among the grasses handfuls of beans carefully stored by the prairie mice.
- When they returned, each woman carried approximately three pounds of purloined beans.
- After two years among the Indians, Corabelle was invited to a new Indian Center among the Cheyenne, at the Cheyenne River Reservation in Nebraska.
- This time, her parents were proud of her decision and repeatedly said so during a round of Washington, DC, parties given in her honor.
- Language continued to be a major issue: instruction was in English only at the government schools, while the vernacular was permitted at the schools in which Corabelle taught.
- But the tide had firmly turned: Indians would only be successful in American society when they abandoned their old ways.
- When she arrived in Nebraska, Corabelle was met by a platform filled with cowboys and Indians eager to get a glimpse of "the new schoolmarm."
- "The fellow bowed with his hand over his heart and offered me an elbow. As I reached to take it, thinking he had been sent to meet me, he fired a pistol above my head. At this signal, the mob swirled about the end of the coach, pistols popping, war whoops ringing."

*Corabelle married Samuel Campbell, son of a trader and Sioux woman.*

- The Indians were reluctant to attend school because scalp locks and painted faces were not permitted, so Corabelle taught three teens—Dog Bear, Gray Bear, and White Owl—at night when others were not around.
- They were asked not to wear frightful paint because Corabelle thought it was ugly.
- In addition, she had to fight off a marriage proposal—and virtual kidnapping—which she accidently encouraged because she didn't understand the traditional rituals.
- "The white blanket is worn by the Cheyenne man who seeks a mate. I had spoken to him; therefore, I approved of him. I left my house alone, and after sunset—final proof of my approval and interest—and he'd been in his own right to attempt to carry me off. I retraced his trail the next day. He had carried me to within possibly 200 feet of his tepee. Had he once entered it with me, by the law of the Cheyenne, I would have been his lawful squaw property from that hour forward."
- Corabelle's time as a teacher drew to a close after she worked briefly at a boarding school at Fort Benning, where she met Samuel Campbell, the son of a trader and a Sioux woman who was raised by an Episcopal priest.
- On March 15, 1888, Corabelle Fellows married Samuel Campbell, ending her teaching career, but not her time in the West.

*Marriage ended Corabelle's career.*

## Life in the Community: The Dakotas

- Prior to Corabelle Fellows' arrival, the Lakota people had lost most of their land in Minnesota through treaties signed in 1837, 1851 in 1858.

- The terms of the Treaty of Fort Laramie in 1868 granted the Lakota a single large reservation that covered parts of North Dakota, South Dakota, and four other states.

- After the conclusion of the Indian Wars in the 1870s, the U.S. Government confiscated about one-half of this reservation; the Great Sioux Reservation was reduced from 60 million to less than 22 million acres.

- Reservation treaties sometimes included food and supply stipend agreements, in which the federal government would grant a certain amount of goods to a tribe yearly.

- The implementation of the policy was erratic, however, and in many cases the stipend goods were not delivered.

- These treaties were often established by Executive Order and rarely pleased anyone.

- All the while, missionaries were urging the Indians to abandon traditional ways and adopt the white culture.

- Progress among the Dakota people was defined as "interest in speaking the English language, monogamy replacing polygamy, houses that incorporated windows and doors, and an interest in agriculture."

- The creation of American Indian reservations began in earnest during the administration of President James K. Polk (1845-1849), who believed in the establishment of "colonies" for the Indian natives in the region beyond the Mississippi River.

- The establishment of reservations, or "permanent" Indian frontiers, was also indelibly tied to the policy of Indian removal from lands now desired by white settlers east of the Mississippi.

- In most cases, the West's reservation policy either reduced the homeland of the native people or required that they move to a new location where they had less land that needed to be protected from white immigrants flooding the area.

- In 1851, Congress passed the Indian Appropriations Act, which authorized the creation of Indian reservations in modern-day Oklahoma.

- Relations between settlers and natives continued to deteriorate as the settlers encroached on Indian territory and consumed the natural resources in the West.

- By the late 1860s, President Ulysses S. Grant pursued a stated "Peace Policy" as a possible solution to the conflict.

- The policy included a reorganization of the Indian Service, with the goal of relocating various tribes from their ancestral homes to parcels of land established specifically for their habitation.

- The policy called for the replacement of government officials by religious men, nominated by churches, to oversee the Indian agencies on reservations in order to teach Christianity to the native tribes.

- The Quakers were especially active in this philosophy for reservations; their "civilization" policy was aimed at eventually preparing the tribes for citizenship.

*Promoting Indian culture, including Native dress, was strongly discouraged by the US government.*

- White settlers objected to the size of land parcels; various reports submitted to Congress found widespread corruption among the federal Native American agencies, and many tribes who ignored the relocation orders were then forced onto their limited land parcels.
- Enforcement of the policy required the U.S. Army to restrict the movements of various tribes by force, leading to a number of Native American massacres and some wars.
- The most well-known conflict was the Sioux War on the northern Great Plains, between 1876 and 1881, which included the Battle of Little Bighorn.
- By the 1880s, government officials, military officers and congressional leaders were unanimous in their agreement that allowing tribal landholdings and promoting tribal culture should end.
- They also believed that reservations should disappear along with Indian identity.
- In 1887, Congress undertook a significant change in reservation policy with the passage of the Dawes Act, which began the policy of granting small parcels of land to individuals, not tribes as a whole.
- The government's policy continued to assume that the road to salvation followed the white road to the church, school, and the farm.
- This belief remained firm even when the dry Plains proved difficult or even impossible to farm.

## HISTORICAL SNAPSHOT
# 1888

- The 91-centimeter telescope was first used at Lick Observatory
- In January, blizzards hit the Dakota Territory, as well as Montana, Minnesota, Nebraska, Kansas, and Texas, leaving 235 dead
- In Washington, DC, the National Geographic Society was founded
- Thomas Edison met with Eadweard Muybridge to discuss plans for sound film
- The Agriculture College of Utah was founded in Logan, Utah
- The Football League was formed

- The Brighton Beach Hotel in Coney Island was moved 520 feet using six steam locomotives by civil engineer B.C. Miller to save it from ocean storms
- Congress established the Fort Belknap Indian Reservation, covering 1,014,064 square miles in north central Montana
- "Casey at the Bat," a baseball poem written by Ernest Thayer, was published in *The San Francisco Examiner*
- The Republican Convention in Chicago selected Benjamin

Harrison and Levi Morton as its nominees for president and vice president, respectively
- Handel's *Israel in Egypt* was recorded onto a wax cylinder at The Crystal Palace, and became the earliest known recording of classical music
- The British Parliament permitted bicycles on the roads, on condition that they were equipped with a bell that should be rung while on the carriageway
- Berta Benz drove 40 miles in a car manufactured by her husband, Karl Benz, completing the first "long-distance" drive in the history of the automobile
- George Eastman registered the trademark "Kodak" and received a patent for his camera, which used roll film
- Dead bodies attributed to Jack the Ripper began appearing in London
- The Washington Monument, begun in 1848, officially opened to the general public as the world's tallest structure
- Presidential incumbent Grover Cleveland won the popular vote, but lost the Electoral College vote, and the election went to Republican challenger Benjamin Harrison
- Delta Delta Delta sorority was founded at Boston University
- Richard Wetherill and his brother-in-law discovered the ancient Indian ruins of Mesa Verde in southwestern Colorado
- John Robert Gregg published his method of taking dictation quickly and accurately
- Susan B. Anthony organized a Congress for Women's Rights in Washington, DC

## Selected Prices

Baking Powder………………………………………………$0.20

Bicycle Skirt………………………………………………$2.50

Civil War Picture Book……………………………………$7.50

Coffee, Pound……………………………………………$0.25

Corset.........................................................................$3.00

Dental Fees, Gold Filling…………………........................$1.00

Horse's Hoof Ointment, Jar………………………………$1.00

*Ladies' Home Journal*……………………………………$1.00

Men's Lace Shoes…………………………………………$0.98

Sewing Machine……………………………………………$9.00

## "Child Life, Curiosity and Other Matters," *Ballou's Monthly Magazine,* July 1886:

Many a child goes astray, not because there is a want of prayer or virtue at home, but simply because the home lacks sunshine. A child needs smiles as much as flowers need sunbeams. Children look little beyond the present moment. If a thing pleases, they are apt to seek; if it displaces, they are apt to avoid it. If home is the place where faces are sour, and words harsh, and fault finding is ever in the ascendant, they will spend as many hours as possible elsewhere.

## "Things Pleasant and Otherwise," *Ballou's Monthly Magazine,* July 1886:

David Key, of Tennessee, told a good story of a man in the mountain region of his state, who was a stereotyped candidate for local offices of all descriptions, but who would never give a decided opinion upon any question. On one occasion when he was a candidate for the position of Sheriff, there was great excitement on the enforcement of the school tax. He addressed quite a gathering at a muster, but evaded the only question the audience wanted to hear about, and just as he was closing a fellow shouted:

"Tell us about your school tax. Are you for it or are you not?"

The crowd cheered, and the orator, thus pressed for a declaration of opinion, said:

"Gentlemen, you have a right to ask for an answer. I have no concealment to make. I am a frank man, and to you I say in all frankness, if it is a good thing I am for it, if it is a bad thing I am against it."

Wanted Immediately: A Sober diligent Schoolmaster capable of teaching READING, WRITING, ARITHMETICK, and the Latin TONGUE... Any Person qualified as above, and well recommended, will be put into immediate Possession of the School, on applying to the Minister of Charles Parish, York County.

—*The Virginia Gazette*, August 20, 1772

## "Among the Wild Indians," Corabelle Fellows, *The Word Carrier,* January 1886:

The sight that grieves me most is to see women doing work that is much too hard for them, when they have children that need their care and strength. It is hard to sit by and see the men allow their wives to bring great heavy wood upon their backs, while they (the men) idle their time away, generally preparing for a dance in the evening, with paint, ornaments, and feathers. I hope the day will come when these heathen customs will be done away with, and the man will learn that his first Christian duty is to his wife and children; to shield them from these things, and be noble enough to do the hard work. The women will have to learn to be more cleanly, and out of scanty material have their homes pleasant and neat. Oh, how much there is for most of them to learn.

The Indian children were all most anxious to be noticed. "He Mye" ("This is I") was their constant phrase. It was their way of showing they could answer the question, that they wanted to be invited to my room, that they were standing at my desk and wanted me to acknowledge their value and presence. The smallest girls were a constant delight. I marveled at their patience and ability in sewing. Before the year was out, they were making all manner of undergarments.

One day one of them came to me and furtively asked me for "wasena." I questioned her and found out this time of the favorite dish of the Sioux, made of bone marrow, pounded with cherry pits and cherries and lean meat. I wrote a letter or two, and when the delicacy finally came from her home, she shared it with me. I found it excellent food. These children would sigh, when pleased or impatient or disappointed, just as their elders sighed. The little sewers never returned a word when a seam must be ripped and done over; they only sighed, a weary long-drawn sigh.

—Corabelle Fellows, Blue Star, Caxton Printers. Ltd., Caldwell, Idaho, 1938

Since about 1872 efforts had been put forth by every agent to make agriculturalists of these Indians, but the soil and the climate will not allow it.... It may be said that the Indian has been furnished with an occupation to employ his time; but I see no good in keeping these Indians employed at what they cannot make a living in this country.

—United States Office of Indian Affairs, Annual Report, 1887

# 1896 NEWS FEATURE

**"Law, Women in the Professions," Mrs. Theodore Sutro, *The Delineator*, April 1896:**

Why should women embrace the profession of law as a means of livelihood? For the same reason that men embrace it, for the same reason that has induced women to become physicians, artists, scientists, ministers, educators, financiers, editors, and to engage in almost all pursuits which a few generations ago were considered the exclusive property of men. Because we have arrived at the point in our civilization when their mental subordination, merely because they are women, has become almost inconceivable.

Why should women not study law? This question could be answered far more readily. The reason women have so long been disbarred from this particular profession may be partly explained because precedent more than anything else holds sway over the minds of judges and lawyers, and it has become almost a matter of tradition that a woman should not become a lawyer.

It may also be partly explained through a misconception on the part of the public of the character of the profession. Among the laity, the lawyer is pictured as a person who must constantly engage in the strife and turmoil of the forum, whose stentorian voice must terrorize witnesses and impress juries, and who must move about in all the highways and byways of life like a whirlwind in order to ferret out and discover material which he may use in the trial of the case. No one knows better than members of the profession how remote such an idea is from the facts. The main business of a lawyer, insofar as his time is occupied at all with litigation, is performed in the seclusion of his private office and in the careful analysis of the facts of his case and the study of the law bearing upon it. Especially in our generation, however, the main portion of his work consists in advising and counseling, and in performing such labor as rather tends to prevent and avoid litigation, and then to conduct it when it is unavoidable. Surely in this branch of the profession, it is a question of intellect and training solely, and not one of sex, as to whether the person pursuing it is fitted to be successful or not.

Actual experience has proved that in the classes which have now been open to women for the study of law (as since time immemorial they have been to men), women take as high a rank as men, if not higher. There are a hundred avenues in the profession outside of actual court practice in which women, providing they have the necessary qualifications and training, may be equally successful with men.

To succeed in certain legal fields, woman is no doubt particularly fitted and adapted by Nature. There is many a subject which a sensitive woman would shrink from revealing to a lawyer of the sterner sex, and, therefore, rather bears her cross in silence, which she would only be too glad to confide to a woman lawyer upon whose womanly sympathy, instincts and comprehensions she could rely. Certainly in everything that pertains to office advice and counsel, the preparation for trial and laying out plans for conducting litigations where the interest to women and young children are involved, one is especially qualified so far as natural abilities go....

At all events, women are now entitled to admission to the bar in New York as well as in several other states. Paragraph 56 of the Code of Civil Procedure of New York provides that "Race or sex shall constitute no cause for refusing any person examination or admission to practice."

The chief drawback to the study of the profession of law by women as compared to men is their greater lack of general education training, a lack proportional to the small number of colleges for women in comparison to those open to young men. While exceptional brilliant examples exist of success in almost every profession without ample preliminary general training, there can be no doubt that, as a rule, such training is necessary in law. I would not advise any young woman to undertake the study of law with a view to making it a means of livelihood unless she has at least a thorough high school education; properly, it should be a college education. The profession being for women as yet a novelty, many of them are tempted to think they must be adapted for it simply because so many men are engaged in it. These young women, however, forget that while, as Daniel Webster said, "There's always room in the upper story," the upper story nevertheless has its limits, and of the thousands of men who undertake to practice law, the percentage of those who actually succeed is almost insignificant. Not only does the practice of this profession require thorough preliminary mental training, but also the possession of that peculiar type of an intellect known as the "legal mind."

Moreover, the exactions of the profession are enormous, and unless able to bear an almost unlimited amount of work and possessing a constitution which can surmount the wear and tear of incessant mental anxiety, no man can succeed in this pursuit; how much less, then, a woman! While I fully believe in throwing open the avenues of every profession to my sex, I think it is also proper to point out to its members the danger of spending years and large sums of money in pursuing a mere fad. Let a young woman pause and well consider whether she has the educational and physical qualifications required for the pursuit of this exacting profession, and, over and above these, whether she has the peculiar mental traits which adapt her to make a success of it.

# 1898 PROFILE

Jarrett Winston grew up in Atlanta, Georgia, committed to entering the ministry, until an accident at age 16 caused him to consider becoming a teacher.

## Life at Home

- Even though Jarrett Winston had shared the stress that permeated his household during important religious holidays, at times of great conflict in the church, or at the death of a beloved parishioner, he accepted his calling at an early age.
- The third of eight children, he was called "little preacher man" by the time he was seven, thanks to an impromptu religious service he conducted one morning among the hens.
- History will record that none of the chickens sought conversion at the end of his talk, but the rooster remained to the end of the service.
- Jarrett's long-planned career was literally crushed when he was 16; a wagon fully loaded with grain rolled over his legs, rendering them unusable.
- As he recovered, he grew more and more despondent; convinced that no one would want a cripple around, he even contemplated suicide.

*A crippling accident pushed Jarrett Winston to consider teaching.*

*Jarrett did not enjoy teaching younger children.*

- In his darkest hour, it was his mother, not his father, who shone a light on a possible future.
- On the front page of the *Atlanta Journal* was a two-column picture of a legless Civil War veteran teaching a college class in biology.
- "Here," his mother said, "is a profession that focuses only on the mind and not on the body. With two years of college," she said, "you could become a college professor."
- He could even use his position in the front of the class, she whispered conspiratorially, to pick out his wife.
- It was the first time he had laughed out loud since the accident.
- His timing was excellent.
- As the nineteenth century was drawing to a close, America's increasing role as a world power had bolstered its confidence and accelerated the changing status of professionals in an increasingly industrialized world.
- One of the clear winners was college professors, whose prestige was rising along with the emergence of the modern university.
- In addition to a plethora of existing traditional denominational colleges and large universities, libraries with laboratories and endowments had begun taking their own place in American education.
- With these advances came professional schools, higher salaries and increased prestige.
- At the same time, the clergy were losing ground as molders of opinion; as more farmers became city dwellers and factory workers, multigenerational ties to a particular church faded as transportation became more sophisticated.
- Despite the constant pain in his back and legs, Jarrett shifted his focus to the study of math—a subject he had always enjoyed, but shunned as unimportant to a minister.
- As his mother predicted—and helped orchestrate—Jarrett was admitted to Emory College, whose motto was *Cor Prudentis Possidebit Scientiam*: The wise heart seeks knowledge.
- Conceived in 1836, Emory was located in remote Oxford, Georgia, and named after Rev. John Emory, an American Methodist bishop whose broad vision for education incorporated the development of the character as well as the mind.
- The first year Jarrett attended Emory, the 1891-1892 catalogue banned students from attending any ball, theater, horse race or cock fight; from imbibing intoxicating drinks, playing cards, playing any game for stakes, keeping firearms or any deadly weapon, a horse, a dog, or a servant; from engaging in anything forbidden by the faculty, associating with persons of known bad character, visiting points beyond the limits of Oxford without permission from some member of the faculty, and visiting points more distant without written permission from parents or guardians and the permission of the president of the college; visiting any place of ill repute, or at which gaming was practiced or intoxicating liquors were sold; engaging in any "match game," or "intercollegiate" game of football, baseball, etc.
- Jarrett blossomed in the intellectually challenging atmosphere of Emory.
- He also found romance with Naomi Arthur, a student at nearby Covington Female Academy.
- Both then found jobs as teachers in a school outside Atlanta: Jarrett taught 23 children, aged 11 to 14; Naomi was assigned 33 first graders.
- Despite being at the top of his class academically at Emory, Jarrett found instructing 11- to 14-year-olds intimidating and unfulfilling.

- Once the students had become accustomed to Jarrett's crutches and no longer asked inappropriately personal questions, they began to take advantage of his lack of mobility.
- One overly large 14-year-old farm boy walked out of class and dared Jarrett to do something about it; math lessons were sometimes lost in the wake of classroom turmoil.
- Jarrett lasted a year and was more than ready to give up on teaching when he received a letter from Rev. Samuel Lander inviting him to interview for a math professor's job at Williamston Female College, located in Williamston, South Carolina.
- Jarrett was offered the position in 1896.

*Jarrett married Naomi Arthur, who taught first grade.*

## Life at Work

- After Jarrett Winston had completed his two-day buggy ride from Atlanta to Williamston, South Carolina, Rev. Samuel Lander explained that "the leading peculiarity of our plan is that we do not give a pupil three or four difficult studies at once, as is usual in other institutions."
- He said, "We devote special attention, though not quite exclusive, to one principal subject for five weeks, then lay that one down and take up another in the same way for five weeks more."
- Jarrett was impressed with the seriousness of the college's intent and the industry of its students.
- Williamston Female College had been created through a joint stock company composed of friends of education, mostly citizens of Williamston.
- Its published objective was to "furnish young ladies, at low rates, a thorough education as far as its course extends, giving them opportunity, encouragement, and help, to lay deep and well the foundation, and erect there and on, with care and patience, the beauteous superstructure of accurate scholarship, combined in symmetrical proportions with physical vigor, cultivated manners, and sanctified affections."
- Founded in February 1872 by Rev. Lander, Williamston Female College and its founder had much to offer Jarrett.
- Rev. Lander was also the son of a Methodist minister, and education had been an important part of his upbringing.
- As important, Rev. Lander embraced Jarrett's physical handicap and even made plans for several of the female students to assist him to and from class.

*At Williamston Female College, Jarrett encouraged students to pursue teaching.*

- Jarrett's wife Naomi swiftly put an end to that scheme, declaring that she would be her husband's legs.
- By 1898, when the upstart college had gained the support of the South Carolina Conference of the Methodist Episcopal Church, South, Jarrett and Naomi were a familiar sight at the college's hotel-turned-classroom.
- Jarrett, still endowed with a religious zeal, wanted to devote his energy to training young women to be teachers.
- Even though important steps were being taken to provide college opportunities for teachers, South Carolina student funding was scant.
- By 1896, the per-pupil spending for whites stood at $3.11, while spending on black pupils was $1.05.
- As a result, the teachers assigned to educate children were often fresh from the schoolroom themselves—quite often town girls with a high school education who taught for diversion and a $75.00-a-month salary.
- Jarrett had come to believe that if teaching was to attain the distinction of a profession, raising the quality of the personnel in the classroom was essential.
- South Carolina's English settlers in the 1700s brought with them the belief that education was a private, voluntary matter.
- Families of the upper and middle classes were expected to pay for the education of their children, most of whom attended private or church schools, or were taught by tutors.
- Public support for education was reserved for orphans and pauper children "in limited numbers and a limited time."
- The state's educational heritage was best summed up: "The business of the lower classes is to serve rather than to think."
- Early educational efforts were focused on spreading rudimentary learning among the population, both for humanitarian reasons and to foster civilized behavior among the working class.
- Following the American Revolution, a new philosophy emerged based on the belief that a democratic government could not succeed if the masses were denied an education.
- This outlook—which was embraced by some of the progressive thinkers among the aristocracy—eventually led to a new school law in 1811.
- The bill to Establish Free Schools throughout the State was aimed at placing at least one public school in each of the state's 44 election districts.
- From a budget standpoint, each district received $300 per state representative.
- The legislature gave no consideration to the number of students who might attend a school, or the need for more schools in thinly populated areas.

- Lowcountry leaders were generally wealthy, with enough education to value learning, and with a greater willingness to support the government through taxes.
- With the advent of universal male suffrage in 1810, many Lowcountry leaders felt it imperative to improve the education of the Upcountry majority.
- Although the law allowed any white child to attend the free schools, it gave first preference to the poor, so most working families were too proud to participate in the "pauper schools" and kept their children at home.
- The South Carolina College Faculty presented a report that cited two school deficiencies: physical and moral.

- The physical deficiency was sparseness of the program, while the moral shortcoming was stated as follows:

  - the carelessness of the poor about the education of their children
  - the selfishness which leads them to prefer their children's labors to their children's improvement
  - the foolish pride, which prevents them from receiving as a bounty that which they cannot procure in any better way.

- It was also reported that "the attendance of each individual is short, irregular and inadequate to secure proficiency."
- Some pupils attended no more than a few days, and at best, some attended a few weeks of the year.
- In the Upcountry, many districts had no free schools at all, spending the meager aid instead on private tuition for a select few.
- The law also failed to appropriate state aid according to the needs of each area.
- Despite population shifts toward the Piedmont, the law's system of distribution tended to favor wealthier counties in the Lowcountry—establishing a pattern of unequal school finance that has plagued the state ever since.
- The school terms were seasonal—in session only when the children could be spared from farm work.
- Despite the structural gaps in South Carolina, Jarrett began to make progress—firmly supported by Rev. Lander's working philosophy on the college's standard scholarship.
- "We are frequently asked by anxious parents when their daughters will graduate. This we can never answer, for one might be disappointed on the work of one "section," even the last one in her course," Rev. Lander wrote to his students.
- "We carefully avoid mere surface work. By frequent reviews, by extra problems and exercises, independent investigations, actual use of apparatus, and written examinations, in short, by every means in our reach, we enjoy a credible acquaintance with each subject as the essential condition of advancement."
- Indeed, Jarrett found that his pupils embraced the arithmetic courses he taught with enthusiasm; many stayed after class to ask questions and listen to his ideas—occasionally remaining long enough to solicit a jealous remark from his wife.
- Jarrett was encouraged to demand high quality from his students and be a tough grader.
- Three of his four math classes rose artfully to the challenge; in response, respect replaced sympathy in Jarrett's mind—several of his students had the potential to be great teachers.
- As Rev. Lander had said, "We point with pride to the small number of our alumnae; our object is not to graduate young ladies, but to conduct their education as well as we can for the time they remain in our care; we dwell on these facts, not in the spirit of boasting, but principally to prevent misunderstandings and dissatisfaction."
- To make its goals perfectly clear, Williamston Female College began running a notice within its bulletin stating, "Young ladies sometimes attend boarding school merely for the sake of spending a few months in pleasant circumstances, and of referring to their school days in after-life. We kindly warn all such they would not be pleased within our school."

## Life in the Community: Williamston, South Carolina

- The founding of the town of Williamston was a dream-come-true for West Allen Williams, whose discovery of a mineral spring—with healing properties—on his property turned the tiny farming town near Anderson, South Carolina, into a tourist attraction.
- As news of the medicinal water spread, the town grew more rapidly—especially after the railroads arrived in 1851.

- Some local promoters even attempted to dub the community the "Saratoga of the South," a reference to the famous spring waters in New York that had been an attraction for decades.
- To accommodate the influx of newcomers, the Mammoth Hotel was built near the spring and was the largest building in the state at that time, featuring 150 rooms plus a bowling alley and several ballrooms.
- Initially, the town was known as Mineral Springs, but was changed to Williamston in 1852 to honor its founder; West Allen Williams had set aside property to preserve the spring and to build schools and churches.
- In 1872, Rev. Samuel Lander established a girls' school; the first-term enrollment was 36 students, and by the end of the first year, 60 young women were enrolled.
- Within a decade, the school boasted 159 students, 71 from Williamston, 73 from other parts of South Carolina, and the remainder from six additional states.
- Rev. Lander was also instrumental in prohibiting the sale of liquor in Williamston—anticipating the passage of the Eighteenth Amendment two decades later.
- As the century was ending, cotton mills settled near the river and played major roles in shaping the communities.
- Farmers, eager to abandon the uneven economy of Southern agriculture, flocked to the industrial mills—most based on cotton—for the opportunity to be paid regularly.
- Mill owners actively recruited entire families to work in the textile mills—believing that school was not a necessity for farm children whose future was in the mills.
- The settlers of the area were mostly Scots-Irish who came from Virginia and Pennsylvania to farm.
- Farmers grew corn and raised hogs and later, cotton.
- By the late nineteenth century, the Anderson County area was filled with numerous textile mills.

*Mill owners discouraged schooling for farm children who were needed to work in the mills.*

- Thanks to the innovation of Anderson engineer William Whitner, electricity could be conducted by wire to mills throughout the county.
- Anderson was the first city in the United States to have a continuous supply of electric power, which was supplied by a water mill located in the high shoals area of the Rocky River in Anderson County.
- Local historians bragged that the first cotton gin in the world to be operated by electricity was built in Anderson County in 1897; as a result, the city of Anderson became known as "The Electric City."

# HISTORICAL SNAPSHOT
## 1898

- New York City annexed land from surrounding counties, creating the City of Greater New York, geographically divided into five boroughs: Manhattan, Brooklyn, Queens, the Bronx, and Staten Island

- Emile Zola published *J'Accuse*, a letter accusing the French government of anti-Semitism and wrongfully placing Alfred Dreyfus in jail

- The Reverend Charles Lutwidge Dodgson, better known as Lewis Carroll, author of *Alice in Wonderland, Through the Looking-Glass*, and other classic works of children's literature, died of pneumonia at age 65

- The USS *Maine* exploded and sank in Havana Harbor, Cuba, killing 266 men and igniting the Spanish-American War between the United States and Spain

- Robert Allison of Port Carbon, Pennsylvania, became the first person to buy an American-built automobile when he purchased a Winton automobile that had been advertised in *Scientific American*

- Annie Oakley promoted the service of women in combat situations with the United States military, offering "the services of a company of 50 lady sharpshooters' who would provide their own arms and ammunition should war break out with Spain"

- In the Battle of Manila Bay, Commodore Dewey destroyed the Spanish squadron, leading to the American capture of the Philippines

- Secondo Pia took the first photographs of the Shroud of Turin and discovered that the image on shroud itself appeared to be a photographic negative

- The Trans-Mississippi Exposition World's Fair opened in Omaha, Nebraska

- Marie and Pierre Curie announced the discovery of a substance they called "radium"

- John Jacob Abel isolated epinephrine (adrenaline)

- As a result of the merger of several small oil companies, John D. Rockefeller's Standard Oil Company controlled 84 percent of American oil and most U.S. pipelines

## Selected Prices

Artificial Leg……………………………………………………………$75.00

Carriage, Wire or Wooden Wheels………………………………$12.35

Flour, Half Barrel…………………………………………………………$2.50

Folding Bed………………………………………………………………$15.00

Fountain Pen…………………………………………………………………$3.50

Hair Curler………………………………………...........................................$1.00

Man's Shirt…………………………………………………………………$1.50

Piano Lessons, 24…………………………………………………………$8.00

Tooth Extraction………………………………..…………………………$0.25

Woman's Bicycle Costume………………………………………………$7.50

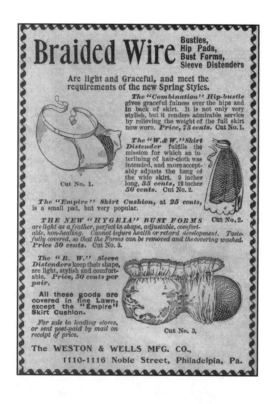

## Rates per Section of Five Weeks at Williamston Female College

| | |
|---|---|
| Board, exclusive of washing: | $15.00 |
| Regular tuition in primary class: | $3.00 |
| Regular tuition in class A, B, or C: | $4.00 |
| Regular tuition in first, second, or third class: | $5.00 |
| Regular tuition in fourth, fifth or sixth class: | $6.00 |
| Incidental tax: | $0.25 |
| Instrumental music: | $5.00 |
| Use of instrument: | $0.75 |
| Local music, individual lesson: | $5.00 |
| Graduation fee: | $7.50 |

Books and stationery are furnished at reasonable rates; or else books are rented to advanced pupils at one third of their retail price for section's careful use.

Pupils furnish their own doilies, towels, sheets, pillow-cases, and toilet soap

Each boarding pupil will pay two sections' expenses in advance, and at the end of her second section, two sections more.

Daughters of Christian ministers who are devoted to the actual work of the ministry enjoy special rates, which will be made known at application.

## "Young Ladies And Dress," *The Naiad,* Williamston, South Carolina, December 1884:

A lady who had taught for over 30 years once gave the writer some very interesting information. "When a new scholar was introduced," she said, "I always look first at her dress. If it was plain, neat, and tidy, I was pretty confident that I had good material to work with. For the first two or three years of my teaching, I was in the habit of scrutinizing the features, and the formation of the heads, but these came at last to be quite secondary considerations. One school was so expensive that none but the daughters of the wealthy could possibly enter it; so when a young lady came to the classroom in a plain dress, I was sure that it was on account of her idea of the fitness of things. This argued common sense. Common sense is always in direct antagonism to vanity, and, where there is no vanity, there is seldom self-consciousness. So, you see, a plain dress came to mean a great deal to me. I learned never to expect anything from a girl whose school dress was silk or velvet. I shall always retain the impression made upon me by a quiet little body in a blue flannel dress, and plain trimmings. She came from one of the first families in wealth and culture, and was the most unobtrusive child I ever knew, as well as the most brilliant. When she told me on graduation day that she had decided to study for a physician, I was not in the least surprised, and I was sure she would succeed, and she certainly has the most marvelous manner. She carried off every honor, and, though the girls in 'purple and fine linen' sneered at her plain attire, and lack of style, there was not one who could ever compete with her."

*Continued*

## "Young Ladies And Dress," . . . *(Continued)*

Certainly, on the whole, the deductions of this teacher are correct. It takes time to array oneself in elaborate garments, and the girl whose mind is occupied with loops and trimming and general furbelows cannot, for philosophical reason, have room for much else. Then there is the reason deeper than this, even. The girl whose tastes are in the line of dress and display has not an intellectual development. She may be imitative and intuitive to a degree, but she will generally be superficial in her learning and shallow in character.

A very good story in this connection is told of a prominent musician in New York. A young lady went to him for a course of "finishing off" lessons. "Let's see what you can do," said the teacher, and placed before her a simple aria of Mozart's. She played a few measures, and was interrupted. "Take off your rings," said the great man. A few measures more, and another interruption. "Take off your bracelets." A little further on, she was stopped again. "Your sleeves are too long. I cannot see your wrists." She stopped and penned up her sleeves with a face on fire. At last she succeeded in finishing the selection.

"Do you want me to teach you?" the instructor asked, as she took her hands from the keys.

"Yes, sir."

"Very well. Come tomorrow at this hour, without any jewelry, and in some sort of a dress you can breathe in. I don't know at all how you have played this aria, because of the rattling gew-gaws, and the distracting noise you make in getting your breath. I am afraid you haven't the instinct of a musician. A musician thinks first of his art, and the last of his appearances; but it seems to me you think first, last, and always of how you look."

SAILOR BLOUSE.—
d. or 20 cents.

Now this may seem to some rough and very uncalled for, but he was an honest soul and a grand musician. His words prove true. This young lady had not the musical instinct, and, after a fair trial, was dismissed. Her teacher proved that her practice had been superficial, and all that she had done had been spoiled by vanity and self-consciousness.

A schoolgirl who dressed very plainly, but in good taste, was once asked why she did not "rig up" more.

"Because," she said, "I haven't time to fuss about clothes, and learn, too, and then I should like to have something new to wear when I was older. Velvets and brocades, and diamonds and pearls, and all those fine things will be new to me by and by, and there's nothing left for you girls to anticipate."

As South Carolina's public education system stumbled into the twentieth century, State Superintendent of Education John McMahan handed down this summary judgment of its condition in his 1900 report to the General Assembly:

"It is a misnomer to say that we have a system of public schools. In the actual working of the great majority of schools in this state, there is no system or orderly organization. Each county supports its own schools with practically no help from the state. Each district has as poor schools as its people will tolerate—and in some districts, anything will be tolerated."

### "Miss Armstrong Exonerated, the Teacher Freed of Horsewhipping Charges, But Complainant Is Bitter Against School Trustees," *The New York Times,* May 17, 1895:

WHITESTONE, L.I. At a meeting of the Board of Education held here tonight, the committee appointed at the request of Miss Edith Armstrong, a teacher in the public school, to investigate the horsewhipping charge made against her by William Joyce, rendered a report exonerating the teacher.

In his complaint, Mr. Joyce alleged that his son, William, and Edward Gleason were severely horsewhipped by Miss Armstrong, and were held during a part of such whipping by Principal William M. Peck, that the teacher was in the habit of flogging the pupils before the classes, and that on numerous occasions she had thrown the boys on the floor, and, holding them by placing her knee on their chests, pounded them with books.

Miss Armstrong admitted having whipped the boys, but claims that the whipping was not unduly severe, and says that she only struck them on the necks and bodies when they attempted to disarm her.

Trustee Robert S. Munson, chairman of the committee made to investigate the charges, and Principal Peck reported that they and trustee L.W. Ensign had made a preliminary examination in Mr. Joyce's presence, and they were agreed that the charges were without foundation and that no public investigation was necessary. The report was accepted and the committee discharged.

William Joyce this evening said he was far from satisfied with the investigation made by the committee appointed by the Board of Education. He said he was hastily summoned to the school a few days ago, and arrived as the session was over. He alleges that Mr. Peck conducts the school in the most undignified manner. Mr. Joyce says he will demand an examination into the charges specific to his complaint. He will use other means, he said, to have the facts of the case brought out that the school trustees refused to properly investigate.

It was with that first class that I became aware that a teacher was subservient to a higher authority. I became increasingly aware of this subservience to an ever growing number of authorities with each succeeding year, until there is danger today of becoming aware of little else.

—Marian Dogherty, Teacher, Boston, 1899

## Norton, John and Levona Page. *A Special Report: Our Schools, The State*, January 1984:

Much of the 300-year history of our public schools is a tragic tale of fits and starts, marked at times by inspired leadership, but too often marred by problems of class, race, war, poverty and geography.

Ten Reasons for Slow Growth of the Statewide Public School System

1. A strong tradition brought from England that public support for education should be limited to the poor

2. Education was seen as more of the responsibility of the Church than the State

3. Attitudes of those outside the wealthy class that worked against a unified system, including low regard for learning, reluctance to accept charity through free tuition, and the need to keep children in the family labor force

4. The very high cost in the 1700s and 1800s to provide quality schools outside the cities and coastal areas, where population was sparse and transportation poor

5. Strong resistance to local taxation for schools until the late 1800s

6. Interruption of a burgeoning "common school movement" in South Carolina by the Civil War, and the subsequent disruption of a tax base

7. Increased white resistance to the public school idea following the Reconstruction government's attempts to open schools to all races

8. An attitude on the part of some twentieth-century leaders that too much education would damage the state's cheap labor force

9. The slow growth of state supervision of the schools due to strong sentiments toward local control

10. The financial burden of operating a racially segregated system, and the social and educational impact of combining two unequal systems in the late 1960s

The Society of Propagating the Gospel, which sent out missionaries not only to preach but also to encourage establishment of schools. The Society's schoolmasters were required to do the following:

- take especial care of the manners of the pupils in and out of school
- warn them against lying and falsehood and evil speaking
- love truth and honesty
- be modest, just and affable
- receive in their tender years that sense of religion which may render it the constant principle of their lives and action

The teacher was an Irishman, Mr. Quigley, a man about 55 years old, and a rigid disciplinarian, altogether very tyrannical and sometimes cruel. This teacher had one remarkable peculiarity in regard to the admission of small boys to his school. It made no odds whether a boy was good or bad; he invariably got a flogging on the first day. The teacher always sought some pretext to make a flogging necessary and when he began, he seldom stopped until the youngster vomited or wet his breeches.

—Dr. J.M. Simms wrote of attending in 1819, at age six, a "boarding school" six or eight miles from his Lancaster home

# 1900–1909

The first decade of the twentieth century was marked by dramatic innovation and keen-eyed energy as America's men and women competed to invent a better school, a better automobile, mass-market soft drinks, or configure the right land deal that would propel them into the millionaire's mansion so frequently described by the press. While architects attempted to create "cathedrals of learning," communities voted for universal high schools while continuing to debate whether the purpose of education was preparation for an occupation or the development of a well-disciplined mind capable of pondering larger questions such as the meaning of life and happiness. More attention was being paid to the status and training of teachers, teacher's unions were forming, and the writing and publication of curriculum-based textbooks was becoming big business.

At the same time, the number of inventions and changes spawned by the expanded use of electricity was nothing short of revolutionary. Factories converted to the new energy force, staying open longer. A bottle-making machine patented in 1903 virtually eliminated the hand-blowing of glass bottles; another innovation mechanized the production of window glass. A rotating kiln manufactured in 1899 supplied large quantities of cheap, standardized cement, just in time for a nation ready to leave behind the bicycle and fall madly in love with the automobile. Thanks to this spirit of innovation and experimentation, the United States led the world in productivity, exceeding the vast empires of France and Britain combined.

In the eyes of the world, America was the land of opportunity. Millions of immigrants flooded to the United States, often finding work in the factories of the New World—many managed by the men who arrived only two generations before from countries like England, Germany, or Wales. When Theodore Roosevelt proudly proclaimed in 1902, "The typical American is accumulating money more rapidly than any other man on earth," he described accurately both the joy of newcomers and the prosperity of the emerging middle class. Elevated by their education, profession, inventiveness, or capital, the managerial class found numerous opportunities to flourish in the rapidly changing world of a new economy.

At the beginning of the century, the U.S. population, comprising 45 states, stood at 76 million, an increase of 21 percent since 1890; 10.6 million residents were foreign-born and more were coming every day. The number of immigrants in the first decade of the twentieth century was double that of the previous decade, exceeding one million annually in four of the 10 years, the highest level in U.S. history. Business and industry were convinced that unrestricted immigration was the fuel that drove the growth of American industry. Labor was equally certain that the influx of foreigners continually undermined the economic status of native workers and kept wages low.

The change in productivity and consumerism came with a price: the character of American life. Manufacturing plants drew people from the country into the cities. The traditional farm patterns were disrupted by the lure of urban life. Ministers complained that lifelong churchgoers who moved to the city often found less time and fewer social pressures to attend worship regularly. Between 1900 and 1920, the urban population increased by 80 percent compared to just over 12 percent for rural areas. During the same time, the non-farming work force went from 783,000 to 2.2 million. Unlike farmers, these workers drew a regular paycheck, and spent it. With this movement of people, technology, and ideas, nationalism took on a new meaning in America. Railroad expansion in the middle of the nineteenth century had made it possible to move goods quickly and efficiently throughout the country. As a result, commerce, which had been based largely on local production of goods for local consumption, found new markets. Ambitious merchants expanded their businesses by appealing to broader markets. In 1900, America claimed 58 businesses with more than one retail outlet, called "chain stores"; by 1910, that number had more than tripled, and by 1920, the total had risen to 808. The number of clothing chains alone rose from seven to 125 during the period. Department stores such as R.H. Macys in New York and Marshall Field's in Chicago offered vast arrays of merchandise along with free services and the opportunity to "shop" without purchasing. Ready-made clothing drove down prices, but also promoted fashion booms that reduced class distinctions of dress. In rural America, the mail order catalogs of Sears, Roebuck and Company reached deep into the pocket of common people and made dreaming and consuming more feasible.

All was not well, however. A brew of labor struggles, political unrest, and tragic factory accidents demonstrated the excesses of industrial capitalism so worshiped in the Gilded Age. The labor reform movements of the 1880s and 1890s culminated in the newly formed American Federation of Labor (AFL) as the chief labor advocate.

The reforms of the labor movement called for an eight-hour workday, child-labor regulation, and cooperatives of owners and workers. The progressive bent of the times also focused attention on factory safety, tainted food and drugs, political corruption, and unchecked economic monopolies.

Progress was, however, not being made by all. Women were still not allowed to vote. For black Americans, many of the gains of Reconstruction were being wiped away by regressive Jim Crow laws, particularly in the South. Cherished voting privileges were being systematically taken away.

The decade ushered in the opening of the first movie theater, located in Pittsburgh, in 1905. Vaudeville prospered, traveling circuses seemed to be everywhere, and America was crazy for any type of contest. The decade marked the first baseball World Series, Scholastic Aptitude Tests, Albert Einstein's new theories concerning the cosmos, and the Brownie Box camera from Eastman Kodak.

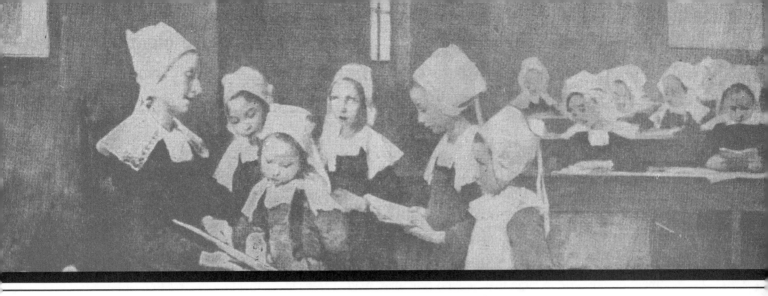

# 1902 News Feature

**"The School and Social Progress,"** *The School and Society*, **John Dewey, University of Chicago Press, 1900:**

We are apt to look at the school from an individualistic standpoint, as something between teacher and pupil, or between teacher and parent. That which interests us most is naturally the progress made by the individual child of our acquaintance, his normal physical development, his advance in ability to read, write, and figure, his growth in the knowledge of geography and history, improvement in manners, habits of promptness, order, and industry—it is from such standards as these that we judge the work of the school. And rightly so. Yet the range of the outlook needs to be enlarged. What the best and wisest parent wants for his own child, that must the community want for all of its children. Any other ideal for our schools is narrow and unlovely; acted upon, it destroys our democracy. All that society has accomplished for itself is put, through the agency of the school, at the disposal of its future members. All its better thoughts of itself it hopes to realize through the new possibilities thus to open to its future self. Here, individualism and socialism are at one. Only by being true to the full growth of all the individuals who make it up, can society by any chance be true to itself. And in self-direction, nothing counts as much as a school, for, as Horace Mann said, "Where anything is growing, one former is worth a thousand reformers."

Whenever we have in mind the discussion of a new movement in education, it is especially necessary to take the broader, or social, view. Otherwise, changes in the school institution and tradition will be looked at as the arbitrary invention of particular teachers, at the worst transitory fads, and at the best, merely improvements in certain details—and this is the plane upon which it is too customary to consider school changes. It is as rational to conceive of a locomotive or telegraph as personal devices. The modification going on in the method and curriculum of education is as much a product of the changed social situation, and as much an effort to meet the needs of the new society that is forming, as are changes in modes of industry and commerce.

It is to this, then, that I especially ask your attention: the effort to conceive what roughly may be termed the "New Education" in the light of larger changes in society. Can we connect this

"New Education" with the general march of events? If we can, it will lose its isolated character; it will cease to be an affair which proceeds only from the over-ingenious minds of pedagogues dealing with particular pupils. It will appear as part and parcel of the whole social evolution, and, in its most general features of these, as inevitable. Let us then use activism as the main aspect of the social movement; and afterward turn to the school to find what witness it gives an effort to put itself in line.

And since it is quite impossible to cover the whole ground, I shall for the most part confine myself in this chapter to one typical thing in the modern school movement—that which passes under the name of manual training—hoping, if the relation of that to changed social conditions appears, we shall be ready to concede the point as well regarding other educational innovations.

I make no apology for not dwelling at length upon the social changes in question. Those I shall mention are writ so large that he who runs may read. The changes that comes first to mind, the one that overshadows and even controls all others, is the industrial one—the application of science resulting in the great inventions that have utilized the forces of nature on a vast and inexpensive scale: the growth of a worldwide market as the object of production, of vast manufacturing centers to supply this market, of cheap and rapid means of communication and distribution between all its parts. Even as to its feebler beginnings, this change is not much more than a century old; in many of its most important aspects, it falls within the short span of those now living. One can hardly believe there's been a revolution in all history so rapid, so extensive, so complete. Through it, the face of Earth is making over, even as to its physical forms; political boundaries are wiped out and moved about, as if they were indeed only lines on a paper map; population is hurriedly gathered into cities from the ends of the earth; habits of living are altered with startling abruptness and thoroughness; the search for the truths of nature is indefinitely stimulated and facilitated, and their application to life made not only practicable, but commercially necessary. Even our moral and religious ideas and interests, the most conservative because they are the deepest-lying things in our nature, are profoundly affected. That this revolution should not affect education in some other than the formal and superficial fashion is inconceivable.

In back of the factory system lies the household and neighborhood system. Those of us who are here today need to look back only one, two, or at most three generations, to find a time when the household was practically the center in which were carried on, or about which were clustered, all the typical forms of industrial occupation. The clothing worn was, for the most part, made in the house; the members of the household were usually familiar also with the shearing of sheep, the carding and spinning of the wool, and the plying of the loom. Instead of pressing a button and flooding the house with electric light, the whole process of getting illumination was followed in its toilsome length from the killing of the animal and the drying of fat to the making of wicks and dipping of candles. The supply of flour, of lumber, of foods, of building materials, of household furniture, even of metal ware, of nails, hinges, hammers, etc., was produced in the immediate neighborhood, in shops which are constantly open to inspection and often centers of neighborhood congregation. The entire industrial process stood revealed, from the production on the farm of the raw materials till the finished article was actually put to use. Not only this, but practically every member of the household had his own share of the work. The children, as they gained in strength and capacity, were gradually initiated into the mysteries of these several processes. It was a matter of immediate and personal concern, even to the point of actual participation.

We cannot overlook the factors of discipline and character building involved in this kind of life: training in habits of industry, and the idea of responsibility, of obligation to do something, to produce something, in the world. There was always something which really needed to be done, and a real necessity that each member of the household should do his own part faithfully and in cooperation with others. Personalities which became effective in action were bred and tested in the medium of action. Again, one cannot overlook the importance for education purposes of the close and intimate acquaintance with nature at first hand, with real things and materials, with the actual processes of their manipulation, and the knowledge of their social necessities and uses. In all this there was a continual training of observation, of ingenuity, constructive imagination, of logical thought, and of the sense of reality acquired through first-hand contact with actualities. The educational forces of the domestic spinning and weaving, of the sawmill, the grist mill, the cooper shop, and the blacksmith forge, were continuously operative.

No number of object lessons, put up as object lessons for the sake of getting information, can afford even the shadow of a substitute for acquaintance with the plants and animals of the farm and garden acquired through actual living among them and caring for them. The training of sense organs in school, introduced for the sake of training, can begin to compete with the alertness and fullness of sense-life that comes through daily intimacy and interest and familiar occupations. Verbal memory can be trained in committing tasks, a certain discipline of the reasoning powers can be acquired through lessons in science and mathematics; but, after all, this is somewhat remote and shadowy compared to the training of attention and judgment that is acquired having to do things with a real motive behind and a real outcome ahead. At present, concentration of industry and division of labor have practically eliminated household and neighborhood occupations—at least for educational purposes. But isn't it useless to bemoan the departure of the good old days of children's modesty, reverence, and implicit obedience, if we expect merely by bemoaning and by exhortation to bring them back? It is radical conditions which have changed, and only an equally radical change of education suffices. We must recognize our compensations—the increasing in toleration, the breadth of social judgment, the larger acquaintance with human nature, a sharpened alertness in reading signs of character and interpreting social situations, greater accuracy in adapting to different personalities, contact with various commercial activities. These considerations mean much to the city-bred child of the day. Yet there is a real problem: how shall we retain these advantages, and yet introduce into the schools something representing the other side of life—occupations which exact personal responsibilities and which train the child in relation to the physical realities of life?

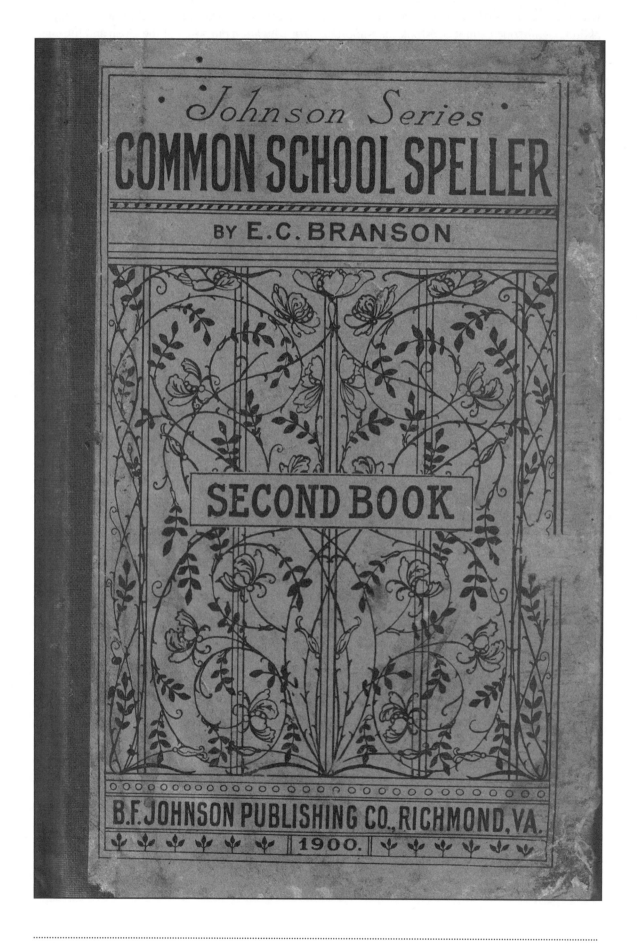

# 1903 PROFILE

Even though Irish immigrant Sarah O'Connell could not read or write, she worked as a nanny teaching four children in the new style of "learning by doing."

## Life at Home

- Until recently, life had not been kind to Sarah O'Connell.
- Sarah was born in Dublin, Ireland, in 1884; her mother died in childbirth, and her father abandoned the family a year later.
- Her mother's sister, Aunt Martha, raised Sarah and two brothers for five years before abruptly leaving for America.
- Her older sister accepted the mother's role before marrying at 16.
- As a teen, Sarah lived in a different house from week to week before emigrating to America, where she was hired as a nanny.
- Irish immigrant women often found work as servants of the upper class in America.
- The "simple-minded" Irish servant girl was so familiar that she became a stock character in nineteenth-century plays, and often inspired cruel ethnic jokes.
- Three years and two jobs later, Sarah was well situated in Hartford, Connecticut, as the childcare giver to a brood of four children—ages two, five, nine and 13.

*Nanny Sarah O'Connell taught her charges much, despite not being able to read or write.*

- Her employers were fourth-generation New Englanders with deep ties to manufacturing and land speculation; her job required that she live in the same house as the children.
- In some ways, she was always on duty.
- In exchange, she was paid, fed, housed and appreciated by both the children and the parents.
- Sarah was rapidly learning to love back.
- Her employers did not yet realize that Sarah could not read or write—a fact discovered by the two older girls almost immediately.
- It was their secret.
- Now, it was her job to learn quickly enough to preserve the finest home life she had ever known.
- The secret was kindergartens and toys that could teach.
- In the wider world, scholars, writers and child-rearing experts had begun to move away from the widely held Victorian concept of absolute innocence of children.

*Two of Sarah's four "children."*

- Born pure and perfect, children were corrupted by the world; as such, they were to be protected and shielded from the contaminated world.
- Now that attitude was changing; modern parents wanted their children to be more independent and self-assertive; they saw complex environments as a stimulating channel for useful energy.
- Mischief, according to this view, was natural, normal and healthy, especially in the development of young boys.
- The progressive-minded parents had come to believe that intellectual stimulation was best derived from physical activity, and that play would help children adapt and mature.
- Believing children could benefit from their own mistakes, the parents wanted to relax the rules under which they had been raised.
- As a result, clothing became looser, long dresses gave way to rompers which did not become tangled when crawling or climbing, and rough play clothes were gaining acceptance.
- Boys who had worn dresses similar to their sisters were freed to wear short pants in the summertime.
- Some children even wore "play clothes" designed for that purpose.
- Playpens replaced the restricted environment of the baby jumper; children were allowed to sit, stand and crawl as they wished.
- Popular magazines encouraged mothers to make their homes child-safe and allow their children to roam more freely, and use more of the house than ever before.

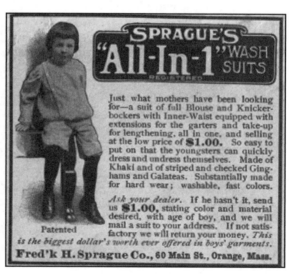

- The *Ladies' Home Journal* published a description of an ideal playroom for children, containing a full-size tent, a sandbox, a small pond of water in which to sail toy boats, a four-sided swing and an aquarium.
- For Sarah, the thought of her own bed to sleep in as a child, without getting kicked by others, was beyond imagining; to think that entire rooms could be set aside for play was unthinkable.

## Life at Work

- Sarah O'Connell was determined to teach her four charges through doing while hiding her inability to read or write.
- What she lacked in reading skills could be accommodated for through sewing, woodworking or craft building.
- The four children were ready converts to the emerging school of "learning by doing"; they embraced adventures outside the classroom and even some exercise.
- This type of child-centered thinking was being promoted by academic John Dewey; Sarah was simply playing to her strengths to hide her weaknesses.
- The opening years of the twentieth century had produced a dramatic expansion of the American public schools as annually, millions of immigrants arrived in New York.
- Schools were called upon to teach the skills and knowledge needed for participation in the democratic industrial society to a rapidly growing and diverse population.
- Industrialist Malcolm Brown was recently elected to the school board and felt an obligation to send his children—at least temporarily—to public school.
- His wife was horrified, but he prevailed.
- Besides, the most important learning of the day was taking place in his upstairs playroom every afternoon after class, he believed.
- Sarah was bringing a different kind of enlightenment to his children's education.
- He sensed it when he watched the children's very energetic puppet show—directed by Sarah—with costumes sewn by his older girls and the sets built by hand.

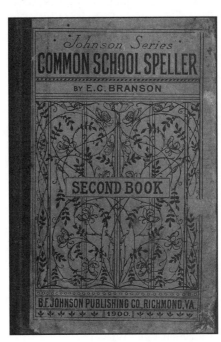

- Next, Sarah taught his daughters how to take their goat wagon apart, grease the wheels, repair a slat and then reassemble.
- All the while, the two youngest children were being taught to read and write by the older girls—with Sarah serving as pupil/teacher.
- Her crowning moment arrived when the circus came to town and Sarah, with the help of all four children, won the community essay contest entitled, "Why I love the circus."
- His third child, the only boy, was becoming a preschool engineer, thanks to the mountains of wooden blocks, logs and tin toys he used to arrange entire cities.
- He also saw that the wooden blocks that had letters stamped into their sides were always arranged in alphabetical order within the design.
- Clearly, the old philosophy "One size (education) fits all" was outmoded; in the modern world, houses could blaze with light at the push of a button and automobiles could take entire families from one city to another without having to stable the horse.

## Life in the Community: Hartford, Connecticut

- Hartford, located at the end of the navigable portion of the Connecticut River, was settled in 1623 as a Dutch trading post called House of Hope.

- Thirteen years later, a group of English settlers led by the Reverend Thomas Hooker left Massachusetts and formed a colony.

- The new settlers made peace with the local Algonquin Indians, who called the town Saukiog, and renamed it after Hertford, England.

- The Fundamental Orders adopted by the colony in 1639 were the first document in history to establish a government by the consent of the people.

- Their pattern was followed by the framers of the U.S. Constitution, giving Connecticut its nickname, "The Constitution State."

*Hartford evolved into an important trading center.*

- Begun as a farming community, Hartford evolved into an important trading center on the Connecticut River, handling molasses, spices, coffee and rum, which were distributed from warehouses in the city's thriving merchant district.

- Trade ships connected the city to England, the West Indies and the Far East.

- The insurance industry was created when groups of merchants began to share the risks associated with deep-water shipping, pirates and severe weather.

- The arrangement was formalized with the creation of the Hartford Fire Insurance Group in 1810, which set the stage for Hartford to become the home of many of the nation's largest insurance companies, such as Aetna and Travelers.

- Pioneering manufacturers like Samuel Colt also called Hartford home.

- Colt's experiments with interchangeable parts created the basis for today's assembly line manufacturing methods.

- New techniques employed in his firearms factory made mass production possible and laid the groundwork for Hartford's pre-eminence in the area of precision manufacturing.

- Authors like Mark Twain and Harriet Beecher Stowe were drawn to the area, because, as Twain said, "Of all the beautiful towns it has been my fortune to see, this is the chief."

- In 1867, Hartford was also the first city in the United States to erect a building designed for use of the Young Women's Christian Association (YWCA).

*The Young Women's Christian Association (YWCA) building in Hartford.*

## HISTORICAL SNAPSHOT
# 1903

- The first west-east transatlantic radio broadcast was made from the United States to England
- The Oxnard Strike of 1903 became the first time in U.S. history that a labor union was formed from members of different races
- Morris and Rose Michtom introduced the first teddy bear
- El Yunque National Forest in Puerto Rico became part of the U.S. National Forest System as the Luquillo Forest Reserve
- Cuba leased Guantanamo Bay to the U.S. "in perpetuity"
- In New York City, the Martha Washington Hotel was opened, the first hotel exclusively for women
- The Hay-Herran Treaty, granting the U.S. the right to build the Panama Canal, was ratified by the Senate over the objections of the Colombian Senate

- Maurice Garin won the first Tour de France
- Dr. Ernst Pfenning of Chicago became the first owner of a Ford Model A
- The first stockcar event was held at the Milwaukee Mile
- The Wreck of the Old 97 engine at Stillhouse Trestle near Danville, Virginia, which killed nine people, inspired a ballad and a song
- The Boston Americans of the American League won the first modern World Series against the National League's Pittsburgh Pirates
- With the encouragement of the United States, Panama proclaimed itself independent from Colombia
- The Hay-Bunau-Varilla Treaty was signed by the U.S. and Panama, giving the U.S. exclusive rights over the Panama Canal Zone
- Colorado Governor James Hamilton Peabody sent the state militia into the town of Cripple Creek to break up a miners' strike
- Taj Mahal Palace & Tower opened its doors to guests
- Orville Wright flew an aircraft with a petrol engine at Kitty Hawk, North Carolina, in the first documented, successful, control-powered, heavier-than-air flight
- A fire at the Iroquois Theater in Chicago killed 600
- The Lincoln-Lee Legion was established to promote the Temperance Movement through the signing of alcohol abstinence pledges by children
- The first box of Crayola crayons was made and sold for $0.05; it contained eight colors: brown, red, orange, yellow, green, blue, violet and black

## Selected Prices

| | |
|---|---|
| False Teeth, Set……… | $3.00 |
| Home Heater, Coal……………… | $9.55 |
| Lead Paint, Pound……………… | $0.07 |
| Liver Pills, Bottle……………… | $0.12 |
| Mattress…………………… | $10.00 |
| Radiator……………………… | $9.45 |
| Rubber Teething Ring……………… | $0.10 |
| Shotgun……………………… | $27.75 |
| Tombstone, Marble……………… | $7.65 |
| Tool Chest…………………… | $5.40 |

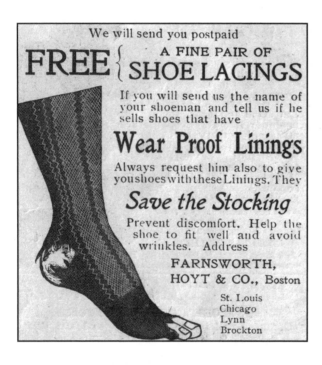

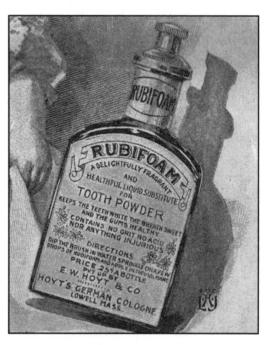

## Letter to the Editor, Mrs. H. L. William, *Homestead*, Des Moines, Iowa, July 4, 1901:

I am pleased to be able to give my opinion in regard to sending children to school. They should go by all means, even if they have to make sacrifices and work harder; it is only doing our duty by our children. Education is better than wealth. I would rather give my children a good education and no money than money and no education, no matter what station in life they filled. Knowledge is necessary. If a farmer has a good education, he understands how to conduct his own business, keep his accounts, do his own writing, drafting and, best of all, manage his farm in a scientific manner. If a child of mine did not want to go to school, I would reason with him and talk kindly, and even hire him to go. As a rule, children who did not like to go to school are those who have difficulty in getting their lessons, or, perhaps, do not like to obey the teacher's rules. Now, I think if parents would take more interest in helping their children with their lessons, there would be less trouble in getting them to go to school. I have an honor roll at home. I tell my children, "Keep up your lessons good and your deportment and I will reward you at the end of each month." Help them every way you can and encourage them. When parents ask them to read their lessons or spell, it helps them. Help them with their essays and it will also help you. I can learn much while helping them. It is a good way to spend the evening, and the time will come when you will be glad that you did so.

## "A Heroine of the Storm, How a Young Nebraska School Teacher Saved Her Pupils," *The New York Times*, January 18, 1888:

Mr. J. H. Ager of Ord, Nebraska, one of the secretaries of the State Board of Transportation, tells an interesting tale of the pluck and good judgment exhibited by a young lady schoolteacher of Valley County.

Not many miles from the town of Ord is situated the schoolhouse of the Mira Valley school district. The house is a small, frame structure, and the nearest dwelling to it is at least half a mile's distance. Thursday morning, January 12, when the blizzard came, there were in the little schoolhouse Miss Minnie Freeman, the teacher, yet in her teens, and 13 pupils between the ages of six and 15 years. The children were wrought up to the highest pitch of excitement by the fury of the storm. In the midst of the teacher's assurance that all would be well, a terrible gust of wind struck the building, the windows rattled, the house shook, and the door of the structure was torn from its hinges. It was then the young teacher realized the necessity of preparing for emergencies. With an exhibition of rare judgment, she gathered her little brood together, and, securing a coil of strong, heavy twine, began with the largest ones and tied the children together by the arms and bodies, three abreast. This completed, she huddled her charges around the stove and awaited the pleasure of the storm king. Its furious work came sooner than expected. The terrific gale, sweeping everything before it, struck the building and carried it away in the twinkling of an eye, the entire roof of the structure leaving the frightened little ones exposed to the elements. The time for prompt action had arrived, but the plucky teacher was equal to the emergency. Taking the youngest and the frailest of her charges in her arms, she tied the remaining end of the twine around her own body, and

*Continued*

## "A Heroine of the Storm . . . *(Continued)*

with all the words of encouragement she could muster, the courageous teacher started with her "team," the frightened little ones, out into the fury of the storm. Those who have braved the terrors of the Nebraska blizzard need not be told that it required courage to enable a young girl to breast these furies, having in her keeping alive the 13 little ones and the happiness of 13 homes. Those who felt and suffered from the effects of Thursday's storm need not be told that the act of that young girl was one from which strong men might quail. Selecting her way carefully, following in the course of the storm, the brave girl led her little charges through snowdrifts and blinding blizzard, now cautioning them about their steps, now encouraging them to cheerfulness, and all the way, herself bearing an additional burden of someone's darling, urging them into renewed efforts. And thus it was that after a wearisome journey of three-quarters of a mile, through all the storm could muster, the little band reached the threshold of a farmhouse, where they received a hearty welcome. At the house where they found shelter, one of the children made its home, and if the eyes of a loving mother filled with tears as she pressed her little one to her heart, they were not dried when she gave to the brave young teacher an embrace in which was embodied all the love and gratitude within a mother's heart. It is safe to say that the subsequent reception of Miss Freeman at all the homes whose little ones she had rescued perhaps from death was equally as warm as that afforded in the first instance.

Miss Minnie Freeman is only 19 years of age, and is teaching her first term of school in the Mira Valley district.

## New Toys: 1903

### Teddy Bears

These cuddly toys were inspired by a hunting trip in 1902. When President Theodore Roosevelt refused to shoot a captured black bear, political cartoonist Clifford Berryman from the *Washington Star* used that incident in a cartoon. New York store owner Morris Michtom was so taken by the sketch, he created a stuffed bear for his store. Michtom then got permission from the president to use his name on the toy, and used the proceeds from those sales to start the famous Ideal Toy Company in 1903.

### Lionel Trains

In 1901, the first trains were used to attract customers through the famous New York City window displays, but it was not long before consumers wanted them in their own homes. The Electric Express, Joshua Lionel Cowen's first model train, was created in 1901 by fitting a small motor under a model of a railroad flatcar. The motor was powered by a battery and the *Electric Express* ran around 30 inches of track.

### Crayons

Crayola Crayons debuted their first box of eight crayons in 1903 by creators Edwin Binney and C. Harold Smith. Their new product would become a necessity in every classroom in the country.

### Tin Toys

Tin toys had been produced in Germany for years, but it was not until the turn of the twentieth century before American companies began producing these toys, thus making them available on a wide scale throughout the country. These toys were made from metal covered with tin and painted. They also had the name "wind-up toys."

### Tiddlywinks

Tiddlywinks creator Eugene Tiedler owned a clock-making shop where his workers used disc-shaped scraps of wood to flip into their co-workers' drinking cups. This developed into a simple game played with small discs, called winks—because the cutouts came from the eye area of the wooden clock owls. He marketed the game as "Tiedler's Winks," and was so successful he stopped making clocks by the year 1889. By the turn of the twentieth century, Tiedler's Winks had spread across the country.

## "The Jubilee of the University of Wisconsin," *The Outlook*, June 18, 1904:

One of the significant events of this year's Commencement season was the jubilee celebration, last week, at the University of Wisconsin, the chief feature of which was the formal inauguration of Professor Charles R. Van Hise, the distinguished geologist, as President of the University. The Commencement of 1904 marks the 50th anniversary of the graduation of the first university class. From a feeble, sparsely attended frontier College, with a faculty consisting of three instructors, the institution has grown, nourished by the bounty of a growing State, into a strong and wisely administered University, with a student body numbering over 3,100 and a faculty of 250, with great technical schools which make it unnecessary for the Wisconsin boy or girl to come East to obtain an education, and with libraries and other facilities for research which are attracting graduate students from other parts of the country. Following the example of Michigan, her neighbor on the east, Wisconsin has built up a system of public instruction in which Huxley's "education ladder" is the embodied ideal. From kindergarten to professional school, the State provides a schooling to all her children. The high schools in the various cities of the state are fitting schools for the University. Nowhere do we find a closer approach to the educational democracy that Jefferson preached. Pres. Van Hise is himself a product of the system. The first graduate to be entrusted with the administration of the University, he is also the first native of Wisconsin to be thus honored. With the exception of Pres. Bryan, of Indiana University, there has been, we believe, no previous instance of any of the middle Western states conferring upon a "native son" the headship of her highest educational institution. The celebration of this jubilee reminds us that these vigorous State Universities, beginning with Michigan, and projecting themselves westward across the continent, have reared up bodies of alumni who may be expected in the future to take an increasingly active part in directing the affairs of their Alma Mater. So far as the corps of instructions are concerned, dependence on the Eastern colleges and universities is growing noticeably less from year to year.

# 1907 PROFILE

Margaret Haley began her autobiography with a simple phrase: "I never wanted to fight," even though she was both worshipped and demonized for the battles she waged on behalf of Chicago's teachers.

## Life at Home

- Margaret Haley spent most of her career on "hectic battlefronts of the unending war" to bring power to teachers when few thought they deserved respect.
- It was her lot to come into maturity just when women were struggling for political, economic and social independence.
- It was also in her nature to stand up to a challenge.
- Margaret was born in 1861 at the cusp of the Civil War in Juliet, Illinois, the home state of the War President, Abraham Lincoln.
- Juliet was also the locale of Elijah Lovejoy's murder by a pro-slavery mob determined to shut down his abolitionist printing press.
- Margaret was one of eight children born to immigrant parents of Irish descent; her mother came from Ireland and her father from Canada.
- He had moved his growing family to Illinois after he witnessed the anti-immigration, anti-Irish, anti-Catholic political party known as the Know Nothings burn a convent to the ground in the East.

*Margaret Haley worked tirelessly on behalf of her fellow teachers.*

- During her early years, Margaret attended a little school near the farm, primarily in the summer and fall; during the winter, impassable roads and heavy snows kept the school closed.
- Her mother taught the children to follow through on anything they started, and firmly believed in the value of education, an opportunity denied the Irish-Catholics in their homeland.

*Financial hardship on her family's farm forced Margaret to start teaching at age 16.*

- Margaret recalled that her mother "knew by experience the truth of the old Irish maxim, "Educate in order that your children may be free."
- By the time Margaret turned 16, economic turmoil and her father's refusal to pay a bribe brought financial distress to the family and forced her to turn from student to teacher.
- Almost immediately, she began to experiment with new ways of teaching, including the emerging emphasis on phonics, a method of sounding out words that propelled a five-year-old boy into one of the best readers in the class.
- At home, she continued to listen to her politically active father talk about the economic impact of the Panic of '73, the personality of presidential candidate James G. Blaine, the work of the Molly Maguires, and the railroad strike of 1877.
- She also learned how to stand up for what she believed in.
- Teachers were badly paid and lacked pension benefits or job security.
- Moreover, they were spied upon in their community, and the women were expected to resign if they married.
- Teaching positions were dispensed through political patronage.
- Immigration, urbanization and westward expansion had both swelled and changed the face of the student population.
- Teachers in urban schools were asked to lift up children from impoverished families who spoke little English.

- They taught in overcrowded, dark and poorly ventilated classrooms; expectations were low, yet America was thirsting for an educated but pliable workforce.
- To become prepared for teaching, Margaret attended the Cook County Normal School and the Buffalo School of Pedagogy, where she received instruction from progressive educators Francis Wayland Parker and William James.
- Normal schools were created to train high school graduates to be teachers; a primary goal was to establish teaching standards, or "norms"—hence, their name.

- As a rural schoolmarm, Margaret was paid $35 per month in 1880, compared to $124 for men and $48 for women in city schools.
- She moved to Chicago in 1882 to teach in the Cook County school system; in 1884, she took a position as a sixth grade teacher.
- In cities such as Chicago, City Boards of Education, which were increasingly composed of business and professional men, promoted teacher reform as a way to ensure real student achievement—and better workers.
- In 1900, few students expected to attend school beyond the sixth grade; that year, elementary schoolteachers constituted 94 percent of Chicago's teachers.
- At the same time, the Boards of Education wanted to impose uniformity and efficiency on classrooms of restless children, so they discouraged individual initiative by teachers, whom they considered too limited to enact worthwhile change.
- Margaret's goals focused on teachers themselves.
- Teachers deserved respect for the task of educating the nation's citizens.
- But her entry into newspaper fame and court dramas was through the Women's Catholic Order of Foresters, a fraternal insurance society established in Chicago to provide death benefits to its members.
- Even though she had never attended a convention of the Order and was not involved with its politics, Margaret was willing to oppose the decision of the chairwoman to award herself a lifetime appointment.
- "I didn't know much about the organization, I knew nothing of its politics, but I knew the principle of election for life was wrong, un-American, autocratic."
- Margaret went to the convention and challenged the lifetime appointment; for her effort, she was expelled from the Order, slapped with an injunction, and introduced to the legal system; it was her first taste of adversarial politics.
- Later, when the Order offered to reinstate her if she would simply apologize, Margaret left the hall and its "mob" behind.
- The Chicago Teachers Federation was established in 1897 toward the end of a major economic depression that had rocked America during the 1890s.
- The school system was the city's largest employer and required the biggest share of the budget, even though teachers earned less than unskilled workers.
- In addition, Chicago was rapidly growing as immigrants from Greece, Poland and Italy stampeded to the Midwestern Mecca for employment.
- Margaret believed that the survival of democracy in America rested upon organized teachers, which she called the "fifth estate."
- She defined democracy as "freedom of activity directed by freed intelligence," and was increasingly concerned about the concentration of wealth into the hands of the few.
- Margaret believed that the "fifth estate" must play a role in the war being waged by the privileged against the people in the lower classes.

## Life at Work
- Under Margaret Haley's leadership, the Chicago Teachers Federation fought for better pay, better conditions, and the right of "the teacher to call her soul her own."
- She was opposed to the "factorization" of the schools and the constraints placed on teachers by bureaucracies.
- And, since nearly 75 percent of America's teachers were women, she wanted them to have a seat at the decision-making table—even though only a tiny percentage of women were eligible to vote in general elections.

*Margaret was one of Chicago Teachers Federation's five district vice presidents.*

- Women made up a small percentage of administrators, and their power decreased with each higher level of authority.
- Their deportment was closely watched; their work in the schoolroom was not only scrutinized, but rigidly controlled.
- Teacher autonomy—always limited—was on the decline, and teachers resented it.
- In urban districts, teachers had the advantage of numbers, and thus cities became the centers for the teachers' associations that eventually grew into unions.
- In Chicago, Margaret and Catherine Goggin of the Chicago Teachers Federation rallied their peers for improved pay, retirement benefits and tenure.
- Margaret was teaching at the Hendricks School in the rough Stockyards district on Chicago's South Side when the Chicago Teachers Federation was organized in 1897.
- Because many teachers considered teaching a genteel, white-collar occupation, joining a union was an anathema to them.
- Margaret was less squeamish.
- Unlike the traditional state teachers' organizations which annually held respectable meetings to pass resolutions, the Chicago Teachers Federation was designed for battle in the courts and the political system for teacher tenure and improved salaries as a means of increasing the quality of teaching applicants.
- Margaret joined the Chicago Teachers Federation in 1898, and was one of the organization's first district vice presidents, just in time to challenge the Harper Commission.
- William Rainey Harper, president of the University of Chicago, headed a commission that proposed a complete restructuring of the Chicago school system.
- The Harper Report called for increased power for the superintendent, the instilling of corporate-like efficiency in the schools, the reduction of the School Board's size, the increase of "experts" in educational leadership positions, and the introduction of a salary system based on merit that favored male high school teachers and administrators over the mostly female elementary school teachers.
- In addition, the Harper Commission promoted the concept of issuing 99-year land leases on school property, which were not subject to taxation.
- This was at a time when school revenues and salaries were falling because the tax base of Chicago was not expanding quickly enough to keep pace with the growing number of schoolchildren.
- Once revealed, the 99-year lease plan looked like another of Chicago's corrupt kickback schemes in which everyone was rewarded except the city and its schoolchildren.

- The tax fight launched Margaret's career as she helped the public link tax reform and corporate arrogance with declining school budgets.
- Her efforts shone a spotlight on five major utility and streetcar companies, and returned $600,000 in tax dollars back to the schools.
- After the Chicago teachers turned back the tax-free land grab by business, *Review of Reviews* reported that "A very great lesson lies in the fact that this splendid triumph over hideous fraud and corruption has now been carried through by energetic women school teachers."
- Then, in 1902, the Chicago Teachers Federation made a second critical move—it linked its activities to a traditional union—The Chicago Federation of Labor—composed of working class men who had the right to vote based on their gender.
- The Chicago Teachers Federation's use of the courts and effective political campaigns to impact change got them branded as the most militant of the teachers' organizations.
- Their activities shocked the Chicago establishment and many teachers.
- Margaret preached from every forum that school reform was fundamental to social reform.
- By 1904, Margaret clambered onto the national stage as president of the Teachers Federation when she became the first elementary school teacher to speak before the National Education Association at the St. Louis Convention.
- Her speech, "Why Teachers Should Organize," demanded that more women have leadership roles at the local and national levels of teachers' unionization.
- In 1905, the teachers were able to elect a city mayor sympathetic to their plight; Margaret joined a "kitchen cabinet" of advisors to assist the mayor—resulting in three women among the first seven appointees.
- The women teachers of Chicago were finding their voice.
- It also meant that the Chicago Teachers Federation was tying its fortunes to city politics.
- Chicago Mayor Edward Dunne, like Margaret, favored the municipal ownership of streetcar lines and the principle of popular control.
- During Dunne's first two-year stint as mayor, the power of "administrative progressives" over teachers diminished.
- By the time Dunne left office, the Chicago Teachers Federation had built a national reputation for aggressive support of teachers.
- Margaret repeatedly challenged the establishment of Chicago and the traditional role of women.
- It made the men she opposed furious.
- When she challenged one male speaker at a national conference, he retorted, "Pay no attention to what the teacher down there has said. I take it she is a grade teacher, just out of her classroom at the end of the school year, worn out, tired out, and hysterical. I have repeatedly said these meetings held at this time of year are a mistake. If there are any more hysterical outbursts after this, I shall insist these meetings be held at some other time of year."

*Chicago Mayor Dunne supported Margaret's ideas.*

- Then, pointing his finger at Margaret, he said, "Chicago is no criterion for other parts of the country…Chicago is a morbid, cyclonic and hysterical place that is in no way representative of the rest of the country."

## Life in the Community: Chicago, Illinois

- The rapidly growing Chicago boasted a population of three million people, over 70 percent of whom were foreign born or the children of foreign-born parents.
- "It is a veritable Babel of languages," a Frenchman observed. "It would seem as if all the millions of human beings disembarking year after year by the shores of the United States are consciously drawn to make this place their headquarters."
- After the fire of 1871, Chicago rebuilt its commercial center buildings with brick, stone and concrete—the consequence of a city ordinance passed in the wake of the great inferno.
- Nationwide, Chicago was known as a railroad center; within its limits the elevated rail system effectively linked workers to factories in different parts of the city.
- The rise of activity among women, both professional and recreational, drove the demand for more simplified clothing; working women, particularly those in the cities, were a prominent part of the consumer culture fostered by women's magazines and those who advertised in them.

- Mass-produced versions of the latest styles and clothing were increasingly available and affordable to the working class.
- Previously, there had been a marked difference between the dress of working women and that of the upper class; by 1907, the key distinction of a well-off patron was quality, not design.
- Marshall Fields, Chicago's leading department store, encouraged workers of all ethnic and economic stations to visit the store, and distributed rules to the sales force stipulating that they be "polite to rich and poor alike."
- While projecting this egalitarian attitude, department stores also reinforced the notions of bourgeois good taste and propriety, emphasizing the correct clothes for every occasion.
- Chicago also boasted hundreds of nickelodeons, or moving picture theaters, most of which were basically converted street front stores.
- Across the country, 10,000 of the tiny theaters had been opened to meet demand; most films lasted less than 10 minutes but enjoyed a high level of audience participation, including laughing, cheering and boisterous commentaries.
- Approximately 19 percent of Chicago's manufacturing workforce was female, typically women in their teens and early twenties earning money to supplement their families' income before they married.
- By 1907, Chicago was teeming with newcomers from Southern and Eastern Europe, especially Greece, Italy and Poland; their arrival was in direct competition with earlier immigrants from Northern and Western Europe, particularly Germany, Ireland and Scandinavia.

# HISTORICAL SNAPSHOT
## 1907

- The first Montessori school and daycare center for working class children opened in Rome

- The Second Hague Peace Conference was held

- A record 1.2 million immigrants arrived in the United States; Congress raised the head tax on immigration to $4

- *Harper's Weekly* warned of "nickel madness," referring to the growing popularity of nickelodeons throughout the country

- The passenger liner *RMS Lusitania* made its maiden voyage from Liverpool, England, to New York City

- The average salary of an American worker was $495 a year; teachers earned $453 a year, while the average factory worker earned $598 per year

- Ringling Brothers bought out Barnum & Bailey as the former continued to grow in popularity and size; railroad caravans carried 1,000 performers or more

- Guglielmo Marconi initiated commercial transatlantic radio communications between his high-power long-wave wireless telegraphy stations in Clifden, Ireland, and Glace Bay, Nova Scotia

- The Forest Preservation Act set aside 16 million acres in five states

- The Protestant Episcopal Convention condemned the removal of "in God we trust" from new gold coins

- Professional baseball player Honus Wagner won his fifth batting title

- Residents of New York City's Lower East Side, eager to read the news in their own language, had more than 50 newspapers and periodicals published in Yiddish

- Surgeons discovered that patients recovered faster and with fewer complications if they became mobile shortly after surgery

- The Diamond Sūtra, a Buddhist scripture from 868 CE, was discovered in the Mogao Caves and dated as the earliest example of block printing

- Lee DeForest invented the triode thermionic amplifier, which began the development of electronics as a practical technology

- Popular songs included, "When a Fellow's on the Level with a Girl That's on the Square," "I'd Rather Be a Lobster Than a Wise Guy," and "I Just Can't Make my Eyes Behave"

## Selected Prices

Automobile, Graham Roadster..............................................$850.00

Baseball Calendar.................................................................$0.30

Bookcase.............................................................................$18.25

Castor Oil Tablets, Box.......................................................$0.10

Dental Filling......................................................................$1.00

Iron Stove...........................................................................$19.50

Motor Oil, Gallon...............................................................$0.60

Rolltop Desk.......................................................................$37.50

Stockings, Women's............................................................$0.25

Tooth Cleanser, Tube..........................................................$0.25

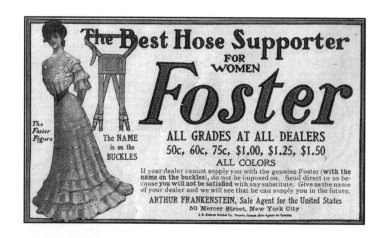

## *How the Rest of the World Goes to School*, "Teachers' Everyday Plans,"
## F.A. Onen Publishing Company, 1907:

In the west this is the age of children. Children have been loved in all ages; but never before have children been so considered, so studied. New systems of education have been carefully devised for them. Their amusement, pleasure, and dress have been as great a study as have those of the adults.

Free schools, free textbooks and commodious buildings are the rule in the United States and wherever her power has extended. And really, is it not wise? We may try to reform the criminal, elevate the degraded, but to really want to do anything for a nation, we must begin with the children.

It is through the study of them, too, that we learn to understand other peoples, for the grown-ups look upon us with the eyes of suspicion in cold distrust, but child nature is essentially the same the world over, trusting and frank, and unconscious; not even racial difference raises any barrier between them and us.

Whenever the ruling class has come into power, the first thought has been to investigate the schools and model them on the plan of their own.

In Hawaii, people were essentially children in nature, living in houses of leaves, and stems and grasses, as are the birds. Their lives were as free and happy and careless as the birds' until the missionary and the schools came.

Hawaiian children are the heritors of little or no literature, and yet they speak and write— those of them who can write—in the language of poetry. They are apt pupils of nature in the land where the flowers flaunt their splendid beauty and thousands of coffee trees lift their handsome heads packed with fragrant scarlet berries.

The people express themselves in many superlatives and with much force and directness.

But education does not agree with Polynesians, at least not Western education, for they were being educated away and the race is rapidly decreasing. The curriculum of the modern school seems not intended for this tropical flower used only to their open air and the warm water of the southern seas. Hawaiian parents never coerce their children, and enforced obedience seems like hothouse flowers.

The Hawaiian children excel in music and poetry, and are very deft in feather work and doing things that are useful in that southern climate.

They are adept swimmers, many of the children swimming to school, with their few garments held in one hand as they paddle along with the other. They are very careful of their bright, pretty clothes.

*Continued*

### *How the Rest of the World Goes to School . . . (Continued)*

Sometimes the teacher and the children sit under the shadow of the pepper tree or beneath the sandal woods. Most of the teachers are men, and if they are natives, they often bring their children to school and tend to them, for in Hawaii the men monopolize many branches of work we associate with women. Men tend all the babies and children—the little they need tending—while the mothers go riding or visiting.

## The President's Letter to the American School Children

To the School Children of the United States:

Arbor Day (which means simply "Tree Day") is now observed in every State in our Union—and mainly in the schools. At various times from January to December, but chiefly in this month of April, you give a day or part of a day to special exercises and perhaps to actual tree planting, in recognition of the importance of trees to us as a Nation, and of what they yield in adornment, comfort, and useful products to the communities in which you live.

It is well that you should celebrate your Arbor Day thoughtfully, for within your lifetime the Nation's need of trees will become serious. We of an older generation can get along with what we have, though with growing hardship; but in your full manhood and womanhood you will want what nature once so bountifully supplied and man so thoughtlessly destroyed; and because of that want, you will reproach us, not for what we have used, but for what we have wasted.

For the nation, as for the man or woman and the boy or girl, the road to success is the right use of what we have, and the improvement of present opportunity. If you neglect to prepare yourselves now for the duties and responsibilities which will fall upon you later, if you do not learn the things which you will need to know when your school days are over, you will suffer the consequences. So any nation which in its youth lives only for the day, reaps without sowing, and consumes without husbanding, must expect the penalty of the prodigal, whose labor could with difficulty find him the bare means of life.

A people without children would face a hopeless future; a country without trees is almost as hopeless; forests which are so used that they cannot renew themselves will soon vanish, and with them all their benefits. A true forest is not merely a store house full of wood, but, as it were, a factory of wood, and at the same time a reservoir of water. When you help to preserve our forests or to plant new ones, you are acting the part of good citizens. The value of forestry deserves, therefore, to be taught in the schools, which aim to make good citizens of you. If your Arbor Day exercises help you to realize what benefits each one of you receives from the forests, and how by your assistance these benefits may continue, they will serve a good end.

THEODORE ROOSEVELT
The White House,
April 15, 1907.

# Planting Suggestions

The proper season for planting is not everywhere the same. Where spring is the best season—north of the thirty-seventh parallel generally—the right time is when the frost is out of the ground before budding begins.

The day to plant is almost as important as the season. Sunny, windy weather is to be avoided; cool, damp days are the best. For this reason it is well to leave the date for Arbor Day unfixed. All exercises are better deferred until the planting is done.

Trees cannot be thrust into a rough soil at random and then be expected to flourish. They should be planted in well-worked soil, well enriched. If the trees cannot be set out immediately after being secured, the first step is to prevent their roots drying out in the air. This may be done by standing the roots in a "puddle" of mud or "heeling-in" the trees by burying the roots deep in fresh earth.

In planting, they should be placed from two to three inches deeper than they stood originally. Fine soil should always be pressed firmly—not made hard—about the roots, and two inches of soil at the top should be left very loose, to act as a mulch to retain the moisture.

Small seedlings may be secured easily and cheaply. If these are set out in good numbers after the pattern of a commercial plantation, they will become in due time a true forest on a small scale. No matter how few the trees, they may be made to illustrate planting for some useful purpose.

The scope of planting may sometimes be broadened by securing permission for the children to plant a small block of trees in some field unsuited for crops, and in this way the work can be done just as it would be done on a larger scale by the forester.

Outside the scope of the actual planting, it is well to bear in mind that Arbor Day is not the only day in the year on which trees deserve to be remembered and cared for. They need care throughout the season. Watching the plantation thrive under the right treatment greatly adds to the educational value of the work, and to its success, which should be its best lesson.

It is all important that the plantation should serve as a model of what can be accomplished along these lines. Then, when the children are grown men and women, they will find great satisfaction in the work of their school days.

Approved:
James Wilson,
Secretary.
Washington, D.C., March 28, 1907.

To win rudimentary justice, women had to battle with brain, with wit, and sometimes even with force. If you happen to be born wanting freedom for yourself, for your group, for people at large, you had to fight for it and you had to fight hard. Those of us who were flown on the frontier of the war for human rights had little choice of weapons or battleground. We had to make our own slings and arrows. If we have won with them anything of lasting value and, in a way, I think we have, it was because we knew that we were never fighting for ourselves alone. Always with us marched the army of the silent, but poor, the oppressed, the shackled. If we faltered, we had to remember them and keep on fighting.

—*The Autobiography of Margaret Haley*

God seems to have made woman peculiarly suited to guide and develop the infant mind, and it seems...very poor policy to pay a man 20 or 22 dollars a month for teaching children the ABCs, when a female could do the work more successfully at one third of the price.

—Littleton School Committee, Littleton, Massachusetts, 1849

### "Teachers Favor Flogging, Say Corporal Punishment Is Necessary for Discipline," *The New York Times*, December 12, 1907:

That corporal punishment is a necessity in the public schools to protect the women teachers from degrading insults, the children from the demoralizing influence of bad companions, and to save, if possible, the few bad boys from utter ruin by the only power they will understand was the unanimous voice of the school Principals and Commissioners who met at the call of the Public Education Association at the house of Mrs. James A. Scrymser, 107 West Twenty-first Street, last evening. The subject for discussion was the conditions that have led to the demand for corporal punishment.

The speakers also acknowledged frankly that corporal punishment is actually in use in the public schools, brought about by conditions that make it practically unavoidable. "The grossness of insult to which the women teachers suffer I could not recite in your presence," said John Doty, Principal of the Rivington Street school. "They suffer daily from indignities to which I do not think any human being could submit and keep their temper and their hands off the perpetrator. That is the very worst kind of corporal punishment; it is not punishment, but retaliation, but I do not blame the teacher.

"I asked President Burlingham of the Board of Education what he would do if a boy of fourteen did thus and so to him. 'I would knock him down,' he answered. Then think of the effect of this disrespect for the law upon the other children.

*Continued*

## "Teachers Favor Flogging . . . *(Continued)*

"In 1872 or 1873, when corporal punishment was given up, we had two methods of redress, expulsion or elimination by a process of stipulation. In 1894, when the compulsory education law was put in force, we lost that power, and I tremble to think what would happen if the law was really enforced. It is that which has led to the present conditions in the schools. All punishment is more or less corporal. The reform school is corporal punishment, and to my mind a flogging does less harm. There is no corporal punishment for men, but if a man resists arrest he is clubbed until he submits. Surgery does not cure, but it saves life and gets rid of the evil, that good may come.

We cannot leave punishment to the parents. I have known a father to knock his boy down and kick him in the ribs until I took him away. Flogging should only be resorted to in a few instances, but I have never known any punishment by God or man that was not based on the corporal."

Commissioner Nathan Jones, Chairman of the committee to investigate the subject of corporal punishment, told of the difficulty there had been even in having the commission appointed against the wishes of the City Superintendent. He told of a personal experience, where a young woman teacher in one of the schools had been sent to him by her Principal. One of her boys had used such vile language to her that she had felt obliged to punish him, and had gone to the Commissioner as a matter of self-protection to tell him the story.

"I thought if that were the case with her," said the Commissioner, "there must be many others. Of all the Superintendents to whom I have written to ask about corporal punishment, the majority have been overwhelmingly in favor of it. The others have said that if they did not have corporal punishment, there must be some method to preserve discipline.

Commissioner McDonald read extracts to be presented to the Board of Education asking for corporal punishment. William McAndrew of the Washington Irving High School said that he was theoretically and sentimentally opposed to corporal punishment, but from his experience with boys' schools he considered it necessary.

In a letter from Miss Lida Williams, she said: "The chief cause of the demand for the return of corporal punishment is the persistent lessening by the Board of Education and the Superintendents of the authority of the school Principal, a consequence of the effort to administer every detail of this enormous system from 500 Park Avenue.

"There is a fourth right that a boy has besides that of life, liberty and the pursuit of happiness: that is the right to be led by compulsion or persuasion to obey where it is for his own usefulness and happiness."

The Public Education Association was not represented among the speakers for corporal punishment.

# 1909 PROFILE

Chicago architect Dwight Heald Perkins—a charter member of the "Prairie School" of architects that included Frank Lloyd Wright—designed more than 40 schools for the Chicago Board of Education and redirected American thinking about school space.

## Life at Home

- Dwight Heald Perkins believed that a school building should serve as the social center of a community and be associated with parks and exercise.
- He also thought the buildings should be architecturally pleasing, such that the building appeared natural to the place where it was built.
- Born in Memphis, Tennessee, in 1867, Dwight moved as a child with his family to Chicago, where his father died when Dwight was 12.
- Dwight attended only three months of high school before dropping out to find work to help support his family; initially, he worked at the

*Designing schools, Dwight Heald Perkins re-educated American thinking about school space.*

Chicago Stockyards and later at several Chicago-based architectural firms.
- He was accepted to study architecture at the Massachusetts Institute of Technology in 1885; a family friend, Mrs. Charles Hitchcock, helped finance his education.
- He studied at MIT for two years and was preparing to drop out for lack of funds when the school, impressed by his skills and eager to assist, invited him to serve as an instructor and complete his third year.

- Also while in Boston, he met writer Lucy Fitch, who would become his wife.
- In January 1889, he interviewed at one of the top firms in the country, Burnham & Root in Chicago, and was employed in early February of that year.
- Two years later, he was placed in charge of the Burnham & Root downtown office when the firm opened its Southside office to oversee the World's Columbian Exposition, which lasted through 1893.
- On January 1, 1894, with a commission from the Steinway Piano Company to design a new building for them, Dwight established his own office in downtown Chicago.
- After completion of the Steinway Hall in Chicago's Loop, he moved his office to the eleventh floor and opened the attic as a drafting studio where he invited some of his friends to share the space with him.
- There in Steinway Hall, the Prairie School of Architecture had its beginnings.
- The first to join him was a friend from M.I.T., Robert C. Spencer, who also brought his close friend Frank Lloyd Wright.
- They were soon followed by Myron Hunt, Walter Burley Griffin, and Marion Mahony Griffin, the first licensed female architect in the world.
- The result was a vigorous intellectual and artistic exchange that would create the Prairie School style.
- The dominant horizontality of Prairie School style construction echoed the wide, flat, treeless expanses of the Midwestern United States.
- Frank Lloyd Wright promoted an idea of "organic architecture," the primary principle of which was that a structure should look as if it belongs on the site, as if it naturally grew there.
- The group shared a secretary and they each had a screened workspace in the attic, but it was also an office where they participated in each other's work.
- According to Frank Lloyd Wright, "Dwight had a loft in his new Steinway building—too large for him. So we formed a group—outer office in common—workrooms screened apart in the loft of Steinway Hall. These young men, newcomers in architectural practice like myself, were my first associates in the so-called profession of architecture."

*The Prairie School style of architecture was predominantly horizontal.*

- Dwight's association with Mrs. Hitchcock also helped him secure a commission at the University of Chicago to design the Hitchcock Hall dormitory building in 1902.
- In order to design the building in accordance with the English Gothic style used by Henry Ives Cobb for most of the other university buildings, Mrs. Hitchcock sent Dwight and his wife Lucy to England for six months for a firsthand study of Gothic architecture.
- With greater visibility, Dwight's early involvement in the social issues of housing for the poor emerged, along with his desire to increase the number of public parks and playgrounds in Chicago.
- At one point, the forward-thinking Dwight predicted that in 50 years, schools would be exclusively built in the country where the air was fresher; the schoolchildren would be transported to and fro by pneumatic tubes.

- Based on an open-space plan prepared by Dwight and noted Prairie landscape architect Jens Jensen in 1903, the groundwork was laid for the formation of the Chicago Park District and the Cook County Forest Preserves—which played a central role in his work.
- In 1905, after scoring 99 on a civil service exam, Dwight was appointed as the chief architect for the Chicago Board of Education by Mayor Edward F. Dunne.
- During his tenure, he designed more than 40 schools for the Board, with Carl Schurz High School being the most famous of his Prairie School designs.

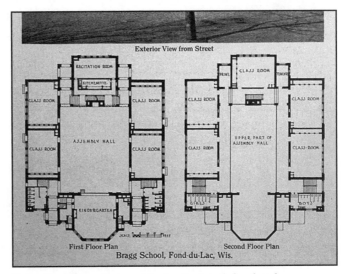

*School building designed in the Prairie School style.*

- For decades, the architectural needs of Chicago's schools had been dictated by a desperate need to house as many students as possible at the lowest cost.
- Since the beginning of public education in the city, the schools had struggled to keep pace with Chicago's phenomenal growth, and to provide places for all its eligible children.
- The result had been large classes and a strictly utilitarian architecture with dark, daunting spaces that were often drafty and cold.
- Infectious diseases spread quickly in the atmosphere, causing some parents to fear for their children's safety.
- The World's Columbian Exposition of 1893 was supposed to herald Chicago's rise from the ashes, but Dwight was disturbed by the Greek and Roman classicism of nearly every building constructed for the fair.
- In his new position, he was ready to establish a true American look to Midwestern architecture, with schools a focal point of the new concepts.

*Before Dwight was appointed chief architect for the Chicago Board of Education, many of the city's schools were dark, drafty and cold.*

## Life at Work

- The innovations of the "Chicago School" of architecture were first applied to public school buildings in 1905, with the appointment of Dwight Heald Perkins as head of the schools' architecture department by a reform-minded Board which included community organizer Jane Addams.
- Schools were generally three-story red brick buildings that resembled factories; they were poorly ventilated and dimly lit, and lacked adequate playgrounds.

- Classrooms had blackboards on two sides and seats for 54-63 students.
- One of the first buildings Dwight was asked to design was the Albert G. Lane Technical High School.
- Chicago already had several manual training schools; now the School Board wanted a facility between high school and the technical universities which conferred degrees.
- As envisioned, the Lane School graduates could directly enter any university which carried technical education into its higher theoretical branches; as important, the new school would produce graduates who would serve as foremen and supervisors in manufacturing plants throughout the region.
- The Board wanted to see whether Dwight could synthesize the functionalism of the Chicago school with the social agenda and aesthetics of the Arts and Crafts Movement.
- The visibility of new schools allowed him to promote the concept of the school building as a community social center and create pleasing space distinguished by its large, airy rooms flooded by daylight coming through banks of windows.

*The Carl Schurz School was designed as a community social center with airy rooms flooded by daylight.*

- The centerpiece of this concept was the stunning Carl Schurz School at 3601 North Milwaukee Road.
- Started in 1908, the building demonstrated Dwight's assertion that a school should be so solidly designed that it would serve a larger purpose than just the housing of classrooms.
- In the process of implementing this philosophy, Dwight elevated the Prairie School style in a public Chicago building, in the heart of the great Midwestern prairie.
- The style emphasized a natural integration between building and landscape, horizontal lines, hipped roofs with broad eves, windows assembled in horizontal lines, and restraint in the incorporation of decoration.
- He eliminated excess details and demonstrated a respect for natural materials.
- It was an architecture style independent of historical and revivalist influence, and developed in tandem with the ideals and design philosophies of the Arts and Crafts Movement started in the late nineteenth century in England by John Ruskin, William Morris, and others.
- Dwight saw it as an alternative to the Classical Revival influence, with a refocus on a style that worshipped simplicity and function.
- Like Arts and Crafts, the Prairie School embraced handcrafting and craft guilds as a response to the new assembly line, which they felt resulted in mediocre products and dehumanized workers.
- Dwight also considered the horizontal orientation of the Prairie style to be a distinctly American design idea; America had much more open, undeveloped land than in most ancient, urbanized European nations.
- The Prairie School was heavily influenced by the Transcendentalist philosophy of Ralph Waldo Emerson and the Idealistic Romantics, who believed that better homes would create better people.
- Gymnasiums and large auditoriums were always important elements in Dwight's designs.
- The innovative design of the Carl Schurz High School embraced 160,000 square feet of brick and terracotta, 1,200 windows, and clay tiles on the roof.

## Life in the Community: Chicago, Illinois

- By the late 1890s, the existing parks could no longer satisfy the needs of Chicago's growing population; the city's tremendous industrial expansion had enticed vast numbers of European immigrants to settle there.

- By 1900, nearly 750,000 people—almost half of Chicago's population—resided in the central part of the city, more than a mile away from any park.

*Chicago, Illinois*

- There were 846 city residents per acre of parkland; living and working conditions were intolerable, and in order to survive, many immigrant families had to put their children to work.

- If children were lucky enough to have time off, there were few clean or safe places in which to play.

- In 1898, reformer and photojournalist Jacob A. Riis of New York City addressed this issue at a meeting of the Municipal Science Club held at Hull House, Jane Addams' influential settlement house in Chicago.

- Focusing on the need for additional breathing spaces in Chicago's tenement districts, the club inspired the creation of a Special Park Commission by Mayor Carter Harrison the following year.

- Early commission members included social reformers Graham Taylor and Charles Zueblin; businessman Clarence Buckingham; architect Dwight Heald Perkins; and landscape architects Jens Jensen and Ossian Cole Simonds.

- The Special Park Commission sought to study Chicago's existing open spaces, create playgrounds in the city's most densely populated neighborhoods, and develop a systematic plan for parks and recreational areas throughout the metropolitan area.

- Over a one-year period, Jensen and Dwight Perkins conducted an exhaustive study, recommending a whole series of new parks and playgrounds and the protection of thousands of acres of forest, prairie and marshland.

- Their influential report, published in 1904, led to the formation of the Forest Preserve District of Cook County a decade later.

- The Special Park Commission at first created municipal playgrounds in the city's most densely populated neighborhoods; a major budget reduction in its second year, however, severely limited the commission's ability to acquire and improve land.
- In response, the agency began working cooperatively with the Board of Education and the three park commissions in order to achieve its goals.
- The South Park Commission took the lead, acquiring a site near the stockyards and opening experimental McKinley Park.
- It provided ball fields within a beautiful landscape, as well as features that had not previously existed in the South Park System, such as a playground, swimming lagoon, and changing rooms.
- When it came time to build a new high school on the city's northwest side, it was only natural that the name of Carl Schurz be chosen for the new facility.
- At the time the new school was planned, 470,000 Germans lived in Chicago.
- One out of four Chicagoans in 1900 was either born in Germany or had a parent who had been born there.
- The original building was a magnificent combination of the Prairie School and the Arts and Crafts style of architecture as they applied to a large institution.
- Carl Schurz, a German-American born near Cologne in 1829, came to the United States and was admitted to the bar in 1858; by 1860, he was the spokesman for the Wisconsin delegation at the Republican National Convention held in Chicago that nominated Abraham Lincoln for the presidency.
- Lincoln sent Schurz to Spain as ambassador in 1861, and it was his efforts that kept the Spanish from supporting the Confederacy.

# HISTORICAL SNAPSHOT
# 1909

- The last U.S. troops left Cuba after being there since the Spanish-American War

- The national economy was rebounding strongly from the Panic of 1907

- The Audubon Society continued to protest hats decorated with bird feathers

- Hit songs included, "I Wonder Who's Kissing Her Now," "By the Light of the Silvery Moon," and "Squeeze Me Tight"

- Einar Dessau used a short-wave radio transmitter, becoming the first radio broadcaster

- Rocky Mountain fever was shown to be transmitted by woodland ticks

- College tuition varied from $40 at the University of Michigan to $150-$250 at Harvard, Columbia, and Princeton

- Matthew Henson and four Eskimo explorers came within a few miles of the North Pole

- An estimated one million people attended various ceremonies commemorating the centennial of Lincoln's birth

- The Anglo-Persian Oil Company, now BP, was incorporated

- Jane Addams worried that "thousands of young people in every industrial city are going into the show [theatre]" so often it was becoming a daily and potentially dangerous habit

- The U.S. Army Signal Corp Division purchased the world's first military airplane, a Wright Military Flyer, from the Wright Brothers

- The concept of pH was introduced as a measure of acidity and alkalinity

- President Howard Taft confessed that whenever he heard the words "Mr. President," he looked around for Teddy Roosevelt

- The movie industry agreed to use the 35 mm format as the standard

- Filtered water produced dramatic reductions in death rates

- The automotive industry produced 127,000 cars, twice the production of 1908

- Ice cream sales topped 39 million gallons, up from five million in 1899

- The Lincoln penny replaced the Indian Head, which had been in circulation since 1864

- The cork-centered baseball was introduced into the major leagues

- President Taft gave recreational golf a boost when he said the game helped him control his weight

## Selected Prices

| | |
|---|---|
| Camera, Kodak | $50.00 |
| Carburetor | $18.00 |
| Children's Woolen Hosiery, Pair | $0.25 |
| Hotel Room, Chicago, The Plaza, per Day | $2.50 |
| Ice Box | $16.50 |
| Motorcycle | $275.00 |
| Petticoat | $1.39 |
| Potatoes, Sack | $2.50 |
| Snake Fight Ticket | $2.00 |
| Suitcase, Leather | $3.00 |

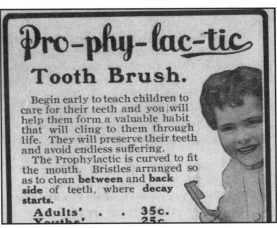

In these days of difficulties with servants and of inadequate and inexperienced help, more and more women are learning to depend upon themselves to keep the household machinery running smoothly."

—Gustav Stickley, 1909

## "When Patty Went to Boarding-School," Jean Webster, *The Ladies' Home Journal*, April 15, 1911:

"I'm tired of Women's Rights on Friday afternoons," said Patty disgustedly. "I prefer soda water!"

"This makes the third time they've taken away our holiday for the sake of a beastly lecture," Priscilla grumbled as she peered over Patty's shoulder to read the notice on the bulletin board in Miss Lord's perpendicular library hand.

It informed the school that instead of the usual shopping expedition to the village, they would have the pleasure that afternoon of listening to a talk by Prof. McVey, of Columbia University. The subject would be the strike of the women laundry workers. The tea would be served in the drawing room afterward, with Mae Van Arsdale, Harriet Gladden and Patty Wyatt as hostesses.

"It's not my turn!" objected Patty, as she noted the latter item. "I was hostess two weeks ago."

"That's because you wrote an essay on the Eight Hour Day." Lordy thinks you will ask the professor man intelligent questions and will show him that St. Ursula's is not a common boarding school where only superficial accomplishments are taught."

"And I did want to go shopping!" Patty mourned. "I need some new shoestrings. I've been tying a knot in my old ones every day for a week."

"Here she comes," whispered Priscilla. "Look happy or she will make you translate the whole 'Good morning, Miss Lord! We were just noticing about lecture. It sounds extremely interesting.'"

The two smiled a perfunctory greeting and followed their teacher to the morning's Latin.

Miss Lord was the one who struck the modern note at St. Ursula's. She believed in militant suffragism and unions, and boycotts and strikes; and she labored hard to bring her little charges to her own advanced position. But it was against a heavy inertia that she worked. Her little charges didn't care a rap about receiving their rights in the dim future of 21, but they were very much concerned about losing a present half-holiday. On Friday afternoons they were ordinarily permitted to draw checks on the school bank for their allowances, and march in a procession, with a teacher forming the head and tail, to the village stores, where they laid

*Continued*

### "When Patty Went to Boarding-School," . . . *(Continued)*

in their weekly supplies of hair ribbons, soda water, and photograph films. Even had a girl acquired so many demerits that her weekly stipend was eaten up by fines, still she marched to the village and watched the lucky ones disburse. It made a break in the monotony of six days of bounds.

But every cloud has its silver lining.

Miss Lord preceded the Virgil recitation that morning by a discussion of the lecture to come. The laundry strike, she told them, had marked an epoch in industrial history. It proved that women as well as men were capable of standing by each other. The solidarity of labor was a point she wished her girls to grasp. Her girls listened with grave attention, and by eagerly putting a question whenever she showed signs of running down, they managed to stave off the Latin recitation for three quarters of an hour.

The professor, a mild man with a Van Dyke beard, came and lectured exhaustively upon the relations of employer and employed. His audience listened with politely intelligent smiles, but with minds serenely occupied elsewhere. The great questions of Capital and Labor were not half so important to them as the fact that they lost the afternoon, nor as the essays which must be written for tomorrow's English, nor even that this was ice cream night with dancing class to follow.

But Patty, on the front seat, sat with wide, serious eyes fixed on the lecturer's face. She was absorbing his arguments and storing them for use.

Tea followed according to schedule. The three chosen ones received their guests with the facility of long-tried hostesses. The fact that their bearing was under inspection, with marks to follow, did not appreciably diminish their ease. They were learning by the laboratory method the social graces that would be needed later in the larger world. Harriet and Mae presided at the tea table, while Patty engaged the personage in conversation. He commented later to Miss Lord upon her student's rare understanding of economic subjects.

Miss Lord replied that she endeavored to have her girls think for themselves. Sociology was not a field in which lessons could be taught by rote. Each must work out of her own conclusions and act upon them.

Ice cream and dancing restored the balance of St. Ursula's after the mental exertions of the afternoon.

At half past nine (school did not retire until 10 on dancing nights), Patty and Pricilla dropped their goodnight curtsies, murmured a polite "Bon soir, Mam'selle," and scampered upstairs still very well wide awake. Instead of preparing for bed with all dispatch, as well-conducted schoolgirls should, they engaged themselves in practicing the steps of their new Spanish dance down the link to the south corridor. They brought up with a pirouette at Rosalie Patton's door.

*Continued*

## "When Patty Went to Boarding-School," . . . *(Continued)*

Rosalie, who was still in the pale blue fluffiness of her dancing frock, was sitting cross-legged on the couch, her yellow curls bent over the open pages of a Virgil, tears spattering with dreary regularity on the line she was conning.

The course of Rosalie's progress through Senior Latin was marked by blistered pages. She was a pretty, cuddling, helpless little thing, deplorably babyish for a Senior, but irrevocably appealing. Everyone teased her and protected her and loved her. She was irrevocably destined to bowl over the first man who came along with her feminine irresponsibility. Rosalie very often dreamed—when she ought to have been concentrating upon Latin grammar—of that happy future state in which smiles and kisses would take the place of gerunds and gerundives.

Taste is not only a part and index of morality; it is the only morality. The first, and last, and closest trial question to any living creature is, 'What do you like?' Tell me what you like; I'll tell you what you are.

—John Ruskin, *Seven Lamps of Architecture*, 1849

## "Big School Building, Chicago to Have One Unlike Any Other in the United States," *Waterloo Daily Courier* (Iowa), January 9, 1919:

School architect Dwight H. Perkins of Chicago recently completed his first drawings of the proposed $2 million commercial high school and school office building erected at Harrison Street in Plymouth Court, Chicago. The structure as planned is unlike any other school building in the United States, having 17 stories above ground and four basements.

The basement stories will have the school supply department and the heating and ventilation apparatus. Above these will be, in succession, a great assembly hall for teachers' meetings and school exercises, the commercial high school, and the offices of the Board of Education and its various departments. A unique feature of the plans is a truck elevator, which will lower the largest coal wagon bodily to the last of the four basements.

## "To School by Air Tube," *The Logansport Pharos* (Indiana), January 17, 1909:

"Fifty years from now there will be no schools in Chicago," said architect Dwight H. Perkins of the Chicago Board of Education the other day. He meant conditions in Chicago, particular transportation, will have changed to such an extent that the schools will be 30 or 40 miles beyond the school city limits, far from its smoke, dust, dirt and turmoil and close to nature.

"We will shoot children out through pneumatic tubes every morning into the fields, groves and parks to school," said the architect's enthusiastic prophecy. "In the evening we will shoot them back again."

# 1910–1919

America was booming during the second decade of the century. More than one million immigrants a year were flooding into the United States in search of economic opportunity. Once again, schools were called upon to manage social change by "Americanizing" the foreigners. Urban kindergartens were organized with the expressed purpose of teaching the children who would "reform" the home. Instead of creative play, kindergartens stressed order and discipline. After World War I erupted in Europe, classes taught in German rapidly declined and "English only" curricula became more prominent.

Economically and politically, anything seemed possible. America's upper class enjoyed the world's finest transportation—by train and automobile—and spent considerable time discovering new forms of entertainment. Opera continued to grow in popularity, and church music expanded its reach and sophistication. An emerging middle class was showing that it was capable of carrying a greater load of managerial decisions, freeing factory owners and stockholders to travel, experiment, and study ways to cure the ills of the poor. Millions of dollars were poured into libraries, parks, and literacy classes designed to uplift the immigrant masses flooding to American shores.

During the decade, motorized tractors changed the lives of farmers, while electricity extended the day of urban dwellers. Powered trolley cars, vacuum cleaners, hair dryers, and electric ranges moved onto the modern scene. Wireless communications connected San Francisco to New York and New York to Paris; in 1915, the Bell system alone operated six million telephones, which were considered essential in most middle class homes as the decade drew to a close. While the sale of pianos hit a new high, more than two billion copies of sheet music were sold as ragtime neared its peak and the patriotic spirit ignited by America's entry into World War I resulted in dozens of rousing or romantic songs. Thousands of Bibles were placed in hotel bedrooms by the Gideon Organization of Christian Commercial Travelers, reflecting both the emerging role of the traveling "drummer" or salesman and the evangelical nature of the Progressive Movement.

Immigration continued at a pace of one million annually in the first four years of the decade. Between 1910 and 1913, some

11 million immigrants—an all-time record—entered the United States. The wages of unskilled workers fell, but the number of jobs increased dramatically. Manufacturing employment rose by 3.3 million, or close to 6 percent, in one year during the period. Earnings of skilled workers rose substantially and resulted in a backlash focused on protecting American workers' jobs. As a result, a series of anti-immigration laws was passed, culminating in 1917 with permanent barring of the free flow of immigrants into the United States. From the beginning of World War I until 1919, the number of new immigrants fell sharply while the war effort was demanding more and more workers. Accordingly, wages for low-skilled work rose rapidly, forcing the managerial class to find new and more streamlined ways to get the jobs done.

In the midst of these dynamics, the Progressive Movement, largely a product of the rising middle class, began to shape the decade, raising questions about work safety, the rights of individuals, the need for clean air and fewer work hours. The results were significant and widespread. South Carolina prohibited the employment of children under 12 in mines, factories, and textile mills; Delaware began to frame employer's liability laws; the direct election of U.S. senators was approved; and communities argued over the right of women to vote and the lawfulness of alcohol consumption.

Yet in the midst of blazing prosperity, the nation was changing too rapidly for many—demographically, economically, and morally. Divorce was on the rise. One in 12 marriages ended in divorce in 1911, compared with one in 85 only six years earlier. The discovery of a quick treatment for syphilis was hailed as both a miracle and an enticement to sin. As the technology and sophistication of silent movies improved yearly, the Missouri Christian Endeavor Society tried to ban films that included any kissing. The rapidly expanding economy began producing marked inequities of wealth—affluence for the few and hardship for the many. The average salary of $750 a year was rising, but not fast enough for many.

But one of the biggest stories was America's unabashed love affair with the automobile. By 1916, the Model T cost less than half its 1908 price, and nearly everyone dreamed of owning a car. Movies were also maturing during the period, growing rapidly as an essential entertainment for the poor. Some 25 percent of the population, including many newly arrived immigrants, went weekly to the nickelodeon to marvel at the exploits of Charlie Chaplin, Mary Pickford, and Douglas Fairbanks, Sr.—each drawing big salaries in the silent days of movies. The second half of the decade was marked by the Great War, later to be known as the First World War. Worldwide, it cost more than nine million lives and swept away four empires—the German, the Austro-Hungarian, the Russian, and the Ottoman—and with them the traditional aristocratic style of leadership in Europe. It bled the treasuries of Europe dry and made the United States the richest country in the world.

When the war broke out in Europe, American exports were required to support the Allied war effort, driving the well-oiled American industrial engine into high gear. Then, when America's intervention in 1917 required the drafting of two million men, women were given their first taste of economic independence. Millions stepped forward to produce the materials needed by a nation. As a result, when the men came back from Europe, America was a changed place for both the well-traveled soldier and the newly trained female worker. Yet women possessed full suffrage in only Wyoming, Colorado, Utah, and Idaho.

The war forced Americans to confront one more important transformation. The United States had become a full participant in the world economy; tariffs on imported goods were reduced, and exports reached all-time highs in 1919, further stimulating the American economy.

# 1910 PROFILE

Abraham Flexner authored the groundbreaking 1910 Flexner Report, which revolutionized medical education and radically reduced the number of medical schools in the United States.

## Life at Home

- Abraham Flexner's study, which was funded by the Carnegie Foundation, triggered reforms in the standards, organization and curriculum of North American medical schools.
- The Flexner Report caused more than 100 medical schools to close down, and most of the remaining schools were reformed to conform to the Flexnerian model.
- The number of medical schools fell from 155 to 31 as the American Medical Association took steps to eliminate uncertified for-profit medical schools.
- Abraham Flexner was not a doctor but a secondary school teacher and principal in Louisville, Kentucky.
- Abraham's father Moritz was born in Neumark, Bohemia, in 1820; he spent his teenage years in Strasbourg where he lived with an uncle, a rabbi.

*Abraham Flexner's study of medical schools revolutionized medical education.*

- Abraham's mother was born in 1834, one of six children, in the village of Roden near Saarlouis in the Rhineland; getting an education meant she had to share her textbooks with her brothers and sister.
- After immigrating to America, Moritz first tried New Orleans and then settled in Louisville, Kentucky.
- Abraham was born in 1866, the sixth of nine children, to the German-Jewish immigrants.
- Abraham's father Moritz was a hat merchant, and his mother, Esther Abraham, was a seamstress.
- Education for their children was at the heart of their ambitions; Abraham's parents repeatedly said, "Our children will justify us."

- Severe financial losses in the Panic of 1873 forced the Flexners to abandon their dreams of sending all their sons to college; to simply make ends meet they were forced to move several times into smaller and smaller homes.
- To help support the family, the teenage Abraham worked at the Louisville library six days a week from 2:30 p.m. to 10 in the evening; he made $16 a month.
- He used the time to read hundreds of books and keep up with national affairs through *Nation*, the *Saturday Review* and several city newspapers.
- He also wrote to the editors, including one letter that championed the secret ballot and its adoption by Kentucky.
- He prepared himself carefully for each project; he liked to quote Pasteur's remark, "opportunity favors the well-prepared mind."
- Following a pattern going back two generations, Abraham delighted in reading aloud his favorites: Shakespeare's *Hamlet*, Keats' *Ode on a Grecian Urn*, and Wordsworth's *Ode: Intimations of Immortality*.
- The older boys took menial jobs to help support the household, while Abraham and his three younger siblings were able to remain in school.
- Abraham was the first of the children to finish high school.
- With assistance and encouragement from his older brother, Abraham attended Johns Hopkins University in 1884 at age 17.
- Revered institutions such as the University of Virginia and Vanderbilt University were impoverished and still hobbled as a result of the Civil War.
- In Baltimore, Maryland, merchant Johns Hopkins had left $7 million, nearly his entire fortune, to endow a university and to fund the building of a hospital—which he wanted to be associated with the university.
- Abraham fully understood that his money would run out after two years, so he graduated in two years by taking a double load of courses.
- Johns Hopkins stressed postgraduate education—then very rare in the United States—and Abraham hoped to continue his studies, but the fellowship he sought eluded him.
- He returned to Louisville to teach Latin and Greek at Louisville High School before founding, in 1890, an experimental school, which had no formal exams or grades, but excelled at preparing students for prestigious colleges.
- He wanted a place to test his ideas about education.
- He believed that education should be marked by small classes, personal attention, and hands-on teaching.
- With the success of his school, Flexner was able to help his older brother Simon in attending Johns Hopkins and to support his sister Mary so that she could attend Bryn Mawr College.
- In addition, his wife, playwright Anne Crawford, a former pupil in his school and a graduate of Vassar College, had found financial success on Broadway with the production of her play "Mrs. Wiggs of the Cabbage Patch."

*Harvard Medical College circa 1878.*

- This, too, enabled Abraham to pursue a master's degree in psychology from Harvard and spend a year at the universities of Berlin and Heidelberg.
- Despite his initial enthusiasm, he left Harvard after a year, disappointed in his professors and assistantship.
- Never to earn an advanced degree, Flexner embarked instead upon an extended period of observation of all types of schools and universities, in both New York and Europe.
- In 1908, Abraham published his first book, *The American College: A Criticism.*
- Strongly critical of many aspects of American higher education, it was especially scathing in regard to the university lecture as a method of instruction.
- According to Abraham, lectures enabled colleges to "handle cheaply by wholesale a large body of students who would be otherwise unmanageable, and thus give the lecturer time for research."
- This book received little notice except by the president of the Carnegie Foundation for the Advancement of Teaching, Dr. Henry S. Pritchett.
- Pritchett soon offered Abraham the opportunity to conduct a survey of medical schools, even though Flexner had never set foot inside a medical school.
- Thus, he joined the research staff at the Carnegie Foundation in 1908.
- Two years later, he published the Flexner Report, which examined the state of American medical education and led to far-reaching reforms in the way doctors were trained.

## Life at Work

- When Abraham Flexner stepped into the role of medical school evaluator, he had never attended a medical school, had not been inside a medical school or had any affiliation with a one.
- He knew he was vulnerable to attack, especially if his reports were negative, and most of them were.
- During an American Medical Association convention in Chicago, he said that two-thirds of America's medical schools were dangerous to the profession and the public.
- His report caused an uproar of protest.

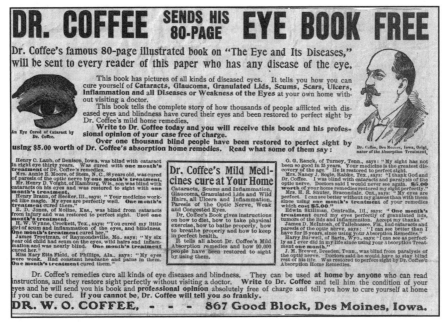

*These dangerous claims were rampant when Flexner began his research of medical schools.*

*Given the opportunity by the Carnegie Foundation to evaluate medical schools, Flexner reported on entrance requirements, faculty, financial support, laboratories, and relationships with hospitals.*

- But that was why Henry Pritchett had wanted Abraham to take the lead—he was smart, incorruptible and beholding to no one.
- To Pritchett, Abraham Flexner was a "layman educator" capable of completing a key assignment in the Carnegie Foundation's larger institutional classification scheme, such as differentiating colleges from secondary schools, and universities from colleges.
- He was paid $5,000 a year.
- Abraham began in Chicago, where he found that the reports of the American Medical Association were credible, painstaking documents that went to great lengths to be diplomatic.
- Prepared by a committee of physicians from medical schools, the reports were tactful and cautious, but Abraham was not a doctor and under no obligation to be cautious or diplomatic.
- His next trip was to Tulane University in New Orleans; keenly conscious of his own ignorance and inexperience, he wanted make his start in a location well removed from New York.
- His assignment was to view it from an educational standpoint: its entrance requirements, number and training of the faculty, financial support for the institution, the quality of laboratories, and the relationship among medical school hospitals.
- Abraham found that entrance requirements were often ignored, and that many of the faculty were local doctors and not college professors.
- Equipment was often inadequate and poorly maintained, and many students were pronounced to be medical doctors even though they had had little practical experience because of minimal access to hospital patients.
- Abraham was fearless.
- After a trip to St. Louis to see the medical school of Washington University, where Dr. Pritchett had been a professor of astronomy, Abraham said, "its medical department is entirely out of

harmony with the spirit and equipment of the rest of the university. Unless this department is to be a drag and a reproach, one of two courses should be adopted: The department must be either abolished or reorganized."

- At Bowdoin College in Maine, he produced similar scorched-earth reports, even though the president of the college was a trustee of the Carnegie Foundation.
- He found that many of the schools were "essentially private ventures, moneymaking in spirit and in object."
- He was widely criticized that his inspection tours, which rarely took more than a few hours, were inadequate and superficial.
- He was accused of trying to reduce the number of new doctors and remove competition for current physicians.
- Abraham became known as "the severest critic and the best friend American medicine ever had."
- The Flexner Report led to the closure of most rural medical schools and all but two of America's African-American medical colleges.
- It also set the stage for modern American medical education.

## Life in the Community: Louisville, Kentucky

- Louisville was struggling to be a cosmopolitan city at the dawn of the twentieth century.
- One hundred years earlier, the growing popularity of the recently invented steamboat had brought new life to Louisville via the Mississippi River.
- Until then, most of the cargo was going downstream.
- In 1815, the *Enterprise*, captained by Henry Miller Shreve, became the first steamboat to travel from New Orleans to Louisville, showing the commercial potential of the steamboat in making upriver shipping practical.
- Industry and manufacturing flocked to Louisville; its population grew rapidly, tripling from 1810 to 1820.
- By 1830, its growth would surpass Lexington to become the state's largest city.
- The completion of the Louisville and Portland Canal in 1830 allowed boats to circumvent the Falls of the Ohio and travel through from Pittsburgh to New Orleans.
- In 1831, Catherine Spalding moved from Bardstown to Louisville and established Presentation Academy, a Catholic school for girls; she also established the St. Vincent Orphanage, which was later renamed St. Joseph Orphanage.
- In 1839, a precursor to the modern Kentucky Derby was held at Old Louisville's Oakland Race Course.
- Over 10,000 spectators attended the two-horse race, in which Grey Eagle lost to Wagner—36 years before the first Kentucky Derby.
- The Kentucky School for the Blind was founded in 1839, the third-oldest school for the blind in the country.
- Following the 1850 Census, Louisville was reported as the nation's tenth largest city, while Kentucky was reported as the eighth most populous state.

*Louisville, Kentucky*

*Louisville Colonials baseball team thrived in the growing city.*

- The Louisville and Nashville Railroad (L&N) Company was founded in 1850 by James Guthrie, who also was involved in the founding of the University of Louisville.
- When the railroad was completed in 1859, Louisville's strategic location at the Falls of the Ohio became central to the city's development and importance in the rail and water freight transportation business.
- Part of that business was the slave trade.
- Louisville conducted one of the largest slave markets in the United States before the Civil War; shifting agricultural needs had produced an excess of slaves from parts of the Upper South to the Deep South.
- Kentucky slave traders sold 2,500-4,000 slaves annually; the expression "sold down the river" originated as a lament of eastern slaves who were sold in Louisville and shipped south on the Mississippi River.
- Kentucky officially declared its neutrality early in the Civil War, but heavily supported the Union army.
- The first Kentucky Derby was held on May 17, 1875, at the Louisville Jockey Club track (later renamed Churchill Downs).
- One year later, professional baseball launched the National League, and the Louisville Grays were a charter member.
- In 1877, the Southern Baptist Theological Seminary relocated to Louisville from Greenville, South Carolina, where it had been founded in 1859.
- Its new campus, at Fourth and Broadway downtown, was underwritten by a group of Louisville business leaders eager to add the promising graduate-professional school to the city's resources.
- It grew quickly, attracting students from all parts of the nation, and by the early twentieth century, it was the second largest accredited seminary in the United States.
- On August 1, 1883, President Chester A. Arthur opened the first annual Southern Exposition.
- Exhibitions included the largest to-date installation of incandescent light bulbs, having been recently invented by Thomas Edison, a former resident.
- Downtown Louisville began a modernization period in the 1890s, with Louisville's second skyscraper, the Columbia Building, opening on January 1, 1890.
- One year later, landscape architect Frederick Law Olmsted was commissioned to design Louisville's system of parks.
- Two Louisville sisters, Patty and Mildred J. Hill, both schoolteachers, wrote the song "Good Morning to All" for their kindergarten class; the song did not become popular, and the lyrics were later changed to the more recognizable, "Happy Birthday to You."
- Early in the twentieth century, controversy over political corruption came to a head in the 1905 mayoral election, called the most corrupt in city history.
- The Waverly Hills Sanatorium was opened in 1910 to house tuberculosis patients.

## HISTORICAL SNAPSHOT
# 1910

- The 1910 Los Angeles International Air Meet at Dominguez Field was the first aviation meet to be held in the United States

- The average worker earned $15 for a 58-hour week; 42 percent of his income went to food

- Halley's comet was visible from Earth

- The illiteracy rate dropped to 7.9 percent; 4 percent of Americans had a college education

- African-American boxer Jack Johnson defeated American boxer James J. Jeffries in a heavyweight boxing match, sparking race riots across the United States

- To stem illegal drug trafficking, attempts were made to control the sale of morphine

- Missouri's Christian Endeavor Society tried to ban all silent movies that featured kissing

- Rule changes divided football games into four quarters instead of two halves; players who were replaced would now return in a subsequent quarter

- William Bragg discovered that x-rays and gamma rays act like particles

- Francis Rous discovered that viruses cause some animal cancers

- Popular songs included, "Let Me Call You Sweetheart," "Down by the Old Mill Stream," "Plant a Watermelon on My Grave and Let the Juice Soak Through" and "Come, Josephine, in My Flying Machine"

- The Vatican introduced a compulsory oath against modernism, to be taken by all priests upon ordination

- Wright Brothers pilot Philip Parmalee initiated the first commercial freight flight in the United States between Dayton and Columbus, Ohio

- France and Italy continued to lead the world in movie film production

- Henry Ford's Ford Motor Company sold 10,000 automobiles

## Selected Prices

| | |
|---|---|
| Baby Walker | $2.75 |
| Cake Turner | $0.02 |
| Egg Incubator and Brooder | $10.00 |
| Inlaid Linoleum, per Yard | $2.35 |
| Phonograph Record | $0.65 |
| Piano, Steinway Baby Grand | $2,000.00 |
| Toilet Paper, Six Rolls | $0.27 |
| Trunk | $16.95 |
| Tuition, Harvard University, per Year | $150.00 |
| Umbrella | $2.74 |

### "Medical Education in America, Rethinking the Training of American Doctors," Abraham Flexner, *Atlantic*, June 1910:

The American medical school is now well along in the second century of its history. It began, and for many years continued to exist, as a supplement to the apprenticeship system still in vogue during the seventeenth and eighteenth centuries. The likely youth of that period, destined to a medical career, was at an early age indentured to some reputable practitioner, to whom his service was successively menial, pharmaceutical, and professional; he ran his master's errands, washed the bottles, mixed the drugs, spread the plasters, and finally, as the stipulated term drew toward its close, actually took part in the daily practice of his preceptor—bleeding his patients, pulling their teeth, and obeying a hurried summons in the night. The quality of the training varied within large limits with the capacity and conscientiousness of the master. Ambitious spirits sought, therefore, a more assured and inspiring discipline. Beginning early in the eighteenth century, having served their time at home, they resorted in rapidly increasing numbers to the hospitals and lecture-halls of Leyden, Paris, London, and Edinburgh. The difficulty of the undertaking proved admirably selective, for the students who crossed the Atlantic gave a good account of themselves. Returning to their native land, they sought opportunities to share with their less fortunate or less adventurous fellows the rich experience gained as they "walked the hospitals" of the old world. The voices of the great masters of that day thus reechoed in the recent western wilderness. High scientific and professional ideals impelled the youthful enthusiasts, who bore their lighted torches safely back across the waters.

Out of these early assays in medical teaching, the American medical school developed. As far back as 1750, informal classes and demonstrations, mainly in anatomy, are matters of record. Philadelphia was then the chief centre of medical interest. There, in 1762, William Shippen the younger, after a sojourn of five years abroad, began, in the very year of his return home, a course of lectures on midwifery. In the following autumn, he announced a series of anatomical lectures "for the advantage of the young gentlemen now engaged in the study of physic in this and the neighboring provinces, whose circumstances and connections will not admit of their going abroad for improvement to the anatomical schools in Europe; and also for the entertainment of any gentlemen who may have the curiosity to understand the anatomy of the Human Frame."

From these detached courses, the step to an organized medical school was taken at the instigation of Shippen's friend and fellow student abroad, John Morgan, who in 1765 proposed to the trustees of the College of Philadelphia the creation of a professorship in the theory and practice of medicine. At the ensuing Commencement, Morgan delivered a noble and prophetic discourse, still pertinent, upon the institution of medical schools in America. The trustees were favorable to the suggestion; the chair was established, and Morgan himself was its first occupant. Soon afterwards, Shippen became professor of anatomy and surgery. Thirteen years previously, the Pennsylvania Hospital, conceived by Thomas Bond, had been established through the joint efforts of Bond himself and Benjamin Franklin. Realizing that the student "must Join Examples with Study, before he can be sufficiently qualified to prescribe for the sick, for Language and Books alone can never give him Adequate Ideas of Diseases and the best methods of Treating them," Bond now argued successfully on behalf of bedside training for the medical students. "There the Clinical professor comes in to the

*Continued*

## "Medical Education in America, . . . (Continued)

Aid of Speculation and demonstrates the Truth of Theory by Facts," he declared in words that a century and a half later still warrant repetition; "he meets his pupils at stated times in the Hospital, and when a case presents adapted to his purpose, he asks all those Questions which lead to a certain knowledge of the Disease and parts Affected; and if the Disease baffles the power of Art and the Patient falls a Sacrifice to it, he then brings his Knowledge to the Test, and fixes Honour or discredit on his Reputation by exposing all the Morbid parts to View, and Demonstrates by what means it produced Death, and if perchance he finds something unexpected, which Betrays an Error in Judgement, he, like a great and good man, immediately acknowledges the mistake, and, for the benefit of survivors, points out other methods by which it might have been more happily treated."

The writer of these sensible words fitly became our first professor of clinical medicine, with unobstructed access to the one hundred and thirty patients then in the hospital wards. Subsequently, the faculty of the new school was increased and greatly strengthened when Adam Kuhn, trained by Linnaeus, was made professor of materia medica, and Benjamin Rush, already at twenty-four on the threshold of his brilliant career, became professor of chemistry.

Our first medical school was thus soundly conceived as organically part of an institution of learning and intimately connected with a large public hospital. The instruction aimed, as already pointed out, not to supplant, but to supplement apprenticeship. A year's additional training, carrying the bachelor's degree, was offered to students who, having demonstrated a competent knowledge of Latin, mathematics, natural and experimental philosophy, and having served a sufficient apprenticeship to some reputable practitioner in physic, now completed a prescribed lecture curriculum, with attendance upon the practice of the Pennsylvania Hospital for one year. This course was well calculated to round off the young doctor's preparation, reviewing and systematizing his theoretical acquisitions, while considerably extending his practical experience....

Since that day medical colleges have multiplied without restraint, now by fission, now by sheer spontaneous generation. Between 1810 and 1840, twenty-six new medical schools sprang up; between 1840 and 1876, forty-seven more; and the number actually surviving in 1876 has been since then much more than doubled. First and last, the United States and Canada have in little more than a century produced four hundred and forty-seven medical schools, many, of course, short-lived, and perhaps fifty still-born. One hundred and fifty-six survive to-day. Of these, Illinois, prolific mother of thirty-nine medical colleges, still harbors in the city of Chicago fourteen; forty-two sprang from the fertile soil of Missouri, ten of them still "going" concerns; the Empire State produced forty-three, with eleven survivors; Indiana, twenty-seven, with two survivors; Pennsylvania, twenty, with eight survivors; Tennessee, eighteen, with eleven survivors. The city of Cincinnati brought forth about twenty, the city of Louisville eleven.

These enterprises—for the most part, they can be called schools or institutions only by courtesy—were frequently set up regardless of opportunity or need, in small towns as readily as in large, and at times, almost in the heart of the wilderness. No field, however limited, was

*Continued*

## "Medical Education in America, . . . (Continued)

ever effectually pre-empted. Wherever and whenever the roster of untitled practitioners rose above half a dozen, a medical school was likely at any moment to be precipitated. Nothing was really essential but professors. The laboratory movement is comparatively recent, and Thomas Bond's wise words about clinical teaching were long since out of print. Little or no investment was therefore involved. A hall could be cheaply rented, and rude benches were inexpensive. Janitor service was unknown and is even now relatively rare. Occasional dissections in time supplied a skeleton—in whole or in part—and a box of odd bones. Other equipment there was practically none.

The teaching was, except for a little anatomy, wholly didactic. The schools were essentially private ventures, money-making in spirit and object. Income was simply divided among the lecturers, who reaped a rich harvest besides, through the consultations which the loyalty of their former students threw into their hands. "Chairs" were therefore valuable pieces of property, their prices varying with what was termed their "reflex" value; only recently a professor in a now defunct Louisville school, who had agreed to pay three thousand dollars for the combined chair of physiology and gynecology, objected strenuously to a division of the professorship assigning him physiology, on the ground of "failure of consideration," for the "reflex" which constituted the inducement to purchase went obviously with the other subject. No applicant for instruction who could pay his fees or sign his note was turned down. State boards were not as yet in existence. The school diploma was itself a license to practice. The examinations brief, oral, and secret—plucked almost none at all; even at Harvard, a student for whom a majority of nine professors "voted" was passed. The man who had settled his tuition bill was thus practically assured of his degree, whether he had regularly attended lectures or not. Accordingly, the business throve….

In the wave of commercial exploitation which swept the entire profession, so far as medical education is concerned, the original university departments were practically torn from their moorings. The medical schools of Harvard, Yale, Pennsylvania, became, as they expanded, virtually independent of the institutions with which they were legally united, and have had in our own day to be painfully won back to their former status. For years they managed their own affairs, disposing of professorships by common agreement, segregating and dividing fees along proprietary lines. In general, these indiscriminate and irresponsible conditions continued at their worst until well into the eighties. To this day, it is as easy to establish a medical school as a business college, though the inducement and tendency to do so have greatly weakened.

Meanwhile, the entire situation had fundamentally altered. The preceptorial system, soon moribund, had become nominal. The student registered in the office of a physician whom he never saw again. He no longer read his master's books, submitted to his quizzing, or rode with him in the countryside in the enjoyment of valuable bedside opportunities. All the training that a young doctor got before beginning his practice had now to be procured within the medical school. The school was no longer a supplement; it was everything. Meanwhile, the practice of medicine was itself becoming quite another thing. Progress in chemical, biological, and physical science was increasing the physician's resources, both diagnostic and remedial. Medicine, hitherto empirical, was beginning to develop a scientific basis and

*Continued*

## "Medical Education in America, . . . *(Continued)*

method. The medical schools had thus a different function to perform; it took them upwards of half a century to wake up to the fact. The stethoscope had been in use for over thirty years before its first mention in the catalogue of the Harvard Medical School in 1868-69; the microscope is first mentioned the following year.

The schools simply had not noticed at all when the vital features of the apprentice system dropped out. They continued along the old channel, their ancient methods aggravated by rapid growth in the number of students, and by the lowering in the general level of their education and intelligence. Didactic lectures were given in huge, badly-lighted amphitheatres, and in these discourses the instruction almost wholly consisted. Personal contact between teacher and student, between student and patient, was lost. No consistent effort was made to adapt medical training to changed circumstances. Many of the schools had no clinical facilities whatsoever, and the absence of adequate clinical facilities is, to this day, not prohibitive. The school session had indeed been lengthened to two sessions; but they were of only sixteen to twenty weeks each. Moreover, the course was not graded, and the two classes were not separated. A student had two chances to hear one set of lectures—and for the privilege paid two sets of fees. To this traffic, many of the ablest practitioners in the country were parties, and with little or no realization of its enormity at that! "It is safe to say," said Henry J. Bigelow, professor of surgery at Harvard, in 1871, "that no successful school has thought proper to risk large existing classes and large receipts in attempting a more thorough education."

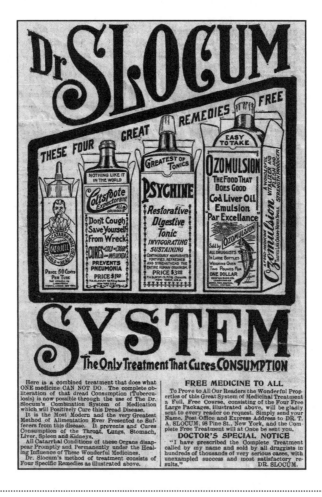

I recall that on one occasion, when I was in high school, I came home and complained to [my father] of what I conceived to be the injustice of one of my teachers. He heard me out patiently and then walked away without a word. I was greatly puzzled.

After breakfast he said to me, "I'll walk to school with you today." We left our home together on Sixth Street near Broadway, walking a block to Chestnut Street and then down to the old high school building at Ninth Street. Nothing was said, but I continued to wonder what he intended to do. On reaching the school, he went to the office of the principal, Prof. Ashley B. Hurt, a very competent school executive and excellent Greek scholar. Prof. Hurt greeted us and asked us to be seated. My father said, "I need only a few moments, Prof. Hurt. My son has complained to me of what he regards as the injustice of one of his teachers. I should like you and all the teachers to know that if any question arises between my son and his teachers, I shall always regard his teachers as being in the right."

Not a word was said in explanation. My father arose, shook hands with Prof. Hurt, bade me good-by, and left. It was no wonder that I never complained again. On the contrary, I became more assiduous in my studies and made a very credible record as a high school student. I should not say that this mode of procedure is necessarily correct in all cases, but it shows a strain of common sense capable of very wide application.

—Abraham Flexner: *An Autobiography*

## "Making Children Mind," Elise Morris Underhill, Formerly Instructor in the Kindergarten Department of the Normal College, New York, *Munsey's Magazine*, February 1911:

Marian's mother stands in the doorway of the kindergarten room, facing Miss Blank, a frown of perplexity creasing her brow.

"I'd like to ask your advice, Miss Blank," she says. "It's about Marian. I want to know how you manage her in school. She's a good enough child at home, only we can't make her mind!"

And Marian, clinging to mother's hand, hears that she cannot be made to mind, and swells visibly with pride at the smartness of her small self.

Another time it is Henrietta's mother who comes with her tale of disobedience, to drink of the well of Miss Blank's wisdom.

"I just don't know what to do with Henrietta," she says. "She is so impudent to everyone, and answers back so, that I have to send her away from the table almost every meal. I told her," continued the mother blandly, "that you are coming to visit us some time, and you won't like her if she is naughty at the table. I wish you would tell her so, too, and ask her not to be so saucy at table. She would do it for you!"

*Continued*

## "Making Children Mind," Elise Morris Underhill, . . . *(Continued)*

As there was no invitation to a meal following this request, Miss Blank wonders how long her influence over the somewhat troublesome child would last if she, too, should seek to discipline Henrietta by means of lies....

When all teachers of little children can duplicate such cases many times over, there is a significant fact concealed somewhere in the evidence. For, without doubt, the first, most important lesson a child has to learn is to obey—and to obey immediately and unquestionably.

Now, the modern child does not obey immediately and unquestionably. That is beyond dispute. This failure to do so would seem to be due to the modern parent's inability to command wisely, for the reason of a child's misbehavior may nearly always be found in the attitude of the people who have authority over him. There is too little examination into the motives of his acts, too little relation to the punishment to the offense. Too often, discipline means physical coercion, or futile threats which the mother or nurse has no power or intention of carrying out.

How wearily often have we heard, in streetcar, ferry, or train, an anxious mother in a rasping voice commanding Willie to "come away from the window," or she will "throw him out"? How many times have we seen small arms almost dragged from their sockets, small hands slapped, even spanking administered publicly, not because of the real disobedience, but because Willie or Johnny or Mary wished to gratify some perfectly legitimate interest which did not appeal to the adult!

As corporal punishment has the sanction of history and the weight of custom behind it, it is not to be passed over lightly and unadvisedly. "Spare the rod and spoil the child" is a doctrine that has been adhered to militarily through many generations—though, be it said, often times with such untoward results that it usually seems that the parent or guardian is aiming not at the betterment of the child, but the easiest way to rid herself a troublesome duty.

The net result of whipping in all its forms is not to create a better, more amenable spirit in the child, for which he will learn to right for the love of the right, but on the contrary, when the child does respond to this physical discipline, it is from fear—the lowest of the motives and the farthest removed the ideal one.

If we recall our own whipped selves, I fancy that most of us will admit that our first feeling on those sad occasions of reproof was one of flying rage—rage that someone who was bigger

*Continued*

## "Making Children Mind," Elise Morris Underhill, ... *(Continued)*

and stronger than ourselves was taking advantage of our weakness and getting the best of us in the only way it was possible to get the best of us. Our will was as strong as her or his hands. If it wasn't, the issue would never have been raised, so on the face of it, spanking is a confession of failure.

It is as if the one in authority said to the child, "I am master this way, at any rate," and any normal child is just as well aware of this as you are. You were quite well aware of it in your early days, and though you may have minded if the punishment hurt enough, your resulting emotion was not sorrow for the fault and a determination "not to do so anymore." It was, in all probability, a fierce sullenness and rage at your own powerlessness to hit back. These feelings, I imagine, must form a large part of the mental context of every whipped child, and it is hardly necessary to point out that they are neither healthy nor constructive feelings.

There is also the sense of loss of dignity—how painful a feeling to a sensitive child!—which he takes long to forgive. I remember one little boy who refused to speak to his mother for a week after she given him his first—and only—spanking, because he felt his pride and self-respect had been hurt beyond repair. These are delicate matters to tamper with in the growing child, and he who does so is laying up for himself lack of esteem and loss of authority, if not actual feelings of dislike. We none of us love him who makes us lose our self-respect.

Is corporal punishment never to be practiced, then? Must we always "spare the rod and spoil the proverb"?

Never, we should say, upon a child more than three or four years old. Previous to the age, the child is somewhat like a small animal, and immediate physical reaction is often the best way to correct the baby's faults, as immediate present is all that interested it. But this does not necessarily mean a whipping. If your child is in a tantrum, you'll bring him around far sooner if you take his two arms in yours and holding so firmly be used for power. The very fact that he is in the grasp of someone stronger than he, will have a soothing effect.

But, of course, this presupposes control within you, and how pitifully seldom this scene in one administering punishment! How often the red face and flashing eyes, a loud voice and intemperate speech, tell of a judgment in abeyance and a spirit in the worst possible case for the dealing out of justice!....

The fact that so many parents fail where so many teachers succeed in representing these things to a child is, I think, for a very simple reason, and that is that the child has absolute faith in the justice of the teacher. He means what he says, but she says what she means, but a given order must be obeyed, and that she carries out which she promises. Certainly this in the mind of the child is fruitful in two ways. It establishes the right attitude toward obedience and develops a child respect for rightful authority.

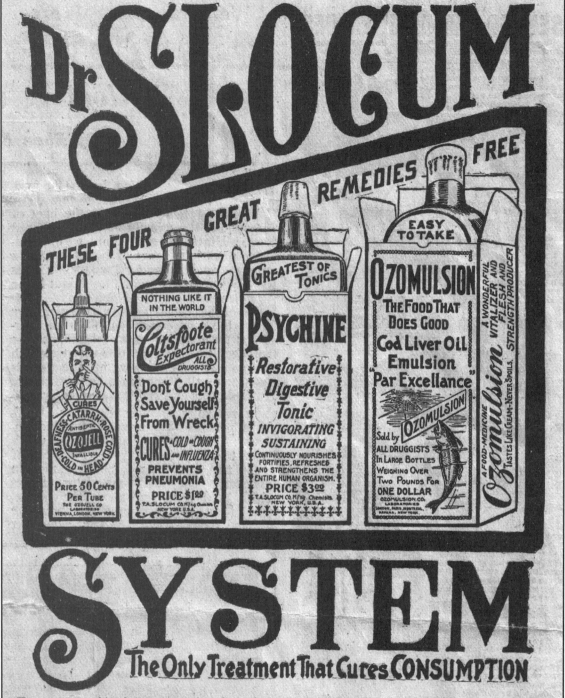

# 1913 NEWS FEATURE

**"The Home Training of Children," H. Addington Bruce, *The Outlook*, March 29, 1913:**

There are important and scientifically established reasons for beginning the education of a child far sooner than is commonly the rule—for beginning it, in fact, while he is still a mere infant crooning to himself in his cradle or playing about on the floor of his nursery.

It is not alone, or chiefly, mental growth that should be aimed at in the scheme of early home training. If it is well to habituate a child from the very dawning of his intelligence to the proper role of his reasoning powers, it is still more essential to apply to his education methods that will result in a stable moral development. As Professor M. E. Sadler has tersely but truly said: "The question of moral education is the heart of the educational problem. If it is neglected, education is in peril." This has long been recognized, and it has been recognized that the prevailing educational system is conspicuously inefficient in this respect. It was Horace Mann's observation that for every man who fails from intellectual defect, there are 10 who fail from moral defect. Or, as Dr. Morton Prince said to me not long ago, "What the world really needs is not more brains but more character."

Now, just a story of Karl Witte, which I have already told in part in *The Outlook*, contains many hints valuable to parents who wish to see their children develop into men and women mentally alert and vigorous as possible, so also is it helpful from the point of view of character building. For primarily it was not the elder Witte's purpose to make his son a "learned" man. What he wished to do was make him an all-around man, strong physically and morally as well as mentally. If he rightly believed that the boy's reasoning powers could not be properly developed unless they were trained from earliest infancy and the principles of sound reasoning, he was quite as firmly convinced that the process of moral development should likewise begin in the earliest possible moment. He believed this because he instinctively appreciated the truth of a law on which modern scientific investigators are nowadays laying ever-increasing stress—the so-called law of psychological determinism.

Stated briefly, this law, with which all parents ought to be acquainted, affirms that every occurrence in the moral life of a man is indissolubly associated with, and determined by, previous occurrences, especially by the occurrences and influences of early childhood. "If you have the happiness to be a well living man," said Dr. Paul Dubois, one of the foremost exponents of the philosophy of determinism, "take care not to attribute the credit of it to yourself. Remember the favorable conditions in which you have lived, surrounded by relatives who loved you and set you a good example; do not forget the close friends who have taken you by the hand and led you away from the quagmires of evil; keep a grateful remembrance for all the teachers who have influenced you, the kind and intelligent schoolmaster, the devoted pastor; realize all these multiple influences which have made of you what you are. Then you remember that such and such a culprit has not in his sad life met with the favorable conditions, that he had a drunken father or a foolish mother, and that he has lived without affection, exposed to all kinds of temptation. He will then take pity upon this disinherited man, whose mind has been nurtured through malformed mental images, begetting evil sentiments, such as a modern desire or social hatred."

In the case of the "spoiled" child, equally with that of the neglected one, the determinist sees the implanting of the seeds certain soon or late to ripen into a harvest of moral flabbiness. And this cry, consequently, is for the beginning of moral education in the first years of childhood, so that by the time the child reaches school age he will have acquired a viewpoint and strength of character sufficient to enable him to resist the allurements of companions of perhaps vicious, or at all events morally weak, tendencies.

So convinced was Witte of the same supreme importance of environment as a factor of moral development that he even laid down rules to be strictly observed by the maid-of-all-work, a simple but goodhearted peasant girl, in her dealings with the child. The whole family life, in fact, was regulated with a view to "suggesting" to the child ideas which, taking root in the subconscious region of his mind, would tend soon or late to affect his moral outlook and exercise a lasting influence on his conduct. Hasty words, disputes, discussion of unpleasant subjects, all these things were scrupulously avoided. In their relations with one another, as with the little serving-maid and all who visited the Witte home, the parents displayed only those characteristics with which they wished to imbue their son. They were unfailingly genial, courteous, considerate, and sympathetic. Over and above all this, they set him a constant example of diligence, of that earnest activity which is of itself a most forceful form of moral discipline.

# 1916 PROFILE

Emily Strandhope thought that, if Americans were not careful, the Greeks, Italians and Russians would overrun the United States and reduce English to a minority language.

## Life at Home

- Emily Strandhope heard the call at an early age; in retrospect, the vision arrived while she was at the open-air market not far from her home in Brooklyn, New York.
- She was 15 and had been sent to the market for some carrots, cabbage and flour.
- None were in sight, and when she asked the vendor, he replied in German that he didn't understand her request; she turned to the next vendor and he, too, spoke no English.
- That's when Emily decided that she was being called to Americanize the immigrant hordes flocking to the United States.
- Fixing the immigrant problem would save America from the anarchists and Bolsheviks, and the best way to do that was to teach the "foreign parts" out of their heads.
- The quicker they learned to speak nothing but English, the better off everyone would be.
- From 1870 to 1916, 27 million immigrants arrived at America's shores to find work, education and opportunity.
- The lure of American-style education was so great that, on days after a steamship landed in New York Harbor, the city's schools would often experience an enrollment hike of 125 pupils.
- Education was necessary if the American way of life was to be preserved.
- Emily attended college at Columbia with this goal in mind.
- There, she learned that the emerging idea called "kindergarten" could not only educate the very young, but also serve as a

*Emily Strandhope*
*Americanized immigrants.*

substitute for the moral training not taught to the children by their parents in the slums of New York.

- Under this theory, children could be taught in school disciplines such as cleanliness, politeness, obedience and regularity; some schools even installed showers to meet the needs of the dirty, neglected unban children.

- These steps were all necessary, experts said, because among the immigrants, critical influences like the family, church and community had collapsed.

*Immigrants lived in poor, neglected neighborhoods.*

- Emily knew in her heart that the child who lived for years in the misery of a crowded tenement home would become too comfortable with corruption and immorality as an adult.

- She was, in effect, saving America from itself, and was often disappointed that her friends did not fully comprehend how important her work was, and how much she was sacrificing for the country.

- She didn't hesitate to scrub a child clean when he arrived dirty, she washed children's hair to reduce lice infestations, and she regularly swatted children on their backsides when she heard them speaking in their native language.

- Emily was one of five children born in Upstate New York in 1880.

- Her parents owned so many books—possibly as many as 300—the neighbors used the Strandhope home as a lending library.

- Emily always made sure every book was returned on time—sometimes without a lot of finesse.

- Early in her career, she had read *The Atlantic Monthly* that called for adoption of business organization by schools.

- The author identified the ideal teacher as one who would rigidly "hew to the line."

- His ideal school was a place strictly adhering to rigid routine, and repeatedly stressed in his article a need for "unquestioned obedience."

- Emily did not wish to be well liked by her students—popularity was a dangerous game that helped no one; she was going to Americanize the foreigners before they took over.

- While her parents were enormously proud, her sisters thought her a fool.

- When she was 24, she turned down a marriage proposal from

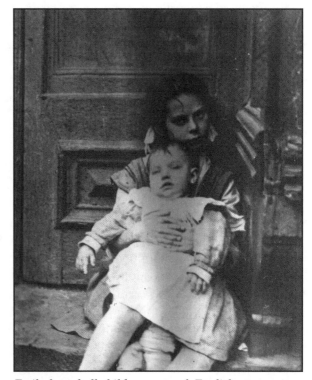
*Emily forced all children to speak English.*

*Emily's students adhered to rigid routines and did not question her.*

a solid working man so she would not have to give up teaching—as married women were expected to do.

- Now, at 36, she was an "old maid" with no prospects on the horizon.
- At least with the onset of World War I, Europe had radically reduced the number of new immigrants coming to America; now was the time to pull the welcome mat, extinguish the symbolic welcome flame on the Statue of Liberty, and deal with what they had already.
- One of the answers was kindergarten and the chance to "straighten the crooked sticks" while they were young.
- Emily had even helped several young children by changing the spelling of their names to make them more American; when one parent objected, Emily told her "it was for her own good."
- The first public school kindergarten in the United States opened in St. Louis, Missouri, in 1873, with the specific purpose of dealing with urban poverty.
- Forty-three years later, the educational reform movement had evolved, and now included the improvement of parenting skills—especially those of the urban poor immigrant mothers.

## Life at Work

- Emily Strandhope knew in her bones that the Gary Plan was destined to fail in New York City, where the student population was diverse, multiple languages were embedded in the culture, and the children were less manageable.
- First established in 1906 in Gary, Indiana, the Gary Plan curriculum kept students in motion; children moved from class to class, learned automobile repair and took physical education classes.
- Superintendent William Wirt wanted his students to be busy.
- He viewed the self-sufficient family farm as containing all of the characteristics necessary for a student's development, particularly vocational training, physical activity, and character growth.
- Work and productivity characterized rural life, and Wirt believed that the rapid urbanization occurring in the early twentieth century threatened the rural values necessary for the total development of children.
- Wirt maintained that the public schools should provide an oasis to instill the values of family, work and productivity among urban students and produce an efficient, orderly society of solid, productive citizens.
- He pioneered nature classes, animal care and husbandry, an auto mechanics shop and businesses to run.
- All the space was used all the time; he called it "Work-Study-Play."
- Gary students helped to run the school from the print shop to the cafeteria.
- Wirt's goal was to "make every working man a scholar and every scholar a working man."

- Emily considered it an invitation to bedlam; children learned best when they were sitting still, facing forward and paying attention.
- When their hands got too busy, the brain went dead.
- Besides, if farming was so great, why were so many people flocking to the cities?
- There was only enough time to help the promising ones, she declared proudly, and that is how she wanted to spend her time—no matter what crazy fad some status-seeking superintendent had foisted on the public.
- She had learned to read people's characters at an early age.

*Children learned best when they were sitting still.*

- Now that she had taught for more than 16 years, she could spot a loser from across the room.
- Classes with 45 children were too big, and making teachers instruct in only one subject robbed the teacher of the opportunity to engage the whole student.
- While the Gary Plan was still being tested on children, it was merchandised from the newsstand, pulpit, and lecture circuit, lauded in administrative circles, and soundly praised by John and Evelyn Dewey in their 1915 book, *Schools of Tomorrow*.
- It was quickly adopted as gospel by the proponents of the scientific management movement, while *Elementary School Teacher* in 1912 published a piece titled, "Elimination of Waste in Education."
- Teaching, it said, was slated to become a specialized scientific calling conducted by pre-approved agents of the central business office.
- Classroom teachers would teach the same thing over and over to groups of traveling children; special subject teachers would deliver their subjects to classes rotating through the building on a precision time schedule.
- Early in 1914, the Federal Bureau of Education endorsed the Gary Plan, which was installed in dozens of schools in Brooklyn.
- New York City parents, especially the guardians of the city's Jewish students, staged a spontaneous rebellion against extension of the Gary Plan.
- A program that looked like a complete and comprehensive education in Gary, Indiana, looked like a government-paid training program for New York City factory workers.
- In addition, the size of the schools envisioned by the Gary Plan would reduce the personal touch and turn neighborhood schools into education factories.
- New-fangled ideas about education were not going to produce moral, educated children—only strict discipline would do that.
- And Emily was sure—without question—that she had been called to Americanize the filthy masses and protect America's shores from foreign invaders.

THE SCHOOL AND
SOCIETY

*and*

THE CHILD AND THE
CURRICULUM

JOHN DEWEY

INTRODUCTION BY PHILIP W. JACKSON

*A Centennial Publication
of the University of Chicago Press*

THE UNIVERSITY OF CHICAGO PRESS
CHICAGO & LONDON

## Life in the Community: Brooklyn, New York

- The Dutch were the first Europeans to settle in the area on the western end of Long Island, also inhabited by a Native American people, the Lenape.
- The Dutch lost the area they called Breuckelen in the British conquest of New Netherland in 1664; over time, the name evolved from Breuckelen, to Brockland, Brocklin, Brookline, Brookland and, eventually, Brooklyn.
- During the first half of the nineteenth century, Brooklyn experienced significant growth along the economically strategic East River waterfront across from New York City; Brooklyn's population expanded more than threefold between 1800 and 1820, doubled again in the 1820s, and doubled yet again during the 1830s.
- Then, in 1854, the City of Brooklyn annexed the City of Williamsburg, an event that allowed Brooklyn to grow from a substantial community of 36,236 to an influential city of 96,838.
- The building of rail links, such as the Brighton Beach Line in 1878, heralded explosive growth, and, in the space of a decade, Brooklyn annexed the towns of New Lots in 1886; Flatbush, Gravesend, and New Utrecht in 1894; and Flatlands in 1896.
- The Brooklyn Bridge, completed in 1883, linked Manhattan to Brooklyn, and in 1894, Brooklyn residents voted by a slight majority to join with Manhattan, The Bronx, Queens, and Richmond (later Staten Island) to become the five boroughs of the modern New York City.
- But Brooklyn continued to maintain a distinct culture.
- Many Brooklyn neighborhoods were enclaves where particular ethnic groups and cultures predominated.
- When the Williamsburg Bridge opened in 1903, it was the largest suspension bridge in the world.
- Five years later, in 1908, the city's first subway began running trains between Brooklyn and Manhattan; in 1909, the Manhattan Bridge was completed.

*Brooklyn, New York*

# HISTORICAL SNAPSHOT
# 1916

- Ebbets Field opened in 1913, and the Brooklyn Dodgers, formerly known as the Bridegrooms and then the Trolley Dodgers, had a new home
- During World War I, Paris was bombed by German zeppelins for the first time
- In the court case of *Brushaber v. Union Pacific Railroad*, the U.S. Supreme Court upheld the national income tax
- The Royal Army Medical Corps staged the first successful blood transfusion using blood that had been stored and cooled

- Tristan Tzara "founded" the art movement Dadaism
- Emma Goldman was arrested for lecturing on birth control
- The Baltimore Symphony Orchestra staged its first concert
- President Woodrow Wilson sent 12,000 troops over the U.S.-Mexico border in response to Pancho Villa leading about 500 Mexican raiders against Columbus, New Mexico, in an attack that killed 12 U.S. soldiers
- The light switch was invented by William J. Newton and Morris Goldberg
- The U.S. Marines invaded the Dominican Republic
- During the secret Sykes-Picot Agreement following the conclusion of World War I, Britain and France agreed how to divide Arab areas of the Ottoman Empire into French and British spheres of influence
- The *Saturday Evening Post* published its first Norman Rockwell cover
- President Wilson signed a bill incorporating the Boy Scouts of America
- In Seattle, Washington, William Boeing incorporated Pacific Aero Products, later named Boeing
- German agents caused the Black Tom explosion in Jersey City, New Jersey, an act of sabotage destroying an ammunition depot and killing at least seven people
- Woodrow Wilson signed legislation creating the National Park Service
- D. W. Griffith's film *Intolerance: Love's Struggle Through the Ages* was released
- Margaret Sanger opened the first U.S. birth control clinic, a forerunner of Planned Parenthood
- The 40-hour work week began in the Endicott-Johnson factories of western New York
- Woodrow Wilson narrowly defeated Republican Charles E. Hughes
- Republican Jeannette Rankin of Montana became the first woman elected to the U.S. House of Representatives
- Woodrow Wilson married Mrs. Edith B. Galt in Washington
- Oxycodone, a narcotic painkiller closely related to codeine, was synthesized in Germany
- The Summer Olympic Games in Berlin, Germany, were cancelled
- Ernst Rüdin published his initial results on the genetics of schizophrenia

## Selected Prices

Automobile, Franklin Runabout ...................................................$1,900.00

Campbell's Condensed Soup, Can......................................................$0.12

Cookware, Aluminum, 25 Pieces.......................................................$10.95

Doll ..........................................................................................$0.98

Doublemint Gum, 25 Pkgs.................................................................$0.73

Food Jar, One Gallon ......................................................................$10.00

Rum, Bacardi, Fifth..........................................................................$3.20

Theater Ticket, including War Tax ....................................................$2.20

Victrola.......................................................................................$125.00

Woman's Hose, Artificial Silk............................................................$0.35

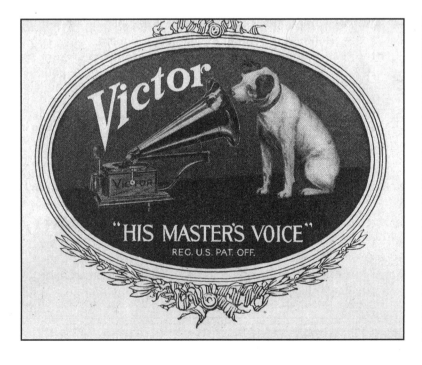

## Letter to the Editor: "The Gary Plan: A Backward S," Isidore Springer, Principal, Public School 25, Brooklyn, *The New York Times*, January 6, 1915:

Very few educational movements have aroused so much interesting discussion among the public and education circles as the Gary Plan. We find editorials and newspapers advocating very strenuously its adoption. Directors of educational associations seem to find it a cure-all for all educational ills. In view of this constant agitation, I believe it is time to consider the Gary Plan, not in the light of partnership, but in view of educational history and practice, and seek to find whether this movement or plan is in harmony with the trend of educational thought during the past two decades.

I do not wish to be considered as an opponent of the Gary Plan, nor an exponent of the Ettinger or any other plan. It is simply my purpose to consider this plan in light of the various educational movements that had been discussed and proved worthy to be incorporated as a part of the educational program. I beg, therefore, to make a brief summary of the various movements that have been occupying the public attention and discussion for the past 20 years: to note, if possible, the common tendency or meaning; to examine, in such a light, the Gary Plan, and so determine whether this plan is a step forward and therefore in harmony with the main currents of educational history, or whether, on the contrary, this plan is not an about-face to what has gone before and practically nullifies educational progress for the past 20 years.

The graded class, which was called into being by the organization of large city schools, presented many problems which soon demanded solution. An attempt to solve the problem of mass instruction, with its attendant evils of disregard of the individual, was by formation of special classes, such as the "C" classes, or, English to foreign classes; "E" classes, classes which should help the backward pupils; and the ungraded classes, which would take care of the mentally unfit. A further attempt at this solution took the form of the organization in every class of groups, and the provision of the educational busy work for the members of the group not reciting.

In 1912, the Committee of Inquiry of the Board of Estimate and Apportionment began an investigation of the city schools with a view of determining wherein these schools were inefficient and uneconomical. This inquiry had been called forth by the then public discussion as to the prevalence of overage and retarded children in schools of the city of New York. It will be remembered by even the general reader that this question of overage became so heated as to, at times, assume an acrimonious stage. Conferences were called by the city superintendent, various committees were appointed, and important progress was made to solve the problem of retardation. It was seen that retarded and overage children were an economic loss to the city, and the prevention of retardation would result in a gain to the city, both economically and socially. The committee appointed by the Board of Estimate and Apportionment presented a report that showed that part-time and overcrowded classes were causes of retardation.

*Continued*

**Letter to the Editor . . .** *(Continued)*

If we examine carefully, then, these various movements which have been deemed worthy of being incorporated as part of the educational practice of the day, I think it will be found that all these agitations seemed to have a basis, whether consciously or not, in a desire that the interests of society are best served when the needs and capacity of the individual are considered and developed....

In other words, the past two decades will be known in educational history as the period of the individualization of instruction.

Now let us consider the relation of the Gary Plan to this movement. The Gary Plan calls for the economical and wider use of the school plan by providing for schools of large size and large numbers of children in each class. Fundamentally considered, the Gary Plan is a plan for part-time schools, with many of the objectionable features of part-time schools culminating by incorporating ancillary activities, such as swimming pools, libraries, shops, etc. The Gary Plan does not present a single innovation in school methods or show a new approach toward individual instruction, but is simply a departmental schedule so drawn up as to accommodate two groups of classes in one building, a scheme which was attempted for many years in New York under the part-time school.

The Gary idea, and planning for large schools, from 64 to 128 classes, creates such a tremendous educational machine that the individual is lost. The direct relation between the supervisor in the class is reduced to a minimum. The close personal touch that should exist between principal and children must disappear. The supervisor becomes administrative officer, a business manager. The school becomes an educational factory.

The greatest danger, however, is the overcrowding of classrooms. The question of the number of children in the class that makes for efficient instruction has been the subject of a number of experiments recently. It has been proved almost conclusively that the ideal class should have 30 to 35. The Gary Plan, fundamentally a plan of economy, calls for classes of 45 and more. The possibility of a close study of the individual with the view of determining his needs and issues, teaching, instead of becoming an art based on scientific pedagogy, degenerates into the peddling of information....

Finally, the Gary Plan, however attractive it may be made, is a double session plan, or part-time plan, and therefore brings with it the attendant evils of retardation and overage. Our evaluation of the Gary Plan leads us to the conclusion that it is a distinct backward step in educational history. The problems for retardation and overage which promised to be solved again become in imminent danger. The process of individualized education, the process of the study of the individual, to know his capacities, and to adopt himself to the service of society according to its needs, is halted, and American education becomes reactionary because of a policy of financial entrenchment.

### "Working Women and Wages," *The Outlook*, March 29, 1913:

The employment of girls and women in factories, department stores, and all such out-of-the-home industries is comparatively new, says *Life*. "It has nearly all come with the immense development of machinery during the last two generations and with the demand for cheap labor which has followed. Commercial organizations such as has given us the department stores is a form of machinery and has come along with all the other machines," *Life* adds.

At present, girls are the cheapest article in the labor market, and are used enormously in industrial exploitation. If it gets around that girls have a potential value to society which makes it uneconomic to use them up in service and scrap them like worn-out machines, it may raise hob with a lot of industries that are run by cheap girl-power at present.

When Jane Addams enlisted in the Progressive Movement sometime prior to the formal opening of the last presidential campaign, says the Los Angeles *Express*, her critics demanded that she confine her activities to the field of accredited philanthropy. "Her answer to these critics was an appeal for relief for the victims of an industrial system that refused to take account of the right of working girls and children to food, shelter, and safety." The Progressive National platform calls for "minimum wage standards for workingwomen to provide a living wage in all industrial occupations." But the New York *Sun* warns us that "a generous concern for the underpaid or the unfortunate should not blind the great mass of us to the fact that any artificial system of wages must result in cruel displacements of labor."

### "Vocational or Trade Schools," *Croonborg's Gazette of Fashions*, August 1915:

In this country, broad, educational systems are in a transitional stage. The best schools are discarding the narrow traditions of the past and are adjusting their activities to the needs of the present. The old subjects with the exception of the Three R's are being changed to meet new conditions which confront a nation of workers.

A careful examination of the records of those who have graduated from the grammar schools will show that a very small percentage enter into the High Schools, and their destination may be classified as 1) business, 2) trades, 3) domestic life. Greatly changed social conditions have transformed what were formerly parental obligations into school obligations.

These changed conditions have led the Legislatures and School Boards to revive their systems, in order that the rising generations may be enabled to fit themselves with a trade or profession which will bring them a competency ample and sufficient to take them through life.

There was a time when a boy or a girl was enabled to serve an apprenticeship with those who are qualified to teach them a trade or profession, but that is a thing of the past, and today we are made aware that the average tradesmen or mechanic has neither the inclination nor the time and patience, and more often than not, the means, to do this great work. Furthermore, we have learned that the best method of education is that laid down in our public school system where all partake of the same source and are paid for out of one common purse.

The citizen is awake to this, and with that in mind, the systems are being made over to conform with the needs of the hour. This work should have the endorsement of every employer and employee giving such assistance and aid to those interested with this work.

First, find out the ideas in the child of tender age, and then put them in operation through manual training. This may be described as the means of education through the hand and eye by work with tools and materials of industry. This will bring up the pace and attitude of those different branches of industry.

Second, this should be followed by the occasional work in higher grades with the result that when graduation takes place, the pupils are apt to go to work as soon as the law allows, and take with them what will be of use through life, viz., "the ability to earn their living no matter where they may be, and not be turned down and out and doomed as unskilled laborers."

Much thought and attention must be given to the subject during the next few years, and we as Merchant Tailors can do a large share of this work, by doing it in each locality, wherever that may be.

Yours truly,
Harry Fisher

# 1919 PROFILE

Before Joshua Blevins got a contract to construct small homes for out-of-town teachers, he had never heard of a teacherage or even realized they were needed.

## Life at Home

- Joshua Blevins loved the sights, sounds and smells of France in the closing days of World War I, but it was great to get back to central Texas, where the air was sweet and the sunsets uniformly spectacular.
- During the previous 18 months, Joshua had led a seven- to 12-man construction crew in a small village outside Paris, attempting to build or rebuild housing for the American troops and the flood of refugees pouring through the area.
- As a result of wartime conditions, he learned how to adapt quickly to changing situations, build buildings with the existing material, and be flexible when emergencies arose.
- It was the perfect combination of skills and training for a third-grade school dropout whose new job was the construction of 32 teacherages across central Texas.
- By 1919, more than 3,000 teacherages had been constructed.
- The movement was ignited in 1905 after a young female teacher, who could not afford proper

*Joshua Blevins built teacherages – small houses for out-of-town teachers.*

housing, commandeered a cookhouse wagon in Walla Walla County, Washington, for her living quarters.
- The 20-foot wagon, covered only in canvas, let in the rain and snow and attracted newspaper stories concerning this unusual housing arrangement, much to the embarrassment of the community.

- With the backing of the school board, a two-room cottage was built on school property, sparking a national movement to assist rural communities by building teacherages.
- By 1919, Texas was one of the nation's leaders in providing housing for its rural, predominately female teachers.
- At the center of this movement were the General Federation of Women's Clubs and its 100,000 members who embraced school reform as a natural extension of their role as mothers.
- The women's clubs lobbied for improved teacher training, the end to political patronage in the selection of school superintendents, school consolidations, better facilities, and quality instructional materials for students.
- Much of their focus was on rural schools, where facilities lagged and the instruction was often poor; typically, illiteracy was twice as great in rural areas as it was in urban ones.
- Teacher pay was frequently an unlivable wage—one of the reasons that teacherages became necessary.
- Women routinely were paid 50 percent less than men.
- A primary concern was that poor rural schools would continue to drive a flood of ill-prepared youth into the city streets in search of jobs; this would weaken both the urban and the farm economies.

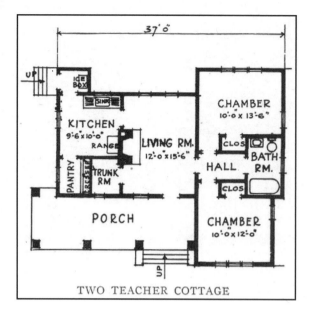

TWO TEACHER COTTAGE

*Accommodations for rural teachers were often makeshift and unsatisfactory.*

- Good schools were seen as the best way to shore up the American tradition of family farms in the agricultural economy; that demanded changes in teacher recruitment and school-lesson hours.
- The average school term nationally lasted 150 days; in rural Texas, the average number of school days totaled 106, while some schools only operated 63 days of instruction a year.
- Approximately 60 percent of all rural children were still educated in one-room schoolhouses.
- Plus, everyone was tired of the practice of boarding 'round,' whereby the teacher moved from house to house every few weeks, sleeping on whatever the home provided.
- The practice discouraged teachers and angered parents, who resented the presence of another adult in their cramped house.
- Even when the teacher paid for her accommodations, conditions could be dreadful—young teachers often had to wait for the man of the house to run "errands" in the barn so she could have enough privacy to get dressed.
- In some parts of the country, the teacher paid the home's owner for the privilege of sleeping four to a bed with schoolchildren; teacher privacy was non-existent, possessions few, and instability high.
- Teacher turnover was equally shameful; in a typical year, two-thirds of the rural teachers were new to the profession.

- In the years following the Civil War, the average age of a teacher was 15 years, and she possessed just enough knowledge to stay ahead of the oldest child,
- The average age was now 19 years; the average pay of a female teacher was $43 per month.
- Women's groups fully understood that a good rural education demanded quality teachers and living conditions that protected the morality and good name of the teacher; already a dozen states had passed legislation to fund teacherages.

*Teacherages were often two or three stories on school property.*

- As many as 1,000 teacherages were under construction nationwide—most built in a two- or three-room fashion on school property.
- In some cases, the teacherage comprised three-story dormitories capable of rooming five or six teachers.

## Life at Work

- When Joshua Blevins began construction of his first teacherage in a town 20 miles from his home in Marlin, Texas, he had a clear vision of how to construct two- and three-room cottages for under $100 if he was to make a profit.
- But that was before he fully understood how much help he was to receive.
- When he arrived for the first morning of work—hauling all his tools and supplies in a 12-foot cart pulled by a horse—he was met by a committee of women representing the School Superintendent's Office.

*A livable home for teachers was something to be proud of.*

- They were so excited about the prospect of a livable home for their teacher; they had brought a gaggle of sullen teenage boys and several elderly servants to assist.
- Against all objections from Joshua, the menagerie of helpers pulled everything from the wagon.
- Joshua was beside himself in anguish; he was a precise man and his years of experience had taught him that setting up properly was as critical to the exacting work of building a house as was using quality lumber from a tree he had just cut down.
- It didn't matter; the welcoming committee was immensely proud of it—even when the boys picked up several very precise and proud tools to use in mock sword fights.

- Joshua had a contract to build 32 units in cities stretching across central Texas the summer before school began again after Labor Day.
- Joshua took a deep breath and mumbled to himself, "Yes. I survived bombs and buffoons in France. I will survive even this."
- As World War I had drawn to a close, women's confidence was up and admission to colleges grew at the phenomenal rate of 75 percent.
- The majority of the female graduates left with teaching certificates despite the skills displayed by women in factories and office buildings supporting a war—teaching was still one of the few occupations reliably available to them.
- In many rural communities teachers were subjected to small-town scrutiny when it came to dating, in addition to an expectation that teachers should socialize by attending every community event.
- At the same time, local expectations demanded that teachers not smoke, drink, dance, play cards, wear certain types of clothing or take weekend trips.
- Joshua discovered that many of the club ladies disapproved of him smoking, too, but lacked the courage to ask him to stop.
- As far as Joshua was concerned, the automated cigarette rolling machine was one of the greatest inventions in the history of man.
- On the second day of the job, Joshua was greeted by schoolchildren and their mothers who possessed a world of knowledge—albeit little experience—about how he should proceed, but had no inclination to keep their children out of his wood pile and away from his tools.
- Day two, like day one, went more slowly than planned; day three brought the teacher occupant herself with a list of preferences, including her ideas about window dressings, the height of steps, and the location of the outhouse.
- All Joshua could say was, "One down and 31 to go."
- It was a process that was repeated over and over.
- By the time he built the ninth teacher's home, he fully realized that Texas communities wanted to offer good education, and that his building was a visible symbol of that desire.
- Church ladies brought picnic baskets of food for lunch, amateur architects showed him various improvements to his design, and several times, truly talented carpenters came to help construct a wall or fashion some steps.
- Of course, the other delight was meeting a bevy of young women teachers who thanked him profusely as though it were his idea.
- After several attempts to deflect credit failed, he started simply saying, "You're welcome" in a quiet voice.
- By the time he finished his last house—a four-room house for two teachers, the townspeople were mailing him letters asking him to come and see what they had done—some paint, some trim and some curtains allowed each school to take ownership of the teacherage.
- In Marlin, his hometown, Joshua discovered that a phone had been installed in the teacherage— even though most of the student homes were still phoneless.
- The local, family-owned phone company donated the phone as a promotion, designed to help people understand the value of a phone in emergencies.

## Life in the Community: Marlin, Texas

- Marlin, Texas, the county seat of Falls County, was experiencing a tourism boom thanks to the hot springs discovered nearby and the town's excellent train connections.
- Located near the falls of the Brazos River, the town was incorporated in 1867 and named to honor John Marlin, a pioneer patriot.

*Marlin, Texas*

- Samuel A. Blain, his son-in-law, laid out the streets and lots and drafted a map around a square; lots for Presbyterian, Methodist, and Baptist churches were the first to be chosen.
- Zenas Bartlett's General Store was the first business, and its brick building was used as a school for a short period.
- When the Houston and Texas Central Railway completed its line in 1871, the population of Marlin tripled from 500 to 1,500 within a decade.
- Marlin also had a freighting business, a tavern, a law office, and later the Green-Bartlett Mercantile Business.
- The first courthouse was a log cabin used for county business and court, as a school taught by Dr. Giles W. Cain, as a church, as a meeting place for political and community meetings, and as a dance hall.
- In 1901, a second railroad, the International-Great Northern, laid its tracks in the town and dredged a lake in what became the City Park, which is still used as a recreation area, a site for Marlin Festival Days, and as a Youth Center for its Falls County Future Farmer, 4-H Club, and Future Homemaker annual shows.
- In 1871, a tuition school, Marlin Male and Female Academy, was located on Ward Street north of the public square.
- Fire destroyed the public school building in 1900, and a new brick school was constructed in 1903.
- Two community Black schools, dependent on state funds, were organized in 1875 and met in the Baptist and African Methodist church buildings.
- In 1916, the City Council voted to build a school for African-Americans.
- The Bank of Marlin was chartered in 1892, followed by Marlin National Bank and the First State Bank.
- The Marlin Compress and Cotton Seed Oil Mills were established in 1892 by a board of directors headed by J. A. Martin.
- That same year, hot mineral water was found during the search for an artesian well, prompting Dr. J. W. Cook to promote Marlin as a health center.
- Bethesda Bathhouse, Majestic Bathhouse, the Imperial Hotel, Torbett Hospital, and the pavilion for the flowing hot water fountain were all founded soon after.
- Conrad Hilton built the Falls Hotel, with a tunnel to a mineral bath, to accommodate the business generated by the hot springs.

# HISTORICAL SNAPSHOT
# 1919

- Theodore Roosevelt, the 26th president of the United States died in his sleep at the age of 60
- A literal wave of molasses released from an exploding storage tank swept through Boston, killed 21 and injured 150
- The League of Nations was founded in Paris
- Oregon placed a one-cent-per-gallon tax on gasoline, the first state to levy a gas tax
- Congress established most of the Grand Canyon as a national park
- Edsel Ford succeeded his father as head of the Ford Motor Company
- Hit songs included "Swanee," "The World Is Waiting for the Sunrise," and "Oh, What a Pal Was Mary,"
- Eugene V. Debs entered the Atlanta Federal Penitentiary in Georgia for speaking out against the draft
- Scientist Robert Goddard proposed using rockets to send a vehicle to the moon
- Babe Ruth hit a major league record of 29 home runs
- The Treaty of Versailles with the League of Nations provision was signed, ending World War I
- More than 30,000 Jews marched in Baltimore to protest pogroms in Poland and elsewhere
- Labor unrest was its most severe since the 1890s
- When 45,000 strikers threatened to paralyze Seattle, Washington, the mayor set up machine guns to ward off anyone threatening municipal functions
- Congress approved the Nineteenth Amendment to the Constitution, which guaranteed suffrage to women, and sent the amendment to the states for ratification
- Boxer Jack Dempsey knocked down challenger Jess Willard seven times in the first round of a heavyweight fight before winning in the third round with a technical knockout
- Afghanistan gained independence from the United Kingdom
- The American Communist Party was established
- Herbert Hoover was named director of the relief organization for liberated countries
- President Woodrow Wilson suffered a serious stroke
- Congress passed the Volstead Act over President Wilson's veto and Prohibition went into effect on January 19, 1920, under the provisions of the Eighteenth Amendment
- The first Palmer Raid was conducted on the second anniversary of the Russian Revolution; over 10,000 suspected communists and anarchists were arrested in 23 U.S. cities
- Cartoon character Felix the Cat appeared for the first time in "Feline Follies"
- The first national convention of the American Legion was held in Minneapolis
- John Maynard Keynes' book *The Economic Consequences of the Peace* was published
- John Moses Browning finalized the design for the M1919 .30 machine gun, the first widely distributed air-cooled medium machine gun used by the U.S. military

## Selected Prices

Egg Incubator and Brooder.............................................................$10.00

Electric Radiator ...........................................................................$5.75

Farmland, per Acre........................................................................$20.00

Hair Curlers...................................................................................$0.25

Inlaid Linoleum, per Yard .............................................................$2.35

Phonograph Record........................................................................$0.65

Radium Water, 50 24-Ounce Bottles.............................................$25.00

Shampoo .......................................................................................$0.33

Trunk.............................................................................................$16.95

Woman's Hose, Artificial Silk.......................................................$0.35

### "After the Christmas Dinner, Bright Things of All Times That People Have Laughed Over," *The Ladies' Home Journal,* December 1918:

**Couldn't Faze Ethel**

Ethel had her quick wit working that minute! She was sitting, after the Christmas dinner, with a gallant captain in a charmingly decorated recess. On her knee was a diminutive niece, placed there pour les convenances. In the adjoining room, with the door open, were the rest of the company. Finally the little niece was heard to say in a jealous and very audible voice: "Auntie, kiss me, too."

"Certainly, dear," returned Ethel. "But you should say twice, dear; two was not grammar."

**A Prodigy**

A gentleman living outside of Chicago went into the city of his office each day. When he was leaving home in the morning before Christmas, his wife said she would like him to bring a banner for her Sunday school class to use at an entertainment that evening, but that she did not know the wording and size needed. They agreed that she should send him a telegram during the day, giving him these two items. Consequently, before starting for home in the afternoon, he went to the nearby telegraph office and found quite an excitement over the message which had just been received and which read: "Unto us a child is born. Three feet wide and six feet long."

**Much Better**

"Is your father's stomachache better?" asked the teacher, the day after Christmas.

"Yessum," replied the boy, "It isn't aching half as loud as it did."

**She Knew, Sweet Dear**

The young bride went to the grocery store to do her Christmas marketing. She was determined that the grocer should not take advantage of her youth and inexperience.

"These eggs are dreadfully small," she criticized.

"I know it," he answered. "But that's the kind the farmer brings me. They are just fresh from the country this morning."

"Yes," said the bride, "and that's the trouble with those farmers; they are so anxious to get their eggs sold that they take them off the nest too soon!"

**Faith and Works**

One Monday morning two little girls, aged seven and nine, were on their way to school. Fearing they would be tardy, the seven-year-old said to the nine-year-old: "Let's kneel down and pray that we won't be late."

The nine-year-old said to the seven-year-old: "Let's keep hiking and pray as we hike."

*Continued*

**"After the Christmas Dinner, . . .** *(Continued)*

**Better the First Time**
A man asked a friend, who was hard of hearing, if he would lend him five dollars, to tide him over Christmas.

"What?" asked the friend.

"Will you lend me 10 dollars?"

"Oh, yes," replied the friend, "but I wish now I had heard you the first time."

**Revenge**
The druggist danced and chortled until the bottles danced on the shelves.

"What's up?" asked the soda clerk. "Have you been taking something?"

"No. But do you remember when our water pipes were frozen last Christmas?"

"Yes, but what?"

"Well, the plumber who fixed them has just come to have a prescription filled."

**One on the Teacher**
Boy: "Can a person be punished for something he hasn't done?"

Teacher: "Of course not."

Boy: "Well, I haven't done my geometry."

**"Colored Night School Still Making Progress,"** *The Asheville Times* **(North Carolina), March 30, 1919:**

At the close of the second week, the enrollment at Catholic Hill colored night school has increased to 125 pupils. The grownups in attendance show deep interest in their studies, and utilize every chance to progress. The teachers report that the interest shown by these people is really remarkable, and they are making rapid advances in securing the elements of an education.

During the absence of Principal W. S. Lee, who is at Atlanta attending the YMCA training school, W. K. Level has conducted both day and night schools, and everything has passed off without friction under his management.

## "The Evolution of the School," *American Social Problems,* The MacMillan Company, New York, 1920:

One evidence of educational readjustment is the growing content of the curriculum. We have already mentioned the great development of natural and social sciences. Since the sum total of human knowledge is constantly increasing, each age must decide for itself what knowledge is of most worth. Educational readjustment is one indication of intellectual progress, for static societies abhor educational changes. Again, methods of teaching and progress in school administration must keep pace with the growth of the science of education. A third factor in educational readjustment is the spread of the spirit of democracy. Education for all is the modern ideal, for education is both a cause and a result of democracy. The need of "the classes" is not that of "the masses"; the educational ideals of the aristocracy of yesterday are not the democratic ideals of those of to-day. Consequently, the curricula and the courses of modern schools have expanded far beyond the straight and narrow path of antiquity that led to "culture" and a "liberal education." We have seen that the anonymous commercial and industrial development of the past century has reflected itself in educational changes. Industrial society feels the need of intelligent workers, and the present generation asked for that type of education which will best prepare for the practical duties of everyday life. Therefore, vocational courses are demanded for the workaday world.

## Letter to the Editor: Why Girls Go Wrong, One of the Unskilled Class Tells Her Story, *The New York Times*, March 13, 1913:

I have for some time been reading in the papers and listening to men from the pulpits and platforms argue and express their opinions as to "Why girls go wrong," and while some of these opinions and arguments are the result of guessing, others, such as low wages, dismal home surroundings, etc., are true, but I have been waiting to read or hear of the greatest and most tragic of all causes why girls go wrong, and find that even the costly investigation at Chicago has failed to bring it out....

For an unskilled working girl it is difficult enough to find employment except at a job paying $4 or $5 a week, but when she is also unfortunate enough to not have a home and applies to a storekeeper or any businessman for a least responsible position that pays near a living wage, she makes an unfortunate impression and is turned away. The longer she is out of work, the more she appears a doubtful character to those to whom she applies for work, and she is often asked, "How have you been living, being out of work and having no home?" These continual insults when seeking work are alone enough to suggest to a girl to do what she is suspected of having done. Is it any wonder if, after tramping the streets searching for work in a dispirited mood, girls yield to the temptations held out to them by flirts, mashers, white slavers, and others who seek their prey among this class of girls? And it is this class that is inevitably doomed to the underworld.

Though I have stood on the brink of the precipice for the last five years, the reason I have not yet fallen is the fact that I have a power of endurance which thousands who do fall have not, to prove that those who may be skeptical I am compelled to relate some of my own experiences.

*Continued*

## Letter to the Editor . . . *(Continued)*

When I was 17 I lost my only friend, and it was necessary for me to get employment at once. Not having been taught any kind of work, the best job I could get was in the office of a department store at five dollars per week. I cooked my own coffee in the morning, which cost about two cents a cup, and purchased three rolls for two cents, one of which I had for breakfast and two for lunch, and another cup of coffee for which I paid three cents at the store lunch counters....

Having no one to depend on in case of emergency, I managed to save a least one dollar weekly. In the month of November another department store offered me seven dollars per week. Then I looked as big as all New York to me, and, of course, I accepted the job, but I did not know that help taken in that time in the year was laid off on Christmas Eve. While working there I learned of that fact, so I lived even more economically than before and walked about 40 blocks to and from work in order to save.

After a few days I had taken a place in a restaurant on West Street as cashier, but had to leave it at the end of a few weeks on account of the talk and insults I heard from sailors, drunkards, and ruffians who patronized the place.

Though I was awake most of the night and up at 5 a.m. daily scanning the advertisements, everywhere I went I found a large army of girls, young and old, applying to answer an advertisement that called for one person, and one who lived at home and was neat and cheerful was the one always taken on. It was about four months before I was successful in getting another job, which was in another department store at six dollars per week. While I was out of work, though I cut out the $0.12 suppers and lived on $0.10 or less a day, all I had saved was spent.

Because of these experiences, I decided to take up a course in bookkeeping at night. In order to do this, I tried more than ever before to save, and after attending school for two months I was compelled to leave, as I became sick, according to the doctors from lack of nourishment, and had to pay doctors what I saved on food to pay a tuition fee, and Christmas Eve I was again laid off in the next store to which I went. It was then again after three months before I got another job in a department store, for these stores did not take on help after Christmas and Easter season. Then, because of my worried state of mind, I made errors in my work and was dismissed. It now became almost impossible for me to work, even in department stores, or when a superintendent looked over my application he would remark, "How is it you have worked in so many places for so short a time and each only to be laid off, dismissed? And you are not living at home. We want people with better records." So the only time I can get work now is during the busy seasons, Christmas and Easter, and I have to exist on what I save then for the rest of the year and do odd jobs occasionally, such as addressing envelopes and making $0.75 per thousand.

Domestic work has at times been suggested to me, but until recently I regarded it as very humble work, and since I have changed my opinion I have not any more the strength for such work. Thus have I been existing for the last six years, during which time I had more than one offer from gentlemen with money to be a friend to me. As I have said above, while I possess the power to endure misery, as well as my higher ideals which have kept me from falls, hundreds situated as I am and to whom society is cold and cruel have fallen.

A victim of existing social conditions
New York

I board where there are eight children and parents, and only two rooms in the house. I must do as the families do about washing, as there is but one basin, and no place to go to wash but out the door. I have not had the luxury of either lamp or candle, their only light being a cup of grease with a rag for a wick…. I occupy a room with three of the children, and a niece who boards there. The other room serves as a kitchen, parlor, and bedroom for the rest of the family.

—Letter to activist Catharine Beecher

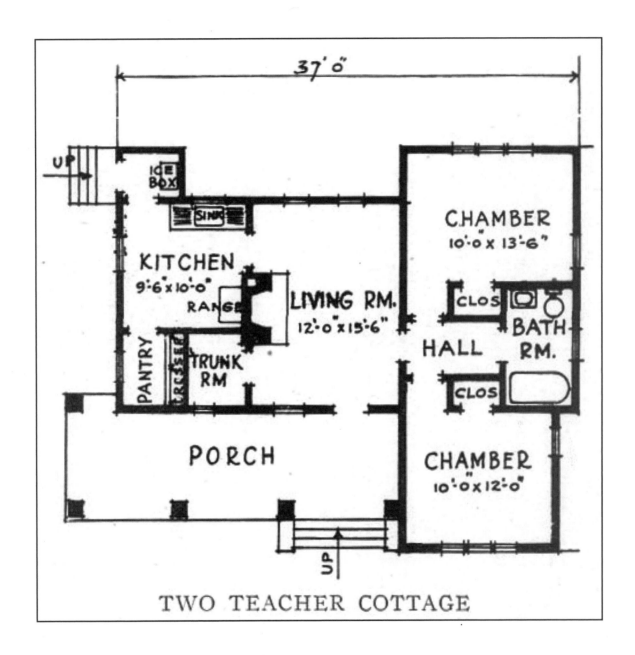

TWO TEACHER COTTAGE

# 1920–1929

In the decade following the Great War, America was dividing itself into a society that embraced change, consumerism and new adventures, versus a society resistant to new freedoms for women, new inventions, and shifting social ethics. Parents demanded that progressive educational efforts be branded "fads" and tossed aside in favor of teaching basic skills. New concerns were raised that too many men were attending college unnecessarily. A movement to halt immigration reduced new students from foreign lands.

By mid-decade, the IQ test—forerunner to standardized testing that would later shape America's educational curriculum—was firmly entrenched in educational philosophy. The 1920s were marked by a new nationalism symbolized by frenzied consumerism. By 1920, urban Americans had begun to define themselves—for their neighbors and for the world—in terms of what they consumed. The car was becoming universal—at least in its appeal. At the dawn of the century, only 4,192 automobiles were registered nationwide; in 1920, the number of cars had reached 1.9 million. Simultaneously, aggressive new advertising methods began appearing, designed to fuel the new consumer needs of the buying public. And buy, they did. From 1921 to 1929, Americans bought and America boomed. With expanded wages and buying power came increased leisure time for recreation, travel, and even self-improvement. Advertising reinforced the idea that the conveniences and status symbols of the wealthy were attainable for everyone. The well-to-do and the wage earner began to look a lot more alike.

Following the Great War, the attitude of many Americans was expressed in President Calvin Coolidge's famous remark, "The chief business of the American people is business." The role of the federal government remained small during the period, and federal expenditures actually declined following the war effort. Harry Donaldson's song "How Ya Gonna Keep 'Em Down on the Farm after They've Seen Paree?" described another basic shift in American society. The 1920 Census reported that more than 50 percent of the population—54 million people—lived in urban areas. The move to the cities was the result of raised expectations, increased industrialization, and the migration of millions of Southern blacks to the urban North.

The availability of electricity expanded the universe of goods that could be manufactured and sold. The increased use of radios, electric lights, telephones, and powered vacuum cleaners made them essential household items. Construction boomed as—for the first time—half of all Americans now lived in urban areas. Industry, too, benefited from the wider use of electric power. At the turn of the century, electricity ran 5 percent of all machinery, and by 1925, 73 percent. Large-scale electric power also made possible electrolytic processes in the rapidly developing heavy chemical industry. With increasing sophistication came higher costs; wages for skilled workers continued to rise during the 1920s, putting further distance between the blue-collar worker and the emerging middle class.

Following the war years, many women who had worked in men's jobs in the late teens remained in the work force, although at lower wages. Women, now allowed to vote nationally, were also encouraged to consider college and options other than marriage. Average family earnings increased slightly during the first half of the period, while prices and hours worked actually declined. The 48-hour week became standard, providing more leisure time. At least 40 million people went to the movies each week, and college football became a national obsession.

Unlike in previous decades, national prosperity was not fueled by the cheap labor of new immigrants, but by increased factory efficiencies, innovation, and more sophisticated methods of managing time and materials. Starting in the teens, the flow of new immigrants began to slow, culminating in the restrictive immigration legislation of 1924, when the number of new workers from Europe was reduced to a trickle. The efforts were largely designed to protect the wages of American workers—many of whom were only one generation from their native land. As a result, wages for unskilled labor remained stable, union membership declined, and strikes, on average, decreased. American exports more than doubled during the decade, and heavy imports of European goods virtually halted—a reversal of the Progressive Movement's flirtation with free trade.

These national shifts were not without powerful resistance. A bill was proposed in Utah to imprison any woman who wore her skirt higher than three inches above the ankle. Cigarette consumption reached 43 billion annually, despite smoking being illegal in 14 states and the threat of expulsion from college if caught with a cigarette. A film code limiting sexual material in silent films was created to prevent "loose" morals, and the membership of the Ku Klux Klan expanded to repress Catholics, Jews, open immigration, make-up on women, and the prospect of unrelenting change.

The decade ushered in Trojan contraceptives, the Pitney Bowes postage meter, the Baby Ruth candy bar, Wise potato chips, Drano, self-winding watches, State Farm Mutual auto insurance, Kleenex, and the Macy's Thanksgiving Day Parade in New York City. Despite a growing middle class, the share of disposable income going to the top 5 percent of the population continued to increase. Fifty percent of the people, by one estimate, still lived in poverty. Coal and textile workers, Southern farmers, unorganized labor, single women, the elderly, and most blacks were excluded from the economic giddiness of the period.

In 1929, the other fifty percent appeared to be in an era of unending prosperity. U.S. goods and services reached all-time highs. Industrial production rose 50 percent during the decade as the concept of mass production was refined and broadly applied. The sale of electrical appliances from radios to refrigerators skyrocketed. Consumers were able to purchase newly produced goods through the extended use of credit. Debt accumulated. By 1930, personal debt had increased to one-third of personal wealth. The nightmare on Wall Street in October 1929 brought an end to the economic festivities, setting the stage for a more proactive government and an increasingly cautious worker.

# 1920 News Feature

**"Going to College,"** *The High School Boy and His Problems*,
**Thomas Arkle Clark, 1920:**

I am convinced that far too many boys go to college. It is not that I undervalue the worth of a college education—far from it—but too many fellows go who have no appreciation of what college education means, no special interest, no impelling motive, no desire for what college gives. When I entered college, it was a great event in our country community for a boy to break away from his environment and go off to a higher institution of learning; the neighbors all turned out to see me off. Now everybody goes; it is as common a thing for a boy to go to college as it is for him to take a summer vacation. I often ask the young fellows in our freshman class who come in to see me why they are in college, but I seldom get a very thoughtful or very specific answer.

I asked Parker the other day. He is a boy of good brains and attractive physique. He has plenty of money, and every chance to do well, but his work is ragged and commonplace, he gets no pleasure out of books, he has no enthusiasm for study; he is quite as likely to fail as to pass when the test of final examination comes.

"It wasn't because I wanted to come," was his reply. "My brother George finished here two years ago, and he wanted me to come. Father would've been disappointed if I had not done so, so what was I to do?"

He showed about as much animation and pleasure as a young man might do who was taking a dose of cod liver oil to please his grandmother.

Down the street a block or so was another boy to whom his college course is a source of constant joy. He has been an orphan for many years, he has no resources but those which come from the labor of his own hands. Ever since he was a small boy, he had looked forward to being in college as one of the hoped-for but nearly impossible things. It was to him like a dream of fairy-land not likely to come true.

He worked his way through high school, he got a good job the following summer, he won a scholarship by examination, and then he began to feel that possibly his dream might be realized. He is in college now, and he finds it all a delight. He has no money and few pleasures, but he is full of enthusiasm, he laughs at the sacrifices he must make, he counts it a privilege to be able to pursue the subjects which he enjoys, and he knows very well why he came to college. His four years in college will be full of hard toil, but they will bring him constant and keen pleasure.

Too many boys go to college for the same reason that scores of fellows went into the Army in 1917—it is the easiest thing to do; it is the thing which a large number of his friends are doing. To others it seems more attractive, perhaps, and more likely to result in a hilariously good time than going to work. There is a generally accepted belief extant, also, that the man who goes to college is likely in some way to have an easier time than the fellow who does not do so. No one seems to appreciate the fact that the man who secures an education is also sure to follow heir to pretty heavy responsibilities.

Why should a boy go to college? Not to any large extent because other fellows are doing so, though of course, custom is not a thing to be wholly ignored even in following educational practices; not so much as most people think to acquire information or to acquaint oneself with facts, though the accumulation of facts is a necessary detail in any system of education. More than anything else, one should go to college for the symmetrical training of the mind, for the learning of self-control, for the disciplining of all the faculties, for the development of ideals.

I studied calculus and conic sections while I was in college; I pored over Anglo-Saxon texts, and spent considerable time in the chemistry laboratory working out experiments and developing formulas. Most of those these things I have forgotten, and few if any of them have I had any occasion to use in the routine business which has engaged my attention since I left college. I do not for this reason, however, in any way underestimate the permanent value of these subjects to me. They developed my brain, they caused me to think cosmic things, they helped me to draw conclusions quickly and gave me a broader and clearer outlook on life, and these powers have helped me every day of my life since, in every relation which I have formed to my fellow men. It is seldom that I have needed the specific information which I derived from the subjects, but all through the years I've depended upon the training which I thus received. It is this training and discipline which in my mind is the most viable thing that college gives.

# 1921 PROFILE

Mildred Gambon decided that it was her job to teach her students English—in English only—if they were going to learn how to be Americans.

## Life at Home

- Mildred Gambon knew in her bones that the time of reckoning had finally arrived.
- After years of having to listen to her students jabber in a foreign language, English-only instruction was going to be the law of the land.
- Thirty-four states had passed, or were considering, legislation mandating English instruction.
- German was not even a pretty language; why in the world would second- and third-generation immigrants cling to something so foreign to the American way?
- Now they couldn't talk behind her back and call her ugly names.
- Nope—those days were over.
- Without English, they would never be real Americans, she knew in her heart, so why did they keep speaking German?
- Well, it was out of their hands now: English-only instruction was on the horizon and they couldn't do a thing about it.
- Mildred had lost count of the number of children who had arrived at her first-grade class without a world of English on their breaths.
- Their parents had not bothered to Americanize them properly, and proudly spoke only German at home.

*Mildred Gambon taught English to German immigrants.*

- She wouldn't have handicapped her three children in that way.
- She never ceased to be amazed at the way some parents treated their children.
- During the century preceding the First World War, a well-established German-language culture existed in America that formed the readership of a vast array of German-language newspapers and publications.
- America's reaction to these German-cultural enclaves was mixed.
- While some states mandated English as the exclusive language of instruction in the public schools, Pennsylvania and Ohio in 1839 were first to permit German to be used as an official alternative.
- Some public and many private parochial schools, primarily in rural areas, taught exclusively in German throughout the 1800s.
- In a few large cities, such as Baltimore, Cleveland, and Cincinnati, bilingual public schools were available.
- According to the 1910 Census, in a total U.S. population of 92 million, nine million people in the country still spoke German as their dominant language.
- Following the onset of the First World War in Europe, the power erosion of German-Americans accelerated, especially after America entered the war in 1917.
- Rocks were thrown through the windows of the Germania State Bank in South Carolina; the name "frankfurters" gave way to the term "hot dogs," and works by German composers—living and dead—were erased from the upcoming season of classical music.
- The ban of German hit some groups particularly hard.
- For the Missouri Synod Lutherans, the war and postwar hysteria discouraged the teaching of Lutheran Bible exegesis in German.
- In the words of the state legislature of Nebraska in April 1919: "No person, individually or as a teacher, shall, in any private, denominational, parochial or public school teach any subject to any person in any language other than the English language."
- One state representative spoke for many when he said, "If these people are Americans, let them speak our language. If they don't know it, let them learn it. If they don't like it, let them move…."

## Life at Work

- Mildred Gambon had to admit that many German families were trying especially hard to become Americans now that the American doughboys had smashed Germany's dreams of world domination.
- German-Americans, especially immigrants, were blamed for the aggression of the German Empire; in many places, speaking German was seen as unpatriotic.
- Some families Anglicized their last names (e.g., from Schmidt to Smith, Schneider to Taylor, Müller to Miller, etc.), and German disappeared nearly everywhere from the public arena.
- Mildred was now able to fully implement her "sink or swim" program—total submersion, she called it privately—that required her first- and second-graders to learn English and how to read simultaneously.
- One of her sons had returned with scarred lungs from fighting in France during World War I—the result of German mustard gas—and it was about time someone paid for his disability.
- Her first-grade class of 27 included five German-speaking-only students—four boys and one girl.
- On day one, she placed the five in the back corner near the punishment stick and told them to be silent.
- It was their job to learn English, and she was not about to hold the rest of the class back.
- She had an obligation to her other students, and saw no reason to penalize the majority for the faults of the few.
- For two weeks, the terrified girl cried quietly and then disappeared.
- The quietest boy was moved to the slow class, and three boys learned enough to pass the first semester.
- Besides, it was obvious to anyone with a brain that humanity could be improved by encouraging the ablest and healthiest people to have more children.
- If America was to be a great nation, it needed positive breeding.

*Mildred required her first and second graders to act like Americans.*

- It was time more people supported Charles Fremont Dight, a physician in Minneapolis who launched a crusade to bring the eugenics movement to Minnesota.
- He believed that the state should actively improve the stock within its borders through eugenics education, changes in marriage laws, and the segregation and sterilization of what he called "defective" individuals.
- The issue of multiple languages had ricocheted across public opinion throughout American history.
- As a result of the Louisiana Purchase in 1803, the United States acquired French-speaking populations in Louisiana.
- Following the Mexican-American War, the United States acquired about 75,000 Spanish speakers in addition to several indigenous language-speaking populations.
- In 1849, the California Constitution recognized Spanish-language rights.
- In 1868, the Indian Peace Commission recommended English-only schooling for Native Americans.
- In 1878-79, the California Constitution was rewritten: "All laws of the State of California, and all official writings, and the executive, legislative, and judicial proceedings shall be conducted, preserved, and published in no other than the English language."
- In the late 1880s, Wisconsin and Illinois passed English-only instruction laws for both public and parochial schools.
- By 1896, under the Republic of Hawaii government, English became the primary medium of public schooling for Hawaiian children.

- After the Spanish-American War, English was declared "the official language of the school room" in Puerto Rico.
- In the same way, English was declared the official language in the Philippines, after the Philippine-American War.
- During World War I, widespread sentiment against the use of the German language in the U.S. included removing books in the German language from libraries.
- The Nomenclature Act of 1917 authorized the renaming of 69 towns, suburbs or areas that had German names.
- ProEnglish, the nation's leading advocate of "Official English," summarized their belief that "in a pluralistic nation such as ours, the function of government should be to foster and support the similarities that unite us, rather than institutionalize the differences that divide us. Therefore, ProEnglish "works through the courts and in the court of public opinion to defend English's historic role as America's common, unifying language, and to persuade lawmakers to adopt English as the official language at all levels of government."

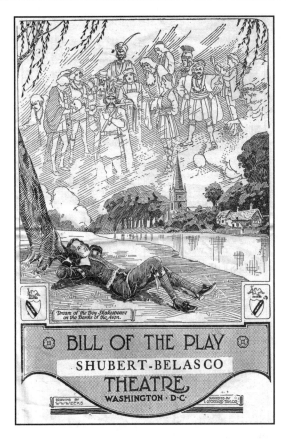

- Another "Official English" advocate group, U.S. English, summarized their beliefs: "The passage of English as the official language will help to expand opportunities for immigrants to learn and speak English, the single greatest empowering tool that immigrants must have to succeed."
- Most states had enacted laws that required the use of English in specific situations, such as in testing for occupational licenses.
- During World War I, the idea of expulsion as an alternative to assimilation was frequently discussed; in 1916, the National Americanization Committee, which had close ties to the Federal Bureau of Education, sponsored a bill in Congress to deport all aliens who did not apply for citizenship within three years.

## Life in the Community: Minneapolis, Minnesota

- Minneapolis and Saint Paul are collectively known as the "Twin Cities," and fostered a rivalry during their early years, with Saint Paul being the capital city and Minneapolis becoming prominent through industry.
- The term "Twin Cities" was coined around 1872 after a newspaper editorial suggested that Minneapolis could absorb Saint Paul.
- Residents decided that the cities needed a separate identity, so people coined the phrase "Dual Cities," which later evolved into "Twin Cities."
- Minnesota became a part of the United States as the Minnesota Territory in 1849, and became the thirty-second state on May 11, 1858.
- After the upheaval of the Civil War and the Dakota War of 1862, the state's economy started to develop when natural resources were tapped for logging and farming.

- Minnesota became an attractive region for European immigration and settlement as farmland.
- Minnesota's population in 1870 was 439,000; this number tripled during the two subsequent decades.
- The Homestead Act in 1862 facilitated land claims by settlers, who regarded the land as being cheap and fertile.
- The railroad industry, led by the Northern Pacific Railway and the Saint Paul and Pacific Railroad, advertised the many opportunities in the state and worked to get immigrants to settle in Minnesota.
- In 1890, the railroad, now known as the Great Northern Railway, started building tracks through the mountains west to Seattle. Other railroads, such as the Lake Superior and Mississippi Railroad and the Milwaukee Road, also played an important role in the early days of Minnesota's statehood.
- The power of the waterfall first fueled sawmills, but later it was tapped to serve flour mills.
- In 1870, only a small number of flour mills were in the Minneapolis area, but by 1900, Minnesota mills were grinding 14 percent of the nation's grain.
- Advances in transportation, milling technology, and water power combined to give Minneapolis dominance in the milling industry.
- Technological improvements led to the production of "patent" flour, which commanded almost double the price of "baker's" or "clear" flour, which it replaced.
- Pillsbury and the Washburn-Crosby Company became the leaders in the Minneapolis milling industry.

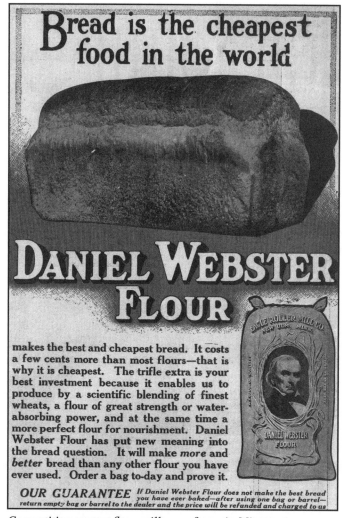

*Competition among flour mills was fierce in Minnesota.*

## HISTORICAL SNAPSHOT
# 1921

- The first religious radio broadcast was heard over station KDKA AM in Pittsburgh, Pennsylvania

- Henry E. Huntington bought Gainsborough's *The Blue Boy* and Reynolds' *Portrait of Mrs. Siddons* for $1 million

- Books included John Dos Passos' *Three Soldiers*; *Symptoms of Being Thirty-Five* by Ring Lardner; *The Outline of History* by H.G. Wells, and *Dream Psychology* by Sigmund Freud

- The DeYoung Museum opened in Golden Gate Park, San Francisco

- The Mounds candy bar, Eskimo Pie, Betty Crocker, Wise potato chips, Band-Aids, table tennis, and Drano all made their first appearance

- The Allies of World War I Reparations Commission decided that Germany was obligated to pay 132 billion gold marks ($33 trillion) in annual installments of 2.5 billion

- The Emergency Quota Act was passed by Congress, establishing national quotas on immigration

- Cigarette consumption rose to 43 billion annually despite its illegality in 14 states

- A Massachusetts jury found Nicola Sacco and Bartolomeo Vanzetti guilty of first-degree murder following a widely publicized trial

- The first vaccination against tuberculosis was administered

- Researchers at the University of Toronto led by biochemist Frederick Banting announced the discovery of the hormone insulin

- Adolf Hitler became Führer of the Nazi Party

- Harold Arlin announced the Pirates-Phillies game from Forbes Field over Westinghouse KDKA in Pittsburgh in the first radio broadcast of a baseball game

- Sixteen-year-old Margaret Gorman won the Atlantic City Pageant's Golden Mermaid trophy to become the first Miss America

- Literature dealing with contraception was banned; a New York physician was convicted of selling *Married Love*

- Centre College's football team, led by quarterback Bo McMillin, defeated Harvard University 6-0 to break Harvard's five-year winning streak

- Albert Einstein was awarded the Nobel Prize in Physics for his work with the photoelectric effect

- During an Armistice Day ceremony at Arlington National Cemetery, the Tomb of the Unknowns was dedicated by President Warren G. Harding

- Hyperinflation was rampant in Germany after the Great War, where 263 marks were needed to buy a single American dollar

## Selected Prices

Alarm Clock.................................................................$2.50

Apartment, Sacramento, Five Rooms .............................$70.00

Bathing Suit, Men's .....................................................$5.00

Carpet Sweeper ...........................................................$5.00

Crib .........................................................................$17.50

Handkerchiefs, Dozen....................................................$1.80

Hen...........................................................................$25.00

Hotel Room, New York, per Day ...................................$3.00

Poker Set, 100 Chips...................................................$6.25

Typewriter, Remington.................................................$60.00

We have room for but one language in this country and that is the English language, for we intend to see that the crucible turns our people out as Americans, of American nationality, and not as dwellers in a polyglot boarding house.

—President Theodore Roosevelt, 1907

## Letter to the Editor, *Forward*, New York, 1907:

Worthy editor,

Allow me a little space in your newspaper and, I beg you, give me some advice as to what to do.

There are seven people in my family, parents and five children. I am the eldest child, a 14-year-old girl. We have been in the country two years and my father, who is a frail man, is the only one working to support the whole family.

I go to school, where I do very well. But since times are hard now and my father earned only five dollars this week, I began to talk about giving up my studies and going to work in order to help my father as much as possible. But my mother didn't even want to hear it. She wants me to continue my education. She even went out and spent $10 on winter clothes for me. But I didn't enjoy the clothes, because I am doing the wrong thing. Instead of bringing something in the house, my parents have to spend money on me.

I have a lot of compassion for my parents. My mother is now pregnant, but she still has to take care of the three borders we have in the house. Mother and father work very hard and they want to keep me in school.

I am writing to you without their knowledge, and I beg you to tell me how to act. Hoping you can advise me, I remain your reader.

ANSWER: The advice to this girl is that she should obey her parents and further her education, because in that way she will be able to give them greater satisfaction than if she went out to work.

## "Courses Offered in the Second Term, State Normal School," Virginia Teacher, March 1921:

113. Elementary Education

The first 25 days of the course will be based on LaRue's *The Science and Art of Teaching*. Topics: nature teaching; method as determined by the nature of the child; method as related to the teacher; teaching as conditioned by subject matter; administrative organization of schools; specific school problems, the first day, the daily program, children's textbooks, attendance, grading, children's monthly reports, promotion; how to get acquainted with school and regulations; how to get needed repairs and equipment; how to get a school library; monthly and term reports to superintendents; duties of teachers to children, the community, politicians, to fellow teachers, to superior officers, to profession.

116. Methods in Reading for Primary Grades, First Year

General topic for term, the introduction of the child to reading. Topics: meaning of reading; elements in reading, problems in beginning reading, the best approach, units of reading, material. (A.) children's poems, (D.) stories, (C.) nature, (D.) plays and games, (E.) school activities; mechanical elements, essentials in phonic study, drill, devices; relationship between oral and silent reading in first grade; critical study of primers and first readers, including those which are on the State list.

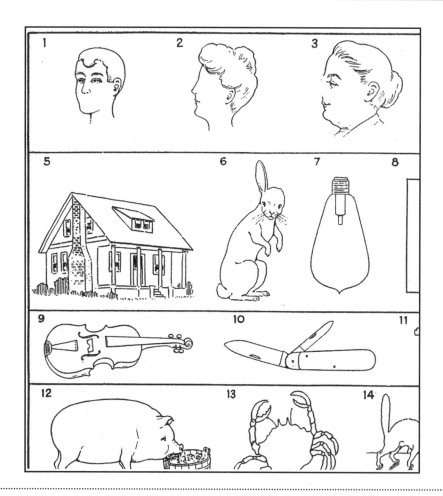

## "English Only in Schools," *Mills County Tribune* (Glenwood, Iowa), March 20, 1919:

The bill of Representative Dean of Osceola County requiring that English only be used in the public and private schools of Iowa for elementary instruction passed the House Wednesday noon by a vote of 63 to 40, after being amended to permit the use of foreign language for religious worship or instruction. The bill as passed reads as follows:

"That the medium of instruction in all secular subjects taught in all of the schools, public and private, within the state of Iowa should be the English language, and the use of any language other than English in secular subjects in said schools is hereby prohibited; provided, however, that nothing herein shall prohibit the teaching and studying of foreign languages as such, as part of the regular school course in any such school in all courses above the eighth grade."

## EDITORIAL: America or Americans, *Twin Falls Daily News* (Idaho), February 9, 1919:

The action by the Idaho Legislature in adopting Sen. John D. Robertson's bill making it a felony to hoist, carry or display a red flag or other emblem of anarchy, will be endorsed by every loyal citizen of the state and nation who believes with the late Col. Theodore Roosevelt that there should be in this country only one flag and one language.

It is in order now for the Idaho lawmakers to follow the lead of Washington and some other states in adopting a measure to abolish the study of the German language from our public schools. No adequate excuse has existed for the introduction of the study of German into our curriculums. It is of service and value to not one in 100 pupils who are instructed in it, and it enfolds no treasure of literature, or sciences that would suffer its translation into the English language. Only upon easygoing, unsuspecting Americans could the harbor for enemies within our boundaries have a potent implement for insidious propaganda afforded by the foreign tongue has been imposed.

If a foreign language must be taught in our schools, let it be Spanish, which is the language of the southern hemisphere, or French, which is so thoroughly established that, reports tell us, many of the sessions incidental to the peace conference are carried on in that tongue. At least some satisfactory reason must be found than can be induced to the language of the enemy.

Another thing, and one perhaps more essential than the eradication of the red flag for the elimination in the enemy tongue, is a necessity for greater caution and care being used in the selection of the textbooks in our schools. A cursory examination of some of the textbooks here for use in American schools yielded the trail of the propagandist.

Determined and relentless warfare must be waged against foreign graphs in the development American ideals wherever they are to be found.

America must be made safe for Americans.

# 1927 PROFILE

When Scott Kelly took a deep breath and reflected on the future—his future—he envisioned a world with more order, less waste and a better trained workforce.

## Life at Home

- In the modern world of 1927, where automobiles, telephones and radios were virtually everywhere, Scott Kelly knew that testing of schoolchildren would produce scientific efficiency in the nation's classrooms, better workers for America's factories, and early identification of students with high IQ potential.
- Scott believed that, once people understood that IQ testing was for their own good, all the barriers would fall, and that would make him a millionaire.
- The 29-year-old super salesman had just been awarded the right to sell the Cooperative Test Service, a sophisticated form of IQ testing, in southern California.
- The product would make him a fortune.
- He already had his eye on a wonderful stretch of beach to buy and develop—once he hit a home run in school sales.
- The future of education was grouping or tracking students based on their IQ—determined by his test—and Scott was in the vanguard of that movement.
- The established market included both elementary schools and colleges—and that was just the beginning.
- Scott figured that before too long, people would want to know their IQ—a number as integral to life as their favorite radio show.
- Intelligence testing received its greatest boost when the French government commissioned psychologist Alfred Binet in 1905 to find a method to differentiate between children who were intellectually normal and those who were inferior.
- The purpose was to put the slow students into special schools, where they would receive more individual attention and the disruption they caused in the education of intellectually normal children could be avoided.

*Scott Kelly sold IQ tests to California schools.*

*IQ tests were designed as a guide for identifying students who needed extra help in school.*

- This led to the development of the Binet Scale, which tested children by asking them to follow commands, copy patterns, name objects, and put things in order or arrange them properly.
- Since Paris schoolchildren were used to initiate the program, they also became the standard; if, for example, 70 percent of eight-year-olds passed a particular test, then success on the test represented the eight-year-old level of intelligence.
- After Binet's work was adopted by American promoter Lewis Terman of Stanford University, the phrase "intelligence quotient," or "IQ," entered the vocabulary.
- The IQ was defined as the ratio of "mental age" to chronological age, with 100 being average. So, an eight-year-old who passed the 10-year-old's test would have an IQ of 10/8 x 100, or 125.
- Although it constituted a revolutionary approach to the assessment of individual mental ability, Binet himself cautioned against misuse of the scale or misunderstanding of its implications.
- According to Binet, the scale was designed with a single purpose in mind; it was to serve as a guide for identifying students who could benefit from extra help in school.
- His assumption was that a lower IQ indicated the need for more teaching, not an inability to learn; the test was not intended to be used as "a general device for ranking all pupils according to mental worth."
- Binet even complained that some researchers had begun falsely claiming that an individual's intelligence was a fixed quantity, a quantity that could not be increased: "We must protest and react against this brutal pessimism; we must try to demonstrate that it is founded on nothing."
- Binet's scale had a profound impact on educational development in the United States and elsewhere; however, the American educators and psychologists who championed and utilized the scale and its revisions ignored Binet's caveats concerning its limitations.
- Soon, intelligence testing, critics charged, assumed an importance and respectability out of proportion to its actual value.
- Private industry gave the IQ test a test drive in a hunt for the best workers, but the first major test was America's entry into the Great War.

- In 1917, with the war in Europe well underway, America was being asked to sort through the skills of the 24 million men registered by the nation's draft boards, of which almost three million were to be inducted into the armed forces, where the underprepared U.S. had supplies for an army of only 500,000 men.
- To assign them to appropriate army units was also a gigantic task.
- Psychologists, especially those with prewar applied personnel management experience, thought they had the answer: intelligence testing.
- A specially formed Committee on the Classification of Personnel in the Army (CCPA) applied a prewar Rating Scale for Selecting Salesmen with minimal modification as a Rating Scale for Selecting Captains, and also constructed proficiency tests for 83 military jobs.
- Character, not just intelligence, loomed large in official army documents regarding the acceptability of recruits.
- Eventually, the Vineland Training School for Feebleminded Girls and Boys in New Jersey became a site that the Army "Alpha and Beta" mental tests were worked out.
- The main issue under consideration was simply one of working out which technical and statistical devices could be employed to best balance the needs of the Army.
- They found a way to transform the examinees' answers from highly variable, time-consuming oral or written responses into easily marked choices among fixed alternatives, quickly scored by clerical workers with the aid of superimposed stencils.
- The Army "Alpha and Beta" tests were marketed as a means to root out those who could not understand or follow orders; assess the trainability potential of recruits and predict what rank a soldier might be expected to attain; and administratively balance the average intellectual of military units.

## Life at Work

- Scott Kelly paid little attention to the critics who charged that the IQ tests subscribed to the "cult of efficiency," which tended to rule out individuality and creativity.
- The efficiency was as "American as the assembly line, and perhaps as alienating," one critic charged.
- By 1927, the tests had shown their value, Scott insisted.
- American educators became increasingly convinced of the need for universal intelligence testing, and the efficiency it could contribute to school programming—based on the notion that intelligence tests were accurate and scientific.
- As a result, the assigning of an IQ score took on an exalted position as a primary, definitive, and permanent representation of the quality of an individual, and became entrenched in the schools over the next several decades.
- Many of the founding fathers of modern testing also advocated eugenics, a movement concerned with the selective breeding of human beings.
- Selected human beings would be mated with each other in an attempt to obtain certain traits in their offspring, much the same way that animal breeders worked with champion stock.
- The eventual goal of eugenics was to create a better human race, in part by eliminating inferiors—including retarded children or adults, and any individuals with genetic defects.
- Eugenics was also used by some to target entire races of people as inferior and not worthy of bringing new children into the world.

*Selective breeding of humans was the goal of some test developers.*

- One test founder, Henry Goddard, preached his belief in the inalterability of intelligence levels: "If mental level plays anything like the role it seems to, and if in each human being it is the fixed quantity that many believe it is, then it is no useless speculation that tries to see what would happen if society were organized so as to recognize and make use of the doctrine of mental levels… It is quite possible to restate practically all of our social problems in terms of mental level…. Testing intelligence is no longer an experiment or of doubted value. It is fast becoming an exact science…. Greater efficiency, we are always working for. Can these new facts be used to increase our efficiency? No question! We only await the Human Engineer who will undertake the work."

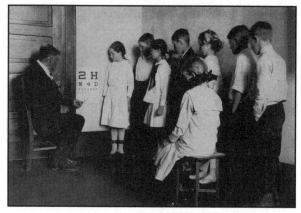

*By the 1920s, IQ testing had become a multi-million dollar industry.*

- This logic contributed to a movement toward more restrictive immigration laws, aided by Goddard's "discovery" that all immigrants except those from Northern Europe were of "surprisingly low intelligence."
- Little mention was made of the fact that the tests were in English, with questions based on American cultural assumptions, to people who could barely speak English, if at all.
- By the 1920s, mass use of the Stanford-Binet Scale and other tests had created a multimillion-dollar testing industry as Americans grew increasingly alarmed about foreigners and of "un-American" doctrines such as socialism.
- And the debate concerning the area of education was wide open.
- Comprehensive schools were being advocated as a way of safeguarding the U.S. economy, while two-thirds of those entering high school were still failing to graduate.
- Stepped-up enforcement of the attendance laws and widening of curriculum choices were simply not enough to ensure success in climbing the newly democratized educational ladder.
- But within the context of the classroom, blame was plentiful and free flowing; was it the teacher's fault that children did not meet their potential or that of the student and his or her failure to achieve?
- In addition, academics viewed the high failure rates—especially in mathematics, science, and language arts—as the result of the personal failings of students, separate and apart from the institutional structure or teaching emphasis of progressive public schooling.
- Once again, testing seemed to be the answer—specifically, that schoolchildren should be tested in their first half-year of school and during the fourth grade, with additional testing of pupils who scored very high or very low in the yearly group examination.
- Standards evolved that called for a formal multiple-track plan made up of five psychometrically defined groups: gifted, bright, average, slow, and special.
- While the "road for transfer" between tracks must be left open, the abilities measured by the tests were considered largely constant and determined by heredity.
- Scott didn't hesitate to tell school-based prospects about the importance of testing as an "instrument for further research" into important psychological questions such as mental growth, potential for re-education, individual differences, and of changes to the typical pattern of mental organization.
- Scott also played up the fact that California had been a proving ground for the IQ tests.
- These student evaluations and predictors of success were homegrown, he would always mention to an elementary school principal.

- Scott's sales pitch included a new opportunity for administrators to deal with the ongoing issue of immigrant Mexican schoolchildren.
- According to the tests on 12-year-old pupils of Latin ancestry, 42 percent of the students were behind their grade level, and such "retardation" was nearly twice as high in Latin schools as it was in the northern European schools.
- This "scientific proof" that the Latin children were "decidedly inferior" would mean it was easier to group students of similar intelligence.
- In order to avoid a rise in failure rates of these students, it was decided to put into place a program of "vocational guidance" at the beginning of the seventh grade.

*Mexican children scored lower than their classmates of European descent.*

- Scott could then argue that the increasingly complex nature of society and its occupational structure would guide students toward appropriate paths based on their skills.

## Life in the Community: Alta, California
- When the Alta Territory in California became part of the United States in 1850 following the U.S. victory in the Mexican-American War, it included the small village of San Diego.
- The U.S. Census reported the population of the town as 650 in 1850 and 731 in 1860.
- Thousands stopped briefly in San Diego on their way to the San Francisco Gold Rush, but few stayed.
- Investors such as William Heath Davis saw the potential of San Diego and spent $60,000 constructing a wharf near the property he had purchased near the foot of Market Street, but it was a financial disaster.

*San Diego business harbor circa 1911.*

- By 1860, many of the enterprises that had been established during the early 1850s had closed.
- The remaining businesses that survived suffered from water shortages, high costs of shipping, and a declining population.
- Fifty-three-year-old Alonzo Horton was the visionary San Diego needed in 1867.
- Although his first view was of barren, mesquite-covered land with a few decaying structures, he was awed, saying, "I have been nearly all over the world and it seemed to me to be the best spot for building a city I ever saw."
- Less than a month after his arrival, he had purchased more than 900 acres for only $265, an average of 27.5 cents an acre.
- He began promoting San Diego by enticing entrepreneurs and residents alike; he built a wharf and promoted development there.
- By 1878, San Diego was staking a claim as a rival of San Francisco's trading ports.
- In 1885, a transcontinental railroad transfer route came to San Diego, and the population boomed, reaching 16,159 by 1890.
- In 1906, the San Diego and Arizona Railway of John D. Spreckels was built to provide San Diego with a direct transcontinental rail link to the East by connecting with the Southern Pacific Railroad lines in El Centro, California.
- San Diego hosted the Panama-California Exposition in 1915, and left a lasting legacy in the form of Balboa Park, the San Diego Zoo.
- A significant U.S. Navy presence began in 1901, with the establishment of the Navy Coaling Station in Point Loma, and expanded greatly during the 1920s.
- Camp Kearny was opened in 1917 and eventually became the site of Marine Corps Air Station Miramar.

*The Southern Pacific Railroad connected San Diego with the East.*

## HISTORICAL SNAPSHOT
# 1927

- The U.S. Federal Radio Commission began to regulate the use of radio frequencies
- In New York City, the Roxy Theater was opened by Samuel Roxy Rothafel
- The first armored car robbery was committed by the Flatheads Gang near Pittsburgh, Pennsylvania

- Bell Telephone Company transmitted an image of Herbert Hoover, the Secretary of Commerce, which became the first successful long-distance demonstration of television
- The first Volvo car rolled off the production line in Gothenburg, Sweden
- The new Ford Model A was offered in four colors, and with a self-starter and a shatterproof windshield
- The Great Mississippi Flood of 1927 impacted 700,000 people in the greatest natural disaster in American history at that time
- American Philo Farnsworth transmitted his first experimental electronic television pictures, as opposed to mechanical TV systems that others had tried before
- The novel *To the Lighthouse* was finished by Virginia Woolf
- The Academy of Motion Picture Arts and Sciences was founded
- Charles Lindbergh made the first solo, nonstop transatlantic flight, from New York City to Paris in his single-seat, single-engine monoplane, the *Spirit of St. Louis*
- The Food, Drug, and Insecticide Administration (FDIA) was established
- Leon Trotsky was expelled from the Soviet Communist Party, leaving Joseph Stalin with undisputed control of the Soviet Union
- The Holland Tunnel opened to traffic as the first vehicular tunnel under the Hudson River linking New Jersey with New York City
- The Mount Rushmore Park was re-dedicated, and President Calvin Coolidge promised national funding for the proposed carving of the presidential figures
- The Al Capone gang netted him $100 million in the liquor trade, $30 million in protection money, $10 million in vice, and $10 million in the rackets
- The Columbia Phonographic Broadcasting System (later CBS) was formed and went on the air with 47 radio stations
- A treaty signed by the League of Nations Slavery Commission abolished all types of slavery
- Harold Stephen Black invented the feedback amplifier
- The Voluntary Committee of Lawyers was founded to bring about the repeal of Prohibition in the United States
- World population reached two billion
- The success of the movie *The Jazz Singer* signaled the end of the silent movie era
- Frank Heath and his horse Gypsy Queen completed a two-year journey of 11,356 miles to all 48 of the states
- The musical play *Show Boat*, based on Edna Ferber's novel, opened on Broadway

## Selected Prices

| | |
|---|---|
| Alarm Clock | $3.25 |
| Baseball Bat | $2.00 |
| Corn Popper | $1.75 |
| Girls' Camp, Virginia, Eight Weeks | $225.00 |
| Grave Marker | $1.50 |
| Pistol | $12.00 |
| Sewing Machine | $33.95 |
| Ticket, Ringside, Heavyweight Title Fight | $27.50 |
| Toaster, Pop-up | $12.50 |
| Vacuum Cleaner, Hoover | $75.00 |

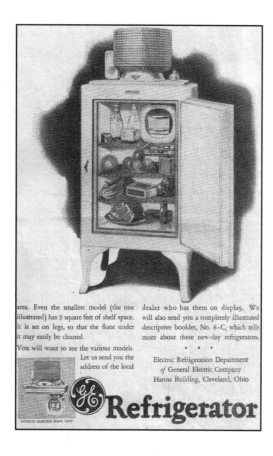

area. Even the smallest model (the one illustrated) has 9 square feet of shelf space. It is set on legs, so that the floor under it may easily be cleaned.

You will want to see the various models. Let us send you the address of the local dealer who has them on display. We will also send you a completely illustrated descriptive booklet, No. 8-C, which tells more about these new-day refrigerators.

• • •

Electric Refrigeration Department
of General Electric Company
Hanna Building, Cleveland, Ohio

**GE Refrigerator**

Ask for **Horlick's** The ORIGINAL Malted Milk

**Safe Milk** and **Food**

*For INFANTS, Children, Invalids and for All Ages*

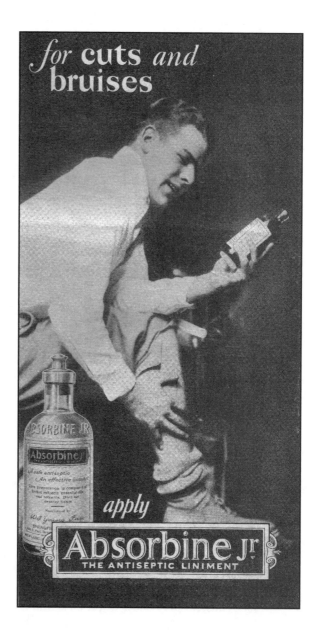

*for* **cuts** *and* **bruises**

*apply*

**Absorbine Jr.**
THE ANTISEPTIC LINIMENT

## "Democratic Tendencies in Education, Two Outstanding Advances in the United States," James R. Angell, *These Eventful Years*, 1924:

In the United States, undoubtedly the two outstanding features of educational development in this century have been the unprecedented growth of the public high schools and, especially since the World War, the extraordinary increase in attendance of colleges and universities. In 1900, there were 696,000 high school students. In 1922, there were 2,371,000. Nor does this mere increase in numbers at all convey the real situation, for partly as cause and partly as effect there has occurred in parallel with this growth in attendance, an amazing growth in physical appointments of many of the schools and the educational opportunities offered. Millions of dollars have been expended upon school buildings, certain of which challenge in beauty and convenience any educational buildings ever erected. In many cases, they have become centers for civic interest related to the schools: for example, the development of music, art and general public education. The pride felt by towns and cities in these buildings and their equipment reflects a radical change in the community attitude toward education....

The change in the curriculum which had begun long before the opening of the twentieth century, but which has gone on rapidly since then, is attributable chiefly to two circumstances, the first of which has affected higher education as well as secondary, and Europeans as well as American.

1) A few generations ago, the scope of American education beyond the elementary school was fundamentally comprised of Latin, Greek and mathematics. Presently, the natural sciences (astronomy, chemistry, geology, physics and biology), modern languages, including English itself, history, both modern and ancient, and the social and economic sciences, all came knocking at the door and all were admitted, with the result that, where half a dozen subjects formerly covered the entire educational offering, there are now four or five times as many, each of which can present some cogent claim to replace certain of the older subjects, hard pressed to stand upon a par with them. Some of these subjects, especially those of laboratory character, require much more elaborate and costly equipment for their proper presentation than the older and more bookish subjects. Moreover, instruction in them requires a large number of teachers who are more or less specialists and who will be difficult to secure in requisite numbers until the demand has induced a sufficient number of candidates to get the necessary preparation.

2) Again, the high school movement has been fundamentally affected by the natural desire to give students who complete their former education at this level, opportunity to acquire training which it is hoped and believed they can make immediately available in earning a livelihood and taking up the practical duties of citizenship. Considerations of this character have resulted in the establishment of new commercial and technical high schools and the introduction of many essentially vocational studies into the programme of the ostensibly non-technical schools. High schools, state colleges and state universities have all been affected by federal legislation such as the Smith-Hughes Bill of 1917, which appropriates large sums for vocational training on the condition that the state contribute dollar for dollar with the Central Government. The invasion of this material has called for the construction of costly shop laboratories of various kinds. The same motive has in part controlled the criteria offered in the continuation schools, whose pupils pursue there some fraction of the time, when they are not engaged in business or industrial employments, the school training which they interrupted to seek such remunerative occupation.

*Continued*

## "Democratic Tendencies in Education, . . . *(Continued)*

One notable circumstance deserves special emphasis. Never before has any country entered seriously a program of free education of high school grade for literally every child who may apply his intelligence and permits the pursuing of the course of study, and with the expectation that a large proportion of the eligible children will take advantage of the opportunity. This programme carries with it the necessity of providing trained teachers and physical facilities on a scale never before undertaken. The cost of the enterprise is staggering, and many communities are at present proceeding under the greatest financial embarrassment in the maintenance of their schools.

Side-by-side with the increase of the number of high schools and the number of pupils has naturally been a great increase in the number of children in the primary schools, of whom there were 20,383,222 in 1920. This increase which has been in general most marked in urban centers, has reflected in part the tremendous growth in population, and in part a better enforcement of compulsory educational laws, to say nothing of some growth in the ambition of parents to have their children educated to meet the more exacting demands of modern life.

The steps that should be taken to preserve or increase our present intellectual capacity must, of course, be dictated by science and not by political expediency. Immigration should not only be restrictive but highly selective. And the revision of the immigration and naturalization laws will only afford a slight relief from our present difficulty. The really important steps are those looking toward the prevention of the continued propagation of defective strains in the present population. If all immigration were stopped now, the decline of American intelligence would still be inevitable. This is the problem which must be met, and our manner of meeting it will determine the future course of our national life.

—Carl Campbell Bingham, professor of psychology at Princeton University's
Department of Psychology and pioneer in the field of psychometrics

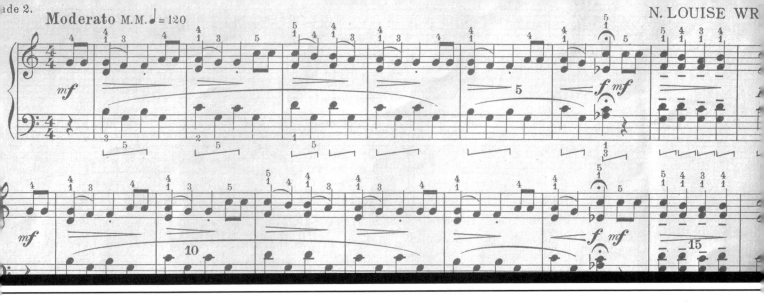

# 1928 PROFILE

Warren King knew from experience that the essence of teaching children was the delicate process of molding a given personality toward a set of ideals, goals and objectives.

## Life at Home

- The third of five children, Warren King had no desire to compete with his athletic older brothers and his artistic younger sisters.
- He first played the piano while sitting on his father's lap; at the age of three he would sneak into the music room and attempt to pick up notes he had heard his brother play during his weekly lesson.
- One day, he was caught standing on the piano bench composing a little musical ditty; lessons were started the next day.
- His father was a successful contractor who had made a fortune prudently riding the economic wave of the 1920s; Baltimore, Maryland, was doing great and that meant the King family was doing well.
- Two major office buildings in the center of town and a 3,000-acre subdivision on the edge of town all bore the mark of King Construction.
- The Kings were considered trendsetters; they were among the first to get a radio, install a telephone in their home, and invest in an electric toaster.
- The latest model car was always parked in the family garage, protected from the weather, beside a children's motor bike and the most inventive toys.
- Warren's mother led a ladies' group discussion on the first Tuesday of the month, intellectually wrestling with some major issues of the day.

*Warren King taught piano with passion and seriousness.*

- The city's leading women were debating the rights of professional women to receive equal pay as men.
- Warren was educated in private schools and tutored each afternoon in music, Greek, Latin and fine art.
- Pampered most of his childhood because of severe asthma and an early childhood episode with whooping cough, Warren learned early that playing the piano brought him the most attention.

*Warren was tutored as a child in music and art.*

- Although he was accepted at half a dozen elite colleges, Warren elected to attend the University of Maryland.
- There he came to understand—through good examples and bad—that the characteristic that distinguished a talented teacher was an incessant desire for learning.
- He compared this trait to the natural curiosity of children who were forever bubbling over with wonder and curiosity at all the things around them.
- This sense of curiosity was often blocked through faulty teaching, unsympathetic parents, the child's environment, and other factors.
- This caused children to grow into maturity with a dull and stunted interest in the world about them and therefore be concerned only with their own personal advancement.
- Following college, Warren went to work in the family construction business.
- It was Warren's job to attend civic functions to meet the city's most influential players, prospect for new business and create a marketing department.
- His father and two older brothers were to focus on the actual construction projects, estimating the cost of each project and negotiating the final contract price.
- Warren tried hard to fit into the macho world of heavy construction, but after three years it became clear that four Kings at King Construction was one King too many.
- At the insistence of his highly talented and super competitive brothers, King Construction bought out Warren's financial interest in the company, thereby locking Warren out of the company forever.
- He couldn't have been more pleased: no more construction, no more brotherly competition, plenty of money to live on and a chance to test his teaching theories on dozens of developing talents.

*Warren struggled to keep up with his highly competitive brothers.*

- Baltimore possessed a long history of artistic tradition; all he had to do was lift the city's talent to the next level by properly training both the fingers and the minds of piano students.
- In early 1923, he opened a ground-floor studio for piano lessons that featured a sweeping view of the harbor and the early morning sounds of birds calling in the day.
- After five years of intense work, he understood that teaching was indirect and subtle.
- Any direct effort to mold another's personality was apt to meet with strong resistance; people did not wish to feel that someone else was prying into their inner beings.
- In fact, the more he taught, the more he believed that the word "teach" should be dropped when discussing how to shape an effective piano personality.
- As a teacher, Warren worked at a disadvantage; he was a child prodigy who never dreamed of doing anything except playing the piano.
- Practice was play, performance an award, and bicycles and games of cowboys and Indians with his friends held little competition to the piano.
- Some days it was difficult for him to understand that everyone did not live to play the piano.

## Life at Work

- Now 28, Warren King got up each morning with optimism; he looked forward to working with young talent and influencing their musical decisions.
- Highly motivated music teachers were responsible for building the foundation of America's musical future; they secretly believed they would soon discover the next Bach or Mozart.
- Warren's teaching style emphasized the need to mold both the personality and talent of his piano students.
- Success could not be achieved unless both areas were addressed.
- "The type of person that the teacher is gradually penetrates the pupil according to his sensitivity, and he comes to strive to be likewise in some manner," Warren said.
- It was a form of education called "contagion," in which results could be achieved simply by being in the presence of another who was interested in the student's welfare.
- Parents had a very strong influence on the children over and above the education they attempted to impart, simply by their presence.
- Warren believed that the parents' very attitudes and habits often had more of an effect on the lives of their children than anything they directly attempted in the way of instruction.
- The same principle applied to teaching the piano and to the piano teacher.
- Warren believed his ideals, goals, his essence, seriousness of purpose, love of music, and sincerity all had a culminating effect on his pupils as time went on.
- Warren fully understood that most piano teachers would think him foolish; but considering the number of children who started and stopped playing the piano, then dropped out completely, Warren was justified in believing he had the answer.

*Warren's teaching style incorporated his students' personality and talents.*

- To top it all off, a sense of humor could make the lessons delightful as well as absorbing.
- As important, Warren believed, was the style the teacher exhibited.
- "Treating all pupils alike connotes a lack of ability to distinguish essential differences in personalities; the greater the lack, the less talent one may be said to have for teaching."
- Warren believed students were so different it was impossible to make each and every one follow an identical set of coursework.
- The best teacher, he believed, worked for the day when his pupils could stand on their own two feet.

## Life in the Community: Baltimore, Maryland

- Founded in 1729, Baltimore was the largest seaport in the Mid-Atlantic United States and is situated closer to Midwestern markets than any other major seaport on the East Coast.
- Baltimore's Inner Harbor was the second leading port of entry for immigrants to the U.S. and a major manufacturing center.
- Named after Lord Baltimore, a member of the Irish House of Lords and the founding proprietor of the Maryland Colony, Baltimore was an Anglicization of the Irish Gaelic name *Baile an Tí Mhóir*, meaning "town of the big house."
- Baltimore played a key role in events leading to and including the American Revolution.
- The Second Continental Congress met in the Henry Fite House from December 1776 to February 1777, effectively making the city the capital of the United States during this period.
- The port city was the site of the Battle of Baltimore during the War of 1812.
- After burning Washington, DC, the British attacked Baltimore on the night of September 13, 1814.
- Francis Scott Key, a Maryland lawyer, was aboard a British ship where he had been negotiating for the release of an American prisoner, Dr. William Beanes.
- Key witnessed the bombardment from his ship and later wrote "The Star-Spangled Banner," a poem recounting the attack.
- Following the Battle of Baltimore, the city's population grew rapidly.
- The construction of the federally funded National Road and the private Baltimore and Ohio Railroad (B&O) made Baltimore a major shipping and manufacturing center by linking the city with prominent markets in the Midwest.
- Maryland did not secede from the Union during the Civil War; however, when Union soldiers marched through the city at the start of the war, Confederate sympathizers attacked the troops, which led to the Baltimore Riot of 1861.
- In 1904, the Great Baltimore Fire destroyed over 1,500 buildings in 30 hours, leaving more than 70 blocks of the downtown area burned to the ground; damages were estimated at $150 million.
- The city grew in area by annexing new suburbs from the surrounding counties, the last being in 1918, when the city acquired portions of Baltimore County and Anne Arundel County.

*Baltimore, Maryland*

# HISTORICAL SNAPSHOT
# 1928

- Charles Jenkins Laboratories of Washington, DC, became the first holder of a television license from the Federal Radio Commission

- The first regular schedule of television programming began in Schenectady, New York, by General Electric's television station W2XB

- The animated short *Plane Crazy* was released by Disney Studios in Los Angeles, featuring the first appearances of Mickey and Minnie Mouse

- Aviator Amelia Earhart was successful in her attempt to become the first woman to cross the Atlantic Ocean; Wilmer Stultz was the pilot

- At the Democratic National Convention in Houston, Texas, New York Governor Alfred E. Smith became the first Catholic to be nominated for president by a major political party

- The first machine-sliced and machine-wrapped loaf of bread was sold in Chillicothe, Missouri, using Otto Frederick Rohwedder's technology

- The U.S. recalled its troops from China

- Paul Galvin and his brother Joseph incorporated the Galvin Manufacturing Corporation, later named Motorola

- The moat at the Tower of London, previously drained in 1843 (and planted with grass), was completely refilled by a tidal wave

- An iron lung respirator was used for the first time at Children's Hospital, Boston

- In the U.S. presidential election, Republican Herbert Hoover won by a wide margin over Democrat Alfred E. Smith

- The Boston Garden opened

- Congress approved the construction of Boulder Dam, later renamed Hoover Dam

- Coca-Cola entered Europe through the Amsterdam Olympics

- Eliot Ness was placed in charge of enforcing Prohibition in Chicago

- Margaret Mead's influential cultural anthropology text *Coming of Age in Samoa* was published

- The Episcopal Church in the U.S. ratified a new revision of the Book of Common Prayer

- The first patent for the transistor principle was registered in Germany to Julius Edgar Lilienfeld

- Russian leader Joseph Stalin launched the First Five-Year Plan

## Selected Prices

| | |
|---|---|
| Airplane, Single Engine | $2,000 |
| Bathing Suit | $8.50 |
| Camera | $80.00 |
| Handbag, Leather | $2.98 |
| Pocket Watch | $63.50 |
| Radio, Six Tubes | $65.00 |
| Railroad Ticket, Chicago to San Francisco | $89.00 |
| Stationery, 24 Sheets and Envelopes | $0.50 |
| Tennis Racket | $15.00 |
| Traveling Bag | $10.50 |

### "Child Labor vs. Children's Work," *Child Labor*, Julia E. Johnsen, The H. W. Wilson Company, New York, 1925:

Nothing could be further from the truth than the rather widespread notion that child labor reform is predicated on the assumption that children should have no work whatever to do. It must be said, however, that the belief that children should have work is responsible for a good deal of child labor. Though much has been done by society to abolish child labor, little has been done to establish children's work on a proper basis. Society has made no serious constructive attack on the children's work problem, but sooner or later we must come to grips with this problem. The school has not done its part toward answering the true work needs of children; neither has the home, and the urban home is under heavy handicap in this regard. Instead of enough children's work, we have had too much child labor. As part of the solution of the child labor problem, as a means to the abolition of child labor and the breaking down of opposition to reform, we must give attention to the work that children should have and see that they have it. To establish children's work is quite as important as to establish children's play or to abolish child labor. These are all aspects of a single problem.

Let us consider for a moment some of the supposed values of child labor. In defense of it, we have heard the assertion that it furnishes training in the sense of responsibility and in the habit of thrift, and that it affords the discipline of self-subordination to unpleasant tasks. However, there is abundant opportunity for developing the sense of responsibility in the home and the school through household duties, home projects under school auspices, schemes of self-government and so on. The same is true of thriftiness. Moreover, thrift is not merely a matter of money, and the virtues connected with it may be developed in relation to school supplies, home possessions, food and clothes. Child laborers have not yet been shown to be especially thrifty with their earnings. As to the disciplinary value of child labor, modern psychology teaches that the only discipline that is worthwhile is that which accords with the child's own nature, his instincts and desires—not all of them, of course, but a selected few. It is not the discipline that runs counter to his nature, resulting in nothing more than sullen obedience or strained submission. This latter kind weakens or breaks what we sometimes, rather inaccurately, call the will. The activity that develops the will is willing activity. The work performed in accordance with the child's own purposes and desires has far more disciplinary value than drudgery, which stifles initiative, individuality and expressiveness, all of which may be enlisted in the service of character building, and without which there is no character.

### "Lowell Attacks Secondary Schools, Harvard Head Tells Teachers That They Waste Time, Effort and Money," *The New York Times*, February 28, 1928:

President A. Lawrence Lowell of Harvard, in an address today at the opening session of the convention of the National Education Association, declared that American public schools cost too much and are ineffective, that their courses are superficial, that they waste years of pupils' time and that at the end they leave to the college the job of giving high school work.

They scatter their power in trying to teach too many things and end by teaching nothing well, he said, and in trying to make studies pleasant, has made them easy and they need to be hard.

Dr. Lowell's speech anticipated the express purpose of many of the educators who came here to open fire upon the traditional interest requirements of Harvard, and during its convention counted on persuading New England colleges to their point of view. The leading candidate for the presidency of this organization is making his campaign on the issue of "domination of the high school by the college."

Dr. Lowell began by figuring out how much faster public school salaries, figured on a per-pupil basis, have increased in the past 15 years more than have Harvard salaries on the same basis. He insisted that Harvard got more for its money. The difference in increased cost was between 67 percent for Harvard salaries and 167 percent for public school teacher salaries.

He thought the problem of the next generation will be to make universal education "equally good and less expensive."

Then he stepped to "the more immediate question of effectiveness," and wanted to know why American schools could not finish the job of secondary education at the age of 19, as European schools do, without putting a couple of years of work preparation upon the colleges. If they could not do the job right, they ought to knock off those two years of time, he declared.

"To some aspects of education we seem to have paid insufficient attention," Dr. Lowell continued. "One of these is selective function. We hear much in the present day of vocational guidance, the determination of the pursuits for which students and schoolchildren are best adapted by somewhat artificial devices for discovering their natural abilities. But all true education is a sifting process.

"What we need is good mental training, an accurate and thorough habit of mind, not a frittering away in the attention by a multitude of small matters, of which the pupil does not get enough to develop consecutive thought."

Dr. Frank D. Boynton, Superintendent of Schools in Ithaca, replied later to Pres. Lowell's charges of high school inefficiency.

*Continued*

## "Lowell Attacks Secondary Schools, . . . *(Continued)*

"President Lowell seems to think the main function of the American high school is to send its pupils to college," said Dr. Boynton to newspapermen during the general meeting of the Department of Superintendents tonight. "In fact, the preparation of boys and girls for college is a mere detail in the broad program of the great high school.

"President Lowell compares American schools with European schools. That comparison is just as unfair as it would be to compare the American Constitution to the aims of government in Europe. Our objective is not to train a chosen few for higher education, but to prepare all our students for the American conditions of life."

Turning to the charge of excessive costs, he said: "The expenses per pupil of the public schools are negligible compared to those of the institutions of higher learning. You will observe that there are no empty buildings and costly monuments on the campus of the American high school."

# 1930–1939

Few Americans—including the very rich—escaped the devastating impact of America's longest and most severe depression in the nation's history. Banks failed, railways became insolvent, unemployment factories closed and the upper class moved out of the biggest houses in town. Economic paralysis gripped the nation. Promising businesses and new inventions stagnated for lack of capital and customers. By 1932, one in four Americans were jobless. One in every four farms was sold for taxes. Five thousand banks closed their doors, wiping out the lifetime savings of millions of Americans—rich and poor.

As the stock market sank into the doldrums, Americans looked to their schools as a source of hope. Putting aside several decades of debate concerning the role of education, Americans demanded that schools prepare their pupils for employment, even as the middle school and high school dropout rates increased dramatically. Libraries increasingly accepted their mandate to provide lifelong learning opportunities, while politicians decided that rounding up thousands of Mexican-Americans for transport to Mexico—where they had never lived—would help reduce the unemployment rate. Bread lines had become a common sight. The unemployed wandered from city to city seeking work, only to discover the pervasive nature of the economic collapse. In some circles, the American Depression was viewed as the fulfillment of the Marxist prophecy—the inevitable demise of capitalism.

Backed by New Deal promises and a focus on the "forgotten man," Franklin D. Roosevelt produced a swirl of government programs designed to lift the country out of its paralytic gloom. Roosevelt's early social experiments were characterized by relief, recovery, and reform. Believing that the expansion of the United States economy was temporarily over, Roosevelt paid attention to better distribution of resources and planned production. The Civilian Conservation Corps (CCC), for example, put 250,000 jobless young men to work in the forests for $1.00 a day. By 1935, government deficit spending was spurring economic change. By 1937, total manufacturing output exceeded that of 1929; unfortunately, prices and wages rose too quickly and the economy dipped again in 1937, driven by inflation fears and restrictions on bank lending. Nonetheless, many roads, bridges, public buildings, dams, and trees became part of the landscape, thanks to federally employed workers. The Federal Music Project, for example, employed 15,000 musicians during the period, giving 225,000 performances to millions of Americans. Despite progress, however, 10 million workers were still unemployed in 1938 and farm prices lagged behind manufacturing progress. Full recovery would not occur until the United States mobilized for World War II.

While the nation suffered from economic blows, the West was being whipped by nature. Gigantic billowing clouds of dust up to 10,000 feet high swept across the parched Western Plains throughout the 1930s. Sometimes the blows came with lightning and booming thunder, but often they were described as being "eerily silent, blackening everything in their path." All human activity halted. Planes were grounded. Buses and trains stalled, unable to race clouds that could move at speeds of more than 100 miles per hour. On the morning of May 9, 1934, the wind began to blow up the topsoil of Montana and Wyoming, and soon some 350 million tons were sweeping eastward. By late afternoon, 12 million tons had been deposited in Chicago. By noon the next day, Buffalo, New York, was dark with dust. Even the Atlantic Ocean was no barrier. Ships 300 miles out to sea found dust on their decks. During the remainder of 1935, there were more than 40 dust storms that reduced visibility to less than one mile. There were 68 more storms in 1936, 72 in 1937, and 61 in 1938. On the High Plains, 10,000 houses were simply abandoned, and nine million acres of farm turned back to nature. Banks offered mortgaged properties for as little as $25 for 160 acres and found no takers. The people of the 1930s excelled in escape. Radio matured as a mass medium, creating stars such as Jack Benny, Bob Hope, and Fibber McGee and Molly. For a time it seemed that every child was copying the catch phrase of radio's Walter Winchell, "Good evening, Mr. and Mrs. America, and all the ships at sea," or pretending to be Jack Benny when shouting, "Now, cut that out!" Soap operas captured large followings and sales of magazines such as *Screen* and *True Story* skyrocketed. Each edition of *True Confessions* sold 7.5 million copies. Movie theaters prospered as 90 million Americans attended the "talkies" every week, finding comfort in the uplifting excitement of movies and movie stars. Big bands made swing the king of the decade, while jazz came into its own. And the social experiment known as Prohibition died in December 1933, when the Twenty-first Amendment swept away the restrictions against alcohol that had been enacted in 1920.

Attendance at professional athletic events declined during the decade, but softball became more popular than ever, and golf began its drive to become a national passion as private courses went public. Millions listened to boxing on the radio, especially the exploits of the "Brown Bomber," Joe Louis. As average people coped with the difficult times, they married later, had fewer children, and divorced less. Extended families often lived under one roof, and opportunities for women and minorities were particularly limited. Survival, not affluence, was often the practical goal of the family. A disillusioned nation, which had worshipped the power of business, looked instead toward a more caring government during the decade. United Airlines hired its first stewardess to allay passengers' fears of flying. The circulation of *Reader's Digest* climbed from 250,000 to eight million before the decade ended, and *Esquire*, the first magazine for men, was launched. The early days of the decade gave birth to Hostess Twinkies, Bird's Eye frozen vegetables, windshield wipers, photo flashbulbs, and pinball machines. The opening of the 1939 New York World's Fair gave millions a peek into the future and a momentary respite from the unrelenting anxiety of the Great Depression. By the time the Depression and the 1930s drew to a close, Zippo lighters, Frito's corn chips, talking books for the blind, beer in cans, and the Richter scale for measuring earthquakes had all been introduced. Despite the ever-increasing role of the automobile in the mid-1930s, Americans still spent $1,000 a day on buggy whips.

# 1933 PROFILE

Laura Hargrove, whose older, bossy sister was a schoolteacher, never considered that profession until she was asked one day to do research at the library concerning a local business; it opened up a whole new world for her.

## Life at Home

- Laura Hargrove grew up in bustling Danville, Virginia, and had always wanted to be a telephone operator, a job that would pay well, give her prestige and make her father proud.
- The fourth of five girls, Laura knew early that her father had desperately wanted her to be a boy.
- When she could barely walk, she learned to carry tools to her father as he repaired cars, and later was his congenial companion during the long walks he liked to take along the Dan River.
- Considered the plain daughter by nearly everyone, Laura knew she would work for a living—at least until she was married, if anyone asked her.
- Telephone operating was considered a respectable, white collar occupation for unmarried, mostly native-born women; the Bell Telephone System, along with its subsidiaries, had become the largest employer of women in the United States.
- In the years just before the Great War, local businesses routinely paid telephone operators a $50 Christmas bonus to guarantee better phone service; by the time Laura applied for a job as a telephone operator in 1928, scientific management ideas and systematized work processes had been rigidly put in place.

*Laura Hargrove's unexpected love for libraries led her to becoming a librarian.*

*Laura worked as a telephone operator before discovering her passion.*

- Bonuses were out, while elaborate manuals covering any situation were in.
- Some offices had as many as 15 operators sitting at an exchange; Danville had six, not counting the chief operator, who stood behind them and evaluated their ability to follow rules quickly and courteously.
- Laura was proud to tell her dad that she had been promoted to senior operator after only a year; the job was essentially the same, but the pay was higher.
- She credited her success to studying the operator's manual and knowing how to handle every situation; her employers were also impressed by her diction and ability to pronounce numbers and words clearly.
- By her third year on the job, she could anticipate whom the caller was attempting to connect with and answer questions before she was asked.
- No chitchat was allowed, but her supervisor—a second cousin on her mother's side—trusted her to help customers even when it meant breaking the strict rules of the manual.
- Bell Telephone was the only company in the area that provided its employees with sick pay.
- For the girls who worked the textile mills, Laura was considered lucky because she dressed nicely, didn't get lint in her hair during work hours, and was performing an indispensable public service.
- She was happy to have made her father proud; that's why the visit to the library was so unsettling—and exciting.
- Her supervisor had asked her to research a local business, and she was told she had all afternoon to complete her work.
- With plans of finishing early and purchasing an ice cream cone on the way home, Laura set to work reading books, magazines and newspapers provided by the librarian.
- The librarian seemed to know everything—where to find the information and how to compile it; she appeared organized, flexible and resourceful.
- It was a life-changing day; for the rest of the month, Laura found an excuse to visit libraries as often as possible—even volunteering to do research.
- She had found a place that was capable of feeding her curiosity and enhancing her knowledge.

- To learn more, she began using the "Reading With a Purpose" courses provided by the Carnegie Corporation which were distributed through the nation's library system.
- Each "course" was a short volume introducing a specific subject with specifically recommended books and commentary on that subject.
- She sampled English Literature, Alexander Meiklejohn's Philosophy, and Everett Martin's Psychology.
- In all, a total of 54 courses had been prepared: topics included foreign languages, classics, English, history, mental hygiene, and journalism. Nationwide, the librarian was being viewed no longer as "the jealous guardian of sacred treasures almost too sacred to be touched by the hand of the vulgar" but rather "the enthusiast inflamed with missionary zeal."
- The prospect thrilled Laura and horrified critics.
- After a few months, the librarian—an older woman who had grown up with Laura's mother—asked Laura why she didn't think about becoming a librarian herself.
- She obviously liked to do the work, and with her sharp mind would be able to guide others; the woman even volunteered to train her in the special skills and techniques of being a librarian.
- "You are already curious, detailed and tenacious," Laura was told. "Now all you need are a few tricks of the trade."
- Besides, the increasing number of high schools in the area had spawned the need for librarians in the public school system.
- It didn't pay as well as the telephone company, but it might be the answer to a deep desire to do more with her life.
- The thought elicited an emotion that surprised her.
- In the nineteenth century, the rise of school libraries was intertwined with the rise of public libraries.
- In 1835, New York State allowed school districts to use tax funds to purchase library books, and in 1839, the local districts were permitted to establish district libraries.
- By 1876, 19 states—nearly half the number of states in the Union—passed laws allowing school libraries to be developed.
- By 1913, the U.S. Office of Education reported about 10,000 public school libraries, many doubling as community libraries.

## Life at Work

- It was pure celestial music to Laura's ears to hear state education leader C. W. Dickinson announce at the annual meeting of the Virginia Education Association that libraries were a high priority in Virginia.
- She had already applied for a job as the Danville High School librarian; friends had told her the job was hers, but it had not been formally offered.
- Dickinson said, "If I were allowed to name the single requisite for effective school-library service, my unhesitating choice would be the school librarian, one who has a vision of the increasingly important role which the library must play in the modern, progressive school and who has the personality and professional training to make her vision a reality."
- The successful school librarian, he said, needs the professional training required of both teacher and librarian; she must use tact, sympathy, initiative, patience, and much common sense to win the position of leader among the teachers.

- Her knowledge of the course of study and the contents of the basic textbooks must be proved to teachers by helpful suggestions as to how they may make wider use of library materials.
- "It is most important to the librarian to secure the friendly support and cooperation of the teachers at the very beginning of the school term," he said.
- The ability to select materials wisely is important, he told the assembled audience.
- Knowledge of children's books and children's literature should have been gained by wide reading and practical work with them as a student teacher in the model school library.
- William Learned, staff member of the Carnegie Foundation and author of the book *The American Public Library and the Diffusion of Knowledge* (1924), had prophesied that the city library had the potential to "be an institution of astonishing power—a genuine community university bringing intelligence systematically and persuasively to bear on all adult affairs."
- If properly organized nationwide, "it would immediately take its place as the chief instrument of our common intellectual and cultural progress."
- Learned continued, "We cannot abandon our education at the schoolhouse door; we must keep it up through life; the success of a democracy depends upon an educated and intelligent citizenship."
- Laura believed in her heart that democracy could last on just one condition: getting everyone educated.
- Three days after the library conference, Laura was offered the position of librarian at the high school.

## Life in the Community: Danville, Virginia

- Danville, Virginia, located on the south side of the commonwealth, was proud of its national reputation as a tobacco and textile center.
- Boasting a population of 30,500, Danville was recognized for its 48 manufacturing plants, with investing capital of $21 million capable of producing new business revenues of $52 million a year.
- The city was home to 10 tobacco auction warehouses which employed 319 people and represented annual sales of $11.8 million.
- The city advertised itself as the "Gateway to the industrial section of the Piedmont," providing "good schools, good health, good government, good people—all combining to make a good city."
- The Clarke Electric Company declared in its advertisements that electricity was one of the greatest services to all of mankind, making it possible to offer the Frigidaire automatic refrigerator.

*Danville, Virginia*

- In 1728, Colonel William Byrd visited the area as a member of the joint commission to establish the exact boundary between Virginia and North Carolina, and declared it to be the "Land of Eden."
- During the American Revolution, soldiers gathered in the area to witness sturgeon leaping high into the air at Wayne's Falls on the Dan River.
- Danville was founded by an act of the legislature in November 1793, and incorporated in 1833.
- By 1856, the Richmond and Danville Railroad was established to transport tobacco and other agricultural products.
- Danville largely escaped the destruction of the Civil War, though it did serve as the last capital of the Confederacy.
- With the fall of Petersburg, Virginia, in April 1865, Confederate President Jefferson Davis and his Cabinet were forced to evacuate Richmond and retreated to Danville.
- The executive offices of the Confederacy were then maintained in an old school building on Wilson Street until word of General Robert E. Lee's surrender reached Danville on April 10.
- During Reconstruction, the city was occupied by Wright's Sixth Army Corps and became the military district until the end of the "re-adjuster movement" in 1883.
- With the aid of steam power to operate hydraulic tobacco presses, Danville enjoyed prosperity in the run-up to the new century.
- At one time, 24 independent tobacco manufacturers engaged in making cigarettes, chewing tobacco and smoking tobacco.
- Many carried the Danville name—further promoting the city.
- Textile mills added to the industrial base of the community, particularly the manufacture of yarns.
- According to a 1933 special report by the *Danville Register*, the city "turned the corner of the new century on two wheels, and has been rapidly forging ahead ever since, nearly doubling its population and increasing its manufacturing output by 85 percent since 1900."
- During America's entry into the Great War, Danville continued to prosper; the Liberty Loan quotas assigned to the city were always oversubscribed, and its Red Cross was one of the most active in the South.
- The city's textile industry supplied clothing and materials essential to the success of the Allied cause, while Danville itself provided its share of soldiers.
- In the early days, when most of the highways were terra-cotta ribbons stretching over hill and dale, it was a day's journey to Greensboro, North Carolina.
- With the advent of the automobile and good roads, the 45-mile journey took only a few hours.

*Danville Yarnworks employees were part of the city's growing textile industry.*

# HISTORICAL SNAPSHOT
# 1933

- Construction of the Golden Gate Bridge began in San Francisco Bay
- Congress voted for independence for the Philippines, against President Hoover
- The Twentieth Amendment to the United States Constitution was ratified, changing Inauguration Day from March 4 to January 20, starting in 1937
- *The Lone Ranger* debuted on the radio
- The New York City-based Postal Telegraph Company introduced the first singing telegram
- In Miami, Florida, Giuseppe Zangara attempted to assassinate President-elect Franklin D. Roosevelt; Chicago Mayor Anton J. Cermak was killed
- *Newsweek* was published for the first time
- *King Kong*, starring Fay Wray, premiered at Radio City Music Hall in NYC
- Mount Rushmore National Memorial was dedicated
- President Franklin Roosevelt proclaimed, "The only thing we have to fear, is fear itself."
- Frances Perkins became U.S. Secretary of Labor and the first female Cabinet member
- Dachau, the first Nazi concentration camp, was opened
- The Civilian Conservation Corps was established to relieve unemployment
- Karl Jansky detected radio waves from the Milky Way Galaxy, leading to radio astronomy
- The Tennessee Valley Authority was created
- The Century of Progress World's Fair opened in Chicago
- Walt Disney's *Silly Symphony* cartoon *The Three Little Pigs* was released
- The first drive-in theater opened in Camden, New Jersey
- The first electronic pari-mutuel betting machine was unveiled at the Arlington Park race track near Chicago
- The first Major League Baseball All-Star Game was played at Comiskey Park in Chicago
- Army Barracks on Alcatraz was acquired by the Department of Justice for a federal penitentiary
- Albert Einstein arrived in the United States as a refugee from Nazi Germany
- The Civil Works Administration, designed to create jobs, was launched
- The Dust Bowl in South Dakota stripped topsoil from desiccated farmlands
- The Twenty-first Amendment officially went into effect, legalizing alcohol in the U.S.
- The first doughnut store, Krispy Kreme, opened in Nashville, Tennessee

*Frances Perkins was the first female Cabinet member.*

## Selected Prices

Bed Sheet .................................................................................$0.65

Bell Telephone, NY to London, Three Minutes............................$30.00

Book, *Popular Chemistry*...........................................................$0.50

Electric Washer .........................................................................$79.85

Ice Box .......................................................................................$18.75

Lawn Mower ...............................................................................$5.49

Mattress.......................................................................................$4.65

Microphone .................................................................................$1.00

Motor Oil, Gallon........................................................................$0.49

Percolator ...................................................................................$1.00

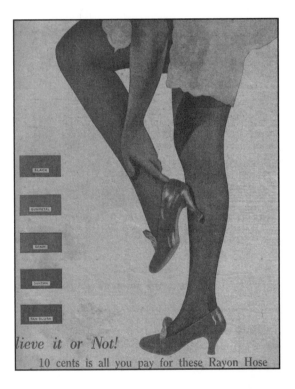

...lieve it or Not!
10 cents is all you pay for these Rayon Hose

HOTEL DANVILLE, DANVILLE, VA.

Danville's Newest and Most Modern Hotel

Wishes full measure of success to the industrial survey project and offers every possible co-operation in the development of this good city.

**ALL FOR DANVILLE**
AND
**DANVILLE FOR ALL**

**When In Danville Stop at the Hotel Danville**

*"Danville's Only Fireproof Modern Hotel"*

Question to Carl Milam, secretary of the American Library Association, from H. L. Woolhiser, city manager in Illinois, during a 1933 radio broadcast called *How to Reduce the Library Budget*:

Wages are down, and the incomes from every business and every property have been drastically reduced. In many cases the income from property is not sufficient to pay taxes, much less living expenses of the owner.... In a time of depression we have to stop considering what is good for a well-organized social structure and consider what is necessary for continued existence of the people. In my town, we have been spending $90,000 per month for poor relief and that is not enough. Our public library spends about the same amount each year. Suppose we are reduced to the necessity of eliminating one of these functions; which will it be, Mr. Milam?

The public library is maintained by democratic society in order that every man, woman, and child may have the means of self-education and recreational reading.

—*Standards for Public Libraries*, 1933

### *The Library and Adult Education*, Alexander Meiklejohn, 1924:

Democracy is education..... Insofar as we can educate the people, insofar as we can bring people to understanding of themselves and of their world, we can have a democracy. Insofar as we cannot do that, we have got to have control by the few.

### *Survey of Danville and Pittsylvania County*, P. H. Batte, 1928:

The first and only industrial survey ever made of Danville and Pittsylvania County comes at a time when Danville's future appears brighter than ever. The new spirit of Danville is in line with the new progressive spirit of the Old Dominion, and Danville, one of Virginia's oldest cities, charted 136 years ago, is presenting today a comprehensive survey of her realization of past ambitions, as well as her objective of future greatness.

Danville is a good city—solid as the Rock of Gibraltar. Unlike many ambitious cities, Danville is out of its experimental stage. Confidence in the future is just led by marvelous achievements in the past.... This city, like many others, may not fully appreciate the many other industries because of the unusual size of their largest industry. The cotton mills have 467,000 spindles and are equal to 24 of the average-size North and South Carolina cotton mills. The number of bails of cotton consumed in 1927 was 91,569, or 46,439,753 pounds. The production in yards was 158,565,440, in miles 90,094, or enough cotton to go around the world 3 1/2 times.

*Continued*

## *Survey of Danville and Pittsylvania County, . . . (Continued)*

Danville has many other large industries. The Danville Knitting Mills, manufacturers of stable and fancy hosiery, is the largest knitting mill in Virginia. This mill was organized in 1899 by Danville citizens, and enjoys a tremendous business. Then we have a number of other substantial industries, such as the Morotock Manufacturing Company, manufacturers of overalls, children's suits and men's work pants; the Anderson Brothers Consolidated Company, manufacturers of tropical linen suits, overalls and work shirts; the Dan City Silk Mills, manufacturers of broad silks; Boatwright Furniture; the Westbrook Elevator Manufacturing Company; Dan Valley Mills, manufacturers of flour; and the Waddill Printing Company.

The tobacco industry has been another great factor in the development of Danville. Since 1869, the market has shown a steady yearly increase in tobacco handled here. Danville is recognized throughout the world as the premier tobacco market. It offers better facilities, more experienced tobacconists, and all-round marketing conditions unlike any other market in the United States....

The modern Danville offers the advantages of a well-planned city. In its desire to grow, it reflects a spirit infused with progressive ideas.... Danville is not a "one industry" city. On the other hand, the city has 48 thriving industries engaged in the manufacturing and tobacco industry. If anyone should ask the writer to give some of the chief contributory factors in the development of Danville, he would put at the top of the list "Type of Citizens." Men of character, vision, ability and all-round progressive citizens have made Danville the kind of town men like to do business in. The largest industries of Danville were founded by and are still directed by home men and money.

## Survey of Danville and Pittsylvania Co.

## "Library on Wheels Takes Books to Readers," *The New York Times*, June 24, 1934:

Booklovers living in rural parts or outlying districts of the city, far from a branch of the public library, need not despair of obtaining reading material. The "traveling library" has been put into operation for the purpose of circulating books in the more sparsely populated regions of the country which do not warrant the installation of regular branch libraries.

One such library on wheels [was] designed by H. J. Gumpolt, bursar of the New York Public Library, and R. E. Rohne of the Expando Company of Chicago.... Its outward appearance resembles that of any other commercial vehicle except for the books which line both sides.

Through specially constructed mechanical contrivances, the side walls of the bus are expanded 13 inches, the roof is raised 11 inches, at the same time exposing the side panels which supply

*Continued*

## "Library on Wheels Takes Books to Readers," ... *(Continued)*

additional light and ventilation to its interior. A tire box at the rear of the car is lowered and becomes a platform with steps on either side, giving access to the librarian's window.

Every inch of the interior is ingeniously utilized. There are facilities for carrying 2,000 books each trip. The compact arrangement leaves sufficient room for the selection of books by 15 persons at a time.

According to Mrs. Ruth E. Wellman, head of the extension division of the New York Public Library, the traveling library has proved a successful venture. There are 8,000 enrolled readers, most of them young people. The bus takes a different route each day, stopping for an hour at each station.

## "First Free Library in the United States Observes Its 100th Birthday," *The New York Times*, April 2, 1933:

PETERBOROUGH, N.H.—The 100th anniversary of the first free public library in the United States to be supported by taxation is to be observed this spring and summer by the people of this town, where on April 9, 1833, the Peterborough Town Library, by vote, was declared "free" to every citizen.

During the week of April 9, the Peterborough churches, clubs and schools will commemorate the event, and the Peterborough Stamp Club is sponsoring a cachet that will be mailed out on the library's anniversary. It will bear the stamp of one of New Hampshire's most famous sons, Daniel Webster. On August 22, the people of Peterborough will take further recognition of America's first free library when it will give a special program with members of the New Hampshire Library Association and others as guests.

The movement to establish the Peterborough Town Library resulted from the division of the State Literary Fund, established in 1821 and raised by an annual tax on the capital stock of banks for an endowment of the State University. This project was abandoned, and a little later on this money was divided annually among the towns of the State of New Hampshire "for the support of common free schools, or other purposes of education." Peterborough was the first town to realize the significance of the later clause and the educational importance of a free library.

In 1833, Rev. Abiel Abbott, D. I., then Minister of the Peterborough Unitarian Church, with others, conceived the idea of a free library, which was carried into execution. Since April 9, 1833, by vote at the Peterborough annual town meeting, the library was owned and wholly supported by an annual town appropriation.

The catalog of America's first free library made its appearance in February 1834. It was written in longhand by the Rev. Dr. Abbott, and a copy is still in existence. This was followed

*Continued*

**"First Free Library in the United States Observes
Its 100th Birthday,"** ... *(Continued)*

in 1837 by a catalog printed by John Prentiss of Keene, a 16-page pamphlet, listing 579 volumes. In 1834, the policy of keeping open Sundays was adopted and this has been continued without interruption down to this day.

The library had many religious books 100 years ago, but others were not overlooked, and on the shelves were found the lives of Bonaparte and Mohammed, the travels of Capt. Cook and of Lewis and Clark. For fiction, one could read Robinson Crusoe, the works of Goldsmith, Miss Edgeworth or Washington Irving. There were, also, a number of books for the young.

Miss Susan N. Gates was the first woman librarian of the library supported entirely by taxation, and to her fell the honor of making the first individual gift of money to the library. It was $20 and represented her entire salary for eight months.

In 1873, the lot upon which the library stands was purchased by 10 public-spirited men, who contributed $77 apiece. The present library was built in 1892 through the generosity of Mrs. Nancy S. Foster of Chicago, George S. Morison of New York, and William H. Smith of Alton, Ill.

# 1938 PROFILE

John Andrew Rice, Jr., founded Black Mountain College in Asheville, North Carolina, based on his belief that higher education should emphasize emotional and intellectual maturity, as well as academics.

## Life at Home

- John Andrew Rice, Jr.'s educational concepts had played a role in his firing from a Florida college and assured his status as a maverick.
- His strong ideas both placed him in the center of numerous debates concerning the role of higher education, while the college attracted many important artists as contributing lecturers and mentors, including John Cage, Robert Creeley, Willem de Kooning, Robert Rauschenberg, and Franz Kline.
- John was born February 1, 1888, the son of a Methodist minister, in Lynchburg, South Carolina.
- His mother grew up at Tanglewood, a plantation in South Carolina, where the family would spend its summers.
- The Rice family had three sons, of which John was the oldest.
- During his childhood summers at Tanglewood, John enjoyed the company of his cousins and the families of freed slaves who still lived on the plantation.

*John Rice founded Black Mountain College.*

- During these years, John became unsettled by the dichotomy of race relations on the plantation; he puzzled over the apparent equality of black and white children at playtime which gave way to segregation and white privilege in the home and at mealtimes.
- John believed it was his Southern heritage that inclined him toward human observation and "a fascination with people, their actions, and their motivations for acting."

*John spent summers at Tanglewood, his family's plantation in South Carolina.*

- His first interlocutor was "Uncle Melt," a former slave who resided on the family plantation.
- Uncle Melt, John claimed, was his first instructor in the art of dialogue.
- He would pose questions to the young John then patiently listen to the boy's answers.
- These conversations were not undertaken with a specific end, but simply for the sake of them, for the joy of the conversation, which John grew to love.
- John's formal education began at the Webb School in 1905, a highly regarded boarding school in Bell Buckle, Tennessee, where the curriculum included Greek, Latin, and mathematics.
- The school was founded and staffed by the Webb brothers.
- The elder, William R. "Sawney" Webb, was a Civil War veteran—a Confederate, with a hardscrabble, rural character.
- His younger brother, John Webb, was the more gentle and scholarly of the two.
- The Webb School was reputed to be both a reformatory and a prestigious preparatory school—a contradiction which stemmed from the school's philosophy that every child deserved another chance at education, and no student should be refused admission.
- The school's prestige likely resulted from the high number of Rhodes Scholars among its alumni.
- The curriculum was demanding and the rules were designed to instill self-discipline in the students, who were responsible for their own learning.
- John would later say of the school, "The teacher … it seemed, was not, strictly speaking, a teacher at all: he was kind of a referee."
- Matriculating to Tulane University, following his time at Webb, he received a B.A. from the college in 1911.
- He attended Queens College, Oxford, on a Rhodes Scholarship.
- There, he studied jurisprudence and admired the tradition of extensive reading with tutors.
- Oxford was an ideal: the environment was given to lengthy conversation and the circulation of ideas, where "all were teachers and taught."
- Moreover, John, having left the South for the first time, was able to regard his homeland as never before.
- In so doing, he saw himself in a new light and came to the conclusion that "Oxford was a man's world as the South was a woman's."
- While at Oxford, John met Nell Aydelotte, who would become his wife.
- She was the sister of his friend, Frank Aydelotte; the couple married in 1914 during the winter holiday.

- John pursued a doctorate in English Literature, which he did not complete, at the University of Chicago.
- He had little appreciation for scholarly research, his friends said, and displayed an unwillingness to persevere in tasks he did not enjoy.
- He taught first at the Webb School from 1914-1916, followed by a stint as a professor of Classics at the University of Nebraska, where he proved himself brilliant in the classroom and in counseling students but a consistent irritant to the administration.
- From the University of Nebraska, John took his unique teaching techniques to the New Jersey College for Women.
- He was forced to resign after two years amid a faculty controversy.
- He then landed a faculty position at Rollins College in Winter Park, Florida, where faculty and students found him to be either brilliant and charismatic, or divisive and argumentative.

*John married Nell Aydelotte in 1914.*

- At Rollins, he advocated a truly liberal arts college that rejected the traditional rules and regulations such as required courses, grades, and boards of trustees.
- In John's opinion, the ideal college would create the potential result of life in a democracy.
- His vision of education embraced both practical work and intellectual development.
- Moreover, this development would be the result not only of traditional methods of study, but would also come as the natural result of the experience of experimentation, and life in a challenging and supportive community.
- John became dedicated to those modes of learning that originated out of sight, hearing, and everyday human experience, rather than from the written word.
- In 1933, John was fired from Rollins College as a result of a conflict regarding academic freedom arising from a 1930 Conference on Curriculum for the College of Liberal Arts for the purpose of scrutinizing Rollins' own curriculum and possibly developing models for other schools.
- Those in attendance included the conference's chair, John Dewey, an educational theorist whose ideas had been influential for more than three decades.
- Dewey himself issued an "appeal for a curriculum that recognizes student interests and abilities."
- The issue of specific subject area incited heated discussion.
- The conference therefore turned its attention to "curricular philosophies."
- In the end, the conference proposed a collegiate model that featured a lower division, for the purpose of "imparting required knowledge and prescribed information," and an upper division, devoted to "immersion in an area of in-depth learning."
- The final recommendation of the conference stated: "There should be less emphasis on the acquisition of mere facts, and more emphasis upon generalization, thinking, application of knowledge and awareness of gaps in knowledge. Prerequisites for entrance and within [Rollins] College have been too rigid, too formal, and not fully justified."
- Rollins College president Hamilton Holt approved of the conference recommendations and sought to incorporate them into the life of the college.

- He advocated the idea of upper and lower divisions, formally stating, "Courses in the Upper Division will be adjusted to the needs of the individual. Instead of limiting the teaching schedule of the instructor on the basis of time, alone, Rollins has assigned each instructor a given number of students only.... In lower divisions the student will fill in gaps in [her] preparation, and lay a broad foundation for the specialized work [she] is to do later in upper divisions."
- A committee of Rollins faculty members, of which John was a part, was assembled and charged with working out the inception of the new curriculum and schedule.
- Chief among the difficulties in implementing the new plan was trying to make it compatible with the eight-hour-day "conference plan" already in place.
- The "conference plan" involved four two-hour class sessions per day, during which students would receive general instruction and engage in independent study, and have one-on-one conferences with instructors.
- Holt was very much in favor of the "conference plan."
- John and his colleagues on the committees agreed that the conference plan could not be reconciled with a new curriculum geared towards individual achievement, rather than doing time in a classroom.
- An infuriated Holt rejected the committee's suggested changes and called John to his office to demand the Classics professor's resignation.
- When John refused to resign his tenured position, he was fired.
- In addition to his dissatisfaction with John's input as a member of Curriculum Committee, Holt had grievances that included his objection to John's characteristic candor in his remarks to faculty, students, and, especially, wealthy donors to the college.
- John had the habit of making negative remarks in the wrong company about the wrong things.
- For instance, he persisted in his criticism of the chapel building and the required services held within, into which Holt had put much of his fundraising efforts.
- Further, John was outspokenly critical of the tradition of sororities and fraternities on campus, claiming that they "prevented a wide variety of friendships."
- He was also critical of debating, since, in his opinion, it "encouraged participants to try to win rather than to search for truth."
- The complaints against John included:
  He had called a chisel one of the world's most beautiful objects.
  He had whispered in chapel.
  He had proposed that male and female students be paired off on arrival at college.
  He had labeled debates "a pernicious form of intellectual perversion."
  He had put "obscene" pictures on the walls of his classroom.
  He had an "indolent" walk.
  He had left fish scales in the sink after using the college's beach cottage.
  He had helped alienate one young lady from her sorority.
- The AAUP investigating team, Arthur O. Lovejoy of Johns Hopkins University's philosophy department, and Austin S. Edwards professor of psychology from the University of Georgia were nonplussed by the litany of offenses.
- Ultimately, they concluded that John "was dismissed upon charges which, insofar as they are substantiated, would in most American institutions of higher education not be regarded as grounds for that action in such a case."
- Beyond simply vindicating John, the committee went as far as to praise him, saying, "he had shown himself an unusually stimulating and effective teacher, peculiarly adapted to the informal method of instruction in use in the college."
- In the subsequent investigation into the matter by the American Association of University Professors, the conclusion was that John's dismissal was "unwarrantable," and a "violation of his personal and professional rights."

*Hailed as an "unusually stimulating teacher" John's goals focused on emotional and intellectual maturity, rather than on memorization and classroom attendance.*

- Upon his dismissal, he became instrumental in the 1933 founding of Black Mountain College, in the mountains of western North Carolina.
- It was said of the educator "safe did not suit John Andrew Rice. Characteristically, he determined to earn his hemlock. He earned it...by venting large doses of candor that could be viewed accurately as insulting or honest, outrageous or courageous."
- John's mental acuity was matched, if not surpassed, by his tendency to be physically idle.
- Students rushing past his house to arrive at his class on time would notice him in repose on his porch, reading in his bare feet.

## Life at Work

- In 1933, John Rice set out to create the ideal higher education environment which he had advocated for decades—Black Mountain College—and it opened with 21 students, eventually growing to nearly 100.
- His innovations soon caused the tiny college to be recognized nationally; he was particularly critical of courses based upon memorization, overreliance on Great Books, and classroom attendance.
- Accompanying John in opening the college were Ralph Lounsbury, Frederic Georgia, and Theodore Dreier, all of whom had been fired from Rollins College or resigned.
- Within three months, the necessary $14,500 was raised for the opening of the college; John and Dreier traveled north in pursuit of funding, prospective students, and the support of friends who had academic influence.
- Lounsbury and Georgia remained in North Carolina to negotiate the lease, correspond with potential students, and prepare the official documents pertaining to the incorporation of the college.

- The State of North Carolina issued a certificate of incorporation for the college on August 19, 1933.
- Thus, Black Mountain College was initiated as a coeducational school "where students may receive instruction in those branches of learning which will aid in qualifying them for honorably and effectively discharging their obligations to society and their duties as citizens."

*John, second from right, with his students.*

- Characterizing the college's inception, John Rice's biographer, Katherine Chaddock Reynolds, said, "The founding of Black Mountain College was to become one of the most remarkable start-up sagas in American higher education, punctuated by a series of small victories and substantial setbacks in the race to develop programs, policies, and financial and human resources."
- The college was housed in buildings leased from Blue Ridge Assembly, a YMCA facility near Black Mountain, North Carolina.
- The college comprised 13 faculty members and 26 students.
- The faculty of Black Mountain College organized the institution as a nonprofit corporation from which they elected members of the governing Board of Fellows, which elected college officers from among the faculty.
- There was no formal president of Black Mountain College.
- A presiding officer was elected for brief periods, an assignment which rotated among faculty members.
- In place of deans and other administrative officers, faculty members organized themselves into committees to address specific needs.
- The governing structure was based on the "European Plan," rather than the traditional American model.
- The common structure of governance in American colleges placed the ultimate control over the institution's administration in the hands of a board of trustees, the members of which may or may not have specific educational concerns.
- At Black Mountain College, the faculty had complete authority in matters of the school's methodology, rather than being beholden to the directions of an external governing body.
- Grades were recorded only for transfer purposes, and were otherwise unknown to students.
- Instead of defining students conventionally as members of one of four classes, the college was organized into two divisions—the Junior College and the Senior College.
- The Junior College was devoted to the exploration of and introduction to a variety of subjects and interests, which were guided by advisory instructors.
- While in the Junior College, students were to develop an attention to a particular subject, which they would subsequently spend the majority of their time pursuing while in the Senior College.
- The intention was to formulate individual programs of study for each student.
- Programs were meant to be flexible enough to accommodate changes arising from the different needs of students and the inevitable development of new interests.
- Student consultation with instructors was a thorough and constant process.
- The goal was that the students develop a level of maturity and intelligence that would lead them to choose an appropriate "field of specialization" in the Senior College.

- Before moving on to the Senior College, a student had to complete an in-depth study sufficient to demonstrate competency on comprehensive oral and written exams, which were set by the board of admissions to the Senior College.

- In the Senior College, a student was required to choose a field of concentration and pursue it with competent mastery.

- Students and tutors collaboratively devised a plan of work; the tutors, working closely with students, oversaw the execution of the plan.

*Black Mountain operated a farm in an effort toward greater self sufficiency.*

- Both the students and the tutors decided when the work outlined in the plan of study was complete.

- Mastery was assessed by means of thorough, comprehensive exams that were administered by experts in the pertinent field from outside the college, such as professors from Duke, the University of North Carolina, Clemson, and Yale.

- The college was devoted to belief in the "centrality of artistic experience to support learning in all disciplines, the value of experiential learning, the practice of shared democratic governance by faculty and students, the value of social and cultural endeavors outside the classroom, and the elimination of oversight from outside trustees."

- To that end, Black Mountain College was developed as an experiment in "education in a democracy," with the concept that the creative arts and practical responsibilities are of the same value in the development of the intellect.

- John conceived an "education for democracy" such that "education should address the capacity of citizens to act responsibly in a democratic setting."

- Believing that the ends of education should correspond with the means, John championed the belief that "responsible democratic action" must be the experience within the educational environment if any wished to achieve such action as an educational goal.

- John's idea of a "responsible actor in a democracy" was "an individual of both intellectual and emotional maturity, whose actions were informed by feelings and knowledge."

- The thematic attention at Black Mountain College was to interaction, relativity, process, nature of forms, commitment to a democratic form of government, and an abhorrence of totalitarian systems.

- Tuition was factored on a sliding scale, and it was not uncommon for it to slide to zero.

- The collectivist spirit and communalist nature of the college extended to every aspect of education.

- Students and faculty were to share in the tasks necessary for maintaining the college, clearing tables, sweeping floors, cutting firewood, and shoveling furnace coal.

- The college leased and operated a 25-acre farm in an effort toward greater self-sufficiency.

- Produce from the farm was either served in the dining hall or sold at market.

- At its height, the farm provided 50 percent of the vegetables used in the dining hall.

- Students were encouraged, but not required, to share in the work of maintaining the farm.

- Other projects aimed at greater self-sufficiency included raising pigeons, harvesting apples, and running a school for children and local youths.

## Life in the Community: Western North Carolina

- In 1933, John Andrew Rice and his colleagues opened Black Mountain College in Black Mountain, North Carolina, just east of Asheville.
- The college was set in the remote and breathtaking southern slopes of the Blue Ridge Mountains.
- Here, the topography of North Carolina rises to its summit, sloping westward from the Atlantic Ocean in the east to the mountainous region of the Eastern Continental Divide, where tree-covered foothills converge into gentle ridges.
- Henry Miller, visiting the college, said of its vistas: "From the steps of Black Mountain College in North Carolina, one has a view of mountains and forests which makes one dream of Asia."
- The years 1910-1930 were spectacular in terms of the growth of real estate development, tourism, and population.
- In the years between 1920 and 1930, Buncombe County's population increased from 64,000 to 98,000.
- On September 23, 1928, the Dutch Manufacturing company, American ENKA Corporation, which specialized in rayon production, became the largest employer in Buncombe County.
- Along with Beacon Manufacturing, ENKA would comprise the region's driving economic force for much of the twentieth century.
- Each of these companies employed more than 1,000 workers, with hundreds more working for retail affiliates.
- The heights to which the region's economy soared would be proportionate to its plunge, which began in 1930.
- On November 30, 1929, the Central Bank and Trust Company's failure to open for business led to the sudden collapse of the national economy.

*Dutch Manufacturing, specializing in rayon, was the region's largest employer.*

- Among the depositors were city and county governments, with deposits totaling more than $8 million.
- The year 1933 saw the region that was home to Black Mountain College reeling in the aftermath of economic catastrophe.
- This dismal economic condition was precipitated by the national circumstances affecting the Great Depression, and exacerbated by the localized economic extremes seen during the preceding boom years.
- The majority of the banks in Asheville closed, including the Asheville Central Bank and Trust, which struggled and ultimately failed in 1933.
- The region's economic center, Asheville, was saddled with the highest debt per capita of any city in the nation.
- The excessive burdens placed on the real estate market, in the forms bad loans and investments, were unable to be recovered.
- Buncombe County, however, did encounter a surge in the production of tobacco, giving the rural economy of the region a boost.
- The Civilian Conservation Corps and the Public Works Administration programs offered some support to those in rural locales.
- As a result, those dwelling in such places fared better than the urban workforce.
- Construction on the Great Smoky Mountain National Park began in 1931.
- The State of North Carolina purchased approximately 150,000 acres of land, which it relinquished to the United States Government as a contribution to the park.
- Lumber companies and some local residents were strongly opposed to the development of the park, as they were forced to relocate outside of the park's boundaries.
- In 1938, the plans for the Blue Ridge Parkway began to take shape. Another scenic byway would trace a path through the Southern Appalachians from Great Smoky Mountain National Park in Tennessee to Shenandoah National Park in Virginia.

*The Blue Ridge Parkway in 1938.*

# HISTORICAL SNAPSHOT
# 1938

- The Merrie Melodies cartoon short *Daffy Duck and Egghead* was released, becoming the first cartoon to give Daffy Duck his current name
- The March of Dimes was established by Franklin Delano Roosevelt
- Thornton Wilder's play *Our Town* was performed for the first time
- The Niagara Bridge at Niagara Falls, New York, collapsed due to an ice jam
- Walt Disney's *Snow White and the Seven Dwarfs*, the first cel-animated feature in motion picture history, was released
- A nylon bristle toothbrush became the first commercial product to be made with nylon yarn
- Comic book icon Superman made his first appearance in Action Comics #1
- U.S. Secretary of State Cordell Hull rejected Russia's offer of a joint defense pact to counter the rise of Nazi Germany
- *Information Please* debuted on NBC Radio
- László Bíró patented the ballpoint pen in Britain
- Heavyweight boxing champion Joe Louis knocked out Max Schmeling in the first round of their rematch at Yankee Stadium in New York City
- The Civil Aeronautics Act was signed into law, forming the Civil Aeronautics Authority in the United States
- The Evian Conference on Refugees was convened in France, noting that "no country in Europe is prepared to accept Jews fleeing persecution and the United States will only take 27,370. The prospect for European Jewry looks bleak"
- Howard Hughes set a new record by completing a 91-hour airplane flight around the world
- General Ludwig Beck, convinced that Hitler's decision to attack Czechoslovakia would lead to a general European war, resigned his position as Chief of the Army General Staff
- In Nazi Germany, Jews' passports were invalidated, and those who needed a passport for emigration purposes were given one marked with the letter J
- The minimum wage was established by law in the U.S.
- DuPont announced the name for its new synthetic yarn: "nylon"
- Orson Welles' radio adaptation of *The War of the Worlds* was broadcast, causing panic in various parts of the United States
- In an effort to try to restore investor confidence, the New York Stock Exchange unveiled a 15-point program aimed to upgrade protection for the investing public
- In horse racing, Seabiscuit defeated War Admiral by four lengths in their match race at Pimlico Race Course in Baltimore, Maryland
- On the eve of Armistice Day, Kate Smith sang Irving Berlin's "God Bless America" for the first time on her weekly radio show
- John L. Lewis was elected as the first president of the Congress of Industrial Organizations
- President Roosevelt agreed to loan $25 million to Chiang Kai-shek, cementing the Sino-American relationship and angering the Japanese government
- Adolf Hitler was *Time* magazine's "Man of the Year" as the most influential person

## First Lecture of Marriage Course [excerpt], Dr. Alfred C. Kinsey, Indiana University:

The culture which we have received is responsible for the prudish ideas which have done so much more than any other single factor to undermine the home. Studies indicate that some 34 percent of the whole married population is in trouble sexually at some time. The same studies indicate that 68 percent of the religiously devout and the highly educated have marital maladjustments. It is the development of ideas as to what is proper and what is not, what is fine and what is not, which interferes with the consummation of the biological relationship in marriage. Specifically, sexual difficulties in marriage originate through ignorance of sexual anatomy and physiology. In an uninhibited society, a 12-year-old would know most of the biology which I will have to give you in formal lectures as seniors and graduate students. It is to make amends for the interference our social organization has imposed that a course like the marriage course is necessary. Sexual maladjustment in marriage originates also because of the ignorance in this day and generation of adequate contraceptives, and above everything else, originates because of prudish ideas of both men and women.

## "Anti-Lynch Bill Insult to South, Harrison Says: Warns Senators From North Measure May Cause Party Split," *Asheville Citizen-Times*, January 11,1938:

Southern Senators fighting the anti-lynching bill warned Northern Democrats today that their support of the measure might produce a party split.

"Beware, gentlemen, beware," deep-voiced Senator Harrison (D-Miss.), advised Democrats supporting the proposal. "Your action may be most momentous. Is the faith of the South to be broken? Is its love for the Democratic party to be shattered?"

Senator Miller (D-Ark.), joined Harrison in the discussion to assert that the Southern people would "revolt" if the "long hand of the federal government" reached into their communities. They would do so, he said, "because they love their Constitution."

Harrison also advised presidential and Supreme Court aspirants in the Senate to "stop, look and listen" before voting for the anti-lynching bill. He said the South had been loyal to the Democratic Party because it believed the Party would cooperate in "protecting the white civilization of the South."

"But now," he thundered, "we see the terrible situation of a Democratic majority betraying the trust of the Southern people and destroying the things they have idolized and in which they believed."

Harrison wiped his brow frequently and paced up and down in front of his desk. The bill was an "insult" to the Southern people, he charged.

The Mississippian poked fun at "the sweet, amiable, gentlemen" who, he said, "answered with fluttering hearts" when called from the Senate chamber because they believed the call might mean news of their nomination to the Supreme Court. These men had best beware, he declared, adding that they would not "add anything to their standing as lawyers or their qualifications for the highest court" by voting for "such a legislative monstrosity" as the anti-lynching bill.

The bill "would ravish the Constitution, violate every principle of local self-government, and rob the sovereignty of the states," he said.

Harrison declared that advocates of the measure did not attempt to defend it because their attitude was, "Why speak? We've got the votes."

Miller said there was "no demand or reason to support its enactment.

"I don't believe a member of this Senate believes this bill is constitutional," he added. Miller told the Senate that the bill was not aimed at the South any more than it is aimed at our form of government." It would sound the death-knell of the right of states to regulate their own affairs," he said, continuing:

"It is inconceivable to me that those who profess to follow Jackson and Jefferson are willing to say that the federal government may reach its hand into your community and regulate its affairs."

*Continued*

## "Anti-Lynch Bill Insult to South, Harrison Says . . ." *(Continued)*

Action of the Democratic leadership in endorsing the bill was "camouflage," Miller continued. "At the first opportunity, the Democratic party has had to return this government to the principles of Jackson and Jefferson, senators are yielding to the black pressure and willing to surrender their birthright," he said. "Return this government to a constitutional basis and stop further consideration of this bill."

## "House Group Is Named to Write Wage-Hour Bill," *Asheville Citizen-Times*, March 2, 1938:

The House Labor Committee turned over to seven of its members today the task of writing a wage-hour bill which will overcome congressional opposition and comply with President Roosevelt's demand for legislation to end "starvation wages and intolerable hours."

Chairman Norton (D-N.J.) named Representative Ramspeck (D-Ga.) head of the subcommittee. She asked all House members with ideas on the subject to communicate them to the subcommittee.

Ramspeck said the group would start work tomorrow "without any preconceived ideas." Other members said, however, the new bill would have to be flexible to stand the test of constitutionality and also to meet the objections of the House Rules Committee. That group blocked the legislation for months last year.

Representative Thomas (D-Tex.), a member, said the subcommittee probably would include in a new bill some of the features of several conflicting proposals received by the full committee.

## "Pass This Test You Are Sober, Doctor Asserts,"
### *Asheville Citizen-Times*, February, 1938:

If you can write the numerals from 20 to 1 and the alphabet backwards you are not drunk, Dr. John W. Winston testified today in police court.

Dr. Winston said Talbot Smith, 37, of Norfolk, Virginia, charged with being drunk in an automobile, "did both and didn't make a single mistake one hour after his arrest." The physician exhibited the pad on which he said the tests had been made.

Justice Clyde H. Jacob dismissed the charge.

## "Men Love Peppy Girls!" Advertisement, 1938:

If you are happy and peppy and full of fun, men will take you places. But if you are cross and always tired out, men won't like you. Men don't like "quiet" girls. They want girls who are full of pep.

For three generations one woman has told another how to go "smiling through" with Lydia E. Pinkham's Vegetable Compound. It helps Nature tone up the system, thus lessening discomforts from the functional disorders which women endure in the three ordeals of life: 1. Turning from girlhood to womanhood. 2. Preparing for motherhood. 3. Approaching "middle age."

Pinkham's compound, made especially for women from Nature's wholesome herbs and roots, has helped women for over 60 years.

## "The Killer-Diller: The Life and Four-Four Time of Benny Goodman,"
### *The Saturday Evening Post*, May 7, 1938:

"Radio people claim that three nights a week, 2,000,000 people are listening to the Benny Goodman broadcast. If you ever heard him, chances are you would not forget him. His chief characteristics are definition and power, the rhythm instruments piano, drums, bass sound and sure, solidly thumping out the time, while the melody, carried by the concerted brasses and reeds, pulses just a fraction ahead to give off-beat the brasses a fine strong burr and the reeds swirling with improvisations on the tune. And then Goodman's clarinet, clear and unhurried and artful, playing a song that was never written and may never be heard again. No other band of this quality has ever had such popular acceptance. In the past year and half

*Continued*

## "The Killer-Diller . . . *(Continued)*

it has sold more records, played longer runs and scored higher radio ratings than any band of its kind in the history of American popular music. When you hear it play in a dance hall or hotel ballroom, you want to dance. In an auditorium, the audience reaction is almost pure violence...

[T]he director of the New York School of Music prepared a bill for the legislature making swing music illegal, and a New York University psychologist turned the light of pure science on the audience reaction. "It's simply that a combination of circumstances has made them one-minded and their inhibitory checks have been broken down," he explained. "Some individuals are more suggestible than others, and those individuals start then piling into the aisles...."

The man who causes all this excitement is a highly talented, very effective and richly likable bundle of contradictions just past his twenty-eighth birthday. That makes him and jazz about the same age. In fact, they grew up together.... [E]xposure to the classical tradition is just now beginning to take full effect, with the result that, while Goodman plays the music of each well enough to excite critics of serious music, he frankly states that, whereas Mozart was a cat, for him Brahms is not in the groove.

But in 1921, Benny was not under the influence of dead Germans but live American Negroes. King Oliver had come up from New Orleans several years before the general migration of American syncopation was up the Mississippi and turned right, and his protégé, Louis Armstrong, had his name in lights out in front of the Black Belt's famous Plantation. These two colored trumpeters strongly influenced all the musicians who listened to them. And Benny listened to them all he could...Jimmy Dorsey had come out west from Davenport, there was Bix Beiderbecke, whose improvisations on the trumpet were often pure lyric poetry. He was not only interested in the colored men but hung around the College Inn a lot, listening to Tony Panico. The town was full of young musicians, and some a little older, who were showing them which way to go. Jazz music, in spite of the big, sweet, suffusing, movie-house bands, was on its way to its second pinnacle....

In the Dixieland era and just after the war, it was called jazz. Scott Fitzgerald used the word to describe an age. In the feverish late '20s it was hot music that Pollack's and Don Voorhees' and Goldkette's and Red Nichols' bands were playing. Now they call it swing, but it's the same kind of music.

*Typical class discussion group at Black Mountain College.*

# 1938 NEWS FEATURE

*Report to the President on the Economic Conditions of the South: Education*

Great numbers of Americans are continually moving from one region to another. This makes poor schooling in any region a matter of national concern. The illiteracy, poor training, lack of education, go along with those migrating people who have not had schools. The fact that the South is the source of a considerable part of the rest of the nation's population makes the South's difficulty in providing school facilities a national problem.

In the United States as a whole, it is more possible than ever before to supply training for children and young people. The child population has only doubled since 1880, while the adult population has increased more than threefold. Too, the productive capacity per worker today is far in excess of what it was 50 years ago. In the South, however, owing to the higher birth rate and to the migration of adult workers, the proportion of productive workers to schoolchildren is much lower than elsewhere in the country. A study of this condition in the 1930s showed that there were 10 adults to six children, as compared to 10 adults for four children in the North and West.

In the rural regions of the South, particularly, there is a marked disparity between the number of children to be educated and the means for educating them. For example, in 1930, the rural inhabitants of the Southeast had to care for 4,250,000 children of school age of the country's total, although they received an income of only about two percent of the nation's total. In the nonfarm population of the Northeast, on the other hand, there were 8,500,000 children in a group that received 42 percent of the total national income—21 times as much income available to educate only twice as many children.

This disparity in this educational load, which bears so heavily on the South, continues. In 1936, the rate of natural increase in the population was greatest in the southeastern and southwestern sections of the United States, precisely where a lack of educational opportunity is already most pronounced.

The Southern regions are affected by population shifts more than other sections because the greatest proportions of movers originate there. In the 1920s, the states south of the Potomac and Ohio Rivers and east of the Mississippi lost about 1,700,000 persons through migration, about half of whom were between 15 and 35 years of age. These persons moved at the beginning of their productive life to regions which got this manpower almost free of cost, whereas the South, which had borne the expense of their care and education up to the time when they could start producing, suffered an almost complete loss of its investment. The newcomers to the South did not, by any means, balance the loss. The cost of rearing and schooling the young people of the Southern rural districts who moved to cities has been estimated to be approximately $250,000,000 annually.

The South must educate one-third of the nation's children with one-sixth of the nation's school revenues. According to the most conservative estimates, the per capita ability of the richest state in the country to support education is six times as great as that of the poorest state.

Although Southern teachers compare favorably with teachers elsewhere, the average annual salary of teachers in Arkansas for 1933-34 was $465, compared to $2,361 for New York State for the same year, in no one of the Southern states was the average salary of teachers equal to the average of the nation. In few places in the nation, on the other hand, is the number of pupils per teacher higher than as in the South. Overcrowding of schools, particularly in rural areas, has lowered the standards of education, and the short school terms of Southern rural schools further reduce their effectiveness.

In the South, only 16 percent of the children enrolled in school are in high school, as compared to 24 percent in states outside the South.

Higher education in the South has lagged far behind the rest of the nation. The total endowments of the colleges and universities of the South are less than the combined endowments of Yale and Harvard. As for medical schools, the South does not have the facilities to educate sufficient doctors for its own needs.

Since adequate schools and other means of public education are indispensable to the successful functioning of a democratic nation, the country as a whole is concerned with the South's difficulty in meeting its problem with education.

Illiteracy was higher in 1930 in the Southern states than in any other region, totaling 8.8 percent. The North Central states had a percentage of 1.9. New England and the Mid-Atlantic States combined had a percentage of 3.5. In the South, the percentages ranged from 2.8 in Oklahoma to 14.9 in South Carolina. Every state in the South except Oklahoma had a percentage higher than 6.5 percent.

But poor educational status of the South is not a result of lack of effort to support schools. The South collects in total taxes about half as much per person as the nation as a whole. All Southern states fall below the national average in tax revenues per child, although they devote a larger share of their tax income to schools. For the Southern states to spend the national average per pupil would require an additional quarter of a billion dollars of revenue.

Between 1933 and 1935, more than $21,000,000 in federal funds were necessary to keep rural schools open, and more than 80 percent of this amount was needed in the South, where local and state governments were unable to carry the burden.

In 1936, the Southern states spent an average of $25.11 per child in schools, about half the average for the country as a whole, or a quarter of what was spent per child in New York State. In 1935-36, the average school child enrolled in Mississippi had $27.47 spent on his education. At the same time, the average school child enrolled in New York State had $141.43 spent on his education, or more than five times as much as was spent on a child in Mississippi. There were actually 1,500 school centers in Mississippi without school buildings, requiring children to attend school in lodge halls, abandoned tenant houses, country churches, and, in some instances, even in cotton pens.

# 1939 PROFILE

Sister Mary Henry was a good and enthusiastic teacher who was admired by her students, though some of the other nuns complained that her classes were noisy and her curriculum strayed from the agreed-upon courses—like her plans to take her class on a field trip to the 1939 New York World's Fair.

## Life at Home

- Every fiber of Sister Mary Henry tingled with excitement over the chance to explore the "World of Tomorrow"—as the 1939 New York World's Fair advertised itself—and she was especially eager to see how her seventh-grade class would react to the spectacle.
- She had told everyone who asked that the daylong trip was the educational experience of a lifetime.
- Field trips of this kind were normally discouraged— read, prohibited—but no one wanted to oppose Sister Mary Henry when she was this determined; the fair was just a subway ride away and Sister Mary Henry insisted that the outing would cost the school nothing.
- It was a teacher's dream.
- They would not go anywhere near the much-criticized girly show; Sister Mary Henry said she simply wanted her class to drink in the "Dawn of a New Day" as the fair's official slogan boasted.

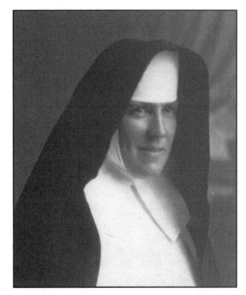

*Sister Mary Henry was a popular, though sometimes unorthodox, teacher.*

- Her friend and prayer partner, Sister Ann Seton, had joined 206,000 people on opening day and had had plenty to say about its magnificence and importance.
- Sister Mary Henry had been stirred up ever since.
- President Franklin D. Roosevelt gave the opening day address, which was not only broadcast over the various radio networks, but also was televised.

- NBC used the event to inaugurate regularly scheduled television broadcasts in New York City over their station W2XBS, viewed by approximately 1,000 people on 200 television sets scattered throughout the New York area.
- Sister Mary Henry was raised Catholic in a home that neither discussed nor expected either of its two daughters to become nuns.
- Sister Mary Henry—whose birth name was Edna Wolfe—shocked her parents when she returned from church shortly after turning nine and declared that she was destined to become a nun and planned to enter a convent.
- "It came out of the blue one morning when I decided to go to church on my own before school started. It's very difficult to explain, but as I lit a candle in church and stayed behind for a little while on my own, I suddenly felt a calling to be a nun. When I got home, I asked my mother to promise not to laugh, and then told her that I wanted to be a nun when I grew up. I realized that it was an unusual choice."

*The opening of the 1939 New York's World's Fair was televised throughout New York.*

- In 1922, shortly after turning 17, she joined the Society of the Sacred Heart in New York, carrying all her worldly possessions in a suitcase in one hand.
- Founded in 1881 by the Society of the Sacred Heart, a Roman Catholic congregation established in France in 1800, the convent was New York City's oldest private school for girls and was originally housed in a Manhattan brownstone on Madison Avenue at E. 54th Street.
- Life in the convent was a huge culture shock, made easier by her close friendship with the novices and her Polish roommate, Renata, who grew up in Chicago.
- The pair often chatted into the small hours, taking sips from a bottle of vodka that Renata had brought with her.
- Mornings started at 6 a.m. with an hour of meditation in the chapel, followed by mass and prayers.
- In addition to studying the meaning of chastity, poverty and obedience, Edna, dressed in a novice's uniform consisting of a long blue skirt and blue jumper, was expected to help the nuns with the cleaning and gardening.
- Then there was an hour of private prayer before evening prayers.
- The youngest of 150 nuns, Edna was happy.
- "Life was certainly regimented, but it wasn't miserable or austere," she recalled.
- After three years, Edna was ready to take her vows as a fully professed nun.
- This meant writing to the Mother Superior and undergoing psychometric tests to ensure she was emotionally and psychologically ready for such a huge step.

*Edna shocked her parents by announcing, at age 9, that she wanted to be a nun.*

- For the past dozen years, Sister Mary Henry had been teaching, praying, and telling children to spit out the gum at a parochial high school that accepted both boys and girls.
- The daydream that became the New York World's Fair began in 1935, at the height of the Great Depression.
- A group of New York City retired policemen decided to create an international exposition to lift the city and the country out of depression.
- Not long after, these men—along with the city's leading businessmen and investors—formed the New York World's Fair Corporation.
- For the next four years, the committee—working out of offices on one of the higher floors in the Empire State Building—organized the fair and its exhibits, and recruiting countries around the world to take part in creating the biggest international event since World War I.
- Robert Moses, New York City Parks Commissioner, saw great value to the city in having the World's Fair Corporation transform "a pestilential eyesore with a great capacity for mosquito breeding in Queens" into the exposition site, and later into a park at the World's Fair's end.
- A Greyhound Bus brochure bragged that the 1,216-acre fairgrounds were "3 1/2 miles long, and, in some places a mile wide."
- To lend the largely commercial venture a cultural air, it was decided to make the fair's opening day correspond to the 150th anniversary of President George Washington's first inauguration.
- Previous World's Fairs had left behind the Crystal Palace in England, the Eiffel Tower in Paris, and memories of the Great White Way in Chicago.
- The symbol immediately attached to the New York World's Fair was "The Theme Center," which consisted of two all-white, landmark monumental buildings named the Trylon and the Perisphere, which were entered by a moving stairway and exited via a grand curved walkway named the Helicline.
- The most popular exhibit was General Motors' Model City of Tomorrow that Sister Mary Henry and her class viewed as soon as possible.
- The 36,000-square-foot Futurama exhibit transported visitors over a huge diorama of a section of the United States that was designed with a stunning array of miniature highways, towns, 500,000 individually designed homes, 50,000 miniature vehicles, waterways, and a million miniature trees of diverse species.
- As the visitors seated in moving chairs continued through the exhibit, the diorama gradually grew larger until the cars and other elements became life-size.
- At the end of the Futurama exhibit, fair visitors were given a pin reading: I HAVE SEEN THE FUTURE.

## Life at Work

- Sister Mary Henry's immediate impression of the fair was of water: fountains shooting water, alabaster statues surrounded by falling water, and fountains bubbling with energy.
- Her normally rambunctious seventh graders were awestruck.
- Millions of visitors had already flowed through the gates, millions more would attend before the show closed in 1940, and many would come back dozens of times.
- Attending the fair was not inexpensive: admission was $0.75; bus rides around the fair cost $0.10, and hotdogs and hamburgers were each a dime.
- "A nickel is a coin no one recognizes at the fair," friends told her.
- For years she had been receiving "mad" money from her father and had been saving it for something special—taking her class to the 1939 World's Fair seemed pretty special.
- At the General Motors building, Sister Mary Henry grew anxious with excitement as she and her gaggle of seventh-graders snaked their way up through the tremendous crowds toward the gentle slope of the ramp leading to the huge red and silver facade towering over them.
- "The line behind is a sea of bobbing hats a happy crowd."
- Inside was Futurama—specifically, the exotic world of 1960—seen from moving chairs that glided through a futuristic landscape featuring narration and sound.
- At the Chrysler exhibit, Sister Mary Henry experienced air conditioning for the first time, and the entire class watched a Plymouth being assembled right before their very eyes.
- Days later, the class discussed at length the Westinghouse Time Capsule, which was not to be opened until 6939 AD.
- Inside the capsule was a tube containing writings by Albert Einstein and Thomas Mann, copies of *Life* magazine, a Mickey Mouse watch, a Gillette safety razor, a kewpie doll, a dollar in change, a pack of Camel cigarettes, millions of pages of text on microfilm, and much more.
- The capsule also contained seeds of foods in common use: wheat, corn, oats, tobacco, cotton, flax, rice, soy beans, alfalfa, sugar beets, carrots and barley, all sealed in glass tubes.

*Sister Mary Henry took her class to the World's Fair.*

- When the students prepared their own list of time capsule markers, the list included a "Catholic ruler" to rap students' knuckles, student uniforms, essays on life in 1939 and a fiction story called, "How to Kill Your Big Sister Without Getting Caught."
- The author figured that his secret would be safe for 5,000 years.
- Sister Mary Henry wished she'd had the courage to go on the fair's popular parachute ride, described as "packs more thrills in 90 seconds than any wings-in- sky interlude since Icarus, with landing a lot safer."
- But she knew that it was a poor ride to undertake in a long habit.
- Two Sisters at the school, both with an artistic bent, had insisted that she visit the fair's highly publicized art exhibition—a collection assembled from around the world—headlined by Vermeer's painting *The Milkmaid* from the Rijksmuseum in Amsterdam.
- In all, 300 priceless works of the Old Masters—from the Middle Ages to 1800—were on exhibition: works from Leonardo da Vinci and Michelangelo to Rembrandt, from Hals to Caravaggio and Bellini.
- One of her musically oriented students wanted to see the keyboard-operated speech synthesizer, but Sister Mary Henry was especially drawn to the British Pavilion where a copy of Magna Carta belonging to Lincoln Cathedral was on display.
- "Imagine," she told herself as she peered at the contract from 1215, "getting to personally view the document that had shaped Western civilization, including a direct influence on the United States Constitution."
- The Jewish Palestine Pavilion introduced the students—and much of the world—to the concept of a modern Jewish State.
- The fair was the first public demonstration of several lighting technologies, especially the first fluorescent light and fixture.
- The class heard predictions that in the "World of Tomorrow," automobiles would be available for purchase at $200 in 1960, America's new interstate highway system would incorporate lookout towers every five miles, and radio controls within automobiles would help them maintain a proper distance from each other.
- The emergence and role of the American middle class was represented by the Middleton family enjoying the new products being manufactured to make life easier and affordable: the automatic dishwasher and Elecktro, a seven-foot-tall talking robot.
- At the IBM pavilion, the class discussed the merits of electric typewriters, and an electric calculator that used punched cards.
- Other firsts at the fair included color photography, nylon, the View-Master, and Smell-O-Vision.

## Life in the Community: New York City

- When the New York World's Fair opened in 1939, New York City's population was 7.5 million, the second-largest city in the world behind London.
- New York City's diverse, immigrant-charged population exceeded every state in the union.
- This teeming mass of energy supported eight major daily newspapers and 35 foreign-language dailies including three in Italian and four in Yiddish.
- The modern City of New York was formed 1898 with the consolidation of Brooklyn, Manhattan, the Bronx and outlying areas.
- Throughout the first half of the twentieth century, the city became a world center for industry, commerce, and communication.
- Interborough Rapid Transit (the first New York City subway company) began operating in 1904, and the railroads operating out of Grand Central Terminal and Pennsylvania Station thrived.
- As the city's demographics stabilized, labor unionization brought new protections and affluence to the working class; the city's government and infrastructure underwent a dramatic overhaul under Fiorello La Guardia; and his controversial parks commissioner, Robert Moses, ended the blight of many tenement areas, expanded new parks, remade streets, and restricted and reorganized zoning controls.

Life in the Community: New York City

- The skyscraper epitomized New York's success of the early twentieth century; the city was home to the tallest building beginning in 1908.
- The Harlem Renaissance flourished during the 1920s and the era of Prohibition, coincident with a larger economic boom that saw the skyline develop with the construction of competing skyscrapers.
- For a while, New York City became the most populous city in the world starting in 1925, overtaking London, which had reigned for a century.
- The 1930s saw the building of some of the world's tallest skyscrapers, including numerous art deco masterpieces that set the tone for vast areas of the city to be reshaped by the construction of bridges, parks and parkways.
- Catholic parochial schools were instituted in the United States in the 1840s as a reaction against a growing publicly funded school system that was essentially Protestant.
- In 1900, an estimated 3,500 parochial schools existed in the U.S.
- By the time Sister Mary Henry was preparing to teach, the number of elementary schools had reached 6,551, enrolling 1,759,673 pupils taught by 41,581 teachers.
- Secondary education likewise boomed.
- In 1900, there were only about 100 Catholic high schools, but by 1920 more than 1,500 were in operation.

*Catholic schools were on the rise in New York City.*

# HISTORICAL SNAPSHOT
# 1939

- The Hewlett-Packard Company was founded

- Aviation pioneer Amelia Earhart was officially declared dead after her disappearance

- Adolf Hitler ordered Plan Z, a five-year naval expansion program intended to establish a huge German fleet capable of crushing the Royal Navy by 1944

- British Prime Minister Neville Chamberlain stated in the House of Commons that any German attack on France would be automatically considered an attack on Britain

- The Golden Gate International Exposition opened in San Francisco

- Sit-down strikes were outlawed by the Supreme Court

- Billie Holiday recorded "Strange Fruit," the first anti-lynching song

- Major League Baseball's Lou Gehrig, the legendary Yankee first baseman known as "The Iron Horse," ended his 2,130 consecutive games played streak after being diagnosed with amyotrophic lateral sclerosis

- Pan-American Airways began transatlantic mail service

- The sculpture of Theodore Roosevelt's face was dedicated at Mount Rushmore

- Albert Einstein wrote to President Franklin Roosevelt about developing the atomic bomb using uranium, leading to the creation of the Manhattan Project

- MGM's classic musical film *The Wizard of Oz*, based on L. Frank Baum's famous novel and starring Judy Garland, premiered

- German ships fired on the fortress Westerplatte, a Polish army installation at the mouth of the port of Danzig

- The United Kingdom, France, New Zealand, and Australia declared war on Germany; President Roosevelt advocated neutrality

- Gerald J. Cox, speaking at an American Water Works Association meeting, proposed the fluoridation of public water supplies in the United States

- *The Time of Your Life*, a drama by William Saroyan, debuted in New York City

- Roosevelt ordered the U.S. Customs Service to implement the Neutrality Act of 1939, allowing cash-and-carry purchases of weapons to non-belligerent nations

- The nearly four-hour film *Gone with the Wind*, starring Vivien Leigh, Clark Gable, Olivia de Havilland and Leslie Howard, premiered

- General Motors introduced the Hydra-Matic drive, the first mass-produced, fully automatic transmission, as an option in 1940 model year Oldsmobiles

## Selected Prices

| | |
|---|---|
| Flashlight | $0.55 |
| Fountain Pen | $1.00 |
| Lawn Mower, Power | $69.50 |
| Movie Camera | $49.50 |
| Movie Ticket | $0.25 |
| Nylons | $1.95 |
| Pocket Telescope | $1.00 |
| Seat Covers, Sedan | $5.85 |
| Toothpaste | $0.25 |
| Wall Clock | $6.98 |

## "The World of Tomorrow" The Official New York World's Fair Pamphlet, 1939:

The eyes of the Fair are on the future—not in the sense of peering toward the unknown nor attempting to foretell the events of tomorrow and the shape of things to come, but in the sense of presenting a new and clearer view of today in preparation for tomorrow; a view of the forces and ideas that prevail as well as the machines. To its visitors the Fair will say: "Here are the materials, ideas, and forces at work in our world. These are the tools with which the World of Tomorrow must be made. They are all interesting and much effort has been expended to lay them before you in an interesting way. Familiarity with today is the best preparation for the future.'"

## "President Cites U.S. as World Peace Pattern," *Salt Lake Tribune* (Utah), May 1, 1939:

President Roosevelt told a war-frightened world Sunday the United States stood united in a desire to "encourage peace" and expressed for "all the Americans" the hope that the years to come will "break down many barriers of intercourse" between nations in Europe.

Opening the mammoth New York World's Fair on the Flushing Meadows of Long Island, the chief executive avoided any reference to Chancellor Hitler's Reichstag address, but re-dedicated America to the cause of international goodwill and declared her wagon was "hitched to a star."

"But it is a star of goodwill, a star of progress for mankind, a star of greater happiness and less hardship, a star of international goodwill, and above all, the star of peace," he said.

"May the months to come carry us forward in the rays of that hope."

The president spoke in the outdoor "court of peace."

On the speaker stand were the President's wife and mother and other members of his family. Representatives of many of the 60 nations exhibiting at the fair were present, as were some members of the Supreme Court and cabinet....

## "Here's the Set Up of the New York Fair," *Salt Lake Tribune* (Utah), May 1, 1939:

Here are a few pertinent facts about the New York World's Fair, which opened Sunday.

Cost: $160 million

Area: 1,216 and 1/2 acres

Participants: 60 foreign governments, 35 states, 747 concessions, 1,500 exhibitors

Personnel: 41,750

Buildings: Fair exhibits, 20; other major structures, 32; foreign flooring, 23; states, 17

Heights: Trylon, 700 feet; Perisphere 200 feet in diameter

Distance From Times Square: a half-mile

Gates: Capacity, 11 gates, total of 160,000 persons an hour

BRITE

# 1940–1949

The dramatic, all-encompassing nature of World War II dominated the economy and the lives of working Americans in the 1940s. Teacher shortages were pervasive as America's industries ramped up to fight the Nazis and the Japanese. Overcrowded classrooms were the result of teachers and administrators joining the service and large numbers of experienced teachers abandoning the classroom for the higher pay available in industry. One of the most lasting impacts of the war was the creation of the GI Bill, which helped fund vocational training and college for returning veterans. The opportunity for a large number of former soldiers and sailors to receive advanced degrees fueled innovation and the size of the middle class. During the seven years that these benefits were provided, 7.8 million veterans received some form of post-secondary education.

Business worked in partnership with the government; strikes were reduced, but key New Deal labor concessions were expanded, including a 40-hour work week and time and a half pay for overtime. As manufacturing demands increased, the labor pool shrank, while wages and union membership rose. Unemployment, which stood as high as 14 percent in 1940, all but disappeared. By 1944, the U.S. was producing twice the total war output of the Axis powers combined. The wartime demand for production workers rose more rapidly than for skilled workers, reducing the wage gap between the two to the lowest level in the twentieth century.

From 1940 to 1945, the gross national product more than doubled, from $100 billion to $211 billion, despite rationing and the unavailability of many consumer goods such as cars, gasoline, and washing machines. Interest rates remained low, and the upward pressure on prices remained high, yet from 1943 to the end of the war, the cost of living rose less than 1.5 percent. Following the war, as controls were removed, inflation peaked in 1948, and union demands for high wages accelerated. Between 1945 and 1952, confident Americans—and their growing families—increased consumer credit by 800 percent.

To fight inflation, government agencies regulated wages, prices, and the kinds of jobs people could take. The Office of Price

Administration was entrusted with the complicated task of setting price ceilings for almost all consumer goods and distributing ration books for items in short supply. The Selective Service and the War Manpower Commission largely determined who would serve in the military, whose work was vital to the war effort, and when a worker could transfer from one job to another. When the war ended and regulations were lifted, relations between labor and management became strained. Massive strikes and inflation followed in the closing days of the decade, and many consumer goods were easier to find on the black market than on the store shelves until America retooled for a peacetime economy. The decade saw the flowering of composer Irving Berlin, the development of bebop, and the stirrings of rock 'n' roll. By 1948, the long-playing record was introduced, and the following year, *Billboard* substituted the phrase "rhythm and blues," for "race records."

The 1940s made America a world power and Americans more worldly. Millions served overseas; millions more listened to broadcasts concerning the war in London, Rome, and Tokyo. Newsreels brought the war home to moviegoers, who numbered in the millions. The war effort also redistributed the population and the demand for labor; the Pacific Coast gained wealth and power, and the South was able to supply its people with much-needed war jobs and provide blacks with opportunities previously closed to them. Women entered the work force in unprecedented numbers, reaching 18 million. The net cash income of the American farmer soared 400 percent.

But the Second World War exacted a price. Those who experienced combat entered a nightmarish world. Both sides possessed far greater firepower than ever before, and within those units actually fighting the enemy, the incidence of death was high, sometimes one in three. In all, the United States lost 405,000 men and women to combat deaths; many suffered in the war's final year, when the Army spearheaded the assault against Germany and Japan. The cost in dollars was $350 billion. But the cost was not only in American lives. Following Germany's unconditional surrender on May 4, 1945, Japan continued fighting. To prevent the loss of thousands of American lives defeating the Japanese, President Truman dropped atomic bombs on the Japanese cities of Hiroshima and Nagasaki, ending the war and ushering in the threat of "the bomb" as a key element of the Cold War during the 1950s and 1960s.

Throughout the war, soldiers from all corners of the nation fought side by side and, through this government-imposed mixing process, refined nationalism and what it meant to America. This newfound identity of American GIs was further cemented by the vivid descriptions of war correspondent Ernie Pyle, who spent a considerable time talking and living with the average soldier to present a "worm's eye view" of war. Yet, despite the closeness many men and women developed toward their fellow soldiers, discrimination continued. African-American servicemen were excluded from the Marines, the Coast Guard, and the Army Corps. The regular army accepted blacks into the military—700,000 in all—only on a segregated basis. Only in the closing years of the decade would President Harry Truman lead the way toward a more integrated America by integrating the military. Sports attendance in the 1940s soared beyond the record levels of the 1920s; in football, the T-formation moved to prominence; Joe DiMaggio, Ted Williams, and Stan Musial dominated baseball before and after the war; and Jackie Robinson became the first black in organized baseball. In 1946, Dr. Benjamin Spock's work, *Common Sense Baby and Child Care*, was published to guide newcomers in the booming business of raising babies. The decade also discovered the joys of fully air-conditioned stores for the first time, cellophane wrap, Morton salt, Daylight Saving Time, Dannon yogurt, the Everglades National Park, the Cannes Film Festival, Michelin radial tires, Dial soap, and Nikon 35 mm film.

# 1943 NEWS FEATURE

**"Against That Day!" Dorothy Brooks Paul,** *American Home*, **January 1943:**

Your government has created a War Damage Corporation and now, through the facilities of the fire insurance companies in the country and their representatives, you can obtain war damage insurance on your home and property for as little as $0.10 per $100 per year. This insurance is not obligatory, but your government wants you to know that it is available for you to purchase and urges you to do so for your own protection. It is interesting to note that in the first two months after the War Damage Corporation was created, more than 3.5 million policies were issued, involving $100 million worth of coverage.

This coverage is something with which every housewife, homeowner and tenant should be very familiar. You can obtain the insurance by contacting your insurance agent or broker. The War Damage Corporation is an agency set up by the federal government to offer protection to property owners in the event of damage to their property which may result from enemy attack, including any action taken by the military, naval and air force of the United States in resisting the enemy attack. The insurance companies in the country have offered their cooperation and the facilities of their services in writing this coverage. The premium is payable with the application and, in the event of loss, the claim will be paid within 60 days after applicable proof of loss is received by the War Damage Corporation. Your policy will cover your home and its contents, your automobile and practically every form of personal property. The minimum premium for which you can obtain it is $3.00.

In whatever part of the country you live, you must be aware of the precautions being taken against enemy air raid attack. If you live in any of the coastal areas, blackouts and dimouts are familiar occurrences and you have taken the necessary steps to prevent fires caused by incendiary bombs. You have been urged to provide yourself with pails of sand, a shovel, in some cases a stirrup pump, and if you live in a section where dimout regulations are in force for the duration of the war, you probably have provided your home with blackout curtains. But have you made more preparation, or even giving any further thought to the matter?

Our entire country is vulnerable to enemy attack. It is entirely conceivable that, instead of, or in addition to, sending bombers to the coastal areas, the enemy might send planes into the Hudson Bay area by boat and from there fly them into various industrial centers of the Middle West. The tactics of the enemy are not only to destroy defense plants, airfields and army concentrations, but to terrify the citizens and break down the morale of our country. Moreover, bombs do not always reach their objectives, but sometimes hit defenseless residential areas. Consequently, there is no part of the country that would be absolutely safe from enemy attack—not even the deep interior.

We hope that the blitz will never come to the United States. But if it should, are you protected? You do not buy fire insurance on your property in anticipation of a fire, but as a precaution should fire come. For the same reason, you should buy war damage insurance. It is not expensive—it is, in fact, cheap, for a $5,000 policy on your home costs only $5.00, and you'd really be protected.

# 1945 PROFILE

In times of war, everyone had to make sacrifices, but Martha Deaton was convinced that her high school students would not be prepared for the world they were about to enter.

## Life at Home

- When Martha Deaton took a long look at her ninth-grade history class, she had but one conclusion: America's schools were one of the primary casualties of the current World War.

- Thirty-nine students were crammed into a space designed for 28; children in shock over the recent deaths of brothers and fathers were being asked to dispassionately study the Peloponnesian War; rationed food, blaring headlines of even more fighting, and a total lack of qualified teachers were ever present.

- In her senior American history class, overcrowding was less an issue: within a week, two young men volunteered for the Army, while three more boys were anticipating their induction notices.

- And now that Martha was also teaching a class in world literature—to cover for a teacher whose son was recently wounded— her preparation time had doubled and her one free period had vanished.

*Teaching during war time was challenging for high school teacher Martha Deaton.*

- The same war that had disrupted family life and heightened emotional tensions had placed an additional responsibility on schools to guide the younger generation toward self-reliance.

- Between 20,000 and 25,000 teaching positions had been abandoned in the name of patriotism and war, resulting in overcrowded classrooms and dispirited teachers.
- Martha began her teaching career on the farm when, at the age of four, she corralled a gaggle of chickens into one end of the barn where she proceeded to teach them to count.
- Grades went unrecorded as the hens scratched their way to giggly, gleeful success.
- The second of four children, Martha learned to read when she was three, preached a "youth sermon" at church on her seventh birthday, and tutored eighth-graders in math when she was only 10.
- Martha's mother constantly talked about her precocious daughter; Martha's father, a structural engineer, rarely spoke at all, yet made prodigious efforts to attend piano recitals, district-wide writing contests and school plays.
- Martha attended a local teacher's college on a scholarship, fell in and out of love several times before discovering Mr. Right, and accepted her first job as a special education teacher in one of the toughest schools in Ohio.
- There she learned a lifetime's worth of lessons about standing her ground and looking beyond stereotypes; the administration had been ordered by the Board of Supervisors to institute the program.
- Martha's principal wanted the program to fail, Martha to quit, and the handicapped children to go away from his school.
- He received his wish, with a twist: after a year the principal was asked to leave, while Martha and the children stayed.
- She then tried teaching third-graders, followed by a stint with seventh-graders before finding her home with high school teenagers, whose influence on cultural and economic society was being recognized, advertised and highlighted in every major newspaper.
- Now that high school graduation rates had jumped from 10 percent in 1900, when high schools were in their infancy, to 30 percent in 1930, Martha thought that the 50 percent now being attained would go even higher.
- Already a greater emphasis was being placed on the teens.
- *Seventeen*, an American magazine for teenagers created in 1944, was squarely aimed at young girls and women.
- Article headings such as "What You Wear" and "Having Fun" were clearly aimed at expanding the American consumer market beyond adults.

## Life at Work

- Thirty-one-year-old Martha Deaton wished that the foreman at the Cincinnati weapons plant would stop recruiting teachers to work in the factory.
- Plainly, women with teaching degrees could do more to service the cause of peace by staying in the schools.
- Besides, once the war ended—as it surely would one day—the factories would turn their backs on women again; it happened after World War I and it would happen this time, too, Martha believed.
- The only time women received any respect was when men needed something.
- More than any war in history, World War II was a battle of production.
- After all, the Germans and the Japanese had had a 10-year head start on amassing weapons, so rapid production of military equipment was essential to victory, and women were the last labor reserve.
- When President Franklin D. Roosevelt asked in 1940 for 50,000 airplanes a year, critics lampooned the goal, but by 1944, the U.S. was producing 120,000 planes annually.
- Half of the aircraft were built in plants where more than half of the employees were female; ammunition plants, shipyards and equipment factories recorded similar gender employment.

- To meet the aggressive goals, industry recruited educated, middle-class housewives who had never dreamed of working outside the home.
- They were willing to serve their country, but not under dirty, dangerous conditions.
- First-generation immigrant women spurned the environment thrust upon them; working conditions improved for all and harsh disciplinary techniques were abandoned for more positive incentives.
- Shortages were so acute, women were recruited from surrounding states and counties to fill job openings and were provided buses for commuting or dormitories for those who needed housing.
- In some rural locations, the new women workers had never used telephones or flush toilets, but their pay gave them access to independence, skills and confidence they had never experienced before.
- In 1940, 12 million women were working; five years later there were 19 million in the workforce.

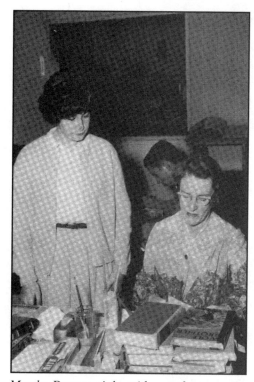

*Martha Deaton, right, with a student.*

- It was time for firsts for many women— including teachers who benefited from the competitive atmosphere for workers.
- For more than 100 years, school boards—mostly composed of men—had imposed onerous rules on teachers' behavior—including where they could live, how they might socialize, the color of the clothes they could wear and how ashes from the schoolhouse fire must be removed.
- Women who married often had to stop teaching; married teachers who became pregnant were asked to step down.
- Now that industry was sniffing around for help, married women were suddenly acceptable and some school boards even made exceptions for childbirth.
- One national survey showed that 39 percent of school superintendents approved of the marriage prohibitions for teachers and 52 percent disapproved.
- But if highly vocal, tax-paying citizens opposed married teachers, many superintendents found it too risky to confront them.
- Men were considered the breadwinners and a wife's pay purely supplemental.
- It was generally believed that teachers were more likely than blue-collar women to be married to white collar men, and as such, had more economic flexibility to resign their jobs when they married.
- Some middle-class husbands simply would not allow their wives to work.
- In October of 1939, there were virtually no teaching jobs available nationwide; by October 1943, 7,000 jobs went unfilled and 57,000 had been filled by teachers who could not meet regular certification.
- U.S. Commissioner of Education John W. Studebaker said that during the course of the national emergency, as many as 115,000 teachers had left the nation's classrooms to help the war effort in one way or another.

**WAR**

**needs the wires**

**this Christmas**

War can't wait—not even for Christmas. So please don't make Long Distance calls to war-busy centers this Christmas unless they're vital.

BELL TELEPHONE SYSTEM

*U.S. Commissioner of Education John Studebaker, standing, worried that recruiting teachers for the war effort resulted in understaffed schools and overcrowded classrooms.*

- "Every community can testify to the competent and unselfish job teachers have done both at their posts and in voluntary wartime tasks of rationing, salvaging and bond sales. But the fact remains that at this critical time in our history, between 20,000 and 25,000 positions have been abandoned and thousands of classes are overcrowded."
- Rights had come begrudgingly slowly to teachers.
- The question of whether married women could still teach was litigated in 1937 when a New Jersey tenured teacher was asked to sign a contract that reduced her pay to a level designated for married teachers; the State Supreme Court ruled the classification "unreasonable and thus invalid."
- Society as a whole believed women could be superior teachers, especially for the lower grades, because of biological predestination and the natural affinity for children.
- Ironically, motherhood was often the reason a teacher was asked to step aside.
- A bevy of studies concerning the competence of married women scrutinized everything from the number of sick days they could have to what they did on Saturdays, the number of dependents, their service participation, and whether eighth-graders liked them more than single women.
- Teachers found "no distinct differences in social, recreational, and professional life of married and single women as teachers."
- Yet reformers saw working women as dangerous to the family ideal, while feminists considered employment a prerequisite for female independence.
- What was also true was that the higher the visibility of a job, the more likely it was to encounter societal discrimination; considerably less was said about female factory workers and domestics.

- Suddenly, the war presented female teachers with a unique bargaining position; once shortages occurred, teachers' viewpoints became more important.
- Martha had faced similar challenges through the years, and though they were not pleasant, she had been allowed to continue teaching.
- She was also determined that her daughter would not be subjected to similar economic discrimination.
- If men could change the rules when a war necessity dictated, they could keep the reforms once the danger had passed.
- After World War II broke out, Wellesley College assistant professor of education Isabel Stephens studied the opportunities provided by teaching versus the expanded job market.
- For college-educated women, she found five reasons to leave the field of education: 1) lack of community support, 2) lack of intellectual interchange, 3) petty gossip in the schools, 4) a system where scientific efficiency was valued over ideas, 5) the practice of firing women if they married.

## Life in the Community: Cincinnati, Ohio

- At the dawn of the 1940s, Cincinnati was the 14th biggest city in the United States, bustling with life and still proud of its title as the Gateway to the West.
- During World War II, gas and rubber were tightly rationed for everyone in the United States, and in Cincinnati, the streetcar became a popular means of transportation.
- Rationing seemed to suit the people of the Queen City, and the 1940s in the tri-state area were constantly hopping with development, art and culture.
- Cincinnati sweetheart Doris Day was just beginning her famous career in the city in the 1940s, performing as a vocalist for local bands and building her reputation just as the city was beginning to fade.
- Cincinnati's public schools ranged from nursery schools to a municipal university.
- In addition, several elementary and 16 parochial high schools and academies were scattered throughout the city, along with two Catholic colleges in three theological schools—Catholic, Protestant, and Jewish.
- Settled in 1788, by the early nineteenth century, Cincinnati was the first American boomtown in the heart of the country and rivaled the larger coastal cities in size and wealth.
- As one of the first major inland cities, Cincinnati earned a reputation as "the first purely American city."
- It was originally named "Losantiville" from four terms, each from a different language, meaning "the city opposite the mouth of the Licking River."
- In 1790, Arthur St. Clair, the governor of the Northwest Territory, changed the name of the settlement to "Cincinnati" in honor of the Society of the Cincinnati, of which he was a member.
- The Society honored General George Washington, who was considered a latter-day Cincinnatus, the Roman farmer who was called to serve Rome as dictator, an office which he resigned after completing his task of defeating the Aequians in no less than 16 days, and was considered the role model dictator.
- Cincinnati was incorporated as a city in 1819; the introduction of steam navigation on the Ohio River in 1811 and the completion of the Miami and Erie Canal helped the city grow to 115,000 residents by 1850.
- To protect its growth, the city began paying men to act as its fire department in 1853, creating the first full-time, paid fire department in the United States and the first in the world to use steam fire engines.

- Six years later, in 1859, Cincinnati laid out six streetcar lines, making it easier for people to get around the city.
- By 1872, Cincinnatians could travel on the streetcars within the city and transfer to railcars for travel to the hill communities.
- The Cincinnati Red Stockings, a baseball team whose name and heritage inspired the Cincinnati Reds, began their career in the nineteenth century as well, and became the first professional team in the country in 1869.
- In 1879, Procter & Gamble, one of Cincinnati's major soap manufacturers, began marketing Ivory Soap. It was marketed as "light enough to float."
- By the end of the nineteenth century, with the industrial shift from steamboats to railroads, Cincinnati's growth had slowed considerably and was surpassed in population and prominence by Chicago.
- Cincinnati weathered the Great Depression better than most American cities of its size, largely because of resurgence in river trade, which was less expensive than rail.
- The rejuvenation of the downtown area began in the 1920s and continued into the next decade with the construction of Union Terminal, the post office, and a large Bell Telephone building.
- The flood of 1937 was one of the worst in the nation's history; afterwards, the city built protective flood walls.

## HISTORICAL SNAPSHOT
# 1945

- Franklin D. Roosevelt was inaugurated to an unprecedented fourth term as president

- In the Philippines, 121 American soldiers and 800 Filipino guerrillas freed 813 American POWs from the Japanese-held camp at Cabanatuan City

- The Soviet Union agreed to enter the Pacific War against Japan once hostilities against Germany were concluded

- President Roosevelt, Prime Minister Winston Churchill, and Soviet leader Joseph Stalin held the Yalta Conference

- Chile, Ecuador, Paraguay, and Peru joined the United Nations

- In the Battle of Iwo Jima, approximately 30,000 U.S. Marines landed on Iwo Jima

- Dutch diarist Anne Frank died in the Bergen-Belsen concentration camp

- The film *Les Enfants du Paradis* premiered in Paris

- American B-29 bombers attacked Tokyo with incendiary bombs, killing 100,000 citizens

- The 17th Academy Awards ceremony was broadcast via radio for the first time; the Best Picture award went to *Going My Way*

- American bombers numbering 1,250 attacked Berlin

- Sylvester the cat debuted in *Life with Feathers*

- Adolph Hitler, along with his wife Eva Braun, committed suicide on April 30, 1945

- President Roosevelt died suddenly at Warm Springs, Georgia; Vice President Harry S. Truman became the thirty-third president

- Rodgers and Hammerstein's *Carousel* opened on Broadway

- Poet and author Ezra Pound was arrested by American soldiers in Italy for treason

- The Trinity Test, the first test of an atomic bomb, used about six kilograms of plutonium and unleashed an explosion equivalent to that of 19 kilotons of TNT

- Winston Churchill resigned as prime minister after his Conservative Party was soundly defeated by the Labour Party in the 1945 general election

- The United Nations Charter was ratified by the U.S., the third nation to join the new international organization

- The Zionist World Congress approached the British government to discuss the founding of the country of Israel

- Emperor Hirohito announced Japan's surrender on the radio; the United States called that day V-J Day for Victory over Japan

- Writer Arthur C. Clarke advanced the idea of a communications satellite in a *Wireless World* magazine article

- The Detroit Tigers won the baseball World Series against the Chicago Cubs

- At Gimbels Department Store in New York City, the first ballpoint pens cost $12.50 each

## Selected Prices

Ashtray ............................................................................$8.50

Automobile, De Soto .................................................$2,200.00

Deep Freezer .................................................................$225.00

Fountain Pen ..................................................................$15.00

Home Permanent Kit.........................................................$1.40

Radio Phonograph.........................................................$199.95

Record Cabinet..............................................................$13.50

Records, Four 12" ...........................................................$4.72

Silk Stockings ..................................................................$0.98

Wrenches, Set of Six.........................................................$2.85

### "Education," *1944 Britannica Book of the Year*, 1944:

#### The Shortage of Teachers

The shortage of teachers, which had already begun to make itself felt in 1942, increased during 1943, when it was estimated that more than 100,000 teachers had left the profession to join the armed forces or to enter defense industries. It was anticipated that this number would continue to grow, particularly since steps were not taken immediately to adjust teachers' salaries to the increasing cost of living. With 40 percent of the teachers receiving less than $1,200 a year and 8 percent less than $600 a year, the temptation to enter well-paid positions in defense industries could not be resisted. The exodus of teachers was in the main from rural and village schools; teachers who left the urban schools were chiefly those whose special training was needed in defense industries and by the armed forces. The effect on all schools—rural and urban—was serious. In rural schools it was estimated that about 6,000,000 pupils would be taught by inexperienced teachers, assuming that the schools were open at all. In urban schools, serious difficulties were encountered in replacing teachers of mathematics, chemistry, physics, and industrial and physical education. The War Manpower Commission, as a result of pressure brought to bear upon it by school officials and educational associations, declared teaching an essential occupation and sought, under its stabilization plan, to regulate the transfer of teachers from one position to another for increased pay. Nevertheless, the turnover of teachers was nearly double that of any normal year (189,000 as compared to 95,000).

In an effort to check the migration from the profession, a variety of schemes were tried. Attention was directed to the importance of education in a democracy; parent-teacher associations conducted publicity campaigns among the public and among teachers; promises of better conditions of service, tenure and old-age security were made; promising candidates were encouraged to enter the profession; and emergency training classes were established for inexperienced teachers or for those who had been out of the profession for some time and wished to help during the emergency....

#### The Exodus From School

It was estimated by the middle of 1943 that at least 2,000,000 boys and girls between the ages of 14 and 18 had left school to enter wage-earning occupations, and that of these, 25 percent were under 15. This was a consequence of the labor shortage and the high wages which could be earned after a very short period of training. To some extent, the disruption of school organization due to the shortage of teachers and lax enforcement of compulsory attendance laws may have exercised some influence. The situation became sufficiently serious for the War Manpower Commission, the Children's Bureau of the Department of Labor, and the U.S. Office of Education to issue an announcement to urban communities stating that "The first obligation of school youth is to take advantage of their educational opportunities in

*Continued*

## "Education,". . . *(Continued)*

order that they be prepared for citizenship and for service to the nation ... school authorities, employers, parents and other interested parties should recognize the obligation to safeguard the physical and intellectual development of youth." The Educational Policies Commission of the National Education Association issued a similar recommendation: "School attendance until graduation is the best contribution to the war effort which school age youth can make." Both groups urged that arrangements be made to combine part-time work in war occupations with the continuation of regular schooling until high school graduation. Not only was the academic education of youth being sabotaged, but young workers were being exploited and were not being paid the "wages paid to adult workers for similar job performances."

### Federal Aid for Education

The effort to secure federal aid for education, which began during World War I, was continued during 1943, but was again defeated. Since 1917, the need for federal aid to implement the American ideal of equality in educational opportunity was believed by some educators to be greater than ever. The war revealed differences in educational provisions in the country as never before. Under the selective draft systems, large numbers of draftees were shown to be wholly or functionally illiterate, and another large number were rejected on physical grounds. The shortage of teachers revealed the low standards of remuneration which prevailed in the country.

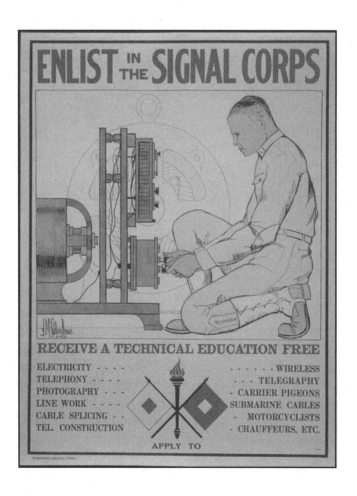

**"Bible Teacher for Elementary Schools Named,"**
*The Asheville Times* **(North Carolina), January 14, 1946:**

Miss Mary Ann Dendy of Weaverville has been elected teacher of Bible for Asheville elementary schools and will assume her duties tomorrow, it has been announced.

A graduate of Weaverville high school and Mars Hill College, Miss Dendy received a bachelor of arts degree in religious education from Erskine College, Due West, South Carolina, in 1945 and did graduate study work in Bible at Columbia Seminary in Decatur, Georgia....

Miss Dendy's appointment was announced by L. T. New, chairman of the Bible in the Schools executive committee.

Mr. New pointed out that the committee launched a campaign last August to raise funds to make employment of a fourth Bible teacher for the city schools possible, and that, since a teacher was not available for the first semester of school work, the $1,006 raised from the campaign was held in trust until a teacher could be obtained.

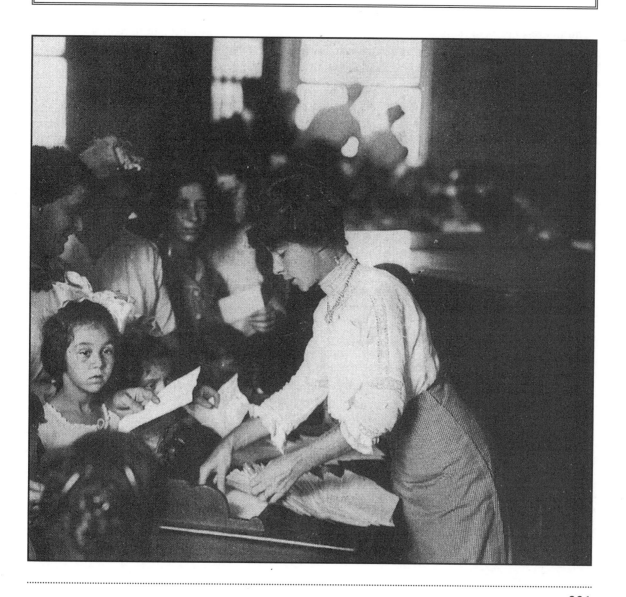

## "Major Problems: Teacher Shortage,"
### *Waukesha Daily Freeman* (Wisconsin), September 10, 1949:

Any discussion of the problems facing schools must start, of course, with the teacher shortage. For in the final analysis, the teacher is the school; the teacher is the curriculum.

A district may have an excellent building and the finest equipment available, but if the teacher is poor, the school is poor. On the other hand, a good teacher can often provide a good school despite numerous handicaps.

Because the nearest state Teachers College has virtually stopped preparing rural teachers, we here in Waukesha County have been very seriously hampered by the teacher shortage. The recruitment of teachers has become one of the major duties of the county office. After tremendous efforts throughout the summer, we finally filled all vacancies. But then our real problems began, for many of these new teachers were unprepared and must be given detailed, continuous guidance in educational policies and methods. Thus, in addition to being an employment bureau, the Office of County Superintendent has become a sort of a mobile college for on-the-job training of teachers.

This year, we have in the county 66 special emergency permit teachers, which is the same number as last year. This would indicate that we are holding our ground, but in reality we are not, and unless conditions change suddenly it will probably be several years before the supply of teachers balances the demand, especially in the elementary field.

Our factory superintendents complain that the high turnover of workers impairs and slows down production. This is, of course, true, but the turnover of a Waukesha industry comparable in size to our school system was only 20 percent last year, whereas the turnover of teachers in our county was 33 percent.

It is, therefore, clear that the problem of labor shortage is much more intensive in education than in industry. It is also more serious, for the production by the schools of an inferior product has a much more dramatic and lasting effect upon our civilization than the production by industry of an inferior motor or refrigerator.

In fact, we have ample evidence to support the argument that the teacher shortage is one of the most perplexing problems facing America today.

### The Handicapped Child

It is fitting and proper that we improve the education of normal children, but at the same time we must not neglect the mentally and physically handicapped. These children who, through the force of circumstances, are not able to meet the standards set up for normal boys and girls need special attention for their own sake and for the sake of society in general.

Years ago, when Dr. G. O. Banting was president of the Wisconsin Education Association, he made a significant speech on this problem at the State Teachers Convention. In his speech he pointed out that just as one weak rail can wreck the midnight express, so one misguided boy can bring chaos to humanity.

*Continued*

## "Major Problems . . . *(Continued)*

For years, the State of Wisconsin has appropriated a large sum of money to eight cities in the employment of special teachers of handicapped children. Through action on the last legislature, these funds are now available to counties. Under this new arrangement, several counties are employing or taking the steps to employ special teachers. Here in our county we need:

1. A speech correctionist to work with stutterers, children with cleft palates, etc.
2. A specially trained instructor to assist mentally retarded children and establish and supervise opportunity rooms.

As the state bears three-fourths of the cost of these workers, and as the problem of the handicapped child is becoming more and more acute in our overcrowded schools, Waukesha County cannot for long put off the employment of such educational specialists.

## "We Stick Our Neck Out," *Predictions of Things To Come*, March, 1943:

- Dried eggs will become an increasingly important food commodity.
- Women's fashion reflecting an African influence will be promoted next fall.
- If and when razor blades are rationed, American men will cultivate beards and mustaches.
- Because of the increasing number of women engaged in war work, the wearing of slacks will become more and more popular.
- Metal and plastic screw caps for tubes of drug and toilet goods will shortly be replaced by caps made of tough, fibrous stock covered at the end with a printed label.
- The Alcan Highway (which is the official name of the new Alaska-Canada highway that has just been completed) will become, after the war, one of the greatest tourist attractions of the age. Scenery, as well as the hunting and fishing en route, will be incomparable.
- Most colleges will drop intercollegiate football next fall for the duration.
- Next summer, the percentage of women who will go stockingless will increase many times.
- Rudolph Hess will be put on trial after the war, but not until then. It will be one of the most sensational trials in the history of the world.
- Pennies will be made of steel and coated with zinc to release copper for war industries as soon as Congress passes permissive legislation.
- Double movie features will decline, especially during the war. The government is discouraging them, because there is a shortage of film and because it wishes to increase the use of one-reel films which contribute towards civilians' morale and the war effort.

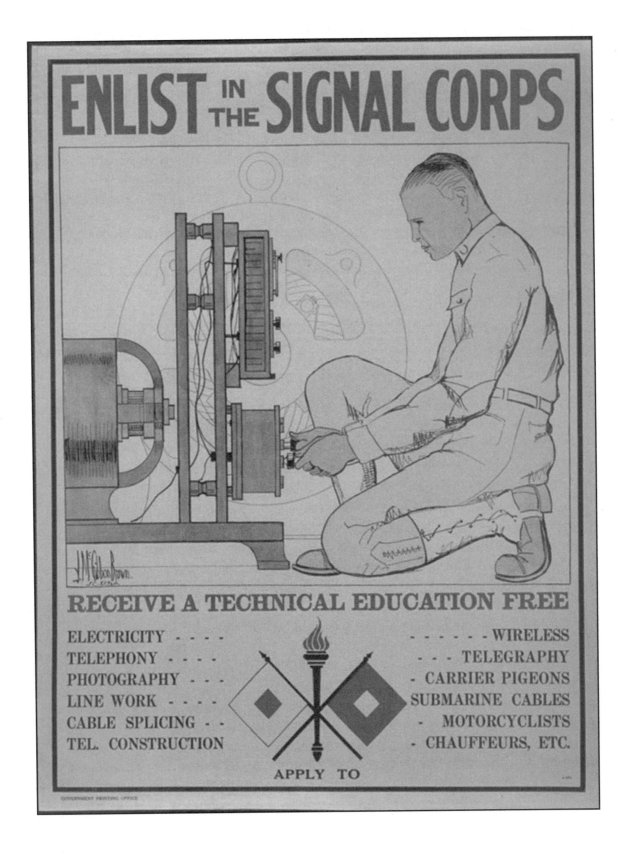

# 1948 PROFILE

Steven Diner's proudest moment as a fifth-grader was being selected as a member of the Junior Safety Patrol, a club for future leaders, organized in cooperation with the Seattle Police Department.

## Life at Home

- Steven Diner—known as Rocky to his friends— was pleased that grades were not the only criterion used for selection in the Schoolboy Patrol; not all subjects were created equal, and sometimes turning in all your homework was a royal pain.
- The Schoolboy Patrol was an exclusive club at Loyal Heights Elementary School in Seattle, composed of students believed to be future leaders.
- No girls were allowed; the Patrol was organized by the school in cooperation with the Seattle Police Department.
- It provided trained crossing guards at two intersections near the school grounds.
- Besides, everyone at school recognized that Rocky was the best kickballer around and was frequently picked to captain a team; he even picked a few younger kids to play on his team— something his older brother taught him to do.
- After Rocky's big brother died during the Bataan Death March in the Philippines, his father was in an automobile accident that forced his mother to give up her nursing job; money had been scarce ever since.

*Steven "Rocky" Diner proudly served on the Junior Safety Patrol.*

- Rocky was convinced his older brother would have been very proud of his selection as a member of the Patrol.
- Rocky also attended church and sat in the same pew his brother had occupied; the weekly gesture would not bring his brother back, but seemed fitting somehow.
- The minister had asked Rocky to be a member of the choir, but that sounded too goody-goody for Rocky.
- After all, since his nickname was borrowed from one of the greatest boxers of all time, it would not be appropriate to go too soft.
- The idea for the Junior Safety Patrol first emanated from The Chicago Motor Club in the 1920s.

*Rocky's older brother died in the Philippines.*

- According to Charles Hayes, who had been president of the club since 1914, "A child was being killed every other day and something had to be done."
- The patrols promptly reduced accidents around Chicago school areas, and within six years there were 70,000 patrol members in 500 American cities.
- The American Automobile Association Club in Western Washington began a Safety Campaign Plan in the 1920s, which included a variety of events in many communities to emphasize and teach safety on highways and streets.
- Schoolteachers and children were a particular focus.
- Among other things, essay contests were sponsored and safety posters distributed to schools.
- When schools opened in September 1928, the Schoolboy Patrol program was begun in Seattle schools.
- It was sponsored and equipped by the AAA Club; the idea quickly spread around the state.
- In May 1930, the second annual Schoolboy Patrol picnic was held at Woodland Park with 1,000 boys and 150 adults attending.
- In the early 1920s, about the time Charles Hayes envisioned the Junior Safety Patrol, the automobile industry was overtaking steel as the most important sector of the American economy.
- Approximately 10 percent of Americans' annual income was used for purchasing cars and trucks and buying gas, oil, parts, repairs and other auto-related items.

ROCKY MARCIANO
Heavyweight Champion of the World

*Rocky wanted to be tough, just like the fighter he was named for.*

- The automobile industry, led by the big three companies, General Motors, Ford, and Chrysler, fueled the upswing in the economy in the latter half of the 1920s.
- By 1929, the industry set a record by selling more than five million vehicles; the next year, even after cutting prices in the wake of the market crash, sales dropped by two million cars and trucks.
- In 1932, when the number of vehicles sold had plummeted to 1.3 million, a drop of four million from the 1929 record, half the male population in Detroit and Flint was unemployed.
- The Depression was especially hard on the independent carmakers, including Pierce-Arrow, Peerless, Stutz, Marmon, Du Pont, Durant, Duesenberg, Auburn, Hupmobile, and Kissel, all of which virtually disappeared.
- Many were manufacturers of luxury cars, which experienced a declining market in the tough times of the 1930s.

## Life at Work

- Steven "Rocky" Diner's responsibility as a member of the Junior Safety Patrol was to help students safely cross NW 80th Street and also 24th Avenue NW, the two nearby arterial streets.
- Students living east of 24th were not permitted to cross either street at any point other than the intersection of 80th and 24th. Students living west of 24th and north of 80th were not allowed to cross 80th anywhere except at 26th.
- The rules were designed to ensure the safety of students crossing these busy arterials, and were enforced by the school.
- Most often, Rocky was assigned along with at least one other student to the intersection of 24th and 80th, which was two blocks east of the school.
- The immediate area was vacant land with no traffic light, but there was a stop sign.
- Many students crossed both 24th and 80th on their way home.
- The Junior Safety Patrol also served at the 26th crossing; the school building was at the southeast corner of this intersection with houses on the other three corners.
- Rocky's role was to teach safety; he was taught to "direct children, not traffic."
- He understood that he did not have any authority over vehicular traffic on the streets; "We were trained to keep students out of the street and on the sidewalk until there was no approaching traffic."
- Poles with bright red STOP flags were used to stop students from entering the street until the patrol had determined it was safe to do so.

*Rocky was assigned to help students safely cross the street.*

- As students crossed, Rocky stood on one end of the crosswalk and held up STOP flags; "This was a warning to any vehicular traffic that might suddenly appear where students were crossing."
- He was especially proud of his badge and crossing guard belt.
- With the help of the older guys, Rocky learned how to fold and roll up his Sam Browne belts so he could hook them on his belt with the badge still attached.
- Rocky dreamed of being appointed captain one day and get the chance to wear a special blue-trimmed badge.

- This was the perfect training for someone who wanted to become an officer in the Army Air Corps.

## Life in the Community: Seattle, Washington

- Throughout its history, Seattle experienced a cycle of booms and busts, a common fate for cities near extensive natural and mineral resources.
- Logging was Seattle's first major industry, but hardly its only economic opportunity.
- By the late nineteenth century, the city had become a commercial and shipbuilding center as a gateway to Alaska during the Klondike Gold Rush.
- By 1910, Seattle was one of the 25 largest cities in the U.S.
- The growth of shipbuilding during World War I produced even more expansion and helped lead the Seattle General Strike of 1919, the first general strike in the country.
- The Great Depression severely damaged the city's economy, but growth returned during and after World War II, due partially to the local Boeing Company, which established Seattle as a center for aircraft manufacturing.
- Seattle enjoyed a noteworthy musical history.
- Starting in 1918, nearly two dozen jazz nightclubs flourished along Jackson Street in the current Chinatown District, launching the careers of Ray Charles, Quincy Jones, Ernestine Anderson and others.

## HISTORICAL SNAPSHOT
# 1948

- Warner Brothers showed the first color newsreel, featuring the Tournament of Roses Parade and the Rose Bowl

- Mahatma Gandhi was assassinated by Nathuram Godse

- The Soviet Union began to jam *Voice of America* broadcasts

- The stock car racing series NASCAR was founded by William France, Sr.

- In the court case *McCollum v. Board of Education*, the Supreme Court ruled that religious instruction in public schools violated the U.S. Constitution

- The Hells Angels motorcycle gang was founded in California

- Renowned Italian conductor Arturo Toscanini made his television debut, conducting the NBC Symphony Orchestra in an all-Wagner program

- Scientists Ralph Alpher and George Gamow published the Alpher-Bethe-Gamow paper describing the big bang theory

- President Harry Truman signed the Marshall Plan, which authorized $5 billion in aid for 16 countries

- The Land Rover was unveiled at the Amsterdam Motor Show

- The RAND Corporation was established as an independent nonprofit policy research and analysis institution

- Laurence Olivier's film version of *Hamlet* made its world premiere

- The British Mandate of Palestine was officially terminated; expeditionary forces from Egypt, Transjordan, Syria and Iraq invaded Israel and clashed with Israeli forces

- Columbia Records introduced the LP (long-playing) 33 1/3 rpm phonograph record

- William Shockley filed the original patent for the grown junction transistor, the first bipolar junction transistor

- President Truman signed Executive Order 9981, ending racial segregation in the Armed Forces

- The House Un-American Activities Committee held its first-ever televised congressional hearing, featuring "Confrontation Day" between Whittaker Chambers and Alger Hiss

- In professional baseball, the Cleveland Indians defeated the Boston Braves to win the World Series, four games to two

- In the presidential election, Democratic incumbent Harry Truman defeated Republican Thomas E. Dewey and "Dixiecrat" Strom Thurmond

- In Tokyo, an international war crimes tribunal sentenced seven Japanese military and government officials to death, including General Hideki Tojo, for their roles in World War II

- Alfred Kinsey published *Sexual Behavior in the Human Male*

## Selected Prices

| | |
|---|---|
| Baby Food | $0.59 |
| Car Seat | $1.98 |
| Carpet Sweeper | $19.95 |
| Jaguar Sedan | $4,600.00 |
| LP Record | $1.25 |
| Portable Phonograph | $27.50 |
| Record of Handel's *Messiah* | $1.25 |
| Scooter With Rubber Tires | $1.59 |
| Toaster | $15.05 |
| Whiskey, Fifth | $3.98 |

## "The Oldest School Safety Patrol Boy, For 31 Years a Man in Chicago Has Helped the Nation's Youngsters Help Themselves to Safety," *Colliers*, May 16, 1953:

On the morning of March 4, 1953, a well-filled school bus stopped on U.S. Route 12, two miles east of Michigan City, Indiana, to pick up a small group of children. A gasoline truck stopped behind the bus. Suddenly, as the youngsters were getting aboard, a cattle truck rumbled out of nowhere and ripped into the gasoline truck. The peaceful morning scene became a roaring, crackling blur of flame. The rear of the school bus caught fire. It looked like certain death for the screaming children. But almost instantaneously with the explosion, the bus driver, Bernard Jakubowski, drove forward, sweeping the flames backward and preventing them from invading the vehicle. Immediately, 13-year-old James Hart organized a crew of older boys and girls and set to work moving the younger children forward in the bus, calming them until they could be let out. No child suffered anything greater than shock.

Why was Jimmy Hart so alert to danger? He's a safety patrol boy, one of 500,000 boys and girls throughout the U.S. whose job it is to guard the traffic lanes around schools.

Every spring, usually on the second Saturday in May, representatives of the half-million Patrollers meet in Washington, DC, to celebrate National School Safety Patrol Rally Day. It's an exciting occasion, but few get more pleasure out of it than 76-year-old Charles M. Hayes of Chicago, who might be called the oldest Safety Patrol Boy in the U.S.

*Continued*

## "The Oldest School Safety Patrol Boy . . . *(Continued)*

Mr. Hayes has been president of the Chicago Motor Club since 1914. He began to worry about school children in traffic in 1922. "A child was being killed every other day," he recalls, "and something had to be done." Hayes did something.

He convinced Congress, the police department, and public school authorities that it might be a good idea to let older schoolboys protect the younger ones as they travel to and from school. They agreed to try the plan. The patrols reduced accidents in Chicago school areas, and within six years there were 70,000 patrol members in 500 American cities. Today, besides the half-million or more boys and girls in the U.S., there are tens of thousands in Canada, Germany, Sweden, Brazil, New Zealand, the Azores, India, and Japan.

While Hayes gave the Patrol Boy project its initial impetus, civic associations of every type now play leading roles in furthering its function in local communities. And the patrols have chalked up an enviable record. For instance: statistics over the past 25 years show that traffic accidents involving children under 16 were cut in half in New York State; Missouri hasn't had a single death or injury where a School Safety Patrol Boy was on duty during the last 24 years; and Flint, Michigan, has had only one accident at guarded crossings since 1927.

The rest of the remarkable list could literally fill a book. But the School Safety Patrol youngsters on guard in 9,000 cities and towns in the nation don't think much about statistics. They are too busy saving lives: just the way Charles Hayes planned it.

## EDITORIAL: "Service Station Man Champions Part of Big Business," *Martinsville Bulletin* (Virginia), October 23, 1949:

"Oil Progress Week" ended in Martinsville and Henry County yesterday, and as it ended, the thought struck us: "Have you ever considered how available certain types of oil and gas are?"

Well, we think it should. You could travel the county over and the nation as well and find that on the average, you'll encounter a service station every time you drive 12 miles along the road. The total for the nation is 250,000.

To any one of these retail outlets you can say "Fill 'er up" and usually it is done in a matter of seconds with a lot of extra windshield wiping and water checking thrown in. The average motorist might never think of it, but in back of that swiftly executed order is one of the most complex and highly developed industrial organizations in the world. A large part of it exists to have gasoline and other oil products available for the motorist when he wants it.

Last year 37,000 oil wells were drilled within the United States. The oil enters a vast distribution system of roads, motor cars, then barges and pipelines. In laboratories, about $1 billion a year is spent on research to develop new products and to improve old ones.

*Continued*

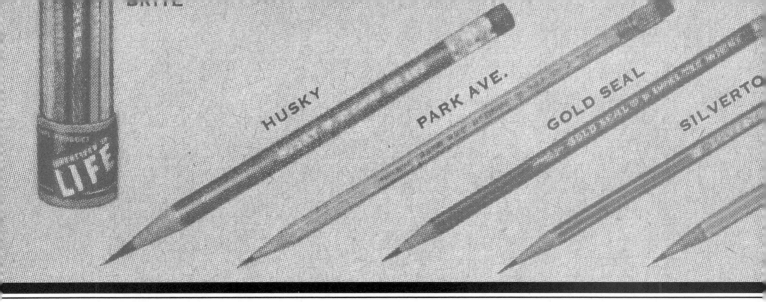

HUSKY  PARK AVE.  GOLD SEAL  SILVERTO

# 1949 PROFILE

Dr. Delaney Burris taught engineering at the college level for 30 years, but was totally unprepared for the ingenuity, hard work and maturity of the GI Bill students.

## Life at Home

*Delaney Burris taught engineering at the University of Denver.*

- Dr. Delaney Burris was prepared to be disappointed, but not dumbfounded, by the hordes of GI Bill students flooding the classrooms of the University of Denver.
- The hilltop beautiful campus had quickly been tagged GI Tech because so many returning World War II soldiers were enrolled there.
- Same predicted that the tidal wave of new students fresh from the war would seriously dilute the quality of higher education, saying the legislation failed to "distinguish between those who could profit most by advanced education and those who cannot."
- After all, a large proportion had never planned to attend college, and few had parents who had; critics of the mass education bill predicted that yesterday's soldier class was ill prepared to meet the academic challenges of tomorrow.
- The thousands of ex-soldiers marching into Delaney's classroom were part of a government wager against economic disaster if the returning troops grew disgruntled over employment, housing and a sense of appreciation.

- A *New Republic* columnist called the potential economic crisis "a Pearl Harbor of peace, not of war."
- After the soldiers' experience of war, however, all night drinking parties, fraternity hazing, and even panty raids seemed to hold little interest; many were married, some were wounded, and most were very interested in proving that they were "college material."
- After all, college was an opportunity they never thought would be theirs.
- One of Delaney's students calculated he was one of only 18 soldiers out of 570 infantrymen in his company who were not wounded, captured or killed in the bloody fighting across Italy, France and Germany.

*College parties held little interest for the soldier students.*

- The Servicemen's Readjustment Act of 1944, better known as the GI Bill, transformed education, the cities, suburbia, cultural geography and, most important, the expectations and aspirations of millions of veterans and non-veterans alike.
- The most visible benefits of the program were financial assistance for education and housing.
- With the financial aid and encouragement of the federal government, America's colleges were transformed; many rapidly abandoned the traditionally elite model of education to embrace a more egalitarian student body.
- College was no longer going to be the exclusive realm of the rich; in 1910, 2.7 percent of eligible men nationwide received a college diploma; by 1940, the rate before the passage of the GI Bill had grown to only 4.6 percent of eligible men.
- At the same time, the favorable mortgage conditions contained in the legislation propelled the U.S. from a nation of renters to a country of homeowners.
- Delaney was born in 1896, the same year William McKinley defeated Democrat William Jennings Bryan for the presidency; that same year, most of America experienced a dramatic solar eclipse that both frightened and dazzled the nation.
- His father, a blacksmith and entrepreneur, who recognized early the potential of the automobile, proudly wore a political campaign button showing McKinley's head eclipsing the fading Bryan.
- While many of his friends were learning the economics of farming in central Illinois, Delaney was repairing equipment, rebuilding automobile engines and staging mock arguments with his dad concerning ways to create greater efficiency and combustion using a gasoline engine.
- Despite the Panic of 1907, times were good for Delaney growing up in Rantoul, Illinois.
- The blacksmith business evolved into an automobile dealership and repair facility that sold everything a modern motorist might need.
- When Delaney turned 16 in 1912, he was given two broken-down cars and a welder.
- "Invent something that people will want to drive," his father said.
- One year later he unveiled the "Burris Beauty," with a four-cylinder engine, shock absorbers modeled after those used in the railroad industry, and a sleek look that mimicked a small bird in flight.

The greatest

**BUICK**

in 50 great years

- The teenager's innovative ideas got his photograph in the Chicago papers, numerous offers to buy the car, and a letter from the University of Illinois—just up the road—inviting him to apply for admission to the engineering school.
- Delaney accepted the invitation and then hung around long enough to earn both an undergraduate and master's degree.
- His graduate work was focused on boosting the efficiency of the internal combustion engine, and by the time he graduated he had opportunities at three Michigan-based auto manufacturers.
- After four years of high-pressure research so secret he couldn't discuss it with his wife, he got an offer from the University of Denver to earn his doctorate while teaching at the college.
- Delaney couldn't get to Denver fast enough.
- He discovered very quickly that he loved teaching and energizing motivated students; he displayed little patience for dullards just trying to get a grade.
- Thus, he developed a reputation as a tough grader to be avoided by all but the best students.
- That suited him fine.
- When he learned that his precious classroom was soon to be overrun by ex-soldiers, he was horrified.
- After all, one out of every eight Americans had served in the military, most of whom had already been judged to be "not college material," and Delaney saw little about military life and getting shot at that would make them more capable.
- Now, at the end of his career—nearly 30 years—why did he have to endure the invasion of the hordes? Why make a social problem into an education issue?
- Colleges should be, he felt, temples of learning, not a hothouse laboratory to quiet a potential rebellion.

## Life at Work
- Dr. Delaney Burris was fully aware that government planners were concerned about the need to create a "peacetime economy."
- Following the Japanese bombing of Pearl Harbor, the entire nation suddenly stopped manufacturing cars, washing machines and refrigerators and took on the tasks of building tanks, planes and bombs.
- Now that these soldiers, sailors, airmen and Marines were once again becoming civilians and returning home in search of jobs, America could not afford a return to the Depression that consumed most of the 1930s, or permit an atmosphere in which a demigod could rise to power based on the discontent of the soldiers.
- It had happened before.

*A military education did not take place in a typical classroom.*

- Delaney knew that in 1783, impoverished, inflamed soldiers surrounded Philadelphia's Independence Hall after promises of back pay and pensions were broken by the brand new, cash-strapped nation; Congress would not fully pay its debts to its Revolutionary war veterans for 49 years.
- The Civil War pension program, designed to compensate the two million Union soldiers who had fought against the Confederacy, was so wracked with fraud, graft and patronage, it eventually had to be scrapped.
- The five million veterans of World War I who returned from France received no consideration for lost income, lost jobs, financial sacrifices and a peek at hell.
- It took six years for Congress to agree to payments of up to $625 each, payable in 1945—which satisfied few and resulted in the Bonus Army's march on Washington in 1932.
- In all, 40,000 veterans played a role in the march; 20,000 made it to the Capitol in Washington and established tent cities that came to be known as Hoovervilles.
- Eventually, the army had to be called out to drive away the World War I veterans—an embarrassing scene for everyone.
- This time the federal government was determined to avoid high unemployment, dissatisfaction and fear.
- With the war ending, President Roosevelt envisioned "winning the peace" with "a second Bill of Rights that included giving every citizen the right to a rewarding job, living wage, decent home, home healthcare, education, and a pension."
- The extremely popular American Legion lobbied for a different form of compensation to the servicemen of World War II: for their lost time and opportunity.
- What the Legion didn't anticipate was how eager America's fighting men were to have a new start—especially the opportunity to attend college.
- An unprecedented 51 percent of GIs took advantage of the educational provision, allowing 2.2 million veterans to attend college and 5.6 million vets to receive vocational training.

*Many veterans were married.*

- Government budget planners had anticipated that 8 to 12 percent of GIs would be interested in additional education; the influx of veterans overloaded America's higher education system.
- Despite serious shortages of student housing and faculty, U.S. colleges expanded to meet the increased demand.
- Educational benefits included tuition payments of up to $500, book allowances, and stipends of $50 a month—$75 for married vets.
- The war, Delaney was convinced, had changed an entire generation.
- America was the one major participant whose landscape and infrastructure had not been destroyed by bombs and marching armies; the United States was the sole country whose economy had improved since 1941, boasting a rising standard of living, better wages, better productivity and an improved stock market.
- Unlike World War I, whose completion ushered in a renewed call for pacifism and isolationism, the Second World War was a catalyst for establishing a global economy in the emerging Cold War with the Soviet Union.
- For several semesters, Delaney was convinced the vets in his class—via a mercy admission—would wash out quickly.
- They didn't.
- Many did not possess all of the higher-level math skills he demanded, so they banded together to work harder and longer.
- They requested extra tutoring, demanded additional assignments, and displayed a deep resentment to any suggestion that they were given special privileges.
- Unlike many undergraduates, they recognized that school was their primary responsibility; they were focused on the future and already understood hardship.
- By 1947, half of all college students—including seven of 10 male students—were enrolled through the GI Bill.
- In general, the veterans earned higher grades than their civilian counterparts.
- Delaney fully understood the impact of the GI Bill when he heard a traditional student berating a vet for "messing up the curve" with high scores.
- *The New York Times* reported in 1947, "The GIs are hogging the honor rolls and the Dean's lists; they are walking away with the top marks in all their courses…. Far from being an educational problem, the veteran has become an asset to high education."
- So many male veterans demanded college spots, civilian female applicants were disproportionately excluded.
- Nor did the program ensure that African-American veterans would gain equal access to higher education.
- At the same time, many veterans were taking advantage of a different provision in the GI Bill that was designed to spur homeownership: low interest, zero-down-payment home loans for servicemen that enabled millions of American families to move out of urban apartments and into suburban homes.

*The GI Bill allowed many veterans to buy their own homes.*

- Prior to the war, the suburbs tended to be home to the wealthy and upper middle class.
- Another provision was known as the 52–20 clause that enabled all former servicemen to receive $20 once a week for 52 weeks a year while they were looking for work.
- Less than 20 percent of the money set aside for the 52–20 Club was distributed; rather, most returning servicemen quickly found jobs or pursued higher education.
- By 1949, the Cold War was shifting into high gear as the Soviet Union was conducting nuclear tests.
- Eight million American workers were jobless in 1939, an employment rate of close to 15 percent; in 1949, the problem was replaced by worker shortages.
- After the war, the "American dream" included a new car, job security, a television set and homeownership.

## Life in the Community: The University of Denver, Colorado

- The University of Denver was founded by John Evans as the Colorado Seminary in 1864.
- In the beginning, 30 male students and three instructors tackled a classical curriculum of algebra, rhetoric, French, Latin, music, and theology.
- Battling an anemic economy, the college lasted three years, only to be resurrected in 1880 and then rejuvenated by Henry Buchtel, a prominent Methodist minister and friend of industrial magnate Andrew Carnegie.
- The campus quickly became recognized as one of the few possessing a major refracting telescope and a coeducational policy open to all races and religions.
- The campus had expanded sufficiently by 1928 to handle 3,500 students.
- When the Great Depression hit, enrollment dropped and budgets in all areas were cut.
- Enrollments, nationwide, further decreased with the outbreak of World War II, from 1.4 million students in 1939 to 750,000 in 1943.
- During the war years, female enrollment increased dramatically; women began occupying 75 percent of the seats in the engineering program, 60 percent of the slots in the pharmacy program, and a 14 percent increase in those seeking architectural degrees.

- Liberal Arts colleges were the hardest hit by the onset of war, with some experiencing enrollment declines of between 50 and 70 percent.
- Even elite colleges such as Yale University experienced enrollment declines, finding it with only 565 students in 1944; traditionally a typical freshman class alone comprised 800 students.
- Colleges accelerated many of their programs to allow graduation in two and a half years, while others revamped their curriculum to emphasize war-related needs.
- At Yale, the isolationist, "No War, America First" programs had gained deep support prior to the bombing of Pearl Harbor.
- After the surprise Sunday morning attack, seven of the school's 10 residential colleges were turned over to the military.
- Despite serious shortages of student housing and faculty, the University of Denver expanded to meet the increased demand; at its peak, the number of students swelled to 13,000—more than double its prewar enrollment.

<table>
<tr><td>

## HISTORICAL SNAPSHOT
# 1949

</td></tr>
</table>

- President Harry Truman unveiled his Fair Deal program

- KDKA-TV became the first local, on-air television station in the U.S.

- The first VW Type 1 to arrive in the United States, a 1948 model, was brought to New York by Dutch businessman Ben Pon; first year sales totaled two cars

- The first Emmy Awards were presented at the Hollywood Athletic Club

- *Death of a Salesman* by Henry Miller opened at the Morosco Theatre on Broadway

- Ezra Pound was awarded the first Bollingen Prize in poetry by the Bollingen Foundation at Yale University

- The B-50 Superfortress *Lucky Lady II* under Captain James Gallagher completed the first non-stop around-the-world airplane flight

- Rodgers and Hammerstein's *South Pacific*, starring Mary Martin and Ezio Pinza, opened on Broadway

- Albert II, a rhesus monkey, became the first primate to enter space, on U.S. Hermes project V-2 rocket *Blossom IVB*, but died on impact at its return on June 19

- Glenn Dunnaway won the inaugural NASCAR race at Charlotte Speedway, but was disqualified due to the car owner having shored up the chassis by spreading the rear springs; Jim Roper was declared the official winner

- The U.S. Air Force ended a two-year investigation of flying saucer reports by denying the authenticity of UFOs

- Eight essential amino acids for human use were described

- The first television Western, *Hopalong Cassidy*, aired on NBC

- President Truman announced that the USSR had the atomic bomb

- Phonograph records were issued in three different speeds—33.3, 45, and 78—causing customer confusion

- The Polaroid Land camera, capable of producing a picture in 60 seconds, went on sale for $89.75

- The U.S. postwar Baby Boom reached 3.58 million live births

- The minimum wage was increased from $0.40 per hour to $0.75 per hour

- *All The King's Men* won the Academy Award for Best Picture

## Selected Prices

Adding Machine..............................................................$120.00

Annual Tuition, Harvard ............................................$600.00

Clock Radio ....................................................................$36.95

Hairdryer .........................................................................$9.95

LP Record ........................................................................$1.25

Man's Shoes ...................................................................$10.95

Movie Ticket ...................................................................$1.00

Tattoo ...............................................................................$0.25

Whiskey, Fifth.................................................................$3.98

Woman's Blouse, Crepe.................................................$4.95

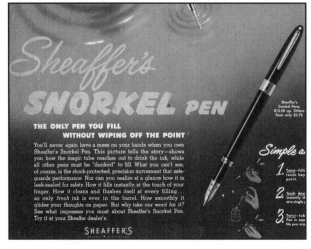

## "Revised GI Bill Okayed by Senate," *The Danville Register* (Virginia), November 9, 1945:

A revised "GI Bill of Rights," easing the way for veterans to get government-backed schooling or loans, received Senate approval today after a proposal to extend its benefits to widows of veterans was shouted down.

Passage on a voice vote sent the measure to the House, which approved GI amendments last summer. The Senate bill is a complete substitute, however, retaining only the House title.

Sen. Johnson (D-Colo.), floor manager for the bill, estimated the changes would make the GI Program cost the treasury $9 billion over the years of its operation.

He said the cost of the original GI Bill, enacted in June 1944, was estimated at $7,635,000,000.

Sen. Magnuson (D-Washington) offered the amendment to give widows of veterans benefits for the bill. "It probably will involve only a very minimum, particularly younger, women," he argued.

He was thinking in particular, he said, that younger widows were the breadwinners for families and might want to improve their job opportunities by schooling at government expense.

Johnson replied that the finance committee had considered that proposal as well as a suggestion by Sen. Wheeling Wheeler (D-Montana) that benefits be extended to the children of veterans, but decided against both.

The Colorado senator noted that widows received a pension and suggested that any additional aid for them should be through legislation amending the pension laws rather than to the GI measure. The amendment lost on a voice vote.

Here are the chief changes the legislation would make:

Give any veteran of World War II, regardless of age, the right to go to school with the government paying expenses of tuition, books, etc., up to $500 a year. Present law applies to veterans whose schooling was interrupted by service and declares that it presumed to be the case of those who were under 25 when they entered the Army or Navy.

Increase from $50 to $65 the monthly allowance for student-veterans without dependents, and from $75 to $90 allowance for those with dependents.

Bring under the program short technical training courses and correspondence courses if the cost does not exceed $500 a year.

Authorize Veterans Administrators to make agreements with state institutions for payments in lieu of tuition. (Some state institutions charge no tuition or very little.)

*Continued*

## "Revised GI Bill Okayed by Senate," . . . *(Continued)*

Permit government guarantees up to one-half, or not more than $2,000, of loans to veterans to buy homes, businesses and farms, provided the property purchased had a "reasonable value...."

Permit guaranteed loans to cover working capital, seeds and farm machinery as well as real estate.

Increase the amortization period for non-farm loans from 20 to 25 years, and for farm loans from 20 to 40 years.

## "Let's Train Our Youth, NOW!" Frank Knox, Secretary of the Navy, *The Reader's Digest*, July 1944:

It is my belief that our country should adopt now, as a permanent policy, the universal military training of all young men. I believe that a minimum of 12 months of continuous training should be given every American boy of 17 or 18 who is not mentally deficient or immobilized by physical handicap.

I state my proposition thus baldly as an invitation to general discussion. I believe the system of national military training would pay swift dividends in a healthier, more unified, more democratic nation, and one able to defend itself more quickly and efficiently should we ever again be attacked. If we are to profit by our mistakes in past wars, if we are at last to adopt a long-range, non-political, fixed policy of national defense, then we must erect its structure upon the foundation of the military training of all our youth. There are in addition so many more benefits of practical value for the individual and to the nation, that I have no doubt we shall ultimately endow ourselves with the system.

If ultimately, why not now? We shall shortly have urgent use for such corps of trainees. If there were no other reason, we should undertake the program at once to speed the return of our fighting men when the war ends.

Our armed forces cannot be demobilized when the last enemy lays down his gun. The United States will have to remain, for an indefinite period, with armies of occupation and national patrols and overseas supply lines, as the areas of occupation expand to the final inclusion of Britain and Tokyo. For years afterward, self-interest alone will dictate that we maintain military and naval police forces the world around.

That the men who are now doing the fighting—mature men long absent from home—shall be required to stand by their arms abroad, while there exists in this country a vast supply of potential replacements, is unreasonable and detrimental. They should be replaced in outpost duty by younger man who can conclude their year of military training in actual, practical national service.

Win Your Wings
U. S. AIR FORCE

RECRUITING

U.S. ARMY    U.S AIR FORCE

If you are single, between the ages of 20 and 26½, with at least two years of college, this is your opportunity for U. S. Aviation Cadet training as pilot or navigator.

Get your application *today* at your local Recruiting Office or U. S. Air Force Base, or write Chief of Staff, U. S. Air Force, Attention: Aviation Cadet Branch, Washington, D. C.

*Continued*

## "Let's Train Our Youth, NOW!" . . . *(Continued)*

As a nation, we tend to put noisy emphasis on the privileges we inherit with American citizenship, and to shirk the duties. In peacetime, the only duties the federal government compels from its law-abiding citizens are the payment of taxes and rare calls to serve on a jury.

But suppose we gave all our young men of 17, the age of bodily maturity and mental receptiveness, a year's demonstration in duty? Duty to the nation, to their fellow men, to themselves? Military training does definitely more for young men than to make them potential soldiers or sailors; afterwards they would go back to work, or to college, be better citizens and healthier human beings than their fathers had a chance to be.

The American Legion lists five benefits of national military service:

1) It will create so great a body of effective reserves that this nation will be forever safe from attack. 2) Every young man who has earned the privileges of citizenship by being trained to defend them will have a greater appreciation of their worth. 3) Discipline learned during service will reduce crime. 4) Unemployment will be reduced. 5) The nation's health will be improved.

Health is not a standard of physical robustness alone. Close to 50 percent of the men answering the call of National Selective Service were being rejected, the greatest single cause being mental health. Of the 56,000 persons invalidated out of the Navy for noncombatant disabilities in the first 21 months of the war, 14,000 were dropped for mental and nervous disorders.

What is the cause? The experts differ; but may I, as a layman, contribute the thought that misdirected, aimless youth in an exceedingly complex and competitive civilization are more susceptible to mental and nervous disorders than young man who are helped to build up a rugged body and find a purpose in life?...

If there was one factor in Hitler's calculation—and Tojo's—which convinced the warlords that they could win, it was the conviction that the "decadent democracies" would not fight or could not. Suppose we had military training in the United States since the last war. Would the axis powers have risked war with a nation whose every man between 18 and 40 was a trained sailor or soldier? Would they have risked their strength against the nation which was not only rich with raw materials and industrial capacity, but had upward of 20 million men trained to shoot, to fly, to sail, to fight?

Let us suppose we have the common sense not to scrap our Navy and military equipment again, including the training centers and technical schools we have acquired since 1941. Then let us utilize this magnificent establishment not only for defense of the nation and for preservation of the peace, but to train young men during their year of military service and a later refresher course. What Hitler or Tojo of 1965 would challenge a United States thus prepared?

## "Loan Machinery for Vets Is Speeding Up!" Maj. Thomas M. Niol, *Syracuse Post Standard,* March 17, 1946:

Some of the letters to me about GI Bill loans have gone so far as to say that most lenders would rather make any kind of loan except a GI loan!

That's because these letters claim getting a GI Bill loan has been taking too much time and effort, and involving enough red tape to take care of your Christmas wrapping for years.

Perhaps, as time passed, the GI Bill loan provisions would have become as unused as a guest towel. But changes have now been made, so let's keep our fingers crossed while we wait to see if the new amendments to the loan section of the GI Bill actually make it easier for U.S. veterans to get loans.

Under the old plan, the first big time waster was getting from the Veterans Administration a certificate of eligibility for a loan.

A vet with an honorable discharge and 90 days' service knew he was eligible to apply for a loan. Everybody else knew it. The law made it as clear as excellent flying weather. Still he had to use up time getting a certificate of eligibility.

But not anymore. Now, an honorable discharge automatically becomes your certificate of eligibility. So, if you have an honorable discharge, you can go right to work on a deal with an authorized lending institution….

And here's number two. Last summer, when the Veteran's Committee of the House of Representatives went to work on a vision of the GI Bill, it wanted to take away from the VA all authority to approve loans. It wrote the loan provisions of the new bill that way and the House approved. But the Senate wouldn't agree to that; once the lender and the veteran made a deal on a loan, the VA would have to guarantee part, without any check on the thing at all. It argued it would be the first time the government guaranteed anything while blindfolded.

So the House and the Senate got together and came up with a compromise.

Under the loan provisions, the VA still retains authority of the GI Bill loans to use the VA approved local appraisers.

The result of these two changes is that now, if you want a GI Bill loan, you don't have to wait for a certificate of eligibility. If you have an honorable discharge or satisfactory Certificate of Service, you're automatically eligible.

Next, if you find the lending outfit willing to make the loan, then a nearby appraiser can decide without delay if it's a reasonable loan. If he nods, then the loan is made and the VA must guarantee, following the terms of the new GI Bill.

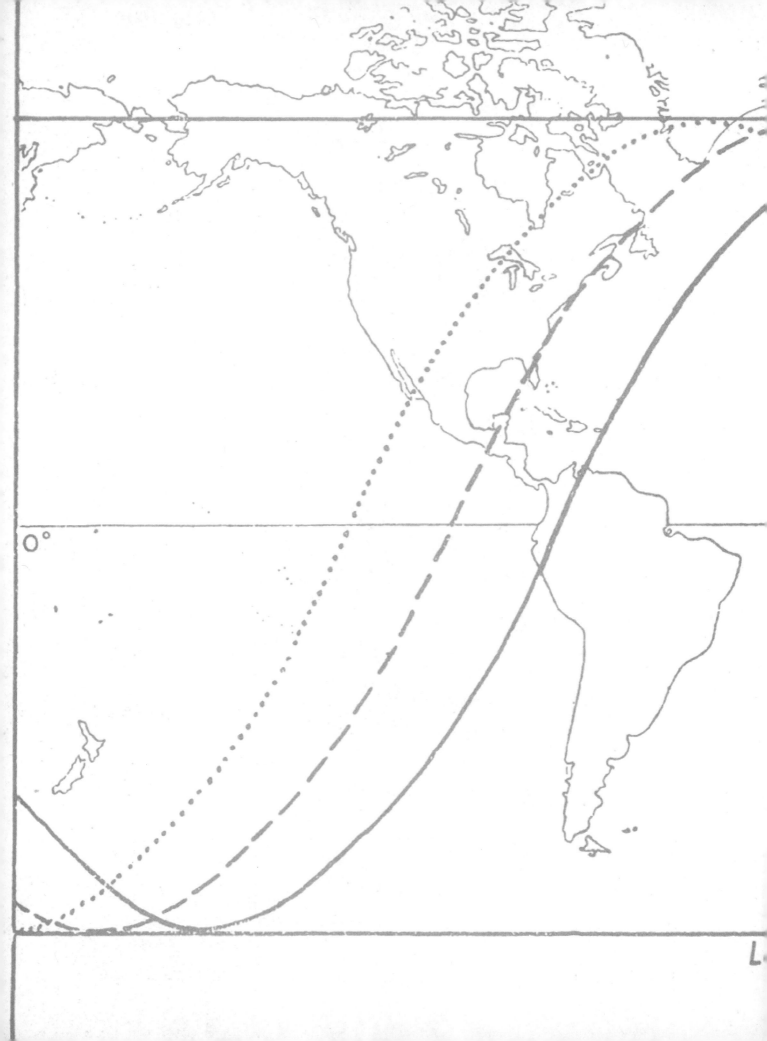

0°

L.

# 1950–1959

As the 1950s began, the average American enjoyed an income
15 times greater than that of the average foreigner. Optimism
and opportunity were everywhere. The vast majority of families
considered themselves middle class; many were enjoying the
benefits of health insurance for the first time. Air travel for the upper
class was common. America was manufacturing half of the world's
products, 57 percent of the steel, 43 percent of the electricity, and 62
percent of the oil. The economies of Europe and Asia lay in ruins,
while America's industrial and agricultural structure was untouched
and well oiled to supply the needs of a war-weary world.

   After World War II, American schools were increasingly tied to
the policy needs of the federal government. The Cold War between
the United States and the Soviet Union spawned demands for more
science and math. The expanding role of the federal government
was also felt after the Supreme Court ruled against the continuation
of racially segregated schools and called for integration "with
all possible speed." Americans debated the need for a mandatory
one-year universal service for all youth, while educators once
again proposed that the nation's superior students receive a more
demanding curriculum—overtly allowing schools to be a social
sorting machine focused on meeting the employment needs of
American corporations. Men's high school sports became more
prominent during the decade, federal funding for schools expanded,
and businesses of all kinds prospered. Rapidly expanding families,
new suburban homes, televisions, and, most of all, big, powerful,
shiny automobiles symbolized the hopes of the era. During the
1950s, an average of seven million cars and trucks was sold
annually. By 1952, two-thirds of all families owned a television set;
home freezers and high-fidelity stereo phonographs were considered
necessities. Specialized markets developed to meet the demand
of consumers such as amateur photographers, pet lovers, and
backpackers. At the same time, shopping malls, supermarkets, and
credit cards emerged as important economic forces.

Veterans, using the GI Bill of Rights, flung open the doors of colleges nationwide, attending in record numbers. Inflation was the only pressing economic issue, fueled in large part by the Korean War (in which 36,500 American lives were lost) and the federal expenditures for Cold War defense. As the decade opened, federal spending represented 15.6 percent of the nation's gross national product. Thanks largely to the Cold War, by 1957, defense consumed half of the federal government's $165 billion budget.

The economic prosperity also ushered in conservative politics and social conformity. Tidy lawns, "proper" suburban homes and buttoned-down attitudes concerning sexual mores were certainly "in" throughout the decade as Americans adjusted to the postwar years. The planned community of Levittown, New York, mandated that grass be cut at least once a week and laundry washed on specific days. A virtual revival of Victorian respectability and domesticity reigned; divorce rates and female college attendance fell while birth rates and sales of Bibles rose. Corporate America promoted the benefits of respectable men in gray flannel suits whose wives remained at home to tend house and raise children. Suburban life included ladies' club memberships, chauffeuring children to piano and ballet classes, and a newly marketed product known as tranquilizer whose sales were exploding.

The average wage earner benefited more from the booming industrial system than at any time in American history. The 40-hour work week became standard in manufacturing. In offices, many workers were becoming accustomed to a 35-hour week. Health benefits for workers became more common, and paid vacations were standard in most industries. In 1950, 25 percent of American wives worked outside the home; by the end of the decade, the number had risen to 40 percent. Communications technology, expanding roads, inexpensive airline tickets, and an unbounded spirit meant that people and commerce were no longer prisoners of distance. Unfortunately, up to one-third of the population lived below the government's poverty level, largely overlooked in the midst of the prosperity.

The Civil Rights Movement was propelled by two momentous events in the 1950s. The first was a decree on May 17, 1954, by the Supreme Court ruling that "in the field of public education the doctrine of 'separate but equal' has no place. Separate educational facilities are inherently unequal." The message was electric but the pace was slow. Few schools would be integrated for another decade. The second event established the place of the Civil Rights Movement in society. On December 1, 1955, African-American activist Rosa Parks declined to vacate the white-only front section of the Montgomery, Alabama, bus, leading to her arrest and a citywide bus boycott by blacks and some whites. Their spokesman became Martin Luther King, Jr., the 26-year-old pastor of the Dexter Avenue Baptist Church. The yearlong boycott was the first step toward the passage of the Civil Rights Act of 1964.

America's youths were enchanted by the TV adventures of *Leave It to Beaver*, westerns, and *Father Knows Best*, allowing them to accumulate more time watching television during the week (at least 27 hours) than attending school. TV dinners were invented; pink ties and felt skirts with sequined poodle appliqués were worn; Elvis Presley was worshipped; and the new phenomena of *Playboy* and Mickey Spillane fiction were created. The ever-glowing eye of television killed the "March of Time" newsreels after 16 years at the movies. Sexual jargon such as "first base" and "home run" entered the language. Learned-When-Sleeping machines appeared, along with Smokey the Bear, Sony tape recorders, adjustable shower heads, *Mad Comics*, newspaper vending machines, Levi's faded blue denims and pocket-size transistor radios. Ultimately, the real stars of the era were the Salk and Sabin vaccines, which vanquished the siege of polio.

# 1955 PROFILE

Dee-Dee Kliebard, heiress to a fortune, decided to use her wealth to create a scholarship program for talented New Jersey girls who wanted a college education.

## Life at Home

- Her real name was Jesse Elaine Torrey Kliebard, but everyone called her Dee-Dee.
- Through the years the origin of her nickname had changed dozens of times—predicated on Dee-Dee's mood and the circumstances at hand.
- For years, she told friends that her first words were "Dee-Dee" instead of "dada."
- In high school, after her mother died leaving behind a fortune amassed in the condiment industry, she claimed Dee-Dee was her mother's middle name.
- To her dates in the 1930s, she shyly "confessed" that a previous boyfriend had christened her Dee-Dee based on the new method of measuring brassiere cup size.
- By the time her aristocratic father died in 1945 when Dee-Dee was 35, she started telling anyone who asked that the moniker had started out as "darling daughter" and evolved into Dee-Dee.
- When Dee-Dee reached the age of 45—10 years after her father had died—she made an evaluation of her life.
- She was rich—that was clear.
- Her mother's ketchup fortune had been carefully invested, which, in combination with her architect father's real estate holdings, made her one of the wealthiest women in New Jersey.

*Dee-Dee Kliebard founded a scholarship for college-bound girls.*

- She had been married once—for 31 days—which she noted to friends was not enough time to use up a whole bar of soap.
- Her ex-husband liked her money and loved other women, a combination that failed to stir Dee-Dee's passion.
- Her time at Sweet Briar College lasted longer—three semesters—where she acquired a taste for Kentucky bourbon, tall men with Southern accents, and the rousing music played at country honky-tonks—any one of which could get her suspended from school.

*Head of Sweet Briar College, left, from which Dee-Dee was expelled.*

- Three out of three was worthy of immediate dismissal, especially when a 1948 red Chevrolet coupe was added to the mix.
- After several years of touring Europe, learning to fly a plane, and a near-death experience to Antarctica, Dee-Dee had an epiphany.
- She realized that she was simply a custodian of the oodles of money sitting in her accounts; wealth had been given to her so she could help others.
- But as she had known most of her life, the world was full of hopeless causes eager to be rescued by her wealth.
- The key was picking out the recipients before they knew they were being examined.
- That way, the least and the lost would have just as good a chance to get help.
- Her goal was helping young women get an education, including graduation from high school and an opportunity to attend college—no matter their financial condition.
- The creation, fostering and growth of universal, free high school education was one of America's successes.
- Until the late 1800s, an eighth-grade education was customary for most Americans; in 1870, only two percent of 17-year-olds had received a high school diploma.
- In 1875, a lawsuit was filed in Kalamazoo, Michigan, affirming the right of towns to use taxes to support the village high school.
- Thanks to expanded taxing power, hundreds of new buildings were erected nationwide; by 1910 the percentage of high school graduates had increased to nine percent, of which 60 percent were female.
- Progressively more and more cities expanded the opportunities for its citizens to go beyond the completion of the eighth grade.
- In 1940, more than half the U.S. population of all ages had completed no more than that, and only six percent of males and four percent of females had completed four years of college.
- Immediately after the Second World War, the high school graduation rate attained 70 percent.
- But clearly, in the postwar environment of the 1950s, a high school education was not going to be enough; college would be vital for American world leadership.

- Dee-Dee believed that women should be included in the educational bonanza underway thanks to the thousands of men being educated through the G.I. Bill.
- Women, simply because they were not called up to be soldiers, should not be thrown on the economic trash heap.
- Therefore, she decided that she would find, select and finance the next generation of female leaders by giving a large number of women the opportunity to compete independently in the world—supported by a fully paid four-year scholarship to the college of their choice.

*Unless supported by rich families, many women were not given the opportunity to attend a four-year college.*

- Many, if not most, college educations prior to 1900 were privately financed, and thus, only open to the wealthy; despite that, both men and women born prior to 1910 had attended college in almost equal numbers.
- But women, who were almost universally enrolled in two-year teachers' colleges, were expected to resign their teaching jobs when they married—which devalued the educational experience.
- The number of students from the working classes who could raise the tuition was usually kept in check by the expenses of living during the years of study.
- A typical family could not afford educating a son, let alone a daughter, even if the education itself was free.
- After World War II, more working-class students were able to receive a degree, resulting in the inflation of education and an increased middle class.

## Life at Work

- The idea of creating a scholarship program for talented New Jersey girls was so exciting; Dee-Dee Kliebard could not sleep at night.
- At first, she hired a team of educators and charity professionals to help her select the first crop of recipients from Trenton, New Jersey.
- The educators talked in theories and carefully coded messages, and the others mostly talked with their hands.
- Both groups quickly decided that they could succeed best if they told her little, believing that her millions did not make her an expert.
- Undaunted, Dee-Dee ordered books and met with experts to decide the purpose of education: to get a job, to create better citizens, to establish a foundation for lifetime learning, to find a mate, or to develop a business network.
- Educational theories abounded; everyone had opinions but no one had the answer.

*The first recipients of Dee-Dee's scholarships were chosen without her input.*

- Should education stick to the basics? Should the curriculum be broad and wide to excite the interests of students? Should students be divided by potential or class or IQ to make the classroom more efficient?
- Then there were the questions concerning the role of administrators versus teachers, and even disputes between colleges and high schools over how students could be best prepared for the challenges of life.
- The first 10 girls were selected without Dee-Dee's input.
- When she met with the winners, most understood little about Dee-Dee's aspirations for them, and most could not pronounce her last name during the congratulatory reception.
- In addition, most looked like the daughter she never had, fully understood what to do during a formal tea, and planned to attend Ivy League schools.
- Dee-Dee managed to wait until the last recipient had left before she fired everyone in sight.
- The sanctimonious educators and experts had not listened to her at all.
- Her scholarships were to be about opportunity for those who were struggling—not the perpetuation of the ruling, wealthy class.
- America had made tremendous educational progress in the prior 55 years, and Dee-Dee planned to accelerate that achievement, even if she had to interview every high school principal in the state of New Jersey personally.
- In 1900, 50 percent of children five to 19 were enrolled in school; by 1930, the enrollment rate was 69 percent, and by 1955, enrollment stood at 86 percent of eligible children.
- The number of girls in school and the percentage of African-Americans were also in the mid-80s.

- The number of days devoted to school was also increasing: from 78 days per year in the decades after the Civil War compared to an average 152 days in 1950.
- The illiteracy rate, which was at 10.7 in 1900, had fallen to 2.2 percent.
- At the same time, many educators had declared that 20 percent of students were being well served by the college entrance programs, and 20 percent were gaining benefit from vocational classes.
- But the remaining 60 percent of high school students should be educated and prepared for the working world, marriage and supporting democracy through life-adjustment classes.
- Dee-Dee wondered how many of her potential recipients were being hidden by the new system, and how many believed they were not college bound because they couldn't afford more education.
- This time, Dee-Dee hired three teachers and one principal to be her advisors.
- She invited them to her home for a week of training and then visited the first eight schools with each one of her teacher-investigators.
- Then she turned them loose to find 25 girls capable of changing the world.
- Under no circumstance were the investigators allowed to discuss where the money originated; Dee-Dee didn't want to experience back channel lobbying efforts and planned to swear each girl to secrecy after her selection.
- After seven months, she was presented with the candidates, each driven to Dee-Dee's home with her parents for a personal interview.
- Dee-Dee was terrified that she would not know what to ask, but found the process pleasing and the high school seniors enchanting.
- Two of the girls had given up on going to college, even before they entered high school; the grades of three more were marginal and six had not started applying to schools.
- What they had in common was spunk and a mentor.
- In nearly every case, a teacher, coach or principal had spotted potential hidden from the rest of the world.
- Of the 25 candidates, Dee-Dee selected 23 for full scholarships.
- One girl bragged that she had a trust fund and didn't need anyone else's money, while another confessed that she was pregnant and not planning to attend college for a while.
- After that, Dee-Dee decided that future classes would also contain 23 winners, and that each year she would stage a reunion of "her girls" to celebrate their successes.
- A total of 19 college students returned in 1955 to receive their second year's tuition and scholarship money.
- One of her favorites, a tall dark-haired Italian who was attending Sweet Briar College, even brought a small bottle of Kentucky bourbon that tasted as good as Dee-Dee remembered.

*Nineteen of 23 first year scholarship girls returned for their second year's tuition.*

## Life in the Community: Trenton, New Jersey

- The first New Jersey settlement, which would become Trenton, was established in 1679 by Quakers, who were being persecuted in England at this time; North America provided the perfect opportunity to exercise their religious freedom.
- By 1719, the town adopted the name "Trent-towne," after William Trent, one of its leading landholders who purchased much of the surrounding land.
- During the Revolutionary War, the city was the site of the Battle of Trenton, George Washington's first military victory.
- On December 26, 1776, Washington and his army, after crossing the icy Delaware River to Trenton, defeated the Hessian troops garrisoned there.
- After the war, Trenton was briefly the national capital in November and December of 1784.
- The city was considered as a permanent capital for the new country, but the Southern states favored a location south of the Mason-Dixon Line.
- Trenton became the state capital in 1790, but prior to that year the Legislature often met here.
- Growth was rapid throughout the nineteenth century as Europeans came to work in the city's pottery and wire rope mills.
- Trenton was a major industrial center in the late nineteenth and early twentieth centuries, earning the slogan "Trenton Makes, The World Takes" for its role in the manufacture of rubber, wire rope, ceramics and cigars.

WASHINGTON AT THE BATTLE OF TRENTON.

## HISTORICAL SNAPSHOT
# 1955

- Marian Anderson became the first African-American singer to perform at the Metropolitan Opera in New York City

- The game Scrabble debuted

- Congress authorized President Dwight D. Eisenhower to use force to protect Formosa from the People's Republic of China

- Ray Kroc opened a McDonald's fast food restaurant (the company's ninth since it was founded in 1940), and oversaw the company's worldwide expansion

- Eisenhower sent the first U.S. advisors to South Vietnam

- The Broadway musical version of *Peter Pan*, which had opened in 1954 starring Mary Martin, was presented on television for the first time by NBC-TV with its original cast

- KXTV of Stockton, California, signed on the air to become the 100th commercial television station in the country

- Evan Hunter's movie adaptation of the novel *Blackboard Jungle* premiered in the United States, featuring the famous single, "Rock Around the Clock," by Bill Haley and His Comets

- The Salk polio vaccine received full approval by the FDA

- The TV quiz program *The $64,000 Question* premiered on CBS-TV with Hal March as the host

- *Lady and the Tramp*, the Walt Disney Company's fifteenth animated film, premiered in Chicago

- The first edition of the *Guinness Book of Records* was published in London

- *Gunsmoke*, *Alfred Hitchcock Presents*, and *The Mickey Mouse Club* all debuted on TV

- Disneyland opened to the public in Anaheim, California

- Racial segregation was outlawed on trains and buses in interstate commerce

- The Montgomery Improvement Association was formed in Montgomery, Alabama, by Dr. Martin Luther King, Jr., and other black ministers to coordinate a boycott of all city buses

- General Motors Corporation became the first American corporation to make a profit of over $1 billion in one year

## Selected Prices

Acne Cream ........................................................................................$0.59

Automobile, Chrysler New Yorker...............................................$4,243

Face Powder ......................................................................................$1.38

License Plate ....................................................................................$1.00

Mattress, Serta King Size................................................................$79.50

Paneling.............................................................................................$47.00

Pocket Radio .....................................................................................$75.00

Race Car Kit......................................................................................$2.75

Railroad Fare, Chicago to San Francisco.......................................$63.12

Razor Blades, 20 ..............................................................................$0.79

## "Teenomania," by Marion Walker Alvado, *Woman's Day*, September 1952:

I want to make it perfectly plain that I have nothing whatsoever against teenagers. Some of my favorite people are teenagers, including my oldest son. But I can't help wondering if there isn't currently much too much commotion about them.

I wonder if the teens haven't come to be considered too much an age apart, age completely different from any other. I wonder if the teenager isn't too continually in both the public and family limelight. And, at the risk of being put summarily in my place by the experts, I wonder if parents are those long-suffering clay pigeons of the shotguns in How-To-Bring-Up-Your-Children books about this particular stage in the offspring's development.

The teenager is a fairly recent discovery. Twenty years or so ago, if you were between 12 and 17, you were referred to rather vaguely as being "at that age" or "in between." There were no clothes designed especially for you; you wore little girl dresses until the waistlines were under your armpits, and then you were graduated abruptly into your mother's kind of clothes. If you were a boy, you were promoted to long pants when your legs got long enough. No one considered your patois amusing. No one considered your problems important. You were low man on the social totem pole.

This was a deplorable state of affairs and clearly needed improvement. But now the pendulum seems to have swung as far the other way. Today the teenager, also known as the teenster, the teener, the subdeb, the prep, and the Junior Miss, is a national celebrity. He, or she, is society's most publicized and pampered pet. Magazines feature his problems. Novels, plays, comic strips, movies, radio serials, and television programs are based on his escapades and his wit. Fashion experts vie to design his clothes. And the general public views him with a flattering mixture of affection that used to be reserved for collegians in a raccoon coat.

At home, a teenager used to be treated like an ordinary member of the family. Today it is considered de rigueur to treat him like visiting royalty. The family kitchen and the family living room should be at his instant disposal, the experts tell us. Authorities suggest that we remodel an entire section of the family residence for his exclusive use. According to the experts, it is a teenager's privilege to monopolize the family radio and the family telephone. It is also considered his privilege to monopolize practically all of his parents' time, effort, patience, energy, and attention.

You can always identify a teenager's parents. There is a stoop to their shoulders. There is a harried look in their eyes. "Isn't it awful!" They are likely to murmur hollowly when you happen to meet. "If you think that is strenuous," they warn you while your own children are still in pin-up lingerie, "just wait till they're teenagers!"

Yes, you can always identify teenagers' parents, that is, if you can catch up with them. They haven't time to come to dinner. They haven't time to play bridge, they have been warned of sinister evils that would befall their young unless they maintained an all cylinder program supervision and entertainment. They have been made to feel that they are failing in their

*Continued*

**"Teenomania,"... *(Continued)***

duty as parents unless they spend every possible moment conveying their children and their children's friends to movies, club meetings, ball games, and parties, and retrieving them afterwards.

This vogue of lionizing the teenager is based on good intentions. Its purpose is to give him a fair share of social prominence, to help him avoid some well-known pitfalls, and to help him solve the problems of growing up. But does it really accomplish what it sets out to do? In my opinion, it is being carried to such extremes, it creates new problems instead of solving old ones, in my opinion, and it's unfair to everyone concerned....

Keeping your teenagers happy and well adjusted is a commendable achievement. Keeping parents happy and well adjusted will never make sensational copy, but there are those among them who feel it deserves some thought.

From the very end of a very long limb, I should like to suggest that our whole conception of what the parent-child relationship should be is in serious danger of getting out of kilter. Years ago, duty to one's parents was a recurrent and silent topic of discussion. Today, nobody talks about duty to his parents. Today, everybody talks about duty to children. Parents are held responsible for every physical and emotional anomaly that children develop, for every mistake they make, for every problem they have to face. Years ago, children were virtually the slaves of parents. We seem to be progressing a good deal faster than the law demands toward the exact reverse.

Religion, morality and knowledge being necessary to good government and the happiness of mankind, schools and the means of education shall forever be encouraged.

—The Northwest Ordinances of 1787 that authorized grants of lands for the establishment of educational institutions

**Annual Cost of University of Pennsylvania Undergraduate Schools:**

**1900**
College and the Wharton School:
Tuition: $150
Minimum: Room and Board: $185; Text-books: $10
Maximum: Room and Board: $250; Text-books: $50

**1930**
College, School of Engineering and Applied Science (SEAS) and the Wharton School:
Tuition: $400, which included the General Fee
Room and Board: $520; Text-books: $35; Clothing and miscellaneous: $260

**1955**
College, College of Liberal Arts for Women, School of Engineering and Applied Science (SEAS), the Wharton School, the School of Nursing, and the School of Allied Medical Professions (SAMP)
Tuition: $800
General Fee: $135; Room and Board: $835; Books: $50

# 1957 PROFILE

Martha Gardner had been reading to her son Scott since he was three, and he knew all the words in every book they read together, so she couldn't understand why he had so much trouble reading new material.

## Life at Home

- At long last, Martha Gardner had the answer to why her son Scott was not the top reader in his third-grade class.
- Everyone Martha met commented—with only a little prompting—on what a bright boy he was.
- So why didn't the school recognize his brilliance and award him better grades?
- The answer was phonics.
- Martha had suspected that Scott's problems were the school's fault, and now she had the evidence—Rudolf Flesch's best-selling book, *Why Johnny Can't Read*.
- America was in a crisis, thanks to the constant threat of communism and nuclear war, and it was America's schools that would lead the way to security.
- If only America's children were taught to read properly, the country would be safer.
- Martha had grown up in rural Georgia near Macon, and was married in 1945 to a military officer she met at the USO club at Warner Robins Air Force Base.
- He was tall, soft spoken and almost exotic with his Yankee background and mysterious way of smiling rather than talking.
- Not that anyone had a real opportunity to say anything when Martha was around.

*Martha Gardner blamed the schools for her son's reading problems.*

*Sally worked hard in school and always did her homework,*
*while Scott couldn't contain his energy long enough to pay attention.*

- She had the ability to speak in gusts of 60 miles per hour with sustained winds of 50 mph.
- Scott was the second child and was into everything; excess energy was his middle name.
- His older sister Sally mostly ignored her little brother, except when she wanted something; Scott could ask for anything, she had concluded, and get it.
- Sally worked hard, paid attention to the teacher and did her homework; Scott only took his brain to school a few days a week and rarely did his homework.
- But now everyone was in a lather over his grades when it was entirely his own fault, Sally was convinced.
- Sally knew that Scott was capable of learning—even memorizing—anything he wanted, no matter how complex—if he would simply slow down long enough to pay attention.
- Dating back to the colonial period, the alphabet was the focal point of reading instruction.
- Noah Webster's *Blue Backed Speller*, the first true reading textbook, sold 24 million copies, second only to the Bible, and served as the foundation for phonics.
- This was followed by the work of Favell Lee Mortimer, who employed phonics in the early flashcard set, *Reading Disentangled* in 1834, and *Reading Without Tears* in 1857.
- Then, in the middle of the nineteenth century, innovator Horace Mann criticized the repetitive drills in reading education and advocated that phonics not be taught at all.
- Since then, debates—or reading wars—had raged.
- John Dewey, the father of progressive education, noted the "drudgery" of the phonics method.
- What evolved was the commonly used "look-say" approach ensconced in the *Dick and Jane* readers popular in the mid-twentieth century, which dominated the field of early reading education.
- In 1955, Rudolf Flesch re-awakened the debate over phonics instruction and the prevailing preference for whole language teaching.
- In the opening chapter of his book *Why Johnny Can't Read*, he wrote that, after surveying American schools, "What I found was fantastic. The teaching of reading—all over the United States, in all the schools, in all textbooks—is totally wrong and flies in the face of all logic and common sense. Johnny couldn't read until half a year ago for the simple reason that nobody showed him how. Johnny's only problem was that he was unfortunately exposed to an ordinary American school....
- "Reading means getting meaning from certain combinations of letters. Teach the child what each letter stands for and he can read."
- The "whole language" approach to reading used in schools across America was predicated on the principle that children could learn to read given proper motivation, access to good literature, focus on meaning, and instruction to help them use meaning clues to determine the pronunciation of unknown words.

- The whole language method emphasized using words in context and focusing only a little on the sounds.
- For some advocates of whole language, the parsing of words into small chunks and reassembling them had no connection to the ideas the author wanted to convey.
- All Martha knew was that she had been reading to her son since he was three.
- Why did he have so much trouble reading new material, and why wasn't he able to read like his father did?

## Life at Work

- As the wife of an Air Force pilot, Martha Gardner endured long periods during which her husband was away when she raised the two children alone.
- Their current assignment was Homestead Air Force Base in Homestead, Florida, which housed a fleet of B-52 bombers under the control of the Strategic Air Command.
- After she completed reading, *Why Johnny Can't Read*, she was eager to discuss her conclusions with her husband, and was enormously frustrated that he was overseas on assignment.
- So she read parts of the book a second time, especially the letter to parents that opened the book, and Martha decided she must talk to Scott's teacher; surely she would understand that he could be her best student if only her method of teaching reading could be changed.
- Mrs. Mildred Greene had been teaching for 17 years to both town children and military kids who flowed through the city for a year or two, never to return.
- She had been trained in both whole language and phonics, and preferred phonics, but the school district endorsed the look-say methodology.
- Mrs. Greene knew from experience that education theories swing in and out of favor on a regular basis; phonics would have its day again, she knew.
- Besides, Martha Gardner was not the only parent who had read *Why Johnny Can't Read* and concluded a change was needed.
- When the book first appeared in 1955, it was serialized in newspapers across the country, igniting significant debate.
- Long ago, Mrs. Greene had blended phonics- and whole language-based reading in her class, but officially she followed the curriculum laid out by the district.
- She even owned a vintage collection of early McGuffey Readers, some of the first textbooks developed to teach reading.
- The McGuffey Readers included stories that emphasized the sounds of letters in words and contained stories that emphasized values like the rich helping the poor and being kind to animals.

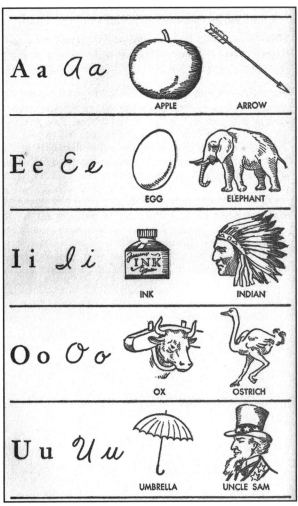

*Mrs. Greene used both the phonics (above) and whole language approach.*

- At the beginning of the twentieth century, the Progressive Education Movement pushed for instruction that focused more on the interests of students, using a more scientific approach to learning.
- In the 1950s, the *Dick and Jane* Readers published by Scott Foresman used a "whole word" approach to teaching reading, where words were repeated on each page enough times that students could remember them.
- Phonics advocates charged that the whole word approach fell apart when students began reading children's stories that did not have carefully controlled vocabularies.
- With phonics, they said, the reader had the necessary tools to sound out words based on how they were spelled.
- Phonics allowed students—especially those with large vocabularies—to go to the library and read a wide variety of children's literature.
- The history of reading instruction resembled a pendulum swinging between the two approaches.
- Whole language was considered a "top down" approach in which readers construct a personal meaning for a text based on using their prior knowledge to interpret the meaning of what they are reading.
- As soon as Martha came through the door, Mrs. Greene knew it was going to be a contentious meeting; Scott was a delightful young man when he settled down and paid attention—which wasn't often.
- Martha began politely enough, by first thanking Mrs. Greene for her skills and patience with Scott.
- Then she paused and produced the book *Why Johnny Can't Read*.
- The flaw of this method, Martha said, practically quoting the book word for word, was that it required learners to memorize words by sight.
- "These textbooks are not about reading, but word guessing."
- According to Flesch's book, when confronted with an unknown word, the learner became confused, and the only logical conclusion was a revival of the phonics method, the teaching of reading by teaching learners to sound out words.
- Mrs. Greene was patient and worked hard to wait Martha out.
- Her research had shown her that different children learn differently.
- The phonics model drew heavily from behaviorist learning theory associated with the work of the Harvard psychologist B.F. Skinner, while the whole language emphasis drew from constructivist learning theory and the work of the Russian psychologist Lev Vygotsky.
- Behaviorist learning theory was based on extrinsic rewards like money, grades, and gold stars rather than intrinsic rewards like feeling good about successfully accomplishing a difficult task.
- Constructivist learning theory was based on the idea that children learn by connecting new knowledge to previously learned knowledge.

---

## Chapter I

### A LETTER TO JOHNNY'S MOTHER

*A page from "Why Johnny Can't Read."*

- If children cannot connect new knowledge to old knowledge in a meaningful way, they may with difficulty memorize it (rote learning), but they will not have a real understanding of what they are learning.
- Mrs. Greene began quietly: "Learning to read is not a natural process," only to be interrupted by, "Scott started reading when he was three."
- Mrs. Greene began again: "Young children can memorize words rapidly in a way that gives the illusion of reading."
- Like many teachers, her approach was a systemic decoding of words blended with a literature-rich environment, a key aspect of the whole language approach.
- Martha listened carefully before asking again, "Why isn't Scott your best student? If only he could sound out the words, he would improve overnight. This book proves it."
- Mrs. Greene smiled, "Scott will learn to read the day he decides to settle down and pay attention. Not before. Phonics is not the problem, he is."
- Martha was unprepared for such a raw rendition of the problem and began to weep.
- Scott's older sister was an enthusiastic reader, her husband was a dedicated and consistent reader, so why wasn't her son following that path?
- Mrs. Greene listened patiently and then suggested that Martha use a phonics book to help Scott, and she would reinforce those lessons in the classroom.
- "In my experience," Mrs. Greene said, "you can't force feed children to learn; all you can do is create the right environment and opportunity."

## Life in the Community: Homestead, Florida
- Homestead, Florida, located 35 miles south of Miami, is nestled between Biscayne National Park to the east and Everglades National Park to the west.
- Homestead was incorporated in 1913 as the second-oldest city in Miami-Dade County, after the city of Miami.
- Its name originates from when the Florida East Coast Railway extension to Key West was being built.
- When the rail line was passing through an area, it was opened up for homesteading, and as the construction camp at the end of the line did not have a particular name, construction materials and supplies for the workers were consigned to "Homestead Country," shortened to "Homestead."
- Homestead Air Force Base was resurrected from the palmetto scrub of South Dade County in the early days of World War II.

*Martha's husband was in the Air Force.*

- In September of 1942, Lt. Col. William L. Plummer, with a handful of officers and enlisted men, assumed control of an isolated airstrip located about a mile inland from the shore of Biscayne Bay.
- The airstrip had been turned over to the government by Coconut Grove-based Pan American Ferries, Inc., which had carved it out of the rocky terrain in the early 1940s.
- With the attack on Pearl Harbor a vivid memory, the Army Air Corps commandeered the site as a maintenance stopover point for aircraft being ferried to the Caribbean and North Africa.
- In September, officers with the Caribbean Wing of the Air Transport Command (ATC) sent Colonel Plummer to the site to begin construction of a fully operational military base.
- During its first six months of existence, the newly established Homestead Army Air Field (AAF) served as a scheduled stop on a well-traveled air route from the northeastern United States.
- On January 30, 1943, the base assumed a more vital role with the activation of the 2nd Operational Training Unit (OTU).
- The mission of the permanently assigned cadre of nine officers, 15 enlisted men, and 12 civilian flight instructors was to provide advanced training for aircrew members who would one day pilot C-54s, C-87s and C-46s along the 188,000 miles of the ATC's globe-spanning routes.
- By 1945, Homestead AAF represented the largest four-engine transport training operation in the entire ATC.
- The 2nd OTU had graduated 2,250 C-54 pilots, 14,505 copilots, 224 navigators, 85 radio operators, and 1,375 flight engineers.
- On September 15, 1945, three years to the day after the base's founding, a massive hurricane roared ashore, sending winds of up to 145 mph tearing through the Air Field's buildings.
- Enlisted housing facilities, the nurses' dormitory and the Base Exchange were all destroyed.
- The roof was ripped from what would later become building 741, the "Big Hangar."
- The base laundry and fire station were both declared total losses.
- The few remaining aircraft were tossed about like leaves.
- Following an evaluation of the damage, officials announced on October 25, 1945, that Homestead AAF would be shut down, with a target date for complete closure of December 1, 1945.
- When the Air Force was created as a separate service on September 18, 1947, the old Homestead Army Air Field lay in ruins.
- In June of 1948, when the Soviets began the total land blockade of Berlin, the Air Force responded with an unprecedented airlift effort known as Operation Vittles.
- Twenty-four hours a day, seven days a week, for 16 months, Air Force C-54 "Sky Masters," many of them piloted by Homestead graduates, flew in and out of Berlin, keeping one of the world's great cities alive.
- In the early 1950s, as the Korean conflict was winding down, defense officials once again looked toward Homestead with an eye to making the site an integral part of the U.S. continental defense.
- In mid-1954, an advance party arrived at the old base to begin the cleanup effort, and on February 8, 1955, the installation was reactivated as Homestead Air Force Base.
- The base quickly became home to the 823rd Air Division, an umbrella organization encompassing the 379th and 19th Bomber Wings.
- By the end of the decade, Homestead housed more than 6,000 permanently assigned members, twice the size of its busiest World War II days, and a fleet of B-47 "Stratojet" bombers.

## HISTORICAL SNAPSHOT
# 1957

- The San Francisco and Los Angeles stock exchanges merged to form the Pacific Coast Stock Exchange
- Hamilton Watch Company introduced the first electric watch
- Wham-O Company produced the first Frisbee
- Ku Klux Klan members forced truck driver Willie Edwards to jump off a bridge into the Alabama River, where he drowned
- The FBI arrested union leader Jimmy Hoffa and charged him with bribery
- Elvis Presley bought Graceland on 3734 Bellevue Boulevard, Memphis, Tennessee, for $100,000
- Rodgers and Hammerstein's *Cinderella*, the team's only musical written especially for television, was telecast live and in color by CBS, starring Julie Andrews in the title role
- IBM sold the first compiler for the FORTRAN scientific programming language
- Allen Ginsberg's poem *Howl*, printed in England, was seized by U.S. Customs officials on the grounds of obscenity
- Brooklyn Dodgers owner Walter O'Malley agreed to move the team from Brooklyn, New York, to Los Angeles
- Oklahoma celebrated its semi-centennial statehood by burying a brand-new 1957 Plymouth Belvedere in a time capsule, to be opened 50 years later on June 15, 2007
- John Lennon and Paul McCartney met for the first time as teenagers at Woolton Fete, three years before forming the Beatles
- Marine Major John Glenn flew an F8U supersonic jet from California to New York in three hours, 23 minutes and eight seconds, setting a new transcontinental speed record
- The International Atomic Energy Agency was established
- *American Bandstand*, a local dance show produced by WFIL-TV in Philadelphia, joined the ABC Television Network
- President Eisenhower announced a two-year suspension of nuclear testing
- Senator Strom Thurmond (D-SC) set the record for the longest filibuster with his 24-hour, 18-minute speech railing against a Civil Rights bill
- The Ford Motor Company introduced the Edsel on what the company proclaimed as "E Day"
- The first edition of Jack Kerouac's *On the Road* went on sale
- President Eisenhower sent federal troops to Arkansas to provide safe passage into Central High School for the Little Rock Nine
- *West Side Story* premiered on Broadway and ran for 732 performances
- The Soviet Union launched *Sputnik 1*, the first artificial satellite to orbit Earth
- The comedy sitcom *Leave It to Beaver* premiered on television
- Toyota began exporting vehicles to the U.S., beginning with the Toyota Crown and the Land Cruiser
- Gordon Gould invented the laser
- The first U.S. attempt to launch a satellite failed when the rocket blew up on the launch pad
- The movie *The Bridge on the River Kwai* was released and captured the Academy Award for Best Picture
- The Boeing 707 airliner was introduced

## Selected Prices

Candygram, Western Union, Pound....................................................$2.95

Clearasil ............................................................................................$0.59

Fruit Cocktail ....................................................................................$0.93

Hamburger, Burger King Whopper....................................................$0.37

Hotel Room, Ritz-Carlton, Boston.....................................................$9.00

Man's Shirt, Arrow............................................................................$5.00

Movie Projector ..............................................................................$89.95

Theatre Ticket, New York ................................................................$3.85

Vodka, Smirnoff, Fifth ......................................................................$5.23

Woman's Suit...................................................................................$17.95

### "Two Years Wasted," Rudolph Flesch, *Why Johnny Can't Read*, 1955:

If you are a mother of a child in the second or third grade who can't read and spell, you'll sooner or later go to the school and complain that your child isn't taught the letters and sounds. You will then be told, one way or the other, that phonics is utterly out of date; just wait, your boy or girl will suddenly catch on.

But if your child is in first grade, the answer you'll get will be considerably shorter, strongly resembling a brush-off. The teacher will tell you, with a rather indulgent smile: "He isn't ready, you know."

When you get to the subject of "readiness," you approach the holy of holies, the inner sanctum of the whole "science" of reading. In each of the fat tomes on how to teach reading, pages and pages are filled with profound discussions of what makes a child ready for reading, when does he get ready, how to tell whether he is or not, how to speed him up or slow him down, what to do with him before he gets ready, how to instill readiness, how to make it grow, how to use it, treat it, protect it, diagnose it, improve it, ripen it, and direct it. Deep mystery covers this whole recondite subject, and work has been going on for decades to explore its recesses.

One of the "authorities," in fact, went so far as to devote a whole book to the subject of "reading readiness." I went through that whole book in search of the definition of "readiness," being sincerely curious to know what was meant by the word. But there was no definition that could be found. So, since the experts didn't seem to help us, I'll offer my own definition. "Reading readiness" means the readiness of the teacher to let the child start reading.

If ever there was an example of reasoning in a vicious cycle, this is it. You take a six-year-old child and start to teach him something. The child, as often happens, doesn't take to it at once. If you use a common-sense approach, you try again and again, exert a little patience, and after some time the child begins to learn. But if you are a twentieth-century American educator, equipped with the theory of "readiness," you drop the whole matter instantly and wait until the child, on his own, asks to be taught. Let's wait until he's seven, until he's eight, until he's nine. We've all the time in the world; it would be a crime to teach a child who wasn't "ready."

**"Johnny Can Read!" Dr. Arthur F. Corey, State Executive Secretary, California Teachers Association, *Humboldt Standard*, Eureka, California, May 28, 1955:**

San Franciscans and Northern Californians should know that, contrary to Mr. Flesch's contention that phonics are being disregarded, actually phonics are being used in almost all schools in their areas. On May 13, telegrams asking about the use of phonics to 20 Northern California school districts brought forth a response from everyone. All are using phonics….

Is it any wonder, then, that people everywhere are surprised, not to say shocked, at the bland conclusion of Mr. Flesch that phonics are taught either "not at all or only incidentally."

Every manual prepared for the guidance of teachers of reading that I have seen emphasizes that no one method of teaching reading is sufficient to the needs of a classroom of children; that more than one method is necessary if the varying capacities of all the children are to be, from the reading standpoint, properly nurtured.

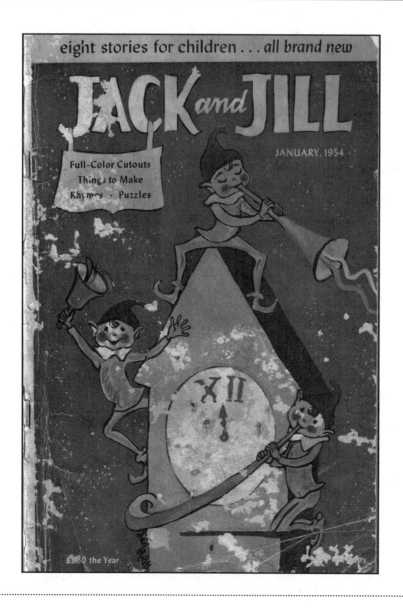

# 1958 NEWS FEATURE

*How Children Fail*, **John Holt, Perseus Books, 1964:**

**May 10, 1958**

Children are often quite frank about the strategies they use to get answers out of the teacher. I once observed a class in which the teacher was testing her students on parts of speech. On the blackboard she had three columns, headed Noun, Adjective, and Verb. As she gave each word, she called on a child and asked in which column the word belonged.

Like most teachers, she hadn't thought enough about what she was doing to realize, first, that many of the words given could fit into more than one column and, second, it is often the way a word is used that determines what part of speech it is.

There was a good deal of the tried-and-true strategy of guess-and-look, in which you start to say a word, all the while scrutinizing the teacher's face to see whether you are on the right track or not. With most teachers, no further strategies are needed. This one was more poker-faced than most, so guess-and-look wasn't working very well. Still, the percentage of hits was markedly high, especially since it was clear to me from the way the children were talking and acting that they hadn't a notion what nouns, adjectives, and verbs were. Finally, one child said, "Miss, you shouldn't point to the answer each time." The teacher was surprised, and asked what she meant. The child said, "Well, you don't exactly point, but you kind of stand next to the answer." This was no clearer, since the teacher had been standing still. But after a while, as the class went on, I thought I saw what the girl meant. Since the teacher wrote each word down in its proper column, she was, in a way, getting herself ready to write, pointing herself at the place where she was soon to be writing. From the angle of her body to the blackboard, children picked up a subtle clue to the correct answer.

This was not all. At the end of every third word, her three columns came out even, that is, there were an equal number of nouns, adjectives, and verbs. This meant that when she started off a new row, you had one chance in three of getting the right answer by a blind guess; but for the last word you had one chance in two, and the last word was a dead giveaway to the lucky student who was asked it. Hardly any missed this opportunity; in fact, they answered so quickly that the teacher (brighter than most) caught on to their system and began keeping her columns uneven, making the strategist's job a bit harder.

In the midst of all this, there came a vivid example of the kind of thing we say in school that makes no sense, but only bewilders and confuses the thoughtful child who tries to make sense out of it. The teacher, who specially, by the way, was English, had told these children that a verb is a word of action—which is not always true. One of the words she asked was "dream." She was thinking of the noun, and apparently did not remember that "dream" can easily be a verb. One little boy, making a pure guess, said it was a verb. Here the teacher, to be helpful, contributed one of those "explanations" that are so much more hindrance than help. She said, "But a verb has to have action; can you give me a sense, using dream that has action?" The child thought a bit, and said, "I had a dream about the Trojan War." Now it's pretty hard to get much more action than that. But the teacher told him he was wrong, and he sat silent, with an utterly baffled and frightened expression on his face. She was so busy thinking about what she wanted him to say, she was so obsessed with the *right answer* hidden in her mind, that she could not think about what he was really saying and thinking, could not see that his reasoning was logical and correct, and that the mistake was not his but hers.

At one of our leading prep schools I saw, the other day, an example of the way in which a teacher may not know what is going on in his own class.

This was a math class. The teacher, an experienced man, was doing the day's assignment on the blackboard. His way of keeping attention was to ask various members of the class, at each step, "Is that right?" It was a dull class, and I found it hard to keep my mind on it. It seemed to me that most in the class had their minds elsewhere, with a little mental sentry posted to alert them when their name was called. As each name was called, the boy who was asked if something or other was right answered yes. The class droned on. In time, my mind slipped away altogether; I don't know how long. Suddenly something snapped me to attention. I looked at the teacher. Every boy in the class was looking at him, too. The boy who had been asked if what he'd written on the board was right, was carefully looking at the blackboard. After a moment he said, "No, sir, that isn't right, it ought to be so-and-so." The teacher chuckled appreciably and said "You're right, it should be." He made the change and the class and I settled back into our private thoughts for the rest of the period.

After the boys had left, I thanked the teacher for letting me visit. He said, "You notice I threw in a little curve ball there. I do that every now and then. Keeps them on their toes." It didn't seem the time or place to tell him that when he threw his little curve ball, the expression of his voice changed enough so that it warned not only the boys, but also a complete stranger, that something was coming and that attention had better be paid.

**July 27, 1958**

It has become clear over the year that these children see school almost entirely in terms of the day-to-day and hour-to-hour tasks that we impose on them. This is not at all the way the teacher thinks of it. The conscientious teacher thinks of himself as taking his students (at least partway) on a journey to some glorious destination, well worth the pains of the trip. If he teaches history, he thinks how interesting, how exciting, how useful it is to know history, and how fortunate his students will be when they begin to share this knowledge. If he teaches French, he thinks of the glories of French literature, or the beauty of the spoken French, or the delights of French cooking, and how he is helping to make these joys available to his students. And so for all subjects.

Thus, teachers feel, as I once did, that their interest in their students is fundamentally the same. I used to feel that I was guiding and helping my students a journey that they wanted to take but could not take without my help. I knew the way looked hard, but I assumed they could see the goal almost as clearly as I and that they were most eager to reach it. It seemed very important to give students the feeling of being on a journey to a worthwhile destination. I see now that most of my talk was wasted breath. Maybe I thought the students were in my class because they were eager to learn what I was trying to teach, but they knew better. They were in school because they had to be, and in my class either because they had to be or otherwise they would have had to be in another class, which might be even worse.

Children in school are like children at the doctor's. He can talk himself blue in the face about how much good the medicine is going to do them; all they think of is how much it will hurt them and how bad it will taste. Given their own way, they would have none of it.

So the valiant and resolute band of travelers I thought I was leading toward a much-hoped-for destination turned out instead to be more like convicts in a chain gang, forced under threat of punishment to move along a rough path leading nobody knew where. School feels like this to children: it is a place where *they* make you go and where *they* tell you to do things and where *they* try to make your life unpleasant if you don't do them or don't do them right.

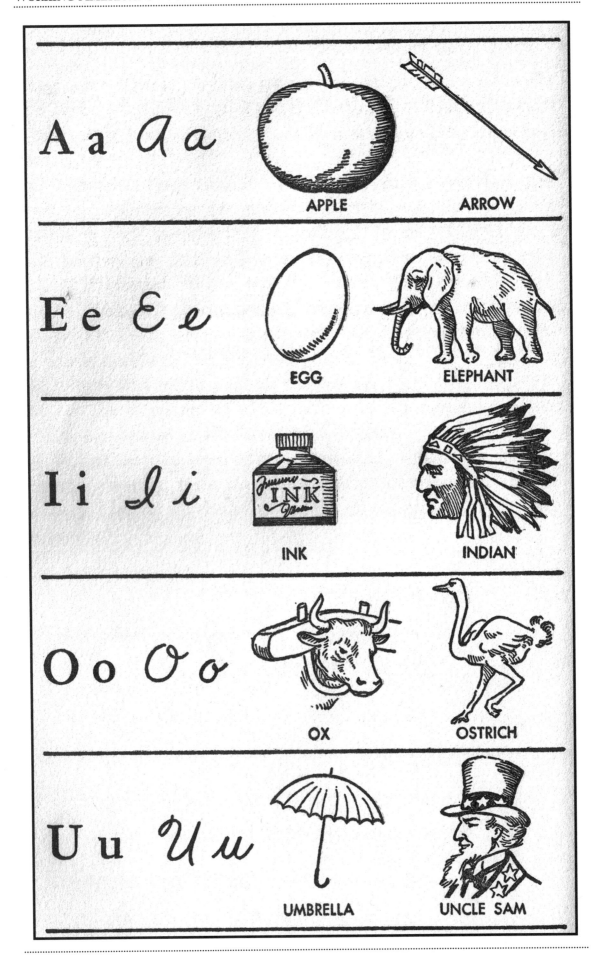

- These loans ranged from $1,000 to $5,000, to be repaid within 10 years after the student had graduated.
- The legislation also prohibited federal control over curricula, administration, or personnel.
- To Carl's way of thinking, Sputnik also brought to the surface many of the issues raging within the education community.
- Should progressive, child-centered education or basic, discipline-centered education have precedence in the schools?
- Should a priority be given to building the nation's scientific capability or to creating nationwide science literacy?
- Who should decide what students were supposed to learn? Teachers, school administrators and trustees, parents, or university scholars?
- What should the balance be between the stability that comes with maintaining traditional content and the confusion and inefficiency that accompanied the introduction of major changes?
- Carl discovered that projects founded in the Sputnik years—linking teachers and scientists—accomplished more.
- Most scientists knew little about the realities of precollege education, and few educators had a firm grasp of the practice of science.
- The greatest result of Sputnik, Carl believed, was the way it stimulated additional science-oriented activities.
- Prior to Sputnik, little science was taught in the lower grades; now children were being exposed to the fundamentals at an earlier age, and Carl could push them further when they reached his class.

*The Russian satellite was launched into orbit in 1957.*

## Life in the Community: Oklahoma City, Oklahoma
- Oklahoma City, the capital and the largest city in Oklahoma, was founded during the Land Run of 1889, and grew to a population of over 10,000 within hours.
- As the town continued to grow, the population doubled between 1890 and 1900.
- During the opening decades of the twentieth century, Oklahoma City developed one of the largest livestock markets in the world, attracting jobs and revenue from Chicago and Omaha.
- Oklahoma was admitted to the Union in 1907.
- Oklahoma City was a major stop on Route 66 during the early part of the twentieth century.
- With the 1928 discovery of oil within the city limits, it became a center of oil production.
- Natural gas, petroleum products and related industries became the largest sector of the local economy; oil derricks dotted the city, including the capitol grounds.
- Bisected by the North Canadian River, Oklahoma City experienced flooding every year until the 1940s, when a dam was built on the river to control the water.

*Oklahoma City was a center for oil production.*

## HISTORICAL SNAPSHOT
# 1959

- CBS Radio eliminated four soap operas: *Backstage Wife*, *Our Gal Sunday*, *The Road of Life*, and *This is Nora Drake*
- Alaska was admitted as the forty-ninth state; Hawaii became the fiftieth
- The U.S. recognized the new Cuban government of Fidel Castro
- Motown Records was founded by Berry Gordy, Jr.
- Walt Disney released his sixteenth animated film, *Sleeping Beauty*, which was the company's first animated film to be shown in 70 mm with modern, six-track stereophonic sound
- A chartered plane transporting musicians Buddy Holly, Ritchie Valens, the Big Bopper, and pilot Roger Peterson went down in foggy conditions near Clear Lake, Iowa, killing all four occupants
- At Cape Canaveral, Florida, the first successful test firing of a Titan intercontinental ballistic missile was accomplished
- The United States launched the Vanguard II weather satellite
- Racecar driver Lee Petty won the first Daytona 500
- Recording sessions for the album *Kind of Blue* by Miles Davis began at Columbia's 30th Street Studio in New York City
- The Marx Brothers made their last TV appearance in *The Incredible Jewel Robbery*
- The Barbie doll debuted
- The Busch Gardens amusement park in Tampa, Florida, was dedicated and opened its gates
- The Dalai Lama fled Tibet and was granted asylum in India
- NASA selected seven military pilots to become the first U.S. astronauts
- The St. Lawrence Seaway linking the Great Lakes and the Atlantic Ocean officially opened to shipping
- The USS *George Washington* was launched as the first submarine to carry ballistic missiles
- Charles Ovnand and Dale R. Buis became the first Americans killed in action in Vietnam
- The first skull of Australopithecus was discovered by Mary Leakey in the Olduvai Gorge in Tanzania
- The Soviet rocket Luna 2 became the first man-made object to crash on the moon, and Luna 3 sent back the first photographs of the far side of the moon
- Rod Serling's classic anthology series *The Twilight Zone* premiered on CBS
- MGM's widescreen, multimillion dollar, Technicolor version of *Ben-Hur*, starring Charlton Heston, was released and won a record 11 Academy Awards
- The Henney Kilowatt went on sale in the U.S., becoming the first mass-produced electric car in almost three decades
- Plants discovered after this year could only be named in a modern language rather than in Latin

## Selected Prices

Candygram, Western Union, Pound.................................................$2.95

Clearasil ....................................................................................$0.59

Fruit Cocktail ............................................................................$0.93

Hamburger, Burger King Whopper................................................$0.37

Hotel Room, Ritz-Carlton, Boston.................................................$9.00

Man's Shirt, Arrow......................................................................$5.00

Movie Projector .........................................................................$89.95

Telescope, 80 mm .......................................................................$59.99

Theatre Ticket, New York ............................................................$3.85

Vodka, Smirnoff, Fifth ................................................................$5.23

*Philosophiae Naturalis Principia Mathematica*, **Sir Isaac Newton, 1687:**

If a leaden cannon ball is horizontally propelled by a powder charge from a cannon positioned on a hilltop, it will follow a curving flight path until it hits the ground.... You can make it turn 10 degrees, 30 degrees and 90 degrees before it touches the ground. You can force it to circle the Earth and even disappear into outer space, going away to infinity.

---

I saw the bright little ball, moving majestically across the narrow star field between the ridgelines. I stared at it with no less rapt attention than if it had been God Himself in a golden chariot riding overhead. It soared with what seemed to me inexorable and dangerous purpose, as if there were no power in the universe that could stop it. All my life, everything important that had ever happened had always happened somewhere else. But Sputnik was right there in front of my eyes in my backyard in Coalwood, McDowell County, West Virginia, U.S.A. I couldn't believe it.

—Fourteen-year-old Homer H. Hickam, Jr., describing Sputnik

---

**"Spudnik's [sic] Beeps Continue But Tones Varying,"**
*Hamilton Journal* **(Ohio), October 10, 1957:**

Fog over the U.S. northeast coast today blanked out a major effort to get a visual fix on the Soviet Earth satellite hurtling through the skies.

Scientists and moon watchers of a Cambridge team man the telescopes atop the Harvard College Observatory as the moonlet sped on a southeasterly course above Nova Scotia, northeast of Boston, at 6:40 AM. But the fog hit the target, as clouds had done when the Cambridge observers made their first effort Wednesday.

Monitoring stations in the Western Hemisphere and Europe reported signals from the speeding sphere were coming in strong, although with varying tones.

There was some difference of opinion among scientists whether the satellite is maintaining its rate of speed and its altitude.

But broadcasts from Moscow said the man-made moon will stay aloft for a long time.

*Continued*

**"Spudnik's [sic] Beeps Continue But Tones Varying,"** . . . *(Continued)*

Canada's Dominion Observatory at Ottawa said Wednesday night the Russian moonlet, launched last Friday, was photographed over Alberta. Earlier, it was reported that the photograph had been taken at Auckland, New Zealand....

The signals emitted by the sphere were reported by listening posts in various places to have changed from the original beep-beep sound.

The U.S. Naval Research Laboratory said it was receiving a hum interspersed with an occasional beep. Radio operators in Mazatlan, Mexico, told of hearing a signal that sounded like "psst, psst, psst."

A spokesman for the Naval Research Laboratory said the difference in signals might be explained by a variation in receiving equipment, or perhaps the location of the sets in relation to the path of the satellite.

Two Moscow radio broadcasts, both for home listeners, gave conflicting views on the moonlet's speed. One said it was speeding up. The other said it was slowing down. There was no attempt to explain the conflict.

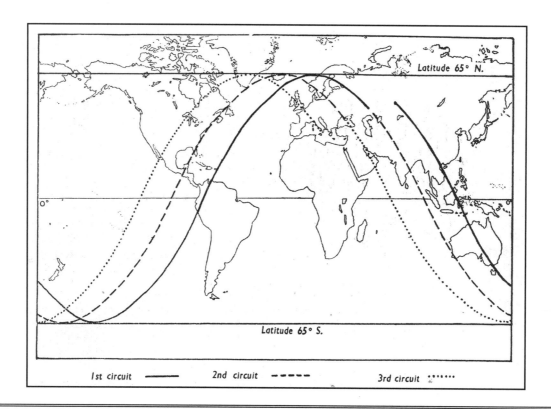

## "The Russian Earth Satellite," *The Space Encyclopedia*, November 1957, Supplement, 1958:

On the evening of October 4, 1957, the first of a series of artificial satellites was successfully placed into an orbit by the scientists of the Soviet Union. Being the most outstanding feature of this achievement are the unexpectedly great weight of the satellite, the speed with which the Russian project has been put into practice, and the inclination of the orbit….

The Russian satellite is only two inches longer than the Vanguard sphere, but about nine times as heavy. This means that the original launching vehicle must have been about nine times the weight of the Vanguard three-stage rocket, or that Russian scientists have made remarkable advances in rocket propulsion techniques. It is most unlikely that so heavy a rocket was fired from a balloon in the manner of the Far Side rockets. It is far easier to double the height attained by the rocket than to double the payload it can carry, and the Russian success on this point is most significant, especially when one remembers that from military applications, it is the payload, i.e., the weight of the warhead, that matters.

The Russian satellite carries little instrumentation other than a strong radio transmitter, and its weight is therefore mostly taken up by heavy batteries which supplied the necessary power for three weeks. It has been said that because of its lack of other instrumentation, the Russian satellite has been of little scientific use compared with one being prepared in the U.S., but it has already provided a wealth of information and paved the way for later, more elaborate models, in which solar energy may be used to power the transmitter so that the batteries can make room for a number of instruments and telemetering equipment.

**"Political and Military Implications of Sputnik Throw Screen Around Scientific Value of Moon,"** *Hamilton Journal* (Ohio), October 10, 1957:

The political and military implications of Sputnik are throwing a smokescreen around the scientific value of the man-made, man-controlled Earth satellite.

While the West mourns a race lost, Sputnik spins merrily on, its stuttering beeps apparently transmitting scientific data to its earthbound makers.

What information is Sputnik transmitting?

The Soviets have said it is counting meteor hits and collecting data on the South Magnetic Pole. One Russian scientist has hinted it also is measuring temperatures in space.

That's only one part of what Earth satellites—Russian and American—were expected to do this International geophysical year. Six to 10 planned by the United States will study meteors, magnetism, and temperature as well as cosmic and sun rays, air density, space pressure, even the shape and composition of the earth.

These things have been studied before but never outside the atmosphere, the dense layer of air that envelops the earth and obscures the secrets of space.

Data gathered by the prying satellites probably will not have immediate practical value. But it will provide a foundation on which future practical results may be built.

A half-century ago, Albert Einstein formulated a basic theory that matter can be converted into energy. It was 40 years before practical atom energy grew up on that platform.

The satellite reports can answer questions like these:

What effect do temperatures in the line of severe electric current have upon wind velocities on the surface of the earth?

What does this mean for weather forecasters?

What is the connection between sunspots, those vast, turbulent storms on the face of the sun, and the auroras that frequently rob an earthly radio communication?

What does this hold for the future of radio?

What is the source of cosmic rays, powerful and penetrating electromagnetic radiation, which create energy as they pass to the atmosphere?

Can they be harnessed to serve mankind?

Satellites, of course, are man's first tentative steps toward space travel.

*Continued*

### "Political and Military Implications of Sputnik Throw Screen Around Scientific Value of Moon . . . *(Continued)*

The artificial moons reach a balance at 18,000 miles an hour between the possessive pull of the earth's gravity and centrifugal force tending to hurl them into outer space.

A relatively not much faster push would allow them to break out of this hold and possibly reach the moon, and they hope to hit within the next decade.

# Federal Legislation Supporting Education

**1787 and 1788**
Land Ordinance Act and Northwest Ordinance: These ordinances provided for the establishment of public education first in the territory between the Appalachian Mountains and the Mississippi River, requiring that one square mile of every 36 be reserved for support of public education and then in new states be encouraged to establish "schools and the means for education."

**1862 and 1890**
Morrill Land Grant College Acts: These acts established 69 institutions of higher education in various states.

**1917**
Smith-Hughes Act: This act provided funds for teacher training and program development in vocational education at the high school level.

**1944**
Servicemen's Readjustment Act: This Act paid veterans' tuition and living expenses for a specific number of months.

**1958**
National Defense Education Act: In response to Sputnik, funds were allocated for student loans, the education of school counselors, and the strengthening of instructional programs in science, mathematics and foreign languages.

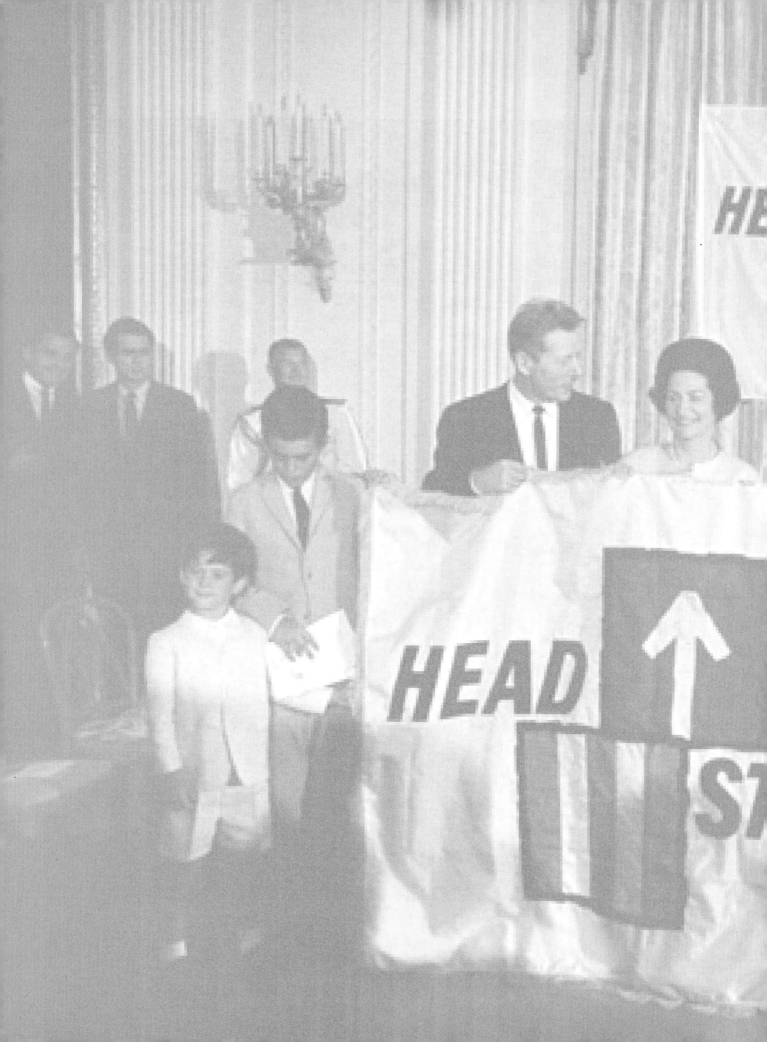

# 1960–1969

The 1960s were tumultuous. Following the placid era of the 1950s, the seventh decade of the twentieth century contained tragic assassinations, momentous social movements, remarkable achievements in space, and the longest war in American history. Civil Rights leader Martin Luther King, Jr., would deliver his "I have a dream" speech in 1963, the same year President John F. Kennedy was killed. Five years later, in 1968, King, along with John Kennedy's influential brother Bobby, would be shot.

The Cold War became hotter during conflicts over Cuba and Berlin in the early 1960s. Fears over the international spread of communism led to America's intervention in a foreign conflict that would become a defining event of the decade: Vietnam.

From 1960 to 1964, the economy expanded; unemployment was low and disposable income for music, vacations, art, or simply having fun grew rapidly. Internationally, the power of the United States was immense. Congress gave the young President Kennedy the defense and space-related programs Americans wanted, but few of the welfare programs he proposed. Then, inflation arrived, along with the Vietnam War. Between 1950 and 1965, inflation soared from an annual average of less than 2 percent (ranging from 6 percent to 14 percent a year) to a budget-popping average of 9.5 percent. Upper class investors, once content with the consistency and stability of banks, sought better returns in the stock market and in real estate.

In addition to its stated objective of educating the nation's youth, America's local public schools were placed at the center of the nationwide war on poverty. More and more studies had linked years in school to lifetime earning potential or the confluence of dropouts and prison. A major report on education read, "The school must play a larger role in the development of poor youngsters if they are to have, in fact, equal opportunity." All the while, educators were coping with student threats to protest the Vietnam War, parental threats to protest sex education classes, meeting the mandate for school integration, and reshuffling declining school tax revenues impacted by inflation, rising gasoline prices, and white flight from America's cities.

Military involvement in Vietnam grew from advisory status to full-scale war. By 1968, Vietnam had become a national obsession, leading to President Lyndon Johnson's decision not to run for another term and fueling not only debate over the country's role in Vietnam, but also more inflation and national division.

The antiwar movement grew rapidly. Antiwar marches, which had drawn but a few thousand in 1965, grew in size until millions of marchers filled the streets of New York, San Francisco, and Washington, DC, only a few years later. By spring of 1970, 448 colleges made ROTC voluntary or abolished it.

The struggle to bring economic equality to blacks during the period produced massive spending for school integration. By 1963, the peaceful phase of the Civil Rights Movement was ending; street violence, assassinations, and bombings defined the period. In 1967, 41 cities experienced major disturbances. At the same time, charismatic labor organizer César Chavez formed the United Farm Workers and led a Civil Rights-style movement for Mexican-Americans, gaining national support which challenged the growers of the West with a five-year agricultural strike.

As a sign of increasing affluence and changing times, American consumers bought 73 percent fewer potatoes and 25 percent more fish, poultry, and meat, and 50 percent more citrus products and tomatoes, than in 1940. California passed New York as the most populous state. Factory workers earned more than $100 a week—their highest wages in history. From 1960 to 1965, the amount of money spent on prescription weight-loss drugs doubled, while the per-capita consumption of processed potato chips rose from 6.3 pounds in 1958 to 14.2 pounds eight years later. In 1960, approximately 40 percent of American adult women had paying jobs; 30 years later, the number would grow to 57.5 percent. Their emergence into the work force would transform marriage, child rearing, and the economy. In 1960, women were also liberated by the FDA's approval of the birth control pill, giving both women and men a degree of control over their bodies that had never existed before. During the decade, anti-establishment sentiments grew: men's hair was longer and wilder, beards and mustaches became popular, women's skirts rose to mid-thigh, and bras were often discarded. Hippies advocated alternative lifestyles; drug use—especially marijuana and LSD—increased; the Beatles, the Rolling Stones, Jimi Hendrix, and Janis Joplin became popular music figures; and college campuses became major sites for demonstrations against the war and for Civil Rights. The Supreme Court prohibited school prayer, assured legal counsel to the poor, limited censorship of sexual material, and increased the rights of the accused.

Extraordinary space achievements also marked the decade. Ten years after President Kennedy announced he would place a man on the moon, 600 million people around the world watched as Neil Armstrong gingerly lowered his left foot into the soft dust of the moon's surface. In a tumultuous time of division and conflict, the landing was one of America's greatest triumphs and an exhilarating demonstration of American genius. Its cost was $25 billion and set the stage for 10 other men to walk on the moon over the next three years. The 1960s saw the birth of Enovid 10, the first oral contraceptive (cost $0.55 each), the start of Berry Gordy's Motown Records, felt-tip pens, Diet Rite cola, Polaroid color film, Weight Watchers, and Automated Teller Machines. It was the decade when lyrics began appearing on record albums, Jackie and Aristotle Onassis reportedly spent $20 million during their first year together, and the Gay Liberation Front participated in the Hiroshima Day March, the first homosexual participation as a separate constituency in a peace march.

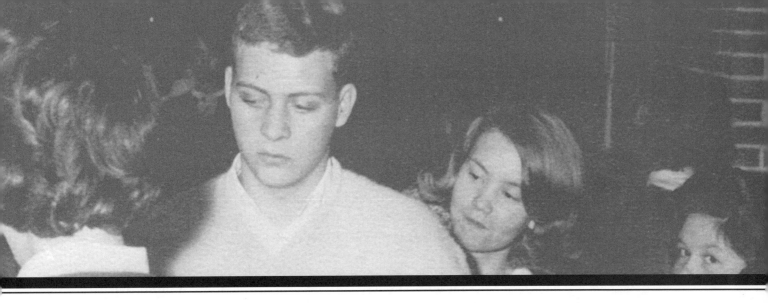

# 1960 News Feature

**"Improving Textbooks," Russell Kirk, *National Review*, September 10, 1960:**

Anyone who has bothered to save school and college textbooks over the past 40 or 50 years—or who will go to the trouble of turning over such textbooks as have accumulated in the attics of an old house—can see for himself there has been a dismaying deterioration of quality with the passing of the decades. The paper, binding, illustrations, and typeface all have improved; but in style and substance, the text itself, in nearly all disciplines, has been reduced to boring and deceptive generalizations. Really first-rate textbooks for high schools now are difficult to obtain: The educationist pressure-groups have persuaded every big publisher in the field to adopt his textbooks to "progressive" and "permissive" standards.

What is equally disheartening, there has crept into textbooks a sermonizing indoctrination in "socially approved attitudes," at the expense of straightforward instruction in the particular discipline. This is true not only of "social studies" textbooks, but of many in the humanities. "Socially approved attitudes" usually include enthusiasm (quite indiscriminating) for the United Nations Organization, zeal for promoting equality of economic condition, fondness for the centralized welfare state, a favorable view of federal aid to schools, and all that. Until very recent years, sweet sympathy for the aims of the Soviet peoples was on this list of approved attitudes in many textbooks, but in recent editions, that socially approved attitude has been stricken out or modified.

Sometimes the authors of these textbooks are so candid as to declare their aim of indoctrination. Take, for instance, the foreword "To Teachers" in a high school textbook entitled *Geography and World Affairs*, by Stephen Jones and Marion Fisher Murphy (Rand McNally and Company, 1957). Jones and Murphy declare roundly that "an important part of our objectives is the development of socially desirable understandings and attitudes. Evaluating these intangibles is more difficult. *Geography and World Affairs* sets up a series of subjective tests as one means by which the student's personal and social reactions can be gauged. These ... may be used in pre-testing as a legitimate part of the evaluation process...." In short, indoctrination and conditioning are fine and dandy with Prof. Jones and Mrs. Murphy. It should be said for them, however, that their "socially approved attitudes" toward world affairs and geography are merely part and parcel of a muddled and sentimental humanitarianism.

**Distorted History**

To effect some reform of substance and style in these textbooks, frank and fair criticism is necessary. Secondary school and high school textbooks are reviewed almost nowhere; college textbooks only in the journals of learned societies. Educational administrators, professors, teachers, school board members, and college trustees scarcely know where to turn for evaluation of textbooks, even when they are aware that the books used in their classrooms are anti-intellectual and propagandistic.

At a Michigan high school, a student's mother came to complain to the superintendent about the tenth-grade textbook in American history. Yes, the superintendent agreed, it was a superficial and opinionated book. About Benjamin Franklin, for instance, all the textbook authors said was that he was senile at the Constitutional Convention and had been over fond of women. The superintendent knew and regretted this. But where could one find a better one? He had tried and failed. The whole level of history textbooks was low, and textbooks used in the schools have to be in a list approved by the state educational authorities, so he was limited in his choice.

Lest I sink my readers irrecoverably deep in the Slough of Despond, I hasten to add that rescue is at hand: Two tax-exempt foundations are taking action in this matter and are about to make standard evaluation of standard textbooks....

If you, gentle reader, desire to aid in the improvement of textbooks, we suggest you give or lend copies of these evaluations to professors, teachers, school board members, and college trustees— aye, even unto administrators. Say not the struggle naught availeth.

# 1961 PROFILE

Civil Rights pioneer Septima Clark taught in the South Carolina schools for 40 years before she was fired for refusing to resign her membership in the NAACP.

## Life at Home

- Septima Poinsette Clark was born on May 3, 1898, in Charleston, South Carolina.
- Her mother, Victoria Warren Anderson, was raised in Haiti and excelled in its challenging educational environment, which was modeled after that of Europe.
- As a young woman, Victoria came to live in the United States, where she met and married Septima's father, Peter Porcher Poinsette.
- Peter, a Muskhogean from the tribes of the Georgia Sea Islands, was born a slave on a coastal plantation.
- Freed at the end of the Civil War, he found work on a steamship, which traveled between Charleston and New York.
- Once married, Victoria and Peter took up residence in Charleston.
- Septima was the second of their eight children.
- Septima's mother, having been reared outside of the American South, had never been a slave and did not allow the prevailing prejudice to inhibit her from demanding opportunities for her children.
- In the first grade, Septima went to a public school called the ABC Gallery under less than perfect conditions.

*40-year veteran teacher Septima Clark was fired for her affiliation with the NAACP.*

- There were approximately 100 other students in her class, the facility had outdoor bathrooms and bleachers for seating, and beatings were administered daily for disciplinary infractions.
- So Septima's mother sent her to a private school in the home of a woman and her niece.
- It was common at the time for black women to run small schools in their homes.
- The woman who ran the school reserved admission for the children of free issues—African-Americans who had never been slaves—as they were considered to be of higher social standing.
- The head teacher was very strict, because she believed that the children of free issues should be held to a higher standard of behavior.
- The school's rules extended beyond the classroom and the school day; children could be whipped for infractions in their spare time away from school.
- For instance, if the teacher saw a student outside a store eating candy from a paper bag, it was considered unacceptable behavior and grounds for a beating.

*Septima's Haitian mother knew the importance of education for her daughter.*

- When she was about eight years old, Septima returned to public school, attending Mary Street School for two years, followed by two years at Burke Industrial School, where she completed the seventh grade.
- Septima recalled, "I shall never forget those years. They were the most important for me, and I shall to the end of my days be grateful to my parents for them. They were hard years, years of struggle for both my father and my mother. There were eight children to feed and clothe, and always there was little money with which to provide even the bare necessities. But love made the household a home, and though constant toil from sunup until the late hours of the night was the year-round routine, it was a happy home. Despite the hardships, the children were able to trudge off each day to school after a hot breakfast and with a lunch, and there were hot meals when they returned from school. Some days there was even a penny with which to buy a piece of candy, for in our childhood days a penny would indeed buy a little treat."
- Upon completion of the seventh grade, Septima had earned a teaching certificate, however the Charleston public schools still were not hiring black teachers.
- Two circumstances—Septima's high scores on an exam, which would make her exempt from having to complete the eighth grade, and her mother's insistence that she continue her schooling—led her to matriculate at Avery Normal Institute in the ninth grade.
- Avery was a coeducational school for African-American students.
- It was developed at the turn of the twentieth century by the American Missionary Association, and sponsored by the Congregational Church.
- Avery was staffed primarily by white teachers from the North, predominately New England.
- In order to pay her tuition at Avery, Septima worked for a couple who lived across the street from her parents, serving as a companion, housekeeper and babysitter for the woman while her husband was away on business.
- Septima and the woman were close in age and became good friends.
- The woman would make lovely dresses for Septima, and the two would go on outings together.
- At Avery, Septima loved the library and astronomy.
- She loved the teachers for their dedication; they taught her how to cook and sew.

- When Septima was a junior at Avery, Benjamin F. Cox, a black man, became president of the institute.
- Cox brought many positive changes to Avery, improving the facilities and expanding the curriculum.
- With Cox came the appointment of black teachers to the faculty.
- The arrangement of black and white teachers living together in the faculty dormitories was unacceptable to the white establishment in Charleston, and the city outlawed this arrangement.
- Thus, Avery Normal Institute had to dismiss its white teachers.
- In her senior year at Avery, Septima passed another teaching exam, earning her a first-grade teaching certificate.
- Her teachers encouraged her to seek enrollment at Fisk College in Nashville, Tennessee, but at $18 per month, Fisk was more than Septima's family could afford, and she began looking for work as a teacher.
- Charleston's public schools did not employ black teachers at the time, so Septima found work at Promised Land School on Johns Island, off the coast of South Carolina.
- Septima met her husband Nerie Clark in January, 1919.
- He was a sailor aboard the USS *Umpqua*, which docked in Charleston Harbor.
- During a three-day leave, Nerie returned in May of 1919 to visit Septima.
- The two were married a year later.
- Septima's family did not approve of or consent to the relationship, because they did not think the two had had sufficient time to become acquainted.
- Septima and Nerie had a daughter, named Victoria after Septima's mother, but the baby died soon after being born.
- Nerie never met his daughter, because he was away at sea when she was born.
- Soon after Nerie's return, he and Septima moved to North Carolina to live with his family.
- There, Septima became pregnant again.
- Nerie got out of the Navy and the couple moved to Dayton, Ohio.
- Septima's second child, a son, was born in a Dayton hospital.
- The child was named Nerie, after his father.
- While Septima was still in the hospital following her son's birth, she found out that her husband had an ex-wife of whom she was unaware.
- Septima also learned of another woman in Dayton with whom her husband had practically been living.
- At this time, Nerie Clark asked his wife to take their newborn child and move away from Dayton as soon as possible.
- Septima moved back to Hickory, North Carolina, to live with her in-laws.
- Ten months later, Nerie was dead from kidney failure.
- Septima transported Nerie's body back to his family home in the mountains of North Carolina, and stayed there to teach for a year.
- Then she moved with her son back to Johns Island and resumed teaching at Promised Land School.
- But the island winters proved to be too harsh for her child, and the rigors of her schedule were too great for her to provide him with adequate care.
- Though it would bring her anguish, Septima entrusted her son to the care of his paternal grandparents.

## Life at Work

- Septima Clark took her first teaching job at a school for African-Americans, called Promised Land School, on Johns Island, off the coast of South Carolina in 1916.
- On the island, there were 14 schools, which were staffed by one or two teachers each, for black students.

- For white students, there were three schools, each staffing one teacher.
- Septima was rated a principal, earning $30 per month from the State of South Carolina, with an additional $5 per month as a supplement from Charleston County.
- She shared the responsibility of teaching 132 students with one other teacher, a fellow graduate of Avery Normal Institute.
- The white teachers on Johns Island were responsible for as few a three and not more than 18 students; those with teaching certification comparable to Septima's were paid $85 per month.
- The school itself was a log cabin-like building with an open fireplace for which the students had to collect their own firewood.
- The only materials provided for the school were an ax, a water bucket and dipper, a table and chair, and some makeshift benches and chalkboards.
- Teachers had to provide their own chalk and erasers.
- Of greater concern was the wide range of children's skills and ages; individual instruction was a daily task.

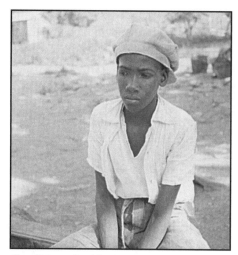

*Conditions for black students and teachers on Johns Island were far worse than for whites.*

- Moreover, those students old enough to work were contractually obligated to labor on the plantations on behalf of their families; attendance at school was erratic.
- In 1918, Septima accepted a job teaching sixth grade at Avery Normal Institute, and moved back to Charleston.
- She was paid $30 per week.
- "The experience of teaching at Avery was one of the most important and formative experiences of my life. It was then that I first became actively concerned in an organized effort to improve the lot of my fellow Negroes. Sometimes I have the almost certain feeling that I was providentially sent to Avery that year."
- During the next decade, Septima held a series of teaching positions and began attending interracial meetings in Columbia, South Carolina.
- In the summer of 1930, Septima went to Columbia University in New York, studying math, curriculum building, and astronomy.
- At Columbia, she learned to incorporate the vernacular of her students into the reading lessons in order to improve their comprehension and teach them new words.
- She studied astronomy so she could include information about, and words pertaining to, the natural world in the lessons she taught.
- In the summer of 1937, Septima went to Georgia to study at Atlanta University; specifically, she wanted to learn more about working with rural populations.
- One of her professors was W. E. B. Du Bois, the intellectual leader of the National Association for the Advancement of Colored People (NAACP).
- Many of Septima's fellow students in Atlanta were from rural places where work on plantations and on contract farms were common.
- Often these students found her attention to the racial inequalities and injustices of the day threatening and controversial.
- "But nevertheless, I went on, and I got to the place where I had to give my concerns regardless of where I was. The problem, I realized, was not only whites against blacks. It was men against women; it was old against young. You had all those things to fight all the time regardless, and it's still a constant fight."

- Working her way through college while teaching, Septima earned a Bachelor of Arts degree in 1942 from Benedict College in Columbia, South Carolina.
- Once she had completed her B.A., she wanted to pursue a master's degree.
- In 1944, she began classes at Hampton Institute in Virginia.
- Over the course of three summers, she worked toward and earned her master's.
- During the 18 years that Septima lived in Columbia, her teaching salary increased from $780 to $4,000 per year.
- In addition to earning two degrees during that time, she also helped to fight for and win equal pay for black teachers.
- Black teachers in Columbia only earned around half of what white teachers with equivalent education and experience made.
- The NAACP took up the cause, sending Thurgood Marshall to represent Septima and her colleagues.
- In 1945, Judge Julius Waties Waring ruled in federal court that teachers with comparable credentials must be compensated equally, regardless of race.
- School officials drafted the National Teacher's Exam for the purpose of evaluating teachers.
- Septima was one of 42 teachers to take the exam the first time it was administered.
- She scored an "A," and with it a raise from $62.50 to $117 per month.
- In 1947, she moved back to Charleston to take care of her mother, who had suffered a stroke.
- She became involved with the Young Women's Christian Association (YWCA), serving as the chairperson of administration for the black YWCA.
- Through her work with the YWCA, she became close personal friends with Judge Waring and his wife Elizabeth.
- It was a friendship anchored by a shared belief in the justice of an integrated society, and their mutual efforts toward building one.
- Judge Waring's court rulings and friendships caused controversy; friends ceased to associate with him and his wife, they were refused service at local businesses, and had to be accompanied by guards in public.
- Ultimately, the Warings were forced to leave Charleston.
- Septima was criticized by her colleagues and her principal for her friendship with the Warings; her neighbors worried that she would bring trouble to the entire neighborhood.
- She was the target of obscene and threatening phone calls, and had to live daily with the reality that her work and her associations made her a target for all those who would resort to violence in an effort to maintain a culture of white supremacy.
- In 1954, Septima went to Highlander Folk School for the first time.
- The school, located in Monteagle, Tennessee, was the only place in the South at that time where interracial education and organization were taking place.
- At Highlander, every aspect of life was communal and integrated; for many it was their first experience in this kind of environment.
- After her initial visit to Highlander, Septima became very active in the work of the school, transporting groups there from South Carolina, leading workshops, and drafting pamphlets.
- In 1954, she collaborated on two pamphlets: "A Guide to Action for Public School Desegregation" and "What is a Workshop?"
- "At Highlander I found out that black people weren't the only ones discriminated against. I found out that whites were against whites. The low-income whites were considered dirt under the feet of the wealthy whites, just like blacks were. I had to go to Highlander to find out that there was so much prejudice in the minds of whites against whites. I didn't dream—I thought that everything white was right. But I found out differently. I found out that they had a lot of prejudice against each other."
- Septima continued to teach elementary school in Charleston and work with local civic organizations as the Civil Rights movement developed throughout the United States, particularly in the South.

- She also kept up her involvement at Highlander, returning in the summer of 1955, at which time she worked with and got to know Rosa Parks.
- Throughout the South, the white establishment—including, in most cases, local government entities such as legislatures and law enforcement—was reacting to the changes being achieved through the coordinated efforts of Civil Rights organizations.
- Following the 1954 *Brown v. Board of Education* decision, in which the Supreme Court deemed segregated schools to be unconstitutional, the white power structure of the South sought to disable the NAACP, the driving force behind much of the legal action and resulting change.
- To this end, the heads of state legislatures in the South called special sessions ruling that the NAACP must make public its membership lists.
- The NAACP refused to do so.
- The individual states reacted in different ways, some obtaining injunctions to stop the operation of NAACP.
- In 1956, the South Carolina legislature passed a law banning all persons employed by either the city or the state from any membership in, or association with, Civil Rights organizations.
- Having been a long-time member of the NAACP, Septima became the vice president of the Charleston Chapter in 1956.
- She refused to sever her ties with the organization despite the state's ruling.
- As a result, she was fired from the teaching position she had held for 40 years and lost the pension she had earned along with it.
- She attempted to organize the teachers of South Carolina to fight the injustice of the new law, but there was little response to her letters and entreaties.
- The culture of intimidation was working, she realized; teachers were afraid for their lives and livelihoods, and would not fight the new law.
- It was at this moment that Septima came to the realization that what she was asking of the people she was trying to mobilize was more than they were prepared to take on.
- She remembered thinking, "I'm going to have to get the people trained. We're going to have to show them the dangers or the pitfalls that they are in, before they will accept. And it took many years."
- She was offered a job at Highlander Folk School as Director of Workshops and moved in June of 1956 to Monteagle, Tennessee, where the school was set on 200 acres of land on the Cumberland Plateau.

"JOIN THE FIGHT FOR FREEDOM" CAMPAIGN of N.A.A.C.P.

Received from............................(Name)

............................(Address)

Paid $............

Signed............ Solicitor

Address............

If you receive no acknowledgement from National Office, write Lucille Black, Membership Secretary, 20 West 40th Street, New York 18, N. Y.

- In this role, she traveled widely and continued to be active in her Charleston community as well.
- While at Highlander, Septima developed the Citizenship School model, which she then implemented throughout the South.
- The objective of the Citizenship Schools was to teach black adults to read and write, and learn the information necessary to become registered voters.

- The first Citizenship School was started on Johns Island, South Carolina.
- It was a collective effort between Septima, Highlander head Myles Horton, and a man from Johns Island named Esau Jenkins.
- Jenkins wanted to run for election to the school board, but he couldn't get elected unless his supporters were allowed to cast ballots.
- Voters told him that if he could help them learn the requisite information to pass the Voter Registration tests, then they would vote for him.

*Septima teaching adult students.*

- Jenkins had attended Highlander and worked with Horton and Septima to develop a curriculum for these adult students.
- When it came time to open the school on Johns Island, no church, school, or civic organization was willing to assume the risk associated with such an undertaking.
- The Progressive Club, a voter education group started by Jenkins, bought a $1,500 building, with financial support from Highlander, in which to hold Citizenship School classes.
- The site housed a cooperative store which operated out of the front of the building, while the Citizenship School classes took place in a windowless room in the back.
- This non-violent, direct action—educating black voters so that they could claim the right of their political voice—had to be concealed to prevent violence.
- The first Citizenship School teacher was Septima's cousin, Bernice Robinson.
- The method of teaching involved students telling stories about their daily activities.
- They would then record the stories and read them back to the class.
- Any challenging words would be used in the spelling lessons.
- Classes were organized with an attention to civic participation and empowerment.
- Following the success of the Johns Island Citizenship School model, Highlander developed a program to train teachers to lead Citizenship Schools all over the South.
- Septima recalled, "Working through those states, I found I could say nothing to those people, and no teacher as a rule could speak with them. We had to let them talk to us and say to us whatever they wanted to say. When we got through listening to them, we let them know that they were right according to the kind of thing that they had in their mind, but according to living in this world, there were other things they needed to know. We wanted to know if they were willing then to listen to us, and they decided that they wanted to listen to us."
- Because of its integrated environment and its work in training and educating blacks and the rural poor to empower themselves, Highlander Folk School was accused of advocating Communist ideals and activities, and was under the scrutiny of the FBI.
- "...anyone who was against segregation was considered a Communist," Septima recalled.

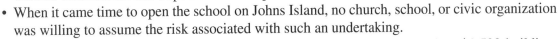

*Anti-segregationists were considered Communists.*

- "White Southerners couldn't believe that a Southerner could have the idea of racial equality; they thought it had to come from somewhere else."
- In 1959, during Highlander's twenty-fifth anniversary celebration, the Rev. Dr. Martin Luther King, Jr. was photographed sitting near a reporter for *The Daily Worker*, a Communist newspaper.
- The reporter had not made her affiliation with the Communist paper known when seeking admission to the celebration.
- Throughout the South, the photograph was used as propaganda to "prove" that Highlander was a Communist training center.
- This prompted the authorities of the State of Tennessee to investigate "the subversive activities" taking place at the school.
- The state legislature met and solicited the district attorney to bring any suit against Highlander so that the school's charter might be revoked.
- Though it was integration on the Highlander campus that Tennessee authorities wanted to end, they couldn't bring that charge against the school with a reasonable expectation of winning because the Supreme Court had already ruled that segregated schools were unconstitutional.
- Ultimately, the state felt most confident that it could successfully charge Highlander with the possession of alcohol and intent to sell it.
- On July 31, 1959, nearly 20 Tennessee police raided Highlander Folk School.
- They detained Septima, and "finding" moonshine at the residence of Myles Horton, they arrested her and some of the students.
- In court, Septima testified that the liquor found the night of the raid had at no time been in her possession.
- Despite incongruence in the statements of the prosecution's witnesses, the court upheld the possession charge.
- The initial consequence was an order that the administration building be temporarily padlocked.
- Subsequently, the Grundy County Circuit Court revoked the school's charter.
- "I wasn't going to let them scare me to death. I just wouldn't let them. But it wasn't an easy thing, because when you'd go home you would keep thinking what they could do and what they might do, because they were very, very harassing and very mean, very much so."
- By early 1961, 82 teachers who had received training at Highlander were conducting citizenship classes in several Southern states.
- In the summer of 1961, the legal status of Highlander was so tenuous that the Citizenship School Program was relocated to the Dorchester Co-operative Community Center in McIntosh, Georgia.
- The project of the Citizenship Schools was taken up by the Southern Christian Leadership Conference (SCLC).

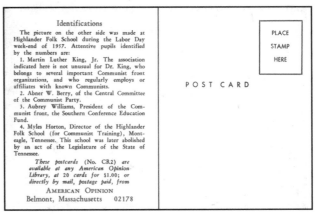

*Propaganda against Citizenship School Programs was mailed.*

- Septima, for a time, was both employed by Highlander and working on behalf of the SCLC.
- She traveled widely in the South and throughout the country recruiting and fundraising for the Citizenship School Program.

## Life in the Community: Charleston, South Carolina

- Charleston is a prominent harbor town with a colonial significance.
- It was originally situated at Albemarle Point, on the Ashley River, and in 1680 moved to its location at Oyster Point.
- Charleston was the original capital of the Carolina Colony.
- It was established to serve as a major port city, an expectation it fulfilled.
- As such, it was the primary location for the unloading and selling of humans captured in Africa, and transported and sold as slaves in the Colonies and later in the United States.
- As a result of its role as a trade center, Charleston became the wealthiest city south of Philadelphia and the fourth-largest in the Colonies by the themed-1700s.
- More than half of its population was made up of slaves.
- In the nineteenth century, black slaves and domestic servants continued to comprise the bulk of the city's population.
- South Carolina grew increasingly adamant that state's rights supersede the power of the federal government.
- In 1832, the state passed an ordinance whereby it could nullify the mandates of the federal government.
- Federal troops were, therefore, dispatched to Charleston's forts to collect tariffs.
- The state's history of conflict with and resistance to the federal government had begun.
- On December 20, 1860, South Carolina's General Assembly voted to secede from the Union following the election of Abraham Lincoln as president.
- Thus began the Civil War.
- Charleston incurred heavy bombardment and severe damage during the war.

*Charleston, after the Civil War.*

- In 1865, Union troops moved into Charleston and took control of many of its areas.
- Federal troops were dispatched to South Carolina following the Civil War to oversee Reconstruction.
- The war had devastated both the economy and infrastructure of the city.
- Freed slaves faced poverty, discrimination, intimidation, and various abuses and other forms of disenfranchisement.
- Many former slave owners refused to free their slaves.
- South Carolina languished economically for the remainder of the nineteenth century.
- Once one of the nation's wealthiest states, by 1890 South Carolina was near the bottom in per-capita income.
- Illiteracy impacted 45 percent of the population; public health was so poor that 44 percent of military volunteers for the Spanish-American War were rejected.
- Cities began aggressively developing textile manufacturing as a sign of progress; the standard work week was 66 hours before a 1907 law reduced it to 60 hours.
- Charleston's public school system was one of the best in the state, but statewide private education continued to play a major role.
- In 1916, one in eight high school students was enrolled in a private school.
- The outbreak of World War I brought a handful of federal military training centers to the state and dramatically increased the activity in the Charleston Naval Yard.
- But agriculture, particularly the growing of cotton, continued to dominate the economy.
- In 1939, approximately 80 percent of the state's male high school and college graduates moved elsewhere in search of better opportunities.
- A survey in 1945 showed that 40 percent of those desiring a college education indicated they plan to go to school out of state.
- Following the Second World War, industrial recruitment accelerated; within nine months, Charleston had attracted 19 new companies employing 812 people.
- This was followed by major investments of federal dollars as a large military presence in the region helped to shore up the city's economy.

# HISTORICAL SNAPSHOT
# 1961

- At the National Reactor Testing Station near Idaho Falls, Idaho, atomic reactor SL-1 exploded, killing three military technicians
- In his farewell address, President Eisenhower warned Americans of the increasing power of a "military-industrial complex"
- Ham the Chimp was rocketed into space aboard *Mercury-Redstone 2* in a test of the Project Mercury capsule, designed to carry U.S. astronauts into space
- The U.S. launched its first test of the Minuteman I intercontinental ballistic missile
- The Beatles performed for the first time at the Cavern Club
- President John F. Kennedy established the Peace Corps
- Max Conrad circumnavigated the earth in eight days, 18 hours and 49 minutes, setting a new world record
- The first U.S. Polaris submarines arrived at Holy Loch
- The Twenty-third Amendment to the Constitution was ratified, allowing residents of Washington, DC, to vote in presidential elections
- Soviet cosmonaut Yuri Gagarin became the first human in space aboard *Vostok 1*
- The Bay of Pigs Invasion of Cuba failed to overthrow Fidel Castro
- Freedom Riders began interstate bus rides to test the new Supreme Court integration decision
- Alan Shepard became the first American in space aboard *Mercury-Redstone 3*
- A bus full of Civil Rights Freedom Riders was fire-bombed near Anniston, Alabama, and the Civil Rights protestors were beaten by an angry mob
- *Venera 1* became the first manmade object to fly by another planet—Venus—but failed to send back any data
- President Kennedy announced before a special joint session of Congress his goal to put a man on the moon before the end of the decade
- Peter Benenson's article "The Forgotten Prisoners" was published in several internationally read newspapers, leading to the founding of the human rights organization Amnesty International
- Russian ballet dancer Rudolf Nureyev requested asylum in France while in Paris with the Kirov Ballet
- President Kennedy delivered a widely watched TV speech on the Berlin crisis, and urged Americans to build fallout shelters
- The Walt Disney anthology television series, renamed Walt Disney's Wonderful World of Color, began telecasting its programs in color
- Baseball player Roger Maris of the New York Yankees hit his sixty-first home run in the last game of the season to break the 34-year-old record held by Babe Ruth
- The Soviet Union detonated a 58-megaton-yield hydrogen bomb, the largest ever manmade explosion
- The *Fantastic Four #1* comic debuted, launching the Marvel Universe
- *Catch-22* by Joseph Heller was first published
- President Kennedy sent 18,000 military advisors to South Vietnam
- Nazi Adolf Eichmann was pronounced guilty of crimes against humanity by a panel of three Israeli judges and sentenced to death for his role in the holocaust
- "Barbie" got a boyfriend when the "Ken" doll was introduced

## Selected Prices

Bedroom Set, Walnut .................................................................$645.00

Coffee Maker, Percolator ...........................................................$16.88

Lipstick, Cashmere Bouquet.......................................................$0.49

Mattress, Serta............................................................................$79.50

Nylons ........................................................................................$1.00

Paneling, 70 Panels ....................................................................$47.00

Refrigerator ................................................................................$259.00

Typewriter, Smith-Corona, Electric ...........................................$209.35

Vacuum Cleaner, Eureka.............................................................$69.95

Watch, Bulova ............................................................................$59.50

## "30 More Virginia Schools to Integrate This Week,"
### *The Martinsville Bulletin* (Virginia), September 3, 1961:

Seventy-three Virginia schools will admit Negro pupils—30 of the schools for the first time—at opening sessions this week.

Negro enrollment in the commonly white schools is estimated at 537, more than double the Negro enrollment in the 1960-61 term.

Last year, 211 Negroes attended 43 white schools in 11 localities, while for the 1961-62 session, that figure has jumped to 73 schools in 19 localities.

Enrollment of Negro pupils in the predominately all-white classrooms is expected to proceed without incident and no special precautions are being taken anywhere in the state.

Heaviest concentration of integration in the state is in the Northern Virginia area across the Potomac River from Washington. These for localities—Alexandria, Falls Church, Arlington County and Fairfax County—account for more than half of the Negroes admitted.

The other localities are scattered from Virginia's Tidewater to the Blue Ridge Mountains.

Most of the Negro students were assigned to the schools by the state Pupil Placement Board, which only last week assigned seven more Negroes to white schools in five localities. Others were ordered admitted by federal judges.

## Reverend Dr. Martin Luther King, Jr.'s Address to the AFL-CIO Convention [excerpt], 1961:

"How can labor rise to the heights of its potential statesmanship and cement its bonds with Negroes to their mutual advantage?

First: Labor should accept the logic of its special position with respect to Negroes and the struggle for equality. Although organized labor has taken actions to eliminate discrimination in its ranks, the standard for the general community, your conduct should and can set an example for others, as you have done in other crusades for social justice. You should root out vigorously every manifestation of discrimination so that some international, central labor bodies or locals may not besmirch the positive accomplishments of labor. I am aware this is not easy or popular—but the eight-hour day was not popular nor easy to achieve. Nor was outlawing anti-labor injunctions. But you accomplished all of these with a massive will and determination. Out of such struggle for democratic rights you won both economic gains and the respect of the country, and you will win both again if you make Negro rights a great crusade.

Second: The political strength you are going to need to prevent automation from becoming a Moloch, consuming jobs and contract gains, can be multiplied if you tap the vast reservoir of Negro political power. Negroes given the vote will vote liberal and labor because they need the same liberal legislation labor needs....

If you would do these things now in this convention—resolve to deal effectively with discrimination and provide financial aid for our struggle in the South—this convention will have a glorious moral deed to add to an illustrious history."

## "Desegregation Developments, Education," *The Americana Annual 1962, An Encyclopedia of the Events of 1961*:

As the eighth school year after the U.S. Supreme Court's desegregation decision began, only three states—Alabama, Mississippi, and South Carolina—continue to have complete segregation at all levels of the public education system.

The number of Negroes attending classes with white children was still small. As of November 1961, according to the *Southern School News*, 7.3 percent of the 3,210,724 Negro children enrolled in schools of the 18 previously segregated states were attending biracial schools. However, of the 233,509 Negroes in mixed classes, 88,881 were in Washington, DC, 47,588 in Maryland, 20,636 in Kentucky, an estimated 35,000 in Missouri and 15,500 in West Virginia, 10,555 in Oklahoma and 8,448 in Delaware. In the rest of the previously segregated states, fewer than 7,000 Negroes were in mixed schools.

*Continued*

### "Desegregation Developments, Education,"... *(Continued)*

The increase of 31 in the number of the segregated school districts in the fall of 1961 was extremely small, and led to the enrollment of only 392 additional Negroes in previously all-white schools. Nevertheless, the segregation steps taken were significant. Three of the largest cities in the south—Atlanta, Dallas, and Memphis—were desegregated, and all fall school openings were without violence....

Outside the South, efforts were being made in 1961 to eliminate what is called de facto segregation. Such moves were underway in Chicago, New York, Pasadena, Montclair, New Jersey, and New Rochelle, N.Y.

### "Special Message to Congress on Urgent National Needs" [excerpt], President John F. Kennedy, May 25, 1961:

Finally, if we are to win the battle that is now going on around the world between freedom and tyranny, the dramatic achievements in space which occurred in recent weeks should have made clear to us all, as did *Sputnik* in 1957, the impact of this adventure on the minds of men everywhere, who are attempting to make a determination of which road they should take. Since early in my term, our efforts in space have been under review. With the advice of the Vice President, who is Chairman of the National Space Council, we have examined where we are strong and where we are not. Now it is time to take longer strides—time for a great new American enterprise—time for this nation to take a clearly leading role in space achievement, which in many ways may hold the key to our future on Earth....

I therefore ask the Congress, above and beyond the increases I have earlier requested for space activities, to provide the funds which are needed to meet the following national goals:

First, I believe that this nation should commit itself to achieving the goal, before this decade is out, of landing a man on the moon and returning him safely to the Earth. No single space project in this period will be more impressive to mankind, or more important for the long-range exploration of space, and none will be so difficult or expensive to accomplish. We propose to accelerate the development of the appropriate lunar space craft. We propose to develop alternate liquid and solid fuel boosters, much larger than any now being developed, until certain which is superior. We propose additional funds for other engine development and for unmanned explorations—explorations which are particularly important for one purpose which this nation will never overlook: the survival of the man who first makes this daring flight. But in a very real sense, it will not be one man going to the moon—if we make this judgment affirmatively, it will be an entire nation. For all of us must work to put him there.

### "Franchise Selling Catches On," 1960:

"We are witnessing a new surge of small, independent, enterprise. But, if we're going to be good, we've got to be good. That's why we're here."

Thus roughly you might paraphrase the thinking at a meeting in New York's Coliseum last week. Representatives of some 40 franchising corporations, blanketing 25,000 franchise holders, gathered to midwife and baptize the International Franchise Assn. According to A. I. Tunick, president of the Chicken Delight chain of carry-out and delivery dinner outlets, and first president of the association, the group has two chief aims: to win recognition for franchising as a major method of merchandising and to set up a code of ethics.

*Continued*

## "Franchise Selling Catches On," ... *(Continued)*

### How It Works

The franchising formula varies from one operation to another. Basically, though, it's a system set up by a manufacturer or purveyor of services, which sets up under a single brand name a chain of small businessmen, who buy some of their equipment and supplies from the franchisers and run their own show—with some strings. To get a franchise, the dealer may pay a franchise fee—most of them under $10,000, some as low as $10—or he may simply make a down payment on the equipment or plan. Usually, too, he pays a fee or royalty on his own sales. Franchising as the association defines it, Tunick says, is not a one-shot deal. A continuing relationship between franchise and franchisee marks the operations of its members.

For the franchising company, this setup offers quick, assured distribution and expansion at relatively low cost—since the franchise holder himself puts up some of the investment. The franchiser keeps title to the name and basic product or service rights. Because the franchise holder runs the business himself, the franchiser gets a dealer who is both cost and sales conscious.

For the franchise holder, the setup gives him some independence with the security of a tested business. His capital investment is relatively small—and financing comes easier with a big concern backing him. In effect, he gets the buying edge of a big chain, the parent's promotion, and management knowhow. In some cases, he gets the plus of direct-from-manufacturer price. Sherwood estimates that bulk buying gives the dealer savings of anywhere from 30 percent to 50 percent. While he is subject to quality and other controls, he is basically a man on his own.

### Postwar Spurt

The first big spurt in franchise selling came right after World War II. During the war, Tunick explains, GIs lived with two dreams: the little white cottage they were going to own, and the prospect of a job with no boss to hound them. With their bonuses in their pockets, they constituted a fine potential for the franchiser.

The 1957-58 recession gave franchising another boost. Men lost their jobs, or got scared. They wanted security—and they wanted it in an easy-to-handle package.

Expanded credit is now a major factor in contributing to franchising's growth, thinks J. J. Connolly, president of Roll-A-Grill Corp. of America, and a director of the association. Credit allows the little man to take part in the kind of enterprise that a Frank Woolworth built up for himself in the old days, he says.

In the last few months, several newcomers—large and small—have moved in. In November, Frank G. Shattuck Co. announced a new Franchise Div., for operation of Schrafft's restaurants, chiefly tied into new motel operations.... And last week, an ad in *The New York Times* urged people to go into the Franchised Art Galleries business.

# 1965 PROFILE

Susan Walton Gray belonged to the generation of psychologists who challenged the belief that a child's genes were his or her destiny; their work provided the inspiration for Head Start, a federal program launched in 1965 to groom preschool children from poor families to succeed in school.

## Life at Home

- Susan Walton Gray was born December 5, 1913, to a wealthy family in the small town of Rockdale in Maury County, Tennessee, about 70 miles southwest of Nashville.
- She was the second of three children.
- The family was originally from New England, where it had a tradition of iron manufacturing stretching back to the 1700s.
- Her uncle, J. J. Gray Jr., owned the Rockdale Iron Company, a pig iron furnace that owned a patented process.
- Her father, Dan R. Gray, Sr., practiced falconry and raised basset hounds; Susan lived around much poverty, especially among African-Americans.

*Susan Gray's work inspired the Head Start program.*

- In later years she would describe her childhood as living in a "feudal society" centered around her uncle's blast furnace.
- Her father was highly individualistic, and she didn't feel pressure to assume traditional female roles.

- "I got the notion as a little child I was just as good as anybody."
- The Grays sold their furnace in 1926 as part of a $30 million merger, and Susan's parents moved into a house in Mount Pleasant, about eight miles northeast of Rockdale.
- She enrolled in Randolph-Macon Woman's College in Lynchburg, Virginia, in the early 1930s, in the midst of the Great Depression.
- She recalled feeling very guilty when an economics professor said, "the trouble with you young ladies is that you don't think an intelligent thought can ever be achieved by someone with dirty fingernails."

*Susan attended Randolph-Macon Woman's College.*

- From then on, she became concerned about social injustice.
- Susan majored in the classics—Latin and Greek—but she also liked math and biology, and took some psychology courses.
- She was intrigued by the work of Mary Margaret Shirley, a psychologist who was writing "The First Two Years," an important work in developmental psychology.
- She graduated with her bachelor's degree in 1936 from the school and taught fourth grade in public schools, but soon realized that was not what she wanted to do for the rest of her career.
- She decided to pursue a higher degree, and was encouraged by some friends and mentors to study psychology.
- Susan came to George Peabody College for Teachers in Nashville, where she earned her master's degree in 1939 and a doctoral degree in developmental psychology in 1941.
- She taught for four years at Florida State College for Women in Tallahassee during World War II, and published research on the vocational aspirations of young black children.
- After the war, the president of Peabody recruited her to return and build the psychology department.
- When she joined the faculty in 1945, she was the only psychologist at the school—male or female; a second woman psychologist arrived in 1958.
- Her most famous work was the Early Training Project, born of her need to have a program where graduate students from Peabody could perform research, her belief that psychologists should perform socially useful work, and the concern of the superintendent of Murfreesboro schools over a decline in achievement scores of black children.
- She never married or had children of her own—not uncommon in her day when a woman's choice was between a career and family.
- "I don't know whether I feel good about it or not," she said in later years.
- She was elected president of the Southeastern Psychological Association in 1963, the first woman to hold this post.
- She was very much a Southern lady, but she had a strong will and great intellectual curiosity—she always asked probing questions.
- She took an interest in photography, and shot thousands of photos of subjects ranging from children living in poverty in Appalachia to close-ups of flowers.

- An Episcopalian, she served tea and cookies in the afternoons; with her knowledge of Latin and Greek, she would play games using obscure words with her colleagues.
- Despite her proper manner, she drove a sporty Ford Thunderbird in the early 1960s; one of her graduate students recalled that Susan received speeding tickets more than once on her frequent drives between the campus in Nashville and Murfreesboro, 33 miles away.

## Life at Work
- Susan Gray said her career path was more a matter of serendipity than planning.
- According to colleague Penny Brooks, "The timing of her work was perfect. The crack in the door was the need for a program for the War on Poverty. And it was the '60s—a time when there was growing emphasis on the social environment as the cause of all ailments…. The Civil Rights Movement was raising awareness of people who were disadvantaged, and these factors aligned to make it a time of hope—race and income are not necessarily destiny…. Enter the Early Training Project. It showed that early training and intervention could make important differences in the future of children."
- A nationwide survey of October 1964 enrollments found that nursery schools were predominately private and generally beyond the reach of low-income families.
- Most kindergartens were public, but were absent in many areas.
- The U.S. Health, Education and Welfare Department released its report in August 1965.
- "Large numbers of American youngsters who are most in need of a hand up in the early stages of the educational processes are not getting it," said Wilbur J. Cohen, who was then the department's acting secretary.
- Among five-year-olds nationwide, the percentage enrolled in kindergarten or other grades hovered around 20 percent from the 1920 through the 1940 Census.
- But five-year-old enrollments rose to 35 percent in 1950, and 45 percent in 1960.
- The South as a whole had a 23 percent enrollment rate for five-year-olds in 1960, while the rate for other regions ranged from 53 percent to 58 percent.
- The rate was 20 percent in Tennessee in 1960.
- Peabody professors Julius Seeman, Raymond Norris, and Susan started Peabody's doctoral program in school psychology in 1957, and won a federal grant to support this emerging branch of education training.

*Susan believed that many children in her kindergarten classes were disadvantaged by poverty and social disabilities.*

- In 1959, Susan started an experimental preschool program called the Early Training Project.
- Many educators at the time believed that a child's intelligence was innate and could not be changed by training.
- Susan believed that poverty and other social disabilities held back children; she believed a child's "educability" could be enhanced by early education of the child and training for parents.

- Contrary to considerable thinking of the times, children from poor families weren't destined to fail, and they could reach their full potential with careful help.
- Four- and five-year-olds from poor, mostly black neighborhoods in Murfreesboro attended a summer school.
- Others involved with the program made regular visits to the children's homes and worked with mothers to share their skills in preschool education.
- In Columbia, Tennessee, a town near where Susan grew up, researchers created a control group to identify a similar group of preschoolers and chart how well they performed over the years with no intervention.
- Susan carefully measured the progress of these students as they started school, and also charted changes within families.
- Her research showed that children from poor families had a better chance of success when they started the first grade if they had participated in a well-designed preschool.
- She also found those around the child—mothers and siblings—also benefited as the methods diffused through families and neighbors.
- "We have been struck by great strengths in most of the homes we have visited," Susan wrote. "One is the deep, underlying concern of the parents for their children. Not only do they have the same goals and aspirations as more affluent parents, they also have a deep reservoir of potential for improving their lives…. This deep concern for the welfare of their children and latent ability to cope with life's demands provide the opportunities for an intervention program working with mothers, a program designed to enable them to become more effective as teachers of their young children.
- "Home visiting is not a panacea for the problems of low-income families in present-day society," she wrote. "Still, if we can enable parents to become more effective educational change agents, we thereby make a lasting contribution toward improved lifestyles and general welfare in such low-income homes, and toward a more satisfying future life for their children."
- Research similar to the Early Training Project was being done by several other researchers across the country.
- Twelve such teams formed a consortium in the early 1960s to be able to pool their data to test their findings more rigorously.

*Home visits helped mothers help their children.*

- President Lyndon Johnson had launched a series of federal programs called the "War on Poverty." In 1964, Sargent Shriver, who was in charge of the new agency overseeing the programs, joined his wife, Eunice Kennedy Shriver, on a visit to Tennessee to present a grant at Peabody for another program and to visit the Early Training Project.
- Only a year before, Eunice's brother, President John F. Kennedy, had been assassinated in Dallas.
- Susan drove the Shrivers to Murfreesboro in her Ford Thunderbird, along with another Peabody psychologist, Carl Haywood, who recalled that they visited facilities and homes where the preschool experiment had been taking place.
- The Shrivers thought they had seen children who were "mentally retarded," but Haywood said the children were picked only for their poverty status—social impediments, not physical ones.
- On the flight back, Sargent Shriver turned to his wife and remarked on the success of the Early Training Project.
- "I could do this with regular children all across America," he said.
- The Shrivers credited that visit as a crystallizing moment for the inception of Head Start; the program was approved by Congress that year, and the first summer program began in 1965.
- Head Start's first program lasted eight weeks in July and August of 1965, involving 561,000 children ages four and five at 13,344 centers across the country.
- The program's first year cost $95 million: 90 percent from federal grants and 10 percent from local matches.
- The centers employed more than 40,000 teachers and other professionals.
- Assistance also came from 45,000 neighborhood residents, most of whom were paid the federal minimum wage of $1.25 an hour, and about 250,000 volunteers.
- Later Susan wrote: "A start has been made for these young people and others like them, but there is still far to go before such young people as a group can realize the potential that is within them."

## Life in the Community: Nashville, Tennessee

- Head Start was founded as America passed through its most turbulent years of the Civil Rights Movement.
- One of the program's motives was to give disadvantaged children, many of them minorities, a better chance to succeed in school as they were desegregated.
- It was part of a pantheon of anti-poverty programs launched as part of Johnson's Great Society Program, whose underlying philosophy said that discrimination and poverty were preventing schools from the proper development of human talent.
- To tackle the issue of poverty in America, Congress passed the Economic Opportunity Act of 1964 and the Elementary Education Act of 1965.
- Contained in the Economic Opportunity Act were both Job Corps and Head Start.

*Young girl in Head Start program.*

- Head Start was seen as a way for children of the poor to enter the social-sorting process of school on more equal terms with children of the middle class.
- Job Corps focused on one of the three areas of emphasis: unemployment and delinquent youth; disadvantaged students for whom education did not provide equality of opportunity; and ways to break the cycle of poverty.
- In many parts of America, race and poverty were intertwined.
- The Civil Rights Movement in Tennessee was more peaceful than in many Southern states, but the road was long and difficult.
- Nashville was one of the crossroads of the movement.
- Tennessee had been a slave state before the Civil War.
- In 1866, one year after the war's end and the abolishment of slavery, the state enacted a law requiring separate school systems for white and black children.
- Laws expanding and stiffening segregation were passed into the 1930s.
- In many counties, it was difficult for blacks to register to vote, and families faced reprisals if they tried.
- Highlander Folk School, founded in east Tennessee in 1932, worked mostly with labor unions for its first 20 years in its efforts to foster education among adults to increase their power in their communities.
- By 1951 it began shifting to establishing "Citizenship Schools" to teach blacks to read and write so they could register to vote.
- Many people who would become prominent in the early Civil Rights Movement attended sessions at Highlander.
- Among them was Rosa Parks, shortly before she and others organized the Montgomery, Alabama, bus boycott in 1955.

*Guy Caraway plays guitar at student workshop at Highlander Folk School.*

## HISTORICAL SNAPSHOT
# 1965

- President Lyndon B. Johnson unveiled his "Great Society" during his State of the Union address
- *Ranger 8* crashed into the moon after a successful mission of photographing possible landing sites for the Apollo program astronauts
- Some 3,500 U.S. Marines arrived in South Vietnam, becoming the first official American combat troops there
- Cosmonaut Aleksei Leonov left his spacecraft *Voskhod 2* for 12 minutes and became the first person to walk in space
- NASA launched the first two-person crew, Gus Grissom and John Young, into orbit around Earth
- Martin Luther King, Jr. and 25,000 civil rights activists successfully ended the four-day march from Selma, Alabama, to the Capitol in Montgomery
- The world's first space nuclear power reactor, *SNAP-10A*, was launched by the United States; the reactor operated for 43 days
- The first Students for a Democratic Society (SDS) march against the Vietnam War drew 25,000 protestors to Washington, DC
- U.S. troops were sent to the Dominican Republic by President Johnson "for the stated purpose of protecting U.S. citizens and preventing an alleged Communist takeover of the country," thus thwarting the possibility of "another Cuba"
- Forty men burned their draft cards at the University of California, Berkeley, and a coffin was marched to the Berkeley Draft Board
- Muhammad Ali knocked out Sonny Liston in the first round of their championship rematch with the "Phantom Punch" at the Central Maine Civic Center in Lewiston
- The U.S. spacecraft *Mariner 4* flew by Mars, becoming the first spacecraft to return images from the Red Planet
- Bob Dylan elicited controversy among folk purists by "going electric" at the Newport Folk Festival
- President Johnson signed the Voting Rights Act and the Social Security Act establishing Medicare and Medicaid
- The Watts Riots ripped through Los Angeles
- The Beatles performed the first stadium concert in the history of rock, playing before 55,600 people at Shea Stadium in New York City
- Congress passed a law penalizing the burning of draft cards with up to five years in prison and a $1,000 fine
- Yale University presented the Vinland map, sparking considerable controversy
- Cuba and the United States formally agreed to start an airlift for Cubans who wanted to come to America
- American generals called for an increase in the number of troops in Vietnam, from 120,000 to 400,000

## Selected Prices

| | |
|---|---|
| Crib, Portable | $22.95 |
| Drill, Black & Decker | $10.99 |
| Film, 35 Millimeter Color Slide | $2.49 |
| Food Processor | $39.95 |
| Hat, Pillbox | $4.97 |
| Pepsi, Six-Pack | $0.59 |
| Radio, Portable Transistor | $12.95 |
| Socket Set, 57-Piece | $56.95 |
| Tape Player, 8-Track | $67.95 |
| Watch, Timex | $9.95 |

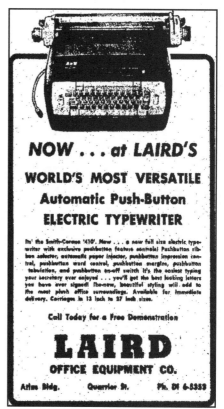

## "The Kindergarten," Elizabeth Palmer Peabody,
### *The New York Times*, August 12, 1873:

The Kindergarten is a method of caring for, developing and instructing little children between the ages of three and eight years, invented or found out by the great German pedagogue, Friedrich Froebel (1782-1852), and which is taught by the most intelligent teachers—indeed, we believe, by all who have any knowledge of it—regarded as a step in education as important to the happiness and development of little children, and their preparation for the more enlightened education of these days, as the telegraph and railroad are to the convenience and successful prosecution of modern commerce.

We do not propose to give a detailed explanation of Froebel's system, but only to say that it keeps the child from books and places him in the hands of an intelligent and loving teacher, whose duty and object it is to repress nothing in the child, but to guide and direct all its energies so that every movement of play shall be both physically and morally, also a movement of discipline and development.

For this purpose, Froebel put into the hands of the teacher a series of inventions made by himself, consisting of building blocks, material for braiding, embroidery, and platting, clay for modeling figures, etc.... With these the child is taught to play in such a manner as to become, during those early years, practically acquainted with all geometrical forms, their lines, angles, planes, and faces, and with many mechanical and scientific facts and principles, while it also acquires manual facility and skill, with judgment in the use of material for the production of all forms of use and beauty.

The child, through all this discipline and development, is conscious only of playing with the most delightful toys. The teacher plays with the child—not in a purposeless, haphazard way, but by a series of carefully devised exercises, all of which tend to lead the child as it plays also to observe and reflect upon the things which are offered to its observation.

Plays of a certain kind are accompanied by music, and this most soothing and agreeable agency might perhaps be called the foundation of the Kindergarten.

*Continued*

**"The Kindergarten,". . .** *(Continued)*

Books are entirely withheld from the child, and all of its operations of mind are left to be free and voluntary. It undergoes no drudgery, but is led to ask questions and derive instruction by the presentation to its mind of interesting objects concerning which the teacher, having prepared herself beforehand, is full of requisite information. Whoever has observed his own mental operation knows that knowledge is acquired with vastly greater ease and effect when the mind is seeking specific information about some concrete thing. This is more true of children than adults—indeed, the child learns in no other way at first.

The object of the Kindergarten by Froebel, for a somewhat whimsical and yet perfectly just reason, is that it treats the little child as the wise gardener treats the plant—bringing to its aid everything that can promote growth, and requiring nothing from it which is not natural to its immature state.

**"Head Start Project May Bring Changes to America's Education,"**
*Delta-Democrat-Times*, **Greenville, Mississippi, November 4, 1965:**

NASHVILLE, Tenn.—The impact of the federal government's hastily conceived Project Head Start may already have caused a permanent alteration in the entire structure of American education, an article in the new magazine *Southern Education Report* said today.

This suggestion by some educational observers was noted by writer Erwin Knoll in a survey of the vast program's activities during the past summer. The SER article is titled "Hasty 'Landmark.'"

The preschool training program, Knoll wrote, "has already established itself, in the view of many observers, as the most formidable weapon in the arsenal of the federal War on Poverty." But its proponents, he said, believe it will reach far beyond the lives of the nation's poor.

Head Start "has encountered its share of administrative problems and political controversy," the article said, including racial conflict in the South, religious friction in the Middle West, salary disputes in New York and enrollment difficulties in Alaska.

"Nonetheless," Knoll [wrote], "the program has enjoyed broader support than most other aspects" of the government's antipoverty campaign.

Knoll's report appeared in the second issue of *Southern Education Report*, published bimonthly in Nashville under a grant from the Ford Foundation to the Southern Education Reporting Service. The objective, fact-finding enterprise is directed by a board of Southern educators and editors.

Head Start's summer program enrolled 561,000 children in communities around the country. As the session drew to a close at the end of August, President Johnson called it "a landmark, not just in education, but in the maturity of our own democracy," and announced the program would be extended on a year-round basis.

*Continued*

## "Head Start Project May Bring Changes to America's Education,"... *(Continued)*

Dr. Julius B. Richmond, dean of the medical faculty at the State University Upstate Medical Center in Syracuse, New York, and director of Project Head Start, said:

"Even at this early date, we can say that gains of the children in widely varying programs have exceeded the expectations of our planning committee. Since the child development centers are comprehensive in nature, we have seen improvement in nutrition and health, and vocabularies have shown striking improvements. The children have gained confidence in their relations with people, and they are much richer in their understanding of the world around them.

"Many long-term observers of the development of young children have been somewhat surprised at the apparent effectiveness of our programs, particularly in view of their brevity. They tend to attribute much of this success to the small groups (a pupil-teacher ratio of 15-to-1) and to the teacher assistants and aides who helped to provide individual attention."

Delegates to the White House Conference on Education in July said Project Head Start presaged a nationwide commitment to universal public preschool education. Reporting on the discussion in a panel session on early childhood education, James E. Allen Jr., New York state commissioner of education said:

"The continuation of Head Start and other such preschool programs was deemed essential. The incorporation of such programs into regular school programs was considered to be highly desirable, with the provision that the co-operation and involvement of the entire community and its whole resources be continued. And paramount in the deliberations on the subject of preschool education was an all-pervading feeling that the momentum of Head Start should not be lost."

# 1969 PROFILE

Known as indefatigable, with a commitment to sexual responsibility, Dr. Mary Steichen Calderone found herself at the center of a controversy about the need to educate elementary schoolchildren about human sexuality.

## Life at Home

- Nationwide, one school district after another was embroiled in angry arguments over sex classes being promoted by Dr. Mary Steichen Calderone through the organization she headed, Sex Information and Education Council of the U.S. (SIECUS).
- Even though the National Education Association had passed a resolution strongly affirming its support of the courses, communities in 35 states were debating the role of the public school in sex education.
- The arguments were not new to Mary; she had championed the cause for more than a decade dating to a time when sex was simply not discussed in public.
- The current controversy revolved around how specific the information should be, to what ages it should be taught, and who should be teaching children about health and human development, including human sexuality.
- As an outspoken advocate for sex education in the public schools, Mary promoted the concept that human sexuality was a multifaceted and vital part of a healthy life that should not be hidden under a shroud of secrecy or limited to smutty magazines.
- Born in Paris on July 1, 1904, Mary never lacked for intellectual stimulation.
- Her bohemian childhood was experienced at the feet of her father, photographer Edward Steichen; her uncle, poet Carl Sandburg; and many of the leading artists of the day.

*Mary Calderone was an outspoken advocate for sex education in public schools.*

- When Mary was six, she berated the family friend and sculptor Constantin Brâncuşi for his horizontal-headed bird pieces, which, she said, would undoubtedly hinder the bird from singing.
- Brâncuşi listened respectfully to the tike and afterward only sculpted birds with more upturned heads.
- Dancer Isadora Duncan asked Mary's father to let the girl join her dance troupe.
- Mary attended the Brearley School in New York City for her secondary education before entering Vassar College, graduating in 1925 with an A.B. in chemistry.
- At graduation, Mary decided to go into theatre and studied for three years at the American Laboratory Theater.
- She married actor W. Lon Martin and had two daughters, Nell and Linda.
- She abandoned acting and divorced in 1933.
- During this period, Mary underwent two years of Freudian analysis.
- In 1934 she took courses at Columbia University Medical School, placing her daughters Nell, eight, and Linda, six, in boarding school in Massachusetts.
- Nell died the next year of pneumonia, plunging her mother into the deepest and most bitter emotional crisis of her life.
- She spent that summer recovering at her father's place in Connecticut.
- "I don't really know what I did except hate the world for taking my child," she said. "Then I felt suddenly that if I reached my hand backward and forward in time, hundreds of thousands of other mothers who had lost children would touch me. I was just one of many."
- "Nell was very much like me," Mary said. "She looked like me and had a powerful personality. I had to come back the week after she died and take my exams. A week later I had a hysterectomy scheduled. That was some three-week period."

*Mary's daughter died from pneumonia.*

- In 1939, she received her diploma from the University of Rochester Medical School, and three years later took a master's in public health at Columbia.
- There she met her second husband, Dr. Frank Calderone, who later served as chief administrative officer of the World Health Organization.
- They married in 1941 and had two daughters.
- Mary worked as a physician in the Great Neck, New York public school system.
- In 1953, Mary joined the staff of the controversial Planned Parenthood Federation of America as its Medical Director.
- Her biggest success at Planned Parenthood came in 1964, when she overturned the American Medical Association's policy against physicians disseminating information on birth control, and transformed contraception into part of mainstream medical practice.
- At the same time, letters kept arriving at Planned Parenthood asking questions, not just about sex, but sexuality in general.
- Mary came to the realization that sex education was sorely lacking from American society.
- She believed that her work should not be limited to preventive measures against pregnancy, but should integrate human sexuality into the field of health.
- That would require a new organization and a renewed commitment.

## Life at Work

- Looking for new challenges, Dr. Mary Calderone co-founded the controversial Sex Information and Education Council of the U.S. (SIECUS), which served teachers, therapists and other professionals. Mary's insistence that sex education should begin as early as kindergarten did not impress religious conservative groups like MOMS (Mothers Organized for Moral Stability) and MOTOREDE (Movement to Restore Decency), who branded her the leader of the "SIECUS stinkpot." Nevertheless, her crusade for sexuality education with a "positive approach and moral neutrality" was launched.

- Although adamant about sexual freedom, she believed that the sex act should be ultimately reserved for marriage, and that sexuality found its peak expression through the "permanent man-woman bond."

- Her extensive work popularizing sexuality education was compared to Margaret Sanger's campaign for birth control and Rachel Carson's support of the environment.

- The human child is sexual even before birth, Mary said during lectures across the nation.

- "We know now that the penis erects in the uterus. And when the infant is born, the parents immediately begin to communicate to the child that it is a boy or a girl. For example, fathers are more gentle handling baby girls. Gender identity is fixed by the age of two.

- "Finally, there is the disapproving attitude of the parents toward the child's discovery that his body is pleasurable.

- "Parents reflect our sexophobic society."

- The 1960s were the launching ground for the wave of controversy over sex education in U.S. schools, but as early as 1912, the National Education Association (NEA) called for teacher training programs in sexuality education.

- In 1940, the U.S. Public Health Service strongly advocated sexuality education in the schools, labeling it an "urgent need."

- In 1953, the American School Health Association launched a nationwide program in family life education.

- Two years later, the American Medical Association, in conjunction with the NEA, published five pamphlets that were commonly referred to as "the sex education series" for schools.

- By 1968, Mary was condemned by the John Birch Society as "an aging sexual libertine."

- She was picketed in Oklahoma: "Tulsa's Shame! Calderone Came!" read one placard.

- Fears about what sex education might do to schoolchildren spread to some parents and church groups.

- "I expected someone to take a potshot at me," she says of those early days.

- A bestselling 1968 pamphlet, *Is the School House the Proper Place to Teach Raw Sex?*, targeted SIECUS, calling Mary the "SIECUS Sexpot" and claiming that she wanted to undermine Christian morality and corrupt children.

- Support for sexuality education among public health officials and educators did not sway its opponents; battles raged between conservatives and health advocates over the merits and format of sexuality education in public schools.

*Parents and church groups protested against sex education in schools.*

- They contended that Mary's promotion of sex education in schools was encouraging a premature and unhealthy participation in sex and usurping the role of parents in guiding their children's lives.
- Her reply was that if parents were doing their job properly, there would be no need for school-based sex education.
- Sex education programs were described by the Christian Crusade and other conservative groups as "smut" and "raw sex."
- The John Birch Society termed the effort to teach about sexuality "a filthy Communist plot."
- Phyllis Schlafly, leader of the far-right Eagle Forum, argued that sexuality education resulted in an increase in sexual activity among teens.
- Sex education programs in public schools proliferated, in large part due to newly emerging evidence that such programs did not promote sex but, in fact, helped delay sexual activity and reduce teen pregnancy rates.
- By the 1960s, the United States was experiencing a powerful and widely publicized sexual revolution following the introduction of the birth control pill.
- The classes took two routes: abstinence education supporters insisted that the best way to help with teen sexuality problems was to teach them not to have sex at all.
- If girls did not participate in sex, then they couldn't become pregnant and were dramatically less likely to get a sexually transmitted disease (STD).
- The supporters of abstinence claimed that not only would abstinence prevent harmful psychological presumptions, but would build skills designed for improving a relationship.
- The second approach focused on safe sex teachings.

*Evidence proved that sex education programs helped delay sexual activity and reduce teen pregnancy.*

- These advocates, including Mary, insisted that since many kids would still decide to have sex, it was more effective to teach them ways to protect themselves while doing so.
- At the same time, she had an expansive view of intimacy.
- During a lecture at Syracuse University's Institute for Family Research and Education, Mary said, "You must remember that, for most people, until very recently, sex was something you did in bed, preferably in the dark in one position ... and fully clothed."
- The students laughed appreciatively.
- Then she said, "You know there is a word ending in 'k' which means intercourse. Do you know what it is?"
- Several in the class gave the obvious answer.
- She then asked, "How about 'talk'? That is sexual intercourse. We never talk to each other as nonsexual people. I am not talking to you as a nonsexual person. I am well aware of my sexuality and very happy with it."
- She stated that parents should not punish their children for doing the things that are part of being human.
- Even though masturbation was considered unhealthy and dangerous when Mary was growing up, most doctors now viewed it as not only acceptable but desirable.
- "What you do is socialize. You teach that these are private things for the child alone. Then when he's older, sex will be with someone else whom he'll choose. Later, parents can teach children how to give and receive love because that is the real role of the family—not just providing shelter, food, education and recreation."
- It was as though she had been trained her entire life for this moment.
- Her theatrical and medical training, coupled with her dignity, poise and authoritative voice, helped her to get her message across that children are born sexual beings and remain so until they die, and that people of all ages need and deserve a proper sexual education.
- Sex education in the schools should start in kindergarten, she said.
- Modern children, she insisted, were in desperate need of sex education because they were sexually vulnerable: "devoid of chaperones, supervision, rules and close family relations and subject to onslaughts of commercial sexual exploitation."

## American Education Trends

- As the 1960s came to a close, America's schools had been handed additional, society-based burdens from endemic segregation, illegal drugs and entrenched poverty.
- Teachers and administrators increasingly inherited the problems that swirled in the community—outside the schoolhouse door.
- Often this expectation was created without the consent of the school or proper training of the teachers.
- In the 1960s, schools were seen as one of the primary weapons in the war on poverty by both politicians and the inner-city families struggling for a larger piece of the American pie.
- Americans came to question the ideology in the institutions of public education; issues of income inequality, teen pregnancy and drug use were laid at the feet of U.S. schools and their teachers.
- Critics questioned whether equality of education was enough to hurt the quality of opportunity for all.
- Teacher unionization, collective bargaining, judicial decrees, student rights and community control competed for time in the classroom.
- Liberals and conservatives argued for alternative structures: vouchers, performance contracting, radical decentralization, free schools, alternative schools, home schools.

- Teachers were deserting the profession in large numbers because of low pay and the downward spiraling of morale.
- Classes were overcrowded, more and more communities were embracing double sessions, and affluent parents were losing confidence in the public schools, fueling a dramatic enrollment increase in private schools.
- Educators focused public attention on the need for growing American talent as a weapon in the Cold War with the Soviet Union.
- As the nation's poor moved to urban areas to seek opportunity, the nation's white middle class—along with their children—fled the cities; Cleveland experienced a drop in white population of 26.5 percent during the decade, Chicago's white middle class declined by 18.6 percent, and St. Louis decreased 31.6 percent in its white residents.
- In its ruling concerning *Brown v. Board of Education*, the Supreme Court reiterated its belief in the "importance of education to our democratic society" as "the very foundation of good citizenship."
- In its ruling, the Court said schooling "is a principal instrument in awakening the child to cultural values, in preparing him for later professional training, and in helping him to adjust normally to his environment. In these days, it is doubtful that any child may reasonably be expected to succeed in life if he is denied the opportunity of an education."

*Student plaintiffs from throughout the South came forth in* Brown vs. Board of Education.

# HISTORICAL SNAPSHOT
# 1969

- The Soviet Union launched *Venera 5* toward Venus
- *Led Zeppelin I*, Led Zeppelin's first studio recorded album, was released
- Richard Milhous Nixon succeeded Lyndon Baines Johnson as the thirty-seventh U.S. president
- After 147 years, *The Saturday Evening Post* ceased publication
- Elvis Presley recorded his landmark comeback sessions for the albums *From Elvis in Memphis* and *Back in Memphis*
- A blowout on Union Oil's Platform spilled approximately 100,000 barrels of crude oil into a channel and onto the beaches of Santa Barbara County in Southern California, inspiring Wisconsin Senator Gaylord Nelson to organize the first Earth Day in 1970
- The Beatles gave their last public performance, on the roof of Apple Records; the impromptu concert was broken up by the police
- Two cosmonauts transferred from *Soyuz 5* to *Soyuz 4* via a spacewalk while the two crafts were docked together—the first time such a transfer took place
- In *Tinker v. Des Moines Independent Community School District*, the Supreme Court ruled that the First Amendment applied to public schools
- In a Los Angeles court, Sirhan Sirhan admitted that he killed presidential candidate Robert F. Kennedy
- NASA launched *Apollo 9* to test the lunar module
- In Memphis, James Earl Ray pleaded guilty to assassinating Martin Luther King, Jr.
- The novel *The Godfather* by Mario Puzo was published
- Dr. Denton Cooley implanted the first temporary artificial heart
- The Harvard University Administration Building was seized by nearly 300 students, mostly members of the Students for a Democratic Society
- An American teenager known as 'Robert R.' died in St. Louis, Missouri, of a baffling medical condition later identified as HIV/AIDS
- *Apollo 10*'s lunar module flew to within 15,400 miles of the moon's surface
- President Nixon announced that 25,000 U.S. troops would be withdrawn from Vietnam
- The Stonewall riots in New York City marked the start of the modern gay rights movement in the U.S.
- Edward M. Kennedy drove off a bridge on his way home from a party on Chappaquiddick Island, Massachusetts, killing Mary Jo Kopechne, a former campaign aide to Robert F. Kennedy

- An estimated 500 million people worldwide watched in awe as Neil Armstrong took his historic first steps on the moon
- The Woodstock Festival was held in upstate New York, featuring some of the top rock musicians of the time
- The first automatic teller machine in the United States was installed in Rockville Centre, New York

## Selected Prices

| | |
|---|---|
| Air Conditioner, 8,000 btu | $189.95 |
| Blender, Proctor | $13.49 |
| Camera, Polaroid | $50.00 |
| Bread, Loaf | $0.20 |
| Gas, Gallon | $0.35 |
| Dishwasher | $119.25 |
| Milk, Gallon | $1.10 |
| New House | $40,000 |
| New York City Ballet Ticket | $4.95 |
| Slide Projector, Kodak | $80.00 |

## "Sex Education Opponents Blast Back," Marilyn Baker, *Montclair Tribune* (California), November 13, 1969:

In this final installment of the sex education series, the spotlight is focused on those who adamantly oppose sex education, and why they feel it is wrong and what they base such opinions on, when voicing them.

Perhaps the most outspoken local critic of sex education is the Stanhope family, Clayton and Cleo Stanhope, and their 10-year-old daughter Susan.

All three have written letters, branding sex education in the least attractive terms, with Stanhope himself declaring that such education does little but cause the problems it allegedly corrects.

Mrs. Stanhope felt that past installments of the series were "a smooth cover-up job for sex education" primarily because the medical terminology for the sex organs was not spelled out in newspaper articles.

She added that such medical terms are apparently "A-OK for the toddlers" in the opinion of this reporter, hence, felt that such terms should be published in the newspaper "for those old fogey adults who never had the opportunity to delve into sex at such a tender age."

Stanhope himself based his blast on sex education on the fact that some 10-year-old children preferred baseball to sex education philosophy or other older pursuits.

His comment was, "Would these sex-crazed, meddling adults allow that to present 10-year-olds the same opportunities that young boys had without indoctrinating them with a mess of sex facts that can do nothing but wreck their young lives."

Ten-year-old Susan Stanhope took exception to a statement made via a letter to the editor which claimed "sex is NOT a communist plot and neither is sex education."

The youngster demands that "the burden of proof is on the writer's shoulders ... his proof should be forthcoming."

The statement from 10-year-old Susan Stanhope was her belief that the series was "just spouting the liberal clichés which one reads in the daily or weekly one-sided newspapers."

Another opponent of sex education is Dr. Richard Parlour and his wife Liz.

Dr. Parlour has prepared a six-page statement, which he titled "The Case Against Family Life Education," issued September 27 of this year.

In his statement, Parlour claims the title "family life education" was "cleverly chosen" to delude the American public about the actual subject matter.

*Continued*

**"Sex Education Opponents Blast Back,"** . . . *(Continued)*

Parlour brands as "fallacious and proven unsound" what he terms is the basic philosophy of family life education, that philosophy being "children should not be taught what to think; instead they should be given all this information so they can think for themselves."

"[This] is the philosophy that has created a generation of unhappy, confused, rebellious youth who have achieved their mark with record rioting, suicide, addiction, sexual promiscuity, epidemic venereal disease and rejection of everything established, even the good things," according to Parlour's statement.

Parlour believes that the classroom family life series undermines the "indoctrination process that parents should have established at home."

In another tack, Parlour also challenges the actual need for sex education, asking "How much is the life of an ordinary person enriched by reading *The Kinsey Report*?"

He adds, "Only rudimentary sexology is really necessary for adult mental health. The importance of sex in healthy living is an American obsession."

The doctor adds that "knowledge about sound family life is sorely needed," but does not feel this family life study should include the manner in which a couple beget a family.

Rather, Parlour supports "the time-honored and proven curriculum for children of reading, writing, and arithmetic, taught to the tune of the hickory stick."

---

**"*The Kinsey Report on Women*, Long-Awaited Study Shows They Are Not Very Interested in Sex," Ernest Havemann, *Life*, August 24, 1953:**

Shortly after Dr. Alfred Kinsey published his famous 1948 report on women's sex habits, he got a letter from a woman who hit a particularly shrill note in feminine indignation. The whole study, she complained, was a foolish waste of Dr. Kinsey's time; reading the book was a total waste of hers. For all the book did was prove what she and every other right-thinking woman had known all along, to wit, that "the male population is a herd of prancing, leering goats."

In his new report on women, to be published September 14, Dr. Kinsey quotes this letter with some amusement. Turns out, however, that the letter is only another proof that many a truth is spoken in jest, deliberate or unconscious. The letter, like James Thurber's sardonic title *The War between Men and Women*, like Peter Arno's cartoon of the woman reading the report on men and asking with horrified sympathy, "Is there a Mrs. Kinsey?" is a fairly accurate reflection of what can now be reported as one great message of the Kinsey sex studies.

*Continued*

### "*The Kinsey Report on Women*, Long-Awaited Study Shows They Are Not Very Interested in Sex,"... (*Continued*)

The surprise in the first Kinsey report, if any, was that man's sexual appetite starts earlier, is stronger and lasts further into old age than some people believed. The surprise in the new report, and it will come as a genuine surprise to most people including the various counselors and psychologists who have pretended the greatest knowledge in the field, is that the average woman's sexual appetite starts later and is considerably weaker than anyone has guessed. The optimists who took for granted that the world is just so well organized that for every male sex urge there must also be a female urge have been in gross error. The new Kinsey book demonstrates that, to the average woman, the average man must indeed seem, simply by virtue of his own physique and glandular system and through no fault of his own, like a "prancing, leering goat." To the average man, the average woman must seem, simply by virtue of her own physiology and through no coyness or stubbornness of her own, disinterested, unresponsive and sometimes downright frigid. So completely different are male and female sexual appetites and tastes, says Dr. Kinsey, it is almost a miracle that "married couples are ever able to work out a satisfactory sexual relationship."

The message, to be sure, will not immediately be apparent to the casual reader of *Sexual Behavior in the Human Female*, and there is indeed considerable danger that it may be lost amidst the turmoil of shock and controversy that is sure to follow publication. The 5,940 interviews obtained by Dr. Kinsey and his assistants constitute a sort of mass confession that American women have not been behaving at all in the manner in which their parents, husbands and pastors would like to think, and doubtless a great many people will even be loath to believe that Dr. Kinsey has got his facts straight. (He can only reply that if he and his assistants, who have now devoted 40 man years to the job of gathering interviews, cannot obtain the truth, the world will never have it.)

What the Kinsey figures show, in the way of bare statistical trees, which may in some cases be mistaken for the forest, is that a great revolution in American women's sex habits occurred in the 1920s. "Flaming youth" was no mere catch phrase; the young men returned from World War I, their girlfriends who were starting a mass move into higher education, and the adolescents who followed their precepts behaved quite differently from the generation before them. Part of the change, Dr. Kinsey believes, was due to the wide popularity of such frank commentators as Sigmund Freud and Havelock Ellis. Part of it was due to the fact that in World War I camps and barracks, a great many upper-class young man, reared under strict moral standards, were thrown into contact for the first time with young men in the lower classes, where the unmarried male's pursuit of the female has always been regarded with a certain amount of equanimity. The young men discovered a much more casual attitude toward sex than they had ever dreamed of—and they passed it on the young women of their class.

One of the great issues of this era is the question of how to reframe our moral values in terms relevant to the needs and conditions of a world that grows more complex and demanding every day. Many of the moral dilemmas relate in one way or another to sexual behavior within, as well as outside, marriage.

—Dr. Mary Calderone, 1968

Mary Steichen Calderone (1904-1998), Smithsonian Institution Archives

# 1970–1979

The Vietnam War finally came to an end, only to spawn spiraling costs and set off several waves of inflation. The result was an America stripped of its ability to dominate the world economy. Acrimonious battles over the forced busing of school children to attain integration—North and South—brought violence and dramatic headlines. Meanwhile, Asian-Americans began to capture attention because of their quality performance in school and lack of upward mobility afterward. Within the classroom, technology was creating a new educational experience—not to the satisfaction of everyone—but innovation was booming. Famously called a wasteland, television programming became focused on the education of preschoolers, resulting in the show *Sesame Street*.

Politically, President Richard Nixon was forced in 1971 to devalue the U.S. dollar against foreign currencies and allow its previously fixed value to "float" according to changing economic conditions. By year's end, the money paid for foreign goods exceeded that spent on U.S. exports for the first time in the century. Two years later, during the Yom Kippur War between Israel and its Arab neighbors, Arab oil producers declared an embargo on oil shipments to the United States, setting off gas shortages, a dramatic rise in the price of oil, and rationing for the first time in 30 years. The sale of automobiles plummeted, unemployment and inflation nearly doubled, and the buying power of Americans fell dramatically. The economy did not fully recover for more than a decade, while the fast-growing economies of Japan and Western Europe, mounted competitive challenges to American manufacturers. The value of imported manufactured goods skyrocketed. The inflationary cycle and recession returned in 1979 to disrupt markets, put thousands out of work, and prompt massive downsizing of companies. A symbol of the era was the pending bankruptcy of Chrysler Corporation, who could not compete against Japanese imports. The federal government was forced to extend loan guarantees to the company to prevent bankruptcy and the loss of thousands of jobs.

The appointment of Paul Volcker as the chairman of the Federal Reserve Board late in the decade gave the economy the distasteful medicine it needed. Volcker slammed on the economic brakes, restricted the growth of the money supply, and curbed inflation. As a result, interest rates went to nearly 20 percent—their highest level since the Civil War, and the sale of automobiles and expensive items decreased.

By mid-decade, disco became the music genre most readily associated with the 1970s. First appearing in dance clubs by the middle of the decade, the style was popularized by the movie *Saturday Night Fever*, released in December 1977. The soundtrack to the movie became the best-selling album of all time. The 1970s also saw the emergence of hard rock, personified by Alice Cooper, Lynyrd Skynyrd, Aerosmith, and Kiss. But it was Don McLean's 1971 song "American Pie," inspired by the death of Buddy Holly, that became one of the most recognizable songs of the rock era.

The decade also was marred by the deep divisions caused by the Vietnam War. For more than 10 years, the war had been fought on two fronts: at home and abroad. As a result, U.S. policymakers conducted the war with one eye always focused on national opinion. When it ended, the Vietnam War had been the longest war in American history, having cost $118 billion and resulting in 56,000 Americans killed and 300,000 wounded, 3.8 million Vietnamese dead, and the loss of American prestige abroad.

In the 1970s, the shift of manufacturing facilities to the South from New England and the Midwest accelerated. The Sunbelt became the new darling of Corporate America. By the late 1970s, the South, had gained more than a million manufacturing jobs, while the Northeast and the Midwest lost nearly two million. Rural North Carolina had the highest percentage of manufacturing of any state in the nation, along with the lowest blue-collar wages and the lowest unionization rate in the country. The Northeast lost more than traditional manufacturing jobs. Computerization of clerical work also made it possible for big firms such as Merrill Lynch, American Express, and Citibank to shift operations to the South and West.

The most striking of all the social actions of the early 1970s was the Women's Liberation Movement, which reshaped American society. Since the late 1950s, a small group of American women had attempted to convince Congress and the courts to bring about equality between the sexes. By the 1970s, the National Organization for Women (NOW) multiplied in size, the first issue of *Ms. Magazine* sold out in a week, and women began demanding economic equality, the legalization of abortion, and the improvement of women's roles in society. A report by the Department of Health, Education, and Welfare commented: "All authority in our society is being challenged. Professional athletes challenge owners, journalists challenge editors, consumers challenge manufacturers, and young blue-collar workers, who have grown up in an environment in which equality is called for in all institutions, are demanding the same rights and expressing the same values as university graduates."

The decade also included the flowering of the National Welfare Rights Organization (NWRO), founded in 1966, which resulted in millions of urban poor demanding additional rights. The environmental movement gained recognition and momentum during the decade, starting with the first Earth Day celebration in 1970 and the subsequent passage of the federal Clean Air and Clean Water acts. And the growing opposition to the use of nuclear power peaked after the near calamity at Three Mile Island in Pennsylvania in 1979.

During the decade, California created a no-fault divorce law, Massachusetts introduced no-fault insurance, and health food sales reached $3 billion. By mid-decade, the so-called typical nuclear family, with working father, housewife, and two children, represented only 7 percent of the population, and the average family size was 3.4 persons compared to 4.3 in 1920.

# 1970 NEWS FEATURE

**"Organizing the High Schools," Judy Penhiter, *WIN Magazine*, May 1970:**

Briefly, I'd like to say a few things about what we at War Resister's League/West in San Francisco are doing in relation to high school work. Over the past two years we have been gradually expanding our various projects concerning high schools. I hope that some of the ideas and techniques which we have implemented will be of help to others who are struggling to create a greater and all-encircling awareness among high school students.

In the beginning, we tried to establish contacts in all schools in the Bay Area. With the help of a few high school students that we knew, we began to compile a list of sympathetic teachers. In the private schools, we contacted principals. We talked to principals and teachers alike about some of our ideas concerning nonviolence, hopes for a better world, and our light/sound show (a show comprised of tapes, films and slides). Sometimes we went in with the approval of the administration and other times we were quietly whisked down the back stairs. It wasn't long before we no longer had to call teachers about the show; they called us. We usually tried not to take gigs if we would not be able to come back the following day to rap about the ideas presented in the films and tapes. The show, while stimulating, needs to be discussed because there are so many topics touched upon which can only be clarified and drawn together in discussions.

This year was barely in full swing when we felt the need to expand into doing more concentrated follow-up. It was hoped that if enough exposure to alternative lifestyles and beliefs could somehow be accomplished, some of them would begin to question their own lifestyles and beliefs which had formerly been taken for granted. Another hope was that people would become involved in working with us, Ecology Action, or similar groups. (This has been accomplished to some degree. Students do help us with some of our projects.) Two people who graduated last year have been with us for close to a year.

To accomplish these goals, we began having weekly high school potlucks where these kids could get together to rap about ideas, problems, future plans, and interesting subjects, and also be exposed to a growing and loving community. High school weekends were also planned to which someone would come to rap about their particular interests (ecology, etc.), or the kids would become involved in action projects such as beach clean-ups. After the lottery came into effect, we made six large posters which stand back to back on three display stands. The posters talk about the lottery, the draft, alternatives, non-registration and War Resisters League. Each day from 2 to 4 we take these displays to school and talk to students and provide relevant literature for them to read. We've just now moved to our second school after being in the first for well over a month. (It looks as though we may get a chance to test the anti-loitering act at the second school. We've been hassled but plan to exhaust all means of verbal communication before taking any further steps.) Day after day, the students saw us and began to identify with us. Now, with the groundwork in place, we are able to go into classes four, five or more times. And so, rather than just scratching the surface of nonviolence in our discussions, we are now able to cover both resistance activities and positive alternatives. Besides the light/sound show and follow-up raps, we have begun to do mock draft resistance trials, which seem to hold the interest of students who take the part of jurors. I think it is quite an informative experience for them, too. We've even ended up with a few acquittals.

In addition to the day-to-day activities, we have planned and carried out some one- to two-day special sessions. Recently, about 30 people got together to decide how to facilitate government operations, health and sanitation, education, postal system, food and water supplies, and so forth in a given situation in the year 1973. The students seem to enjoy it immensely and stated there were many subjects discussed about which they had not previously spent much time thinking. They felt we should plan together. We're in the process of doing just that, along with planning a weekend follow-up action project at a commune. Another exercise in the middle stages is the peace games. About 30 people will take part in this exercise in mid-April. For those who know little about this particular topic, a peace game is a socio-drama in which a group of nonviolent people are invaded by a violent outside group and must determine means for coping with the situation. While it was originally planned to be practice in national defense through nonviolent means, I personally feel it is a help in everyday situations we face today in demonstrations, sit-ins, arrests, riots, and so forth. They do a tremendous job in helping a person to know how to best approach these tense situations.

Another thing which we are planning is a nonviolent fair. There will be displays on Gandhi, King, Dolci, the Czechoslovakian resistance, free schools, etc., free nonviolent food, bead making, god's eyes, bread baking, spinning, and the list continues. We held one last year which was well attended and well liked. This year, we hope to have it on the grounds of one of the two high schools here in San Francisco.

# 1970 Profile

Joan Ganz Cooney found a way to broadcast a show for preschool children that was both entertaining and educational, and *Sesame Street* debuted in the 1969-70 television season.

## Life at Home

*Joan Cooney's passion about educational TV, helped put Sesame Street on the air.*

- Joan Ganz Cooney was born November 30, 1929, in Phoenix, Arizona, to a wealthy banking family with both Jewish and Catholic heritage.
- Her grandfather, Emil Ganz, was a German Jew who came to America just before the Civil War, moved to Georgia and fought with the Confederate Army.
- After the war, he moved west 'and settled in Phoenix, where he opened a liquor store and later became president of a local bank.
- He was a Democrat who was elected mayor of Phoenix three times.
- Joan's mother, Pauline Reardon Ganz, was a Catholic from Michigan; her father, Sylvan Cleveland Ganz, was president of his father's bank for 44 years.
- "I was raised in the most conventional way," Joan said, "raised to be a housewife and mother, to work in an interesting job when I got out of college, and to marry at the appropriate time, which would have been 25."

- Joan grew up within a "country-club atmosphere," but she became concerned about poverty in high school.
- She was inspired by Father James Keller, a Maryknoll priest who founded The Christophers, a group that encouraged people to use their God-given talents to make a positive difference in the world.
- The movement borrowed an ancient Chinese proverb: "It's better to light one candle than to curse the darkness."
- She went to the Dominican College of San Raphael, a Catholic college in California, but transferred to the University of Arizona, where she graduated with a bachelor's degree in education in 1951.
- Joan had no interest in teaching.
- So right after college, she and a friend moved to Washington, DC, to work as clerks using a typewriter to create letters and other documents for the State Department.

*Joan was an enthusiastic 23-year old when she moved to New York.*

- "I just wanted to see what it was like to live in Washington and work for the federal government."
- She returned to Phoenix for a year to work on the local newspaper, *The Arizona Republic*, and save money for her next goal: moving to New York City.
- Her mother said: "You know you are a big fish in a little pond in Phoenix; why do you want to be a little fish in a big pond?"
- Joan's response: "How do you know I won't be a big fish in a big pond?"
- Joan was 23 when she arrived in New York in the fall of 1953.
- "When I came to New York I thought I would probably work in print, but of course this great new medium of television was blossoming."
- Her newspaper work helped her get an entry-level job in RCA's publicity department, which quickly led to her getting a job making $65 a week writing summaries of soap operas for the NBC television network.
- In 1954, she stepped up to a job as a publicist for U.S. Steel Corporation on their show, *The U.S. Steel Hour* (ABC, 1953-55; CBS, 1955-63), which aired a variety of critically praised dramas.
- She was aware of the emergence of educational television, and became "obsessed" with being part of it.
- "It just hit me as exactly what I wanted to do with my life," she said.
- "I wanted to see the medium do constructive things, and I could see that that was really the way."
- When WNDT, Channel 13, established a public television station in New York in 1962, she jumped at the opportunity to join, even though she knew it meant a cut in pay.
- She tried to get a job as a publicist, but the general manager said they didn't need publicists; they needed producers, particularly one for a weekly live debate show called *Court of Reason*.
- She had no experience as a producer, but was undeterred.
- She told the general manager: "I don't know all the people personally that you would have on the air, but I know what the issues are and I know who the people are who espouse what positions on what issues. I can do that show."

- She was hired—and her yearly pay fell from $12,000 at U.S. Steel to $9,000 on Channel 13.
- "I had a thousand dollars in the bank," she said; "I figured I would … need a hundred dollars more a month to live, but by the time I ran out of money, I would get a raise, and that's just the way it worked out."
- Joan graduated to short documentaries.
- One of her suppliers for ideas was Tim Cooney, director of public relations for the New York City Department of Labor.

*Joan's documentary was used to train Head Start teachers.*

- He called her in 1964 to alert her to an experimental reading program underway with four-year-olds in Harlem.
- This experiment—like one being conducted by psychologist Susan Gray in Tennessee—would become a model for the inception of Head Start that year.
- Joan met with researchers Lillian and Martin Deutsch and produced a documentary called *A Chance at the Beginning*.
- After Head Start was launched, the federal program bought 125 prints of the documentary to use as training films for their teachers.
- Joan married Cooney in February 1964.
- Her June 1965 documentary called *Poverty, Anti-Poverty and the Poor* caught the attention of Jack Gould, an influential television critic for *The New York Times*.
- He described the format as similar to a "teach-in" held earlier in Washington, DC, joining public officials, experts and the general public.
- "The floor participants queued up before microphones in the aisles and let fly with statements, criticisms, challenges and, occasionally, questions."
- By early 1966, Joan said she "had become absolutely involved intellectually and spiritually with the Civil Rights movement and with the educational deficit that poverty created; I was not necessarily focused on young children, though."
- That moment came at a dinner party she held at her apartment in February 1966.
- For the next three years, she was involved in a swirl of activity that would bring together the educational experts, television artists and the money that would enable the launch of the first season of *Sesame Street* in 1969-70.

## Life at Work

> "Sunny day, keeping the clouds away
> On my way to where the air is sweet.
> Can you tell me how to get,
> How to get to Sesame Street?"
>
> —Opening lines of the *Sesame Street* theme song composed by
> Joe Raposo and Jeff Moss

- Many Americans were hoping for sunshine and sweetness as the 1969-70 television season opened, and what little there was came from an improbable source: a new television show for preschoolers called *Sesame Street*.

- The show first aired as the Vietnam War and protests against it were reaching a feverish pitch.
- Four protesters were shot and killed on the campus of Kent State University in Ohio in May 1970.
- It was also a time when interest in preschool education was high and disdain for popular television intense.
- "The timing was incredible," Joan said. "Every night the TV set brought you bad news. Finally, it was as if the public was saying 'So do something!' to the TV set, and one day they turned on the TV set and the TV set did something. And everyone understood that, for a change, TV was doing something.
- "There was huge idealism because we were trying to reach inner-city children as well as others."
- The way to *Sesame Street* had begun in the early 1960s when Joan met Lloyd N. Morrisett, who would become the show's co-creator.
- Morrisett was a psychologist and executive at the Carnegie Corporation of New York, which was established by steel mill owner Andrew Carnegie in 1911 "to promote the advancement and diffusion of knowledge and understanding."
- Morrisett was about the same age as Joan.
- He moved to New York in 1959 to work for Carnegie, one of the nation's biggest private funders for educational and social improvement programs.
- He and Joan met a couple years later.
- In the early 1960s, Carnegie became increasingly interested in funding programs that would help children from poor households be successful in school.
- While several projects were funded, all were experiments involving only a few hundred children.
- Morrisett and his wife, Mary, were bemused and not a little worried when they woke up 6 a.m. on a Sunday morning in 1965 and found their three-year-old daughter, Sarah, had turned on the television herself and was intently watching.
- Even more concerning was that the only thing on the screen at that hour was what was a test pattern—a still image that was broadcast when the network was "off the air."
- For Morrisett, it helped reinforce his belief in the "the utter fascination that little kids had with television."
- He brought up the subject at a dinner party hosted by Joan and her husband in February 1966.
- As they chatted, Lloyd Morrisett asked: "Do you think television could be used to teach children?"
- "Lloyd talked about the possibility of Carnegie financing … a little three-month study," Joan said, "where [an] investigator would go around the country talking to various child development people.
- "I didn't know until that moment that I would be interested," Joan said. "I suddenly saw that this was a way of making television do something for the people that needed the help."
- With a $15,000 Carnegie grant to WNDT to cover Joan's salary and expenses, she traveled around the country from June to October 1966 talking with educators and child development psychologists.
- Joan left public television station WNDT in early 1967 and became an employee at Carnegie, where she would continue to shape the show.
- This was just a few years after the 1965 launch of Head Start, and in the peak of the "preschool moment."
- Educators, researchers and parents were keenly interested in early childhood education, not only as a way to help all children succeed in school, but especially to help children from impoverished backgrounds overcome their social obstacles.
- And the poor included a disproportionate number of black households.
- The preschool movement coincided with the Civil Rights movement.
- While Joan knew little about preschool educational theories, she, like many white liberals, supported the efforts of blacks to end segregation and gain equal footing in all spheres of life, from education to housing.

- But specifically targeting minority children had its own dangers.
- Louis Housman, a former commercial TV executive and a federal government advisor on the project, said a minority-oriented show would draw the ire of black parents who would consider it "demeaning" and "patronizing," while driving away the white, middle-class audience.
- Joan and Morrisett were continually asked by potential backers whether television could teach.
- She and Morrisett believed it could.
- After all, preschoolers were memorizing television commercials for products ranging from bread to beer.
- Joan decided that, while the creative people would be the final judges of what went on the air, they would work closely with educators and researchers to test and improve the show at every step.
- They enlisted funders to a show that would be an experiment.
- By early 1968, Joan and Morrisett had lined up $8 million in funding for a two-year experimental project that would produce six months of programs for the 1969-70 season.
- Half came from federal government sources, including $650,000 from Head Start.
- The rest came from Carnegie, the Ford Foundation, and other private sources; Carnegie's $1.5 million grant was one of its largest ever.
- With the funding in place, Carnegie announced in March 1968 the creation of the Children's Television Workshop with Joan as its executive director.
- Joan took to heart a key piece of advice from a public television executive: Keep the goals for the program simple and modest.
- "We would teach the alphabet, the recitation of the alphabet, recognition of letters, recognition of numbers when you see them, certain sounds of letters; because we were phonetic, we believed that phonics was the way to go, that learning the sounds of letters was useful."

*Sesame Street's Big Bird taught the alphabet to a pre-school audience.*

- Joan had hired David D. Connell as executive producer.
- Connell had the same role for 12 years with the company that produced *Captain Kangaroo*, an hour-long children's television show on CBS since 1955.
- How would the show's producers know if they were truly engaging the preschoolers?
- The researchers would watch them.
- Young actor James Earl Jones caught the attention of the test audiences by reciting the alphabet slowly in his deep voice.
- Each letter appeared above his head a moment before Jones pronounced it, and researchers saw the value of repetition as the kids began to shout each letter before Jones said it.
- The insert made it into the show's second episode in 1969.
- The show's street scenes were originally filmed without any puppets—a move intended to clearly separate the show's "real" parts from "fantasy" ones.
- But researchers saw kids' attention fall away on the street scenes, and pick up only when the show switched to animation or puppets.
- "So it turned into a street where Oscar can come out of a trash can or Big Bird can come wandering by," Connell said.
- Jim Henson and his Muppets were hired for the project in 1968, and the Muppets multiplied with researchers' suggestions.
- Suggestion: Children ought to be taught that it's okay not to be happy all the time, and not to be pleasant all the time.
- Result: Oscar the Grouch.
- Suggestion: Show a child being smarter than the adults, so that you're modeling smart kids.
- Result: Bert and Ernie.
- Suggestion: Show a child as a child is—awkward and forever asking questions.
- Result: Big Bird.
- One of the last elements to fall into place was the show's name.
- The Muppets acted out the tortured naming process in a promotional video shown to potential funders in 1968.
- After a board of grousing Muppets came up with a name spanning a few dozen words, Kermit the Frog said, "Why don't you call your show 'Sesame Street.' You know, like 'open sesame.' It kind of gives the idea of a street where neat things happen."
- After the first season, the workshop released a study finding that 90 percent of preschoolers surveyed in a poor neighborhood in Brooklyn had seen *Sesame Street* in its first season.
- The 611 children surveyed lived in households with TV sets, and did not go off to daycare or nursery schools.
- Of them, 60 percent saw the show at least once a day.
- Separately, the independent Nielsen Rating Service estimated that half of the nation's 12 million children ages three to five had watched *Sesame Street* in its first season.
- Studies of 120 children in Maine, New York, and Tennessee showed thinking and reading skills improved more among preschoolers who watched the show compared with those who did not.
- The show won an Emmy award in 1970 for Outstanding Achievement in Children's Programming.
- And there were other signs of success.
- "Rubber Duckie," Ernie's signature tribute song to his beloved bathtub toy, reached No. 16 on Billboard's "Hot 100 Singles" chart in 1970.
- The song was nominated for a Grammy Award for Best Recording for Children, but it lost to *The Sesame Street Book & Record*, which included the song.
- And the weekly news magazine *Time* featured *Sesame Street* in its November 23, 1970, issue.
- "When Big Bird hit the cover of *Time*, I knew we had something that would last forever," Joan said.
- The Workshop didn't want to depend on government for funding.

- Most foundations like Carnegie made large grants to start up projects, expecting that recipients would find their own funds to continue the programs—usually government funds.
- The Workshop sought a new funding model for *Sesame Street.*
- By April 1970, Joan was talking about selling books and records to reinforce the show's lessons—and raise money.
- That month, the Children's Television Workshop broke away from its parent, National Educational Television, and became a non-profit company with Joan as its president.

## Life in the Community: Racial Controversy

- While *Sesame Street* allowed the public to meet the Muppets, it also brought them into a world that was urban and integrated.
- A cast with educated black men and women in prominent roles might have escaped the notice of preschool viewers, but it was one of the most noticeable aspects of the show to older children and adults—both black and white—who had grown up with their own notions of racial identity.
- "It was the first show that really worked at integration—not only black and white men and women, but Muppets and human beings," Joan said.
- "It was a show that really taught kindness to one another."
- The racially mixed cast scared public officials in Mississippi.
- The state was one of the last to start an educational television network, and its first station in the state went on the air February 1, 1970, in Jackson, the state capital.
- Shortly afterward, the state legislature voted to spend $5.3 million to establish stations across the state.
- But the all-white state commission overseeing educational television voted to postpone showing *Sesame Street* even though it cost the state no money to air it.
- *The New York Times* carried a short news story noting that the commission chairman, Jackson banker James McKay, was the son-in-law of Jackson's former mayor, Allen Thompson.
- "Mr. Thompson is president and leading spokesman for FOCUS, a new group in Mississippi that is seeking to re-establish the principle of 'freedom of choice' in public schools."
- But the most telling aspect of the outcry was that some of the loudest voices were Mississippians.
- Newspaper editorials blasted the decision, and WDAM, a commercial station in Jackson, said it would offer airtime for *Sesame Street* if the commission didn't reverse its decision when it met again later that month.
- *The Delta Democratic-Times*, a family-owned newspaper in Greenville whose editor was Hodding Carter III, published two editorials languidly eviscerating the commission for the blocking of Big Bird.
- The May 5 editorial read: "We are penalized again, and our children more than adults, by the official determination to pretend that reality doesn't exist."
- On May 12, the Carters, who were longtime Democrats, took another tack: a tongue-in-cheek appeal to the Republican sensibilities of some of its readers.
- The editorial noted *Sesame Street* had the seal of approval from Republican Vice President Spiro Agnew.
- The editorial suggested, "white Mississippians, who like what he has to say about left-wing intellectuals, radical youths and school busing," should embrace the show and claim victory in the name of President Nixon's goal of bridging the generation gap.
- "We can't think of a bigger gap than between our three-year-olds' world and our own."
- And, by following Agnew, "radicals in the kindergarten would be thwarted."
- In late May, the commission met again and reversed its decision.

# HISTORICAL SNAPSHOT
# 1970

- Pan American Airways offered the first commercially scheduled 747 service from John F. Kennedy International Airport to London's Heathrow Airport
- Black Sabbath's eponymous debut album, often regarded as the first heavy metal album, was released
- A jury found the Chicago Seven defendants not guilty of conspiring to incite a riot, in charges stemming from the violence at the 1968 Democratic National Convention; five of the defendants were found guilty on the lesser charge of crossing state lines to incite a riot
- The Nuclear Non-Proliferation Treaty went into effect, after ratification by 56 nations
- The United States Army charged 14 officers with suppressing information related to the My Lai massacre in Vietnam
- Postal workers in a dozen cities went on strike for two weeks; President Richard Nixon assigned military units to New York City post offices
- The first Earth Day proclamation was issued by San Francisco Mayor Joseph Alioto
- Congress banned cigarette television advertisements, effective January 1, 1971
- Paul McCartney announced that the Beatles had disbanded as their twelfth album, *Let It Be*, was released
- An oxygen tank in the *Apollo 13* spacecraft exploded, forcing the crew to abort the mission and return in four days
- The U.S. military invaded Cambodia to hunt out the Viet Cong; widespread, large antiwar protests erupted in the U.S.
- Four students at Kent State University in Ohio were killed and nine wounded by Ohio National Guardsmen during a protest against the incursion into Cambodia
- The U.S. promoted its first female generals: Anna Mae Hays and Elizabeth P. Hoisington
- *Venera 7* was launched and became the first spacecraft to successfully transmit data from the surface of another planet
- The Women's Strike for Equality took place down Fifth Avenue in New York City
- Elvis Presley began his first concert tour since 1958 at the Veterans Memorial Coliseum in Phoenix, Arizona
- The first New York City Marathon took place
- Guitarist Jimi Hendrix died in London of drug-related complications
- *Monday Night Football* debuted on ABC
- In Paris, a Communist delegation rejected President Nixon's October 7 peace proposal for the Vietnam War as "a maneuver to deceive world opinion"
- Garry Trudeau's comic strip *Doonesbury* debuted in approximately two dozen newspapers in the U.S.
- The crash of Southern Airlines Flight 932 killed all 75 on board, including 37 players and five coaches from the Marshall University football team
- The Soviet Union landed *Lunokhod 1* on the moon—the first roving remote-controlled robot to land on a natural satellite
- The North Tower of the World Trade Center was topped out at 1,368 feet, making it the tallest building in the world
- Alvin Toffler published his book *Future Shock*

## Selected Prices

| | |
|---|---|
| Automobile, Gremlin | $2,196.00 |
| Calculator, Electric Printing | $1,495.00 |
| Circular Saw | $27.77 |
| Electric Shaver | $13.97 |
| Guitar, Electric | $199.95 |
| Ketchup, Hunt's, 14 Ounces | $0.22 |
| Refrigerator, Frigidaire | $208.00 |
| Rider Mower | $352.95 |
| Router | $34.95 |
| Whiskey, Seagram's, Fifth | $5.79 |

### Editorial: "No to Sesame Street," *The Delta Democrat-Times*, Greenville, Mississippi, May 5, 1970:

It is not hard to sympathize with officials at Mississippi's educational television commission. They know the state's political and ideological realities, know that suspicious critics are closely examining everything they do and know that what the legislature gave this year it can take away next year. But when caution gives way to what appears to be panic at the first sign of possible controversy, a logical question arises. Exactly what is ETV supposed to be for?

The question must be asked because of the ETV commission's decision not to run *Sesame Street*, an educational show aimed at preschool children.

*Sesame Street* is an extraordinary venture in the use of television to do a serious job of educating young children rather than merely entertaining them, although it educates through a skillful blend of entertainment, psychology, color and sound teaching methods. Tests have repeatedly shown that the show, sponsored by several foundations through The Children's Television Workshop, does a successful job. One test suggested that children who had watched the show over a six-week period showed 2.5 times as much progress as children who had not.

But Mississippi's ETV commission won't be showing it for the time being because of one fatal defect, as measured by Mississippi's political leadership. *Sesame Street* is integrated. Some of its leading cast members are black, including the man who does much of the overt "teaching." The neighborhood of the "street" is a mixed one. And all that, of course, goes against the Mississippi grain.

It doesn't matter that integration in the schools is now a reality in Mississippi, and segregation is against the law of the land in virtually every field, including housing. Commercial television may portray this fact, but educational television, a state-controlled venture, may not. Thus, we are penalized again, and our children more than adults, by the official determination to pretend that reality doesn't exist.

There is no state which more desperately needs every educational tool it can find than Mississippi. There is no educational show on the market today better prepared than *Sesame Street* to teach preschool children what many cannot or do not learn in their homes. But "we decided it would be best to postpone it in the early days of ETV because some of the legislators might be offended," an ETV commission spokesman told *Democrat-Times* Jackson correspondent Ed Williams.

Mississippi ETV's officials maintain that *Sesame Street* is not being banned, but only postponed. Nevertheless, it is fairly apparent that those who run from anticipated pressure today are not very likely to show backbone when real pressure is applied. As in the case of the ETV decision not to show the award-winning documentary, *Hospital*, deciding against running *Sesame Street* seems to indicate that Mississippi ETV will settle for safe mediocrity every time. If that proves the case, there are strong reasons to ask whether the tax money which is being appropriated for educational television would not better be rediverted to the public schools. There, at least, the realities of 1970 cannot be avoided and the needs are immense.

## Editorial: "Agnew Likes It," *The Delta Democrat-Times*, Greenville, Mississippi, May 12, 1970:

Vice President Spiro T. Agnew has a wide following among white Mississippians, who like what he has to say about left-wing intellectuals, radical youths and school busing.

*Sesame Street* does not have much following in Mississippi's educational television commission.

But the vice president thinks *Sesame Street*, the highly acclaimed educational television show for three- to five-year-olds, is one of the few examples of good television fare on the scene today.

Somehow there ought to be a way to get the vice president and the ETV commissioners together. The commissioners could reverse their earlier decision to reject showing *Sesame Street*, the vice president could laud their action, and his many followers would echo his support.

That way, everyone would win. The vice president, speaking for the "silent majority," would give a majority on the ETV commission enough nerve to risk displeasure from state politicians when they allow *Sesame Street* on the air. That would be a victory for our children and for common sense.

But it would also be a victory for the Nixon administration. Bridging the generation gap has suddenly become one of its major priorities, and we can't think of a bigger gap than between our three-year-olds' world and our own. Knowing that their vice president cares about the level of television they are offered would do wonders for the preschoolers' appreciation of this administration, and thus by indirection[,] of all authority. Radicals in the kindergarten would be thwarted. The American way would be upheld.

And all because the vice president likes *Sesame Street*.

### *"Sesame* Showing Would Be Blunder, Officials Say," Ed Williams, Capitol Correspondent, *The Delta Democrat*-Times, Greenville, Mississippi, May 12, 1970:

JACKSON—Showing the widely praised children's program *Sesame Street* on Mississippi educational television at this time would be a political blunder, according to two members of the state ETV commission who asked not to be identified.

The major reason: Only during the last session did the state legislature begin to show solid support for the ETV project, and scheduling *Sesame Street*, with its racially mixed cast and its Ford Foundation funding, would give intransigent ETV opponents another weapon in future battles.

The ETV commission discussed scheduling the program twice, sources said—in January and on April 17. They decided by an informal vote that the program should not be scheduled now. "We decided it would be best to postpone it in the early days of ETV because some of the legislators might be offended," one commission member said.

"Some of the educators on the commission were a little timid," another member said: "You know they have a colored man and a colored woman—who, by the way, speak excellent English—and they have all these little children around them, some black, some white." The fear of legislative disapproval of the key roles played by blacks "was the primary reason we decided to look at it a little longer," he said.

An article in *PTA Magazine* for May 1970 called the program "a sensation in Mississippi," but for different reasons.

*Sesame Street* had its genesis in a study conducted by Mrs. Joan Cooney, a producer of award-winning TV documentaries in New York. The study, funded by the Carnegie Corp., sought to discover what role television could play in the education of preschool children.

After the study, Carnegie joined with the Ford Foundation and the U.S. Office of Education to fund the Children's Television Workshop in 1968. Other major sponsors were the Corporation for Public Broadcasting, the Markle Foundation, and Project Head Start.

Children's Television Workshop gathered a variety of experts—child-development specialists, psychologists, educators, TV producers, film makers, advertising men, book illustrators, and audience researchers. They approached the idea of using television for preschool education with many questions. How much can you expect preschool kids to learn about numbers, letters of the alphabet, people, places, animals? How can the child's interest in new and varied things be stimulated? What format would hold the child's attention?

Their answers are displayed in *Sesame Street*.

*Continued*

## "*Sesame* Showing Would Be Blunder, Officials Say," . . . *(Continued)*

The setting is a typical American city street. It has a sidewalk, apartment houses, a newspaper-candy store, mailbox, trees, and an excavation site. A wall of doors of various colors surrounds the excavation site. The doors open to transport the children of *Sesame Street* to adventures at farms, lakes, mountains, the seashore. The residents of Sesame Street are children, black and white.

*PTA Magazine* said tests in daycare centers in several states indicate *Sesame Street* is a valuable educational tool. In several skills—recognizing letters, numbers and geometric forms; in sorting out and classifying groups—children who watched the program over a six-week period showed 2.5 times as much progress as children who hadn't watched the program.

*Sesame Street* has all the elements which make a prime target for legislative opponents of ETV. Recall some of the arguments made against the $5.3 million ETV appropriation in the state House of Representatives:

—Rep. Tullius Brady of Brookhaven warned of ETV's "subtle influence on the mind" and noted that the Ford Foundation has a "great deal of influence in educational television, and it has been used for evil purposes, for the most part."

—Rep. Malcolm Mabry of Dublin noted the federal money involved in ETV, and said "if you think the federal government is not going to eventually control what it subsidizes, you're very slow to learn."

*Sesame Street* had its nationwide debut last November. It is offered free to ETV stations, and about 95 per cent of them use it. Mississippians aren't shielded from the program. ETV stations in Memphis, New Orleans, and the state ETV network of Alabama show the program, and it seeps across the state line into Mississippi. The ETV commission isn't against *Sesame Street*, some members say.

"There's no question in my mind that it will be on ETV in Mississippi," one said. "But right now I don't think one program is worth risking what we're trying to build in this ETV system. By not showing this program now, the only people we're depriving are the ones around Jackson. We won't have the statewide system set up until at least the fall of next year. We haven't banned *Sesame Street*—we just decided this isn't the proper time to put it on the air."

The ETV commission is made up of the State Superintendent of Education, the head of the Junior College Division in the State Department of Education, a member of the State College Board, and four persons appointed by the governor.

All the members are white.

### "Educational TV, Still Young, Still Trying," John Horn, *The Progressive*, February 1966:

The state of educational television (ETV) in the United States recalls one of Fred Allen's comments on program ratings. "It's possible to get a minus rating," the comedian said. "Nobody listens to your program, but one guy out in Albuquerque goes around knocking it." A bitter critic of selected sampling and the broadcasting industry's uses of the technique, Allen fired off many such barbs. As an analogue applied to educational television, the quip is slightly exaggerated.

It is not true that no one is listening to and looking at ETV. Nearly 100 stations bring ETV programs within the reach of an estimated 50 million Americans. But the actual audience that tuned in is highly selective, which is as ETV wants it. Some five million individuals watch more than one hour a week. In vivid contrast, the average family among the 55 million families who have access to the almost 600 commercial television stations clocks the staggering total of more than five hours of viewing per day.

*Continued*

## "Educational TV, Still Young, Still Trying," . . . *(Continued)*

In other ways, too, ETV is relatively inconsequential. The commercial television industry—three national networks and 575 stations—reported $1.8 billion in total broadcast revenues last year and $415.6 million in pretax profits. That commercial television profit could keep going the operations of all of ETV for eight years. It would be enough to finance the 100 ETV stations and program-producing National Educational Television (NET) network, sometimes called "the bicycle network" because it is not interconnected electronically as the commercial network stations are. ETV tapes and films are shipped and shared. Being non-commercial, ETV is happy to break even.

The 1964 television budget of the medium's top advertiser—Procter & Gamble's $140,736,000—could have supported three ETV station-network complexes with $20 million left over for mad money. The sum spent by television's fiftieth largest sponsor—Royal Crown Cola's $8,001,000—was almost exactly equal to the 1964 budget of NET, the central production facility of educational television.

Program production costs are just as ludicrously disparate.

NET, a far more lavish spender than any of its stations, splurges up to $20,000 to produce a one-hour program. ETV stations can keep their costs extremely low. WNDT, New York, put on the 1964 Emmy-winning series, *The Art of Film*, for a total of $150 a week in out-of-pocket expenses, which included a modest honorarium for the host, Stanley Kauffmann, film critic for *The New Republic*.

Commercial television's bill, in contrast, averages about $50,000 for a half-hour program. But it has often shot to the heady heights of a half a million and more for network extravaganzas such as *Hedda Gabler*, starring Ingrid Bergman, and *My Name is Barbra*, the 1965 Barbra Streisand special.

In a medium overwhelmingly devoted to entertainment, ETV deals with education, enrichment and enlightenment. Although television, in the words of advertising executives, is the greatest sales medium devised by man's genius, ETV sells no commercial products. In the field of mass communications, it appeals only to minority audiences.

ETV is a marvel of perversity and a triumph of sheer survival. Just what is it that makes it something of value?

In the materialistic jeweler's eye of modern affluent America, nothing. To those who step to the music of a different drummer, everything. ETV's informational and cultural programming during prime evening hours offers American viewers a choice, an alternative to the rampant commercialism, standardized comedy, violence and superficiality that dominate commercial television....

ETV is a second chance for American broadcasting.

*Continued*

## "Educational TV, Still Young, Still Trying," . . . *(Continued)*

The first chance, leased to private enterprise with FCC reins held so loosely as hardly to be felt, has reached a dead end. At the times when most people watch, their commercial television choice is held down to virtually one level—that of the comic book—with their range of choice limited to westerns, soap operas, situation comedies, spy stories, and variety shows.

"Television in the main is being used to distract, delude, amuse and insulate us," Edward R. Murrow said in a 1958 speech that still rings true. "We are protecting the mind of the American public from any real contact with the menacing world that squeezes in upon us.... There is a great and perhaps decisive battle to be fought against ignorance, intolerance, and indifference. The trouble with television is that it is rusting in the scabbard during a battle for survival." He was speaking, of course, about commercial television.

The principal accolade for the far-sighted concept of ETV's potential should go to Frieda Hennock, the thoughtful, liberal FCC commissioner who alone, in July 1949—the FCC "freeze" of station construction while priorities were studied—proposed the reservation of certain television channels for education. Educational groups that had been alerted to what was at issue, including agencies of the Ford Foundation, successfully pleaded before the FCC and won 242 channels for non-commercial educational television when the freeze was lifted in April 1952.

The growth of educational television was understandably slow. An investment of more than $50 million in properties had to be made, and operating funds collected. The first ETV station, KUHT, Houston, went on the air on May 12, 1963. One hundred ETV stations have now been established. From the beginning, the Ford Foundation was the prime organizer, creating committees, agencies, and the Educational Television and Radio Center (which eventually became NET); raising funds; establishing stations; getting them on the air and keeping them there.

Since 1951, the Ford Foundation has given a total of $96.8 million to ETV. Three-fourths of NET's $8 million annual operating cost is borne by the same unflagging source. The Foundation has earmarked $10 million more to provide, over the next four years, matching grants to the public-supported community ETV stations as a stimulus to their own fundraising efforts.

The unevenness of NET's output betrays dispersion of responsibility among diverse sources. Outside firms, program underwriters, individual stations and the NET staff are all in the producing act. Strong leadership, minimum standards, and definite direction are yet to be established.

The loose confederacy nevertheless has yielded good, even great programs, especially those produced for NET by WGBH-TV, Boston, operated by the WGBH Educational Foundation. The Foundation is a partnership of Harvard, the Massachusetts Institute of Technology, the Boston Symphony, and the Lowell Institute, a century-old pioneer in adult education.

*Continued*

## "Educational TV, Still Young, Still Trying," . . . *(Continued)*

A major pioneering contribution of WGBH-TV and of NET was the station's coverage, for the network, of the American Negro's civil rights struggle of 1963. The Boston station was first on the airwaves with quality programs on the subject, programs that aired the views of Negroes and whites, and of official and unofficial leaders from Roy Wilkins to Malcolm X. Following NET's spring lead on the big domestic story of the year, the commercial television networks scheduled their own programs on civil rights before the summer was over, notably NBC-TV's three-hour prime-time Labor Day special.

Prodding the commercial networks was an achievement, but more important was influencing national policy on civil rights. A key event took place after a group of Negroes met in New York City in May 1963 with Attorney General Robert F. Kennedy, who represented [his brother] President John F. Kennedy. Both sides left the meeting frustrated and depressed, feeling they had not really understood each other. James Baldwin, who was present, went to a studio within a few hours to tape a WGBH-TV interview. He was furious that he and his friends had failed to convince the Attorney General of urgency of the problem. Baldwin's impassioned speech was telecast May 28. The eloquent 40-minute television plea—that the future of the Negro and of America "is entirely up to the American people, whether or not they are going to face and deal with and embrace the stranger whom they maligned so long"—persuaded the Kennedys, as the abortive meeting had not, and was a factor leading to President Kennedy's moral commitment of America to equality for all in his speech of June 10.

Coverage of the civil rights story of 1963 remains NET's high-water mark, the time it came closest to its stated objective: "To provide a national program service that tangibly contributes (1) to the knowledge and wisdom of the American people on subjects crucial to their freedom and welfare, and (2) to the continuing cultural growth and renewal that are vital in any healthy society."

Such enterprise on "crucial subjects" has not been exhibited since. The controversy over escalation of the war in Vietnam, demonstrated by a rising tide of protest in the United States, was the big story of 1964. NET muffed or dodged it, except for the telecast of a Washington, DC, teach-in. So did commercial television until late summer, when CBS and NBC finally scheduled major documentaries whose principal contribution was detailing of the Johnson administration's position.

In the NET cultural area, a wide variance of quality persists, with far too many embarrassing examples of amateurism and pretension getting on the air. Muddled in execution as it is, ignored by the big audience, existing hand-to-mouth on handouts, displaying more potential than performance, and unsure of direction or survival—ETV still remains a promise of better television to come. Educational television is America's only hope for a second broadcasting chance, a chance to raise the quality of television at least a few notches above the level of comic books.

# 1973 PROFILE

The day Reggie Earl Highlander was asked, as a student at one high school, to be an assistant coach at a rival school, was the day he became a real coach.

## Life at Home

- In a hospital ward jammed with the latest crop of Baby Boomers, Reggie Earl Highlander looked diminutive to those who were polite, and downright scrawny to those who weren't.
- In 1948, the situation was the same in hospitals across America.
- Reggie's father was an auto mechanic with a wealth of experience keeping Government Issue machinery running down the muddy roads of Europe with a few tricks he had learned at his own father's knee.
- His mother was an English teacher who still believed—when no one else seemed to care—in using adverbs properly, when to use whom instead of who, and what a gerund might be.
- At age six, Reggie was small and skinny, and at 16, he was short and skinny.
- A mediocre but enthusiastic athlete, Reggie tried track, football and basketball.
- He liked basketball best, even though he lacked the proper body dynamics to hit a free throw, drive hard to the basket with his left hand or block out a really big opponent.

*Reggie Highlander became a basketball coach before graduating high school.*

- His gift—and it was truly a gift—was the ability to anticipate his opponent's next move, predict where a teammate would be open, and analyze a player's tendencies.

*Reggie went to a school where football was important as well as basketball.*

- As a teen, Reggie could watch a pickup game for a few minutes and immediately know how to stop a player's jump shot or shut down his next drive.
- Or Reggie could tell his buddies how to set their shoulders, position their feet, or force the opposition to be unable to use his strengths.
- Reggie practiced much of his greatest athletic heroism in his head.
- Even when he was a little boy, everyone called him "Coach."
- Growing up in Grand Rapids, Michigan, Reggie worked just hard enough to avoid periodic "talks" with his parents concerning his "future."
- Reggie already knew his future—coach of the greatest basketball teams in the world.
- How many times had he changed the complexion of a game by crowding the center or forcing the point guard to hurry his passes?
- He would start coaching the mites and midgets in the YMCA, trek from gym to smelly gym in high school, and work his way toward college.
- That was the plan.
- First a small college—for a few years—where he could display his skills before moving into a Division I program eligible to play in the annual NCAA tournament.
- And best of all, UCLA coach John Wooden had demonstrated that a basketball coach can be both a gentleman and a winner.
- At college basketball tournament time, Reggie and the television set were inseparable.
- He watched every nuance and mentally recorded every gesture.
- Coaching at the college level was his destiny, even though he had stopped growing when he reached 5'6" and 148 pounds.
- Then, the unthinkable happened.
- The much-acclaimed and much-loved coach at a rival high school in the area was killed in an automobile crash.
- It was mid-season for a team with state championship potential.
- The team's assistant coach was fully capable of running the team, but he needed help.
- Reggie was flabbergasted when he was invited to a meeting in the boardroom of one of Grand Rapids' largest banks.
- There he was met by his principal, the rival school's principal, several coaches, and the Superintendent of Education.
- In what they admitted was an exceptionally unusual move, they were asking a student at one school to be an assistant coach at a rival school.
- The two teams had already met in league play—with each team winning once—and were unlikely to meet again.

- The delegation of adults reassured Reggie that he was not being disloyal to his school if he took the assignment.
- That was the day Reggie became a real coach.

## Life at Work

- By the time Reggie Highlander entered college, he was well recognized in the coaching circles of the Midwest.
- The high school team he helped coach had not won the state championship, but the skills of three players had improved so markedly they were offered scholarships to play college ball.
- With more tools—especially scouting films of the opposing team—Reggie had proved himself to be a veritable genius at breaking down the tendencies of the opposition.
- At first, Reggie passed along all his advice to the head coach instead of talking with the players themselves.
- Quickly, his ideas paid dividends.
- Once his players knew that the opposing team's point guard always pointed his right foot in the direction he was going to pass, interceptions came more frequently.
- Knowing that a forward liked to dribble deep into the corner before passing made double teaming easier.
- So when Reggie turned his attention to the individuals on his team, they listened.
- One tall, gangly sophomore was taught how to leverage his size by pivoting off the hip of his opponent.
- Reggie taught the team's center that when he blocked out for a rebound, he could control more space if he set up a little farther away from the basket.
- At the annual athletic banquet, Reggie was singled out for his contributions; his future seemed assured.
- Then, at the University of Michigan, he was simply one anonymous freshman among thousands on the gigantic campus.
- His freshman year was spent surviving college in huge lecture halls, noisy dorms, and more free time than he had ever experienced.
- No one at the gym was interested in listening to ways they could be better; who did the short kid with no ball skills think he was, anyway?
- By his sophomore year, he was determined to learn everything about the emerging technology of video, and volunteered to scout games for a local high school.
- But instead of getting schooled in the new VCR format introduced by Phillips or the pioneering work of 3M, Reggie ran into a low-key, no-yelling coach who made it clear that Reggie's job was to teach, not simply to win games.
- His new mentor, Bob Summers, believed that high school was a formative time in the boys' lives.
- He understood how complicated life could be for a young man who looked big and strong, but was still wrestling with personal problems and pressures.
- The job of a coach was to encourage a boy's better self, to let his confidence grow.

*Star players were slow to accept Reggie's advice.*

- Coach Summers preached that every sport had its own special demand for courage—each demanded sacrifice and pain.
- If a player cut the wrong way on a play, it was an opportunity to get better, not humiliated with yelling in the huddle.
- Reggie had seen coaches run their teams until everyone had puked, athletes smacked with a wooden paddle for missing a layup in practice, and visited friends in the hospital after a coach had provoked a fistfight between two players he considered "weak."
- The world according to Coach Summers was not only different, but he also had a winning record that proved it worked.
- He emphasized the fundamentals, and demanded that each player remember he was part of a team and play tenacious defense.
- "No easy points," he would say at the break; "make them earn every point."
- Reggie spent so much time and ate so many meals at Coach Summers' house, the coach joked that Reggie should be a tax deduction.
- Reggie learned from Coach Summers that a coach's greatest reward was not the state championship trophy, but a "thank you" from a graduated player who understood the life lessons he had been taught.
- It was a winning season in many ways, and a home away from home for the next two years.
- When Reggie graduated, securely positioned in the vast middle of his class, he had three job offers.
- One suggested that he become the assistant to a soon-to-retire coach in Chicago; the second proposed that he take the head coaching slot at a small, rural high school; and a third outlined the joys of coaching junior high basketball in the inner city.
- His father urged him to take the coaching job in Chicago, while his mother preferred the opportunities of being the boss in a rural school.
- Coach Summers said simply, "Follow your heart."
- Reggie took the position at a run-down school in Detroit.
- His motivation was simple: He needed to understand how to coach young black boys, who were starting to dominate the college ranks.

*After graduation, Reggie coached at an inner city school.*

- His first practice was a total disaster; he was not ready for his new team of seventh- and eighth-grade kids to challenge his authority on the first day.
- They made jokes about his size, they didn't listen when he explained the schedule, and two players kept randomly running off and dribbling the ball.
- Reggie's greatest temptation was to yell and scream—maybe even toss a few players off the team for effect.
- Instead, he simply locked up the gym and asked the players to meet him on the city's most popular outdoor courts the next afternoon.
- When they all arrived the next day, he suggested they scrimmage any way they wished while he took notes.
- His first target was an immensely talented eighth-grader who was dominating the game.
- Five minutes into the game Reggie assigned a much smaller player to guard the star using specific instructions on where to stand, how to position his hands and when to jump.
- It worked like a charm.
- Reggie's target was thrown out of his rhythm and missed the next six shots in a row.
- Reggie then assigned an even smaller player to play defense.
- The new youngster certainly didn't dominate, but he held his own.
- For the rest of the afternoon, Reggie quietly taught his new team how to void an opponent's strengths; the kids said little to him, but they were clearly impressed.
- When he announced at the end of the day that tryouts would be held in the school gym the following day, all the players looked startled.
- Everyone has to earn his spot, he told the team.
- "I would rather have nine kids who want to be the best than 14 players who don't care to listen and be a part of a team."
- The challenge worked well, resulting in the school's first city championship in 12 years.
- Four of his best players stepped into starting roles at the high school level; suddenly, playing basketball for the white coach was a mark of excellence.
- At the end of his second year, Reggie was ready to move on and move up; a dozen offers flowed in.
- This time he selected a private high school outside Indianapolis, where the latest technology was a phone call away, and the students came from affluent families able to afford basketball camps in the summer and private tutors to hone the most skills.

*Reggie's second coaching job brought him to a select private school.*

- What they lacked was heart; no one played as though his life and happiness hung in the balance.
- Three weeks into the season, Reggie decided to promote two of the team's smallest players to the starting team; the two seniors they replaced were incredulous, but figured it was only temporary.
- Then, when they realized they were not starting at the Friday night game, they were furious and embarrassed.
- When Reggie substituted them back into the game, they played inconsistently, but with heart.
- For the remainder of the season, he jumbled the starting lineup.
- "Make them earn every point," he said repeatedly, and sensed a higher level of aggressiveness in their play.
- The team had made it to the state semi-finals before exiting the tournament in a one-point overtime loss.
- The experience had made it clear that young people needed to be challenged, and desired the same level of attention—black or white, rich or poor.
- Reggie's next challenge, he decided, needed to be a fully integrated team with championship potential.
- Just one more year and he would be ready for the next step.

## Life in the Community: Grand Rapids, Michigan

- Grand Rapids, located on the Grand River about 25 miles east of Lake Michigan, was home to five of the world's leading office furniture companies and was nicknamed the "Furniture City."
- Over 2,000 years ago, people associated with the Hopewell culture occupied the Grand River Valley.
- Around A.D. 1700, the Ottawa Indians moved into the area and founded several villages along the Grand River.
- The Grand Rapids area was first settled by Europeans near the start of the nineteenth century by missionaries and fur traders, who traded their European metal and textile goods for fur pelts.
- In 1826, Detroit-born Louis Campau, the official founder of Grand Rapids, built his cabin, trading post, and blacksmith shop on the east bank of the Grand River near the rapids.
- Campau became perhaps the most important settler when, in 1831, he bought 72 acres of what is now the entire downtown business district of Grand Rapids.
- He purchased it from the federal government for $90 and named his tract Grand Rapids; immigrants from New York and New England began arriving in the 1830s.
- The first formal census occurred in 1845, which established a population of 1,510 and recorded an area of four square miles.
- During the second half of the nineteenth century, the city became a major lumbering center and the premier furniture manufacturing city of the United States.
- After an international exhibition in Philadelphia in 1876, Grand Rapids became recognized worldwide as a leader in the production of fine furniture.
- National home furnishing markets were held in Grand Rapids for about 75 years, concluding in the 1960s.
- The first improved road into the city was completed in 1855.
- This road was a private, toll plank road from Kalamazoo through Wayland, and a primary route for freight and passengers until about 1868.
- This road connected to the outside world via the Michigan Central Railroad at Kalamazoo.
- In 1880, the country's first hydroelectric generator was put to use on the city's west side.
- Michigan's economy underwent a transformation at the turn of the twentieth century.
- Many individuals, including Ransom E. Olds, John and Horace Dodge, Henry Leland, David Dunbar Buick, Henry Joy, Charles King, and Henry Ford, provided the concentration

*The major industry in Michigan was automobiles.*

of engineering know-how and technological enthusiasm to start the birth of the automotive industry.

- Ford's development of the moving assembly line in Highland Park marked the beginning of a new era in transportation.
- More than other forms of public transportation, the automobile transformed people's private lives.
- It became the major industry of Detroit, and of Michigan in general, and permanently altered the socioeconomic life of the United States and much of the world.
- With the growth, the auto industry created jobs in Detroit that attracted immigrants from Europe and migrants from across the U.S., including those from the South.
- By 1920, Detroit was the fourth-largest city in the U.S.
- Residential housing was in short supply, and it took years for the market to catch up with the population boom.
- By the 1930s, so many immigrants had arrived that more than 30 languages were spoken in the public schools, and ethnic communities celebrated in annual heritage festivals.
- Grand Rapids was an early participant in the automobile industry, serving as home to the Austin Automobile Company from 1901 until 1921.
- Michigan held its first presidential primary election in 1910.
- With its rapid growth in industry, it was an important center of union industry-wide organizing, such as the rise of the United Auto Workers.
- In 1920, WWJ (AM) in Detroit became the first radio station in the U.S. to regularly broadcast commercial programs.
- Detroit continued to expand through the 1950s, at one point doubling its population in a decade.
- After World War II, housing was developed in suburban areas outside city cores; newly constructed Interstate Highways allowed commuters to navigate the region more easily.
- Modern advances in the auto industry resulted in increased automation, high-tech industry, and suburban growth since 1960.

# HISTORICAL SNAPSHOT
# 1973

- CBS sold the New York Yankees for $10 million to a 12-person syndicate led by George Steinbrenner, $3.2 million less than CBS paid
- Elvis Presley's concert from Hawaii was the first worldwide telecast by an entertainer and was watched by more people than had seen the Apollo moon landings
- In Super Bowl VII, the Miami Dolphins defeated the Washington Redskins 14-7, in front of 90,182 fans, to complete the NFL's first Perfect Season
- The Supreme Court overturned state bans on abortion in its ruling on *Roe v. Wade*
- George Foreman defeated Joe Frazier to win the heavyweight world boxing championship
- U.S. involvement in the Vietnam War ended with the signing of the Paris Peace Accords; the first American prisoners of war were released from Vietnam
- Ohio became the first state to post distance on road signs in metric measurements
- Following President Nixon's visit to mainland China, the United States and the People's Republic of China agreed to establish liaison offices
- Pink Floyd's *The Dark Side of the Moon*, one of rock's landmark albums, was released
- Watergate burglar James W. McCord, Jr. admitted that he and other defendants had been pressured to remain silent, and named former Attorney General John Mitchell as "overall boss" of the operation
- The LexisNexis computerized legal research service began
- The first handheld cellular phone call was made by Martin Cooper in New York City
- The World Trade Center officially opened
- The Sears Tower in Chicago was finished, becoming the world's tallest building at 1,451 feet
- A 71-day standoff between federal authorities and American Indian activists occupying the Pine Ridge Reservation at Wounded Knee, South Dakota, ended with the surrender of the militants
- A patent for the ATM was granted to Donald Wetzel, Tom Barnes, and George Chastain
- Secretariat won the Belmont Stakes, becoming the first Triple Crown of Thoroughbred Racing winner since 1948
- The Summer Jam at Watkins Glen, a massive rock festival featuring The Grateful Dead, The Allman Brothers Band, and The Band, attracted over 600,000 music fans
- Yankee Stadium, known as "The House That Ruth Built," closed for a two-year renovation at a cost of $160 million
- Spiro Agnew resigned as vice president, after which he pleaded no contest to charges of income tax evasion in federal court in Baltimore, Maryland
- Congress overrode President Nixon's veto of the War Powers Resolution, which limited presidential power to wage war without congressional approval
- Nixon signed the Trans-Alaska Pipeline Authorization Act into law, allowing the construction of the Alaska Pipeline
- Nixon's attorney, J. Fred Buzhardt, revealed the existence of an 18 1/2-minute gap in one of the White House tape recordings related to the Watergate break-in
- *Pioneer 10* sent back the first close-up images of Jupiter
- The Endangered Species Act was passed

## Selected Prices

| | |
|---|---|
| Bathroom Scale | $17.99 |
| Food Processor | $39.99 |
| Hair Dryer | $3.88 |
| Home, Six Rooms, Flushing, NY | $48,500 |
| Ice Bucket | $80.00 |
| Maternity Top | $8.00 |
| Radio, AM | $6.99 |
| Stereo Cassette System | $400.00 |
| Watch, Woman's Movado | $925.00 |
| Woman's Jumpsuit | $32.00 |

## University of Michigan Timeline *(Continued)*

**1898**: "The Victors" was composed by Louis Elbel, a senior music student.

**1904**: The Michigan Union was established for male students, alumni, faculty, and regents.

**1911**: "Varsity" was written by Earl Moore, Class of 1912, and J. Fred Lawton, Class of 1911.

**1919**: The Michigan Union building was opened as a gathering place for men only.

**1923**: The William L. Clements Library of American History was erected.

**1925**: The University Hospital, built by Albert Kahn, was dedicated.

**1928**: The University Museums building was completed.

**1930**: The University of Michigan Press was founded.

**1933**: The Law Quadrangle was completed.

**1935**: The University mandated the preservation of state and University history with the establishment of the Michigan Historical Collections.

**1936**: The Burton Memorial Tower was dedicated.

The International Center was established with J. Raleigh Nelson as director.

**1938**: The Rackham Graduate School Building was completed by the architects Smith, Hinchman & Grylls.

**1946**: The Museum of Art was established in Alumni Memorial Hall.

Willow Run Airport was acquired by the University.

**1955**: The North Campus was recognized as a campus geographic area.

**1957**: The Undergraduate Library (Shapiro) was built by Albert Kahn Associates.

**1959**: The Dearborn Center opened, headed by University Vice President William E. Stirton.

**1960**: On October 14, John F. Kennedy announced the concept of the Peace Corps during a presidential campaign stop on the steps of the Michigan Union.

**1964**: President Lyndon Johnson delivered his "Great Society" address to a crowd of more than 80,000 people gathered for spring commencement in Michigan Stadium on May 22.

*Continued*

## University of Michigan Timeline *(Continued)*

**1965**: Astronaut Edward H. White (MSE AA 1959, Hon ScD 1965) became the first American to walk in space during the *Gemini 4* mission commanded by James A. McDivitt (BSE AA 1959, Hon ScD 1965).

**1971**: Astronauts David R. Scott (1949-50), Alfred M. Worden (MA 1963), and James B. Irwin (M.S. 1957) traveled to the moon aboard *Apollo 15*.

**1973**: The Bentley Historical Library building, home of the Michigan Historical Collections, was completed.

## "Students Strike Against Cambodia," *Iconoclast*, Reading, Pennsylvania, May 1970:

On Thursday evening on May 1, President Nixon went on nationwide TV to announce the intervention of U.S. troops in Cambodia to attempt to drive Communist forces from their Cambodian sanctuaries. His pronouncement was steeped in terms of being a necessary concomitant to the Vietnamization, although he had not felt the move compulsory when he announced the projected withdrawal of 150,000 U.S. troops less than two weeks prior. This move came as somewhat of a surprise to most Americans, who merely expected Nixon to offer Cambodian Premier Lon Nol the logistical support he had requested. However, those Americans, particularly students, who knew that U.S. troops have functioned in Cambodia for several years with CIA fronts, were determined to coordinate a national strike to protest Nixon's deceptive maneuvering. The result: a national student strike against Cambodia.

The strike has already reached some 350 of the 1,500 colleges in the country, closing 225 of them, at least 80 of which will remain on strike for the current academic year. The strike has manifested itself in a variety of forms, both peaceful and violent, both legal and illegal, including teach-ins, picketing, mass rallies, petitions (to the legislators and other government officials), the burning of ROTC buildings and other conspicuous symbols of campus complicity with the War Machine. The most poignant example of the senseless provocation the "pig" presence has created from the student strike is, of course, the massacre of four students at Kent State in Ohio, where National Guardsmen, without an order from their commanding officer, spontaneously fired into a crowd of students that had already begun to disperse from a barrage of tear gas.

With four martyrs, the strike received a renewed impetus so that by Friday night, Nixon, after having consulted eight university presidents, was forced to call a press conference to explain his perspective on the student strike and its repercussions. While commending students who were employing the Constitutional right to express dissent to the extension of the Vietnam War into Cambodia, Nixon condemned any "violent" form of protest. But Nixon did not feel

*Continued*

## "Students Strike Against Cambodia," . . . *(Continued)*

compelled to differentiate between violence toward property and violence to human life. He seemed oblivious to the fact that while the destruction of property has been perpetuated by the student demonstrators, loss of human life can be consistently attributed to the "pigs" at Kent State, on Wall Street, in New York City (where the "pigs" refused to respond to the attack on students by construction workers), and in Washington.

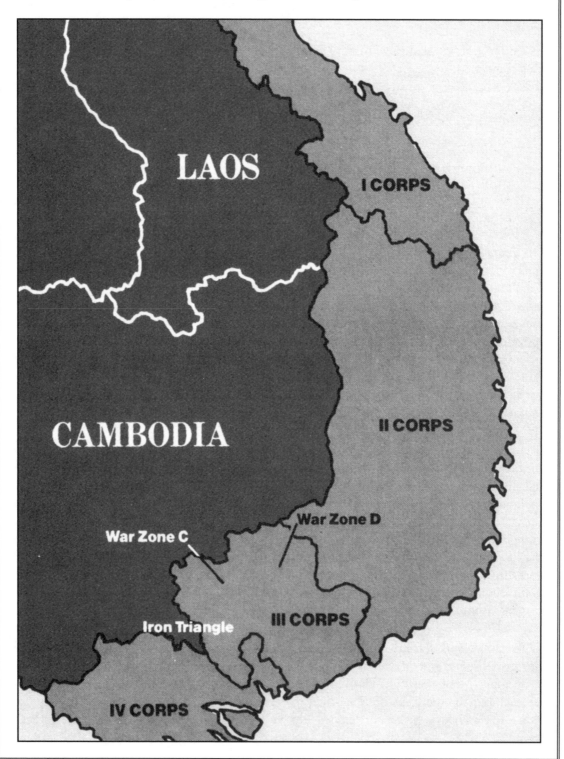

# 1977 PROFILE

Boyd Kesser became the principal of an elementary school just outside of Dallas during the controversial era of school desegregation.

## Life at Home

- For Boyd Kesser, it was a dream come true—and a nightmare waiting to pounce.
- After 11 years as a schoolteacher, he had been named principal of a soon-to-be-desegregated elementary school with the attendant increase in pay, prestige and recognition.
- He and his wife had recently had their third child and they needed a bigger house; now it was possible.
- The nightmare that hovered was not one of his doing; 23 years after the Supreme Court had ruled in *Brown v. Board of Education*, Dallas had elected to move ahead.
- His first year as principal would include the experience of managing a newly integrated school, including a government-ordered busing plan that had divided the community and spawned considerable bitterness.
- Boyd had grown up in Minnesota, where issues of race rarely dominated the political scene.
- When he was 15, his father accepted a new position and moved the family to

*Boyd Kesser's move from teacher to principal was made more difficult by desegregation.*

Dallas, Texas, which his younger sister pledged to hate "with every fiber in her body," but didn't.

- His mother, on the other hand, cheerfully closed her beauty salon, eagerly packed their possessions and pledged to love Texas as long as they both might live—but didn't.
- Seven months later she was gone, leaving behind a fluttering trail of accusations, apologies and demands.
- Boyd stayed with his dad in Texas; his mother and sister headed "home."
- Boyd buried his grief in learning Texas history and collecting bits and pieces of the state's glorious cowboy past.
- His collecting took him into remote areas of the state and taught him the exquisite diversity within its borders.
- High school graduation was followed by four years as a Marine, when he acquired even more skills—and love—for exploring remote locations.
- Shy and quiet, he was nicknamed "The Viper" by his buddies, in recognition of his ability to magically strike silently with lightning speed using deadly force.
- When he left military service, Rice University offered him a partial scholarship which, combined with his military benefits, made college expenses manageable.
- He told himself that coaching would be very fulfilling, especially football and baseball, but every time he entered a classroom his skin came alive, his senses were alert, and he felt the same adrenaline rush he had experienced as a trained sniper.
- He could not deny the truth; he loved teaching kids—no matter the age—and even enjoyed those who had grown a big mouth.
- So when he graduated, he cast his lot in with the schools, landing a math teaching position in a middle school outside Dallas.
- He stayed there for five years, then became an assistant principal/disciplinarian for three years in a high school, followed by three years assisting at an elementary school.
- Finally, he was given opportunity to be a principal in a school constructed outside Dallas whose students had mixed ancestry and which experienced considerable busing.
- Previously, half the kids came from country folk who knew how

*Boyd loved to teach students of all ages and personalities.*

to get things done with their hands; the other half were suburban kids who couldn't open an M&M candy bag without help, but had already been to Europe twice.
- Now the school's mix would include black youths from Dallas who were angry about the hour-long bus ride when there were schools closer to their homes.
- They were not happy about being taken from their schools and teachers, either.
- But Boyd was ready and determined to make it work.
- He understood that it had fallen to the schools—America's youth—to ameliorate and satisfy 200 years of race history.
- Separate housing, separate jobs, separate activities and separate attitudes for blacks and whites were all supposed to disappear through school desegregation.
- Problems that could not be addressed on the adult level were being handed to the children to smooth out.

- It was now part of Boyd's job to bring everyone—including anxious parents—together after all of the social experiments within schools had been attempted for more than two decades.

- It was no accident that the pivotal Supreme Court decision launching the modern Civil Rights Movement was an education case: the 1954 *Brown v. Board of Education of Topeka, Kansas*.

- The drive to end segregated education and put African-American and white children in the same classrooms was the most radical and potentially far-reaching aspect of the Civil Rights Movement.

- That decision—intended to alter the racial attitudes and socialization of children from the youngest age—was necessary to end the inequality inherent in all "separate but equal" facilities, whether they were drinking fountains, public accommodations, or the schools.

- The Civil Rights struggle, Boyd understood, did not arise because someone believed that there was something magical about minority children sitting next to whites in a classroom, but instead was based on a belief that the only way for minority children to get the full range of opportunities was to get access to those schools.

- Since 1954, the struggle for integrated schools had gone through a number of phases—especially as education became the focus of the South's "massive resistance" to the Court's rulings.

- This resistance was symbolized dramatically by Arkansas Governor Orval Faubus and his order that the state's national guard unit block the admission of nine African-American students to Little Rock's Central High School in 1957.

- The nearly month-long confrontation ended when President Eisenhower sent in U.S. troops to protect the students.

- Prince Edward County, Virginia, abandoned its entire public school system, leaving education to private interests that excluded African-American children from their schools.

- Many black children were essentially locked out of school for several years until the Supreme Court ruled Virginia's action unconstitutional.

- Most districts employed delaying tactics; 10 years after the courts called for racial integration of schools at "all deliberate speed," only 2.3 percent of black children in the Deep South attended desegregated schools.

- These tactics tried the patience of both African-Americans and the federal courts.

- In 1966, the Fifth Circuit Court, in *United States v. Jefferson County Board of Education*, ordered school districts not only to end segregation, but to "undo the harm" segregation had caused by racially balancing their schools under federal guidelines.

- A strong federal commitment to enforcement of the Civil Rights Act of 1964 proved critical; by 1968, the percentage of black children attending desegregated schools topped 32 percent.

- By 1976, the South had become the nation's most integrated region, with 55.1 percent of the South's African-American students attending majority white schools, compared with just 27.5 percent in the Northeast and 29.7 percent in the Midwest.

*Armed guards were not an uncommon sight as schools dealt with integration.*

## Life at Work

- The first two weeks as principal were eventful for Boyd Kesser, starting with the mother of a first grader who was convinced her child was being ignored.
- Her first words, "Just because I'm black," told him where the conversation was going, so he went silent and listened to her complaint that her child's white teacher couldn't even pronounce her child's name.
- In the outer room was a white mother with a similar complaint; within minutes they joined together and told their stories, during which they admitted they were both frightened that their first graders would not be successful or happy.

*As schools consolidated, "non-essential" subject teachers lost their jobs.*

- Boyd did little except allow the young mothers to talk; he pledged that the teachers would learn to pronounce the names properly and everyone agreed that first grade was a stressful time.
- After the first month passed, the protestors had stopped showing up, the teachers had settled down, and he could begin evaluating his teachers.
- In other school districts, the consolidation of schools had meant the loss of jobs—frequently those of black teachers—whose skills were prejudged.
- To Boyd's way of thinking, one of the most stabilizing forces in the community was being tossed aside during the consolidation process; in his experience, it was the veteran black teachers who had guided the peaceful desegregation of schools—often encouraging their own children to take a leadership role in integrating the classrooms.
- So he had been very intentional in his hiring of teachers—even when it meant white teachers he had known for years would not be offered contracts.
- This led to at least one embarrassing incident at the grocery store when a longtime teaching associate loudly dissected all the hiring mistakes he had made as they both stood at the produce counter examining cantaloupes.
- The long history of the integration of Dallas' schools did not begin smoothly for those eager to see *Brown* brought to fruition; in a citywide election, Dallasites voted four to one against school integration.
- Powerful business interests then sought to stifle the various lawsuits that ensued.
- Until 1961, Dallas was the largest city in the South with a segregated school system, which drew this criticism from the courts: "Words without deeds are not enough."
- Consequently, in 1961, the Dallas School Board implemented a desegregation plan under the order of the Fifth Circuit Court.
- On September 6, 1961, 18 black children started first grade classes in what had been up until then segregated schools for whites only.
- But was only a token response.
- On October 6, 1970, *Tasby v. Estes* was filed in the U.S. District Court by Sam Tasby of Dallas on behalf of his two sons.
- The class-action lawsuit contended that the Dallas Independent School District was not racially integrated and white schools received more resources than black and "Chicano" schools.
- The greater Dallas community did not welcome this lawsuit, as many felt strongly that it had done its part to implement *Brown.*
- The judge disagreed.

- On July 16, 1971, District Judge William M. Taylor declared, "a dual system still exists," and ordered the Dallas School Board to come up with a plan for integration.
- Taylor's recommended plan included linking two majority-white classrooms with one minority classroom by television for at least one hour each day; less than a month later, the Fifth Circuit Court of Appeals threw out the TV plan.
- In 1971, busing to desegregate the schools began when several thousand black students were bused to predominantly white schools in North and East Dallas.

*"White flight" altered the racial makeup of schools.*

- Several hundred white students were reassigned to predominantly black schools, but the majority stayed home the first day.
- By 1975, the "white flight" out of the district had altered the racial makeup of the schools; white students were no longer in the majority, while black students became the dominant group.
- In March 1976, Taylor ordered the school district to implement a desegregation plan designed by a task force of the Dallas Alliance, an organization of political, civic and business leaders.
- The plan included establishing magnet schools, setting racial quotas for the district's administration, and busing about 20,000 students in grades four to eight.
- In August 1976, the schools opened without major incident under the desegregation plan.
- By the time the Christmas holidays arrived, Boyd knew every child by name and could count on hugs from at least a dozen students during the course of the day.
- The intensity of the joy he experienced was different now, but there was no question that working with young people was the greatest thrill a human could experience.
- These were his kids now, and he was eager to watch them grow.

## Life in the Community: Dallas, Texas
- Dallas, Texas, was founded in 1841 and was formally incorporated as a city in February 1856.
- The city's prominence arose from its historical importance as a center for the oil and cotton industries, as well as its position along numerous railroad lines.
- With the advent of the Interstate Highway System in the 1950s and 1960s, Dallas became an east/west and north/south focal point of the interstate system with the convergence of four major highways in the city, along with a fifth interstate loop around the city.
- Dallas developed a strong industrial and financial sector, and a major inland port, due largely to the presence of Dallas/Fort Worth International Airport, one of the largest and busiest airports in the world.
- The city was the ninth most populous in the United States, and the third most populous in Texas.

# HISTORICAL SNAPSHOT
# 1977

- The world's first personal computer, the Commodore PET, was demonstrated at the Consumer Electronics Show in Chicago
- Apple Computer was incorporated
- In Super Bowl XI, the Oakland Raiders defeated the Minnesota Vikings 32-14 at the Rose Bowl in Pasadena, California
- In the first execution after the reintroduction of the death penalty in the U.S., Gary Gilmore was killed by firing squad in Utah
- President Jimmy Carter pardoned Vietnam War draft evaders
- The television miniseries *Roots* was phenomenally successful on ABC
- Fleetwood Mac's Grammy-winning album *Rumours* was released
- The space shuttle *Enterprise* test vehicle went on its maiden "flight" while sitting on top of a Boeing 747 at Edwards Air Force Base in California
- Tenor Luciano Pavarotti and the PBS opera series *Live from the Met* both made their American television debuts
- A. J. Foyt became the first driver to win the Indianapolis 500 a record four times
- The Portland Trail Blazers defeated the Philadelphia 76ers 109-107 to win the NBA finals 4-2; Bill Walton was named series MVP
- After campaigning by Anita Bryant and her anti-gay "Save Our Children" crusade, Miami-Dade County, Florida, voters overwhelmingly voted to repeal the county's gay rights ordinance
- James Earl Ray, Martin Luther King's assassin, escaped from Brushy Mountain State Prison in Petros, Tennessee
- Oracle was incorporated as Software Development Laboratories by Larry Ellison, Bob Miner, and Ed Oates
- The Supreme Court ruled that states were not required to spend Medicaid funds on elective abortions
- Led Zeppelin played their last U.S. concert in Oakland, California, at the Oakland-Alameda County Coliseum
- The first oil through the Trans-Alaska Pipeline System reached Valdez, Alaska
- Treaties between Panama and the United States on the status of the Panama Canal were signed, agreeing to transfer control of the canal to Panama at the end of the twentieth century
- A nuclear non-proliferation pact was signed by 15 countries, including the United States and the Soviet Union
- Three members of the rock band Lynyrd Skynyrd died in a charter plane crash outside Gillsburg, Mississippi, three days after the release of their fifth studio album *Street Survivors*
- Lockheed's top-secret stealth aircraft project, designated Have Blue, precursor to the U.S. F-117A Nighthawk, made its first flight
- Films released included *Star Wars; Annie Hall; Saturday Night Fever; Close Encounters of the Third Kind; The Goodbye Girl; A Bridge Too Far; Exorcist II: The Heretic; The Turning Point; New York, New York; and Smokey* and *the Bandit*
- John Travolta's role in *Saturday Night Fever* inspired young Americans to wear flared jeans, an updated version of bellbottoms

## Selected Prices

Bicycle .......................................................................$64.99

Cigarette Case…………………………………………..$34.95

Computer, Apple II ..................................................$1,300.00

Hotel Room, St. Moritz, New York....................................$31.00

Ice Cream Machine ..........................................................$24.95

Massage Shower Head ....................................................$26.95

Microwave Oven ..............................................................$168.00

Organic Roast Beef, per Half-Pound ...............................$1.99

Stroller...............................................................................$24.99

Theater Ticket, *A Chorus Line*, New York ......................$17.50

According to a leading Consumer Research Group, this is what each car cost to run for two years, including fuel, maintenance and depreciation: Vega, $1755. Gremlin, $1755. Pinto, $1690. Datsun, $1670. Toyota, $1645. And last, but least, Volkswagen Super Beetle, $1270.

# 1980–1989

The economic turbulence of the 1970s continued during the early years of the 1980s. Rates for both interest and inflation reached a staggering 18 percent. School budgets were stressed and voters were in no mood to vote for increased taxes. College tuition hikes became an annual event at a time when one in 10 Americans was out of work. Yet, by the end of the decade, thanks in part to the productivity gains provided by computers and new technology, more and more Americans were feeling better off than they had in a decade.

Convinced that inflation was the primary enemy of long-term economic growth, the Federal Reserve Board brought the economy to a standstill in the early days of the decade. It was a shock treatment that worked. By 1984, the tight money policies of the government, stabilizing world oil prices, and labor's declining bargaining power brought inflation to 4 percent, the lowest level since 1967. Despite the pain it caused, the plan to strangle inflation succeeded; Americans not only prospered, but many believed it was their right to be successful. The decade came to symbolize self-indulgence.

Defense and deficit spending roared into high gear, the economy continued to grow, and the stock market rocketed to record levels. In the center of recovery was Mr. Optimism, President Ronald Reagan. During his presidential campaign, he promised a "morning in America," and for eight years, his good nature helped transform the national mood. The Reagan era, which spanned most of the 1980s, fostered a new conservative agenda of good feeling. During the presidential election against incumbent President Jimmy Carter, Reagan joked, "A recession is when your neighbor loses his job. A depression is when you lose yours. And recovery is when Jimmy Carter loses his."

The economic wave of the 1980s was also driven by globalization, improvements in technology, and the willingness of consumers to assume higher and higher levels of personal debt. By the 1980s, the two-career family became the norm. Forty-two percent of all American workers were female, and more than half of all married women and 90 percent of female college graduates worked outside the home. Yet their median wage was 60 percent of that of men. For the first time in history, the Naval Academy's graduating class included women. The rapid rise of women in the labor force, which had been accelerating since the 1960s, brought great social change, affecting married life, child rearing, family income, office culture, and the growth of the national economy.

The rising economy brought greater control of personal lives; homeownership accelerated, choices seemed limitless, debt grew, and divorce became commonplace. Two revolutionary changes on the music scene—the advent of MTV and the compact disc—began a technological and financial shift. Music became more diverse, with new wave, heavy metal, rap, techno pop, and alternative rock all mixing with the "new" country sounds. Michael Jackson's *Thriller*, Bruce Springsteen's *Born in the USA* and Prince's *Purple Rain* all registered record sales during the decade. Also, music became a huge marketing tool as filmmakers, TV producers and manufacturers of everything from sneakers to soft drinks used hit songs to sell their products. The collapse of communism at the end of the 1980s brought an end to the old world order and set the stage for a realignment of power. America was regarded as the strongest nation in the world. As democracy swept across Eastern Europe, the U.S. economy began to feel the impact of a "peace dividend" generated by a reduced military budget and a desire by corporations to participate in global markets—including Russia and China. At the end of World War II, the U.S. economy accounted for almost 50 percent of the global economic product; by 1987, the U.S. share was less than 25 percent as American companies moved plants offshore and countries such as Japan emerged as major competitors. This need for a global reach inspired several rounds of corporate mergers as companies searched for efficiency, market share, new products, or emerging technology to survive in the rapidly shifting business environment.

The 1980s were the age of the conservative yuppie. Business schools, investment banks, and Wall Street firms overflowed with eager Baby Boomers who placed gourmet cuisine, health clubs, supersneakers, suspenders, wine spritzers, high-performance autos, and sushi high on their agendas. Low-fat and fiber-rich cereals and Jane Fonda workout books symbolized much of the decade. As self-indulgence rose, concerns about the environment, including nuclear waste, acid rain, and the greenhouse effect declined. Homelessness increased and racial tensions fostered a renewed call for a more caring government. Genetic engineering came of age, including early attempts at transplantation and gene mapping. Personal computers, which were transforming America, were still in their infancy.

The sexual revolution, undaunted by a conservative prescription of chastity, ran head-on into a powerful adversary during the 1980s with the discovery and spread of HIV/AIDS, a frequently fatal sexually transmitted disease. The right of women to have an abortion, confirmed by the Supreme Court in 1973, was hotly contested as politicians fought over both the actual moment of conception and the right of a woman to control her body. Cocaine also made its reappearance, bringing drug addiction and a rapid increase in violent crime. The Center on Addiction and Substance Abuse at Columbia University found alcohol and drug abuse implicated in three-fourths of all murders, rapes, child molestation, and deaths of babies suffering from parental neglect.

Digital clocks and cordless telephones appeared, and 24-hour-a-day news coverage captivated television viewers. Compact discs began replacing records, and *Smurf* and *E.T.* paraphernalia were everywhere. New York became the first state to require seat belts, and Pillsbury introduced microwave pizza. The Supreme Court ruled that states may require all-male private clubs to admit women, and 50,000 people gathered at Graceland in Memphis, Tennessee, on the tenth anniversary of Elvis Presley's death.

# 1985 News Feature

*Still Becoming: A Retired Teacher Reminisces*, **Brenda Monteith:**

I didn't plan on a teaching career. It happened to me. Reaganomics in the 1980s and our children approaching college years nudged me out of my comfortable routine. Leaving my part-time position at our community college, I decided to return to the high school classroom.

I hadn't taught high school English in 17 years. My bachelor's degree from 1963 and my two and a half years of teaching before our daughter was born were vague memories. The daughter was now a high school senior and she had a younger brother. My teacher's persona had smothered under years of carpools, recipes, and church work.

I accepted a half-day position that quickly became full-time, inheriting students from seasoned, overloaded teachers. The students did not want to change teachers, and set out to make every day a challenge for me. One week in October, a daunting female basketball player circulated her less-than-flattering drawing of me around the classroom, a boy in another class told me a dirty joke, and a student made fun of my shoes in front of the whole class. That Friday night, my parents came to dinner. Exhausted and feeling defeated, I stood over my stove, flipped burgers in the pan, and burst into tears.

"I'm not sure I can do this," I told my mother. I felt that I had leapt on a treadmill set at high speed. Mother's eyes darkened with worry and sympathy. Then we all sat down to dinner.

With a weekend's rest and new resolve, I drove to school the following Monday morning as the sun rose. Kool and the Gang sang "Joanna" on the car radio. I sang, too—"take her for a ride/Everything's fine." Everything would be fine, I told myself as I parked and entered the building. Wearing different shoes from last week's pair, and armed with a tighter lesson plan, I plunged into the day. Between classes I stood in the hall beside my door as required and looked out the window at my car. In several hours I could go out there, get in my car and drive home. But first, I must meet with the mother of the loud, uncooperative "artist." It was my first parent/teacher conference. I was nervous.

After school the mother appeared at my door. I saw immediately where the basketball player got her height. We introduced ourselves and sat in student desks. I tried to describe politely her daughter's smart mouth and disruptive behavior. Then I showed her the picture of me. She promised to help me control her daughter and to keep in touch. A school cafeteria worker, she closed our discussion with a bit of philosophy that has stayed with me all these years: "No matter what happens or what somebody has said to me at work, I go back the next day and start all over again. I say, 'Good Morning!' to those people as if there had never been a problem. It's a new day." I had just been counseled.

Week followed week. I conferred with other English teachers and watched what they did. Mae generously shared materials; Mandy, our chairperson, offered ideas; and Joyce, whose room was next to mine, provided me a role model. I noted that she often stood by her door, calm and self-possessed, handing out papers to her students as they entered her room. Her lesson plan seemed to begin right there at the door.

In the afternoons I stopped by my colleagues' rooms, my eyes skimming their walls for bulletin board ideas. The two posters I had bought at Eckerd's looked lonely on my eight-foot expanse of corkboard. "Dare to be different," one said, showing a single green apple among red ones. My favorite poster showed two Lhasa Apso puppies touching noses above the words, "If you love someone, show him."

The other English teachers displayed students' exemplary work and pictures of great writers. Mandy's room even had a wall of butcher block paper, entitled "Graffiti Board," where the kids could scrawl their ideas with magic marker. When I dropped by her room after school, I often found a banner over the door, congratulating a team's winning game or a "Good Luck Tonight!" poster.

As I entered her room one afternoon, she called "How's it going, Girl?"

"Well, okay. I have a couple of questions."

Students had gathered around her desk, wanting help or attention. Browsing among her bookshelves, I waited my turn.

"How do you do short stories, Mandy, as a unit or mixed in?" I asked when the room cleared. "And what about grammar and diagramming?"

"Usage, Honey, that's something they need. You know—correct usage of tenses and agreement. I've got some worksheets. Do your short stories either way you want."

Then we sat down and looked over materials. I noticed that her stylish high heels matched her dress and that she wrote in purple ink. She wore a purple scarf about her neck that nicely complemented her blond hair and blue eyes. Style, experience, charisma.

## I Get Help

I had simply wanted to *be* a teacher, not have to *become* one. While I was beginning to take shape, I lacked a philosophy, a style, and sufficient knowledge in my field. Then a wonderful thing happened. Our school board adopted the new teaching method of Madelyn Hunter, an educator out of California. The countywide mandate required all teachers to attend a many-weeks workshop. We must adopt Hunter's style of teaching and expect to be observed and graded on our mastery of it.

The seasoned teachers complained over losing one and a half hours every week to this requirement. I secretly rejoiced.

Every Wednesday after school, we gathered in a large science lab, where we picked up refreshments and took a seat. Exhausted from the day, I settled into a student chair, enjoyed my chips and Coke, and became a sponge. We saw videos and live demonstrations of classroom procedures. I learned about anticipatory sets, teacher input, guided practice, and feeling tone. Some of these methods did not fit my curriculum, but many did. The training gave me a structure. Seeking more help, I registered for other county workshops.

By spring my principal, Mr. Epperson, called me into his office and handed me a brochure for the California Writing Project Summer Workshop at University of North Carolina at Charlotte (UNCC). He smiled and said, "Consider taking this. I want you to 'do good'."

I latched onto this opportunity and committed four weeks of my summer to this workshop. Twenty-five teachers of all grade levels and subject areas gathered at the university four days a week from 9:00 a.m. to 3:00 p.m. The experience was unlike any I had ever had. University professors shared their knowledge and engaged us in dialogue. They required us to read vast amounts of material, write responses, and finally, present a lesson to the whole group. In the afternoons we met in writing groups and shared personal writing.

By the fall, I entered the school building with confidence and ideas. The teachers' meeting opened with a senior English teacher holding up a copy of the morning newspapers, where an article that I had submitted had been published. Flushed with success and my peers' praise, I left the meeting for the beginning of the most difficult year of my career.

## A New Assignment

I had now been assigned the yearbook.

My yearbook class was a mix of talented leaders, novices, and freeloaders. My student photographer was a charming and talented rogue, who could produce fine pictures one day and get called into the principal's office for infractions the next. He was usually reliable, but he had a part-time job after school and helped care for his younger brother. To help out, I learned to operate a manual camera and to cover sports events and plays in my photographer's absence. At football games, I discovered why camera people run up and down the field—you can't get action shots when the players are running away from you. Half-time was the biggest thrill. My chest vibrated as I stood

*Brenda encouraged action shots in the Yearbook.*

10 feet from the drum line to photograph the band's performance, while the horns blared and the flags and batons flashed by me. At the wrestling matches, I found myself on the floor, supinely positioned to catch the best shot of the pinning hold. Once I even had the chance to catch my own son in a picture when h is school ran cross-country against mine.

That April, we sent in our last proofed galleys and I could relax. A weight lifted. By now I loved my students—well, most of them—and the English classes had progressed. Summer waited tantalizingly as I planned the wrap-up of the school year. I took afternoon walks with Jasper, our family Lhasa, and felt the renewal of spring. Our neighbors' dogwoods and azaleas bloomed about me. Most days the sky reflected my mood in blue and white brilliance.

By May, we received our yearbooks. Though imperfect, they were lovely. Thank goodness for a good student editor and some luck. I was unprepared for the rush I felt each time we popped open a box and distributed books into eager hands. We were published.

The book took over my head the next year. I looked at all school activities through an imaginary camera lens. I worked along with the students on layouts and insisted on certain improvements. By now, I could discuss mosaic layouts, ghost images, tool lines, and bleeding photos.

But there were problems. I stayed in trouble with the former yearbook photography teacher, whose darkroom my less-than-reliable students had to use. I got reports of students off task when they left the room on official business. Sometimes I awoke in the night with sudden reminders, like my 4:00 a.m. stabbing recall of a student memorial page that had been overlooked. The next day, I called our publisher in a panic. Somehow he managed to slip this page in after the last deadline. But some problems could not be solved. There was the girl on the staff who intentionally omitted the picture of a senior girl whom she did not like. Just simply withdrew the girl's photo! I learned about that after the books arrived and I received the mother's irate phone call. All I could do was offer to give her daughter the book.

I sought some way to legitimately rid myself of the yearbook, although I had begun to take some ownership and pride in it. I decided to go to graduate school. Actually, that would be easier than the yearbook, I thought, and would strengthen my knowledge of literature. There is no hubris like that of the untried.

**Lessons in Class Management**

I liked rules. They assured equal treatment and added structure. Our principal, Mr. Epperson, declared in a faculty meeting one day, "I don't make any rules I can't enforce." That made sense, but I wondered how to judge the efficacy of one's rules. What was realistic and worth confrontation? How serious was chewing gum, or wearing a cap during class, or speaking out of turn? Suppose a student refused to do his work or used foul language? Should I confront him and write a discipline referral, or simply warn him?

Every day offered an opportunity to test my rules. No two days were alike, and no two classes were alike. I discovered that each class had a distinct personality and set of management problems. First period was usually sleepy and a little grumpy. I had been up nearly two hours by the tardy bell at 7:20, but many of the students still had wet hair from their showers and gazed about foggily. They dropped their heavy book bags, drew their jacket sleeves over their hands, and sank into their seats. I had to resist the temptation to speak softly, so as not to disturb them, guaranteeing myself an easy 50 minutes.

As the day wore on, the students awoke. They stormed into the classroom in the midst of conversations, carrying their cheer or gloom from the hallway. Some of the students got down to business, and others established roadblocks and strategies to sabotage our lesson. Competing for attention from their peers or from me, they bubbled and fizzed like a shaken Coke. Others sought popularity with their classmates and buzzed about Saturday night's party. A few dragged into the room looking defeated, probably from years of poor grades or home troubles or fatigue after working late the night before. Some students were angry, some were in love, and some sought to please the teacher—bless their hearts.

The second period "regular" class (capable but probably not college bound), in my third year included five boys who organized a whistling plan much like a zone defense on the basketball court. I could not get past them. During independent work, they bent over their desks and the room fell silent. Then a single note, a short whistle, sounded from somewhere near the left center of the room, drawing my attention. As I glanced in that direction, another whistle came from somewhere near the door, then the back center area, then the left again. I walked the aisles and scowled. I admonished, accused, and threatened. The whole independent work time was lost for all of us. I allowed this to continue for enough days to become sure of identities, then admitted defeat to myself, and visited Mr. Dillard, our sympathetic assistant principal.

He nodded solemnly as I confessed my problem with these boys, then simply said, "I'll take care of this, Mrs. Monteith. I'll have a talk with those boys."

The whistling stopped, and while I asked no questions, I noticed our school grounds were litter-free for several days.

## Margy, Tom, Dorothea, and Don

Solutions were not always that easily to come by. In that class of whistlers was Margy, a true magpie. She talked all the time. All the time. We conferred, I scolded, and I put her name on the board. Nothing worked.

Exasperated one day, I said during class, "Margy, what are we going to do? Can you not talk for just a few minutes?"

"Mrs. Monteith, I really can't," she said brightly. "When I was in kindergarten, the teacher had a rule that every Friday the kids in class who had not got their names on the board for talking all week got a cupcake. I never got a cupcake, Mrs. Monteith, not once the whole year."

All of us laughed, even Margy. Perhaps she was doing the best she could. A teacher has to accept the things she cannot change. I would learn more tolerance.

That class filed out as third period entered. These intense personalities filled the room with noise. To get them quiet, I sometimes wrote names of repeated offenders on the board. One day in the middle of a sentence structure lesson, Tom called out, "I want to know why every name on the board is a black person!"

Stunned, I turned to the board and looked. He was right.

"Every name on the board yesterday was black, too," he said.

My throat tightened.

"Well, Tom, these are people I've asked to stop talking. Now is not the time to talk about this. Let's wait till after class."

"I want to talk about it NOW," he said.

This volatile boy ran with a rough crowd. Every day his presence put me on guard. He would take his seat, glance about the room with hooded eyes, and then drift into a reverie. In this moment he was engaged, though. He looked hard into my face. I repeated that we must get on with our work and would discuss the names on the board later. The rest of the class sat still and silent. He persisted until I told him to pack up his things and go to Ms. Yandle's office. Seething, he stalked out.

A tall, handsome African-American woman, Ms. Yandle had my complete trust and confidence in her fairness. I knew she would honor his complaint and my explanation. That afternoon Ms. Yandle approached me in the hall. Her smile eased my concerns somewhat.

"I talked with Tom," she said. "And I told him you are a fair teacher. I said you heard the voices of black students above any others. I told him just to listen in the cafeteria at lunch time and see what I mean. Our voices carry. That's all. I think he'll be okay now."

The class was okay, but Tom was not. He soon dropped out of school and took one too many joy rides with his friends. Late one night, they rode uptown, stopped their vehicle, hopped out, and brutally killed a janitor walking home from work. Tom was just along, but now he was in deep trouble and the concern of our local police department.

Yet Tom taught me more than I did him. He showed me my classroom management through his eyes, and I did not like what I saw. I gave up the names-on-the-board idea forever and became a more sensitive teacher. I wish I had thanked him.

There was the year my health intervened and I had surgery scheduled for mid-May. That was also the year of Dorothea. She entered my class with a scowl on the first day. She sat in the third seat of the middle row and gave me a "Drop dead, Lady" look that she wore every single day all year. She made it clear that our work did not deserve her attention, but she usually passed by the thinnest margin.

Three days before my surgery, she defied me openly in class. She sat there writing a letter and refusing to begin her work. I asked her to put away the letter. She kept writing. Then I insisted she give me the letter or put it away and begin her work. I realize now that she was in charge in that moment as she eased the letter in her book and feigned an effort at the assignment. When I collected the work, she refused to hand me hers, then threw it in my direction. As I picked up the paper, I told her to go to the principal's office. She gathered her things, walked up to me and said softly, "I hope something happens to you next week."

*Brenda was challenged by several defiant students.*

I felt like I had been handed a voodoo doll with a pin stuck in it. Unable to think of a reply, I stood silent as she walked out.

That afternoon, I paid a call on Mr. Dillard. Handing him a referral slip on Dorothea, I explained the incident.

"Can you put her somewhere else during English for the next two days, Mr. Dillard? I just don't think I can look at her again before I leave."

"Oh, yes, Mrs. Monteith. I'll take care of Dorothea," he said. I know he did, because I did not see her again.

My last two school days were delightful. Two classes gave me surprise parties and little gifts, and the service club I advised gave me a generous bookstore gift certificate. One dear boy stopped by my room after school on my last day and handed me a simply wrapped package. Inside was a book of O. Henry's stories. He had written these words in black ink on the inside cover:

"Well, you have taught me personally a lot this year. I enjoyed this book and the way you talked in class, I thought you would like to have this book?[sic] The rest of this year will not be the same. I know some of us in your 4th period class cut up and give you gray, but we're certinally [sic] not boreing![sic] Well, any way from the bottom of my heart I will miss you and I wish you a speedy and full recovery! Love, Don"

That book still stands on the shelf where it has been for many years, between my best copies of *The Scarlet Letter* and *A Farewell to Arms*.

Since school was out before I recovered, I did not get another chance with Dorothea, but I think that several years later I might have handled her better. By then I knew that some students gain attention, even admiration, from their peers by openly defying the teacher. To give them that stage with an audience is to read your lines right off their script. I eventually discovered the quiet, "I'll-need-to-see-you-after-class" approach. Disciplining students one-on-one and following up with a referral slip and a call home give the teacher more control and spoil the student's little scene.

Over time, I determined that those handy rules were guidelines, often most effective when kept flexible. And I learned my own limitations. All I could do was all I could do.

**Growing Pains**

By my fourth year, I was free of the yearbook and wading through Faulkner novels in graduate school when the state Board of Education created a career development program for teachers. Our county received permission to participate in the pilot, and I decided to take the opportunity to enter the program. If I did well, I would gain expertise, receive a salary bonus, and become a mentor to less experienced teachers. The program required designing lesson plans and units according to its six-point outline, meeting certain standards in class management, and documenting student performance assessment. More intimidating were the periodic observations by our principal and by trained county observers.

The observer usually appeared by appointment and began script taping the teacher's words and the students' responses and behaviors the moment the bell rang. I learned that I must monitor all students all the time. If a girl played with her bracelet or a boy dozed, I must address their behavior or lose points. If the students lost focus during transitions, if I failed to state the objective of the lesson, or if all students were not engaged, I lost points. I should call upon or observe the work of all students, give adequate wait time for answers, make sure everyone could hear responses, give directions only once to encourage careful listening, and provide a good feeling tone. At the end of the period, I needed to collect something from the students to check for their understanding or call for hand signal responses to my questions. I was required to close with a quick review of the hour's objective and lesson.

Unannounced observations occurred every semester. On those days, the observer appeared at the door with her briefcase and pen. Ready or not, there she stood. Most of us dreaded those occasions. Some teachers joked about training their students to raise their left hand if they knew the answer to questions, their right hand if they did not. Then the observer would believe everyone was engaged and comprehending.

I thought I was mentally prepared for the first unannounced observation. I was wrong. One day the observer appeared at my door just before the bell for class to start. The sight of her caused near panic in me. I had a good lesson that day and a related newspaper article to share on Thoreau's philosophy of "Simplicity, simplicity, simplicity." Yet my voice shook as I offered the observer a seat and pulled out my roll book. My hands trembled, too, I discovered, as I held up the newspaper article about a lady in Chicago who owned nearly nothing after a house fire and decided she liked the simple life of few possessions.

I got through the lesson. The students responded well, and the lady left.

The next week, I met the observer for the required consultation and my score. She said, "When I walked in your room, you turned pale. I thought, 'What have I done?'"

I admitted my nervousness—no point in denying the obvious. Then we talked. I had received a score of five on a scale of one to six. I wondered how much of that score came from sympathy.

**Art, Craft, and Inspiration**

My summer in the University Writing Project three years earlier had redirected my teaching focus. In my writing groups that summer, I had connected with childhood memories of the 1940s, seeing again my grandmother pedaling the sewing machine or fanning herself in the porch rocker on summer afternoons. I could see my aunt in the back yard, killing a chicken for Sunday dinner, and my mother dyeing her hair at the dressing table the week before my father's furlough. Each workshop I attended brought more memories.

I wanted my students to enjoy the same experiences in writing, so we kept personal journals, did free writes, and wrote memory pieces. They reflected upon their own short lives in class exercises, responding to prompts:

"Think of your earliest memory—jot it down. What were birthdays and holidays like in your home? What was your favorite toy? Draw a floor plan of your childhood home."

Some of the students stared at me slack-jawed and blank, while others bent their heads over their papers and began to scribble. Occasionally, a promising kernel of a story appeared in their work.

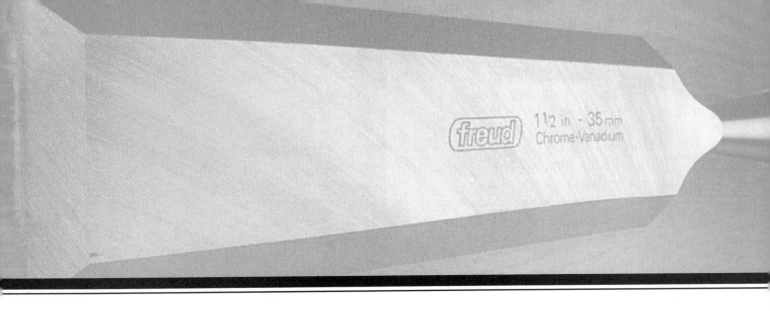

# 1985 PROFILE

Renowned cabinetmaker James Krenov taught the philosophy of wood and the techniques of building fine furniture at the College of the Redwoods in California.

## Life at Work

- At 65 years old, the bearded, long-haired furniture craftsman and teacher Jim Krenov insisted on calling himself "a pre-Kerouac hippie," all the while insisting that he was only an amateur woodworker.

- As the founder of the fine woodworking program at the College of the Redwoods in Fort Bragg, California—one of the most influential programs of its kind in the country—Jim inspired a generation of furniture makers with an aesthetic influenced by organic, subtle details.

- Jim was a philosopher who wrote lyrically about his craft and his reverence for the subtleties of wood.

*James Krenov founded the fine woodworking program at College of the Redwoods.*

- Born on October 31, 1920, in the village of Uelen, Siberia, he was the only child of Dimitri and Julia Krenov.
- He and his family left Russia the following year, and after some time in Shanghai, China, they moved to a remote village in Alaska, where Jim's parents worked as teachers.
- They lived in Alaska for seven years.
- Jim vividly remembered airplane drops of goods and supplies onto the snow for the villagers.
- In one of those bundles was a good steel jackknife.
- "From the time I was six, I was making my own toys with the jackknife; It was a joy to me that I could rely on my hands and my eyes to produce things."
- In the mid-1930s, the Krenovs moved to Seattle, where Jim worked at a boatyard, building yachts and sailing on Puget Sound.

*Working at a boatyard, Krenov developed a love of boats and their design.*

- Thanks to his family roots, he later became an interpreter for the Lend-Lease Program to provide supplies to America's allies, dealing with Russian cargo ships throughout World War II.
- His time surrounded by boats influenced his aesthetic; he loved the lines of boats: "There's hardly a straight line on them, but there's harmony. People think right angles produce harmony, but they don't. They produce sleep," Jim said.
- In 1947, he moved to Sweden and found very unsatisfying work at an electrical appliance factory; whenever he could, he roamed Europe.
- He met his future wife in Paris.
- After they were married on March 2, 1951, Jim and Britta traveled together in Italy and France, and spent many summers in the mountains of Sweden where they liked to hike.
- Jim enjoyed trout fishing in the mountain streams.
- Always a writer, Jim published several articles and a novel chronicling these travels.
- Back in Stockholm, Jim enrolled for two years in the school run by Carl Malmsten, considered by many the father of Scandinavian furniture design.
- After graduating, Jim set up shop in the basement of his home.
- Gradually, his work and philosophy gained recognition among peers and buyers.
- One commission, for a box to contain prized ceramics, came from King Gustav VI of Sweden.
- Toiling anonymously for years, he built a reputation for his simple designs; once established as a master woodworker, Jim also began sharing his expertise.

- He taught at Carl Malmsten's in 1967 and 1968; "Carl would look at your table and he would run his hand around it and he would come to the corner, and he'd stand there a while doing this [rubs his hands together] and he wouldn't say another word. He just walked off. And you'd spend the rest of the day wondering what the hell it was about that particular corner that his hand discovered."
- His international engagements began with an invitation from Craig McArt and Wendell Castle to teach at the Rochester Institute of Technology (RIT).
- Subsequent teaching engagements included the establishment of the program in Wood Artisanry for the Franklin Institute of Boston University, and as a Guest Professor in Graz, Austria, in 1978.
- "I traveled all over the world to talk about my work," Jim said. "These weren't high occasions— just people interested in talking with a craftsman. I'm known as the guy who is always interested in the thing that is both beautiful and useful."
- The response of students at RIT led Jim to try his hand at writing again.
- In 1976, Krenov's first book, *A Cabinetmaker's Notebook*, was published and became so successful that he ended up writing four more books, including one that showcased the work of his students, *With Wakened Hands*.
- His publishers of *A Cabinetmaker's Notebook* sent him on a barnstorming author's tour of the U.S. that led, in turn, to an invitation from the University of California, Santa Cruz, to conduct a workshop.
- Three of the students at that workshop were members of the Mendocino Woodworker's Guild who enticed Jim to conduct a workshop at the Mendocino High School in 1978.
- One lecture led to another in 1979, and again in 1980.
- The Woodworker's Guild members then persuaded the College of the Redwoods, a regional community college with a budding branch in Fort Bragg, to establish a cabinetmaking program.
- "They invited Britta and me up for a dinner and a look around, and we fell for the place, and there were people in the community who wanted to start a school and they finally got the College of the Redwoods to promote it and built the building because I promised I would come.
- "So they said, 'We'll build a school if you'll come.' And I said, 'I'll come if you build a school.'"
- The building was finished with the help of the first group of students in the fall of 1981.

*Krenov's cabinets were known for their simple design.*

## Life at Work
- For the past five years, students from across the globe have attended Jim Krenov's classes at the College of the Redwoods.
- The most recent class included two students from New Zealand, two from London, one from Norway, one from Hawaii, two from Alaska, and a smattering from the remainder of the United States.
- The hands-on, intense classes met six days a week for nine months; most of Jim's students stayed one year, while a few stayed two years.

- Few of his students planned to enter high-end cabinetmaking as a full-time profession.
- Instead, most were part of a national trend that emphasized lifelong learning—including classes in cooking, crafts, foreign languages or the fine points of opera.
- "Krenov really helped re-create an interest in fine woodworking that had largely died out by the 1950s," says Frank Ramsay, president of the Bay Area Woodworkers Association.
- "Krenov introduced a dramatic change from the 'make a box, cover it with plywood and paint it' era of the 1960s."
- One of the first lessons College of the Redwoods students tackled was a requirement to fashion their own tools, starting with a wood plane for scraping very thin strips of wood.
- Jim called the plane "the cabinetmaker's violin," and often suggested that it be made from hornbeam wood because of the way it felt in a craftsperson's hands.

- The class then moved on to cabinet construction and design.
- Jim believed machinery had its place in the shop, especially during the rude stages of stock removal, but thought that power tools often erased the "fingerprints" left on the finished piece that only handwork can leave.
- What distinguished a piece of furniture was not the technical skill or

*Krenov called his plane "the cabinetmaker's violin."*

even the figure of the wood; Jim's credo was "that the work have life in it."
- It wasn't about showing off technique as much as giving the work personality; it wasn't a matter of conquering the wood, he believed, but letting it breathe.
- "Early on, we get into the fact that our tools and materials will respond to our sensitivities; it's the first link in a long chain that gradually becomes a natural way of working. You're no longer worrying about the physical aspects of a tool, but about what you're going to do with it. You're thinking of how it's going to feel and how the results will look."
- Over time, the students were trained to develop an instinct for wood combinations, the colors and textures, melding them to make works with an elegant simplicity.
- "Let us know our wood as we do our hands, and work with it in common respect and harmony," he wrote in *The Fine Art of Cabinetmaking*.
- A favorite wood was pear for its tranquility, its color, and its response to planes.
- His cabinets, rarely more than four feet high and 26 inches wide, were recognizable for their long, slim legs.
- On close examination, the legs reveal a variety of delicate shapes, where Jim's knives and planes adhered to the natural contours of the wood and the patterns of its grain.
- He felt that details such as uniformly rounded edges, perfectly flat surfaces, and sharp corners removed the personal touch from a piece of furniture.
- His books extolled the virtues of clean lines, hand-planed surfaces, unfinished or lightly finished wood, and techniques that Jim referred to as "honest."
- He loved curves, and was known for creating door panels with concave, billowing shapes like sails in the wind.

- For that reason, he avoided the word "design," preferring the language of composing, a continual re-evaluation and improvisation open to wherever the wood takes the composer.
- A self-described "wood nut," he often sought out woods that are rare, highly figured, or contain unique coloration; he liked to keep shavings of Lebanon cedar and sandalwood in a box beneath his bed so he could savor their fragrance.

## Life in the Community: Fort Bragg, California

- Located in coastal Mendocino County, California, along State Route 1, the major north-south highway along the Pacific Coast, Fort Bragg was founded as a military fort prior to the Civil War.
- Fort Bragg became a popular tourist destination, thanks to its picturesque views of the Pacific Ocean and rugged Northern California coastline.
- The town of 6,500 advertised itself as the official Gateway to the California Coastal National Monument, bragging "We've got bookshops for the bookish, thrift stores for the thrifty, shops for the shoppers, art for the artists, camping supplies for the campers.
- "There are no traffic jams, no rush hour (no rushing of any kind) and no parking meters downtown.
- "The air is some of the purest on earth; the blue-green ocean pristine."
- The Redwoods Community College District was formed in 1964 by an election of the people of Humboldt County; a bond issue of $3.6 million was passed for the initial construction phase of the college.
- Instruction began in 1965 and continued into 1967 at Eureka High School.
- Initially, 45 majors were offered, 15 of which were technical-vocational.
- Over 1,800 students registered at the College in 1965-66.
- The founding President/Superintendent, Dr. Eugene J. Portugal, supervised a full-time faculty and administrative staff of 31, with 85 part-time instructors.

Source: www.fortbragg.com

*Fort Bragg, California*

# HISTORICAL SNAPSHOT
# 1985

- In Hollywood, California, the charity single "We Are the World" was recorded by USA for Africa
- William J. Schroeder became the first artificial heart patient to leave the hospital where his surgery had been performed
- Minolta released the Maxxum 7000, world's first autofocus single-lens reflex camera
- The Food and Drug Administration approved a blood test for AIDS to screen all blood donations in the U.S.
- *Amadeus* captured the Academy Award for Best Picture
- WrestleMania debuted at Madison Square Garden
- Coca-Cola changed its formula and released New Coke to an overwhelmingly negative response
- An explosive device sent by the Unabomber injured John Hauser at the University of California, Berkeley
- Scientists of the British Antarctic Survey announced the discovery of the ozone hole
- John Anthony Walker, Jr., was arrested by the FBI for passing classified Naval communications to the Soviet Union, and Thomas Patrick Cavanaugh was sentenced to life in prison for attempting to sell stealth bomber secrets to the Soviet Union
- *Back to the Future* opened in American theatres and became the highest-grossing film of 1985
- Vice President George H. W. Bush announced that New Hampshire teacher Christa McAuliffe would become the first schoolteacher to ride aboard the space shuttle *Challenger*
- In Hiroshima, tens of thousands marked the fortieth anniversary of the atomic bombing of the city
- The wreck of *Titanic* in the North Atlantic was located by a joint American-French expedition led by Dr. Robert Ballard and Jean-Louis Michel using side-scan sonar from RV *Knorr*
- Pete Rose became the all-time hit leader in Major League Baseball with his 4,192nd hit at Riverfront Stadium in Cincinnati
- The Nintendo Entertainment System, including the Super Mario Bros. pack-in game, was released
- The comic strip *Calvin and Hobbes* debuted in 35 newspapers
- Microsoft Corporation released the first version of Windows, Windows 1.0
- President Reagan sold the rights to his autobiography to Random House for a record $3 million
- The Ford Taurus and Mercury Sable were released for sale to the public
- In New York City, Mafia bosses Paul Castellano and Thomas Bilotti were shot dead in front of Spark's Steak House, making hit organizer John Gotti the leader of the powerful Gambino organized crime family
- American naturalist Dian Fossey was found murdered in Rwanda
- NeXT was founded by Steve Jobs after he was fired by Apple Computer
- The Tommy Hilfiger brand was established
- The computer game Tetris was released
- DNA was first used in a criminal case

## Selected Prices

Bicycle, Aero Urban Cowboy ......................................................$600.00

Briefcase, Leather ......................................................................$565.00

Camcorder....................................................................................$994.00

Coca-Cola, Two-Liter ....................................................................$1.00

Doll, Playskool..............................................................................$24.97

Ice Cream, Dove Bar......................................................................$1.45

Martini for Two..............................................................................$1.08

Modem ........................................................................................$119.95

Synthesizer, Yamaha ..................................................................$188.88

Walkman, Sony ..............................................................................$19.95

### "James Krenov, Reflections on the Risks of Pure Craft," Glenn Gordon, *Fine Woodworking Magazine*, November/December, 1985:

The air is charged with Krenov, but the mood of the school is actually pretty loose. It isn't a tyranny. The students are generally good humored and relaxed. A certain amount, not all, of student work bears a resemblance to Krenov's, some of it very closely, which makes it tempting to criticize as merely the work of Krenovian clones, but I think this too conveniently misunderstands it. It's plain to see that some of the students regard the imitation of a master as the price of becoming one oneself, but I also saw work being done that looks nothing at all like what one would associate with Krenov. As long as Krenov feels it is done with sensitivity and skill, he doesn't knock it, but it is clear, from the overall look of things, that Krenov isn't running an art school consecrated on the worship of Design. As independent a spirit as Krenov is, he is still the exponent of an essential conservative furniture tradition. He teaches a craft which has definite and settled criteria in his mind. There is room for experiment, but at heart, the school is committed to the classic way of cabinetmaking, not to the search for profound originality, or to the idea of Design as an activity poised on the edge of the breaking wave of innovation.

## Welcome Letter to College of the Redwoods, James Krenov:

We are a community college accepting students with varying degrees of experience. Our course is organized, but very relaxed. Because the students all have the same beginning point, that is, wanting to be here, we discover that there's a wonderful comradeship and feeling among them; they share a lot.

We try to demystify the process of working wood; we simplify it. We concentrate on the logic and the simple physical and mental relationships in any given process. From the very beginning we work with people, leading them to the realization that wood is a vastly rich material and that different kinds of wood call for different methods of working. Wood also has colors, patterns, and textures that can fit into the work. We help people discover the graphics of wood, and that any shape or proportion can be given additional life through proper use of the wood, whether it's in a cabinet or as something as sculptural as a chair.

We hope that in viewing what we are offering here, you will pay attention to the details, notice the results, and come to realize that if one cares enough, if one pays enough attention to the richness of wood, to the tools, to the marvel of one's own hands and eye, all these things come together so that a person's work becomes that person, that person's message.

In this work, in these details, in these elements, something of a person is included. Their fingerprints or their sense of proportion, line, and detail are there; and what you're experiencing is something very personal from each of these people: something that they've put their heart and soul into.

And we hope some of their enjoyment shows, too.

# 1987 PROFILE

Aaron Slayton learned the facts of life for a smart kid in the third grade; he was always picked first for the spelling bee team and last for the kickball team.

## Life at Home

- Aaron Slayton was the bespectacled smart kid in the class who always did his homework, always did it right, and was willing to share.

- His parents were both college professors; his mother's specialty was Jacobean plays, while his father was known nationally for his research into tenth-century fighting techniques.

*Aaron Slayton was the smart kid who always did his homework.*

- The elder Slayton's research had explained the critical role that horse stirrups played in the changing face of battle; without the stabilizing power of the stirrup, the emergence of the lance would have been impossible.

- Aaron couldn't care less about Ben Johnson or Thomas Kyd—did his mother really need to discuss her work at the dinner table?—he wanted to write novels whose protagonist was a mathematician capable of solving complex crimes using numbers.

- His friend Michael encouraged Aaron's ambition, but secretly believed the concept to be both flawed and stupid.

- Michael's dad was a motorcycle mechanic, which was way cooler than a college professor.

- Nevertheless, Aaron followed the logical steps to join the family business one day.

- His parents loved their jobs—except for the college politics—so all he had to do was avoid the internal battles so common in education and he would have a nice life.
- After several years of public school, Aaron was shipped off to Hotchkiss, an exclusive school in Lakeville, Connecticut, followed by four years at Dartmouth, a graduate degree from MIT, and then a doctorate from Berkeley.
- At 28, he found himself steeped in knowledge, prepared for the future, and totally burned out.
- After three months of hanging out in Kauai, Hawaii, Aaron returned to California to teach.
- Even as an adjunct professor teaching four freshman-level math classes, he was under enormous pressure to publish, participate in college committees, and compete for a tenure track position.
- After four years in academia, he was looking for a change.
- So when a tutor's slot came open at St. John's College in Annapolis, Maryland, he couldn't say "yes" fast enough.
- St. John's College was a four-year liberal arts college with campuses in Annapolis and in Santa Fe, New Mexico.
- Founded in 1696 as King William's School, it received a collegiate charter in 1784, making it one of the oldest institutions of higher learning in the United States.
- Francis Scott Key, author of the "The Star Spangled Banner," was valedictorian of the class of 1796.
- Since 1937, St. John's had followed a distinctive curriculum, known as the Great Books School, based on a four-year discussion of works from the Western canon of philosophical, religious, historical, mathematical, scientific, and literary works.

*Aaron traded his traditional teaching position for tutoring at St. John's College.*

- "The New Program" was developed at the University of Chicago by Stringfellow Barr, Scott Buchanan, Robert Hutchins, and Mortimer Adler in the mid-1930s as an alternative form of education.
- The college was in dire financial straits, and Barr and Buchanan were given nearly free license to develop a new model for the college.
- This took place amidst a milieu of reevaluation and debate regarding pedagogy in the United States.
- World events—including a recent world war, the rise of European fascism, and the fomenting domestic struggles for women's rights and civil rights for black Americans—precipitated questions about the significance of Western traditions and assumptions.
- The inception of the St. John's New Program drew not only attention for its seemingly radical reversion, but also considerable skepticism.
- Aaron knew that tutors, as faculty were called, were expected to lead discussions in a wide variety of topics.
- Small classes dominated, tests were few, and grades largely invisible.
- To Aaron's way of thinking, a better environment for learning could not have been created.

## Life at Work

*Discussion was the heart of St. Johns' programs.*

- Aaron Slayton was mesmerized by the simplistic beauty of St. John's College in the center of historic Annapolis, located one block from the state capitol building.
- The 400-student institution known for its alternative teaching style was located right beside the strait-laced, tall yellow walls of the U.S. Naval Academy.
- The location of the two schools side by side on the Severn River could not have been a finer display of American diversity and attitudes, Aaron thought, and had inspired many a comparison to Athens and Sparta.
- The schools operated on very different schedules, but did carry on a spirited rivalry, seen in the annual croquet match between the two schools on the front lawn of St. John's.
- Aaron was also pleased that—unlike most colleges—St. John's provided a set curriculum for all four years.
- In the campus bookstore, it was clear that St. John's avoided modern textbooks, lectures, and examinations in favor of a series of manuals.
- Every freshman started life as a Johnnie, reading works such as *Nicomachean Ethics* by Aristotle, and every tutor had to be ready every day to accept the challenges of the discussion.
- In a class of eight, in which everyone was expected to participate, there was little room to hide after a night of partying.
- In addition, the discussion format demanded comments in full paragraphs, not simply a bubble mark on a multiple-choice test.
- Aaron especially liked the comprehensive face-to-face evaluation of every student at the end of the semester.
- It was a time to boost some and remove others.
- Students who failed to understand the proper decorum during discussions could be told not to return.
- St John's was not for everyone.
- One of Aaron's first classes focused on Plato and whether virtue was teachable, which logically moved to what constituted virtue.
- He also led a discussion of Ptolemy's *Almagest*, a treatise on planetary movements and atomic theory.
- Every night, Aaron was deep into the lessons until 2 a.m. trying to stay ahead.
- In lab, he had to keep reminding himself that learning evolved from direct observation, and all knowledge was historically linear at St. John's; students couldn't speculate on how the circulatory system worked unless they could prove it themselves.
- Down the hall, another tutor with a Ph.D. in art history and a master's degree in comparative literature stood at the chalkboard drawing parallelograms, constructing angles, and otherwise dismembering Euclid's Proposition 32.
- Clearly, Aaron was not the only tutor who had traded the traditional three-course academic career—writing journal articles, attending conferences, and teaching a specific subject—for the intellectual buffet at St. John's.
- While traditional (A-F) grades were given, the culture of the school de-emphasized their importance, and grades were based largely on class participation and papers, and released only at the request of the student.

- Compared to mainstream colleges, tutors played a non-directive role in the classroom.
- Conversation was at the heart of the St. John's Program.
- Eva Brann, a St. John's tutor, explained, "We are not writing but a speaking school. Conversation is the public complement to that original dialogue of the soul with itself that is called thinking."
- By necessity, class size was small, with a student-to-tutor ratio of 8:1.
- The seminar was the largest class, with around 20 students led by two tutors.
- The rigid structure of New Program's curriculum, based on its historical and cultural focus, was designed to foster open inquiry.
- Developing the educational policy for the college, Buchanan identified three factors, which were intended "to regulate teaching and learning in every part of the program":

  1. The community of the learning effort
  2. The continuity of the learning process
  3. The spontaneity of the learning itself

- The tracing of Western thoughts and currents provided the students—and Aaron—with an understanding of historical content, which was vital to making an informed critique of social, political, and scientific movements of thought, past and present.
- St. John's was not a school where students studied great books, but a community whose members examined life.
- The St. John's Seminar curriculum was unchanging:

  Freshman year: Greek philosophy, poetry, and history

  Sophomore year: The Bible and theology, following some Roman poetry and history, and followed by Dante, Chaucer, and Shakespeare

  Junior and senior year: Modern philosophy from Descartes to Kant, including modern political philosophy

*Sophomores studied Dante, Chaucer and Shakespeare.*

- Seminars always began with a question pertaining to a particular text, and was intended to precipitate discussion, not to direct or confine it.
- Tutorials covered mathematics, language and music.
- Mathematics and language were studied in all four years at St. John's.
- Language was the realm of the St. John's contemplation of and deliberation on the trivium—the study of grammar, logic and rhetoric.
- Greek was the language focus of the freshman and sophomore years, and French that of the junior and senior years.
- Language study began with learning vocabulary and grammar, and progressing to translation.
- The mathematics tutorial was a component of the curriculum in all four years of the St. John's Program, beginning with Euclid's *Elements*, the definitions and propositions of ancient geometry.

## Life in the Community: Annapolis, Maryland

- Incorporated as a city in 1708, Annapolis, from the middle of the eighteenth century until the Revolutionary War, was noted for its wealthy and cultivated society.
- Supported by the slave trade and water trades such as oyster packing, boatbuilding and sail making, Annapolis was known for its theater and sophistication.
- The city became the temporary capital of the United States after the signing of the Treaty of Paris in 1783, and it was in Annapolis, on December 23, 1783, that General Washington resigned his commission as commander-in-chief of the Continental Army.
- During the Civil War, a prisoner-of-war Camp Parole was set up in Annapolis; wounded Union soldiers and Confederate prisoners were brought by sea to a major hospital there.
- In 1900, Annapolis had a population of 8,585.
- Anchoring the historic district, near St. John's College, was Saint Anne's Episcopal Church, erected late in the seventeenth century for the House of Delegates.
- Annapolis maintains many of it finest eighteenth-century houses.
- The names of several of the streets—King George's, Prince George's, Hanover, Duke of Gloucester, etc.—date from colonial days.
- The United States Naval Academy was founded there in 1845.
- During World War II, shipyards in Annapolis built a number of PT boats, and military vessels such as minesweepers and patrol boats were built there during the Korean and Vietnam wars.
- The Maryland State House remains the oldest in continuous legislative use in the United States.
- Construction started in 1772, and the Maryland legislature first met there in 1779; it remains the largest wooden dome built without nails in the country.
- The Maryland State House held the workings of the U.S. Government from November 26, 1783, to August 13, 1784, and the Treaty of Paris was ratified there on January 14, 1784, making Annapolis the first peacetime capital of the U.S.
- St. John's College, a non-sectarian private college that was once supported by the state, was opened in 1789 as the successor of King William's School, which was founded by an act of the Maryland legislature in 1696 and opened in 1701.
- Its principal building, McDowell Hall, was originally to be the governor's mansion, and although £4,000 was appropriated to build it in 1742, it was not completed until after the War of Independence.

*Annapolis, Maryland*

Source: LOC # LC-DIG-highsm-16961

# HISTORICAL SNAPSHOT
# 1987

- Aretha Franklin became the first woman inducted into the Rock and Roll Hall of Fame
- The Dow Jones Industrial Average closed above 2,500 for the first time
- New York Mafiosi Anthony "Fat Tony" Salerno and Carmine Peruccia were sentenced to 100 years in prison for racketeering
- In Super Bowl XXI, the New York Giants defeated the Denver Broncos 39-20
- The last Ohrbach's department store closed in New York City after 64 years of operation
- CBS became the last American network to cease a chime intonation at the beginning of telecasts; satellite feeds had made the tones obsolete
- The U.S. military detonated an atomic weapon at the Nevada Test Site
- American Motors Corporation was acquired by the Chrysler Corporation
- President Ronald Reagan addressed the American people on the Iran-Contra Affair, and acknowledged that his overtures to Iran had "deteriorated" into an arms-for-hostages deal
- In Charlotte, North Carolina, televangelist Jim Bakker, head of PTL Ministries, resigned after admitting having an affair with church secretary Jessica Hahn
- The Fox TV network made its prime-time debut, marking the first time since 1955 that four networks filled the U.S. prime-time television landscape; the network debuted two shows, *Married...with Children* and *The Tracey Ullman Show*
- World Wrestling Entertainment presented WrestleMania III in the Pontiac Silverdome in Detroit, Michigan, attended by over 90,000 that set an all-time indoor attendance record
- Matt Groening's *The Simpsons* debuted as a series of short, animated segments on *The Tracey Ullman Show*
- Andrew Wyeth, with his Helga Pictures, became the first living American painter to have a one-man show of his work in the West Building of the National Gallery of Art in Washington, DC
- Dick Clark's *American Bandstand* aired for the 2,751st and last time on ABC, after 30 years on the network
- During a visit to Berlin, Germany, President Reagan challenged Soviet Premier Mikhail Gorbachev to tear down the Berlin Wall
- In *Edwards v. Aguillard*, the Supreme Court ruled that a Louisiana law requiring that creation science be taught in public schools whenever evolution was taught was unconstitutional
- Michael Jackson released his third solo album, *Bad*
- The first National Coming Out Day was held in celebration of the second National March on Washington for Lesbian and Gay Rights
- Florida rapist Tommy Lee Andrews was the first person to be convicted as a result of DNA evidence and was sentenced to 22 years in prison
- Microsoft released Windows 2.0
- Prozac made its debut in the United States

## Selected Prices

Adirondack Chair and Ottoman ....................................................$119.95

Bicycle, Boy's 20"-Inch Challenger BMX Bike............................$59.99

Camcorder, Sharp 8x....................................................................$1799.99

Cash Register ...............................................................................$179.99

Cereal, per 18 Ounces ..................................................................$1.55

Coffee, per Pound ........................................................................$2.92

Glue Gun.......................................................................................$24.99

Hammer.........................................................................................$10.99

Microwave Oven ..........................................................................$219.99

Sweater, Men's Long Sleeve.........................................................$29.25

## "Clive Davis Blasts Radio," Anthony DeCurtis, *Rolling Stone*, June, 1986:

Clive Davis, president of Arista Records, has attacked rock and pop radio stations for "disenfranchising terrific artists who don't fall into their category, or any category." At a recent conference, Davis condemned radio's tight formatting policies and wondered, How is the next generation of Dylans, Streisands, Coltranes, Bowies going to be heard" if programmers don't open their stations to more diverse sounds?

In his keynote address at the Music Business Symposium in Los Angeles on May 2, Davis complained that radio discourages "large and vital areas of modern music," including music with a social conscience, through a pattern of "conservatism, sterilization and market research," and asked, "Winning a Survivor or a Loverboy record has faded away; what impressions has it left? He dismissed AOR [album-oriented rock] stations as "brand-name radio" for relying on artists whose roots "go back to at least the '70s, and very often the '60s." Davis also took CHR [contemporary hit radio], or top 40, stations to task for limiting the pop ballads on their playlist almost solely to black singers like Lionel Richie or Arista's own Whitney Houston, while shunting white singers doing similar material into the adult contemporary category. Davis praised black stations for their "openness to the new" but lamented the lack of regard for "whole sections of the black-music tradition," including blues, Southern soul and jazz.

Interviewed three weeks after the symposium, Davis explained that he'd wanted to "ventilate" his feelings for some time, adding that he was speaking as "an observer," and that Arista would not be shifting its posture toward radio. "I was just commenting about the sad plight affecting certain areas of music, and hoping that it would stir the imagination of some creative programmers around the country," Davis said. "I can't tell radio how to run its own business, but unless someone identifies the problem, nothing will ever occur.

"The last time something like this occurred," Davis continued, "MTV picked it up and started programming Duran Duran, Culture Club, and a number of English artists who couldn't get arrested except in two or three major cities." Now, he said, "MTV is pretty well reflecting radio. I don't think they're any more or less adventurous.

# 1989 PROFILE

An Dung and Nguyet Nguyen were Vietnamese immigrants who believed that education was the key to being successful in the United States.

## Life at Home

- An Dung and Nguyet Nguyen from Vietnam were part of a revolutionary immigrant tidal wave that struck America's shores in the 1980s.
- From Vietnam alone, two million refugees had uprooted themselves; almost one million of them came to the United States.
- As a result, many American cities were experiencing a cultural makeover.
- Unleashed by the Immigrant Act of 1965, legal immigration expanded from 178,000 new residents a year, under the National Origins System, to one million by 1989.
- Illegal immigration added another 300,000 to 500,000 people each year.
- By 1989, immigration accounted for 60 percent of America's population growth, 82 percent of whom came from Latin American and Asian nations, and 13 percent from Europe.
- Global population had expanded from one billion in 1804 to 5.3 billion in 1989.
- The Immigration Act came just as a worldwide population spike was sending a second great wave of human migration searching for relief from overcrowded, economically damaged nations.

*An Dung steered his son toward a vocational education.*

*Chicago was home to a variety of different cultures.*

- New Americans were being minted from Mexico, the Philippines, China, the Republic Korea, India, the USSR, and Jamaica.
- The Nguyet family had entered the United States legally a decade earlier, shortly after the fall of Saigon, but the new amnesty program brought peace of mind to their cousins who had reached Chicago through Canada.
- The foreign-born population nationwide had reached 8 percent and accounted for one in eight workers, the highest total for foreign-born workers since 1910.
- "Immigration created winners and losers," An Dung told his son Ba.
- Which are we?
- "We don't know yet."
- An Dung had been successful enough during the previous decade to own one small building and a restaurant; children, parents and cousins alike were the labor force that kept it running.
- But schoolwork came first; education was the ticket to the good life in America, along with a good, hardworking spouse, An Dung had preached.
- So when thousands of Asians—from Cambodia, Laos, Vietnam, and China—arrived in Chicago, many were escorted to Argyle Street, home to addicts, pimps and winos, where the newcomers helped push out the drugs, opened small shops, added a new ethnic character to the gang mix and generally participated in an economic turnaround.
- An Dung's greatest concern was the growing number of Mexican and Central American immigrants who were crowding into the area.
- A substantial number of the Hispanic immigrants were illegally in the country; lacking in green cards and vulnerable to deportation, the workers worked for less, possessed little ability to complain about work conditions, and generally made conditions worse for An Dung and his family.
- He was especially concerned about the immigrants' impact on his children's schools.
- His son Ba attended a number of classes with the Hispanic immigrants, whose lack of English skills made the classes progress slowly; the teenage Ba often complained about being bored.
- An Dung couldn't allow others to ruin the American dream for his family—not after all they had gone through.
- Like many of his fellow Southeast Asian immigrants fearing wage competition, An Dung was eager to close the door on additional immigration.
- America's schools were becoming less a melting pot and more of a salad bowl.
- So to protect his children's future, An Dung devoted a considerable amount of his time to improving conditions within the community and steering his children toward vocational education, where they could always make a living.
- The purpose of education was clear to An Dung: to prepare children for the ever-changing workplace in America.
- The study of dead writers like Shakespeare could wait.

## Life at School

- An Dung Nguyen's business background told him that schools should be modeled after corporations so they could be responsive to the workplace.
- Schools should be able to show—through the performance of its children—quality results, or at least measurable progress.
- Every time a school failed to do its job, hundreds of children were impacted—possibly for their entire lives.
- Many high schools with large foreign-born populations already experienced a 50 percent dropout rate—a statistic that was harmful to both the children and the community.
- The reformers who supported "progressive education" and preached the value of allowing children to seek their own interests, avoided an emphasis on grades, and rewarded group efforts had obviously never lived in a world that demanded that their restaurant open at 5:30 a.m. instead of 6:30 to catch one more shift of workers.
- The key was a quality education that prepared people for work.
- For nearly 100 years, business leaders in Chicago and elsewhere had been influencing area schools, their organization, and most importantly, their curricula.
- Business had been demanding that America's schools provide a better-trained workforce.
- As a result, businesses had started schools, helped educators massage their curricula, donated cash and equipment, and persuaded children, parents and teachers of the importance of market economy by subsidizing programs aimed at enhancing teacher knowledge and skill.
- In the public policy arena, business leaders lobbied state and federal officials to guide specific education bills and direct educational funding where it might benefit business.
- An Dung saw his son Ba's future in air conditioning repair and installation—an occupation always in demand, could not be done by cheaper labor in a foreign country, and would not go out of style.
- An Dung, whose Vietnamese upbringing did not include air conditioning, was amazed at how Americans hated sweat or just a little warmth.
- They would never give up air conditioning, even in the worst of times, and Ba would always have a job.
- His thinking meshed with those of American educators since the turn of

*An Dung's son learned the circuitry necessary to succeed in the air conditioning industry.*

the twentieth century when schools were struggling to meet the labor force needs of an America shifting from an agrarian to an industrial economic base.
- In his 1907 address to Congress, President Theodore Roosevelt urged major school reform that would provide industrial education in urban centers and agriculture education in rural areas.
- A powerful alliance supporting federal funding for vocational education was formed in 1910, when the American Federation of Labor (AFL), which had long opposed such programs as discriminatory, gave its approval to the National Association of Manufacturers' (NAM) promotion of trade instruction in schools.

- Federal support for vocational education began with the Smith-Hughes Act of 1917, which established vocational education, particularly agricultural education, as a federal program.
- The act reflected the view of reformers who believed that youth should be prepared for entry-level jobs by learning specific occupational skills in separated vocational schools.
- Vocationalism had its critics, including the American philosopher and educator John Dewey, who believed

*Trade schools were popular in the early 1900s.*

that such specific skill training was unnecessarily narrow and undermined democracy.
- By the 1960s, the vocational education system had been firmly established, and Congress recognized the need for a new focus.
- As a result, the 1963 Vocational Education Act broadened the definition of vocational education to include occupational programs, such as business and commerce, in comprehensive high schools.
- The act also included the improvement of vocational education programs and the provision of programs and services for disadvantaged and disabled students.
- Education reforms focusing on secondary education began in the early 1980s, prompted by concern about the nation's declining competitiveness in the international market, the relatively poor performance of American students on achievement tests, and complaints from the business community about the low level of high school graduates' skills and abilities.
- This reform came in two waves.
- The first wave called for increased effort from the current education system: more academic course requirements for high school graduation, more stringent college entrance requirements, longer school days and years, and an emphasis on standards and testing for both students and teachers.
- Beginning in the mid-1980s, a second wave of school reform arose, based in part on the belief that the first wave did not go far enough.
- The second wave emphasized school-to-work that created closer links between vocational and academic education, secondary and postsecondary institutions, and schools and workplaces.
- The reform movement, particularly its first phase, received major impetus from the publication in 1983 of the National Commission on Excellence in Education's report *A Nation at Risk*.
- This influential report observed that the United States was losing ground in international economic competition, and attributed the decline in large part to the relatively low standards and poor performance of the American educational system.
- The report recommended many of the changes subsequently enacted in first-wave reforms: the strengthening of requirements for high school graduation, including the requirement of a core academic curriculum; the development and use of rigorous educational standards; more time in school or the more efficient use of presently available time; and better preparation of teachers.
- The response to this report and related education reform initiatives was rapid and widespread.

## HISTORICAL SNAPSHOT
# 1989

- Harris Trust and Savings Bank of Chicago settled a government enforcement action by agreeing to pay $14 million in back pay to women and minorities, the largest such settlement ever obtained from a single employer
- President George H. W. Bush named William Bennett as the first Director of the Office of National Drug Control Policy
- Barbara Clementine Harris was consecrated as the first female bishop of the Episcopal Church in the United States
- The first of 24 Global Positioning System satellites were placed into orbit
- Time and Warner Communications announced plans for a merger, forming Time Warner
- Eastern Air Lines machinists and baggage workers walked off the job to protest pay cuts; the airline subsequently filed for bankruptcy protection
- Congress passed a bill to protect the jobs of whistleblowers who exposed government waste or fraud
- Stanley Pons and Martin Fleischmann announced that they had achieved cold fusion at the University of Utah
- In Alaska's Prince William Sound the *Exxon Valdez* spilled 240,000 barrels of oil after running aground
- The 61st Academy Awards awarded *Rain Man* the Best Picture
- More than 300,000 demonstrators marched in Washington, DC, in support of legal abortions
- At the trial of Oliver North on charges related to the Iran-Contra Affair, the jury found North guilty of three criminal charges and not guilty of nine
- In *Texas v. Johnson*, the Supreme Court ruled that burning the U.S. flag was protected under the First Amendment
- The television show *Seinfeld* premiered
- A federal grand jury indicted Cornell University student Robert Tappan Morris, Jr., for releasing a computer virus, making him the first person to be prosecuted under the 1986 Computer Fraud and Abuse Act
- Congress passed the Financial Institutions Reform, Recovery, and Enforcement Act of 1989, which provided a $166 billion bailout to failed savings and loans institutions, and overhauled regulation of the industry
- President Bush and the governors of the 50 states met at the University of Virginia to discuss education policy
- Braniff Incorporated filed for bankruptcy for the second time since 1982
- A jury in Charlotte, North Carolina, convicted televangelist Jim Bakker of fraud and conspiracy
- Douglas Wilder won the Virginia governor's race, becoming the first elected African-American governor in the United States
- David Dinkins became the first African-American mayor of New York City
- Congress passed legislation to raise the minimum wage from $3.35 to $4.25 an hour by April 1991
- In a meeting off the coast of Malta, President Bush and Soviet leader Mikhail Gorbachev released statements indicating that the Cold War between their nations may have been coming to an end

## Selected Prices

| | |
|---|---|
| Apple Macintosh Computer | $2,500.00 |
| Butter, per Pound | $1.99 |
| China, 10-Piece Tea Set | $69.00 |
| Coffee, per Pound | $2.19 |
| Gas Grill | $179.99 |
| House, Four-Bedroom, New York | $156,000 |
| Lawn Mower, Craftsman | $299.99 |
| Screwdrivers, Stanley Set of Four | $26.95 |
| Shotgun, Winchester 12-Gauge | $1,200.00 |
| Woman's Leather Bag | $49.00 |

# "Children of Two Lands in Search of Home," Lisa Belkin,
## *The New York Times*, May 19, 1988:

Growing up in Vietnam, Vinh Doan came to expect rejection. His father was a black American soldier whom he never met. His Vietnamese mother spent years telling him he was ugly because he looked like his father, then gave him to a neighbor when he was seven years old.

When he came to the United States two years ago, he says, he thought he would finally belong. He was wrong. "In Vietnam they called me American," the 19-year-old explained through a translator. "Here they don't know what I am."

### Outcasts in Two Lands

Mr. Vinh's story of hope and disappointment is typical of the disillusionment of nearly 5,000 Amerasian children and their families who have entered the United States over the past 10 years. And it is what faces more than 20,000 more Vietnamese children of American fathers who are expected to arrive in the next 18 months.

"Most of these children have spent their whole lives being discriminated against in Vietnam because they are Americans," said Anna Crosslin, executive director of the International Institute of Metropolitan St. Louis. "Now they come here and people say, 'You don't look American. You don't sound American.'"

The rejection is all the more devastating because "the Amerasians think of this as their country; this is their father's country," said Rose Marie Battisti, executive director of the Mohawk Valley Resource Center for Refugees in Utica, New York, which has settled 360 Amerasians and their families since 1983.

The adjustment problems of Amerasian immigrants have suddenly become a matter of concern to officials and social workers who must prepare for the immigration flood that is expected to result from the Amerasian Homecoming Act. The legislation, passed by Congress last March, marked the end of the tight controls the Vietnamese Government has placed on Amerasian emigration in the last decade.

### Problems Rooted in Chaos

The immigrants will be sent to one of 30 cluster sites around the country, which have not yet been chosen by the State Department but which are likely to include Houston, St. Louis, Utica and Washington.

## "California Faces Teacher Shortage," Louis Freedberg, *The New York Times*, December 15, 1988:

SAN FRANCISCO, Dec. 14—California schools are suffering from a severe shortage of bilingual teachers, leaving many districts unable to find enough qualified teachers to keep up with the sharply rising number of pupils who know little or no English.

Educators and state officials say the shortage means that many of the 625,000 students who the state says need help to learn English before or as they try to learn other subjects are being shortchanged. The number of these students has almost tripled in the last decade, and now accounts for one out of seven pupils in California's public schools. Seventy-five percent of them are Spanish speaking; the rest are spread among 59 languages.

In absolute numbers, the need for Spanish-speaking teachers is greatest, but shortages of teachers who speak languages like Vietnamese or Mandarin are also common.

Texas and New York, among other states with large numbers of immigrant children, also face persistent shortages of bilingual teachers. But the problem seems most acute in California, largely because its education officials have taken a leading position in favor of teaching students first in their native language and in trying new ways to find instructors for them.

### Master Plan Approved

In May, the Los Angeles School Board overwhelmingly approved a master plan for bilingual education, which called for teaching most courses in students' native languages until they learned English. Other state districts followed suit.

Los Angeles acted about a year after Gov. George Deukmejian vetoed an extension of a law that set strict state guidelines for certifying bilingual teachers. School districts are now able to set their own certification standards.

Bilingual certification can take a long time, too.

"You don't learn a language overnight," said Eugene Garcia, chairman of the Department of Education at the University of California at Santa Cruz, which has started a special program to train bilingual teachers. He added that most teachers seeking bilingual certification did not already know a language other than English.

Statewide, 60 percent of California's teachers in bilingual-instruction classrooms lack formal bilingual teaching credentials, according to Policy Analysis for California Education, a research center based at the University of California at Berkeley.

In 1987, 6,500 of 12,000 bilingual-instruction classrooms in elementary schools were staffed by teachers not certified as bilingual, the state Education Department said. Officials say the shortage of certified teachers in junior and senior high schools is probably much worse.

A final reason for California's particular shortage is that student enrollment has exceeded projections by 40 percent over the last decade.

*Continued*

## "California Faces Teacher Shortage," . . . *(Continued)*

### Shortage to Continue

"The bottom line is, no matter what figure you come up with, we don't have enough bilingual teachers, and we won't have enough in the next few years," said Melinda Melendez of the Association of California School Administrators, a professional group.

Dr. David Dolson, assistant manager of the state's Bilingual Education Office, said, "The fact that we are short so many bilingual teachers means that our potential for helping these students academically is greatly reduced."

Many districts are making unusual efforts to find teachers who not only speak a foreign language, but who are also aware of the differences in teaching approaches and cultural backgrounds involving immigrant children.

Many schools have adopted stopgap measures. A common approach is having a bilingual teacher work with another teacher who is not bilingual but who is certified in a specific subject, like science.

Some schools have placed bilingual teachers' aides in classrooms to help teachers who do not speak a foreign language. Still others use "resource teachers," who speak the students' native language and help them in special sessions outside the regular classroom.

### Higher Salary Available

Bilingual teachers have become so dear in some areas that districts offer them higher pay. In Los Angeles, they are already paid almost $2,000 more than regular teachers, and the Board of Education is proposing to increase the bonus to $5,000.

When all else has failed, some school districts with high numbers of Spanish-speaking students have even imported teachers from Spain and Puerto Rico.

But such short-term solutions do not bridge the gap in most cities, officials say. And experts in bilingual education expect the situation to persist for several years at least.

"Those states with the largest concentrations of linguistic minority populations will probably experience a permanent shortage," said Dr. Ramon Santiago, director of the Georgetown University Bilingual Education Center and past president of the National Association for Bilingual Education.

Florida appears to be the exception. It seems to have kept pace with demand in large part because of its established and well-educated Cuban population, and the continuing influx of middle-class immigrants from Nicaragua and other Spanish-speaking countries.

These immigrants provide a greater pool for recruiting bilingual teachers. In addition, their children often know at least some English when they come to the United States, and can be quickly integrated into regular classrooms.

OC OD

OB OC ●D

OA ●B OC OD

15. ●A OB OC OD

16. OA ●B OC OD

17. OA ●B OC O

18. O

# 1990–1999

By the 1990s, largely as a result of the Civil Rights Movement and greater immigration, the debate concerning multicultural education ranged from concerns with empowering oppressed people to creating national unity through the teaching of common cultural values. The public schoolhouse became the battleground for those who wanted the 10 Commandments displayed and cable television to broadcast educational programs. The impact of Title IX was dramatic in women's sports and professional enrollment in medical, religious, and legal schools.

The decade opened with an economic recession, a ballooning national debt, and the remnants of the collapse of much of the savings and loan industry. The automobile industry suffered record losses; household names such as Bloomingdale's and Pan Am declared bankruptcy. Housing values plummeted and factory orders fell. Media headlines were dominated by issues such as increased drug use, crime in the cities, racial tensions, and the rise in personal bankruptcies. "Family values" ranked high on the conservative agenda, and despite efforts to limit Democrat Bill Clinton to one term as president, the strength of the economy played a critical role in his re-election in 1996.

Guided by Federal Reserve Chair Alan Greenspan's focus on inflation control and Clinton's early efforts to balance the federal budget, the U.S. economy produced its best indicators in three decades. By 1999, the stock market produced record returns, job creation was at a 10-year high, and the federal deficit was falling. Businesses nationwide hung "Help Wanted" signs outside their doors, and even paid signing bonuses to acquire new workers. Crime rates, especially in urban areas, plummeted to levels unseen in three decades, illegitimacy rates fell, and every year business magazines marveled at the length of the recovery, asking, "Can it last another year?"

The stock market set a succession of records throughout the period, attracting thousands of investors to stocks for the first time, including the so-called glamour offerings of high-technology companies. From 1990 to the dawn of the twenty-first century, the Dow Jones Industrial Average rose 318 percent. Growth stocks were the rage; of Standard and Poor's 500 tracked stocks, almost 100 did not pay dividends. This market boom eventually spawned unprecedented new wealth, encouraging early retirement to legions of aging Baby Boomers. The dramatic change in the cultural structure of corporations continued to threaten the job security of American workers, who had to be more willing to learn new skills, try new jobs, and move from project to project. Profit sharing, which allowed workers to benefit from increased productivity, became more common. Retirement programs and pension plans grew more flexible and transferable, serving the needs of a highly mobile work force. The emerging gap of the 1990s was not always between the rich and the poor, but the computer literate and the technically deficient. To symbolize the changing role of women in the work force, cartoon character Blondie, wife of Dagwood Bumstead, opened her own catering business which, like so many small businesses in the 1990s, did extremely well. For the first time, a study of family household income concluded that 55 percent of women provided half or more of household income.

In a media-obsessed decade, the star attraction was President Clinton's affair with a White House intern. At the height of the scandal, while American forces were attacking Iraq, the full House of Representatives voted to impeach the president. For only the second time in American history, the Senate conducted an impeachment hearing before voting to acquit the president of perjury and obstruction of justice.

In the music scene, a revival of the singer-songwriter movement of the 1970s brought artists like Norah Jones and Sarah McLachlan to the fore. This movement was well represented by the multi-platinum *Jagged Little Pill* by Alanis Morissette. Grunge remained a local phenomenon until the breakthrough of Nirvana in 1991 with their album *Nevermind*, which also led to the widespread popularization of alternative rock in the 1990s.

During the decade, America debated limiting abortion, strengthening punishment for criminals, replacing welfare with work, ending Affirmative Action, dissolving bilingual education, elevating educational standards, curtailing the rights of legal immigrants, and imposing warnings on the Internet of unsuitable material for children. Nationwide, an estimated 15 million people, including smokers, cross-dressers, alcoholics, sexual compulsives, and gamblers, attended weekly self-help support groups. Dieting became a $33 billion industry as Americans struggled with obesity.

The impact of the GI Bill's focus on education, rooted in the decade following World War II, flowered in the generation that followed. The number of adult Americans with a four-year college education rose from 6.2 percent in 1950 to 24 percent in 1997. Despite this impressive rise, the need for a more educated population, and the rapidly rising expectations of the technology sector, the century ended with a perception that the decline in public education was one of the most pressing problems of the decade. School violence escalated, capturing headlines year after year in widely dispersed locations across the nation.

The 1990s gave birth to $150 tennis shoes, condom boutiques, pre-ripped jeans, Motorola, 7.7-ounce cellular telephones, rollerblading, TV home and Internet shopping, the Java computer language, digital cameras, and DVD players. And in fashion, a revival of the 1960s' style brought back miniskirts, pop art prints, pant suits, and the A-line. Black became a color worn at any time of day and for every purpose. The increasing role of consumer debt in driving the American economy also produced an explosion in personal bankruptcies and a reduction in the overall savings rate. At the same time, mortgage interest rates hit 30-year lows, creating refinancing booms that pumped millions of dollars into the economy, further fueling a decade of consumerism.

# 1992 PROFILE

Gayle Warwick was the first woman in her family to benefit by Title IX by participating in volleyball, track and softball, and by studying advanced science and math.

## Life at Home

- Gayle Warwick had heard all the excuses before; they were disappointedly familiar to what her older sister, mother and grandmother had been told.
- "Playing sports with boys was not only unfeminine but proof of lesbianism."
- "Female athletes were physically unattractive and weren't asked out on dates."
- "Competitive sports would harm reproductive organs as well as a woman's chances of marriage."
- "Girls were too selfish to play team sports; their hearts were too small, tempers too short."
- Girls' teams had to raise their own money through bake sales or carwashes.
- Girls' teams could not afford new uniforms and could only practice when the boys did not "need" the gym.
- Only the newest and worst referees were assigned to the girls' games.
- Cheerleaders received more attention than female athletes.

*Gayle Warwick bucked the trends by excelling in sports, science and math.*

- If the boys' program was cut so that girls could have a team, the entire school would be mad—any decline in the boys' achievements would be the girls' fault.

- Girls played in empty gymnasiums; even parents wouldn't watch their daughters compete.
- Born in 1972—the year Title IX of the Education Amendment was enacted—Gayle was a natural athlete who wanted to take advantage of the law that had changed women's athletics.
- Her older sister had helped blaze the trail in Tampa, Florida, by playing on the boys' soccer team and starring on the newly created girls' squads.
- When it was Gayle's turn to explore the various benefits of playing on girls-only soccer and field hockey teams, she choose to play them both.
- Her father understood; her mother was sure it would end badly.
- In addition to soccer, Gayle wanted to participate in volleyball, track and softball.
- But as important, she also demanded a space in the advanced classes in science and math—avenues that had been considered "boys' activities" and discouraged for girls—prior to Title IX.
- Although Title IX had ushered in athletic opportunities for thousands of girls like Gayle, its impact was far wider, having erased the boys-only label that had been attached to certain academic disciplines, job opportunities and extracurricular activities.

- Hailed as one of the great achievements of the Women's Movement, Title IX states: "No person in the United States shall, on the basis of sex, be excluded from participation in, be denied the benefits of, or be subjected to discrimination under any education program or activity receiving federal financial assistance."

*By the 1990s, more females were participating in organized sports.*

- Gayle considered the law to be "gender-neutral" and not a "gift" to girls like some grown-ups liked to say.
- Title IX simply eliminated the special privileges historically given to boys by providing girls with equal access to higher education, career education, education for pregnant and parenting students, employment, a healthy learning environment, math and science, standardized testing, technology, and laws against sexual harassment.
- Title IX covered all state and local agencies that received federal education funds, including approximately 16,000 local school districts, and 3,200 colleges and universities.
- Prior to the passage of Title IX in 1972, some tax-supported colleges did not admit women, athletic scholarships were rare, and math and science were realms reserved for boys.
- Girls were encouraged to become teachers and nurses, but not doctors or principals; women rarely were awarded tenure and even more rarely appointed college presidents.
- Sexual harassment was excused because "boys will be boys," but if a student became pregnant, her formal education ended.
- Before Title IX, female athletes at the University of Michigan sold apples at football games so that they could compete for the school, which did not have a budget for women, and female gymnasts at the University of Minnesota had to rely on their male counterparts to provide them with leftover tape.
- Graduate professional schools openly discriminated against women; being female was seen as a pre-existing condition that made them unqualified.

## Life at School

- Gayle Warwick was voted the school's most athletic student in her senior year, having earned letters in five different sports and earned three state championships.
- The athletic fields on which she played were considerably better than those provided to her older sister, and the referees who called the games actually liked working the girls' games, without considering it a "punishment."
- In 1972, fewer than 295,000 girls participated in high school varsity athletics, accounting for just 7 percent of all varsity athletes.
- In 1992, female participation exceeded one million, including the traditional male sports of wrestling, weightlifting, rugby, and boxing.
- Parents eagerly watched their daughters on the playing fields, courts, and on television; Gayle's father scheduled his work around her soccer and field hockey games.
- But as far as Gayle was concerned, her greatest achievement was a full-ride scholarship offer from Duke University in Durham, North Carolina, to study biochemistry, not to mention the scholarships offered to her by Florida State, Vanderbilt, and Virginia Tech to play field hockey.
- She had tried to do both sports and biochemistry, and played for Duke's field hockey team her freshman year, but realized that her real interest was in lab research.
- Now a junior with half a dozen science classes under her belt, she had fallen in love with the exploratory study of essential fatty acids such as omega-3s and the role they played in the human inflammatory system.

*Gayle loved to work in the science lab.*

- Considerable information had already emerged concerning infant brain development and fatty acids.
- Now, if science could link omega-3s to the body's inflammatory receptors, Gayle was convinced the impact on medicine would be huge.
- She was convinced this opportunity would have passed her by without Title IX; her success was exactly the result the bill's sponsors had intended.
- The first person to introduce Title IX in Congress was its author and chief Senate sponsor, Senator Birch Bayh of Indiana.
- At the time, Senator Bayh was working on numerous constitutional issues related to women's rights, including the Equal Rights Amendment, to build "a powerful constitutional base from which to move forward in abolishing discriminatory differential treatment based on sex."
- But he was struggling to get the ERA out of committee, and the Higher Education Act of 1965 was on the floor for reauthorization.
- On February 28, 1972, Senator Bayh introduced the ERA's equal education provision as an amendment.
- In his remarks on the Senate floor, he said, "We are all familiar with the stereotype of women as pretty things who go to college to find a husband, go on to graduate school because they want a more interesting husband, and finally marry, have children, and never work again. The desire of many schools not to waste a 'man's place' on a woman stems from such stereotyped notions. But the facts absolutely contradict these myths about the 'weaker sex' and it is time to change our operating assumptions.
- "While the impact of this amendment would be far reaching, it is not a panacea. It is, however, an important first step in the effort to provide for the women of America something that is rightfully theirs—an equal chance to attend the schools of their choice, to develop the skills they want, and to apply those skills with the knowledge that they will have a fair chance to secure the jobs of their choice with equal pay for equal work."
- When President Nixon signed the bill, he spoke mostly about desegregation through busing, which was also a focus of the signed bill, but did not mention the expansion of educational access for women he had enacted.
- Opposition from established men's athletics emerged quickly and powerfully,
- Senator Bayh spent the next three years keeping watch over Health, Education & Welfare (HEW) to formulate regulations that carried out its legislative intent of eliminating discrimination in education on the basis of sex.
- When the regulations were finally issued in 1975, they were contested, and hearings were held by the House Subcommittee on Equal Opportunities on the discrepancies between the regulations and the law.
- Senator John Tower had already tried to reduce the impact of Title IX in 1974 with the Tower Amendment, which would have exempted revenue-producing sports from Title IX compliance.

*Title IX gave girls an alternative to cheerleading.*

- More than 20 lawsuits had been filed challenging the law.
- When HEW published the final regulations in June 1975, the National Collegiate Athletic Association (NCAA) claimed that the implementation of Title IX was illegal, even though America's colleges and universities were given an additional three years to comply.
- Despite the regulatory delays, the concept behind Title IX began having an impact, even in sporting venues not under the aegis of Title IX.
- The Boston Marathon began officially accepting women contestants in 1972; in 1992, 1,893 entrants—nearly 20 percent—in the race were female.
- Women had hardly been welcomed with open arms.
- When Katherine Switzer, a 20-year-old Syracuse University junior, showed up to run the Boston Marathon in 1967, her goal was to prove to her coach that she was capable of running 26.2 miles.
- Women were not allowed to officially run the marathon, but no one had any reason to question "K. V. Switzer" as her name appeared on the application.
- In the middle of the race, Jock Semple, a Boston Marathon official, jumped off a truck, ran toward Switzer and shouted, "Get the hell out of my race."
- Another female athlete, Marge Snyder, said, "I played on my Illinois high school's first varsity tennis team from 1968 to 1970. We were 56-0 over my three years. We were permitted to compete as long as we made no efforts to publicize our accomplishments and personally paid for our uniforms and equipment."
- For Gayle, the celebration of Title IX also embraced a number of less tangible victories, including a study that showed a direct correlation between increased athletic participation and reduced obesity rates.
- In addition, athletics in high school had taught her how to be a member of a team—a valuable skill, for someone determined to collaborate on major science discoveries—and how to handle the personal disappointment of a bad game or a close loss.
- School athletics had given her a strong body frame, which added to her confidence and allowed her to take risks that translated into opportunities.
- "It's a different world now," Gayle told her parents, "and just imagine the opportunities that will be open to my children."

## Life in the Community: Tampa, Florida

- Located on the Gulf of Mexico, Tampa, Florida, experienced dramatic growth during the second half of the twentieth century as both a retirement and vacation destination.
- Once inhabited by indigenous peoples, notably the Tocobaga and the Pohoy, Tampa was briefly explored by Spanish explorers in the early sixteenth century, but there were no permanent American or European settlements within the current city limits until after the United States had acquired Florida from Spain in 1819.
- "Tampa" may mean "sticks of fire" in the language of the Calusa, a Native American tribe, and be a reference to the many lightning strikes that the area receives during the summer months.
- Other historians claim the name means "the place to gather sticks."
- In 1824, the Army established a frontier outpost near the mouth of the Hillsborough River, which provided protection to pioneers from the nearby Seminole population.
- Tampa grew slowly until the 1880s, when railroad links, the discovery of phosphate, and the arrival of the cigar industry jumpstarted Tampa's development.
- In 1891, Henry B. Plant built a lavish 500+ room, quarter-mile long, $2.5 million eclectic/Moorish Revival-style luxury resort hotel called the Tampa Bay Hotel among 150 acres of manicured gardens along the banks of the Hillsborough River.
- The resort featured a race track, a heated indoor pool, a golf course, a 2,000-seat auditorium, tennis courts, stables, hunting and fishing tours, and electric lights and telephones in every

*Luxury hotel in Tampa emphasized the city's importance in the early 1900s.*

room, plus the first elevator in town and exotic art collectibles which Plant had shipped in from around the world.

- Tampa became an important city by the early 1900s and adopted the mantle of "Cigar Capital of the World" long before production peaked in 1929, when over 500 million cigars were hand-rolled in the city.

- During the Depression, profits from the bolita lotteries and Prohibition-era bootlegging led to the development of several organized crime factions in the city.

- The era of rampant and open corruption ended in the 1950s, when the Senator Kefauver's traveling organized crime hearings resulted in sensational misconduct trials of several local officials.

- During the 1950s and 1960s, Tampa saw record-setting population growth spurred by major expansion of the city's highways and bridges, bringing thousands into the city and spawning two of the most popular tourist attractions in the area—Busch Gardens and Lowry Park.

- In 1956, the University of South Florida was established in North Tampa, spurring major development in this section of the city.

- The biggest recent growth in the city was the development of New Tampa, which started in 1988 when the city annexed a mostly rural area of 24 square miles between I-275 and I-75.

- Tampa was part of the metropolitan area most commonly referred to as the Tampa Bay Area that was part of the Tampa-St. Petersburg-Clearwater, Florida Metropolitan Statistical Area (MSA) that embraced 2.7 million residents, making it the fourth-largest in the Southeastern United States, behind Miami, Washington, DC, and Atlanta.

- That population supports a number of sports teams, such as the Buccaneers of the National Football League, the Lightning of the National Hockey League, the Rowdies of the North American Soccer League and the Rays in Major League Baseball.

# HISTORICAL SNAPSHOT
# 1992

- Singer Paul Simon toured South Africa after the end of the cultural boycott

- A Miami, Florida, jury convicted former Panamanian ruler Manuel Noriega of assisting Colombia's cocaine cartel

- Acquittal of four police officers in the Rodney King beating criminal trial triggered massive rioting in Los Angeles that lasted for six days, resulting in 53 deaths and over a $1 billion in damages

- The Space Shuttle *Endeavour* made its maiden flight as a replacement for a lost Space Shuttle

- The first World Ocean Day was celebrated, coinciding with the Earth Summit held in Rio de Janeiro, Brazil

- Boris Yeltsin announced that Russia would stop targeting cities in the U.S. and its allies with nuclear weapons, while George H. W. Bush announced that the U.S. and its allies would discontinue targeting Russia and the remaining communist states

- Iraq refused a U.N. inspection team access to the Iraqi Ministry of Agriculture, said to have archives related to illegal weapons activities

- Nirvana's *Nevermind* album was No. 1 in the U.S. Billboard 200 chart, establishing the widespread popularity of the Grunge movement of the 1990s

- Farm Aid Live took place in Irving, Texas, hosted by Willie Nelson; artists performing included John Mellencamp, Neil Young, and Paul Simon

- The Disney animated movie *Aladdin* was the highest-grossing picture of the year; *Unforgiven* captured the Academy Award for Best Picture

- Dr. Mae Jemison became the first African-American woman to travel into space, aboard the Space Shuttle *Endeavour*

- The average price of gas was $1.05 per gallon

- Green tea was discovered to contain an important anti-cancer agent

- Walter Annenberg donated more than 50 Impressionist paintings worth $1 billion to the Metropolitan Museum of Art in New York City

- Operation Julin was the last nuclear test conducted by the U.S. at the Nevada Test Site

- After performing a song protesting alleged child abuse by the Catholic Church, Sinéad O'Connor ripped up a photo of Pope John Paul II on *Saturday Night Live*, sparking controversy

- NBC Television selected Jay Leno to replace late night talk show host Johnny Carson

- The Church of England voted to allow women to become priests

- A coalition of United Nations peacekeepers led by the U.S. was formed to provide humanitarian aid and establish peace in Somalia

- Extremist Hindu activists demolished Babri Masjid—a sixteenth-century mosque in Ayodhya, India—leading to widespread violence, including the Mumbai Riots, in all killing over 1,500 people

## Selected Prices

Alarm Clock ................................................................................$9.99

Car Seat ....................................................................................$65.00

Christmas Tree, Artificial .......................................................$124.99

Comforter .................................................................................$26.88

Lawn Mower .............................................................................$289.00

Leggings ...................................................................................$15.00

Light Bulb, Halogen .................................................................$8.96

Microwave Oven .......................................................................$99.00

Shower Curtain ........................................................................$19.77

Videotape, Three Blank ...........................................................$8.49

### "High School Football: At Elizabeth High School, It's a Matter of Getting From Here to There," Robert Lipsyte, *The New York Times,* November 27, 1992:

ELIZABETH, N.J.—The sounds and rhythms change at Elizabeth High School as the squeaky slap of leather on hardwood replaces the meaty thud of colliding bodies. The football season ended yesterday and practice begins for the girls' and boys' basketball teams today.

But for the coaches, the purpose of all this noise and sweat remains the same: keep the 4,300 students of New Jersey's largest high school interested and involved until they are prepared to escape this tough port city of 110,000, to college or to meaningful work.

Most coaches here believe, perhaps self-servingly, that a successful athletic program is the secular church of this predominately Hispanic and black school, even for those who only worship. And that the coaches, overwhelmingly white men, are the ministers of a higher order.

Basketball brings particular promise and pressure. The boys' coach, Ben Candeloni, is routinely expected to field a powerhouse. He has sent players to major colleges and the National Basketball Association. The girls' coach, Shannon Luby, may have a harder job: persuading historically oppressed young women from minority groups to assert themselves, even as she fights her own Title IX battles in a department that would prefer a man in her job.

*Continued*

## "High School Football: ... (Continued)

The pressure is still on the football coach, Jerry Moore, who must repay the kids from whom he demanded a season of intensity and pain. He has to help them get into colleges that will pay them to play. The recruiters have been lumbering through the halls all week.

Of his 22 seniors, Moore figures he has six blue-chippers who will quickly go to major schools, another four or five who will be harder sells and another half-dozen who won't be placed, in prep schools or junior colleges, much before February.

The star, six-foot-five-inch linebacker DuLayne Morgan has already been offered admission by Duke, and may also consider North Carolina, U.C.L.A., Rutgers, Florida State, Syracuse, Michigan, and Notre Dame. DuLayne had 980 on the college boards as a junior and a 3.25 average in the advanced honors program. He was rated one of the top 25 prospects in the country.

But there are young men who need Moore to persuade a college to take a chance, to understand that uneven play or erratic grades or low body weight reflects problems that may only be solved by being away at college, away from a violent home, a drunken mother, secure in a place offering three meals a day and a sense of worth.

Moore says that his team, which ended its season yesterday with an anticlimactic 13-12 loss to Cranford, was his most talented ever. So why did it end the season with a 5-4-1 record and two losses to archrival Union?

"Could have been the coaching," snapped Moore, who was pleased to be reminded that he had lost his quarterback and his tailback before the season began and had to depend on the remarkable though raw gifts of a 14-year-old freshman, Al Hawkins. Quarterback Hawkins suffered a sprained shoulder in the next-to-last game, but should be ready to throw his 85-mile-per-hour fastball for the baseball coach, Ray Korn, this spring.

The school's brassy, classy marching band, which often gives the impression that it thinks football is the sideshow to its performance, didn't win the big one, either, finishing third overall in its group at a big competition three weeks ago at Giants Stadium. But its crowd-pleasing "Carmen" routine won best music award.

At Elizabeth, however, victory is often measured not by winning and losing, but by survival, what Jerry Moore calls "getting from here to there," a phrase that has informed his coaching for the past 20 years.

In 1972, as a 30-year-old basketball coach at a suburban, predominately white Somerville High, Moore was far more authoritarian and his West Virginia twang was more pronounced.

When a group of black students defied the principal and stormed out of school to protest what they considered unequal racial treatment, Moore warned his basketball team that anyone who joined the demonstration would never again play for him.

*Continued*

## "High School Football: . . . *(Continued)*

Moore's best player, a black guard named Ken Hayes, said: "Coach, I have to go out because those are the people I pass on the way home. You can help me here, but every day I got to get from here to there."

When Moore hesitated, Hayes said, "If you let me go, I'll bring everybody back into school in 30 minutes."

Moore says now: "I always reflect back on that day. Look at the decision I was forcing on those black players. Give up a shot at a major college scholarship or go against the people in their community. How can I do that?

"My kids at Elizabeth, some of them walk two miles past shootings and drug deals, they have to go from here to there every day, and you got to be sure you don't make too many rules that get in the way of their survival."

Twenty years ago, Moore defied his principal and sent Ken Hayes out to join the demonstration. Hayes, who went on to college ball and is now a law enforcement officer, brought the protesters back inside within 20 minutes. They met with the administration, and the conflict subsided.

"To this day I don't know who was right in all that," says Moore. "I only know it turned me around. When I deal with a kid, I always think first, he's got to get from here to there. How can I stay out of his way? How can I help him get there?"

## Letters, *Syracuse Herald Journal* (New York), October 6, 1992:

**Enough is enough**
When I first read about the boy who was playing girls' field hockey, I kind of laughed. When I heard he might not be able to play anymore, I didn't laugh. Isn't the NHL's Tampa Bay Lightning giving a 20-year-old female a fair chance? Yes, they are. Aren't the men of the NHL physically bigger, stronger? Yes, there are woman who can play with men in the men's game; the boy who wants to play on a girls' field hockey team has to be examined by weight, age, height and be okayed by panel of judges. This is ludicrous. I'm tired of hearing about women's equal rights. Let's put it this way: Holland Patent, you are now much better team and Tampa Bay isn't.

—P. Coleman, Syracuse

**Female athletes deserving**
Should males be allowed to compete in primarily female sports and vice versa? If considered as a "right," there can be no doubt that the potential to ruin female sport dictates disapproval of any such mandate.

*Continued*

## **Letters, . . .** *(Continued)*

In professional sports, male golfers and tennis players could dominate on the women's tour and this sort of thing should not be allowed.

A better way to phrase the question: should upward mobility be allowed for female athletes? For the gifted and competitive-minded female athletes, often the outlets available are more recreational than competitive.

Should the female athletes be allowed to test themselves by moving to more competitive levels? Of course they should.

Males do not belong in women's sports, but allowing women to compete in men's sports is necessary, not only to provide outlets where none exist for female athletes, but also to allow females to test themselves through performance.

—Don Gates, North Syracuse

**Stick to their own teams**

Should boys be allowed to play on girls teams, and vice versa? Certainly NOT.

Feminism or civil rights are not justifiable reasons in the world of sports from the amateur to the professional.

Fifteen-year-old Greg Crumb playing for the Holland Patent High School field hockey team is absurd. It's happened in other school areas, but approval makes a mockery of sports. The object of varsity sports in schools is two divisions. How can one take pride in being, say, the best girls' team if a boy is on the team?

Would you permit a girl in your school to wrestle against boys? Would there be different rules? How does a boy grasp a girl in the chest or crotch? And vice versa?

Football? How can a girl compete against hulking 250-pounders? Boxing: Forget it. Girls would be cut to shreds. And in other contact sports—lacrosse, basketball and soccer—girls or women wouldn't stand a chance.

—Lou Defichy

# 1995 Profile

As a young woman who had grown up with a love for the arts, Scott Shanklin-Peterson became executive director of a South Carolina arts agency that brought more arts into the schools.

## Life at Home

- Scott Shanklin-Peterson was born June 10, 1944, at Eglin Army Air Corps base on the Florida Panhandle, the only child of Ferryle Yeager of Alabama and Edward Henry Shanklin of South Carolina.
- Henry Shanklin's parents died when he was young, so he and his other four siblings were parceled out to relatives; he grew up in Rocky Mount, North Carolina.
- In the mid-1930s, he went to Clemson College, located in the South Carolina countryside between the mid-sized cities of Anderson and Greenville.
- He went there, at least in part, because his older sister, Virginia Shanklin, had been working there since 1925 as secretary to the college's presidents.
- Henry graduated in the late 1930s with a degree in textiles.

*Scott Shanklin-Peterson worked to expand the arts curriculum in South Carolina schools.*

- He went into the Army, and was serving as a major in the Army Air Corps when Scott was born.
- After World War II ended in 1945, he worked briefly at a cotton mill in Danville, Virginia, before returning to Clemson to work for the U.S. Department of Agriculture at its Cotton Quality Research Lab.
- Scott grew up in the small town by the Clemson campus.

- Her Aunt Virginia was still serving as a secretary to the Clemson president.
- Over her 41 years at the college, Virginia served four presidents; one of her jobs was to coordinate all arts activities on campus, including an annual schedule of visiting ballet companies and orchestras.
- Aunt Virginia made sure her niece had tickets, "and she made sure I got there," Scott said.
- "She was a great influence on me for the arts."
- Another influence was Sarah Waikart, an accomplished artist who returned to her hometown near Clemson in 1950.
- Public schools in the area didn't have art classes, but Waikart provided private lessons; Scott was one of her students for two years during elementary school.
- When Scott was a senior in high school, she and her best friend, who also wanted to study art in college, asked the principal to let them take drafting, also called mechanical drawing.
- "They wouldn't let us take it because we were girls," recalls Scott.
- The pair kept insisting, and finally the principal relented.
- Scott went to Columbia College, a small women's college in Columbia, South Carolina.
- She wanted to major in art and business.
- "They told me I couldn't because people who were good in art weren't good in business."
- After being sent to the school psychologist for aptitude tests, she tested fine for both and the college agreed to her request.
- Scott graduated in 1966 with a bachelor's degree in studio art, with minors in business and art education.
- She married Frank Buck Sanders in 1965 and had two children: Buck Henry Sanders, born in 1971, and Stacie Sanders, born in 1975.
- Although Scott and her husband later separated, she continued to use the name Scott Sanders until she married Terry Peterson in the mid-1990s, who was then an advisor to U.S. Secretary of Education Richard W. Riley.
- After college, Scott worked for a few years with the state employment agency, counseling the jobless on how to find work.
- When her husband graduated from University of South Carolina Law School in 1969, Scott moved with him to the Rosebud Indian Reservation in South Dakota, where he provided legal assistance to members of the Sioux tribe.
- Scott helped the tribe set up a co-operative to sell crafts.
- After a year or so, she and Terry moved to Philadelphia, Mississippi, where her husband provided legal aid to the Mississippi band of the Choctaw tribe.
- They then moved to Columbia, South Carolina, in June 1971, shortly after their first child was born.
- When Scott took her baby down to the state employment agency to show him off to her former coworkers, someone remembered her interest in the arts, and mentioned that the South Carolina Arts Commission needed some help.
- The Arts Commission, then only four years old, was looking for someone to set up a program that would place poets into schools to work with students.
- Scott's job application process included being interviewed by three poets and writing several grant proposals.
- She got the job.
- It was considered part-time, and she was paid $3,000 a year—half the salary of an office secretary.
- Her enthusiasm made it full-time.

*Scott encouraged creativity at a young age.*

- Scott initiated her arts education project in the schools with the help of the Springs Foundation, which was interested in the arts and was willing to provide grants for work in three counties.
- Starting in 1973, the program employed painters, poets, potters, printers, and musicians who would work in the schools to expose children to the arts.
- Some teachers' groups feared that employing artists in schools would discourage administrators from hiring full-time arts instructors.
- "The opposite was true," Scott said.
- "Artist residencies developed an interest in having more arts, and the number of art and music teachers expanded."
- It was a lesson that she would carry with her when she was promoted to executive director of the South Carolina Arts Commission in 1980, and over the next 13 years as South Carolina became a national petri dish for a new way of raising the profile and quality of arts in the classroom.

## Life at Work

- When the national "Arts in Education" program began in 1986, Scott Shanklin-Peterson jumped at the opportunity to participate.
- The goal of the NEA-sponsored effort was that students would graduate high school with "with a general understanding of, and elementary literacy in, the major art forms."
- In March 1987, South Carolina was one of 16 states to receive planning grants.
- South Carolina was already ahead of many states in its approach to arts education.
- One reason: Arts educators became angry.
- In the late 1970s, the South Carolina Board of Education issued a regulation saying students in grades 9-12 could use no more than two credits earned in music and visual arts toward their graduation requirements.
- For the first time, visual arts and music educators joined forces through their professional organizations to "right this wrong," said educator Ray Doughty.
- Groups representing arts teachers and students "mounted an intensive campaign which ultimately resulted in the State Board rescinding the so-called two-unit regulation," Doughty said.
- Another factor was that arts education was becoming something students (and their parents) aspired to—at least in Greenville County.
- The county, which borders the mountains in the western end of South Carolina, had one of the state's largest school districts.
- In 1975, it established a Fine Arts Center where gifted high school students would spend half their day working within a given discipline from painting to violin.
- The other half of the day would be spent at their "home" high school, where they would study language, math, science and other required courses.
- This became so popular that a statewide version was established in 1980 as a summer program on the campus of Furman University in Greenville County.
- Then, the Ashley River Creative Arts Elementary School, founded in Charleston in 1984, captured attention by taking arts beyond the domain of the gifted.

*Gifted students thrived in the Fine Arts Center.*

- The magnet school accepted all students in its district, regardless of their artistic abilities.
- While there were special arts classes, it also wove the arts into lessons from science to music; the school's waiting list would swell to 1,500 by 1994.
- Richard W. Riley was elected governor of South Carolina in 1978 on a campaign platform to improve education in the state.
- In 1980, the South Carolina legislature enacted a set of minimum requirements for schools that included arts instruction.
- For every 800 students, schools were supposed to have at least one full-time visual art teacher and one music teacher in grades one through six.
- With funding, an elementary school student spent 40 minutes each week on visual arts and another 40 minutes on music.
- These reforms laid a foundation that made it easier in South Carolina to roll out its proposed Arts in Basic Curriculum project in the late 1980s.
- Nationally, arts were being squeezed out of the schools by shrinking dollars and a clamor for more basics.
- Some educators and the public were concerned about the quality of education basics— reading, writing and arithmetic—being neglected.
- After the election of Ronald Reagan in 1980, newly appointed U.S. Education Secretary T. H. Bell ordered a study to "define the problems afflicting American education."
- In 1983, Bell released a report called "A Nation at Risk" that warned of

*Art class in elementary school.*

"a rising tide of mediocrity that threatens our very future as a Nation and a people."
- The report detailed shortcomings in reading, writing and arithmetic.
- It mentioned the arts in a passage noting that some observers "are concerned that an overemphasis on technical and occupational skills will leave little time for studying the arts and humanities that so enrich daily life, help maintain civility, and develop a sense of community."
- But since the late 1950s, some psychologists, educators and artists had been forming a different way of looking at the place of arts—not just in society but within the human brain.
- One of these was Elliot W. Eisner.
- Growing up in Chicago in the 1930s and 1940s, Eisner had not done well in classes like math and English, but he flourished in the arts and became an art teacher, and then finished his doctoral degree in education.
- He was teaching at Stanford University in 1982 when he was asked to meet with directors from the J. Paul Getty Trust.
- The trust had been established six years after the death of its namesake, one of the nation's richest Americans and an art collector who had founded the Getty Oil Company.
- *The New York Times* reported that the J. Paul Getty Trust planned to establish, in early 1986, partnerships with state arts councils to make the arts an integral part of basic education, from the first to the twelfth grade.

- It was the first time the endowment had encouraged changes in curricula at local schools.
- In the past, the endowment presence in the schools was to provide small salaries for artists who worked within schools for several months.
- The money for the new program would come from cuts in these artists-in-residency programs.
- South Carolina was one of only eight states to win a three-year grant in 1988 to begin rolling out Arts in Basic Curriculum to its first group of 11 schools or school districts.
- "Dismissed as a luxury by school systems fighting even to keep enough textbooks in stock, arts studies have steadily dwindled in recent years," *The New York Times* reported.
- "The National Center for Education Statistics estimates that almost half of all American schools have no full-time arts staff members. The new standards will provide no immediate relief," the paper reported.
- "States or school districts that choose to adopt them will be eligible for some of the $700 million earmarked in the Clinton budget for its Goals 2000 legislation, a broad education bill stressing basic educational goals and including the adoption of voluntary national standards as a central feature."
- Because the goals were voluntary, any chance for implementation depended on cooperation.
- "Local and state arts agencies and organizations, schools and arts educators need to strengthen their partnerships to ensure that quality arts education becomes a reality in all schools," Riley said.
- Among the chief organizers of the partnerships had been Scott.
- Clinton appointed Scott as deputy chair of the NEA in January 1994 on the recommendation of Jane Alexander, Clinton's new NEA chair.
- Alexander was an award-winning actress who had co-starred with James Earl Jones in *The Great White Hope,* an NEA-funded play that opened in 1968.
- It was the first time that a white woman and a black man had played bedroom scenes on stage, a first that brought death threats to both of them.
- "Because Jane's career began with an NEA-funded project, she understood the great value to our country of the NEA," Scott said.
- Meanwhile, Scott's mission was to adapt the model of cooperation from South Carolina to the national stage; her title was Deputy Chair for Partnerships.
- The task would be difficult, with more than 50 groups and agencies representing different segments of arts education, from administrators to teachers unions.
- The key was the support from both Riley and NEA Chair Jane Alexander.
- "People came together, stepped up and did it," Scott said.
- The group spent six months developing a national partnership and a plan to help make the arts part of basic education.
- The success was marked by the creation of the National Arts Education Partnership in 1995 through an unusual interagency agreement between the National Endowment for the Arts and the Department of Education.
- The partnership helps to provide a uniform voice for arts educators.
- Its mission is also to expand arts education to more students, improve arts education practices, and research how art influences and strengthens American education.
- "We created on the national level the same type of partnership we had created in South Carolina," Scott said.

*Elliot Eisner spearheaded Arts in Basic Curriculum.*

- In November 1994, Americans elected more Republicans to the U.S. House than Democrats.
- House Speaker Newt Gingrich of Georgia; Representative Dick Armey of Texas, the majority leader; and Representative John A. Boehner of Ohio had all declared that the federal government had no business making grants to artists and arts organizations.
- "That," Scott said, "was the beginning of the culture wars."

## Life in the Community: South Carolina

- In 1995, South Carolina had 3.7 million people, making it the twenty-sixth-largest of the 50 states and Washington, DC.
- The state's population had grown 18 percent since 1980, slightly faster than the overall growth rate for the nation.
- South Carolina had 38,700 teachers for its 645,000 kindergarten through twelfth-grade public school students in 1995.
- The average class was about 17 students—slightly fewer than the national average.
- The average public schoolteacher earned $30,300 in the 1994-95 school year—18 percent less than the national average of $36,800.
- Taxpayers spent $912 per student per year in a typical district in South Carolina in 1995—21 percent less than the U.S. average.
- By 1990, the state's spending was $2,027 per student—only 6 percent under the national average.
- But the state's spending fell compared with other states through 1995.
- About 174,000 people were enrolled in college in South Carolina.
- That comes out to 4.7 percent of the state's population, ranking South Carolina fortieth by that measure.

*One of South Carolina's mobile arts centers*

# HISTORICAL SNAPSHOT
# 1995

- Valeri Polyakov completed 366 days in space while aboard the Mir space station, breaking a duration record
- Hacker Kevin Mitnick was arrested by the FBI and charged with penetrating some of the country's most "secure" computer systems
- The creative program for children's poetry, "*LITER*~Art" originated in the Valley of the Poets, North Andover, Massachusetts
- In Denver, Colorado, Stapleton Airport closed and was replaced by the new Denver International Airport, the largest in the United States
- Astronaut Norman Thagard became the first American to ride into space aboard a Russian launch vehicle (the *Soyuz TM-21*)
- Mississippi ratified the Thirteenth Amendment, becoming the last state to approve the abolition of slavery; the amendment was nationally ratified in 1865
- In the Oklahoma City bombing at the Alfred P. Murrah Federal Building, 168 people, including eight federal marshals and 19 children, were killed; Timothy McVeigh and one of his accomplices, Terry Nichols, set off the bomb
- More than 170 countries agree to extend the Nuclear Nonproliferation Treaty indefinitely
- In Culpeper, Virginia, actor Christopher Reeve was paralyzed from the neck down after falling from his horse in a riding competition
- Salt Lake City was selected to host the 2002 Winter Olympics
- In response to UNSCOM's evidence, Iraq admitted for first time the existence of an offensive biological weapons program
- Congress passed the Child Protection and Obscenity Enforcement Act, requiring the producers of pornography to keep records of all models who were filmed or photographed
- The Nasdaq Composite index closed above the 1,000 mark for the first time, while the Dow Jones Industrial Average topped 5,000
- Japanese and Americans marked the 50th anniversary of the dropping of the atomic bomb
- Microsoft released Windows 95
- The DVD, an optical disc computer storage media format, was announced
- eBay was founded
- The *Washington Post* and *The New York Times* published the Unabomber's manifesto
- Former professional football player O. J. Simpson was found not guilty of double murder for the deaths of former wife Nicole Brown Simpson and Ronald Goldman
- A budget standoff between Democrats and Republicans forced the federal government to temporarily close national parks and museums, and operate with a skeleton staff
- The Dayton Agreement to end the Bosnian War was reached at Wright-Patterson Air Force Base near Dayton, Ohio
- *Toy Story*, the first full-length computer animated feature film, was released by Pixar Animation Studios and Walt Disney Pictures
- President Clinton signed the National Highway Designation Act, ending the 55 mph speed limit
- Queen Elizabeth II advised "an early divorce" to Lady Diana Spencer and Prince Charles
- The final *Calvin and Hobbes* comic strip was published

## Selected Prices

Art Exhibit, New York..................................................................$8.00
Camcorder.............................................................................$2,700.00
Cell Phone..............................................................................$49.99
Chair, Walnut .........................................................................$195.00
Low-Flush Toilet......................................................................$270.00
Roaster, Calphalon ...................................................................$99.99
Rollerblades ............................................................................$34.97
Shaving Cream..........................................................................$0.99
Soccer Cleats...........................................................................$129.95
Whirlpool Tub........................................................................$1,660.00

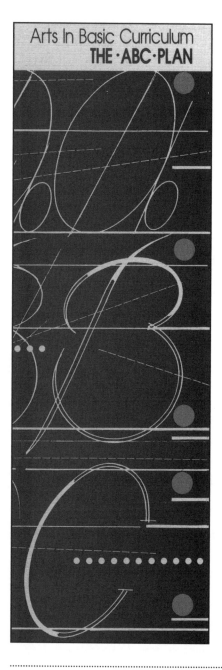

***The Role of Discipline-Based Arts Education in America's Schools,
Elliot W. Eisner, J. Paul Getty Trust, 1988:***

"Any idea that ignores the necessary role of intelligence in production of works of art is based upon identification of thinking with the use of one special kind of material, verbal signs and words. To think effectively in terms of relations of qualities is as severe a demand upon thought as to think in terms of symbols, verbal and mathematical. Indeed, since words are easily manipulated in mechanical ways, the production of a work of genuine art probably demands more intelligence than does most of the so-called thinking that goes on among those who pride themselves on being 'intellectuals.'"

—John Dewey

Why, given the argument developed here, are the arts in such a marginal position in our schools? There are several reasons.

*Continued*

## *The Role of Discipline-Based Arts Education in America's Schools,* . . . *(Continued)*

**ART AND MIND, TALENT AND INTELLIGENCE**
First, there is a long tradition in Western culture that regards the arts as matters of emotional catharsis rather than matters of mind. Art is something you do with your hands, not with your head. To think well requires one to deal with abstraction, not with the qualities of color and space, tone or composition. Intellect is regarded as something that is best cultivated through subjects like mathematics and physics and through the use of language. Since the school's first obligation is to cultivate intellect, and since the arts are believed to deal with emotions, the arts, in this view, are ornamental in education. They are useful as avenues for relief after the serious work of the school has been completed.

This distinction between matters of mind and matters of hand is reflected in the distinctions we make between intelligence and talent. Talented individuals are those who play a musical instrument well, paint a good picture, perform well on the athletic field. Those who are truly intelligent are good at abstract reasoning and solving difficult problems. Intellect and talent are both rare, but it is to intellect that the schools have their first responsibility.

Those who hold this view of mind, intellect, and intelligence fail to understand that the creation of powerful and sensitive images is a matter of mind, a matter that requires inventive problem-solving capacities, analytic and synthetic forms of thinking, and the exercise of judgment. The narrow view of intelligence that has impacted our schools limits our appreciation of the scope of the mind and the many ways in which truly intelligent behavior is displayed.

In recent years, psychologists have broadened our conception of intelligence. They, like cognitive anthropologists, have come to recognize that intelligence comes in many forms and is expressed in different ways both within and between cultures. Some individuals—architects, sculptors, painters—are highly intelligent in dealing with spatial problems. Others display their intelligence best in mathematical and logical reasoning processes. Others are most intelligent in their interpersonal relationships; politicians frequently possess such forms of intelligence in abundance, as do those working with people in clinical settings. One of the major points of the newest research on intelligence emphasizes not only the variety of ways it is displayed, but the factors in the environment that can foster or hamper it. Intelligence, so to speak, is a developmental commodity.

Such views are directly contrary to those that regard intelligence as fixed and limited to verbal and mathematical reasoning. For schools to define intelligence or intellect this way is to disregard the variety of intelligence that children possess and to the place those whose strongest abilities are in the arts in a disadvantaged position. If the only game in town is basketball, those under six feet tall are likely to be handicapped. Education can discriminate through opportunity and recognition denied, as well as through more overt means.

**ART AND ASSESSMENT**
A second reason for the marginal position of the arts in our schools is that, as school programs are now constructed, the arts are not formally assessed and do little to promote the student's

*Continued*

## *The Role of Discipline-Based Arts Education in America's Schools, . . . (Continued)*

academic upward mobility. Until quite recently, the arts did not carry much weight in college admissions decisions. Understandably, parents want their children to succeed in school; they want them to do well so the opportunities beyond school will be open to them. Parents correctly perceive that there is a status hierarchy among the subjects in the school curriculum. Some subjects—math, for example—simply carry more weight than others. Hence, when the instrumental value of a subject is perceived to be low, it is likely to be given low status. If being good at the visual arts, music, theater, and dance are not of much value in the eyes of college admissions committees, and if such areas of work are regarded as "semisolids," the arts are bound to be assigned a marginal place in the structure of schooling.

These practical considerations do not mean that parents, for example, believe the arts to be unimportant in their child's life, only that they are not believed to be particularly useful in terms of short-term academic goals. What we have, then, is a curious separation between what people believe contributes to their child's general educational development and what they regard as important for succeeding in school. As long as our schools' priorities are narrow and limiting, our children will have a hard time pursuing the arts as part of their general education. What we test is what we teach.

### ART AND CREATIVITY

Two other reasons for the current position of the visual arts in our schools have to do with the way we have thought about their role in education. One of these reasons pertains to the long-standing emphasis among art educators and teachers alike that art should be used mainly to develop the child's general creative abilities. For many, art was not something one learned to see, to do, or to understand, but something that unlocked the child's creative potential. As a result, many teachers resisted providing any structure or content in art programs. They thought that structure of any kind would stifle the child's innate creativity and that content, particularly content drawn from the work of adults, would impose inappropriate models for young children. Furthermore, they believed that, in the final analysis, art was not so much taught as caught. This meant, in practice, that the child was to be exposed to a wide variety of art materials, the more the better, since such exposure was thought to stimulate the child's imagination and to provide a rich array of opportunities for self-expression. The results of such policies were often programs with little or no structure, limited artistic content, and few meaningful aims. Such programs were correctly perceived by parents and students alike as lacking substance and left the visual arts in a poor position to claim a serious place in the school's curriculum.

Another factor that has contributed to the marginal status of art in the curriculum is the belief that only a few children are actually talented in art, and that the ability to create requires talent that only a few possess. When it is widely believed that some human abilities are a function of special gifts, the education problem becomes not one of instruction, but of selection. We often hear people claim that they can't draw a straight line without a ruler, implying that no amount of exposure or instruction is likely to make any difference in their ability to draw. With this view, ability in the arts is thought to be the result of a genetically possessed aptitude that one either has or does not have. Yet those who hold such a view would be unlikely to

*Continued*

## *The Role of Discipline-Based Arts Education in America's Schools, . . . (Continued)*

claim that the ability to read or do arithmetic is an ability that one either possesses or does not. Those who hold such a view would not claim that children have, or do not have, the ability to do science or to understand history. Despite this inconsistency, there is a fairly widespread belief that it is futile to teach the arts to the large segment of the population that does not have the genetically determined capacity to understand, experience, or create it.

When such a view becomes persuasive, it creates a self-fulfilling prophecy: one that does not provide meaningful programs or adequate instructional time in the arts. Then the low level of student performance is used to validate one's preconceptions. The fact of the matter is that there are no human abilities that are either present or absent in a population. All of us, to some degree, are capable of learning something in any area, not necessarily to the same extent as others, but to some extent. Education as a process is aimed at converting potentiality to actuality. To relinquish this aim is to significantly diminish our educational aspirations and to guarantee that they will not be achieved.

These views of art in education have a chilling effect on its contributions to our children. As a culture, we have regarded art as a product of emotion rather than mind. We have believed it to be unteachable. We have eschewed programs that have structure, since we were fearful they would stifle the child's creative expression. We have correctly perceived that, as success is now defined in our schools, the arts have limited short-term instrumental utility; they possess little weight in the status hierarchy among the academic subjects we teach or in the academic credit assigned to those subjects. Is art ornamental in education? Given the foregoing views, in most schools it has been and still is. But need it be? Is there some way of conceiving and designing art programs so that the substantial contributions of the arts become an educational reality for our children?

## "Creativity vs. Academic Study: How Should Schools Teach Arts?" Susan Chira, *The New York Times*, February 4, 1993:

The question in Sharon Anderson's drama class was, What do poor people want for Christmas? The answer came in a song.

To the tune of "The 12 Days of Christmas," the students shouted their answers: red roach spray, two dollar bills, three mice traps, and so on, up to 10 food stamps, 11 neck bones, and down to no collard greens. They punctuated each verse with a barked, sardonic "Ho, Ho, Ho!"

In this classroom in Liberty City, one of the poorest and most violent neighborhoods in Miami, children in fourth through sixth grade are learning how to perform and how to think about issues. In rewriting the song at Christmastime, these students were riveted, engaged in a way they might not have been by a straightforward discussion of poverty in social studies class.

*Continued*

## "Creativity vs. Academic Study: . . . *(Continued)*

Such classes, experts say, show how powerful arts classes can be, and how they may even point the way for the rest of education.

"Children naturally learn this way, but teachers don't teach that way," said Ellyn Berk, an educational consultant who is a member of a group drawing up national standards for arts education.

### Capturing Children's Interest

Children usually love classes in art, music, dance and drama, in part because the arts are taught differently from other subjects. The arts demand students' involvement. They capture children's interest in such a way as to motivate them to hone their skills, even if it means accepting the drudgery of practice. And they appeal to those children who learn better when they watch or listen to something than when they read it.

Many educators want to change American schools along these very lines. Yet this is also a time of ferment for arts education. Worried that arts are in danger of vanishing from many American schools, experts are debating what arts education should be. Some argue that the arts' unconventional nature is its strength; others want to see the arts taught more like history, English or math. Should arts teaching focus on creation and performance? Or should it also include more traditional academic study of history, theory and criticism?

*Continued*

## "Creativity vs. Academic Study: . . . *(Continued)*

Very few American schoolchildren, experts say, are getting compelling arts education now. "In drama, it's the spring musical or 'Our Town,'" said Ms. Berk, referring to the ubiquitous Thornton Wilder play. "In dance, it's phys ed with the gym teacher. In music, it's the marching band, and in visual arts, it's make-and-take. This is still what passes for art education."

Some of the most influential and biting criticism has come from the Getty Center for Education in the Arts in Santa Monica, California. In 1982, it stunned the arts education world with a critique, "Beyond Creating," which concluded that art classes had erred in focusing solely on creating art. The report called instead for a "discipline-based art education" that would include history, criticism and esthetics, the last subject directed toward the development of artistic judgment.

The report also argues that art classes' emphasis on making artwork is elitist, in that it favors artistically talented students. A 1988 report by the National Endowment for the Arts echoed this criticism and recommended that all students study and be tested in art, music, dance, drama and design, all under the supervision of full-time art teachers.

But some art teachers believe these criticisms are a misguided attempt to make arts more academic, too much, that is, like other subjects that may already bore or frustrate students.

"Kids who are not making it in school have not been making it for seven or eight years," said Marilyn Polin, who created an arts program that has sent several of her students' grades in other subjects soaring at Cutler Ridge Middle School, south of Miami. "Instead of giving them something different, teachers insist on giving them the same thing that didn't work before." Indeed, when students in her class were asked whether they had studied art history, several shouted out, "Borrr-ing!"

Some answers will come next year, with the expected publication of voluntary national arts curriculum standards. The standards will not specify a complete curriculum, but give broad guidelines. For example, students would be expected to distinguish among Romantic, Classical or Baroque music, and know about music from non-European cultures, said John J. Mahlmann, the executive director of the Music Educators National Conference and a member of the standards group.

### The Purpose of Learning Discipline and Teamwork

Where experts can agree is that the arts, if taught well, can encourage teamwork and self-discipline, promote deeper understanding of other civilizations, bridge cultural gaps between students, reach students who are alienated or discouraged in school, and even, in some cases, help improve students' achievement in other subjects.

In Nan Imbres's class at South Miami Middle School, only the voice of their teacher and the pounding of the beat break the concentration of the young dancers. "I want

*Continued*

## "Creativity vs. Academic Study: . . . *(Continued)*

your heels down," she tells the group of seventh- and eighth-graders as they stretch, bend and flex in a grueling 20-minute warm-up. "You can't be too tall, too thin, too proud or too beautiful in this class." They may groan, but they obey her quickly.

These students, from some of Miami's poorest and richest neighborhoods, competed in citywide auditions for places in this dance program, where they practice two hours a day, five days a week, during school hours. Now, in the rebellious years of early adolescence, they are learning the discipline that dance demands. "We give them seven minutes to put their hair up and dress," said Linda Wills Long, head of the school's dance program. "At this age, they test every rule we make. But we find their grades turn around. They learn how to work."

Those who would improve American schools want children to feel such enthusiasm for all their subjects. And arts advocates say that art classes can lead the way. Name a current educational buzzword, and arts educators point to a way that arts teaches it: multi-culturalism, alternative forms of testing, different learning styles, interdisciplinary curriculum, self-esteem, problem-solving.

In their enthusiasm for the cause of arts education, however, some advocates are accused of going overboard. "We don't want to make extravagant claims about any one discipline," Mr. Mahlmann said. "In other disciplines, we can also talk about creativity and self-esteem."

But if art is not the only model for educational change, many educators do agree that art classes can serve as one model. Educators believe children learn best when they are active rather than passive, when they are asked to find their own answers to questions rather than told to write down information supplied by teachers. Arts educators argue that this is the very way they teach: in classes where students must participate and learn to criticize their own work constructively.

Furthermore, many academics, most prominent among them Howard Gardner, a professor at the Graduate School of Education at Harvard University, say that children learn in different ways; Mr. Gardner calls them "multiple intelligences." Some absorb information best when they read it. Others need to see or hear what they are studying, a need that is often ignored by teachers.

"The arts are natural to a childhood way of learning that is unlike the traditional verbal approaches alone," said Elliott Eisner, a professor at Stanford University and a leading theorist in arts education.

Some arts educators are now drawing on these theories to create different kinds of schools that have art as a unifying theme. The Ashley River Creative Arts School in Charleston, South Carolina, is just one of many new "arts-infused" schools where students, who do not have to be artistically talented to be admitted, study art at least one hour a day, and where teachers integrate arts projects into regular subjects.

# 1999 NEWS FEATURE

**"Report Claims Hispanics Need College Opportunities,"**
*Seguin Gazette Enterprise* **(Texas), October 6, 1999:**

The price that America pays for shortchanging higher education opportunities for its growing Hispanic population is $130 million annually in salaries that would come from higher-paying jobs that require college.

Increasing the ranks of Hispanic college graduates has become a national priority in this knowledge-based economy, which increasingly relies on the skills of the country's fastest-growing minority group, according to a new study by the Educational Testing Service and Hispanic Association of Colleges and Universities. The report, "Education = Success: Empowering Hispanic Youth and Adults," was released recently during a seminar in Washington, DC, sponsored by the ETS/HACU collaboration.

"America loses billions by not improving education for Hispanics," said ETS president Nancy Cole. "But more importantly, it also loses fresh, diverse talents and perspectives."

"Education = Success" not only assesses the Hispanic education gap, but sets out solutions that have as their goal steady improvements in the number of Hispanics that gain college degrees.

"The good news is that Hispanic access to college is improving and that this trend will continue," said HACU president Antonio Flores. "The bad news is that Hispanic youth still trail non-Hispanic white youth in educational achievement." The gap in Hispanic college attendance will grow from the current level of 430,000 to as many as 550,000 Hispanic students still missing out on a college education by the year 2015.

According to the study, among Hispanics age 25 to 64, 13 percent have a post-secondary degree. Of those without a college degree, 18 percent are ready to enroll in a two-year or four-year college, while another 24 percent would be ready to enroll with about 200 hours of basic skills training.

Increasing the number of 18- to 24-year-old Hispanic youth pursuing an undergraduate degree by 10 percentage points would result in Hispanic youth obtaining their proportional share of college enrollments.

That underrepresentation on campus also equals representation in good jobs. "Almost 60 percent of jobs today require college-level skills," said the study's author, Anthony P. Carnevale, ETS vice president for public leadership. "More Hispanic youth will need college to get their first jobs—and more Hispanic adults will need college to keep their current jobs or get better ones."

The Hispanic good-job gap translates to lower wages. On average, non-Hispanic white men earn $17,000 more a year than Hispanic men, and non-Hispanic women earn $6,700 year more than Hispanic women.

"Evidence is mounting that linguistic, racial and class bias differences are limiting the job prospects and incomes of minority workers," said Flores. According to the study, the broader problem-solving and interpersonal skills demanded by the new information-based economy may be more culturally and class bound than the narrower technical and vocational skills characteristic of the old industrial economy.

How do we get from here to there? Carnevale addresses issues ranging from money to Affirmative Action, testing and language skills—but notes that they are only part of the story.

Financial aid has not kept pace with increasing college costs. In addition, since a large number of young Hispanic students entering college are either first-generation Americans or first-generation college students, they need more social support, counseling, college and career planning than is currently available. Hispanic adult students also need more supportive services and flexible course offerings that allow them to meld schooling, work and family.

Carnevale added that to increase Hispanic participation in college through graduation, America needs to substantially expand its focus on college access policies. "We need affirmative development and affirmative outreach for all Hispanic students through the full 5-K system, not just college admissions information provided to relatively few students in the spring of their senior year of high school," he said.

"And better tests can be part of the solution," said Cole. "The ultimate goal is to create tests that establish the linkages of how to improve academic skills in preparation for college," she added.

The bottom line, according to the report, is that America needs to invest in Hispanic social capital to achieve the economic rewards possible. To combat prejudice and low expectations that face Hispanics, Carnevale advocates a strategy of engagement, encouragement, and social support. "Financial investment will be necessary, but even more essential is human investment—showing interest, defining and imparting values, and advising and caring," he said.

"If we focus on these deeper causes of frustrated potential, our policies will be more surefooted," concluded Carnevale.

# 1999 PROFILE

Viola Chadusky's job as a teacher had always been tough, but the challenges of new testing standards led her to wonder whether the stakes for testing were becoming too high.

## Life at Home

- Viola Chadusky was born in Syracuse, New York, on September 17, 1959.
- She was a bright, vivacious girl who grew up wanting to make a difference in the world.
- As a college student, she chose the classroom as a place to start.
- Viola's mother, Anna Fisselbrand, was from nearby Manlius, where the family had lived for generations.
- Anna became a registered nurse and went to work in 1956 at the State University of New York's Upstate Medical Center, where she met Alfred Chadusky, an accountant at the hospital; they married in 1958.
- Al had grown up in Rochester and graduated from Columbia College in New York City in 1955.
- By the time Viola turned five, she had a sister, Anna, and a brother, Tom.
- Viola's parents sent her to a private kindergarten, then to a Catholic school in first grade.
- She was so excited before her first day at school she had trouble going to sleep.
- Girls wore a uniform consisting of a plaid, pleated skirt and a white blouse; boys wore black pants, a white shirt and a plaid bowtie.
- Viola was a good student and liked to play teacher with her siblings.
- Whenever she was alone, she read.

*Teacher Viola Chadusky questioned the value of standardized testing.*

- When her friends came over, they played with Barbie dolls or talked about the Beatles; her best friend Marcia liked Paul, but Viola liked John.
- Soon their musical interests drifted to the Monkees, who had their own television show from 1966 to 1968.
- The intrigue of the made-for-television band was heightened by the fact that the show debuted in color.
- Until then, television shows were almost always in black and white, and color television sets were just becoming available.
- Marcia's parents were the first on the block to get a color TV, so Viola stopped by often.
- Her parents decided in 1969 that it was too expensive to send their kids to Catholic schools, and enrolled them in public schools in the fall.
- For the first time, Viola had to choose what to wear to school each day.
- She didn't think much about "what she wanted to be when she grew up" as she moved from junior high into high school in 1973; she was more interested in hanging out with her friends.
- When they got together, she was often the one to steer them into their evening plans, and had a quick wit and a loud laugh.
- In a group, she wasn't always the one who talked the most, but when she spoke, people listened.
- Viola continued to read, and in tenth grade had an English teacher, Molly Peacock, who opened up her mind to authors new and old.

*In Catholic school, Viola didn't think about what to wear.*

- When Viola first read Shakespeare, she was struck by the oddness of how words were spelled and strung together.
- But as Mrs. Peacock helped untangle the language, Viola marveled as she began to understand English as it was spoken in the 1600s.
- She read John Steinbeck's *The Grapes of Wrath*, in which she saw stark choices faced by many in the Great Depression.
- Watching Mrs. Peacock orchestrating her classroom through lively discussions led Viola to consider teaching as a career.
- While Viola had always earned good grades, she didn't consider herself very smart.
- But when she took her college aptitude tests in her junior year, she was surprised at having scored near the top, with especially high marks in English. Everyone else seemed to be able to write their papers effortlessly, while her first drafts were as painful as pulling fingernails.
- Second and third drafts were another matter; by that point, she could whip her words into shape.
- Her high scores were a big help in getting her a scholarship to New York University, which her family would not have been able to afford otherwise.

- She decided to major in education.
- Some of her classes were extremely dull and filled with a mind-numbing amount of jargon that she believed was more a way of showing status than conveying ideas.
- Her classes became more interesting as she entered her junior year, and her ability to write, speak and use her natural leadership skills helped her excel.
- During her senior year, she did an internship in a third-grade classroom in a New York public elementary school.
- It was an eye-opening experience.
- She met students who couldn't read, some who couldn't even speak English.
- Many were being raised by single mothers, or grandparents, who lacked the skills or time to help them.
- "I'm not in Syracuse anymore," Viola said to herself.
- She was hired in the fall of 1981 to teach fourth grade at a public school in New York City.
- During her first year of teaching, she came home many days and cried.
- The range of students' backgrounds and abilities was dizzying.
- Some of the brightest seemed bored, and she felt she wasn't doing enough to help those who were struggling.
- Discipline problems were constant.
- Administrators didn't seem to care, except when they dropped in to observe her class.
- Many of her fellow education graduates dropped out after their first year of teaching, but Viola persevered.
- As she talked with other teachers, she learned to focus better on her students by not carrying the guilt of all their failings.
- She did the best she could, which turned out to be pretty good, indeed.
- Her writing talent was a help, but she listened closely to other teachers, and when she could, she watched their techniques.
- A few of the other teachers were mediocre, but despite the school's failings, most of the teachers were committed and effective.
- Viola emphasized reading in her classroom, especially nonfiction.
- She kept lists of all the books students were reading during the year, helped organize book clubs, and arranged reading partners so her students could talk about what they read.
- As the years passed, she gained the respect of her peers, and even the administrators.
- She received recognition for her work at the end of her fifth year of teaching in 1997, and also completed her master's degree at the Teachers College of Columbia University in 1998, bumping up her pay to about $35,000 a year.

## Life at Work
- Viola Chadusky accepted that standardized testing had always been part of teaching.
- However, she felt truly challenged when a movement for higher standards and tougher tests gained momentum in New York City in the mid-1990s.
- Viola often thought the tests were measuring the wrong things.
- Worse, the results tended to be used in ways for which the tests were not designed.
- On the other hand, she had seen from her students' work the paucity of their knowledge and the weakness of their skills.
- And, if nothing else, Viola had learned to work within the system to get the job done.
- Whatever tests the administration wanted, she would prepare her students for them.
- Most of her colleagues felt about the same way.
- Elementary schools already were under pressure from the city, with new and more stringent tests that could be used to fire principals or reassign teachers.

*Standardized testing was becomming more important in 1999.*

- But teachers' concerns about testing increased when they learned the State Board of Regents was planning to introduce a new, more rigorous set of language and math tests in 1999.
- Principals held long meetings with teachers in the fall of 1998 on what the new tests would mean.
- The old fill-in-the-blank test about a passage students had read was intended to measure minimum adequacy.
- About two-thirds of Viola's class had passed the test the previous year.
- Fourth-graders across the state would be taking three 55-minute tests over the course of three days starting January 12, 1999.
- This test differed from the usual in that it had an essay component.
- In one segment, students would read an excerpt and write a short essay; in another, teachers would read them a story, after which students would write an essay.
- The January 1999 test would be a practice run for students, but the next year it could be used to flunk and hold back fourth- and eighth-grade students.
- Viola's principal estimated that about 25 percent of the school's fourth-graders were in danger of failing.
- Although Viola didn't show her concern with her fourth-graders, she began spending more time on punctuation, rules of grammar, and—in anticipation of the stress—deep breathing exercises.
- She waited until November to describe the tests to her students.
- "They were stunned," she recalled.
- In the teachers' lounge, one third-grade teacher recounted how one of his borderline students had vowed "from now on I'll study more and I won't talk in class."
- The other teachers at the table laughed, but they also knew how devastating being held back would be on a child.
- Viola remembered the sleepless nights she had in her first years when she knew one of her children was going to be held back.
- She practiced with "Amos and Boris," a story about a mouse who is saved from drowning and carried home by Boris, a whale; years later, Amos finds Boris beached on the seashore and finds a way to return him to the sea.
- After reading the story, she told her students to jot down what each character did, and then to some of those words to write sentences describing the personality traits of the mouse and the whale.

- When two of her most worried students had done especially well, she praised them out loud.
- But many of her students didn't seem to grasp the task, and wrote garbled sentences.
- When Viola finally had a chance to retreat to the teachers' lounge, she could see that other teachers were worried, too.
- "They're not going to do their homework, and they know I can't make them," third-grade teacher Catherine Browne said. "I can't control what happens at home. I can't even reach a parent on the phone half the time."
- "Yeah," Viola said, "the public doesn't seem to get it. They look at our absentee rates and point their fingers at the schools. They wouldn't believe some of the reasons. I had one kid last year who skipped school so he could translate for his dad at the Immigration Office."
- The school remained open three hours in the mornings during most of the holiday break.
- About half the students attended the special sessions.
- In March, the results from the tests given back in January came in.
- Two-thirds of the fourth-graders at the school had flunked the English test, and it was only a small consolation to Viola that the failure rate in her classroom was 52 percent; she had hoped for at least a little more than that.
- She began thinking of new ways to teach that would strengthen her students' comprehension and writing skills.
- As much stress as the state test caused fourth-grade teachers, she heard even more complaints about the city's burgeoning schedule of multiple-choice tests.
- "And I don't know why they're so hot about these tests," a third-grade teacher said. "When was the last time anyone told kids to memorize the 50 states and their capitals? Not in the last 10 years. What's important is teaching the kids how to find the answers. Okay, they get them wrong half the time, but at least they're trying."
- At lunch, when fifth-grade teacher Henry Shekhanna said that the advocates of high-stakes testing would not be satisfied until they could put teachers' names and their performance scores on the school bulletin board, Viola said he was a crazy old man.
- "The union wouldn't stand for it," she said, "and even the regents would know it would backfire. People would never want to be teachers with that hanging over their heads."
- Henry, who was two years from retirement, had to have the last word: "That'll be yours to find out."

## Life in the Community: New York City
- In 1995, big changes started happening in schools in New York City and across the state.
- By 1999, the number of tests students were required to take had increased, the tests became harder, and the stakes for failing higher.
- The changes started at the top.
- In 1995, the New York Board of Regents hired Richard P. Mills as its school superintendent, and Mayor Rudy Giuliani picked Rudy Crew as chancellor of New York City schools, the nation's largest school system, with more than one million students.
- Both Mills and Crew supported more stringent standards, more testing, and an end to "social promotion," the practice of promoting failing students from grade to grade so that they remain with their age group.
- New York became a leader in a national movement to set higher school standards and hold schools and students accountable to them through standardized tests.
- From 1993 to 1998, every state except Iowa had begun setting statewide standards.
- President Clinton wanted to create a national exam, and while states could use or ignore the federal test, it would set a national standard to allow parents, teachers and administrators to compare their schools with similar schools anywhere in the country where the national exam was adopted.

*New York education leaders Rudy Crew, left, and Richard Mills supported stringent testing standards.*

- Crew was able to convince the New York legislature to change a law to give him more power to appoint—and fire—superintendents of the system's 32 school districts—a move designed to curtail cronyism and make schools more accountable.
- He also negotiated a deal with the principals' union to end provisions providing lifetime job protection.
- But the biggest pressure on Crew was that New York City students weren't making the grade.
- They had lower test scores and higher dropout rates than students elsewhere in the state.
- And the pressure mounted.
- As Crew introduced new and tougher tests for students in the city, the state was imposing more stringent tests of its own.
- For Mills, a key piece for creating higher standards would be the New York State English Regents' Exam for seniors, who would have to hit a particular mark to graduate from high school.
- There were also new English tests for grades 4 and 8.
- "For teachers who have long been granted wide latitude in how they structured their lesson plans—especially those weaned on the flexible, child-centered approach popular since the 1960s—adapting to the new standards has required serious adjustment," *The New York Times* reported.
- The first round of the new state tests was set for Tuesday, January 12, 1999—one week after students returned from their holiday break.
- This would be a big change.
- With the old tests, fourth-graders read sentences or short passages, then filled in missing words from a list of multiple-choice answers.

- The new test, developed by a panel of 22 fourth-grade teachers, "moves from a focus on simple reading to an expectation that by the middle of fourth grade, pupils can understand and write about complex passages and about themselves, using correct spelling," *The New York Times* reported on the eve of testing.
- Mills expected the scores to be low because the standards were deliberately higher.
- Schools worked feverishly on writing exercises that fall, and offered special sessions during the holidays.
- The test's inauguration was inauspicious.
- There were complaints about late test deliveries and possible security breaches that might have given some schools an advantage.
- Also, bad weather closed dozens of schools.
- The test answers were scored by committees of teachers, after which the state released the results on May 25, 1999.
- Statewide, 48 percent of fourth-graders passed; in New York City only 33 percent passed.
- "This is an exercise in truth telling," Mills said. "Where do we go from here? We have to go up, obviously."
- An analysis by *The New York Times* showed that city students actually performed slightly better than others in the state when compared to similar groups based on poverty and homes where Spanish or another language other than English was used at home.
- Nevertheless, poor grades on the state test and city tests led Crew to send 35,000 failing students to summer school to give them another chance to pass their tests.
- The city's summer school program was strongly pushed by Mayor Giuliani, who argued that one way to improve schools was to get tough with failing students.
- But city officials flunked, too.
- The company that made the tests goofed in scoring them.
- In September 1999, the city announced that it had to revise results for citywide tests given in grades 3, 5, 6, and 7.
- The correct results showed higher scores, which meant the city had sent about 8,600 students to summer school by mistake.
- The display of incompetence in administering a student competency test was an embarrassment for Crew, even though the mistake was the vender's and was originally flagged by Crew's chief testing advisor.
- Relations between Giuliani and Crew had been worsening since April 1999, when the mayor proposed experimenting with school vouchers.
- Crew, who opposed vouchers because they diverted public money to private schools, fought the mayor's plan fiercely and defeated it.
- The testing problems and other issues made matters worse.
- On December 23, 1999, the city school board voted to end Crew's contract.

# HISTORICAL SNAPSHOT
# 1999

- The Senate trial in the impeachment of President Clinton resulted in acquittal; he had been impeached by the House of Representatives
- In one of the largest drug busts in American history, the Coast Guard intercepted a ship with over 9,500 pounds of cocaine aboard, headed for Houston, Texas
- Rapper Big L was shot to death
- White supremacist John William King was found guilty of kidnapping and killing African-American James Byrd, Jr. by dragging him behind a truck for two miles
- The Supreme Court upheld the murder convictions of Timothy McVeigh for the Oklahoma City bombing
- The Roth IRA was introduced by Senator William V. Roth, Jr., as a retirement tool
- The 71st Academy Award for Best Picture went to *Shakespeare in Love*
- A Michigan jury found Dr. Jack Kevorkian guilty of second-degree murder for administering a lethal injection to a terminally ill man
- During the year, the Dow Jones Industrial Average closed above the 10,000 and 11,000 marks for the first time
- The World Trade Organization ruled in favor of the United States in its long-running trade dispute with the European Union over bananas
- Bill Gates' personal fortune exceeded $100 billion, based on the increased value of Microsoft stock
- In the Columbine High School massacre two Littleton, Colorado teenagers opened fire on their teachers and classmates, killing 12 students and one teacher, and then themselves
- Nancy Mace became the first female cadet to graduate from the Military College of South Carolina
- *Star Wars Episode I: The Phantom Menace* was released in theaters and became the highest-grossing *Star Wars* film
- The U.S. House of Representatives released the *Cox Report*, which details the People's Republic of China's nuclear espionage against the U.S. over the prior two decades
- Texas Governor George W. Bush announced he would seek the Republican Party's nomination for president
- Lance Armstrong won his first Tour de France
- USA soccer player Brandi Chastain scored the game-winning penalty kick against China in the FIFA Women's World Cup
- Off the coast of Martha's Vineyard, a plane piloted by John F. Kennedy, Jr. crashed, killing him and his wife Carolyn Bessette Kennedy and her sister Lauren Bessette
- *Mercury-Redstone 4* raised *Liberty Bell 7* from the Atlantic Ocean floor
- The last Checker taxicab was retired in New York City and auctioned off for approximately $135,000
- Viacom and CBS merged
- The New York Yankees swept the Atlanta Braves to win their twenty-fifth World Series baseball championship

## Selected Prices

Automobile, Volvo Sedan .............................................................$26,895

Bath Towel ....................................................................................$24.00

Breadmaker ..................................................................................$129.99

Cell Phone ....................................................................................$49.99

Computer, Apple MAC Performa .................................................$2,699.00

Digital Camera .............................................................................$800.00

Man's Belt, Italian Leather ..........................................................$42.00

Palm Pilot ....................................................................................$369.00

Wine Bottle Holder ......................................................................$150.00

Woman's Purse, Kenneth Cole.....................................................$148.50

# Take the trouble out of travel. Go Greyhound.®

There are lots of reasons why Greyhound takes the trouble out of travel. Like the convenience of worry-free traveling. When you go Greyhound, you travel safely without the hassles and problems of driving yourself.

Greyhound also has convenient schedules to over 14,000 locations across the continental United States. We go to more places than anyone else. And at great low fares.

Worry-free traveling, low fares, convenient schedules and lots of destinations. They all add up to make going Greyhound no trouble at all. So call Greyhound for more information on schedules and fares.

**GO GREYHOUND**
And leave the driving to us.®

MANY DENTISTS RECOMMEND BAKING SODA. YOU'LL RECOMMEND THE TASTE.

Introducing Colgate® Baking Soda Toothpaste.
Better Tasting Than Arm & Hammer Dental Care® Original Paste Formula.

Many dentists and hygienists recommend baking soda and baking soda toothpaste for clean, white teeth. But unfortunately, the taste leaves something to be desired.

But now there's new Colgate Baking Soda Toothpaste. It's not too gritty, because it's made with extra-fine baking soda. It also has a natural mint flavor. In fact, in a recent test, people preferred the taste of Colgate Baking Soda Toothpaste over Arm & Hammer Dental Care® original paste formula. And, it has fluoride for strong, healthy teeth. So try the baking soda toothpaste with the taste people prefer. New Colgate Baking Soda Toothpaste. It's what

### "In New York, 'Whole Language' vs. 'The Test,'" Diane McWhorter, *The New York Times*, January 3, 1999:

GALLEON BEACH, Antigua—I've been getting the sweats here over making my nine-year-old daughter miss three days of school next week. (All the earlier flights back to New York were booked.) That means she'll have three fewer crucial days of cramming for the controversial new standardized test that all of New York State's public-school fourth graders must take, over three days, soon after our return.

During a recent siesta hour, Lucy attacked a sample test that she was assigned to practice over the holidays, stoically deconstructing a passage about a banana named Joey who regrets ending up in a bowl of cereal rather than a cream pie.

The Test represents an abrupt departure from the old multiple-choice format to an uncharted field of "inferencing," note-taking and essay writing. The students don't seem to be as exercised as their parents and teachers, who see The Test as yet another potentially punishing yardstick in the high-stakes meritocracy. Many in my cohort of two-career, college-educated families think their children are being treated as guinea pigs and worry that a poor test score, by disqualifying their kids from a good middle school, will start a long slide to Mudville.

But there's more at play here than New Yorkers' competitive neurosis. Many parents I know, even if their kids are in one of the "gifted" programs or other high-performance schools (that is, those with rich PTAs) are worked up because The Test will judge their children on skills that have never been a priority in school: what the Board of Education

*Continued*

### "In New York, 'Whole Language' vs. 'The Test,'" . . . *(Continued)*

calls the "conventions" of grammar, spelling, punctuation, and even that hobgoblin of little hands, penmanship.

This brusque shift in testing protocol—and the heroic last-minute lengths to which teachers are going to accommodate it—suggests to me that The Test may be a stealth referendum on the "whole language" method that has been used to teach this generation of children to read and write. With its snubbing of phonics in favor of let-it-all-hang-out written expression through "invented spelling," whole language has long been a battleground in the larger culture war between the forces of tradition on the right and the proponents of fuzzywuzzy 60s-style self-actualization on the left.

But The Test has confused the ideological battle lines. Some of my fellow baby-boom parents, creatures of the 1960s (and victims of "See Spot run") for whom progressive education seemed invented, are not so sure which side of this particular conflict they're on. Our children's rampant run-on sentences and abuse of the apostrophe have made us nostalgic for the days of separate grades for form and content—indeed, for having grades at all—and make us question whether "conventions" can be converted into habit if they are introduced late in the process.

Yet perhaps the most alarming thing about The Test is that it seems to slight the real strength of our children's reformed education. Students who have been taught that writing is an evolutionary process of constant revision—Lucy's classroom "writing workshop" puts a piece through at least seven stages before it is "published"—are now expected to produce camera-ready essays to the ticking of a stopwatch.

Children who have been encouraged to reach beyond their grasp—to improvise the fancy words they did not know how to spell—are being directed toward a "conventional" middle. Lucy was told that if she wasn't sure how to spell the word "select," she should use "pick" or "choose" instead.

I haven't exactly found the practice tests a snap myself. I had trouble keeping all the characters straight in one story, a legend about how orchids came to grow on trees. (Every name seemed to begin with M and end with I.) And Lucy misread the key word as "orchard." It turned out she didn't know what an orchid was, having never received a corsage.

Still, she isn't staying up nights worrying about The Test. She did have trouble getting to sleep the first night we were here, but that was because she was upset about the poor people we saw while taxiing in from the airport.

# 2000–2012

History will record that the new century began in the United States on September 11, 2001, when four American commercial airliners were hijacked and used as weapons of terror. After the tragedies at the World Trade Center in New York, Shanksville, Pennsylvania, and the Pentagon in Washington, DC, Americans felt vulnerable to a foreign invasion for the first time in decades. America's response to the attacks was to dispatch U.S. forces around the world in a "War on Terror." The first stop was Afghanistan, where the terrorist group al-Qaeda had formed. However, finding leader Osama bin Laden and stabilizing a new government proved vexing; the United States shifted focus from Afghanistan to Iraq. Despite vocal opposition from traditional allies such as Germany and France, President George W. Bush launched Operation Iraqi Freedom with the goal of eliminating the regime of Saddam Hussein and his cache of "weapons of mass destruction." The invasion resulted in worldwide protests. The U.S. achieved a rapid military victory, but struggled to secure the peace. When no weapons of mass destruction were found, soldiers continued fighting while an internal, religious civil war erupted and U.S. support for the war waned. By 2012, most American troops were out of Iraq, a timetable for leaving Afghanistan had been established, and Osama bin Laden had been found and killed.

The opening years of the new century produced considerable angst concerning the state of American education. While continuously repeating the mantra that innovation would invigorate the U.S. economy, educators discovered that schoolchildren in dozens of countries were outperforming America's youth. To achieve a course correction, the George W. Bush Administration introduced "No Child Left Behind" to bring measurable accountability to the schools. The result was extensive testing and the measurement of students and teachers. Subsequently, college professors complained that the students who arrived on campus were chock-full of facts, but had little background in problem solving or analytical thinking. This result— once again—ignited a debate concerning the purpose of education.

Despite the cost of two wars, the falling value of the dollar, and record high oil prices, the American economy began to recover by

2004. Unemployment declined, new home purchases continued to surge, and the full potential of previous computer innovation and investment impacted businesses large and small. Men and women of all ages began to buy and sell their products on the Internet. eBay created the world's largest yard sale; Amazon demonstrated that it could be the bookstore to the world; and we all learned to Google. Globalization took on new meaning and political importance as jobs, thanks to computerization, moved to India, China or the Philippines, where college graduates provided cheap and eager workers. American manufacturing companies that once were the centerpiece of their community's economy closed their U.S. factories to become distributors of furniture made in China or lawn mowers made in Mexico. The resulting structural change that pitted global profits and innovation against aging textile workers unable to support their families resulted in a renewed emphasis in America on education and innovation.

After eight years of the George W. Bush Administration, America's economy was in recession—the victim of its own excesses: too much consumer borrowing, extensive speculation in the housing market, and widespread use of "exotic" financial instruments that failed to reduce risk. In the wake of the economic crash, some of the most respected firms on Wall Street disappeared through mergers or collapse, unemployment topped 10 percent, and consumer confidence plummeted. When newly elected President Barack Obama took office in 2009, America's banking system was on the verge of collapse, the automobile industry in desperate need of a governmental bailout, and economists predicted that a major depression was just around the corner. The administration pumped trillions into the system to prevent its collapse, saving millions of jobs, especially in the automotive industry, stabilizing the housing industry, and championing new initiatives in green energy. President Obama made universal healthcare a key element of his first year in office, igniting controversy and exposing the deep divisions existing in the U.S.

Sports became a 24/7 obsession for many. With the dramatic expansion of the Internet, cell phones, the addition of new cable channels and a plethora of new sporting events, America was addicted to sports, including those tinged with danger.

Professional women began to find bigger opportunities in the 2000s. Significantly, the promotion of a woman to a top slot in a Fortune 500 company ceased to make headlines. Yet surveys done at mid-decade showed that more Americans were working longer hours than ever before to satisfy the increasing demands of the marketplace and their own desire for more material goods. In some urban markets, the average home price passed $400,000, average credit card debt continued to rise, and the price of an average new car, with typical extras, passed $20,000.

No industry was rocked more by the Internet than the music industry. The online music decade started with Napster, a free music file-sharing service that eventually morphed into Apple's iTunes, which offered songs for $0.99. MySpace and Facebook became popular hangouts for local bands, especially indie rockers. Bloggers pushed their way to the forefront with the unsanctioned message: the music industry heads were no longer in control of the manufacturing or distribution of music. Nearly 20 years after record stores dumped their records and replaced them with the bright, shiny compact discs, the CD itself was replaced by digital music. Fans could virtually make their own albums. The TV show *American Idol* turned the nation into talent scouts and music judges producing pop culture phenomenon Kelly Clarkson, country heavyweight Carrie Underwood, rocker Chris Daughtry, and fan favorite Clay Aiken. The decade was extraordinarily rough on soap operas. *As the World Turns* and *The Guiding Light* both ended half-century runs as the number of entertainment devices, cable channels, and DVRs exploded.

# 2010 PROFILE

Annie Rosewood left a good job for full-time parenting, and began home-schooling her children when her oldest turned four.

## Life at Home

- Annie Rosewood was born August 23, 1964, in Wilmington, Delaware.
- Her mother suffered from manic depression and divorced soon after Annie was born.
- She couldn't keep a job, had three more children from another failed marriage, and moved the family from apartment to apartment.
- When Annie was five years old, she started watching a new television show called *The Brady Bunch*, which portrayed an upper-middle-class family comprising a mother with three daughters and a father with three sons.
- It was the first time Annie had seen a blended family on television, though their problems were far tamer than those in Annie's family.
- "That's what I want," she recalled thinking. "I want to have money, a car, nice things. The path I was on wouldn't bring me nice things."
- Her own family moved every year until Annie was in the sixth grade.
- In 1974, her mother married Frank Youngblood, who then owned a bakery.
- "He was a terrible businessman, but a good stepdad," Annie said.
- They moved into his home in a white, working-class neighborhood, and stayed there.
- On her first day of class, a boy came up to her and said, "Hey, Annie! I'm Jeff. Remember me?"

*Annie Rosewood's hard work in school laid the ground work to home schooling her children.*

- She looked at him blankly, and saw on Jeff's face a look of hurt, which surprised her.
- When she later thought about it, she realized that she had never really bothered to remember people because faces flowed so quickly through her life—and until that moment, she hadn't realized that this wasn't normal.
- Annie worked from the time she was 10 years old.
- Her first job was as a babysitter, which usually allowed her to do her homework.
- Annie knew she would have to work hard to have a nice life, but for now, the most important thing was to keep her grades up.
- She had gone to public schools all her life, and often spent 45 minutes on the bus to school.
- The public high school she entered in the fall of 1978 was in disrepair; the toilets often clogged up and sometimes there was a roof leak.
- "But the teachers had a lot of heart, and that helped," Annie recalled.
- She didn't get much support in her school years.
- Her mother wouldn't take her to after-school activities, and her stepfather was too busy running his businesses.
- Annie became a cheerleader in high school, but had to beg rides from friends to get home.
- While her friends' parents were always in the stands during games, hers never were; "It was so depressing," Annie said. "They didn't care."
- Needing to work anyway, she quit cheerleading after only a few months.
- When her stepfather's bakery went bankrupt, he bought a pizza parlor in town, where Annie waited tables and ran the cash register.
- Sometimes she worked in the kitchen, but usually only men worked "behind the counter."
- She was very social, too, often riding around in cars with friends until 11 p.m. or later.
- She continued to make A's and B's, and was kept on a college preparatory track in high school.
- One of her favorite teachers was John Johnson, who taught biology.
- While they chatted after class one day, he asked her what she wanted to do after high school.
- "I don't know," she replied.
- She liked science, and knew she wanted to go to college, but didn't know what she wanted to study.
- John showed her a brochure about a new program that was designed to train nurses in radiation therapy at the local junior college, and that classes would run continuously for 27 months until graduation.
- Annie contacted the school, set up an interview, and filled out her application.
- She was one of six students admitted to the program.
- "They took pride in the fact that they had a high dropout rate," Annie said.
- Even so, she was one of three in her class to graduate in 1985, despite delivering pizzas for her stepfather's business in the evenings.
- She could have gone on and earned a bachelor's degree, but decided to go to work.
- "I was so desperate to get my life started, become independent, and live my life on my own," she said.
- The timing was excellent; hospitals were seeking nurses, especially those in specialties like radiology.
- She wanted to go to California, but her younger siblings needed her at home and the family needed some of her income, so she went to work at a local hospital.
- Two years later, she and a friend obtained jobs at a hospital in San Diego.
- They delayed their starting time by four months so they could drive across the country, stay in youth hostels, or camp at national parks along the way.
- They arrived in California in 1989.
- Annie met Sam Jones in early 1990, and a few years later they were married.
- Sam had been in the Navy and was inspired by Annie's job to enlist in the Army in 1994 to train as an X-ray technician.

- After his two-year stint ended, he joined the Army Reserve.
- When Annie became pregnant with their first child, they decided to move to Salem, Oregon, where a couple they knew had moved.
- Sam got a job at a local hospital, and Annie left paychecks and regular employment to be a stay-at-home mom for their new baby, Amanda.
- Their son, Lowell, was born in 1998, and Caleb arrived in 2000.
- Annie's plan had been to be a stay-at-home mom while the children were young, but as Amanda neared preschool age, Annie began talking with some of the home-schooling parents at the playground.
- Besides wanting to be an active parent, she knew a normal school schedule would make it difficult for Sam to spend much time with the children.
- His deployments with the Army Reserve had become longer, more frequent, and more unpredictable; by home-schooling, she and Sam could make their own schedule.
- Annie started home-schooling four-year-old Amanda, and followed suit with her other children.
- Under the standardized tests required in Oregon, her children performed well.
- When friends asked her how long she would continue home-schooling, she joked that her commitment was as deep as it was to natural childbirth: "We'll do it as long as it's comfortable and good for everybody. When it's not, we'll explore other options."
- Caleb had announced: "Mom, I'd like to go to public school for high school."
- That would be fine, she told him, but reminded him of his habit of hanging upside-down over a couch to read.

## Life at Work

- Annie didn't start out planning to home-school her children, but by 2010 she had become a nine-year veteran teacher of her three children: Amanda, 13, Lowell, 12, and Caleb, 10.
- At 7:30 a.m., the kids stumbled out of bed and were expected to finish breakfast by 8 a.m.
- The kitchen, dining area, and den were part of one large room.
- The dining table was by sliding glass doors that overlooked their backyard, and a computer was on a small table by the wall.
- On the floor under the TV were three plastic crates filled with books, markers, pens, scissors and folders; a blue parakeet occasionally flitted across the room.
- After breakfast, Caleb would walk into the den toward his crate, pull out a well-worn spelling notebook, and settle into the recliner.
- Amanda would retreat to her bedroom.
- Lowell and his mother would sit on the couch to go over some math lessons.
- Social studies often involved maps and projects, such as building a fort out of craft sticks.
- After five or eight lessons there would be a quiz.
- When they would break at noon, Annie might suggest they watch something during lunch related to weather.

*Successful home schooling took planning and discipline.*

*The children enjoyed educational trips throughout the year.*

- Lunch ended around 1 p.m. and the school day was usually over by 3 p.m.
- Amid the routine, there were games like Scrabble, chess, and a trivia game designed around the curriculum.
- Science lessons were often the byproduct of discoveries made on excursions.
- Physical education often included trips to a pool, a tennis court or a park; they also played team soccer.
- Music education took the form of instrument lessons; all the children took violin, and Lowell was also taking guitar and considering the mandolin.
- They took art lessons at a museum in town.
- History was studied together.
- And then, there was the public library.
- Annie scheduled trips every Tuesday and tried to avoid overdue fines.
- "We usually had about 60 books out at a time," she explained.
- Annie didn't indoctrinate her children with any particular religion, but she did teach morality.
- One important aspect of home-schooling for Annie was to allow her children to become more aware of politics and the affairs of the world.
- They listened to National Public Radio and watched public television news, and then discussed what they had heard or seen.
- "I want my kids to have their eyes wide open," Annie remarked.

## The Demographics of Home-Schooling
- Home-schooled students are still a small minority, but their numbers have grown rapidly since the 1990s.
- Being taught at home was most common among white, middle-income households with two parents.
- In 2010, about two million school-age children were being home-schooled, or about 4 percent of the K-12 population.
- More than 90 percent of the families were two-parent, one-salary homes, and the mother continued to be the most likely parent to stay home, according to the National Home Education Research Institute in Salem, Oregon.

- Joseph Murphy, associate dean at the Peabody College of Education of Vanderbilt University, said the advocacy group's estimate of home-schoolers might not be precise, but the number is huge compared with 1970, when only 10,000 to 15,000 children were home-schooled.
- As in previous surveys, most home-schooling parents in 2010 were conservative religious parents, predominately Protestants, but more moderate and liberal families have chosen to teach at home, Murphy told *Education Week*.
- Religious concerns were once the top reason for home-schooling, but by 2010 those concerns (30 percent) had been slightly outnumbered by those who cited the social environment of schools—from bullying to teaching practices (31 percent), Murphy said.
- Another change was the increasing variety of ways parents home-schooled, including home-school co-ops, online courses, and even taking some courses from public schools, according to *Education Week*.
- Since compulsory education laws were first passed in the early 1800s, "home school was home school, and school was school," Mr. Murphy said. "Now … it's this rich portfolio of options for kids."
- About half of state legislatures now require school districts to allow home-schooled students to enroll part-time if they want to, allowing these hybrid approaches to become "very, very typical, particularly at the middle and high school level," said Yvonne Bunn, director of home-school support for the Richmond-based Home Educators Association of Virginia.
- "It used to be it was very difficult to get materials; now we have people all over the place who want to sell to home-schoolers because they are such a good market," Bunn told *Education Week*.
- In 2007, the U.S. Department of Education found that 1.7 percent of children ages five to 17 (1.5 million) were being schooled at home, up from about 850,000 in 1999.
- By 2007, nearly 3 percent of school-age children were being taught in the home.
- "Parents give many different reasons for home-schooling their children," according to a 2009 report by the Department of Education's National Center for Education Statistics.
- "In 2007, the most common reason parents gave as the most important was a desire to provide religious or moral instruction (36 percent of students). This reason was followed by a concern about the school environment (such as safety, drugs, or negative peer pressure) (21 percent), dissatisfaction with academic instruction (17 percent), and 'other reasons,' including family time, finances, travel, and distance (14 percent).
- "Parents of about 7 percent of home-schooled students cited the desire to provide their child with a nontraditional approach to education as the most important reason for home-schooling, and the parents of another 6 percent of students cited a child's health problems or special needs," according to the report.
- The report found that white children were nearly five times more likely to be home-schooled than African-Americans.
- The home-schooling rate was 3.9 percent for whites, compared with 0.8 percent for blacks.
- About 60 percent of home-schooled students lived in households with three or more children.
- About 42 percent of regular school students had that many siblings.
- Among home-schoolers, 54 percent had one parent in the workforce and one at home.
- Among in-school students, only 20 percent had two parents with one at home.
- By income groups, the home-schooling rate was highest among students living in households with yearly incomes of $50,001 to $75,000 (3.9 percent), followed by those in the $25,001-to-$50,000 bracket (3.4 percent).
- The home-schooling rate was lower than the national 2.9 percent average for students in households with yearly incomes under $25,000 (2.1 percent) or more than $75,000 (2.7 percent).

# HISTORICAL SNAPSHOT
# 2010

- The sculpture *L'Homme qui marche I* by Alberto Giacometti sold in London for $103.7 million, setting a new world record for a work of art sold at auction

- The Deepwater Horizon oil platform exploded in the Gulf of Mexico, killing 11 workers and resulting in one of the largest spills in history

- *Nude, Green Leaves and Bust* by Pablo Picasso sold in New York for $106.5 million, setting another new world record for a work of art sold at auction

- Scientists conducting the Neanderthal genome project announced that they had sequenced enough of the Neanderthal genome to suggest that Neanderthals and humans may have interbred

- Scientists announced that they had created a functional synthetic genome

- The first 24-hour flight by a solar-powered plane was completed by the Solar Impulse Project

- WikiLeaks, an online publisher of anonymous, covert, and classified material, leaked to the public over 90,000 internal reports about the United States-led involvement in the War in Afghanistan from 2004 to 2010

- The International Space Station surpassed the record for the longest continuous human occupation of space, having been inhabited since November 2, 2000

- President Barack Obama signed into law a landmark financial regulatory reform bill, touted as one of the greatest overhauls of the financial system since the Great Depression

- *Time* magazine named the protester as its Person of the Year to underscore the impact protesters had on dictators and world affairs

- The airline industry continued its process of consolidation when United and Continental announced a $3.2 billion hookup to create the world's largest airline

- The fast-food business got a whopper deal when the Brazilian private equity firm 3G paid $3.3 billion to acquire Burger King

- Researchers at CERN trapped anti-hydrogen atoms for a sixth of a second, marking the first time in history that humans have trapped antimatter

- WikiLeaks released a collection of more than 250,000 American diplomatic cables, including 100,000 marked "secret" or "confidential"

- Scientists announced that antiretroviral drugs have turned the AIDS epidemic around by thwarting the virus in HIV-positive patients and serving as a weapon against infection in healthy individuals

## Selected Prices

Bathroom Scale, Digital..................................................................$49.99

BlackBerry Phone ........................................................................$649.99

Bluetooth Headset.........................................................................$99.99

Computer, Toshiba Laptop............................................................$499.99

GPS Navigator, Garmin ...............................................................$219.99

La-Z-Boy Recliner .......................................................................$499.99

Pampers, 176 Count .....................................................................$48.99

Refrigerator/Freezer, Whirlpool...................................................$471.72

Sole F80 Treadmill.......................................................................$1,999.99

Vacuum, Hoover WindTunnel.......................................................$129.99

## "'Hybrid' Home Schools Gaining Traction,"
## *Education Week*, Published Online August 7, 2012:

Emmy Elkin's school day starts with a cooking show.

The 10-year-old and her mom, Jill Elkin of Peachtree City, Ga., are up at 8 a.m., making breakfast along with "Iron Chef America" and chatting about algebra. Last week, Emmy left home after breakfast to meet a new Japanese tutor, around the time her sister Kayla, 14, dragged herself awake to get her independent mathematics study done before a friend came over for a joint British literature course. The sisters spent the afternoon working through a chemistry course online, with Jill Elkin giving more individual coaching to her younger daughter.

Kayla and Emmy are part of the modern generation of home-schooled students, piecing together their education from their mother, a former Fayette County math teacher, other district and university teachers, parent co-ops, and online providers.

Education policymakers and researchers have largely ignored the tremendous growth in home-schooling, particularly among these sorts of "hybrid" home-schoolers willing to blur the pedagogical and legal lines of public and private education, said Joseph Murphy, an associate dean at Peabody College of Education at Vanderbilt University and the author of *Home Schooling in America: Capturing and Assessing the Movement*. The book, an analysis of research on the topic, is being published this month by Corwin of Thousand Oaks, California.

"Historically, home school was home school, and school was school," Mr. Murphy said. "Now ... it's this rich portfolio of options for kids."

Baywood Learning Center in Oakland, California, a private school for gifted students, has offered hybrid home-schooling programs for the past three years. The school has á la carte classes on individual subjects once a week, as well as a multi-age class that meets on Tuesdays and Thursdays to cover core academics. Director Grace Neufeld said demand for the latter has grown 50 percent in the last year, to about 40 students ages four to 17.

"Parents usually design a patchwork quilt of different classes and activities for their children," she said. "What I see is they sign up for various classes being held in various locations like science centers or museums or different places. They also add things like music lessons, art lessons, sports, or martial arts."

*Continued*

## "'Hybrid' Home Schools Gaining Traction," . . . (Continued)

Similarly, more home-schooling parents are developing formal co-ops, like the Inman Hybrid Home School Program in Inman, Georgia. Founder Holly Longino, a former health teacher at Carver Middle School in Inman, left public teaching to home-school her four children, but last year started the group classes a few times a week with five students and a handful of retired public school teachers. The teachers provide video lectures for students to use as well as in-class projects. Ms. Longino said some parents also take their children to courses at the local college and science museum, but would never consider forming a charter school.

"There's a lot of freedom in home-schooling," she said. "I don't ever want to be a school, because I don't want to lose the parental control we have."

## "The Unfinished Business of Mission," *Virginia Seminary Journal*, Spring 2009:

In 1969, the year that Rich Jones entered *Virginia Theological Seminary (VTS)*, interest in overseas mission was at a low ebb in the national Church and at the Seminary. The focus of the Episcopal Church was on the turmoil in the inner cities, and funding for the overseas work of the Church was greatly reduced.

By that time, the course at VTS in World Mission, once a requirement of all students, had not been taught for several years. Nevertheless, a small but dedicated band continued to uphold and promote the historical vision of the Seminary represented by the words above the chapel altar, "Go Ye Into All the World and Preach the Gospel." Their focus was on two areas of concern:

Virginia graduates had gone overseas in the past; now, descendents of their converts were coming back to Virginia for education. But little was being done formally to help them adjust to life in a strange culture. In the early '70s, special orientation and an International Students' Forum were instituted to help them with the ongoing challenges of life in a foreign land, and to foster theological reflection on how they would take what they had learned in this culture and translate it into the terms of their own home culture when they went back.

The need was also felt to find ways for American students to experience life in the Church outside their own boundaries. This gave birth to a Committee on International Programs, which began organizing internships for seminarians to find out firsthand what it meant to be a Christian and an Anglican in another land.

Meanwhile, concern about the neglect of world mission and the need to find a new formulation for the theology of mission was troubling many minds. An exploratory meeting was held at Berkeley Divinity School at Yale, followed by the formation of a Seminarians' Consultation on Mission, an organization in which *Virginia Theological Seminary* representatives played an active role in the coming years.

*Continued*

## "The Unfinished Business of Mission," ... *(Continued)*

At VTS, consciousness was growing that there was a need for a full-time faculty member to embody these concerns. Someone was needed to not only teach courses in the history and theology of mission, but also oversee the various organizations, programs, and activities related to that discipline—the Seminary's Missionary Society, the programs with international students, the internships for American students overseas, and the Seminary's participation in councils of the national Church concerned with the mission of the Church. Furthermore, in an ecumenical age in which dialogue between Christianity and other world religions was a growing concern, it was felt that the person who occupied such a faculty position should have expertise in at least one other world religion, and be prepared to teach courses introducing VTS students to that religion and to principles involved in interfaith dialogue.

Rich Jones was the ideal candidate for such a position. Prior to seminary, he'd worked in Vietnam teaching English as a second language. After graduation in 1972, he and his wife Jody went to Ecuador to organize and administer the theological education programs for that diocese. Back in the United States, after a period of parish ministry in the diocese in the Central Gulf Coast, Rich and his family went off to Toronto, where he enrolled in a program of doctoral studies. His Ph.D. completed, he and Jodi and their children, Kate and Sam, returned to Virginia and Rich became the Seminary's first Professor of Mission and World Religion.

# 2011 PROFILE

Marie Schnall was up to her eyeballs in excited, giggling teens in one of South Africa's slums on the day she decided the next direction in her life: Teach for America.

## Life at Home

- For almost a year, Marie Schnall had been taking the early morning bus from Cape Town to the Kyliechi Township, where she spent the entire day tutoring a gaggle of energized black students as they prepared for the final matriculation test.

- Those who did well would have opportunities; those who did poorly would sink back into the great mass of workers whose entire future would be stunted by the single test they took at 17 or 18 years old.

- For Marie, the opportunity to give these soon-to-be adults hope for going to college and succeeding in their integrated world was exhilarating.

- Under the terms of her contract, she only worked with children who wanted to work with her; hers was a voluntary class and every day it was overflowing with future scholars drinking up the knowledge they needed to pass the test.

- The needs of the students was so great, she knew she could live in Cape Town for a lifetime and still be meeting embedded, intractable challenges.

*Marie Schnall tutored young children in South Africa.*

- The townships were created during the Apartheid era when black South Africans were forcibly evicted from properties that were in areas designated as "white only" and physically moved into segregated townships.
- Separate townships were established for each of the three designated non-white racial groups: blacks, coloreds, and Indians.
- Once Marie's year was up, the South African government had made it clear it was not interested in extending her visa one more year.

*Marie's tests were hard.*

- As the government saw it, jobs should be reserved for South Africans, not recent imports from Jacksonville, Florida.
- Nevertheless, Marie was beginning to realize the truth of what her friends had always told her: "You're born a teacher."
- Why couldn't she continue this rewarding work in America? she asked herself.
- With her theater background, a college degree, two years of working with children, plus her South African experience, surely someone would want her skills.
- Marie was born in 1984, the third of seven children.
- When the family went anywhere, her father always counted heads twice to make sure no one was left behind; Marie loved to hide during the second count to make her father laugh.
- She was the fireball of the family—a hot-tempered, energetic child who always made her presence known.
- When her parents announced that there was no money for summer camp one year, Marie organized a lemonade fair in her backyard complete with rides, contests of skill, and face painting.
- In one afternoon she made almost enough to afford a week at Camp Kanuga in the North Carolina mountains, and captured the attention of a local entrepreneur who recognized talent when he saw it.
- By the time she was 14, Marie was running a small company he helped create, giving parties and organizing children's events for the parents of Jacksonville, Florida, who were too stressed and too busy to know exactly what their children wanted for their birthday.
- At 16, she was using her creative skills to build scenery a for community theater near her home, where she learned how to handle a radial arm saw, work with others, and know when a design idea was practical and when it was totally outlandish.
- That knowledge did not prevent her from trying the outlandish, but at least she knew when she was near the tipping point of craziness.
- When she graduated from high school, she was attracted to her local college for its theater, innovation, and focus on students.
- Her friendships in the theater had already taught her to avoid colleges that emphasized their research abilities, and where the professors only taught classes because they were required to do so.

- During college, she continued to build scenery, perform when an acting role excited her, and run—with the help of a half-dozen teenage assistants—the birthday party business.
- It wasn't until her senior year that she took time out to think about "the future."
- She was in mid-ponder when she was approached about selling her kids party company—its logo, playbook, and customer list.
- The offer was modest, but more than enough to get her to Germany, Indonesia, and South Africa.
- Each location gave her a taste of the joy ahead.
- Upon returning to the United States after three months, she discovered that her boyfriend had been wandering somewhat wildly among the fairest flowers in the Southland.
- The parting was both swift and loud, largely disappearing from her memory when she met Alex at her next job—a year-round wilderness program for boys who needed a course correction in their lives before they ended up in prison.

*South Africa has a diverse population.*

- The camp's program was harsh, humbling, and largely beneficial.
- In Alex she found a fellow adventure junkie and a man willing to go to South Africa with her, where thousands of black children one generation out of apartheid desperately needed a boost up if they were ever going to catch up.
- The return to Africa was mesmerizing for its beauty and its potential; the paperwork and red tape were equally spectacular and confounding.
- Days could be lost at the passport counter where hundreds lined up every morning before daylight for a chance to stay, leave, or simply travel.
- At the end of the year, she knew that leaving South Africa would feel right only if she had an equally fulfilling goal, such as Teach for America.

## Life at Work

- Marie Schnall believed that she and the 21-year-old Teach for America were a good match.
- Its stated goal was to turn American education on its head.
- Founder Wendy Kopp believed that "only a dramatic restructuring of the American education system will solve the problems in our schools. That restructuring will not come from an infusion of public dollars, but from an infusion of the creativity and energy of human capital. Recruiting highly qualified teachers who are motivated to make a difference is a first priority in improving schooling."
- Kopp was in her senior year at Princeton, totally uninspired by the job hunt, and desperately searching for a senior thesis topic when she came upon the idea for Teach for America.

- Why not make teaching a possibility for all college graduates, not just education majors?
- Kopp decided there had to be a way to allow college students to keep their options open while committing themselves to teach for, say, two years.
- At some point, she became obsessed with the idea of a teacher corps, and it became the focus of her senior thesis.
- Using seed money from a corporation, she was able to assemble what she called a "dynamic, dedicated group of recent graduates," and in a few months they created Teach for America.
- The first Teach for America Corps was composed of 500 carefully selected graduates who then participated in an eight-week institute that introduced them to the theoretical understanding and basic teaching techniques.
- What they learned was that "teaching is the toughest, most challenging, frustrating, stressful, and rewarding experience" they had ever had.
- To be accepted by Teach for America, applicants had to survive a lengthy process, with literally thousands of applicants cut at each step.

*Wendy Kopp founded Teach for America.*

- Marie figured that if she could handle the bureaucracy of South Africa and the bribe-seeking border guards in Zimbabwe, she could handle anything.
- That included an online application; a phone interview; presentation of a lesson plan; a personal interview; a written test; and a monitored group discussion with several other applicants.
- Marie scored well at each stage, even when her fellow applicants grew very aggressive during the group discussion.
- After two decades of battling the achievement gap, Teach for America had become a major enterprise with a $185 million operating budget, two-thirds of which came from private donations.
- According to newspaper reports, Harvard graduates, Fulbright Scholars, and University of Virginia Law School students had all felt the sting of Teach for America rejection.
- In 2010, Teach for America selected 4,500 of America's top college graduates to work at high-poverty public schools and earn $45,000 per year.
- They were selected from a pool of 46,359 applicants.
- That same year, Teach for America hired more seniors at numerous colleges—including Yale, Dartmouth, Duke, Georgetown, and the University of North Carolina at Chapel Hill—than did any other employer.

*Teach for America selected 4,500 college graduates from over 46,000 applicants in 2010.*

- At Harvard, 293 seniors, or 18 percent of the class, applied, compared with 100 seniors in 2007.
- In two decades, Teach for America had become an elite brand.
- But not without its critics—mostly based on the turnover; by the fourth year, one study said, 85 percent of the Teach for America teachers were gone; "These people could be superstars, but most leave before they master the teaching craft," one education expert said.
- Marie was older than many of the applicants, but her time had been used wisely—even impressively—so she had very high expectations as she participated in the final interview.
- Teaching the underserved was something she was called to do—her commitment was clear and her anticipation high.
- Marie was blindsided by the rejection message from Teach for America.
- Was it her age? The types of experiences she had? Did she do poorly in the interview? Too aggressive? Not assertive enough?
- Upon reflection, Marie decided that only one path lay ahead.
- She would simply have to take on the task of transforming the educational process on her own—one kid at a time.

## Life in the Community: Jacksonville, Florida

- Jacksonville was the largest city in Florida in terms of both population and land area; thanks to an aggressive incorporation program in the 1960s, the Greater Jacksonville Metropolitan Area had a population of 1,345,596 in 2010.
- Located on the banks of the St. Johns River, about 25 miles south of the Georgia, the area was originally inhabited by the Timucua people.
- European explorers first arrived in the area in 1562, when French Huguenot explorer Jean Ribault charted the St. Johns River.
- Two years later, René Goulaine de Laudonnière established the first European settlement, Fort Caroline, on the St. Johns.
- On September 20, 1565, a force from the nearby Spanish settlement of St. Augustine attacked Fort Caroline, and killed nearly all the French soldiers; the Spanish renamed the fort San Mateo.
- Spain ceded Florida to the British in 1763, after the French and Indian War.

*Jacksonville, Florida*

Source: LOC # LC-DIG-highsm-12203

- Under British rule, the settlement grew at the narrow point in the river where cattle crossed.
- Britain ceded control of the territory back to Spain in 1783, after its defeat in the American Revolutionary War, and Spain ceded the Florida Territory to the United States in 1821.
- A platted town was established there in 1822.
- The city was named after Andrew Jackson, the first military governor of the Florida Territory and seventh U.S. president.
- During Reconstruction and the Gilded Age, Jacksonville and nearby St. Augustine became popular winter resorts for the wealthy.
- Visitors arrived by steamboat and later by railroad.
- After a devastating fire destroyed most of the city in 1901, more than 13,000 buildings were constructed by 1912.
- In the 1910s, New York-based filmmakers were attracted to Jacksonville's warm climate, exotic locations and excellent rail access; over the course of the decade, more than 30 silent film studios were established, earning Jacksonville the title of "Winter Film Capital of the World."
- The city's deepwater port attracted two U.S. Navy bases and the Port of Jacksonville, Florida's third-largest seaport.
- But the economic heartbeat of Jacksonville was banking, insurance, healthcare, and logistics, including the corporate headquarters of several Fortune 500 firms.
- As with much of Florida, tourism was also important to the Jacksonville area, particularly tourism related to golf and the multicultural history of the area.
- On Black Hammock Island in the National Timucuan Ecological and Historic Preserve, a University of North Florida team discovered some of the oldest remnants of pottery in the country, dating to 2500 BC.
- Political corruption, white flight and urban sprawl all had a negative impact from the 1950s through the 1970s; in 1964, all 15 of the county's public high schools lost their accreditation.
- This added momentum to proposals for government reform.
- By the 1980s, Jacksonville had earned a reputation as a business town where things got done.
- By the 2000s, cities across America were looking to Jacksonville to discover its secret to growth and economic progress.

*Remnants of the Timucuan people were discovered in Jacksonville.*

Source: LOC # LC-DIG-ppmsca-02937

# Historical Snapshot
# 2011

- Former Republican House Majority Leader Tom DeLay was sentenced to three years in prison for money laundering
- A landmark study uncovered a new technique rendering T cells resistant to HIV
- The Super Bowl between the Green Bay Packers and the Pittsburgh Steelers attracted 111 million television viewers; the Packers defeated the Steelers 31-25
- AOL purchased online publisher The Huffington Post in a $315 million deal
- The quiz show *Jeopardy!* aired the victory of IBM's artificial intelligence program, Watson, over two of the show's most successful contestants
- The Wood Brothers Racing Team entrant Trevor Bayne became the youngest winner of the 2011 Daytona 500
- The Space Shuttle *Discovery* was launched from Kennedy Space Center for the final time, carrying the Permanent Multipurpose Module to the International Space Station
- *The King's Speech* won four Oscars including the Academy Award for Best Picture
- America's last surviving World War I veteran—and one of only three verified surviving veterans of the war worldwide—died at the age of 110; Buckles, who lived in West Virginia, served in Europe as an ambulance driver for 11 months until the war's end in November 1918
- The Supreme Court ruled that the controversial protests of the Westboro Baptist Church at fallen military members' funerals were a form of protected speech under the First Amendment
- The world's largest bond fund, PIMCO, dumped its U.S. government-related securities, including Treasury and agency debt
- NASA's *MESSENGER* spacecraft became the first manmade technology to establish an orbit around Mercury
- AT&T announced plans to buy T-Mobile for $39 billion
- Archaeologists found new artifacts in an archaeological site in Texas that indicated human existence in America 15,500 years ago—around 2,000 years earlier than the alleged Clovis culture
- More than 1.5 million websites around the world were infected by the LizaMoon SQL attack spread by scareware
- The 2011 Masters Tournament was won by South African Charl Schwartzel by two strokes over Adam Scott and Jason Day
- Standard & Poor's downgraded its outlook on long-term sovereign debt of the U.S. to negative from stable for the first time in history, citing "very large budget deficits and rising government indebtedness"
- President Barack Obama announced that Osama bin Laden, the founder and leader of the militant Islamist group Al-Qaeda and the most-wanted fugitive on the U.S. list, was killed during an American military operation in Pakistan
- The Supreme Court decided that inventors do not give up their patent rights to their employers if that employer received federal funding; the ruling went against Stanford University in a dispute over a Roche HIV *polymerase chain reaction* (PCR) detection test
- The Supreme Court struck down a California law enacted in 2005 that banned the sale of certain violent video games to children without parental supervision, ruling that video games were protected under the First Amendment

## Selected Prices

Backup Hard Drive ........................................................................$44.71

Book, Paperback ..........................................................................$10.20

Business Cards, 250 Count ..........................................................$19.99

Coffeemaker, Krups .....................................................................$90.00

Combination Router/Modem ......................................................$160.00

Phone Service, Land Line, Monthly .............................................$70.00

Printer Ink, Three-Pack ...............................................................$71.00

Surfboard.....................................................................................$735.00

Toaster, Krups .............................................................................$90.96

Trimline Corded Telephone .........................................................$14.72

## "Class Matters. Why Won't We Admit It?" Helen F. Ladd and Edward B. Fiske, *The New York Times*, December 11, 2011:

Durham, N.C.—

No one seriously disputes the fact that students from disadvantaged households perform less well in school, on average, than their peers from more advantaged backgrounds. But rather than confront this fact of life head on, our policy makers mistakenly continue to reason that, since they cannot change the backgrounds of students, they should focus on things they can control.

No Child Left Behind, President George W. Bush's signature education law, did this by setting unrealistically high—and ultimately self-defeating—expectations for all schools. President Obama's policies have concentrated on trying to make schools more "efficient" through means like judging teachers by their students' test scores or encouraging competition by promoting the creation of charter schools. The proverbial story of the drunk looking for his keys under the lamppost comes to mind.

The Occupy Movement has catalyzed rising anxiety over income inequality; we desperately need a similar reminder of the relationship between economic advantage and student performance.

The correlation has been abundantly documented, notably by the famous Coleman Report in 1966. New research by Sean F. Reardon of Stanford University traces the achievement gap between children from high- and low-income families over the last 50 years, and finds that it now far exceeds the gap between white and black students.

*Continued*

## "Class Matters. Why Won't We Admit It?" . . . (Continued)

Data from the National Assessment of Educational Progress show that more than 40 percent of the variation in average reading scores and 46 percent of the variation in average math scores across states are associated with variation in child poverty rates.

International research tells the same story. Results of the 2009 reading tests conducted by the Program for International Student Assessment show that, among 15-year-olds in the United States and the 13 countries whose students outperformed ours, students with lower economic and social status had far lower test scores than their more advantaged counterparts within every country. Can anyone credibly believe that the mediocre overall performance of American students on international tests is unrelated to the fact that one-fifth of American children live in poverty?

Yet federal education policy seems blind to all this. No Child Left Behind required all schools to bring all students to high levels of achievement, but took no note of the challenges that disadvantaged students face. The legislation did, to be sure, specify that subgroups—defined by income, minority status and proficiency in English—must meet the same achievement standard. But it did so only to make sure that schools did not ignore their disadvantaged students—not to help them address the challenges they carry with them into the classroom.

So why do presumably well-intentioned policy makers ignore, or deny, the correlations of family background and student achievement?

Some honestly believe that schools are capable of offsetting the effects of poverty. Others want to avoid the impression that they set lower expectations for some groups of students for fear that those expectations will be self-fulfilling. In both cases, simply wanting something to be true does not make it so.

Another rationale for denial is to note that some schools, like the Knowledge Is Power Program charter schools, have managed to "beat the odds." If some schools can succeed, the argument goes, then it is reasonable to expect all schools to. But close scrutiny of charter school performance has shown that many of the success stories have been limited to particular grades or subjects, and may be attributable to substantial outside financing or extraordinarily long working hours on the part of teachers. The evidence does not support the view that the few success stories can be scaled up to address the needs of large populations of disadvantaged students.

A final rationale for denying the correlation is more nefarious. As we are now seeing, requiring all schools to meet the same high standards for all students, regardless of family background, will inevitably lead either to large numbers of failing schools or to a dramatic lowering of state standards. Both serve to discredit the public education system and lend support to arguments that the system is failing and needs fundamental change, like privatization.

Given the budget crises at the national and state levels, and the strong political power of conservative groups, a significant effort to reduce poverty or deal with the closely related issue of racial segregation is not in the political cards, at least for now.

*Continued*

## "Class Matters. Why Won't We Admit It?" ... *(Continued)*

So what can be done?

Large bodies of research have shown how poor health and nutrition inhibit child development and learning, and, conversely, how high-quality early childhood and preschool education programs can enhance them. We understand the importance of early exposure to rich language on future cognitive development. We know that low-income students experience greater learning loss during the summer when their more privileged peers are enjoying travel and other enriching activities.

Since they can't take on poverty itself, education policy makers should try to provide poor students with the social support and experiences that middle-class students enjoy as a matter of course.

It can be done. In North Carolina, the two-year-old East Durham Children's Initiative is one of many efforts around the country to replicate Geoffrey Canada's well-known successes with the Harlem Children's Zone.

Say Yes to Education in Syracuse, New York, supports access to afterschool programs and summer camps, and places social workers in schools. In Omaha, Building Bright Futures sponsors school-based health centers and offers mentoring and enrichment services. Citizen Schools, based in Boston, recruits volunteers in seven states to share their interests and skills with middle-school students.

Promise Neighborhoods, an Obama administration effort that gives grants to programs like these, is a welcome first step, but it has been under-financed.

Other countries already pursue such strategies. In Finland, with its famously high-performing schools, schools provide food and free healthcare for students. Developmental needs are addressed early. Counseling services are abundant.

But in the United States over the past decade, it became fashionable among supporters of the "no excuses" approach to school improvement to accuse anyone raising the poverty issue of letting schools off the hook—or what Mr. Bush famously called "the soft bigotry of low expectations."

Such accusations may afford the illusion of a moral high ground, but they stand in the way of serious efforts to improve education, and, for that matter, go a long way toward explaining why No Child Left Behind has not worked.

Yes, we need to make sure that all children, and particularly disadvantaged children, have access to good schools, as defined by the quality of teachers and principals, and of internal policies and practices.

But let's not pretend that family background does not matter and can be overlooked. Let's agree that we know a lot about how to address the ways in which poverty undermines student learning. Whether we choose to face up to that reality is ultimately a moral question.

# 2012 PROFILE

At 38 years old, Anne Mandeville-Long needed something beyond volunteer work at her children's school when she answered an ad from another mother to provide childcare.

## Life at Home

- Born in New Haven, Connecticut, in July of 1959, Anne Mandeville-Long was the third daughter and fourth child of Walter and Joan Robbins.
- With two more brothers arriving after her, Anne grew up in the middle of the pack.
- Life outside the Robbins' house in Fairfield included frequent trips to the beach on Long Island Sound, winter ski trips to southern Vermont, visits to the grandparents on the coast of Virginia, and regular New York Ranger hockey games at Madison Square Garden in New York City.
- Anne started her education at the local public elementary school, and later enrolled in a private day school in a nearby town.
- Following the tradition of her family, she spent her sophomore year in high school at a boarding school in north-central Massachusetts, and returned to finish high school at the local academy.
- Between her junior and senior years, she enrolled in a summer program at the Rhode Island School of Design, where she pursued her passion for design and ceramics.
- Intent on making her own statement in life and choosing her college, she enrolled at Hampshire College in Massachusetts, a school known for its creative approach to higher education.

*Anne Mandeville-Long founded Moss Garden Nursery School.*

- At Hampshire, Anne focused on cultural history, and spent a semester abroad studying in Aix-en-Provence in the south of France.
- Following her graduation from Hampshire, she followed the normal trajectory of many Connecticut young people and moved to New York City; there, she found entry-level positions in advertising and sales.
- Her next move brought her back to her Connecticut hometown, where she married and had her first two sons.
- With toddlers to attend to, Anne juggled child-rearing with several years of designing, constructing and selling unique children's clothing.
- She found the apparel market a difficult and challenging industry in which to succeed.
- In her mid-thirties, Anne and her small family decided to move away from the comfortable and familiar Northeast and settled in Chapel Hill, North Carolina, with almost as much thought as throwing a dart at a map.
- With a degree of serendipity, she and her husband decided to build a house on property located only a short walk from a small private school nestled in the woods on the northern boundary of Chapel Hill.
- Now the mother of three boys, Anne enrolled her two older sons at the nearby Emerson Waldorf School.
- At the age of 38, she delivered her fourth child, a daughter named Stella.
- "I knew that I needed to find something to do beyond volunteer work at the school. My 'a-ha' moment came when I saw an ad in the school newspaper from another mother asking for someone who could provide several hours of childcare each week," Anne recalls.
- Following a meeting with the mother Lauren and her son Andrew, who was the same age as Stella, Lauren set it all in motion when she said, "I want my children to come to you."
- For the rest of the school year, Anne provided childcare for a growing number of children, including Stella.

*"No Child Left Inside" was Moss Garden's philosophy.*

- A typical morning would involved walks in the woods, healthy snacks and other simple activities.
- While Anne and the children were having fun, the parent group approached her with a request for more structure and a more organized program.
- "It was at this point that Moss Garden Nursery School came into being," Anne explained.
- Knowing that she needed to learn more about early-childhood education, Anne enrolled in a series of workshops and conferences at Sunbridge College in Spring Valley, New York.
- "It was at Sunbridge College that I learned about the developmental phases of children from zero to seven years old. We discussed the basics such as how children move and how they benefit from certain sensory experiences. Jumping and climbing trees are excellent activities for young children as they form their sensory awareness of the world."
- All along, Anne's knowledge of the world of young children was being reinforced by her experiences with her older sons.

## Life at Work

- Moss Garden Nursery School, now in its twelfth year, admitted 12 students ranging from two and a half to five years old.
- Anne Mandeville-Long was continuously conscious of balancing her enrollment with a mix of ages, genders, and capabilities.
- "I am amazed at how the right child comes to my program when I need that child. And, of course, with 12 children, I tend to have roughly 24 parents. Sometimes I feel that I am teaching far more than 12 students.
- "Moss Garden's program is based on one goal, which is to protect childhood. Too often in our modern world, children are being robbed of their opportunity to be children. We want our children to be open, not to be fearful, and not to feel undue anxiety. It is based on this that I have a nature-based, play-based program.

*Annes's background helped her provide creative, stimulating childcare.*

- "We like to use the phrase, 'No Child Left Inside'," Anne said.
- "With a program which depends so much on the out-of-doors, it is essential that the children understand that we have very clear boundaries, in spite of the fact that we have no fences. If children feel safe and loved, they can relax and engage in the important work of play."
- A typical day at Moss Garden Nursery School includes the following.
- "The children arrive at 9 a.m. The parents are encouraged to bring the children to the play area and then leave as soon as possible.
- "At around 9:15, with all the children wearing their boots, we walk through the woods, rain or shine, snow or ice. The older kids run ahead, but they know where to stop. Each day we visit the same places.

- "The walk in the woods and the 15 to 20 minutes in and around the garden help the children to connect with a sense of place.
- "Some children have started out being terrified of the woods, or scared of the dogs, or afraid to get their feet or hands muddy. It is a pure delight to see how quickly this changes.
- "After our initial time outside, we go into the house. The rhythm for this next part of the morning is always 'Circle Time.'
- "They don't know it, but it is also the time in which I do my most traditional teaching.
- "As part of Circle Time, we often sing, dance and act out stories. We work with language, diction, counting, rhythm and rhymes, all in the context of a movement journey so they can create an inner picture or an imagining of the experience."
- Along with the daily rhythm of Moss Garden Nursery School, "Miss Anne," as she is

*A typical morning at Moss Garden included a walk in the woods.*

affectionately known by children and parents alike, creates seasonal festivals and regular parent meetings.
- Parent meetings happen on three or four occasions during the school year and are helpful with creating a forum for young and new parents to discuss issues relative to child-rearing and early childhood education.
- Anne says that she tells the parents, "I want the children to be in love with learning and with the stories that go with education."
- She then related the story of Kate, who came to Moss Garden with a large dose of skepticism.
- "She would say, 'Are you telling me the truth, Miss Anne?' This questioning turned into a sense of fear, then transformed beautifully into a sense of confidence."
- With a perspective of over 12 years of teaching and nearly 25 years of parenting, Anne ponders the question, "Why do I do this?"
- The answer is, "For selfish reasons. I love it. It fits with my view of the world, of what we need to do to create the next generation of young minds who will solve the problems that we need to confront."

*Nature was Anne's classroom.*

## Life in the Community: Research Triangle Park, North Carolina

- The Research Triangle Park (RTP) area of North Carolina includes Raleigh, Durham, and Chapel Hill.
- Moss Garden Nursery School is one of a half-dozen preschools in this area that embraces the educational philosophy of Rudolf Steiner.
- Born in Austria, Rudolf Steiner created the philosophy upon which Waldorf education was based.
- This type of education focuses on the developmental milestones and temperaments of the individual child, and emphasizes and utilizes the arts and individual thinking as the narratives through which education is achieved.
- During the economic recession that began in 2008, there was concern that enrollment in these preschool programs would drop, since families had less expendable income, but preschool enrollment has been sustained, in some cases, by the need for both parents to seek employment outside the home.
- An increasing number of studies point to the positive effects of early childhood education and the impact it has on achievement throughout the educational experience of young people.
- The RTP was created over 50 years ago by North Carolina educators and politicians who had observed that the local universities were educating North Carolina's youth for jobs that did not exist in the state.
- Drawing on the strengths among North Carolina's academic, government and industry bases, RTP is a place to attract research and development companies, and helped the state transition from an agricultural economy to one based on business.
- The RTP area is recognized as having the highest concentration of Ph.D. graduates in the country.

# HISTORICAL SNAPSHOT
# 2012

- Hawaii's and Delaware's civil union laws went into effect
- San Francisco raised the minimum wage within its jurisdiction to over $10 per hour, making it the highest minimum wage in the country
- Kansas, Texas, Rhode Island, and Tennessee began requiring photo identification for voters as a measure to combat voter fraud
- Classified documents were leaked detailing a range of advanced non-lethal weapons proposed or in development by the U.S. Armed Forces
- The Supreme Court made a unanimous decision that telephone consumers can gain standing in federal courts to sue abusive telemarketers
- Kodak, known for its camera film for more than 100 years, filed for bankruptcy protection
- The Supreme Court unanimously ruled that the government must obtain a search warrant permitting them to install a Global Positioning System (GPS) on citizens' private property
- Super Bowl XLVI was the most watched program in the history of U.S. television, with 111.3 million viewers who witnessed the New York Giants defeat the New England Patriots 21-17
- Umar Farouk Abdulmutallab, the so-called "underwear bomber," was sentenced to life imprisonment for attempting to detonate a bomb on Northwest Airlines Flight 253 in Detroit
- The Dow Jones Industrial Average closed above 13,000 points for the first time since May 2008
- *The Artist* won five Academy Awards including Best Picture
- Maryland became the eighth state to legalize gay marriage
- BP and plaintiffs reached an agreement over compensation for the Deepwater Horizon oil spill in the Gulf of Mexico
- A study suggested that donor stem cells may prevent organ rejection in imperfectly matched transplant cases
- Chicago, Illinois-based *Encyclopaedia Britannica,* the oldest encyclopedia still in print in English, announced that it will only offer its product online.
- A jury found Virginia Tech guilty of negligence for delaying a campus warning about the Virginia Tech Massacre of 33 students in 2007
- Former Illinois Governor Rod Blagojevich reported to Federal Correctional Institution, Englewood in Littleton, Colorado, to begin serving 14 years for attempting to sell his appointment to Barack Obama's vacated senate seat
- The movie *John Carter* recorded one of the biggest losses in cinema history, forcing Disney to take a $200 million write-down and chairman Rich Ross to resign
- MIT researchers Ramesh Raskar and Andreas Velten demonstrated an augmented reality apparatus which can allow observation of a non-line-of-sight object by means of a non-mirror, reflective surface
- Guggenheim Partners, LLC purchased the Los Angeles Dodgers for $2.1 billion, the most ever paid for a professional sports franchise

## Selected Prices

Bookcase ...........................................................................$119.00

Bottled Water ........................................................................$1.50

Coffee Grinder ...................................................................$60.53

Concert Ticket, The Gregg Allman Band ........................$159.00

Digital Cordless Phone ....................................................$119.99

Kindle, 3G + Wi-Fi ..........................................................$189.00

Phone, Camera Flip Phone ................................................$99.00

Printer, HP All-in-One .....................................................$548.88

Sofa ..................................................................................$899.00

Toolset, 137 Pieces ............................................................$99.99

My stories and puppet plays are usually about the animals, insects, trees and flowers that the children might observe around them. Storytelling can be a very effective teaching tool. It can be used to resolve conflict within the group or to address a challenging behavior. The use of metaphor is vitally important. Children will respond to Truth. Also, storytelling is used to inspire the imagination. Stories can be nourishing to young people on many levels, equivalent to a healthy meal. I observe how the children will reenact these stories with their own interpretations and make them their own. Children will take from these stories what they need and will use them to develop their own lives. One of the most important elements of storytelling for this age group is that, in the end, the children feel love and protection.

—Anne Mandeville-Long, 2012

### "Bracing for $40,000 at City Private Schools," Jenny Anderson and Rachel Ohm, *The New York Times*, January 29, 2012:

There are certain mathematical realities associated with New York City private schools: There are more students than seats at the top-tier schools, at least three sets of twins will be vying head to head for spots in any class, and already-expensive tuition can only go up.

Way up.

Over the past 10 years, the median price of first grade in the city has gone up by 48 percent, adjusted for inflation, compared with a 35 percent increase at private schools nationally—and just 24 percent at an Ivy League college—according to tuition data provided by 41 New York City K-12 private schools to the National Association of Independent Schools.

Indeed, this year's tuition at Columbia Grammar and Preparatory ($38,340 for twelfth grade) and Horace Mann ($37,275 for the upper school) is higher than Harvard's ($36,305). Those 41 schools (out of 61 New York City private schools in the National Association) provided enough data to enable a 10-year analysis. (Overall, inflation caused prices in general to rise 27 percent over the past decade.)

The median twelfth-grade tuition for the current school year was $36,970, up from $21,100 in 2001-2, according to the National Association's survey. Nationally, that figure rose to $24,240 from $14,583 a decade ago.

With schools already setting tuition rates for the 2012-13 school year—The Brearley School is $38,200—parents at Horace Mann, Columbia Grammar, and Trinity are braced to find out whether they will join families at Riverdale Country School in the $40,000-a-year club. (Riverdale actually charges $40,450 for twelfth grade.) In fact, it appears to be a question not of "if," but "when."

"Within one to two years, every independent school will cost more than $40,000," said one board member at a top school, who spoke on the condition of anonymity because the school had not yet set tuition.

And that is before requests for the annual fund, tickets to the yearly auction gala and capital campaigns to build a(nother) gym.

Parents are reluctant to complain, at least with their names attached, for fear of hurting students' standing (or siblings' admissions chances). But privately, many questioned paying more for the same. "The school's always had an amazing teacher-to-student ratio, learning

*Continued*

## "Bracing for $40,000 at City Private Schools," ... (Continued)

specialists and art programs with great music and theater," said one mother whose children attend the Dalton School ($36,970 a year). "It was great a decade ago and great now."

"They are outrageous," said Dana Haddad, a private admissions consultant, referring to tuitions. "People don't want to put a price tag on their children's future, so they are willing to pay more than many of them can afford."

Administrators at several of New York's top schools attributed the tuition inflation to rising teacher salaries, ever-expanding programs and renovations to aging buildings. They noted that tuition still covered only about 80 percent of the cost of educating each child (that is what all the fund-raising is about). As at most companies, a majority of the costs—and the fastest-growing increases—come from salaries and benefits, especially as notoriously low-paying private schools try to compete with public school compensation.

"Some New York schools have had a 5, 10, or as high as 30 percent increase in the cost of their medical plans," said Mark Lauria, the executive director of the New York State Association of Independent Schools.

And paying teachers is only a piece of the puzzle. Léman Manhattan Preparatory School has a gym whose floor is cleaned twice a day. The Trinity School has three theaters, six art studios, two tennis courts, a pool and a diving pool. Poly Prep Country Day School raised $2 million to open a learning center this year that has six full-time employees offering one-on-one help with subjects as varied as note-taking and test-taking....

Unlike public schools, which have faced severe cutbacks in the face of dwindling state and local revenues, private schools seem only to add courses. Take foreign languages. Schools used to offer French and Spanish. Then came German and Russian. Japanese was introduced when that country looked poised to dominate the global economy. A few years ago, Mandarin was a must-have, and now many schools offer Arabic.

"Offering Mandarin is a way to prepare students for the twenty-first-century world we live in," said John Allman, Trinity's headmaster.

## "Beyond SATs, Finding Success in Numbers," Tina Rosenberg, *The New York Times*, February 15, 2012:

In 1988, Deborah Bial was working in a New York City after-school program when she ran into a former student, Lamont. He was a smart kid, a successful student who had won a scholarship to an elite college. But it hadn't worked out, and now he was back home in the Bronx. "I never would have dropped out of college if I had my posse with me," he told her.

The next year Bial started the Posse Foundation. From her work with students around the city, she chose five New York City high school students who were clearly leaders—dynamic,

*Continued*

## "Beyond SATs, Finding Success in Numbers," ... *(Continued)*

intelligent, creative, resilient—but who might not have had the SAT scores to get into good schools. Vanderbilt University was willing to admit them all, tuition-free. The students met regularly in their senior year of high school, through the summer, and at college. Surrounded by their posse, they all thrived.

Today the Posse Foundation selects about 600 students a year, from eight different cities. They are grouped into posses of 10 students from the same city and go together to an elite college; about 40 colleges now participate in the program.

Most Posse Scholars would not have qualified for their colleges by the normal criteria. Posse Scholars' combined median reading and math SAT score is only 1050, while the median combined score at the colleges Posse students attend varies from 1210 to 1475. Nevertheless, they succeed. Ninety percent of Posse Scholars graduate—half of them on the dean's list and a quarter with academic honors. A <u>survey</u> of 20 years of alumni found that nearly 80 percent of the respondents said they had founded or led groups or clubs. There are only 40 Posse Scholars among Bryn Mawr's 1,300 students, but a Posse student has won the school's best all-around student award three times in the past seven years. Posse is changing the way universities look at qualifications for college, and what makes for college success.

Sheyenne Brown went to Adlai E. Stevenson High School in the Bronx, which before its closure in 2009 was one of the worst schools in New York City. Her parents had always worked—her mother as an administrative assistant, her father in sales. But in her junior year, her family was evicted from their home—by marshals—the same day her father lost his job. They moved into a series of homeless shelters, some of them decent, some like prison cells. "We were people who do the right thing and follow the path, and you still end up in a situation you believe only happens to you if you do the wrong thing," she said. Brown went to work at McDonald's, putting in between 20 and 48 hours a week for $5.15 per hour. Her combined SAT score was 1080. She did not seem destined to attend an elite college.

*Continued*

## "Beyond SATs, Finding Success in Numbers," . . . *(Continued)*

But in her senior year, at least one of her teachers nominated her to be a Posse Scholar. She competed against thousands of other New York City students (with 14,000 nominations nationwide for 600 slots, the program is more competitive than Harvard) and won a place with 10 other students at Middlebury, a tiny liberal arts college in Vermont. She had never heard of it.

Starting in January, Brown and the 10 others in her posse began to meet weekly with a Posse staff member. The purpose of the sessions was to solidify the group and teach them what they needed to succeed at Middlebury: how to write at a college level, but just as important, how to negotiate the social world: how to deal with a diversity of race and socioeconomic status, how to communicate with people who were very different—"finding ways to express what you want to say so that people get your point and don't feel disrespected," she said. She was living in the shelter at the time.

"In a way, Middlebury was exactly what I needed," she said. "It was a convenient bubble where everything was safe and okay, and you don't have to tell everybody your business."

The posse was key. "It's so easy to get lost. I couldn't imagine going to college without a group of people I already knew. I don't think I would have made it." They were all studying different things, she said. They didn't do homework together, but they held each other accountable for doing it. "If you needed somebody to get you out of bed and get you to the library, Antoinette [a Posse member] would get you to the library." The Posse members, she said, held each other up to the standard they had set: "How you are doing in class, how you behaved socially, and whether you were supporting people you agreed to support."

Brown graduated in 2009, cum laude. Conscious of her good fortune and eager to give back, she joined Teach for America and taught sixth-grade social studies at a KIPP charter school in Newark. Now she is in graduate school at Columbia, studying theater.

# 2012 News Feature

Shortly after South Sudan voted for independence, after nearly three decades of civil war, The Rev. Dr. Ellen J. Hanckel went to Juba, South Sudan, to teach at the Bishop Gwynne College (BGC). The following are excerpts of her e-mails to friends while she was teaching in Africa's newest nation from February to June, 2012.

*******************

Dear Friends and Family,

This time of year, when the season of Epiphany calls us to carry the light of Christ into the world, I'm glad to be in touch with you. I want you to know about the surprising turn my life is taking.

At this writing, I am traveling to East Africa—to Juba, South Sudan, where I will teach at the Bishop Gwynne College (BGC) during the spring semester. This plan is always exciting and sometimes overwhelming to me. I do believe it is God's call on my life at this time.

You may remember that South Sudan recently came into being by way of a Referendum that took place peacefully on January 9, 2011. A large percentage of the people voted and the results overwhelmingly favored forming a new country.

Their Independence Day, a day of joyful celebration, followed six months later—on July 9. The road to peace and freedom from oppression is still rocky, however, with some serious outbreaks of violence reported in areas near the border.

Even so, I count it a blessing to be joining the faculty of BGC in Juba. Their students are educated and nurtured to be the future clergy leaders of this new country. Yes, the task will be challenging. It will be one full of promise and hope as well. Only by the grace of God do I attempt it.

Last September, I was able to meet with BGC Principal Joseph Taban Lasuba on site in Juba. He assigned three subjects for me to prepare to teach: Paul's letter to the Romans, the Reformation, and an introduction to sociology. Since then I've been studying faithfully in preparation.

Grace and peace to you and yours,
Ellen


\*\*\*\*\*\*\*\*\*\*\*\*\*\*\*\*\*\*\*


"Greetings from Juba"


Hooray, the fan is on and I'm eager to write to you on this Sunday afternoon in Juba. The fan helps a lot, cooling with every turn. Without it, the heat overpowers me, a newcomer to these parts, and saps energy.  So, hooray for the fan.

Electricity during the daylight hours is not a given here. It is more regular at night. Even then, not a certainty. For example, a great shout of jubilation went up last night about 10:30 when the power came back on. Ah, the fan is moving again, thank goodness.

One week ago today was my first full day here, having arrived, travel weary, the day before. I spent the first several days in the guest house of the ECS (Episcopal Church of Sudan), then moved to a room in the nearby Bishop Gwynne College, referred to here as the BGC. The building is rectangular, with the walls a series of rooms, one deep, surrounding an open courtyard. This perimeter style layout maximizes ventilation—a good thing.

Principal Joseph Taban Lasuba, among his many other duties, worked very hard to prepare a comfortable place for me to live during the next four months of the spring semester.

The room that I saw at the beginning of the week was completely transformed by mid-week.

A single bed fits snugly under a window along the width of the room. The mosquito net is the shape of the bed, allowing maximum room for a sleeping person. When I do my morning yoga series, I can do a full body stretch, with my fingertips touching one wall and my feet the other.

The length of the room, about twice the width, accommodates a cabinet holding my clothes and books very nicely, also providing a long mirror on the door. A hat rack for hanging a hat, or clothes, or towels stands in the corner next to the cabinet. A writing table and a comfortable chair occupy the other wall. Graciously hung curtains shield the room from the hot sun and dust, as well as giving privacy.

I like this compact room, for now. To me it gives a feeling of focus, purpose and comfort that is sustaining.

Of course, the purpose for my visit is teaching and classes have already begun. Romans met for the first time on Wednesday morning. Beforehand I was nervous and wondered how it could possibly work. Afterwards I was delighted and realized how much I had enjoyed it. Like riding a bicycle again, I found out it works. Fun!

The students appreciate it so much. It's easy to see in their eyes. Their faces shine as we communicate. Even while we get to know each other, I anticipate it will be a pleasure to journey through Romans together. This journey is not on a map, but in a book, through the words of the letter Paul wrote approximately 2,000 years ago.

Part of the first assignment is to write a letter to someone back home dealing with a conflict, similar to what Paul did when he wrote to the Church in Rome. These Sudanese students assured me they would have no trouble coming up with something to write about. I'm looking forward to reading their responses.

Until the next time, I hope all of you are well. You are in my thoughts and prayers.

Peace,
Ellen

*******************

Dear Friends and Family,

First, the good news: Classes are going well. The students are engaged in their studies and actively participating in class discussions. They inspire me with HOPE.

Take Friday's sociology class, for example. What an outstanding group of young adults! The class size has grown from nine at first to 12 now, adding the last two today. We have 11 men and one woman. I could go on and on about the sociology of the students, but let's get back to Friday (3/2/12).

We picked up from last week's class, which introduced the scientific method as a systematic collection of data, not casual observation. When approaching a question to examine or a statement to explore, we considered the use of variables: Independent (cause); Dependent (results); and Intervening (modifying).

To continue this week, we used the following example taken from a book published in Nairobi particularly for African students of sociology: *Willingness of Parents to Send Their Children to Primary School.*

In this case, the Independent Variables included: Status—which increases when parents fulfill their responsibility for training the child; Economic—balancing the immediate need for child labor within the family against the long-term rewards of education; and Legal—since the government has regulations for compulsory schooling.

The Intervening Variables included: Gender of the child—since boys are more likely to be sent to school than girls; Distance between home and school—"Is it too far to walk?"; and the Value of Education, in the future, for family and community.

The results, dependent on the above variables, would equal the proportion of children in the community who would be sent to school. Hypothetically, it could range from 0 to 100 percent.

This example made for very lively class discussion. All but two of the students are married with children, so most face the issue of "Willingness to Send Children to Primary School" in real life, not as a hypothetical example.

It extends beyond their personal circumstances, however, because all of them have been practicing ministry in their local communities, where they are most likely to return after completing their studies. Each of them, as leaders in the church, can be a positive influence by encouraging others and by setting an example.

One student, we'll call him Thomas, challenged the supposition that boys are more likely to be sent to school than girls. "My grandmother would say that," he said, "because that was true in her time. But now that is changing."

"Good to know that," I said. "Our book was published in 1997, so it's good to know that it's changing during the 15 years since then."

The conversation continued around the different variables.

Someone, we'll call him Benjamin, pointed out that he knew of families where the older siblings would walk an hour or more to school with the younger ones, often carrying them on their backs.

We touched on the legal obligation, and they acknowledged that these regulations were probably in place where they lived. Many times, they are not carried out by the parents, however, and not enforced by the local authorities.

We agreed that it would be interesting to know what percentage of the children in their local communities were in school. I challenged them to contact someone who would know, perhaps a local commissioner, and find out. "It may be an extra credit question on the test next week," I said. With hope, I look forward to seeing those results.

Finally, another student, we'll call him Samuel, said strongly, "I'm so glad we had this example in class, so that when we get back home we can mobilize the parents in our community to send their children to primary school."

"Music to my ears, Samuel, music to my ears," I said. "Any teacher would like to hear that. If you do take these things back home and change people's attitudes—their hearts and minds—that will be the most important thing you can do, since the laws are already in place. Then this class would become more than an academic exercise."

By the grace of God, let it be.

As I give thanks for this—one of many blessings on Friday—now let me tell you that it more than makes up for...the bad news, which comes next.

In the dark hours before Friday morning, I made the following journal entry:

"Well, well, well. If my friends could have seen me just now, they would never have believed it. They'd have seen me up in the middle of the night, standing on a chair that I put on the bed to reach a hole in the ceiling tile and plug it up with a rag. Now I hope that the rat I saw coming out of that hole, will not nibble on me anymore—toe on my foot or hair on my head."

That was round one of the battle with the rats that night. After that came a chase scene that was perfect for the movie *Ratatouille*. Two of those critters were running around the room—one on a pole that holds up the mosquito net, another defying gravity by traveling up and down the curtain.

When I thought that I had chased them away, I'd close my eyes to get some sleep. Then I'd hear them again and wake up enough to rattle the window and scare them off for a little while longer.

As the early light finally came, it slowly dawned on me that 'my little friends' were not after me only, but something else as well. Sure enough, when I checked in the morning, I found out what they really wanted—the bread rolls I had been keeping to snack on from time to time. Yep, they had chewed through the sealed plastic bag where I had put them safely away—until then, of course.

Needless to say, "the bait" went out the door and into the trash right away. As soon as I finished my teaching assignment, I got help to patch the holes that same day. Even if it wasn't easy to find a carpenter on Friday afternoon, it wasn't something I wanted to leave until Monday.

Neither did the staff at BGC. "Madame is upset," one of them said. "She needs her sleep." And they got someone there right quick.

I'm happy to report that the fix seems to be holding. So far, so good. On that note, I'll sign off—until the next time.

Grace and peace to you and yours from Juba,
Ellen

\*\*\*\*\*\*\*\*\*\*\*\*\*\*\*\*\*\*\*\*

Dear Friends and Family,

One morning several weeks ago, I had breakfast under the tent at the ECS Guest House here in Juba. I sat at table with a friend—who is also a bishop of the Episcopal Church of Sudan (ECS). He asked me how the students had done on their tests.

"Well," I said with an eye on the time, knowing that I would need to be leaving soon to make the 10-minute walk to the new BGC campus and arrive on time for morning devotions. The answer would have to be brief.

"Well, you know I teach three courses." He nodded, based on our previous conversations. "In two of the courses, the test results were good and I was pleased, as were the students. On the third test, though," and here I shook my head and wrinkled my nose, "the results were not so good. So the students must study and take the test again." We shook our heads together at the disappointing news. "I don't think the students liked that so much," I said, "but I think they understand after seeing the results."

With understanding, the bishop laughed gently. "You don't think they liked that so much," he said.

"No, but I think they understand that we need to work together. I consider that the test results are as much my responsibility as theirs," I said, wrapping up my bread and boiled egg to take with me and eat later for lunch. I put them in my book bag and looked at the small clock I keep nearby. "Now, I really have to go," I said.

"The clock tells you to go now," he said, and I nodded. We wished each other a good day before I departed for my regular brisk morning walk.

A week or so later, we revisited this topic at another, more relaxed breakfast meeting under the tent at the ECS Guest House. As I expected, the results of the next test were much more positive, enabling us to build on a firm foundation in this course—introduction to sociology—and move forward.

As I mentioned earlier, the other two courses—Paul's letter to the Romans and introduction to the New Testament—are going well. Overall, I believe we're moving in the right direction. I know I'm learning from them, and I trust they are learning from me as well. By the grace of God, I feel sure we are enriching each others' lives as we spend time together learning the assigned material.

# SOURCES

# INDEX

## A

Abdulmutallab, Umar Farouk, 518
Abel, John Jacob, 35
abortion, 358, 386, 398, 402, 437, 444
Absorbine Jr. (advertisement), *158*
abstinence programs, 346
Academy Awards, 227
Academy of Motion Picture Arts and
    Sciences, 157
Addams, Jane, 81
Adler, Mortimer, 424
adrenaline, 35
Advanced Research Projects Agency, 294
advertising, 135
Aerosmith, 358
affirmative action, 444
Afghanistan, 126, 489
African-Americans
    Civil Rights Movement and, 264, 308,
        315–317, 321, 334
    discrimination against, 44, 334
    middle class, 358
    school desegregation and, 393–397
    schools for, 125
    servicemen, 218
"After the Christmas Dinner, Bright Things
    of All Times That People Have Laughed
    Over," 128–129
"Against That Day!," 219–220
Agnew, Spiro, 367, 371, 386
"Agnew Likes It," 371
Agricultural College of Utah, 21
agriculture, 1, 6, 34, 89
AIDS, 349, 402, 418, 496
Aiken, Clay, 490

airline industry, 496
airplanes, 53, 114
air travel, 263
*Aladdin*, 452
Alaska, 297
Alaska Pipeline, 386, 398
Albert G. Lane Technical School, 78
Alcatraz, 178
Alexander, Jane, 463
*Alfred Hitchcock Presents*, 271
Alfred P. Murrah Federal Building, 465
Algonquin Indians, 52
Ali, Muhammad, 335
*Alice in Wonderland*, 35
Alioto, Joseph, 368
Allison, Robert, 35
*All the King's Men*, 253
Alpher, Ralph, 239
al-Qaeda, 489, 507
Alta, California, 155–156
alternative rock, 444
Alvado, Marion Walker, 273–274
*Amadeus*, 418
Amazon, 490
Amerasian immigrants, 439
*American Bandstand*, 283, 428
American Board of Commissioners for
    Foreign Missions, 16
American Communist Party, 126
American diet, 308
American Federation of Labor (AFL),
    44, 433
American GIs, 218
*American Idol*, 490
American Legion, 126, 250
American Medical Association, 94, 345
American Motors Corporation, 428

American music, 1
"American Pie," 358
American prosperity, 43–44
American Red Cross, 8
amino acids, 253
Amnesty International, 321
"Among the Wild Indians," 24
Anderson, Jenny, 521–522
Anderson, Marian, 271
Anderson, South Carolina, 34
Andrews, Julie, 283
Andrews, Tommy Lee, 428
Angell, James R., 159–160
Anglo-Persian Oil Company, 81
Annapolis, Maryland, 427
Annenberg, Walter, 452
Anthony, Susan B., 21
anti-immigration laws, 90, 136
"Anti-Lynch Bill Insult to South, Harrison
    Says: Warns Senators From North
    Measure May Cause Party Split,"
    198–199
antimatter, 496
antiretroviral drugs, 496
anti-segregationists, 317–318
antiwar movement, 308, 335, 364, 368, 489
*Apollo 9*, 349
*Apollo 10*, 349
*Apollo 13*, 368
*Apollo 15*, 391
Apple Computer, 398
appliances, 136, 263
architecture, 75, 76–78, 435
Arlin, Harold, 145
Armey, Dick, 464
armored car robbery, 157
Armstrong, Lance, 484

*Italic* page numbers indicate images. **Bold** page numbers indicate profile subjects

*Italic* page numbers indicate images. **Bold** page numbers indicate profile subjects

*Italic* page numbers indicate images. **Bold** page numbers indicate profile subjects

Italic page numbers indicate images. **Bold** page numbers indicate profile subjects

*Italic* page numbers indicate images. **Bold** page numbers indicate profile subjects

*Italic* page numbers indicate images. **Bold** page numbers indicate profile subjects

*Italic* page numbers indicate images. **Bold** page numbers indicate profile subjects

# S

*Italic* page numbers indicate images. **Bold** page numbers indicate profile subjects

Springsteen, Bruce, 402
"Spudnik's [sic] Beeps Continue But Tones Varying," 299–300
Sputnik, 283, 291–295, 299–303
Stalin, Joseph, 157, 165, 227
standardized testing, 135, 477–483, 486–487, 489
Standard Oil, 2, 35
*Standards for Public Libraries*, 180
"Star-Spangled Banner, The," 164, 424
*Star Wars Episode I: The Phantom Menace*, 484
State Farm Mutual, 136
St. Clair, Arthur, 225
stealth bomber, 418
steamboats, 95
steel, 2, 263
Steinbrenner, George, 386
Stephen F. Austin High School, 8
Stephens, Isabel, 225
Stewart's Duplex Safety Pins (advertisement), *82*
Stickley, Gustav, 83
Stieff Pianos (advertisement), *146*
*Still Becoming: A Retire Teacher Reminisces*, 403–412
St. John's College, 424–426
St. Joseph Orphanage, 95
St. Lawrence Seaway, 297
stockcar racing, 53
stock markets, 136, 401, 443–444, 465
Stonewall riots, 349
Storm Slipper (advertisement), *36*
Storrs Agricultural School, 8
Stowe, Harriet Beecher, 52
Strandhope, Emily, **109–112**
"Strange Fruit," 212
strikes, 53, 60, 126, 217, 218, 308, 368, 437
Studebaker, John, 223, *224*
student protests, 307, 349
Students for a Democratic Society (SDS), 335, 349
"Students Strike Against Cambodia," 391–392
Suave (advertisement), *240*
suburbs, 252, 264, 348
Summer Jam at Watkins Glen, 386
Summers, Bob, 381–382
Sunart Photo Co. (advertisement), *54*
Sunbelt, 358
Super Bowl VII, 386
Super Bowl XI, 398
Super Bowl XLVI, 518
Super Bowl XXI, 428
Superman, 194
Super Mario Bros., 418
supermarkets, 263
superpower, U.S. as sole, 402
surgery, 65
*Survey of Danville and Pittsylvania County*, 180–181

Sutro, Mrs. Theodore, 27–28
Swan, Joseph, 8
swing, 172
Switzer, Katherine, 449
Sykes-Picot Agreement, 114
Sylvania (advertisement), *429*
synthetic genome, 496
syphilis, 90
*Syracuse Herald Journal*, 456–457

# T

Taft, Howard, 81
Taj Mahal Palace & Tower, 53
Tampa, Florida, 449–450
Tampa Bay Hotel, 449–450
*Tasby v. Estes*, 396
Taylor, William M., 397
teacherages, 121–124, *123*
teachers, 4–5, 12, 31–32, 33
    autonomy of, 62
    average age of, 123
    married, 223, 224
    shortages, during WWII, 223–225, 229, 232–233
    shortages, in 1980s, 440–441
    training of, 43, 60
"Teacher's Everday Plans," 67–68
"Teachers Favor Flogging, Say Corporal Punishment Is Necessary for Discipline," 72–73
teacher's unions, 43, 62, 63
Teach for America, 501–505
technology, 357, 401
teddy bear, 53, 57
teenagers, 273–274
"Teenomania," 273–274
telegrams, 178
telegraph, 65
telemarketing, 518
telephone, 2, 89, 136, 357
telescope, 21
television, 157, 165, 253, 263, 264, 364
television stations, 271
Temperance movement, 53
tenements, 110
Tennessee, 333–334
Tennessee Valley Authority, 178
tennis, 8, 507
terrorism, 489
Tetris, 418
Texas, 358, 397
*Texas v. Johnson*, 437
textbooks, 43, 309–310
textile mills, 34, 177
Thagard, Norman, 465
Thater, Ernest, 21
"Things Pleasant and Otherwise," 23

Thirteenth Amendment, 465
"30 More Virginia Schools to Integrate This Week," 323
Thompson, Allen, 367
Three-in-One Oil Company (advertisement), *127*
Three Mile Island, 358
*Thriller*, 402
Thurmond, Strom, 239, 283
tiddlywinks, 57
*Time* magazine, 496
*Time of Your Life, The*, 212
Time Warner, 437
*Tinker v. Des Moines Independent Community School District*, 349
Tin Pan Alley, 1
tin toys, 57
*Titanic*, 418
Title IX, 443, 445–449, 454–457
T-Mobile, 507
Toffler, Alvin, 368
Tomb of the Unknowns, 145
Tommy Hilfiger, 418
Toscanini, Arturo, 239
"To School by Air Tube," 86
*To the Lighthouse*, 157
Tour de France, 53
Tower, John, 448
Tower Amendment, 448
Tower of London, 165
Toyota, 283
toys, 57
*Toy Story*, 465
tractors, 89
trade, 136
trade schools, 433–435
train. *See* railroads
tranquilizers, 264
Trans-Alaska Pipeline Authorization Act, 386
transistors, 165, 239
Trans-Mississippi Exposition World's Fair, 35
travel, 135
traveling salesman, 89
Travolta, John, 358, 398
Treaty of Fort Laramie, 19
Treaty of Versailles, 126
Trenton, New Jersey, 270
Trinity Test, 227
triode thermionic amplifier, 65
Triple Crown, 386
Trojans, 136
Tropical Blend (advertisement), *429*
Trotsky, Leon, 157
Trudeau, Garry, 368
*True Confessions*, 172
*True Story*, 172
Truman, Harry, 218, 227, 239, 253
tuberculosis, 145
Tuskegee Institute, 8

*Italic* page numbers indicate images. **Bold** page numbers indicate profile subjects

*Italic* page numbers indicate images. **Bold** page numbers indicate profile subjects

# X

# Y

# Z